Costs Law Reports

Core Volume

Costs Law Reports

Core Volume

Peter Rogers
LL B
Taxing Master of the Supreme Court

Michael Bacon
MA, AALCD

CLT Professional Publishing
A Division of Central Law Training Ltd

© Editors and CLT Professional Publishing

Published by
CLT Professional Publishing
A division of Central Law Training Ltd
Wrens Court
52–54 Victoria Road
Sutton Coldfield
Birmingham B72 1SX

Core Volume ISBN 1 85811 134 X
Core Volume & 1997 Vol 1 ISBN 1 85811 138 2

Produced by Palladian, PO Box 15, Bembridge.

Typeset by The Setting Studio, Back Newbridge Street, Newcastle upon Tyne.

Printed and bound in Great Britain by
Redwood Books, Trowbridge, Wiltshire

Foreword

Costs excite the interest of the public and the legal profession in equal measure. They are, to both, albeit for different reasons, a ceaseless source of mystery, speculation and surprise.

Accordingly, this work serves an admirable purpose. Its comprehensive reporting, including much which has hitherto gone unreported, will help to inform all those interested about the many considerations which affect costs. In consequence, they will be able to avoid contention when this is possible and, when it is not, to present or resolve a case on a sensible basis in accordance with principle.

I warmly recommend these reports.

The Rt Hon Lord Justice Rose

Preface

It has been a constant complaint of those appearing on taxation over the years, that Masters have decided issues on taxation "in accordance with the principle laid down in a recent review of taxation". Those decisions, given in chambers and largely unreported, were quite simply unavailable to legal representatives whose first inkling that there had been a change in a particular aspect of costs law was when the point was decided against them. Various attempts to remedy this problem have been made, but none have prove very satisfactory. With the introduction of this new work, it is hoped that practitioners will be able to keep up to date with major decisions on costs, some reported elsewhere but here gathered together for ease of reference, as well as being able to keep up to date with the subtle shifts in direction and principle brought about by reviews of taxation.

The work consists of a core volume, containing those decisions which have withstood the test of time and from which all other decisions tend to flow. There is also a supplementary volume which will contain more recent cases and those of transient interest. The Editors have collected together not only relevant civil cases but also cases on criminal costs, where, because of the plethora of regulations, civil principles apply only spasmodically, and very different principles apply to costs payable out of the Legal Aid Fund, and those payable out of Central Funds.

I am sure this is a work which will be of tremendous assistance to all those who have to deal with the law relating to costs, either on a regular basis or from time to time.

P T Hurst
Chief Master

Contents

PART II   CRIMINAL CASE-LAW

Table of Cases

(All references are to page. References in bold are to judgments reproduced in full. Note that within the text, cross references to cases reproduced in this work are cited in bold as, for example, **Costs LR (Core Vol) 1** (i.e. Costs Law Reports (Core Volume) page 1).)

Part I

Civil Case-law

Gundry
v
Sainsbury

King's Bench Division
24, 25 February 1910

Headnote

This, one of the most important costs cases, is the foundation for the well established principle that on an inter partes taxation the receiving party may not recover more from the paying party than he has paid to his own solicitors, the so-called "indemnity principle".

COZENS-HARDY MR: This appeal raises a curious and in one way an important point. The plaintiff, a labourer, commenced an action in the county court claiming damages for injuries sustained by the bite of a dog. The action was fought, the plaintiff recovered damages 15*l*, and the learned county court judge ordered judgment to be signed for that amount and has not given as against the defendant any costs of the action. There are two passages in his judgment which state quite clearly his reasons for adopting that course. He said first that "The question in this case was whether the successful plaintiff was entitled to the costs of the action, he having stated in his cross-examination that he had verbally agreed with his solicitor that he (the plaintiff) should not pay him any costs", and a little further on, "In this case the agreement between client and solicitor was that the client should pay the solicitor nothing in respect of costs". I do not know how you can have better evidence of that matter as against the plaintiff than his own statement, and the learned judge, having had that statement made in the witness-box by the plaintiff on cross-examination, and having reserved the consideration of the question of costs to a subsequent day, no application was made to him at that time to admit further evidence; but at the last moment he was asked to allow further evidence to be given. The learned judge in the exercise of his discretion refused to do so. I think it is impossible for us to interfere with that exercise of his discretion, and I have not the smallest doubt that upon the evidence before him he was amply justified in arriving at the conclusion he did, that there was an agreement between the client and the solicitor that nothing should be paid to the solicitor for costs. That gives rise to the question what is the position of the defendant in the action in consequence of that state of things? I think that the common law point made by counsel for the respondent, which has not been dealt with by counsel for the appellant in his reply, is a good point and is sufficient to dispose of this case. What are party and party costs? They are not a complete indemnity, but they are only given in the character of an indemnity. I cannot do better than read the opinion expressed by Bramwell B in *Harold v Smith* [5 H&N 381 at 385]:

"Costs as between party and party are given by the law as an indemnity to the person entitled to them; they are not imposed as a punishment on the party who pays them, nor given as a bonus to the party who receives them. Therefore, if the extent of the damnification can be found out, the extent to which costs ought to be allowed is also ascertained."

Now in the face of the evidence which the learned county court judge has accepted, and which he was perfectly justified in accepting, if he had ordered the defendant to pay these costs he would have been giving a bonus to the party receiving them. That is contrary to justice and to common sense and also to the law as laid down in *Harold* v *Smith*. That is a decision which has remained undisturbed for fifty years, and I am not prepared to depart from it. On that ground alone I think that this appeal must fail. But a further and difficult point arises under sections 4 and 5 of the Attorneys and Solicitors Act 1870. The agreement, I assume, was a verbal agreement, though there is no evidence upon the point, and it is said that the agreement referred to in those sections is limited to an agreement in writing. The object of that group of clauses beginning at section 4 and going on to section 15 was undoubtedly to favour solicitors by enabling them to make certain bargains with their clients in respect of costs which they could not otherwise have made. [The Master of the Rolls read sections 4 and 5.] It is to my mind apparent that the proviso at the end of section 5, though not purely declaratory, was the application of the settled common law principle to the particular facts of the case there dealt with and was absolutely necessary having regard to the first part of section 5.

In the view of the court below that proviso applies not merely to an agreement in writing, but to any agreement for the solicitor's remuneration which, as was held in *Clare* v *Joseph* [1907] 2 KB 369, the client can take the benefit of, although not in writing. I am not prepared to say that that view of the section is wrong. I feel perhaps more difficulty upon the construction of the statute than my brethren appear to do, but on the common law point I feel no doubt at all that the respondent to this appeal was right. I am not prepared to say he was not right also on the Act of 1870. But on one or other of these grounds I think that this appeal should be dismissed, and dismissed with costs.

FLETCHER MOULTON LJ: I am of the same opinion. The Master of the Rolls has dealt with the common law point which in my opinion is quite sufficient to decide this appeal, because I think the passage which the Master of the Rolls quoted from the judgment of Bramwell B is sound law and is decisive of this case. But I am also of the opinion that the case may be decided in the same way under the provisions of the Attorneys and Solicitors Act 1870. The position of agreements between solicitor and client as to the amount of the solicitor's professional remuneration has been dealt with at length by the Court of Appeal in *Clare* v *Joseph*, but it is not necessary to refer to that case further than to say that I venture to think it clearly laid down the proposition that prior to the Act of 1870 solicitors and clients could enter into such agreements, but that the solicitor could not set them up if they were not favourable to the client. The consequence is that they were of imperfect validity in the hands of the solicitor.

The Act of 1870 purports to alter this. Part I relates to agreements between attorneys and solicitors and their clients with respect to the amount and manner of the solicitor's remuneration and says that an attorney or solicitor may validly make such agreements in writing. It therefore prescribes the formality which must be gone through in order to make such an agreement enforceable in the hands of the solicitor, which it was not in all cases prior to the Act. In other words, I look upon section 4 as dealing with a well-known type of agreement and laying down the formality which is necessary to enable the solicitor to set up such an agreement against his client. Section 5 provides, broadly speaking, that agreements of this kind shall not affect the rights of third parties. It may be a question whether it was necessary that this should be expressed in the Act of Parliament, because the general principles of law would probably have prevented its affecting the rights of third parties not parties to the agreement. But section 5 goes on to say that any person who is bound to pay costs to which such an agreement relates may require the costs payable by him to the client to be taxed according to the rules for the time being in force. That is an enactment which may or may not have been necessary. It may be that under the ordinary law he would have had such a right. But inasmuch as the section expressly provides that he can require the costs payable by him to the client to be taxed according to the ordinary rules of taxation there arises this question: Supposing the costs payable by the client to his solicitor under the agreement are less than those which the taxation shews to be the normal costs, what then? The latter part of the section provides for such a case. The principle that party and party costs are only an indemnity – an imperfect indemnity, it is true, but never more than an indemnity – is so deeply rooted in our law that the proviso is put in for the purpose of preventing the earlier part of section 5 from ever giving rise to a case in which costs could be made a profit. By this proviso it is enacted that the client who has entered into such an agreement shall not recover from the person liable to pay to him the costs a greater sum than he himself is under the agreement liable to pay to the solicitor. This proviso is only declaratory in a special instance of what is the general law as to awarding costs throughout our legal system. Both parts of section 5, in my opinion, relate to all agreements of the class to which section 4 applies, that is to say, agreements between a solicitor and his client respecting the amount to be paid to the solicitor for his professional services, and they apply equally whether the agreement be in writing or not. For these reasons I think that both under the statute and at common law this appeal should be dismissed.

BUCKLEY LJ: We have enjoyed the benefit of a clear and closely reasoned argument by Mr Forbes and I thank him for it. The argument is none the less valuable because it does not succeed. If his contention were right it would result that if there were an agreement between the plaintiff and his solicitor that the solicitor should charge only half costs, then if the agreement were in writing the defendant would by reason of the proviso be entitled to have the benefit of it; but if it were a verbal agreement the defendant would not get the benefit of it, but would have to pay full costs, and that would ensue from a statute whose purpose was, as was said in *Clare* v *Joseph*, to relieve the solicitor from the disability under which he otherwise would lie. It is of course exceedingly improbable that the statute intended any such result. Let us look at the two sections. Section 4 relates to any agreement between a solicitor and his client respecting the amount of the solicitor's remuneration. The language of the section is

> "respecting the amount and manner of payment for the whole or any part of any past or future services, fees, charges, or disbursements in respect of business done or to be done by such attorney or solicitor, whether as an attorney or solicitor or as an advocate or conveyancer, either by a gross sum, or by commission or percentage, or by salary or otherwise, and either at the same or at a greater or at a less rate as or than the rate at which he would otherwise be entitled to be remunerated."

That is a sufficiently long sentence to justify the use of the words "such an agreement" in section 5, those being the words with which that section commences. The words "such an agreement" mean, I think, an agreement such as is described by all those words in section 4. Now, as this court held in *Clare* v *Joseph*, if the solicitor is coming to set up an agreement of that kind he cannot be listened to unless he produces an agreement in writing. But if the client sets up such an agreement it is no objection that the agreement was verbal and not in writing. Here we have to consider a case in which not the client but the defendant whom the client was suing seeks to set up an agreement under which the solicitor was to take less than the full amount of his costs. It is a case, therefore, which falls within the principle of *Clare* v *Joseph*, that it is only where the agreement is being set up by the solicitor that the statute requires that it shall be in writing. So much for the construction of the statute. Secondly, I agree with the ground on which the Master of the Rolls has primarily rested his judgment. Suppose the Act of 1870 does not apply. Then the client comes to the court and says "This is a matter in respect of which I am entitled to get costs because I have been put to expense, and the law as administered in this court allows me in that state of things to be indemnified by the defendant to the extent of party and party costs". But he having come to assert that right, the court says "True, you are entitled to such indemnity, but inasmuch as you have nothing to pay by reason of your agreement with your solicitor there is nothing for which to indemnify you". I confess I feel some regret that the solicitor was not allowed to go into the box and state the real facts relating to the agreement, but that was a matter to be determined by the county court judge. He dealt with it in the exercise of his discretion, and he found as a fact – and his finding is of course binding upon us – that there was such an agreement as was sworn to by the plaintiff in his cross-examination. On both these grounds I think that this appeal fails and should be dismissed with costs.

Appeal dismissed.

Solicitor for appellant: *C F Appleton*.
Solicitor for respondent: *L Tubbs*.

Medway Oil and Storage Co Ltd
Appellants
and
Continental Contractors Ltd and others
Respondents

House of Lords
30 October 1928

Present:
Viscount Dunedin, Lord Shaw of Dunfermline, Lord Carson, and
Lord Blanesburgh

[Note. – *The late Viscount Haldane presided at the hearing and prepared
a written judgment, which was read by Viscount Dunedin.*]

Headnote

This definitive case on costs of counterclaim deals with the
principle that should apply where a successful defendant to an
action has brought in a counterclaim but has been defeated on it
with costs. The Court of Appeal had held, reversing MacKinnon
J, that where evidence is given of facts which are put forward in
respect of both the claim and the counterclaim in common, there
is no reason why the plaintiff who had failed in the action but
had succeeded in defending the counterclaim should not be
entitled to the costs incurred in relation to them when resisting
the counterclaim. It was for the Taxing Master to apportion the
amounts when taxing the entire costs. The House of Lords
reversed the Court of Appeal's decision, favouring the principle
adopted by MacKinnon J in the court below. In such
circumstances only the costs occasioned by the counterclaim
should be allowed as costs of counterclaim. The plaintiff who
successfully defends a counterclaim should be "only entitled to
such extra costs as were occasioned by the counterclaim".

APPEAL from an order of the Court of Appeal [[1928] 1 KB 238] reversing an
order of MacKinnon J.

The facts are fully stated in the report of the case before the Court of
Appeal. The following summary may be found useful.

The respondents sued the appellants for 62,000*l* as damages for
wrongfully repudiating a contract to accept and pay for a large quantity of

kerosene oil which the respondents had sold to the appellants; and the appellants counterclaimed for the difference between the contract and market price of the oil, on the ground that the respondents had themselves wrongfully repudiated the contract of sale.

The respondents did not make the first delivery at the stipulated time, but they alleged (1.) an oral agreement to postpone delivery for a month; (2.) that the appellants' tanks were not ready to receive the oil at the contract date of delivery; (3.) that the giving of a bankers' guarantee called for by a clause of the contract was a condition precedent to the respondents' obligation to ship and deliver; (4.) that a conspiracy had been entered into between the appellants and the respondents' suppliers to defeat the respondents in their efforts to obtain the oil.

The appellants denied these allegations.

MacKinnon J held that the respondents had failed to establish any of their allegations, and dismissed their claim with costs. He also dismissed the appellants' counterclaim with costs, on the ground that, though the appellants were justified in treating the contract as having been repudiated by the respondents, they had suffered no damage.

The judgment of the learned judge on the merits was ultimately affirmed by the House of Lords.

On taxation of the costs of the litigation the Taxing Master, for the purposes of obtaining a ruling as to the principle to be applied, reported that he proposed to tax on the assumption that each party had been completely defeated on his affirmative claims.

MacKinnon J, applying the principle of *Wilson v Walters* [[1926] 1 KB 511], held that the only costs which the respondents could recover as costs of the counterclaim were such costs as they incurred by reason of the counterclaim and would not have incurred apart from the counterclaim, e.g., the costs of calling a witness as to the market price.

The Court of Appeal (Bankes, Atkin and Lawrence LJJ) held, on the principle of *Christie v Platt* [[1921] 2 KB 17], that all the matters in issue arose upon the claim and upon the counterclaim, and that the costs of all must be apportioned.

1928. 30 April; 1, 3 May. *Van den Berg* (with him *R L Parry*) for the appellants. The Court of Appeal were wrong in saying that all the four issues were common to the claim and counterclaim and that therefore there must be an apportionment. All the issues arose solely upon the claim, and the costs of those issues were properly incurred in defeating the claim and should be given to the appellants. The only costs that should be allowed to the respondents on the counterclaim are such extra costs as were incurred by reason of the counterclaim and would not have been incurred but for the counterclaim: *Wilson v Walters* [[1926] 1 KB 511].

Cyril Atkinson KC (with him *Roland Burrows*) for the respondents. The broad proposition laid down in *Wilson v Walters* [[1926] 1 KB 511] is inconsistent with *Christie v Platt* [[1921] 2 KB 17] and ought to be overruled. Where the same matter arises on the claim and counterclaim and one party gets the costs of the claim and the other party gets the costs of the counterclaim the costs of litigating the matter ought to be apportioned between the parties, and it is for the Taxing Master to determine what the apportionment should be. The respondents' costs of litigating the matters in controversy were incurred in resisting the counterclaim as well as in supporting the claim, and the appellants' costs were not incurred solely in resisting the claim but were also incurred in supporting the counterclaim. Where cross-claims arise between two parties the principle on which the costs are to be taxed cannot depend upon which of the two comes in first with his writ. The respondents' contention that the costs of issues common to both claim and counterclaim should be apportioned is supported by *Baines v Bromley* [(1881) 6 QBD 691] and *In re Brown* [(1883) 23 ChD 377].

[He also referred to *Saner v Bilton* [11 ChD 416]; *Mason v Brentini* [(1880) 15 ChD 287]; *Shrapnel v Laing* [(1888) 20 QBD 334]; *Atlas Metal Co v Miller* [[1898] 2 QB 500]; *Haskell Golf Ball Co v Hutchinson* [[1906] 1 Ch 518]; *Jones v Stott* [[1910] 1 KB 893]; *Fox v Central Silkstone Collieries* [[1912] 2 KB 597]; *Crean v M'Millan* [[1922] 2 IR 105].]

Van den Berg replied.

The House took time for consideration.

1928. 30 October. VISCOUNT DUNEDIN: before his lamented death Viscount Haldane had prepared a judgment in this case and, as the conclusion he arrived at is the same as that which will be arrived at by the vote of the House, in accordance with precedent I propose to read his judgment.

VISCOUNT HALDANE: My Lords, I think that the real question in this case in the main is one of law. It relates to the principle which ought to prevail in the taxation of costs when the successful defendants to an action have put in a counterclaim and have been defeated on it with costs. In this action the appellants, who were defendants, succeeded in defeating with costs a claim for a very substantial sum. This was the effect of the judgment of MacKinnon J, who tried the case. His judgment on the merits was reversed by the Court of Appeal, but subsequently restored by this House. There was controversy over the result arrived at by the Taxing Master when taxing the costs under the judgment. There was an appeal to MacKinnon J from his order and subsequently a further appeal to the Court of Appeal. That Court altered the order, and it is from the judgment thus altering it that the present appeal is brought. The costs, as directed in the end to be taxed, appear to have finally resulted in 987*l* 9*s* 11*d* being awarded to the respondents, the plaintiffs who failed, as costs of the trial, and in 1,808*l* 4*s* 3*d* being given to the appellants as like costs. The respondents have been given 288*l* 6*s* 2*d* for the costs of the appeal and the appellants have been awarded 583*l* 19*s* 10*d* for such costs.

The amounts in issue, even as to costs alone, are thus substantial. The large amount of costs awarded to the respondents, who failed in their action, but succeeded on the defence to the counterclaim, arises from the decision given that, no damage having been shown to have been caused by them, they were, although in breach, entitled to judgment on the counterclaim with costs. The amount of the costs ultimately allocated to the counterclaim is the result of the application of a principle which MacKinnon J refused to adopt, but which the Court of Appeal has applied. The view of the Court of Appeal is that where the plaintiff fails with costs in his claim and the defendant with costs in his counterclaim, the proper mode of taxation is not, as MacKinnon J thought, to give the defendant all costs incurred in resisting the claim, depriving him only of any costs which he has incurred exclusively in supporting his defeated counterclaim. In that view no question of what is called apportionment can arise. The Court of Appeal has on the contrary held that where evidence is given of facts which are put forward in connection with the claim and the counterclaim in common, there is no reason why the plaintiff should not be allowed the costs incurred in relation to them when resisting the counterclaim on which he has got judgment, and the duty of the taxing master is to apportion the amounts when taxing the entire costs.

My Lords, there is a real divergence in the working out of the two principles, notwithstanding that there are cases in which it is impracticable to rely on either as an abstract principle standing by itself. One brief may, for instance, be given to counsel on both claim and counterclaim, and it may obviously be necessary that there should be an apportionment of the single inclusive fee paid with it. But in most other cases no such difficulty arises. It is therefore necessary to turn to the character of the litigation in the present case to see whether it comes within the character that is not exceptional, so that the principle adopted by MacKinnon J, if indeed it be right as a matter of law, can be applied.

The respondents sued the appellants to recover damages for an alleged breach of contract to take delivery as purchasers of a large quantity of oil. The appellants succeeded in establishing that the respondents had failed to make delivery of the oil in due time under the contract, and they counterclaimed as damages the difference between the contract and market prices of the oil, alleging that the respondents had themselves wrongfully repudiated their contract of sale. The action was tried before MacKinnon J, who gave judgment on the claim of the respondents as plaintiffs for the appellants (defendants) with costs, and on the counterclaim for the respondents with costs. The respondents appealed to the Court of Appeal, and the appellants cross-appealed against the dismissal of the counterclaim. The Court of Appeal reversed the judgment of MacKinnon J and gave judgment for the plaintiff respondents for 44,738*l* 6*s* 8*d* with costs, including the costs of the appeal as well as of the cross-appeal, which was dismissed. The appellants then appealed to this House, which reversed the order of the Court of Appeal and restored that of MacKinnon J. The judgment of the latter had been that judgment be entered for the defendants (the present appellants) with costs and that judgment be entered for the plaintiffs on the counterclaim with costs of the counterclaim. The ground assigned by MacKinnon J for dismissing the counterclaim was that it was not shown that the defendants had suffered any damage by reason of the plaintiffs having failed to fulfil their contract, and that the latter were therefore entitled to have the counterclaim dismissed and with costs, if there were any separate costs of the counterclaim. [The judgment of this House reversed that of the Court of Appeal and restored the judgment of MacKinnon J.] There was no reversal of the judgment as regards the counterclaim, the dismissal of which by MacKinnon J with costs therefore stands.

My Lords, it becomes necessary to ascertain what the matters put in issue and tried really were. As to this all the Courts are in substantial agreement. The issues were four in number: (1.) Whether there was an agreement, as alleged by the plaintiff respondents, to extend the time for delivery of the oil. This has been finally disposed of in favour of the appellants by the judgment here. (2.) Whether the appellants' tanks were ready to receive the oil at the contract dates of delivery. (3.) The questions arising with reference to the guarantee. (This was an agreement contained in clause 6 of the original contract under which the buyers were, if so required, to give the sellers a floating bankers' guarantee for their payments to their own vendors in respect of a certain amount of the oil to be delivered under the contract.) (4.) The allegation of a conspiracy by which it was said that the appellants sought to arrange with the Russian sellers that the latter should fail to supply the respondents with oil, so that the appellants could get out of their contract, and then deal directly with the Russians. [On this again the appellants have finally succeeded.] All these issues were decided in favour of the appellants. MacKinnon J considered the first, the third and the fourth arose solely on the claim. The second, which related to the tanks being in readiness, he thought was relevant on both the claim and the counterclaim, but that, as the appellants had succeeded on that issue, the respondents were entitled only to such extra costs arising in connection with it as were occasioned by the counterclaim. The appellants were, in his opinion, entitled to the costs of this issue which they had actually incurred in defending the action, and the respondents were entitled only to such costs as they would not have incurred had they not been compelled to meet the counterclaim.

It is at this point that the Court of Appeal overruled the learned judge on the question of taxation. They held that there was a substantial claim and a substantial counterclaim arising out of the same contract, and that, except as to the amount of the damages respectively claimed, all the substantial contentions on either side were common to both claim and counterclaim. There was no reason why the respondents should not be allowed costs incurred in resisting the counterclaim merely because the facts they put forward were common to both claim and counterclaim. The Taxing Master ought, they held, to have apportioned to the counterclaim such portion of the common items as had arisen and been incurred by reason of the counterclaim.

My Lords, there is obviously here a conflict of opinion with MacKinnon J about a point of principle. One view is that as the costs of the issues were, as the Taxing Master found, properly incurred in defeating the claim they should be given to the appellants, the respondents getting only such extra costs as were incurred by reason of the counterclaim and but for it would not have been incurred. The other view is that the proper principle of taxation under a judgment such as the judgment in this case is that when one party has got the costs of a claim and another of a counterclaim, the Taxing Master ought to allow to each party all such costs as he has properly incurred in maintenance or resistance, as the case may be. When therefore the matters in controversy are common to both claim and counterclaim, the costs, so far as common to both claim and counterclaim, should be apportioned.

The question is one which, as might be expected, has on a good many occasions come before the judges, and is of a kind, being one of the practice of the Courts, in which what they have laid down is of much importance, although the decisions are not technically binding in this House. I propose therefore to examine the most important of the authorities.

In 1879 Fry J decided *Saner* v *Bilton* [11 ChD 416]. There the plaintiff's claim and the defendant's counterclaim had, as here, both been dismissed with costs. The question was whether the defendant ought to pay only so much of the costs pertaining to the claim as were occasioned by the counterclaim, or whether the costs of all the proceedings which related to both claim and counterclaim should be apportioned. Fry J consulted some of the most eminent of the Taxing Masters, who advised against apportionment. He afterwards gave a considered judgment, in which he said that analysis of the practice before the Judicature Act threw but little light on the question before him. The true view seemed to him to be that the plaintiff having begun the litigation, and the counterclaim having only arisen in it as a consequence, the claim should be treated as if it stood by itself, and the counterclaim should bear only the amount by which the costs of the proceedings had been increased by it. Special directions might be given by the Court which would vary the application of the rule, but in a case where both claim and counterclaim were simply dismissed with costs, there should be no apportionment, and no question of quantum arose.

In 1880 the Court of Appeal, consisting of Jessel MR and James and Brett LJJ, took the same view in a similar case (*Mason* v *Brentini* [(1880) 15 ChD 287]), Jessel MR saying that he entirely agreed with the decision in

Saner v *Bilton* and with the reasons given by Fry J, and that the judgment of the latter was to be considered as expressing the rule of the Court.

Baines v *Bromley* [(1881) 6 QBD 691] was decided in 1881 by the Court of Appeal, consisting of Bramwell, Brett and Cotton LJJ. The circumstances of the case were different in this respect that the plaintiff had recovered on his claim with costs, and that the defendant had recovered a larger amount with costs on a counterclaim. The Court of Appeal, however, held that, the case not being one of set-off but of counterclaim, the proper course was to take the claim as if it and its issues were an action, and the counterclaim and its issues as though also an action. In such a case Brett LJ observes that if there were items common to both actions the Taxing Master would divide them. But he did not explain what were the sort of items in which this would be so. Bramwell and Cotton LJJ proceeded simply on the ground that the plaintiff being declared entitled to his costs of suit had been wrongly allowed only the costs of the issues on which he succeeded.

In re Brown [(1883) 23 ChD 377] was decided in 1883 by Chitty J and then by the Court of Appeal (Baggallay, Cotton and Fry LJJ). The plaintiff had succeeded on a claim and the defendant on a counterclaim, the latter recovering the larger amount. Each obtained an order for the costs. It was contended before Chitty J that there ought to be apportionment. But that learned judge, whose experience in such matters was very great, held that the principle of *Saner* v *Bilton* [11 ChD 416] applied where the plaintiff who had commenced the litigation was wrong, and that it must also apply where the plaintiff was right and the counterclaiming defendant was also right. The effect of the Judicature Act was to make two writs unnecessary, but the plaintiff was to recover none the less the whole costs of the claim in the action. He referred to the dictum of Brett LJ in *Baines* v *Bromley* [(1881) 6 QBD 691] about the Taxing Master dividing items common to both actions, and said that on inquiry he was unable to find that there had been made any apportionment, notwithstanding the observation in the Court of Appeal. His own view appears to have been that there could be no apportionment in the absence of special direction. The Court of Appeal took the same view as Chitty J. The Lords Justices thought that the principle of *Saner* v *Bilton* [11 ChD 416] applied, just as much where claim and counterclaim both succeeded as where they both failed.

In *Shrapnel* v *Laing* [(1888) 20 QBD 334], decided in 1888, in the Court of Appeal (Lord Esher MR and Fry and Lopes LJJ), the same principle was applied. The plaintiff had recovered on his claim and the defendant on a counterclaim, both with costs. It was sought to deny to the plaintiff the general costs of his action, because the amount recovered on the counterclaim was larger. But the Court ordered the taxation to proceed as though the claim were an action in itself and the counterclaim also an action, to be treated as though there had been no claim. If either of the parties fails in particular issues his costs will be to that extent disallowed, but they will not belong to the other side. Lord Esher MR explained his dictum in *Baines* v *Bromley* [(1881) 6 QBD 691] about the Taxing Master dividing common items as limited to items of which both parties get the advantage. Of these he said there were very few, the costs of the writ which includes the whole of the proceedings might be one.

In *Atlas Metal Co v Miller* [[1898] 2 QB 500] Lindley MR in the Court of Appeal reviewed the authorities in a careful judgment. He threw some doubt on the dictum of Lord Esher MR in *Baines v Bromley* [(1881) 6 QBD 691] about common items, and said there could not be included in the costs of a counterclaim any costs not occasioned by its being a counterclaim but saved by its being what it is. There can be no apportionment of what are properly costs of the action. Such costs where ascertained must be paid by the party ordered to pay them.

This judgment of the Court of Appeal obviously follows the principle of *Saner v Bilton* [11 ChD 416], and makes it clear that "no costs," to use the words of Lindley MR, "not incurred by reason of the counterclaim can be costs of the counterclaim." Lindley MR and Chitty LJ laid down that the cases were in reality in agreement in the following points: (1.) A plaintiff who is to pay or be paid the costs of his action must pay or be paid the whole of such costs as if there were no counterclaim. (2.) The defendant who fails on his counterclaim has to pay all the costs of it, the counterclaim being treated as an independent action. What do these costs include? The costs occasioned by it, and these only. The circumstance, for instance, that if there had been no action the costs of the counterclaim would have been larger, because the defendant would then have had to issue a writ, does not make costs not incurred costs incurred, and the costs saved by not bringing a separate action cannot be regarded as costs incurred. Where there are no separate issues requiring special treatment the costs of the defence will be costs of the action, and so with the counterclaim also. Costs common to defence and counterclaim must necessarily be dealt with on this principle, but to apply it is a very different thing from apportioning what are properly costs of the action.

My Lords, in the authorities which I have now cited successive Courts of Appeal have laid down a principle which is not only intelligible, but capable of being easily applied by the Taxing Master. It may work out apparently harshly in exceptional cases. But when these threaten to occur the remedy is to apply at the trial for special directions as to issues and details. The advantage of the principle is that it is a definite one, which lifts the subject out of the somewhat vague regions of apportionment.

So the law had been settled since 1898, the year of the judgment in the *Atlas* case [[1898] 2 QB 500]. Even the minor questions suggested by Lord Esher MR had been superseded, partly by the decisions of other judges and partly by his own subsequent observations.

But in 1920 a change of attitude seems to have disclosed itself in the Court of Appeal. *Christie v Platt* [[1921] 2 KB 17] was an interlocutory appeal decided by Atkin and Younger LJJ. To a claim by a landlady for rent against her tenant, the latter had pleaded that the demised premises, a furnished house, were uninhabitable. By way of counterclaim the tenant had repeated the allegations in her defence and claimed damages. Judgment was entered for the landlady on her claim for 200*l* and costs, and for the tenant on the counterclaim for 225*l* and costs. On each side the claim and counterclaim were dealt with in one brief. The Taxing Master allowed the plaintiff the fee to counsel at the trial and costs and expenses of witnesses. In taxing the defendants' bill of costs he allowed nothing in respect of these items. The Court of Appeal held that the taxation had proceeded on a wrong principle, and that the costs incurred in supporting the claim and opposing the counterclaim ought to be apportioned, and attributed to the costs of the claim and the counterclaim respectively. So mutatis mutandis with the cost of supporting the counterclaim and opposing the claim.

My Lords, in the particular circumstances of *Christie v Platt* [[1921] 2 KB 17] it was no doubt tempting to deal so with the costs. I share the sense of Atkin LJ that there was something in the result of the taxation which on the face of it must have been wrong. For although the defendant had recovered the larger amount on what was a cardinal question between the parties, the plaintiff was given on her case, which was practically uncontroverted, 214*l*, while the defendant only got 3*l* 0*s* 5*d* to cover the whole of her costs. I agree with Atkin LJ that this must have been wrong. There were obviously costs incurred in common; the single fee on the brief given by the plaintiff is an example. It may be that this fee would not have been too much if there had been no counterclaim to meet. But that does not affect the fact that it was paid to the plaintiffs' counsel to cover his services in both proceedings. It ought therefore to have been divided for the purposes of taxation. The same thing appeared to have been true of a good deal of the evidence put forward on the two sides. There may well be costs which have to be divided. In the *Atlas* case [[1898] 2 QB 500 at 506] Lindley MR at one point uses the word "apportioned," but that is where he is quoting Lord Esher MR on another point. He himself goes on at once to say that while costs common to both claim and counterclaim must necessarily be dealt with in this way, "to do so is very different from apportioning what are properly costs of the action. Such costs when ascertained must be paid by the party ordered to pay them. They cannot have been increased by the counterclaim, and no part of them can properly be regarded as costs of the counterclaim."

My Lords, the distinction between division and apportionment may in certain circumstances be a thin one. But under the rule as laid down by Lindley MR, and by the judges in the earlier case also, the distinction is fundamental. I do not criticize the result reached in *Christie v Platt* [[1921] 2 KB 17] by Atkin and Younger LJJ. But I do find in their judgment some failure to recognize the importance of the distinction and to lay emphasis on it.

In a case in Ireland, *Crean v M'Millan* [[1922] 2 IR 105], the question raised in cases such as *Christie v Platt* [[1921] 2 KB 17] was considered by the Courts, which contained three Lords Justices, the Lord Chancellor and the Master of the Rolls, the case being finally disposed of by them on appeal in what was then the High Court of Appeal for Ireland. O'Connor LJ delivered a judgment which is as valuable as it is instructive, and there were exhaustive opinions expressed by the Lord Chancellor of Ireland and Andrews LJ. They disposed of the question as to how the costs should be borne when there was a counterclaim in accordance with the principle initiated by *Saner v Bilton* [11 ChD 416], and finally laid down by Lindley MR. There are expressions in the judgments which I should myself avoid, such as "apportionment." In using them they were obviously influenced by the expression used in *Christie v Platt* [[1921] 2 KB 17], for they do not lay stress on the difference in principle of the *Atlas* case [[1898] 2 QB 500 at 506] between apportionment and division.

In *Wilson v Walters* [[1926] 1 KB 511] Scrutton and Sargant LJJ, sitting as a Divisional Court only, had the following case before them. The plaintiff brought an action in the country court for damages caused by the negligent driving of the defendant's motor car. The defendant denied negligence and counterclaimed for negligent driving by the plaintiff. The county court judge gave judgment on the claim for the defendant with costs, and on the counterclaim for the plaintiff with costs. The registrar in taxing first gave the defendant the costs of the claim. He then gave the plaintiff only such extra costs as were incurred in defending the counterclaim. Where in the latter case he came to an item which had been already dealt with in the costs of the claim he gave the plaintiff nothing in respect of it. But on appeal to the county court judge the latter held that whenever there was an item common to both claim and counterclaim it should be apportioned, believing that in so holding he was following *Christie v Platt* [[1921] 2 KB 17]. The Divisional Court allowed the appeal. They held that the issues on the claim and the counterclaim were one and the same. The defendant who succeeded was therefore prima facie entitled to the whole costs of determining them. The defendant on the other hand could recover on his counterclaim only such extra costs as represented the costs of the proceedings, as increased by the putting in of the counterclaim. In so holding they treated themselves as following the authorities from *Saner v Bilton* [11 ChD 416] down to the *Atlas* case, and also the judgments of the majority in the Irish case of *Crean*.

My Lords, the principle applied in *Wilson v Walters* [[1926] 1 KB 511] may have consequences in individual cases which would be harsh if the Taxing Master did not supervise the costs of claim and counterclaim closely, and split up the costs of items which are required by both. In such instances he takes an item, a single fee on the plaintiff's brief for example, and splits it into two notional fees, the one attributable to the claim, and the other to the counterclaim. This is not an apportioning, in which the payment is treated as a single item and the question is to what it is attributable. It is in reality a notional division of what on the face only of it is one item. If the principle is not kept in mind confusion will follow, as was pointed out by Lindley MR and other judges.

I now come to the judgment which we have to examine in the appeal before us. The learned judges of the Court of Appeal agreed neither with the Taxing Master nor with MacKinnon J. In their order they expressed the opinion that with the exception of the issue whether or not there was an agreement to postpone deliveries, which the parties admitted to arise solely on this claim, all the other issues raised in the pleadings and at the trial were common to both the claims and the counterclaims. I pause to observe that this is not only contrary to what was found by MacKinnon J who tried the case, but is impossible to reconcile with the judgment of the Lord Chancellor in this House. The counterclaim raised another issue, which there is no need to consider, inasmuch as the counterclaim for wrongful repudiation was dismissed with costs.

The order of the Court of Appeal went on to direct the Taxing Master to allow the respondents (the plaintiffs) all costs properly in fact incurred by them in defending the counterclaim, and to allow the appellants (defendants) all costs properly in fact incurred by them in defending the action, and directed that all common items be apportioned in the discretion of the Taxing Master accordingly. The direction given by MacKinnon J was in effect that when, as here, the defendant has succeeded in his defence but failed in his counterclaim he is entitled to the costs which he has actually and properly incurred in defeating the claim (including in this case the costs of the issues mentioned), but is not entitled to any costs which he would not have incurred had he not counterclaimed. The plaintiffs are only entitled to such costs as they would not have incurred had they not been compelled to meet the counterclaim.

The view taken in the Court of Appeal was very different. "In considering," said Bankes LJ [[1928] 1 KB 238 at 251], "what the real contest between the parties under each of these heads" (the issues) "was, I do not think that justice can be done except by treating the costs of the litigation under each head as costs which must be apportioned if the order as to costs is to be complied with." Atkin LJ [at 255] says that "It appears to me wrong both in law and fact to say that when a man sues for 62,000*l* and is sued in counterclaim for 46,000*l*, and the event is to be determined by consideration of the same evidence, he incurs all the costs of evidence because of the claim. He seems to me obviously to incur the cost because of both; in other words the costs are occasioned by both. And it is quite irrelevant as to such costs to consider what he would have incurred if there were no counterclaim, that is with no other cause operating. The result of the rule now laid down is that where there is a substantial counterclaim involving common evidence, the Master will apportion. But apportion does not necessarily mean divide into equal moieties. He will decide how much in fact should be attributed to the claim; how much to the counterclaim." He thought that the statement of Fry J in *Saner v Bilton* [11 ChD 416] that the plaintiff was to be represented as letting loose the waters of litigation, and therefore if unsuccessful should be in a worse position than an unsuccessful counterclaimant, unsatisfactory.

Lawrence LJ concurred, being of opinion that the authorities disclosed no consensus of view. He followed what was laid down in *Christie v Platt* [[1921] 2 KB 17].

My Lords, the judgments in the Court of Appeal appear to me to go back in spirit as well as in letter on the series of decisions by Fry J, Jessel MR, Lindley MR, and other eminent judges whose opinions I have already examined. The purpose of these opinions was to find a principle which might extricate the law relating to taxation in cases like the present from the hopeless confusion in which Fry J found it. The successive decisions, down to *Christie v Platt* [[1921] 2 KB 17], established a principle which in individual cases may seem a hard one. But it is a clear one, and in most cases will operate justly, as was pointed out by Fry J, while in others the Taxing Master can correct the effect of applying it in isolation as an abstract rule, by dividing items as distinguished from apportioning general costs. Such as it is, the rule was one necessary to lay down in some form, and I think that the form in which it has been laid down here and in Ireland was adopted by the learned judges, who did so because practice and authority alike pointed to it as the proper one.

I am therefore of opinion that we must reverse the judgment of the Court of Appeal and restore that of MacKinnon J. The appellants should have their costs here and below.

LORD CARSON: My Lords, we have the advantage of knowing from the judgment of MacKinnon J who tried the case that his view at the end of the trial was that the plaintiffs should only receive "such costs as are occasioned by the counterclaim," and I am not surprised that when on the order as framed the taxation of costs resulted in 900*l* being awarded to the defendants and 1,700*l* to the plaintiffs the result was, as the learned judge has said, "exceedingly startling." In point of fact the defendants had won on every issue, whether considered as an issue on the claim or on the counterclaim, and only failed in obtaining judgment upon the counterclaim by reason of their being unable to prove any damage flowing from the breach of contract which they had succeeded in proving.

Amongst the issues raised was a charge of fraud against the defendants with reference to what has been shortly described as the conspiracy with the Russians. This issue was found in favour of the defendants, but they have been ordered under the taxation appealed from to pay the whole of the costs of such issue as costs of the counterclaim. The mere statement of such an injustice is of itself sufficient to demonstrate that the taxing officer must have acted upon some erroneous principle. My Lords, I have been unable myself to understand how, after the judgment in *Atlas Metal Co v Miller* [[1898] 2 QB 500] already referred to, which is a judgment of the Court of Appeal and was reported as far back as 1898, any Court felt entitled in such a case as the present one to disregard the principles laid down in that case, and which, so far as I am aware, have been generally applied in cases of the failure of a counterclaim when there were no special directions found necessary. The noble Viscount Lord Haldane examined all the authorities, and it is unnecessary for me to refer to them in detail. I think the judgments referred to by the noble Viscount in *Crean v M'Millan* [[1922] 2 IR 105], which were delivered in a case on all fours with the present one, are well worthy of perusal, and I would like specially to refer to the summary of conclusions arrived at by Andrews LJ, which, taken as a whole, fairly represents the principles to be deduced from the various authorities and apart from special circumstances.

My Lords, I think MacKinnon J stated the principle applicable to this case very shortly when he says: "I think the proper principle to apply is that which is stated in *Wilson v Walters* [[1926] 1 KB 511], namely, that where a matter arises both on the claim and the counterclaim the plaintiffs are only entitled to such extra costs as were occasioned by the counterclaim." I agree with the noble Viscount Lord Haldane that the use of the word "apportion" is likely to be misleading. I am not sure I understand in the present case what it means or on what principle it can be adjusted. For example, upon the issue of fraud to which I have referred, found in favour of the defendants, how are the costs to be "apportioned" as between the plaintiffs and the defendants and so with the other issues? Such a method of dealing with the costs seems to impose upon the Taxing Master a duty in the exercise of which he is afforded no guidance whatever. I agree that this appeal should be allowed and that the judgment of MacKinnon J should be restored.

Lord Blanesburgh: My Lords, I was party with Atkin LJ to the decision of the Court of Appeal in *Christie v Platt* [[1921] 2 KB 17]. I am free, however, to confess that until the full discussion of that case on this occasion I was not conscious that there lurked in its judgments the pronounced departure now suggested from the rule of taxation enunciated in such authorities as *Saner v Bilton* [11 ChD 416]; *Mason v Brentini* [15 ChD 287]; and *Atlas Metal Co v Miller* [[1898] 2 QB 500] – a rule which, for brevity's sake, it may be convenient to refer to as the rule in *Saner v Bilton*. That no departure from the rule was, at least consciously, made in *Christie v Platt* perhaps sufficiently appears from the fact that the three cases just mentioned were all of them cited or referred to by Atkin LJ in his judgment, and on their effect was rested the order then pronounced. I do not, however, at this stage further refer to this aspect of *Christie v Platt*. I reserve that for later consideration. What I desire to call attention to now was the fundamental misunderstanding of the *Saner v Bilton* rule disclosed in *Christie v Platt* and corrected by that decision. *Christie v Platt* so regarded is, in the circumstances of the present case, as I see them, a completely reliable guide to the solution of this appeal.

The action was one by a landlady against her tenant of a furnished house for 200*l* rent due. By her defence, the tenant, after a formal traverse of the tenancy agreement, alleged in a series of paragraphs that the demised premises were uninhabitable. In a counterclaim, she repeated, by reference, these paragraphs of her defence, and concluded with a claim for damages. The defendant's allegations were denied by the plaintiff. By the time of the trial, it had become clear, if indeed it was ever in doubt, that the alleged condition of the premises was no defence to the claim for rent. The plaintiff's case in support of that claim was accordingly confined to proof of the tenancy agreement and of the rent due thereunder. That proof given, and the evidence was not questioned, she left the defendant to make good her allegations if she could. A full hearing ensued, with an examination of witnesses on both sides, and, in the result, Sankey J found it to have been an implied term of the tenancy agreement that the demised premises should be reasonably fit for occupation, that they had not been so in fact, and that the defendant had suffered damage in consequence. He gave judgment for the plaintiff on the claim for 200*l* and costs. On the counterclaim he gave judgment for the defendant for 225*l* and costs. The Master taxed the costs. "To state his conclusion," says Atkin LJ [[1921] 2 KB 24 at 26], "is enough to show that there is some flaw in his reasoning. He has taxed the plaintiff's costs at 214*l* 5*s* and the defendant's costs at 3*l* 0*s* 5*d*; and the defendant, who won on the issue involving nearly all the expense, is allowed 3*l* while the plaintiff who succeeded on an unopposed allegation recovers 214*l*. That must be wrong." How very wrong is perhaps even more strikingly apparent when it is remembered that the bulk of the plaintiff's 214*l* represented her costs of a disputed issue on which she had entirely failed, and that no part of her costs of the same issue on which she had succeeded was allowed to the defendant.

The explanation of the Taxing Master's action (and it was on this that the question before the Court turned) may again be given in Atkin LJ's words: "He reasoned thus: The defendant pleaded the breach of the implied term as a defence to the plaintiff's claim for rent; therefore the expense of proving the breach is attributable to the claim. The result of this reasoning is that he has imputed these costs to an irrelevant plea and has allowed them no part or share in establishing a relevant and substantial counterclaim. This has produced a miscarriage of justice."

The Lord Justice pointed out the remedy. The directions as to taxation given in the cases cited were all subject to this overriding condition which, expressed in the terms applicable to the case in hand, was that there must be ascertained what were the costs really incurred by the plaintiff in establishing her claim and what were those really incurred by the defendant in establishing her counterclaim. The taxation was accordingly referred back to the Taxing Master to ascertain these matters and award accordingly.

My Lords, the effective decision in *Christie v Platt* [[1921] 2 KB 17] emerges, I think, very clearly from this statement. And it is very apposite here. It is that in determining for the purposes of taxation in such a case as this whether a particular issue is an issue on the claim or on the counterclaim or on both the claim and the counterclaim, the Taxing Master is not by any rule in *Saner v Bilton* to be enslaved by the form of the pleadings. The question must be determined as one of substance and not of form – the manner in which the action was fought and in which the issues were dealt with by the parties and the Court not being disregarded. On the facts in *Christie v Platt* the Master was to be entitled, indeed he was invited, to attribute to the counterclaim exclusively all costs really incurred by the defendant in maintaining the disputed issue, although that issue had first appeared in the defence and was introduced to the counterclaim only by reference to the defence.

In that sense of the decision, applying it to the present case, I would, with the liberty thereby conceded to me, inquire with reference to all of the four issues here in debate, whether the costs incurred in relation to them, be they the costs of the appellants or of the respondents, were costs really incurred on the claim or its defence, or on the counterclaim or its defence, and I cannot myself doubt the answer to be that these costs were all of them incurred in relation to the claim and none of them in relation to the counterclaim.

It will of course be remembered that their claim was prosecuted by the respondents not only up to judgment, but as far as the Court of Appeal, and this inquiry must be so directed as to ascertain what in relation to these issues was the position and what was the risk of the two parties litigant, in a case so conducted.

To begin with the appellants, their position, I cannot doubt, was that unless they succeeded at the trial in establishing their allegations with regard to each of the four issues, judgment for the respondents on the claim must follow, while their own counterclaim would never arise. Further, when that counterclaim did become effective it would be a proceeding in which these issues would no longer remain as issues. They would already have been decided in the action in the appellants' favour.

As to the respondents, their position, conversely, may be stated with equal ease. Until they had established their allegations with reference to some one of the issues their claim in the action could not prevail. When however they had so far progressed then not only did their claim in the action succeed but, as a necessary corollary, the counterclaim against them at once disappeared.

The correctness of this view was well illustrated in the fortunes of the respondents' appeal from the judgment at the trial. Before the Court of Appeal they contended that as to one of the issues – that in relation to a guarantee – their view was right, and that by their contract they were under no duty to deliver, until the guarantee had been given. The Court of Appeal accepted that contention, with the result that, without more, the respondents' claim in the action was decreed and the appellants' cross-appeal from the order dismissing the counterclaim, was, without discussion, dismissed. The counterclaim had automatically collapsed.

To me therefore it appears clear that it was impossible, in the litigation as conducted, for these issues to arise on the counterclaim at all.

My Lords, it was on this view, taken by the learned judge at the close of his judgment, that he gave to the respondents their costs of the counterclaim. His assumption was that these costs, apart from any divided costs not here in debate, would carry only their costs of the question as to the appellants' damages which was peculiar to the counterclaim. By his present order he has, although by a somewhat different road, in substance reached the same result. For myself, I would be content to restore that order, for the reasons just given.

But, my Lords, other views of these issues have been taken. Lawrence LJ, for instance, is of opinion that, albeit in differing degrees, they are each one of them common both to the claim and the counterclaim. This also is in substance the view of Atkin LJ. The learned trial judge again is now of opinion that so much may truly be said of one issue, and some of your Lordships may possibly share one or other of these views.

I accordingly proceed to ascertain whether, even so, that ought to affect the result which I have reached on the other footing. The question now is whether on this fresh hypothesis the rule of taxation to be applied is that in *Saner v Bilton* [11 ChD 416], or whether, as the Court of Appeal have held, that rule should now be displaced in favour of one which would apportion, between the claim and the counterclaim, the costs of all issues common to both.

Upon this question it is quite academic to inquire whether it was open to the Court of Appeal, now, for the first time, at least avowedly, to depart in this matter from the rule in *Saner v Bilton* and, in effect, overrule *Wilson v Walters* [[1926] 1 KB 511], which had recently adopted it. I say this, because your Lordships are here quite untrammelled by authority and are in a position to choose for application now and for the future the rule which seems to be best.

And with the rest of your Lordships I am satisfied that no reason had been shown why the rule in *Saner v Bilton*, which has so long stood, should be departed from. Now that I have had the opportunity for full consideration that rule appears to me to be preferable to its proposed substitute. In its application to the present case, for instance, its operation is in every way satisfactory. Apart from any application of Order LXV, rule 2, it gives to both parties their costs of matters in which they have been respectively successful and leaves them liable only for the costs of those in which they have failed, in contrast with what would be the result of the apportionment rule – namely, that of the issues on which the respondents failed, not excepting that of fraudulent conspiracy, they would receive from the appellants a proportion of their costs of defeat while the appellants would themselves have to bear a proportion of their own costs of success. The fresh taxation shows that the modification made by the Court of Appeal on the principle of taxation followed by the Master has greatly qualified the amazing figures reached by him. But the improvement is still one of degree only, and I share with my noble and learned friend opposite his condemnation of the result. Moreover I am satisfied that such an outcome of the application of the apportionment rule would not be peculiar to the present case. It would, in a measure, always result from it.

But to that rule there is, I think, a further fundamental objection. I am not myself satisfied that those who favour its adoption have been sufficiently deterred by the difficulties in the way of its application. It is, as has already been pointed out, one thing to divide as between claim and counterclaim expenses incurred with reference to both, e.g., counsel's fees. It is quite another thing to apportion between the two the costs in relation to an issue common to both. If, as an example, I may again refer to the respondents' costs of the issue of fraudulent conspiracy, how with any result capable of rational justification could their costs of that charge which failed be apportioned between the claim and the counterclaim? I know not. And so, even if in less degree, of the other issues.

My Lords, Mr Atkinson did raise one objection to the rule in *Saner* v *Bilton* [11 ChD 416] which struck me as forcible. A rule, he said, is in principle wrong, which depends for its result so much upon the accident which of the two parties in a case like this, first commences proceedings. So far as regards the present litigation the criticism did not strike me as serious, because it is plain from even a superficial consideration of the learned judge's judgment at the trial that if in this litigation the appellants had, instead of the respondents, been plaintiffs, while he might have dismissed both claim and counterclaim – although I greatly doubt whether in such a litigation he would have adventured to dismiss the claim – it is certain that by reference to issues or in some other way he would have brought about the result as to costs which his judgment shows he intended and which, as at long last appears, he has achieved by the order he made in the action as now framed.

But, my Lords, I cannot doubt that Mr Atkinson's criticism of the *Saner* v *Bilton* [11 ChD 416] rule is well justified in its application to some cases. *Wilson* v *Walters* [[1926] 1 KB 511] may perhaps be referred to as one of these. The objection, however, is less serious than it looks. There is no obligation on the judge in such cases to dismiss both claim and counterclaim *with costs*. For the future he will presumably only do so when he is satisfied that an order in that form when worked out will in substance effect the result he desires. As Fry J said in *Saner* v *Bilton* "the Court can in every case give special directions which may vary the rule" and this appeal will not be without permanent utility if it brings home to learned judges the necessity, in cases like these, of adjusting critically their orders as to costs if these orders are not sometimes to produce results at once unintentional and unjust.

On the whole case I am of opinion that the order appealed from should be discharged and that of MacKinnon J restored.

VISCOUNT DUNEDIN: My Lords, I am glad that in this case there is no difference of opinion between my colleagues who are members of the

English Bar. I should have been sorry indeed to have been compelled to give a casting vote on a point which is essentially one of English practice. I may however permit myself two observations. The result at which your Lordships have arrived seems to me the only result which is consistent with the justice of the case. Further, had the same case arisen in Scotland, where the whole practice as to the form of interlocutors dealing with expenses, and the duties of the auditor thereon arising, is quite different – a practice which it is not hujus loci to describe – the result would have been the same as that which is now attained.

LORD SHAW OF DUNFERMLINE: My Lords, I feel thoroughly satisfied with the analysis of the decisions affecting this point of English practice, made by the noble and learned and lamented Viscount who occupied the Woolsack during the hearing and whose opinion has been read.

In the course of the able address of Mr Van den Berg, counsel for the appellant, I put to him a question in order to test in the concrete what were the real topics of contest between the parties on which cost had been incurred. There is a book of the evidence led and of the documents produced in this litigation. It measures 832 pages. My question was: How much of that was occupied with matter relevant to or necessitated by the counterclaim? The answer was that out of the 832 pages only ten were so occupied. The learned counsel for the respondent very faintly challenged this proportion and thought ten pages to be rather too slender an allowance.

To deal with such a case on the footing adopted by the Court of Appeal would manifestly lead to a state of matters in which the counterclaim costs awarded would bear no real relation to the costs which the counterclaim actually caused. The other course, and that now proposed, will very largely avoid such a result; and it is, I cannot doubt, the course supported by the main body of authority in England. I agree to the motion to be submitted to the House, and I may be allowed to add further that I concur in the observations of Lord Dunedin.

Order of the Court of Appeal reversed, and judgment of MacKinnon J restored. The respondents to pay the costs in the Court of Appeal, and also the costs of the appeal to this House. Cause remitted back to the King's Bench Division to do therein as shall be just and consistent with this judgment.

Solicitors for the appellants: *Cosmo, Cran & Co.*
Solicitors for the respondents: *Dehn & Lauderdale.*

Cope
v
United Dairies (London) Ltd

Queen's Bench Division
15 March 1963

Megaw J

Headnote

The case confirmed that a Taxing Officer could not properly refuse to carry out an order for taxation in whole or in part because he considered it to be wrong or ultra vires. It also considered the position where a legally aided party whose certificate had been discharged after a writ had been issued and pleadings had closed and who thereafter had taken no further part in the proceedings, which were terminated by an order dismissing the action "with costs for want of prosecution and the defendants' costs be taxed and paid by the Plaintiff … ".

---

15 March. MEGAW J read the following judgment: On 26 April 1961, a legal aid certificate was issued to the plaintiff in respect of proceedings by him against the defendants, claiming damages for personal injuries said to have been sustained while he was employed by the defendants. A writ was issued and pleadings were delivered. On 27 April 1962, the plaintiff's legal aid certificate was discharged. The plaintiff thereafter took no further steps in the action, but no application was made by him or on his behalf for discontinuance. On 4 June 1962, a summons was issued by the defendants' solicitors in the following terms. It asked for

> "an order that this action be dismissed with costs for want of prosecution, the plaintiff having failed to issue a summons for directions pursuant to R.S.C., Ord 30, r 1, and that the defendants' costs be taxed and paid by the plaintiff."

The summons was heard by Master Ritchie on 8 June 1962. The plaintiff did not appear and was not represented. The defendants were represented by their solicitors, who fairly and properly informed the master that the plaintiff had had a legal aid certificate and that it had been discharged. The master made an order in the following terms:

> "It is ordered that, unless the plaintiff issues a summons for directions within twenty-one days from the date of this order, this action be dismissed with costs

for want of prosecution and the defendants' costs be taxed and paid by the plaintiff, and that the costs of this application be the defendants' costs in any event."

The plaintiff was thereafter notified of the order and of the intended taxation of costs.

When the defendants' solicitors brought in their bill of costs for taxation, they included therein the whole of the costs of the action, including the costs incurred by them during the period when the plaintiff had his legal aid certificate. The taxing officer refused to allow any items in the bill referable to the period between the granting and the discharge of the legal aid certificate. The balance which he allowed, referable to the period after the discharge of the legal aid certificate, was £46 5s 8d. The defendants raised objections to the disallowances. On review, the senior taxing master overruled the objections. The defendants now ask for a review under rule 35 of the Supreme Court Costs Rules 1959. I have been very much assisted by the careful and able arguments presented yesterday in chambers by counsel for the defendants, and by counsel who was instructed by the Law Society on my suggestion that it would be helpful if counsel were to be instructed as amicus curiae, in view of the nature of the issues raised. At the request of the defendants, I adjourned the application into open court for judgment.

The defendants submit that the senior taxing master exceeded his jurisdiction. They say that the order made by Master Ritchie was clear and unambiguous; and that, even if the taxing master thought that it was wrong or ultra vires, he had no option but to comply. He was not entitled to disallow certain items on the ground that they were wrongly or irregularly made the subject of taxation. If the order were wrong, the only remedy would have been by way of appeal from that order to the judge in chambers. No such appeal had been made. The defendants further submitted that Master Ritchie's order was not wrong, irregular or ultra vires.

Counsel for the Law Society agreed that the taxing master could not properly refuse to carry out an order for taxation, in whole or in part, because he considered it to be wrong or ultra vires, and that the same applies to this court on a review. With that proposition, I agree. Counsel instructed by the Law Society submitted, however, that what the senior taxing master did in this case was right; not because he had any jurisdiction to refuse to carry out a taxation as directed, but because, in the circumstances, on the true construction of Master Ritchie's order of 8 June 1962, it required taxation only of those costs which were incurred outside the period during which the legal aid certificate was in force. In my judgment, that contention is right.

Section 2(2) of the Legal Aid and Advice Act 1949 provides as follows:

"Where a person receives legal aid in connexion with any proceedings ... (e) his liability by virtue of an order for costs made against him with respect to the proceedings shall not exceed the amount (if any) which is a reasonable one for him to pay having regard to all the circumstances, including the means of all the parties and their conduct in connexion with the dispute."

Section 2(3) provides:

"Regulations shall make provision as to the court, tribunal or person by whom the amount referred to in para. (e) of the last foregoing subsection is to be determined and the extent to which any determination thereof is to be final."

Regulation 13(1) of the Legal Aid (General) Regulations 1962, which deals with the position of a person who has once been legally aided but whose certificate has, as here, been discharged, provides:

"Subject to the provisions of this regulation, a person whose certificate is revoked shall be deemed never to have been an assisted person in relation to the claim or proceedings to which the certificate related, and a person whose certificate is discharged shall, from the date of discharge, cease to be an assisted person in the claim or proceedings."

That paragraph is, however, qualified as regards costs by regulation 13(6). The relevant part of that paragraph provides:

"Where a certificate has been discharged ... and where he [that is the person who had the certificate] continues to assert or dispute the claim or to take, defend or be a party to the proceedings to which the certificate related ... (b) those provisions of section 2 of the Act which relate to an assisted person's liability by virtue of an order for costs made against him shall apply in so far as the costs were incurred while he was an assisted person."

The effect is that, in relation to the plaintiff's liability for the defendant's costs incurred in the period in which he was an assisted person, he is to be treated, for the purposes of sections 2(2)(e) and 2(3) of the Act, and regulation 18 made thereunder, as an assisted person. Regulation 18(1) is as follows:

"Where an order for costs is made against an assisted person, the determination of the amount of his liability for costs in accordance with section 2(2)(e) of the Act shall be made at the trial or hearing of the action, cause or matter."

Then there is a proviso which is here irrelevant. I should also read regulation 18(5):

"Where an assisted person serves notice of discontinuance or where an order for costs is made against him by reason of his default of appearance or defence or by reason of summary judgment, or upon application by him for leave to discontinue, he shall be liable for the full amount of the costs, unless he makes an application for determination of the amount of his liability under the provisions of section 2(2)(e) of the Act, in which case the court may make any such order for payment as may be made in determining an assisted person's liability by virtue of an order for costs made against him at a trial or hearing of an action, cause or matter, and shall to the same extent be final."

That paragraph has no direct application here, first, possibly, because it applies to an assisted person and not to one who has ceased to be an assisted person; and, secondly, because, perhaps by inadvertence, it does not refer to the termination of proceedings by an order for dismissal for want of prosecution. There is thus no provision, in the circumstances of this case, making the plaintiff liable for the full amount of the costs unless he makes application for the determination of the amount of his liability under section 2(2)(e) of the Legal Aid and Advice Act 1949. It may well be that such a provision would not be appropriate in the case of a person whose certificate has been discharged, since he might have no legal advice and could not fairly be expected to know of, and assert, his right to seek a reduction of his liability for the full amount of costs incurred while he was an assisted person.

Regulation 18(5) is, however, relevant in one way to the present issue. It throws light on the meaning of "the trial or hearing of the action, cause or matter" in regulation 18(1). Paragraph (5) uses those same words in, I think, deliberate contrast with other methods of putting an end to proceedings, such as discontinuance, default of appearance or summary judgment. That indicates that the dismissal of an action for want of prosecution is not comprehended within the words "trial or hearing of the action, cause or matter" in regulation 18(1). It follows that there never has been a trial or hearing of the action in this case. Therefore, the mandatory provision of regulation 18(1) for the determination of the amount of the plaintiff's liability for costs incurred during the period covered by the legal aid certificate could not be complied with.

Counsel for the defendants submitted that, although there was not a "trial or hearing of the action" on 8 June 1962, when Master Ritchie made the order for dismissal of the action at the end of twenty-one days, unless the plaintiff meanwhile should issue a summons for directions, nevertheless there was a notional "trial or hearing of the action" when the twenty-one days expired and the condition subsequent was fulfilled. He said that "trial or hearing of the action" meant no more than "the final determination of the matter". He pointed out that, if it were otherwise, there would be real difficulties in the way of a non-assisted person, in circumstances such as the present, obtaining a determination of the amount of costs payable by the plaintiff in respect of the legal aid certificate period. He said that the suggestion of counsel for the Law Society that the defendants could have themselves issued a summons for directions and obtained directions and thereafter a judgment by default, was unrealistic. It would necessarily involve the incurring of further, probably irrecoverable, costs. That may, indeed, be so on the regulations as they stand, and it may well be unsatisfactory. But I am unable to hold that the coming into effect of the dismissal of the action twenty-one days after the order of 8 June 1962, was a "trial or hearing of the action". It is inconsistent with any ordinary, or, I think, any possible, meaning of the words. It is inconsistent with the indication of the meaning of the words to be derived from regulation 18(5).

Counsel for the Law Society, rightly as I think, submits that, where there is a determination of costs in an action to which an assisted person is a party, that determination involves two phases, though they sometimes take place at the same time. The first phase is the determination by the court, in its discretion, whether or not it is proper that an order for costs should be made against the assisted person. This phase, by reason of section 1(7) of the Act, is carried out without reference to any consideration as to the party being, or having ever been, an assisted person. The second phase, which arises in relation to a person who is, or has been, assisted, is the separate determination as to the amount, if any, of the liability for costs which the assisted person should be ordered to pay. Frequently, in fact, these two phases fall to be dealt with at different stages. Thus, where costs are awarded against an assisted person on an interlocutory application, the amount must not be assessed at that stage. This is clearly established by *Wozniak* v *Wozniak* [[1953] 1 All ER 1192; [1953] P 179]. The doctrine of the two phases is implicit in the judgment of the Court of Appeal in *Blatcher* v *Heaysman* [[1960] 2 All ER 721]. It is reflected in the opening words of regula tion 18(1), and, I think, in section 2(2)(e) of the Act.

For the reasons which I have given, if Master Ritchie purported to make an order determining the amount of the plaintiff's liability for costs in respect of the period when he had a legal aid certificate, he had no jurisdiction to do so, because this could only be done – and had to be done – "at the trial or hearing of the action". Further, if he purported to do so, I should not regard an order for costs in the form of the order made by the learned master as constituting "a determination of the amount of the plaintiff's liability for costs" in respect of the legal aid certificate period. There is, in the order, no determination of amount. If, indeed, that was the meaning and effect of the order, the taxing master would have been wrong in failing to carry it out, and I should have had no power to uphold the taxing master's decision. The plaintiff's only remedy would be to seek leave to appeal out of time and to ask that the order as to costs be set aside or varied. However, I agree with the submission of counsel for the Law Society that that was not the meaning or effect of Master Ritchie's order. All that the master was asked to do by the defendants' summons, and all that he did and purported to do by his order was, first, to make the general order as to costs, referable to the period subsequent to the discharge of the legal aid certificate; and, secondly, in relation to the costs of the period covered by the legal aid certificate, to deal with the first phase, with which alone he had jurisdiction to deal. He was not invited to make, and could not properly make, and did not purport to make, any determination of the amount of the plaintiff's liability for costs incurred during the currency of the legal aid certificate. Such a determination has never been made, and, in view of the course of the proceedings, could never have been made under the Regulations as they now are. The senior taxing master, therefore, has properly given effect to Master Ritchie's order in accordance with its true meaning. He could not himself determine the amount of the costs during the legal aid period, and he could not properly allow any such costs on taxation, since they had never been assessed as required by the Legal Aid and Advice Act 1949 and the Legal Aid (General) Regulations 1962. Master Ritchie's order did not require him to do so.

I cannot accept counsel for the defendants' argument that, prima facie, an assisted person is obliged to pay the whole costs, and that it is up to him, if he sees fit, to invoke the special protection given by the Act of 1949 to an assisted person. Indeed, there was no time in the course of these proceedings when he could have required such a determination. The special protection is the responsibility of the court, whether or not the assisted person, or previously assisted person, invokes it. It is only by virtue of the special provisions of regulation 18(5) that it ever falls on the assisted person to invoke that protection. Regulation 18(5) is not applicable here. Accordingly, though perhaps for rather different reasons from those given by the senior taxing master, I hold that his disallowance of the items which he disallowed on this bill of costs was right.

I should add that it will be clear from what I have already said that, in my view, the Regulations, and in particular regulation 18(1) and (5), may merit reconsideration, especially with regard to the time and manner of the determination of a previously assisted person's costs where, after the discharge of his legal aid certificate, the action is dismissed for want of prosecution. If I am right in this judgment, the regulations may involve hardship on the non-assisted party. If I should be wrong in this judgment, the formerly assisted person, with no available legal advice, may be deprived of the protection which I think that the Legal Aid and Advice Act 1949 intended that he should have.

Application dismissed. Leave to appeal to the Court of Appeal.

J H Hames as amicus curiae.
A Lipfriend and *Eleanor Platt* for the defendants.

Simpsons Motor Sales (London) Ltd
v
Hendon Corporation (No 2)

Chancery Division
3, 4 November 1964

Headnote

When considering the amount of counsel's fees to be allowed inter partes the Taxing Masters and Judges on reviews of taxation must determine what he considered to be the proper figure taking into account his own knowledge and experience. In particular, one must envisage a hypothetical counsel capable of conducting a particular case effectively but "unable or unwilling to insist on the particular high fee sometimes demanded by counsel of pre-eminent reputation".

Adjourned summons

The following statement of the facts is taken from the judgment of Pennycuick J.

In an action, heard by Buckley J on all or part of four days in January, 1962, judgment was given in favour of the plaintiff company, Simpsons Motor Sales (London) Ltd. The appeal was heard on all or part of eight days in June, 1962, when judgment was given allowing the appeal with costs in favour of the defendant corporation, Hendon Corporation [[1963] Ch 57, CA]. It was those costs to which the present application related. Subsequently the plaintiff company appealed to the House of Lords [[1963] 2 WLR 1187; [1963] 2 All ER 484, HL(E)], and this appeal was dismissed after a hearing which lasted all or part of six days. The issue in the action was whether a certain compulsory purchase order made by the corporation in 1952 remained effective in changed circumstances prevailing in 1959. There was a very considerable mass of documents. Certain facts were agreed and there was no cross-examination of witnesses. It appeared that such issues of fact as arose were in the nature of the proper inferences to be drawn from the documents and from particular facts not themselves in dispute. The issues of law were novel and manifestly difficult. The sum at stake was substantial but not enormous. In the event, the corporation became entitled to acquire for £4,470 a site for which the plaintiff company in 1959 had paid £20,000.

In due course, the corporation brought in its bills of costs for taxation.

Those included, as regards each hearing, i.e., that in the Chancery Division and that in the Court of Appeal, brief fee 500 guineas for the corporation's leader and brief fee 333$^1/_3$ guineas to the junior, with refreshers for the appropriate number of days on the five-hour basis at the rate of 100 guineas a day for the leader and 66$^2/_3$ guineas a day for the junior. The clerks' fees were not in issue. The amount paid to the junior represented two-thirds of that paid to the leader and it was accepted on behalf of the plaintiff company that, whatever figure was allowed in respect of the leader's fees, the two-third ratio should be applied to the junior's fees. The bills included a large number of other items, some of which were disallowed in whole or in part, with which the application was not concerned. The taxing master allowed in full the fees paid by the corporation to its counsel.

The plaintiff company lodged its objections, and these, after a statement as to the general nature and course of the action, the time taken by the hearings, and so forth, proceeded as follows:

"The plaintiffs were represented by [a leader] of the Chancery Bar who was paid (as between solicitor and own client) a brief fee in the court below, Court of Appeal and House of Lords of 400 guineas with refresher fees of 100 guineas and the junior counsel was paid the usual two-thirds. On the taxation of the [corporation's] costs in respect of the appeal to the House of Lords the Clerk of the Parliaments after hearing the arguments put forward in support of and in opposition to counsels' brief fees and refresher fees and due deliberation allowed the brief fee to leading counsel for the [corporation] (as between party and party) of 300 guineas with refreshers of 75 guineas with the usual two-thirds to the junior counsel. The burden on counsel for the [corporation] was no heavier in the court of first instance or Court of Appeal than in the appeal before the House of Lords and it is respectfully submitted that as between party and party the brief fees and refresher fees allowed to leading and junior counsel in respect of the hearing before Buckley J and hearing the Court of Appeal are excessive."

It is not in dispute that the leader's brief fee for the plaintiff company was in fact only 400 guineas or that in the House of Lords 300 guineas only was allowed for the corporation's leader's fees on taxation with an appropriate proportion for the junior. The corporation lodged its answers which did not require to be set out.

On 26 May 1964, the taxing master gave his own answers disallowing the plaintiff company's objections. After reciting the purport of the order for taxation the master proceeded as follows:

"2. Objections.   (1) The plaintiffs object, on the ground that they are excessive, to the allowance of a brief fee of 500 guineas with further fees of 100 guineas a day to leading counsel in both courts ... (2) The plaintiffs' objections are founded on three contentions, namely that: (1) Lesser brief fees were paid to their counsel; (2) Lesser fees were allowed to the [corporation] on the taxation of their costs of the plaintiffs' unsuccessful appeal to the House of Lords; (3) No oral evidence was adduced in the Chancery Division where this witness action was dealt with on the basis of agreed documents with which counsel was solely concerned, and the time occupied by the hearing, including judgment, was only 15 hours 3 minutes; The [corporation] have delivered answers dated 20 February 1964, to the plaintiffs' objections.

3. As to the first contention. (1) The plaintiffs paid their leading counsel 400 guineas on the brief in the Chancery Division, the Court of Appeal and in the House of Lords with further fees of 100 guineas a day but say that these sums were only paid on a 'solicitor and own client' basis. (2) Whilst the fees paid by one party to counsel may be some guide to the fees to be allowed to counsel for the opposing party it is not a sound principle of taxation to use such fees as the appropriate yardstick since many other considerations have to be taken into account. (3) It is an incorrect principle of taxation that on a 'party and party' basis the fee to be allowed to leading and junior counsel must be less than the amount marked on their respective briefs on the ground that the fees marked are on a 'solicitor and own client' basis. To the extent that the fee marked on counsel's brief, with the client's authority, represents the amount the client is liable to reimburse his solicitor that fee is on a 'solicitor and own client' basis. If however it also represents the 'rate for the job' and is not a special fee to secure the services of a particular counsel, which the case did not require, e.g., because of its lack of weight and importance, that fee is the fee to be allowed on a 'party and party' basis.

4. As to the second contention. It is not a sound principle of taxation to adopt the fees allowed or allowable 'inter partes' in the House of Lords as the appropriate yardstick on the taxing of counsel's fees in the High Court of Justice or in the Court of Appeal.

5. As to the third contention. (1) The plaintiffs on the taxation before me stated that this action was a town planning inquiry with no special features and accordingly the proper fee to be allowed to leading counsel on the brief was 300 guineas with further fees of 50 guineas a day and the appropriate two-thirds allowance for junior counsel. If the plaintiffs are correct as to the type of case involved I would have allowed for leading counsel in this case a brief fee of 350 guineas with further fees of 100 guineas a day. (2) I did not accept this contention for the following reasons: – A. The brief delivered to leading counsel in the Chancery Division comprised: – (i) The brief proper, the case to counsel to advise on evidence in which the facts are set out, and the pleadings ... (ii) The agreed bundle of documents ... (iii) The documents disclosed in the [corporation's] affidavit of documents dated 17 May 1960, including those for which privilege has been claimed ... (iv) Various agreed plans, planning applications, documents relating to the planning position and 3 other folders ...

B.   The importance of the matter.

The fact that the plaintiffs pursued their action to the House of Lords is evidence enough of the importance they attached to it. The transcript of the judgment of Buckley J in the Chancery Division illustrates the importance of the case to the [corporation], namely: – Whether by reason first of the indulgence granted by the [corporation] to the plaintiffs ... and subsequently by the acceptance by the [corporation] that there was little likelihood of their being able to develop the North Road, Burnt Oak area, ... the [corporation] had abandoned their intention to make use of the notice to treat and their rights thereunder and were now forced to apply de novo for a compulsory purchase order which, as the result of the change of circumstances that had taken place since 13 August 1952 (when the notice to treat was served), they would not, or would very probably not, be successful in obtaining ...

7. Conclusion.   (1) In reviewing my taxation when the parties appeared before me I concluded: first, that the strength of the objections turned on the validity or otherwise of the submission that this was an ordinary town planning case meriting an ordinary fee by town planning standards, and, secondly, that there was sufficient evidence to enable me, without hesitation, to reject the plaintiffs' submission. (2) For all the above reasons I disallow the plaintiffs' objections."

The plaintiff company applied under the Supreme Court Costs Rules 1959, rule 35, for a review of the taxing master's decision. Neither of the counsel appearing on the present application had appeared in the earlier hearings.

No cases, other than those cited in the judgment, were cited in argument.

[The summons was heard in chambers and judgment was delivered in open court.]

4 November. PENNYCUICK J: This is an application by Simpsons Motor Sales (London) Ltd, the plaintiff in the action with which this application is concerned, to review the taxation of the bills of costs of the Hendon Corporation, the defendant in the action, as allowed by the taxing master, Graham Greene. The application is concerned solely with the amount allowed by the taxing master for the fees of counsel for the corporation in the successive hearings in the Chancery Division and the Court of Appeal.

[His Lordship stated the facts as set out above and continued:] I propose for simplicity to refer henceforward only to the fees of leading counsel. At the hearing before me Mr Harman for the plaintiff company contended that, when one looks at all the relevant circumstances, not more than 300 guineas should be allowed in respect of fees. He relied on the three particular matters set out by the taxing master in paragraph 2 of his answer, but made it clear that these are merely certain of the relevant circumstances and not the sole grounds for his contentions. Mr Bell, for the corporation, supported the taxing master's conclusions but, like Mr Harman, did not confine his contentions to the specific points dealt with by the taxing master.

Taxation of costs is now governed by the Supreme Court Costs Rules 1959. [His Lordship read rule 28, as set out above, and continued:] It will be remembered that under rule 35 a party may now apply to a judge for a review of the taxing master's decision if dissatisfied with the amount allowed in respect of any item. Previously, there was in general no review on amount, and no doubt for this reason there is an absence of judicial authority in connection with the amount of counsel's fees on a party and party taxation. One finds broad statements of principle such as that of Malins V-C in *Smith* v *Buller* [(1875) LR 19 Eq 473 at 475], quoted with approval by Devlin LJ in *Berry* v *British Transport Commission* [[1962] 1 QB 306 at 322; [1961] 3 WLR 450; [1961] 3 All ER 65, CA]. In view of the terms of rule 28(2) the words "or proper for the attainment of justice or for enforcing or defending the rights of the party whose costs are being taxed" must, I think, now be read in after the word "necessary" in the statement of principle made by Malins V-C. I have not been referred to any case upon the amount of counsel's fees on a party and party taxation. *In re Grimthorpe* [[1958] Ch 615; [1958] 1 WLR 381; [1958] 1 All ER 765] and *In re Whitley, decd* [[1962] 1 WLR 922; [1962] 3 All ER 45] are concerned with taxation of the costs of trustees as such.

One must then apply the words of rule 28(2) to the particular circumstances as best one can. Mr Harman contended that the proper measure for counsel's fees is such a fee as counsel competent in the field concerned would be content to take upon the brief. Mr Bell, for the corporation, contended that the proper measure is such a fee as counsel appropriate to the brief would be content to take upon the brief. As used by counsel in argument these expressions come, I think, more or less to the same thing. In other words, one must envisage an hypothetical counsel capable of conducting the particular case effectively but unable or unwilling to insist on the particular high fee sometimes demanded by counsel of pre-eminent reputation. Then one must estimate what fee this hypothetical character would be content to take on the brief. I am prepared to apply this measure as a test in the present case, but it is necessary to emphasise that the rule itself uses the words "necessary or proper for the attainment of justice or for enforcing or defending the rights of the party whose costs are being taxed" and that the same measure may not always be applicable in the infinite variety of cases which can arise. There is, in the nature of things, no precise standard of measurement. The taxing master, employing his knowledge and experience, determines what he considers the right figure. The judge in his turn must, I think, consider whether upon his own knowledge and experience the figure adopted by the taxing master falls above the upper or below the lower limit of the range within which in his view the proper figure would come. If, and only if, it does fall above or below those limits, he should substitute his own figure. Mr Harman adumbrated the contention that every leading counsel practising in a particular field should be regarded as competent to conduct a case in that field however heavy and difficult. That contention is, I think, for obvious reasons which it would be invidious to elaborate, untenable, and Mr Harman did not seriously seek to maintain it. What he did maintain with force and truth is that in any field there may be, and generally are, a number of counsel outside the best known names who are perfectly competent to conduct a heavy and difficult case in that field.

To return to the present case, it is, I think, abundantly clear that it could only have been effectively conducted by leading counsel of high calibre. The corporation like the plaintiff company employed counsel of high calibre. The corporation's leader, or his clerk, required a fee of 500 guineas. That sum the taxing master held, and Mr Bell contends, is to be treated as the proper one to be allowed on taxation. Looking simply at the words of rule 28(2), I have reached the conclusion that in all the circumstances of this case 500 guineas was a proper fee for defending the rights of the corporation. A fee of 500 guineas is by some standards a high one, but the fees charged by counsel of high calibre are indeed, and rightly, high, and it does not seem to me that 500 guineas is beyond what is proper in all the circumstances of this particular case. Mr Harman does not suggest that the corporation's leader's services could have been obtained for a less figure. His contention runs on these lines: the corporation's leader he says, truly, is one of the pre-eminent leaders of the bar and his fees are correspondingly high. It would, he says, have been possible to find a less eminent leader who would be competent to conduct this case and who would have been willing to do so for a much lower fee. He puts the fee at 300 guineas. So, applying the measure which he has propounded, 300 guineas is the proper amount to be allowed. In the nature of things, there is no means of establishing whether in fact a leader of the requisite capacity but less pre-eminent reputation could have been found to take the brief at a lower fee as suggested. One can only proceed by estimation based on such knowledge and experience as one possesses. On the best consideration I can give the matter, I am not myself persuaded that this particular fee is higher than one would expect leading counsel competent to conduct this particular case to charge for his services. Equally, I do not think this fee should be regarded as a particularly high one occasioned by the leader's pre-eminent reputation.

The point does not admit of much elaboration, but I must answer in conclusion certain specific points taken by Mr Harman. First, he naturally stresses the fact that the plaintiff company's leader, who was also counsel of high calibre, was content to accept 400 guineas only upon his brief for the plaintiff company. This is certainly a factor of weight but not, I think, by any means conclusive. In the ordinary course of events it often happens that the clerks to counsel of comparable degree ask for rather different fees, but I do not think that in these circumstances one is justified without more ado in saying that one counsel has asked too much. It can equally be said that the other has asked too little. The truth is that there is no exact figure which can be said to represent the proper fee. I agree with the taxing master's comment that it is not a sound principle of taxation to treat the fee paid by the other party as the appropriate yardstick; indeed, the application of such a principle would lead to obviously undesirable consequences. Secondly, again there is weight in the fact that the Clerk of the Parliaments only allowed 300 guineas on the corporation's leader's brief in the House of Lords taxation. It is not suggested that in this respect the House of Lords taxation has any pre-eminence as such, but one must no doubt give weight to the figure adopted by the officer concerned in the taxation. Notwithstanding the Clerk of the

Parliaments' view, I am myself content to treat the taxing master's figure as right in the present case. Thirdly, it was pointed out that this case may have been, and indeed probably was, of great importance to the corporation in relation to its dealings not only with the plaintiff company but with other land-owners. I agree that the corporation could not properly throw upon the plaintiff company any costs it incurred for a purpose other than the defence of the particular action, but I do not think I should be justified in concluding that the corporation has in fact paid a fee to their leader excessive to the requirements of this particular case. It would really be guess-work to scale down the leader's fee on this account.

I propose accordingly to dismiss this present application. My reasons in great part tally with those of the taxing master though I have expressed them in rather a different way.

Application dismissed with costs.

J L Harman for the plaintiff company.
Ronald M Bell for the corporation.

Re Nossen's Patent

Chancery Division
2, 3, 28 October 1968

Lloyd-Jacob J
sitting with
Master Graham-Green
and Sir Denys Hicks as assessors

Headnote

Re: Nossens' Letter Patent is an important case on the definition
of an expert witness as being a person having appropriate
professional qualifications or expertise who is brought into a case
to give his expert opinion as to matters in issue. The case also
held that the mere fact that the expert is an employee of a party
does not disqualify him from being treated and remunerated as
an expert.

LLOYD-JACOB J: These are cross-applications by summons for the review of
the taxation of costs in an abandoned originating motion made pursuant to
the provisions of section 48 of the Patents Act 1949, in respect of the alleged
user by the United Kingdom Atomic Energy Authority (called the authority)
of the invention, the subject of letters patent no 789,446, in the name of
Ernest Samuel Nossen (called the applicant). In this motion an order was
made requiring the applicant to find security for costs in the amount of
£5,000, and the applicant's eventual inability to comply with such order led
to dismissal of the motion and an order that the applicant pay the authority's
taxed costs.

The authority submitted a bill which included two items to which the
applicant particularly objected, namely: £675 solicitors' charges for perusing
and considering the papers submitted; and £26,864 for expenditure on
research and experiments relating to the preparation of the defence. The
taxing master allowed £600 in respect of the former and £12,201 in respect
of the latter. The applicant urges that the latter amount should be wholly
struck out or alternatively substantially diminished as unnecessary,
premature and extravagant and, as the perusal and consideration to which
the former relates included the matters to which the experimentation figure
relates, this figure of £600 too should be consequentially reduced. By their
cross-summons, the authority seek the restoration of their original figure of
£26,864 in respect of the second item.

The first of these two items presents no real difficulty. The research and experiment item plainly relates to matters relevant to the issue of validity and infringement set out in the authority's pleadings and, wholly irrespective of the objection that the expenditure so incurred was vis-à-vis the applicant premature or extravagant, the material provided by such expenditure was in fact available for submission to the authority's legal advisers and the propriety and timing of such submission of it cannot fairly be questioned. The issues involved the consideration of matters such scientific technicality and complexity and the amount at stake (estimated as being in excess of £500,000) so substantial, that the attention given by the solicitors to the documents in the case was by no means excessive and, subject to the slight reduction he applied to the total charge as a matter of detail and not principle, the master was plainly correct in approving its inclusion. His decision in this respect must be endorsed.

For the consideration of the second item, some account of the history of the whole matter needs to be stated. Initially, the applicant, being minded to submit for consideration by the court the activities of the authority in the thermal decomposition of metallic nitrates which he asserted involved the employment of his patented invention, commenced by writ, dated 7 December 1961, proceedings for infringement of letters patent no 789,446, naming the authority as defendants. The defence, filed on 6 February 1962, by the authority, included the plea that the activities were undertaken pursuant to a written authority given by the Lord President of the Council, a plea which, if established, would, by reason of the provisions of section 46 of the Act, justify the use by the authority of the applicant's invention subject to a right of compensation secured by the appropriate procedure under section 48. By notice dated 6 December 1962, the applicant discontinued the action and incurred an obligation to pay the authority's taxed costs.

During the pendency of this action, the authority had engaged Professor Addison, Professor of Inorganic Chemistry at Nottingham University, as a consultant, who, after consultation with some of the technical staff of the authority, drew up a programme of experimental work intended to investigate: (i) the scope of an exclusion set out in the main claim of the letters patent in suit; and (ii) the accuracy of a representation appearing in the body of the specification. After the commencement of this experimental work, counsel for the authority was consulted and he, aware as he was of the effectiveness of the plea that written authority of the Lord President had been obtained, advised as follows in March 1962:

> "Certain experiments have been suggested that would be both expensive and time consuming; they may be necessary but I would not commit my clients to carry them out until I have had a full technical discussion."

The experimental work having been started it appears that the authority decided to continue it after the action was discontinued in December 1962 in the expectation that proceedings would be brought under section 48 and that the issues of validity and infringement would have to be fought.

So far as can be ascertained from the documents in the case, the initial experimentation was conducted at Nottingham University and the results obtained appeared to confirm the authority's objections. In consequence comparable experiments, but on a pilot plant scale, were carried out at the authority's plant and this disclosed the advisability of still further experimentation on a substantially larger scale, which additional work was pursued at both Springfields and Harwell until it ceased when an order to stay proceedings was made in the originating motion on 22 November 1963. From Schedule D to Mr Peachey's statement of 17 November 1966 the work at Harwell appears to have been mainly concerned with investigation after 6 December 1962. The expenditure on experiments therefore covers three periods: (i) From 20 December 1961 to 6 December 1962, whilst the action was pending; (ii) from 6 December 1962 to 4 March 1963, that is, between the date of discontinuance of the action and the issue of the originating motion; and (iii) from 4 March 1963 to 22 November 1963, when the stay of proceedings was ordered.

So far as concerns the first of these three periods, the experimentation was directly related to the issues of validity and infringement pleaded by the respondents in the action. If the costs thereof can be made chargeable to the applicant, it can only be because they were reasonably and properly incurred in actual or threatened proceedings. As the action was an actual proceeding during that period, the order for costs made in the authority's favour in that action provided the proper opportunity to recover them and failure to take advantage of it cannot now be remedied. The reasonableness of the authority's expectation that the applicant would persist in a claim for user of his invention does not establish the existence of any threat by the applicant of section 46 proceedings at the time when the expense was incurred and the taxing master cannot be criticised for his decision to exclude from the bill the items which fell within this first period.

So far as concerns the second period, the allowance of costs incurred before the actual initiation of legal proceedings is within the discretion of the taxing master, who must of course consider whether such costs were incurred at a time when it was right and proper that the outlay should be made in order to safeguard the position of a threatened potential litigant and was necessary for the purpose of obtaining matter of use and service to the party at the trial. The discontinuance of the action cannot, having regard to the special plea of Crown authorised user made therein, be deemed to amount to a withdrawal of the allegation that user by the authority of the applicant's invention had taken place, and it was plainly reasonable for the authority to avoid the expense and delay of an interruption of a planned programme of experimentation so long as that allegation constituted a threat of proceedings. That it did so is abundantly confirmed by the issuance of the originating motion within three months of the discontinuance. That the results obtained from the experimentation would be of service at the trial is proved by the affidavit of Professor Addison sworn on 9 October 1968, and to the extent to which investigation at Nottingham and Springfields had given a complete picture of the nitrate decomposition in the authority's processing it was in no way extravagant. Counsel's opinion on postponement of experimentation, given at a time when an effective statutory answer to the applicant's claim in the action appeared to have every prospect of success, cannot fairly be accepted as applicable once controversy on the issues of validity and infringement appeared unavoidable, although it should have had a cautionary effect when extension of the initial types of experimentation came to be considered. The main expense attributable to this extension fell in the third period, during which investigation of the mechanism of nitrate decomposition by hydrolysis as distinct from identification of its products required the substantial transfer of the work to the research group at Harwell. It is plain enough that the authority, in the normal development of their activities and because of their concern to understand fully the reactions taking place, could quite fairly and properly decide on research into hydrolysis, but this does not provide any basis for treating the cost or part of it as chargeable to the applicant. Nor, when the opportunity to give the applicant notice of the escalating scale of experimentation was provided by the application for security for costs and supported by evidence, did the authority disclose any intention to treat the additional expense already incurred as properly chargeable to the other party in the event of dismissal of the motion.

Whilst it would not be correct to treat the provisions of RSC Order 103, rule 26(2)(f) which relates to directions proper to be given by the court after a right to give notice of trial in a patent matter has been created, as establishing either directly or by implication any ban on chargeable experimentation prior to the summons for directions, it does indicate not only a mutual interest between the parties in experiments conducted by either for the purpose of eliciting matter intended to be of use and service at the trial, but also the desirability of defining and limiting the issues to which such experiments may be directed. Save, therefore, for such exploratory work as is required for the adequate framing of the pleadings, it is only reasonable to defer or rather to refrain from initiating further experimentation until after a clarification of the technical matters genuinely in issue between the parties has been attempted. This was not done and the investigation at Harwell into the changes undergone in the solid phase of uranyl nitrate hydrate decomposition, if accepted as a proper subject for the purposes of this litigation, must be held to have been premature.

There remain for consideration the submissions which were directed to the scale of charges proper for allowance in respect of the activities of the authority and their advisers between 6 December 1962 and 22 November 1963, excluding the hydrolysis project work of the research group at Harwell. The established practice of the courts has been to disallow any sums claimed in respect of the time spent by the litigant personally in the course of instructing his solicitors. In the case of litigation by a corporation, this has not been strictly applied, for it has been recognised that, if expert assistance is properly required, it may well occur that the corporation's own specialist employees may be the most suitable or convenient experts to employ. If the corporation litigant does decide to provide expert assistance from its own staff, as happened in this case, the taxing master has to determine the appropriate charge to allow. For an outside expert, the normal assessment would be based on current professional standards, and this in suitable cases would include a proper proportion of the overhead costs of running his office or laboratory, that is, of the costs necessarily incurred by him in his capacity as a consultant, as well as a profit element on such expenditure. The taxing master in the exercise of his discretion took the view that it would be an unreasonable burden to place on the chargeable party to include any items in respect of the authority's own overhead expenses or any profit element referable thereto. As he himself expressed it:

> "I allowed, broadly speaking, the fees and salaries of those actively engaged in the experiments. I also allowed the costs of the materials and stores used, and electricity, steam, water, etc. I did not allow the overhead expenses for buildings, plant and equipment, nor did I allow works and group overheads. The expenses in connection with the [authority's] qualified staff carrying out these experiments are allowable only on the basis of qualifying fees in connection with expert evidence necessary to the defence of the action. This I considered right as the experiments would otherwise have been carried out by outside experts. I allowed not only the charges I have indicated for the experiments, but also certain charges of the patents staff on making searches and enquiries."

In this he was plainly right, covering as he did the actual and direct costs of the work undertaken in the sense of indemnifying the authority for the salaries, materials and out-of-pocket expenses of those engaged in the conduct of the experiments. No part of the authority's expenditure on overheads was occasioned by this litigation and it would be unreasonable to transfer to the applicant the burden of meeting some part of it by reason only of the authority's decision to prefer the services of their own staff to those of independent experts.

In summary, and since I have been asked to state the principle involved, it is, as the taxing master appreciated, that: When it is appropriate that a corporate litigant should recover, on a party and party basis, a sum in respect of expert services of this character performed by its own staff, the amount must be restricted to a reasonable sum for the actual and direct costs of the work undertaken.

In the result the taxing master's final figures require modification, as follows: Reduce the sum of £12,201 by £269 from column (b) and £8,217 from column (c), a total reduction of £8,486, leaving £3,715 to be substituted.

The authority have failed on their summons and the applicant has partially succeeded on his summons. The applicant should therefore have three-quarters of his costs of the review on these two summonses.

The matter will therefore be referred back to the master to amend his certificate in accordance with this judgment, to tax the costs of the review, and, if he is so minded, to modify his taxation of the costs of the objections.

In concluding my judgment I would like to say in open court what I have said in chambers: that I desire to express my sense of obligation to my two assessors, who have placed their expert knowledge so fully at my disposal.

Certificate modified accordingly. Leave to appeal to the Court of Appeal granted.

A D Russell-Clarke for the applicant.
V W C Price for the authority.

Treasury Solicitor
v
Regester and another

Queen's Bench Division
5, 21 December 1977

Donaldson J
sitting with
Chief Master Graham-Green and P J Purton as assessors

Headnote

This is a non-contentious costs case where the judge (Donaldson J, as he then was) said that one of the distinguishing features of the particular transaction differentiating it from run of the mill transactions was "clearly the adrenalin factor". The judge also referred to the exercise of "a value judgment", a phrase which is recurrent in assessment of counsel's fees particularly in criminal matters.

21 December. DONALDSON J read the following judgment: In *Property and Reversionary Investment Corpn Ltd v Secretary of State for the Environment* [[1975] 2 All ER 436, [1975] 1 WLR 1504, **Costs LR (Core Vol) 54**] the chief taxing master, Master Graham-Green, Mr P J Purton of Norton, Rose, Botterell & Roche and I sought to give guidance to the profession on the approach to be adopted in determining solicitors' remuneration in high value commercial conveyancing. By chance, the same court is now asked to consider another such taxation and this gives us an opportunity of removing some misconceptions about our previous decision. I will refer to that decision as "the *Reversionary* case".

Before doing so, I should like to say a word about the position of Master Graham-Green and Mr Purton. Technically they sit with me as assessors, because that is what the Rules of the Supreme Court provide. In practice, and I think that this will be a relief to both parties, we sit as a court of three, each bringing our own differing skills and experience to bear on the problem. This judgment, like that which I delivered in the *Reversionary* case, is in fact, if not in theory, the judgment of all three of us.

The bill of costs, dated 12 October 1976, is for professional charges in connection with the preparation, settlement and completion of an agreement for a lease of offices at Andover Road, Winchester, Hants. The client was Hamilton Holdings Ltd, but the prospective lessee and paying party was the

Secretary of State for the Environment.

I can take the facts from Master Wright's answer to objections:

> "The Ministry of the Environment (hereinafter 'the Ministry') were seeking premises in Andover. Hamilton Holdings Ltd ('Hamilton') had been accumulating a block of land in Andover by purchases of and obtaining options on various parcels of land. An informal agreement was made that if Hamilton obtained the necessary planning permissions and redeveloped the block of land by building a structure to the Ministry's requirements, then the Ministry would take a long lease of the land and structure at a rack rent. The parties are agreed that the value of the land with planning permission was approximately £1,000,000 and that the cost of the redevelopment and building work necessary would be approximately £1,000,000. Hamilton instructed solicitors in November 1975 and a written agreement was made between Hamilton and the Ministry on 30 July 1976. The agreement runs to some nine pages and has a draft lease of some 20 pages annexed. The agreement provides that Hamilton will build a structure in accordance with a specification referred to and that thereupon the Ministry will take a lease of the land and structure for a term of 40 years at a rental of £190,035 per annum (subject to review). Clause 11 of the agreement reads: 'The Tenant will on the execution of this Agreement pay the Landlord's Solicitors proper costs and disbursements in connection therewith … ' It is by reason of this clause that the Ministry is taxing this bill under section 71 of the Solicitors Act 1974. Both parties agree that if it had been impossible to complete the agreement by the end of July 1976, then for tax reasons it would not have been profitable for the landlord to make either the agreement or the lease, and that neither would have been made. They further agree that on making the agreement and even before completion of the lease Hamilton had a marketable investment: Hamilton in fact sold the freehold subject to the agreement some three months after the date of the agreement."

The solicitors, Mr Paul Regester and Mr Colin McInerney, partners in Messrs Ward Bowie of Basingstoke, Hants, submitted a bill for £9,085.50, of which £9,000 was in respect of their professional charges and £85.50 was in respect of disbursements. The learned master taxed the bill at £6,935.50, of which £35.50 represented disbursements. Originally there was a further dispute as to the proportion of costs which were payable immediately and the proportion which would become payable when, at a later stage, the lease is completed. The master decided that 75% should be paid now and 25% later. This apportionment is now accepted.

Both parties have appealed on the issue of what should be the total amount of the bill. The solicitors submit that their original bill is fully justified as being fair and reasonable, having regard to all the circumstances and, in particular, the eight specific matters referred to in the Solicitors' Remuneration Order 1972 [SI No 1139]. The Treasury Solicitor, on behalf of the Secretary of State, contends that having regard to similar considerations, fair and reasonable remuneration would fall within the lower end of the £4,000 to £5,000 bracket.

The master arrived at his figure by following what he believed to be the approach adopted by this court in the *Reversionary* case. He said that we had mentioned only two figures. The first was recorded time under factor (iii) in article 2 of the 1972 Order. This was put at £450 [[1975] 2 All ER 436 at 440, 442, [1975] 1 WLR 1504 at 1507, 1510, **Costs LR (Core Vol) 54 at 59**]. The second was £5,500 for all the eight factors together. The learned master then deduced that we had calculated a figure of approximately £5,000 for all factors other than factor (iii).

In the present case the parties were agreed, and the learned master accepted, that an appropriate figure for recorded time was £900 being 60 hours of partners' time at £15 an hour. He then considered all the factors other than factor (iii), asking himself to what extent they differed from those in the *Reversionary* case in the expectation that if they were not radically different he would arrive at a figure which was not far removed from the figure of £5,000 in that case. In the end he arrived at a figure of £6,000 which he added to the £900 giving a total of £6,900 excluding disbursements.

In the *Reversionary* case [[1975] 2 All ER 436 at 439, 440, [1975] 1 WLR 1504 at 1507, **Costs LR (Core Vol) 54 at 57**] Master Horne had arrived at his figure in three stages. First, he took the hourly cost rate at £15 and applied this to 30 hours of recorded time, giving a figure of £450. This disposed of factor (iii). Second, he multiplied this by two to take account of all other factors with the exception of factor (vi), "the amount or value of any property involved". This gave him a figure of £900. In the third stage he applied a percentage, calculated on a regressive scale to the value, and obtained a figure of £3,250. Adding the results of the three stages gave him a figure of about £4,600.

In our judgment we expressly disagreed with applying a multiplier to any figure based on recorded time (factor (iii)), but did not expressly say that such a figure should not be added to some other figure arrived at after a consideration of all the other factors. Clearly, we should have done so and we welcome this opportunity of making it clear that the £5,500 in the *Reversionary* case was not arrived at by any process involving an addition to or multiplication of any other figure. As we said in our judgment and we now repeat [[1975] 2 All ER 436 at 441, [1975] 1 WLR 1504 at 1509, **Costs LR (Core Vol) 54 at 58**].

> "The object of the exercise, whether a solicitor is preparing a bill of costs in relation to non-contentious business, or the Law Society is certifying such a bill, or the court is taxing it, is to arrive at a sum which is fair and reasonable, having regard to all the circumstances and, in particular, to the matters specified in the numbered paragraphs of article 2 of the Order. It is an exercise in assessment, an exercise in balanced judgement – not an arithmetical calculation. It follows that different people may reach different conclusions as to what sum is fair and reasonable, although all should fall within a bracket which, in the vast majority of cases, will be narrow. It also follows that it is

wrong always to start by assessing the direct and indirect expense to the solicitor, represented by the time spent on the business. This must always be taken into account, but it is not necessarily, or even usually, a basic factor to which all others are related. Thus, although the labour involved will usually be directly related to, and reflected by, the time spent, the skill and specialised knowledge involved may vary greatly for different parts of that time. Again not all time spent on a transaction necessarily lends itself to being recorded, although the fullest possible records should be kept."

Having considered all the factors, including factor (iii), we concluded [[1975] 2 All ER 436 at 443, [1975] 1 WLR 1504 at 1512, **Costs LR (Core Vol) 54 at 61**]:

"With these factors well in mind, it is necessary to assess a sum which is fair and reasonable. Each case will always have to be considered on its merits and be subject ultimately to the discretion of the taxing master. In this case various figures will no doubt come to mind. They can be tested relative to the remuneration generally accepted, or previously held to be fair and reasonable, in comparable transactions, due allowance being made for all distinctions. They can also be tested by making hypothetical calculations of what the sum would be if any exceptional factors were excluded and then seeing whether the resulting figure conforms with the accepted views of the profession and of the taxing authorities. But in the end it is a value judgment, based on discretion and experience."

The magnetic attraction of factor (iii) as a foundation for assessment of fair and reasonable remuneration is that, in the absence of an approved scale applied to value, it is the only figure which is readily calculable. It is an attraction which must be sternly resisted in cases of this sort where one or more of the other factors is such as to dwarf it into insignificance.

In the *Reversionary* case [[1975] 2 All ER 436 at 443, [1975] 1 WLR 1504 at 1509, **Costs LR (Core Vol) 54 at 60**] we drew attention to the fact that recorded time on a transaction may be expected to reflect labour, but not skill and specialised knowledge and that in the nature of things not all time spent lends itself to being recorded. As Walton J said in *Maltby v D J Freeman & Co* **Costs LR (Core Vol) 64**:

"No professional man, or senior employee of a professional man, stops thinking about the day's problems the minute he lifts his coat and umbrella from the stand and sets out on the journey home. Ideas, often very valuable ideas, occur in the train or car home, or in the bath, or even whilst watching television. Yet nothing is ever put down on a time sheet, or can be put down on a time sheet, adequately to reflect this out of hours devotion of time."

The truth is that an hourly cost rate applied to recorded time at best only indicates the proportion of the solicitor's overhead expenses which are rightly attributable to the transaction. We say "at best" because (a) hourly rates tend to be round figures which do not necessarily represent an accurate assessment of overheads in terms of man hours, (b) they may not be revised sufficiently often to take account of inflation and (c) different firms regard different expenses as being apportionable, some, for example, including notional basic salaries for partners and others omitting such an item.

This is not to say that the calculation has no value. It has a real value in all cases. Thus, if calculated accurately, it informs a solicitor of the minimum figure which he must charge if he is not to suffer an actual loss on the transaction. Second, it gives him an idea of the relationship between the overheads attributable to the transaction and the profit accruing to him. This latter point is plainly relevant in the broad sense that the nature of some transactions will justify much larger profits than others of a more routine type. But we must stress that it is only one of a number of cross-checks on the fairness and reasonableness of the final figure. The final figure will result from an exercise in judgment, not arithmetic, whatever arithmetical cross-checks may be employed.

We also consider that the learned master erred in his use of the figure which he assumed that we had assessed for the remaining factors in the *Reversionary* case. It is flattering to have our assessment in that case treated as if it were an imperial standard measure, but it is wrong to do. We did say [[1975] 2 All ER 436 at 443, [1975] 1 WLR 1504 at 1512, **Costs LR (Core Vol) 54 at 61**], and we repeat, that provisional figures "can be tested relative to the remuneration generally accepted, or previously held to be fair and reasonable, in comparable, transactions, due allowance being made for all distinctions".

But this is a cross-check. It is not a primary source to be modified in the light of a comparison between the circumstances of the transaction and those which existed in the *Reversionary* case or any other reported case.

We now turn to the eight factors to which our attention is directed by the 1972 Order.

(i) *The complexity of the matter or the difficulty or novelty of the questions raised*
The client was engaged in a property development exercise involving the acquisition of adjacent pieces of land and the disposal of the resulting package on terms that they would build an office for the acquirer who would take the developed site on long lease. The bill did not cover the professional work connected with the acquisition, but covered the rest. Such work is not novel, but it is far from being standardised. From its very nature it will give rise to difficulties and will have some degree of complexity, the difficulty and complexity varying from transaction to transaction. We have no evidence that, of its kind, it was more difficult or complex than usual.

(ii) *The skill, labour, specialised knowledge and responsibility involved*
The solicitors were not, so far as we know, specialists in this type of work, but its very nature calls for a high degree of skill and responsibility. The special feature was the short time available. This stemmed from the late acquisition of some of the properties making up the site, coupled with the

fact that, as a result of the impending introduction of development land tax, the deal was only commercially practicable if it was completed before the end of July. The degree of skill, responsibility and labour required when working to a deadline can be very high and was so in this case.

(iii) *The time spent on the business*
The recorded time was agreed at 60 hours of senior partner's time, but this was clearly a case in which a great deal of unrecorded thinking time must have been involved.

(iv) *The number and importance of the documents prepared or perused without regard to length*
Suffice it to say that there were no unusual features under this head.

(v) *The place where and the circumstances in which the business or any part thereof is transacted*
The work was done by a Basingstoke firm, the unusual features being the expedition and value to the client which are better considered under other heads.

(vi) *The amount or value of any money or property involved*
This head is not concerned with a precise valuation, but rather with establishing in what broad category of value it should be placed. In the *Reversionary* case [[1975] 2 All ER 436 at 443, [1975] 1 WLR 1504 at 1511, **Costs LR (Core Vol) 54 at 60**] we suggested bands of under £^{1}/4m, £^{1}/4m–£1m, £1m–£2^1/2m, £2^1/2m–£5m, £5m–£10m and over £10m. We see no reason to suggest different bands today. However, we should perhaps make it clear that we were not then and are not today concerned with the band below £^{1}/4m which would require subdivision or with that over £10m which would also require to be looked at again in its higher reaches. In broad terms this was a £2m transaction. In fact, the parties agreed that the value of the land with planning permission was £1m and that a further £1m was to be spent by the client in redevelopment. But the same result could have been achieved by valuing the lease. The Council of the Law Society has expressed the view based on respectable valuation practice that the value factor in the grant of a lease at a rack rent can be determined by multiplying half the rent by the term of years not exceeding 20 years. We agree with this view and would only add that for terms exceeding 20 years we would adopt a multiplier of ten applied to the annual rent. In the present case this gives a value of £1,900,000.

(vii) *Whether any land involved is registered land within the meaning of the Land Registration Act 1925*
This was unregistered land, and we would have taken this into account if the bill had related to its acquisition. However, in the context of the solicitors

having recently acted in its acquisition, we do not consider this difference to be significant.

(viii) *The importance of the matter to the client*
The matter did not have a special subjective importance to the client, but its objective importance in terms of value and what would be lost if it was not completed by the deadline was very considerable.

Against this background we found ourselves thinking of figures. We will not specify them save to say that they fell within a £2,500 bracket based on experience of the range of professional charges in major property transactions.

We then looked at the eight factors and asked ourselves what was the factor or factors, if any, which distinguished this transaction from the general run of such transactions. The answer was clearly the "adrenalin" factor. By this we mean that the solicitor had not only to work fast but had absolutely no margin for error. The transaction had to be completed by 31 July, come what might, or their client would have lost not only this deal, but all possibility of avoiding the effects of the development land tax. This caused us to look towards the top rather than the bottom of the bracket. In a different case, we might have found that there was plenty of time and that the transaction was very similar to one with which the solicitors had previously been concerned for the same client. This would have caused us to look in a reverse direction.

We then looked at the only two factors which of themselves can be used to produce a monetary result. They are factors (iii), recorded time, and (vi), value. As we have already pointed out, recorded time does not provide an arithmetical basis for a charge in cases such as this. Its relevance is to check whether the provisional figures for remunerating bear a reasonable relationship to the overheads attributable to the transaction. In this case the figures which we had in mind did not seem to bear an unusual relationship to the overheads in a transaction of this type and we therefore obtained no positive assistance from considering this factor.

Turning now to value, we reminded ourselves that scale fees have been abolished. Nevertheless, it is reasonable and fair to the client that the remuneration should not be disproportionate to the value of the property involved. It was therefore useful to employ a yardstick to assess that relationship.

Various yardsticks with a regressive basis can be suggested and an example will be found in the Oyez Practice Notes [[No 20: Chavasse, Conveyancing Costs (6th Edn, 1975), 33]. The author correctly stresses that this is only an example and each case will have to be considered on its own merits. The fact is that there is no right yardstick, although some may be wrong. For our part we would consider that 1/2% on the first £250,000 in a major transaction and thereafter regressing provides a reasonable method of assessment.

We must also make it clear that we disagree with the suggestion in the Oyez Notes that the purpose of a scale is to arrive at remuneration for the responsibility/risk element which is then to be added to the remuneration for other elements. This is not the case. Remuneration has to be assessed for all the circumstances taken together and the purpose of a regressing yardstick is, as we have said, to check that the provisional figure bears a reasonable relationship to the value of the property. This is not only reasonable but also fair to both parties and in particular to the client.

We also compared our figures with that in the *Reversionary* case, taking account of the distinctions which exist. There are several. The most important is that the *Reversionary* case concerned a part transaction covering only the solicitor's work subsequent to the notice to treat. In the present case the bill covered the agreement for a lease, the lease itself and the building contract. The Treasury Solicitor also submitted that there should be a heavy discount because the *Reversionary* case was concerned with a freehold interest whereas this case concerns a leasehold interest. We reject this submission, which reflects a distinction made in the old scales of remuneration. The nature of the interest is irrelevant as such. What matters is the effect which that nature has on the various factors of skill, work, value, complexity etc. There will be occasions when dealing with a leasehold interest is simpler than with a freehold, but the converse can also be true.

One further submission of general interest should be mentioned. This was that the paying party (for whom it is understood speed was not of the essence in this case) should not be expected to pay for the expedition made necessary by the fact that the client failed to assemble the parcels of land at an earlier date and also found itself up against a fiscal deadline. The short answer to this is that the Secretary of State agreed to pay the client's costs and it is the client's costs which we are called on to tax.

As we said in the *Reversionary* case [[1975] 2 All ER 436 at 443, [1975] 1 WLR 1504 at 1512, **Costs LR (Core Vol) 54 at 61**], in the end we have to make a value judgment, based on discretion and on experience, vicarious in my case but direct and considerable in the case of the assessors. our figure may not be *the* right figure, and indeed such a figure probably does not exist. But we hope that it will be *a* right figure; one which is reasonable in all the circumstances and which is fair both to the client and to the solicitor. Our figure is £8,000 exclusive of any value added tax. Of this figure 75% together with £35.50 for disbursements is payable at once. The balance is payable when the lease is completed.

Order accordingly.

Francis Barlow for the Treasury Solicitor.
Mark Potter for the solicitors.

Re Eastwood (deceased), Lloyds Bank Ltd
v
Eastwood and others

Court of Appeal, Civil Division
1, 2, 3, 12 July 1974

Russell, Stamp and Lawton LJJ

Headnote

This is the case where the "A" and "B" elements in a solicitor's hourly rate representing the actual cost of doing the work in the area at the time (the A factor) and the mark-up to reflect the particular difficulties of the case in question (the B factor) was first mentioned and which is now to be found in Appendix 2 to Order 62.

---

12 July. RUSSELL LJ: The judgment I am about to deliver is the judgment of the court. The circumstances with which this appeal is concerned are set out in the report of the case below [[1973] 3 All ER 1079], to which reference should be made in order to understand this judgment. The question of principle involved is whether the taxing master correctly approached the problem of taxation of costs awarded to the Crown, having regard to the fact that the Crown was represented on the originating summons not by an independent solicitor but by the Treasury Solicitor and his department. The question of principle would apply equally to the case of a local government authority, a nationalised industry such as British Rail, and any industrial concern conducting litigation through its own legal department of which all the expenses, including the salaries of solicitors, assistant solicitors and legal executives, are paid by it, and not by instructing an independent solicitor or firm to act for it.

The provisions of RSC Order 62 relating to taxation of costs awarded to a party to litigation against another party, or as here to be paid out of an estate or trust fund, are at least primarily directed to cases where the party has instructed an independent solicitor: for example, rule 25 requires that the bill of costs of the successful party to be submitted for taxation shall enter "professional charges" in a separate column, and be indorsed with the name or firm of the solicitor "whose bill it is". Now, except no doubt for purposes of internal accounting, the employed solicitor or legal department renders no bill to the employer or organisation; he or it makes no professional charges. It is however quite clear on authority that it is not permissible to say that consequently the party is limited to disbursements specifically referable to the particular litigation on the ground that the salaries of employees and other general expenses of the department would have been incurred by the party in any event.

Until the late 1960s, as we understand it, in such cases, on taxation, the bill was treated in the same manner as would have been the case had an independent solicitor been instructed by the party, the conventional approach now being that stated in the report below in the advice of the assessors to Brightman J in relation to discretionary items such as that in the instant case. And we observe that for very many years there have been examples of organisations such as railways with their own legal departments engaged in considerable litigation resulting in orders for costs in their favour which have required taxation; the system seems to have worked without objection, and without a suggestion that in such cases some detailed and complicated method should be adopted of breaking down the activities of the legal department so as to arrive in some other way at a proper attribution of the total expense of the department to the particular litigation.

In the present case the taxing master arrived at a figure of £45, based on a time rate of £7 per hour, as representing that which was referred to in the assessors' advice as figure A, and decided to allow the addition thereto of what is referred to as figure B, on the ground that figure B in an independent solicitor's bill of costs would reflect or contain the profit element in the case of such independent solicitor; though we cannot think it was intended to suggest that, had it been an independent solicitor, he would have been making a pure £30 profit in an item of profit costs of £75: "profit costs", of course, is a phrase used to denote items in a bill of costs which are not disbursements. It was the view of the taxing master that, since there was no element of solicitor's profit in cases such as the present, item B was not allowable, for otherwise the party would be making a profit, contrary to the well-established principle that taxed costs should not be more than an indemnity.

It should be stated that the taxing master was under the impression, which he stated in his answer to objections, that the Crown had conceded that his figure A was "adequate to cover the actual cost incurred in doing all the work done". If such a concession had been made, and if it was to be taken as an acceptance of the fact that a detailed breakdown and analysis of the activities of the Treasury Solicitor's office would correctly attribute to this item of this litigation £45 as the proportion of the whole expenses thereof, then the decision would be correct, but we were assured that a concession to that effect was not made, and was certainly not intended.

The advice of the assessors on the conventional method of approaching such a discretionary item in taxation of an independent solicitor's bill makes it plain that in arriving via an hourly rate at figure A, in for example a case where the work has all been done by a legal executive or salaried assistant, no consideration is given to the earnings of the partners, whether by attributing to them a notional salary or otherwise. In arriving at the figure of £45, it appears that equally the taxing master would not have brought into consideration, for example, the salary payable to the Treasury Solicitor himself, the judge referring to the quantification by the taxing master of "A" at £7 an hour.

In our view, the fallacy underlying the refusal of the taxing master to allow what is referred to as "B" lies in this: that if you embark on an A B exercise, in which A is really meaningless unless accompanied by B, you cannot stop short with A above. If it were, because it is not a case of an independent solicitor, inappropriate to use the A B exercise at all, some quite different exercise would be called for. Moreover, the method adopted assumes that it costs a party less to engage in litigation when he employs his own salaried solicitor and legal department than if he instructs an independent solicitor to act for him, simply because the independent solicitor makes a personal profit out of the litigation. On that last point an example was given in the course of debate. Suppose a solicitor in independent practice with an assistant solicitor, two legal executives, clerks, and typists and other overheads, who in year one works in fact exclusively for corporation X. For year two it is arranged that his whole office and staff is taken over as a department of corporation X, the solicitor also becoming an employee of the corporation at a salary commensurate with the profit made by him in year one doing the corporation's legal work. Suppose that in year one the corporation was successful in a piece of litigation in which in fact one of the legal executives did all the work: in taxing the corporation's costs the taxing master would apply the A and B conventional method and the figure for the discretionary item would be £75. Suppose in year two the corporation is successful in exactly comparable litigation, again with the legal executive doing the work: if the method of taxation adopted in this case were followed, only A (£45) would be allowed for the item, though the change would not have effected any saving to the corporation, who, instead of paying the profit to the solicitor in respect of that litigation, would have paid to him the equivalent in the form of a proportion of his salary. This example seems to us to demonstrate that there must be something wrong in an approach which uses only the A of the A B conventional method in the case of an employed solicitor. It did not appear to us that counsel for the plaintiffs was able to answer the point.

It was contended before us that in any event there was an onus on the party with its own legal department to produce figures to demonstrate that the operations and expenses of that department, analysed and broken down and apportioned, would throw up a figure properly attributable to the litigation in question which would be not less than the figure of reasonable costs to be allowed had it been a case of the use of an independent solicitor. In the first place, we would have thought it a perfectly sensible presumption as a starting point that it would not be less. Secondly, we view with horror the immensity of the complication which would be introduced into an already complicated system of taxation. It may be said that without such an added complication there may be rare cases in which the taxed costs of a successful party will exceed what is needed to indemnify him. Even so, this is preferable to requiring the successful party to prove in all cases in detail the contrary, that is to say, that the other party has not obtained a fortuitous benefit by the use by the successful party of a salaried solicitor and not an independent solicitor.

In our view, the system of direct application of the approach to taxation of an independent solicitor's bill to a case such as this has relative simplicity greatly to recommend it, and it seems to have worked without it being thought for many years to lead to significant injustice in the field of taxation where justice is in any event rough justice, in the sense of being compounded of much sensible approximation.

In summary, therefore, in our opinion: (1) It is the proper method of taxation of a bill in a case of this sort to deal with it as though it were the bill of an independent solicitor, assessing accordingly the reasonable and fair amount of a discretionary item such as this, having regard to all the circumstances of the case. (2) There is no reason to suppose that the conventional A B method is other than appropriate to the case of both independent and employed solicitors. (3) It is a sensible and reasonable presumption that the figure arrived at on this basis will not infringe the principle that the taxed costs should not be more than an indemnity to the party against the expense to which he has been put in the litigation. (4) There may be special cases in which it appears reasonably plain that that principle will be infringed if the method of taxation appropriate to an independent solicitor's bill is entirely applied: but it would be impracticable and wrong in all cases of an employed solicitor to require a total exposition and breakdown of the activities and expenses of the department with a view to ensuring that the principle is not infringed, and it is doubtful, to say the least, whether by any method certainty on the point could be reached. To adapt a passage from the judgment of Stirling J in *Re Doody* [[1893] 1 Ch at 129] to make the taxation depend on such a requirement would, as it seems to us, simply be to introduce a rule unworkable in practice and to push abstract principle to a point at which it ceases to give results consistent with justice.

Accordingly, we allow the appeal. It would appear that, had the taxing master not deleted item B, he would have allowed the figure of £75 for this discretionary item, and it would therefore seem unnecessary to remit the matter for reconsideration on the basis of this decision. But we will hear submissions on what is the technically correct form of order.

Appeal allowed. Order that taxing master's certificate be amended by substituting the figure of £75 for the figure of £45. Leave to appeal to the House of Lords refused.

C A Settle QC and *Peter Gibson* for the Attorney-General.
Gerald Godfrey QC and *P M H Mottershead* for the plaintiffs.

Property and Reversionary Investment Corporation Ltd

v

Secretary of State for the Environment

Queen's Bench Division
17, 25 March 1975

Donaldson J
sitting with assessors

Headnote

This is another of the few reported cases on the basis for quantification of non-contentious costs (see also *Treasury Solicitor* v *Regester and another* at 42 above). The judge, Donaldson J (as he then was), emphasised that the final figure was at the end of the day an exercise in judgment rather than an arithmetical calculation.

DONALDSON J: How do you determine a solicitor's remuneration for conveyancing work involved in the sale of £2¼m worth of commercial property in central London? This is the problem which confronted Master Horne. On appeal from his decision, this is the problem which now confronts me. Fortunately I have had the assistance of the Chief Taxing Master, Master Graham-Green, and of Mr P J Purton of Norton, Rose, Botterell and Roche sitting with me as assessors. Despite this assistance, which has been of the greatest value, the problem is not an easy one, because the basis of charging is of fairly recent origin and transactions of this value are still relatively rare.

The property concerned is in Parliament Street and Bridge Street, Westminster, and it was acquired as part of the scheme for extending the Parliament buildings. The transaction was effected under the Compulsory Purchase Act 1965, and the agreed compensation was £2¼m for the freehold, together with an additional sum in respect of surveyors' fees and the amount of the vendors' solicitors' costs to be taxed if not agreed. No agreement as to these costs was reached. Hence this taxation.

The difference between the contentions of the parties was startling. The vendors' solicitors put forward a detailed bill of costs on the basis of which they claimed £12,391.50 made up of £11,250 professional charges and £15 disbursements with value added tax ("VAT") in each case at the rate of 10%.

The Secretary of State argued for a figure of about £1,500 plus VAT. The learned master originally taxed the costs at £7,000, but on hearing objections from both parties reduced this to £4,625, plus VAT in each case, and £15 plus VAT for disbursements. The vendors now appeal and the Secretary of State cross-appeals.

Solicitors' charges for conveyancing work were for very many years governed by scales related to the amount of the consideration involved. The scales regressed by stages, but soon reached a fixed percentage which continued without limit. In 1970 these scales ceased to apply where the consideration exceeded £30,000 and as from 1 January 1973 were withdrawn completely. Thereafter solicitors' remuneration for work of this kind has been determined in accordance with the Solicitors Remuneration Order 1972 [SI No 1139]. Article 2 of the order provides as follows:

"A solicitor's remuneration for non-contentious business (including business under the Land Registration Act 1925) shall be such sum as may be fair and reasonable having regard to all the circumstances of the case and in particular to – (i) the complexity of the matter or the difficulty or novelty of the questions raised; (ii) the skill, labour, specialised knowledge and responsibility involved; (iii) the time spent on the business; (iv) the number and importance of the documents prepared or perused, without regard to length; (v) the place where and the circumstances in which the business or any part thereof is transacted; (vi) the amount or value of any money or property involved; (vii) whether any land involved is registered land within the meaning of the Land Registration Act 1925; and (viii) the importance of the matter to the client."

Article 4(1) of the order also provides:

"… it shall be the duty of the solicitor to satisfy the taxing officer as to the fairness and reasonableness of the sum charged."

Accordingly if anything turns on onus, that onus is on the vendors and their solicitors.

The learned master approached this taxation by three cumulative stages. First he enquired into what work was actually done and how long it took. In doing so, he was not concerned with all work done by the solicitors for their clients, the vendors. This was a compulsory purchase and the costs to be taxed and paid by the Secretary of State were limited to those incurred after exchange of contracts – in this case the notice to treat – and thus related almost exclusively to deduction of title and completion of the transfer. Thus the work which would have been done by solicitors in an ordinary sale and purchase of land is excluded to the extent that such work precedes the exchange of the contracts of sale and purchase. The title was in fact registered, but it was common ground that nowadays, when in unregistered cases short title can be made, there is little, if any, saving in time or effort in dealing with a registered title. Accordingly the solicitors' remuneration is not greatly affected by this factor. The sale was not with vacant possession and some consideration had to be given to the rights of occupiers.

The bill of costs showed that the solicitors were engaged for 30 hours in the relevant period. Most of this time was made up of short items spread over a period. This did not mean that what was done was of little importance or required little skill or effort. Far from it. The whole transaction was of great importance and it is in some ways more difficult to have to pick up the thread continually over a period than to do the same work more or less continuously.

To these hours the learned master applied an hourly rate designed to cover the expenses involved in doing such of the work as was capable of being considered on a timed basis. This hourly rate he assessed at £15 – perhaps a very modest rate by central London standards – making £450. The vendors put forward an hourly rate of £20.

The second stage consisted of multiplying this £450 figure by a factor which sought to take account of all the factors mentioned in article 2 of the Order other than (a) the time spent on the matter, which had already been considered in the first stage, and (b) para (vi), "the amount or value of any money or property involved", which was considered in the third stage. The learned master applied a multiplier of two, giving a figure of £900 for this stage.

Finally the learned master considered para (vi). He took the view that, in the circumstances of this transaction, this factor "dominated all other factors to an abnormal extent", and that it could only be translated into remuneration by adopting a percentage scale. He considered that this scale should be regressive and he used 0.5% on the first £250,000 of the consideration and 0.1% thereafter. This gave a figure of £3,250 which, when added to the figures of £450 and £900 resulting from the previous stages, should have amounted to £4,600 but, owing to a minor casting error, came to £4,625 to which VAT had to be added at 10%.

On this appeal counsel for the vendors has submitted that the overriding factor is the importance of the transaction and the risk to the solicitors of making some mistake which may expose them to vast liabilities. In particular he submits that the decision in *Hedley Byrne & Co Ltd v Heller & Partners Ltd* [[1963] 2 All ER 575, [1964] AC 465] and the passing of the Misrepresentation Act 1967, have greatly increased the vulnerability of solicitors. Solicitors are now potentially liable to the other party to the transaction as well as to their own client and, furthermore, since the liability is in tort, time runs from the accrual of damage, postponing the benefit of a defence under the Limitation Act 1939. In counsel for the vendors' submission, where there is a potential liability of at least £2¹/₄m, all other factors pale into insignificance.

He then submitted that the only way in which this factor can be reflected in the solicitors' remuneration is by taking a percentage of the purchase price and he put forward 0.5% as an appropriate rate. There is some support for this approach in an article in The Law Society's Gazette ["A personal approach to Schedule 11" (1972), vol 69, 872] by Mr Thomas Woodcock and in the Oyez Practice Notes on Conveyancing and Other Non-contentious Costs [5th Edn (1973), 30]. The only official Law Society publication on the subject is their Questions and Answers booklet on the 1972 Order which suggests that it would be reasonable to reflect the value of the consideration by a ½% charge in a *typical domestic transaction*. But, of course, this transaction is neither typical nor domestic. Indeed the consideration in the average domestic transaction is less than 1% of what was involved in this case. In truth the typical domestic transaction is a different animal. Counsel for the vendors also relied on a transaction in which the London Transport Executive did not object to solicitors' charges of £6,750, where the consideration was £1,385,000.

Finally counsel for the vendors submitted that taking a percentage of the consideration as an important factor would reduce the cost of transactions of small value and that it was in the public interest that large deals should continue in some measure to subsidise the small, as was undoubtedly the case when there was a scale.

Counsel for the Secretary of State was at pains to stress that the government's prime interest was to obtain a decision on how solicitors' costs should be calculated in compulsory purchase cases. In his submission the basic factor must be the amount of time spent on the transaction. Whilst the degree of responsibility assumed was no doubt an important factor, this was related to complexity and complexity would be reflected in the time spent. He also drew attention to the fact that compulsory purchase transactions had two special characteristics. First, the costs which are to be borne by acquiring authority are limited by section 23 of the 1965 Act. By section 23(2) they –

> "… include all charges and expenses … (*a*) of all conveyances and assurances of any of the land, and of any outstanding terms or interests in the land, and (*b*) of deducing, evidencing and verifying the title to the land, terms of interest, and (*c*) of making out and furnishing such abstracts and attested copies as the acquiring authority may require, and all other reasonable expenses incident to the investigation, deduction and verification of the title."

In the normal transaction of sale and purchase, the solicitors' costs cover a substantial amount of important work which is done at the earlier contract stage. Second, most defects in title which emerge following a compulsory purchase can be corrected by a further compulsory purchase order, which would have the indirect effect of reducing the solicitors' potential liability. Taking all these factors into consideration, counsel for the Secretary of State submitted that the basic figure in the calculation should be £450 (30 hours at £15 per hour) which could be multiplied by three to reflect the element of responsibility and the importance of the transaction, giving a final figure of £1,350. This might be rounded up to £1,500.

Both parties have asked me to deliver judgment in open court and to try to give such guidance to the profession as is possible. This I gladly do. There is not, as yet, a great deal of experience of the operation of the 1972 Order in relation to high value commercial transactions. The Law Society is not the rule-making body and, having regard to the differing circumstances which may apply to each case, it has very properly felt unable to give any firm guidance to the profession. For similar reasons, the vendors' solicitors are in no way to be criticised for the amount of the bill which they have rendered, although I and the assessors have reached the conclusion that it is higher than is justified by the Order, bearing in mind the limited scope of the work, the charges for which fall to be taxed and paid by the Secretary of State, as against the charges for a total transaction. Indeed it is perfectly proper for the solicitors in the present case to render an account to their clients for work done prior to the notice to treat, the cost of which was not recoverable from the Secretary of State.

The object of the exercise, whether a solicitor is preparing a bill of costs in relation to non-contentious business, or the Law Society is certifying such a bill, or the court is taxing it, is to arrive at a sum which is fair and reasonable, having regard to all the circumstances and, in particular, to the matters specified in the numbered paragraphs of article 2 of the Order. It is an exercise in assessment, an exercise in balanced judgment – not an arithmetical calculation. It follows that different people may reach different conclusions as to what sum is fair and reasonable, although all should fall within a bracket which, in the vast majority of cases, will be narrow.

It also follows that it is wrong always to start by assessing the direct and indirect expense to the solicitor, represented by the time spent on the business. This must always be taken into account, but it is not necessarily, or even usually, a basic factor to which all others are related. Thus, although the labour involved will usually be directly related to, and reflected by, the time spent, the skill and specialised knowledge involved may vary greatly for different parts of that time. Again not all time spent on a transaction necessarily lends itself to being recorded, although the fullest possible records should be kept.

This error is compounded if, as an invariable rule, the figure representing the expense of recorded time spent on the transaction is multiplied by another figure to reflect the other factors. The present case provides an illustration of this error. The responsibility and value of the property involved were linked factors, but neither was affected by whether the recorded time spent was 30 hours or 60 hours. Yet the application of a multiplier would double the responsibility/value factor, if the recorded time spent had happened to be 60 rather than 30 hours.

In my judgment the proper approach is to start by taking a broad look at "all the circumstances of the case" and in particular the general nature of the business. This should be followed by a systematic consideration of the factors specified in the paragraphs of article 2 of the Order. This I will do in the context of this taxation, but will comment more generally than is necessary for that purpose in the hope that this course will be of assistance to the profession. The numbers refer to the paragraphs of the Order.

(i) This matter was not of unusual complexity or difficulty, bearing in mind its size and value, and no novel questions were raised. Furthermore – and this is important – being a compulsory purchase it included, so far as the taxation was concerned, only part of what would usually be involved in a sale and purchase, where the solicitor was concerned with all the enquiries which must be made prior to the exchange of contracts. The final figure for the solicitors' remuneration must reflect this fact and bear a reasonable relationship to the remuneration which would be fair and reasonable, if the taxation extended to work done at the earlier stage.

(ii) A reasonable degree of skill and of knowledge of the special problems affecting a conveyance of commercial property was called for, but the labour involved was, to judge from the recorded time spent, relatively small. The major factor under this head was the responsibility involved. The client is entitled to rely, and does rely, on the solicitor to ensure that, when the transaction has been completed, he has obtained all that to which he is entitled and that thereafter there can be no complaint against him by the other party. I say that in this case it was a major factor, because of the value of the property involved (see factor (vi)). In other cases it may still be a major factor, but for other reasons such as that highly specialised knowledge was involved. In yet other cases the client may himself have taken decisions on the basis of his own knowledge or other professional advice. This may limit the responsibility of the solicitor and reduce the effect of this factor, but it will usually be a matter of some importance, for one of the major reasons for instructing a solicitor or other professional man is to be advised by someone who will accept responsibility for the correctness of his advice and for any work done by him. Contrary to the theme which seems to underlie some of the argument, a client does not consult a solicitor in order to obtain an indirect, and possibly incomplete, indemnity against the consequences of negligent advice and action. He consults him to get skilled and careful advice and that is what he pays for. Nevertheless the need of the client may vary from transaction to transaction. In the present case this need may be considered to be less than it might have been in, say, a complicated commercial transaction involving a number of parties and the marriage of conveyancing transactions with share exchange or other contracts.

(iii) The solicitors have recorded 30 hours as having been spent on the business. This should have been divided up into partners' time, solicitors' time and legal executive time as it is appropriate to apply different rates. However, in the context of this transaction, this factor is of relatively small importance and an hourly rate of £15 can be adopted as an average figure applying throughout. The selection of the rate is also affected by para (v).

(iv) This factor has to be construed in the light of the fact that it will usually be reflected in factors (i) complexity, (ii) responsibility, (iii) time spent, and/or (vi) value, and should not be taken into account twice over. On the other hand it may well be significant, if the essence of the work is drafting and perusing. In the present case it is relevant to the work of deducing title and conveying, but has been taken into account under other heads.

(v) The vendors' solicitors are central London solicitors and the work was done in central London. This factor is likely to attract an increased rate of remuneration reflecting the increased expenses inherent in a London based practice, but as the work was done near their offices there will be no increase such as would be appropriate if they had had to travel to distant centres. Conversely, if they had been based in the country other than in a high cost area such as the centre of one of the principle cities, remuneration might well have been lower, but would have been increased insofar as they had to travel to London to do the work. Special expedition, rendered necessary by the nature of the transaction or in response to the client's request, is an important part of the circumstances in which the business is transacted and can justify greatly increased remuneration. A skilful lack of expedition may also on occasion be in the interests of the client, and might on an exceptional occasion justify some increase in the remuneration.

(vi) This is an objective test of the importance of the transaction and strongly influences the responsibility factor (see (ii) above). In the present case it is, without doubt, the weightiest single factor. However, I should utter a word of warning. In taking account of high values, while it is right in principle to apply a value factor this factor will vary according to the particular circumstances and it should be remembered that the burden of responsibility on the solicitor does not increase in direct proportion to the value. The effect of increased value is regressive and the rate of regression increases with the value. Furthermore it is a matter of broad bands of value, rather than precision. Others might select different bands, but I and the assessors would suggest that, in the light of the current value of money, the divisions between the higher bands might be taken as being at £$\frac{1}{4}$m, £1m, £2$\frac{1}{2}$m, £5m and £10m. Finer tuning can be achieved by considering whether the value is at the bottom, the middle or the top of the relevant band and there can be even more refined categorisation, if it was thought appropriate. But the essence of the approach is that it involves classification and not enumeration. In the present case the value falls at the top end of the £1m–2$\frac{1}{2}$m band. It may be right that the consequences of negligent action can be less serious where the client can use compulsory powers to remedy the situation, but in my judgment this does not reduce the responsibility of the solicitor to any significant extent, if it does so at all. Certainly it is no ground for reducing the remuneration to which he would otherwise be entitled.

(vii) As I have already said the distinction between registered and unregistered land is not usually of great significance and was of none in the present case.

(viii) This, in contrast to factor (vi), involves a subjective valuation of the importance of the matter. Usually it will add nothing to factor (vi) and does not do so in the present case. If the matter is of special importance to the client, the responsibility will be increased and higher remuneration will be justified, but the fact that the client regards the matter as of small importance will neither relieve the solicitor of his responsibilities nor reduce the remuneration which can be considered fair and reasonable in the light of its objective value and importance.

With these factors well in mind, it is necessary to assess a sum which is fair and reasonable. Each case will always have to be considered on its merits and be subject ultimately to the discretion of the taxing master. In this case various figures will no doubt come to mind. They can be tested relative to the remuneration generally accepted, or previously held to be fair and reasonable, in comparable transaction, due allowance being made for all distinctions. They can also be tested by making hypothetical calculations of what the sum would be if any exceptional factors were excluded and then seeing whether the resulting figure conforms with the accepted views of the profession and of the taxing authorities. But in the end it is a value judgment, based on discretion and experience. It is for this reason, above all others, that the assistance of the assessors has been invaluable. In the present case in the light of their advice, I have concluded that the sum of £5,500 would be fair and reasonable and the assessors authorise me to say that they agree. To this must be added £15 for disbursements together with such VAT as is appropriate.

Profit costs to be taxed at £5,500 plus value added tax; cross-summons dismissed.

John Balcombe QC and *George Hesketh* for the vendors.
Harry Woolf for the Secretary of State.

Leopold Lazarus Ltd
v
Secretary of State for Trade and Industry

Queen's Bench Division
7 April 1976

Kerr J

Headnote

This case extended the A and B philosophy first propounded in *Re Eastwood* and is believed to be the first case in which the expression "direct costs" was used.

KERR J: In his answer the master helpfully summarised the practice concerning the computation of item 26 in cases such as this. Having considered the weight of the proceedings and the responsibility and skill involved, the practice is then to arrive at a total figure consisting of two elements which are referred to as A and B in the judgment of the Court of Appeal in *Eastwood*'s case [**Costs LR (Core Vol) 50**].

The computation of the A figure involves an assessment of the reasonable direct cost, that is to say the grade of person (senior solicitor, assistant solicitor, legal executive, etc.) whom it was reasonable to employ at each stage; an approximation of the cost of employment of each individual by considering the number of hours for each of them to be reasonably engaged; and assessing a rate per hour sufficient to cover the salary and the appropriate share of the general overheads of each such person. The assessment of the appropriate rate per hour would be based on the taxing master's knowledge and experience of the average solicitor or executive employed by the average firm in the area concerned. The total hours of each person multiplied by an approximate cost per hour, together with an allowance for letters, telephone calls and telex messages, then produces what the Court of Appeal referred to as the A figure.

The B figure is then conventionally assessed by adding a percentage to the A figure which is appropriate in all circumstances to cover matters which cannot be calculated on an hourly basis, that is to say supervision and other indirect expenses, together with what the master referred to in his answer as "imponderables", which reflect the degree of skill, responsibility and the other factors set out in RSC Order 62, Appendix 2, Part X as required by paragraph 1(2) of Part X. As mentioned above, the increase for the B figure claimed in the present case was just under 50%, which would be perfectly normal and certainly not excessive in cases of this type. This is the figure which, in the case of an independent firm of solicitors, is expected to make a contribution to the profits of the firm. The appropriateness of the total of A and B, arrived at in this way, is then considered against the background of the proceedings as a whole and rounded off to a convenient sum which appears in all the circumstances.

Appeal allowed.

Harry Woolf (Treasury Solicitor).
Robert Simpson (Herbert Oppenheimer, Nathan & Vandyk).

Maltby and another
v
D J Freeman & Co (a firm)

Chancery Division
22, 25, 26 July, 25 October 1977

Walton J
sitting with
Master Clews and Mr M D T Loup as assessors

Headnote

Another important case in relation to the assessment of non-contentious costs which suggests that where a large estate is involved the most important of the seven factors to be considered is what is the nature and value of the property involved.

---

25 October. WALTON J read the following judgment: The late Harold Vivian Maltby, the father of the first plaintiff and husband of the second, made his last will and testament on 7 August 1958, and thereby appointed the plaintiffs to be executors and trustees thereof, but as to his son on attaining the age of 21, and with a substitutionary appointment in respect of his widow in case she predeceased him. He made a codicil thereto on 13 October 1967, whereby he appointed the plaintiffs executors and trustees. He died on 18 September 1972, somewhat unexpectedly. The deceased had had a somewhat unsatisfactory history of dealing with accountants, and was, I gather, to some extent reticent about his affairs even with his family. He died worth approximately £1³/₄ million, the vast bulk of his estate being in property.

The plaintiffs instructed the defendants, who are well known as solicitors having great expertise in the world of property, to act for them in the administration of the estate by a letter of 21 September 1972. That firm proceeded to obtain all the necessary details of the estate from the first plaintiff, to whom his mother left the main conduct of the administration of the estate. As the first plaintiff is himself a chartered surveyor, he was in a unique position to assist the solicitors in the preparation of valuations of the various properties owned by his father, and he in fact provided them. However, principally I think because of the reticence to which I have already referred, the solicitors did have to check very carefully and in detail the deceased's private company shareholdings.

Probate was duly obtained on 19 July 1973. On 23 October 1973 the first plaintiff wrote to the defendants terminating their instructions, since, owing to reorganisation of the business affairs of himself and his mother, he now had as one of his employees a chartered accountant specialising in tax matters and estate duty, and the first plaintiff considered that with this assistance he could now personally carry on with the administration in place of the solicitors. The parting was, however, quite amicable; the defendants took the point, and simply invited the first plaintiff to come back to them on any points which arose on which that firm might be able to assist.

The defendants then instructed Messrs Kitchen & Co, costs draftsmen, to prepare a solicitor and own client bill of costs in respect of the work so done by them for the plaintiffs. This this firm did, and for the moment it will suffice to say that the total of profit costs came to £11,175. The plaintiffs were dissatisfied with this bill, and requested the defendants to obtain a certificate from the Law Society that their costs were reasonable. This request was expressed to be under article 3(1) of the Solicitors' Remuneration Order 1972 [SI No 1139], but this was clearly a mistake; the preparation of the bill, and the right to obtain the certificate alike, was governed by the provisions of the Rules of the Supreme Court (Non-Contentious Probate Costs) 1956 [SI No 552]. However, the crucial provisions for this purpose are in identical terms, so that no harm was done. In the event, the defendants duly applied for such a certificate on 20 March 1974, and on 24 May 1974 the Law Society issued a certificate to the effect that £8,500 would be a more appropriate charge in respect of profit costs than the sum of £11,175.

Neither of the plaintiffs was satisfied with this outcome, and they accordingly proceeded to taxation. I need not detail the various procedural steps which occurred, but the master first of all allowed the bill in full in the sum of £11,175; but, on objections to taxation being made, reduced it by the sum of £675 to £10,500. The plaintiffs still not being satisfied, they have applied for a review of this taxation, which is now before me. Pursuant to a direction of Oliver J, I have sat with assessors (Master Clews and Mr M D T Loup, senior partner in Boodle Hatfield & Co) from whose experience and advice I have derived the greatest possible assistance, although I should perhaps make it clear that the decision which I have reached is strictly my own, and that neither of them would have reached precisely the same figure.

First, what principles govern the costs of non-contentious probate work? The answer, as I have already indicated, is to be found in the Rules of the Supreme Court (Non-Contentious Probate Costs) 1956. The crucial rule for present purposes is rule 1, which, so far as material, provides as follows:

> "For work done in respect of business to which these Rules apply a solicitor shall be entitled to charge and be paid such sum as may be fair and reasonable having regard to all the circumstances of the case and in particular to – (1) the complexity of the matter or the difficulty or novelty of the questions raised; (2) the skill, labour, specialised knowledge and responsibility involved on the part of the solicitor; (3) the number and importance of the documents prepared or

perused, without regard to length; (4) the place where and circumstances in which the business or any part thereof is transacted; (5) the time expended by the solicitor; (6) the nature and value of the property involved; (7) the importance of the matter to the client."

I should perhaps add that there are two provisos to that rule to which attention must be directed. The first, proviso (*a*), makes it clear that the client is entitled to require from the Law Society a certificate as to the fairness and reasonableness of the charges. The other, proviso (*d*), states that it is the duty of the solicitor to satisfy the taxing master as to the fairness and reasonableness of the charges.

Now fairness and reasonableness is something which in this kind of situation does not exist in a vacuum; it is impossible to consider whether £X is a fair and reasonable charge without there being some guidelines against which one can consider the extent of the charge. Of course, all such guidelines must of necessity be conventional, since they are not specified in the terms of the rules themselves, but without some guidelines, however loose, it would, in my judgment, become impossible to compare one figure with another, to argue from one case to another, which is what the overall concept of fairness must surely involve.

There is one matter concerning the various headings under the rule which is not, I think, really in contention, and that is that although the various matters therein mentioned are at any rate capable of being cumulative, there must be no overlap in the charge. Thus, for example, if the importance of the matter to the client has already been sufficiently taken care of by the charge made under the "nature and value" heading, then there will be nothing to add under the "complexity" heading. Duplication is never permissible.

Now virtually all the considerations as apply under the Rules with which I am here concerned apply in relation to the Solicitors' Remuneration Order 1972; it is virtually only that, in that Order, head (7) in the Probate Rules becomes head (viii), and that there is a new head (vii), relating to the possibility of the land being registered land. Donaldson J has recently commented in general terms on all those heads in *Property and Reversionary Investment Corpn Ltd v Secretary of State for the Environment* [[1975] 2 All ER 436, [1975] 1 WLR 1504, **Costs LR (Core Vol) 54**], and in general further comment would be superfluous.

When dealing with the various matters mentioned, the easiest to deal with, because, assuming, as indeed ought always to be the case, proper records have been kept, there should be little room for argument, is of course the fifth, the time expended by the solicitor or his employees. In a good many cases, although by no means all, it is also the logical starting point in that it gives in itself a good indication of the weight of the matter as a whole. I would, however, make one gloss; however meticulously time records are kept, this will always, save in the plainest of all possible cases, represent an undercharge. No professional man, or senior employee of a professional man, stops thinking about the day's problems the minute he lifts his coat and umbrella from the stand and sets out on the journey home. Ideas, often very valuable ideas, occur in the train or car home, or in the bath, or even whilst watching television. Yet nothing is ever put down on a time sheet, or can be put down on a time sheet, adequately to reflect this out of hours devotion of time. Thus it will be a rare bill which can be simply compounded of time and value; there must always be a third element, usually under the second head.

The most important head in a large estate will of course always be the sixth "the nature and value of the property involved". The corresponding words in the 1972 Order are "amount or value of any money or property involved". I think the difference in wording arises from this fact, that under the 1972 Order one is primarily concerned with a single subject-matter, of which a single block of property as in the *Property and Reversionary Corpn* case is an excellent example. However, no estate is typically concerned with just one single asset; there are usually a mixed bag of assets for consideration. Often there will be what might be described as a "leading asset", in the ordinary case this will be a dwelling-house, and the other assets will be of comparatively little value. In such simple cases it will be right to apply the traditional method of charging, namely, by cumulative bands, each attracting a diminishing rate of charge, without modification. But it may well be otherwise.

If one considers two estates of very considerable value, one represented by a single monolithic block of shares in a quoted company, and the other represented by numerous small parcels of shares, including some in companies which are not so quoted, it is at once apparent that in their practical implications their same values involve quite different considerations on the part of the solicitor concerned. Hence, I think the introduction into the Probate Rules of the word "nature".

As a severely practical matter, I think that it cannot be very useful to assume that there are an infinite series of percentages applicable varying having regard to the nature of the assets; I think that, for the same reasons, one must, where at all possible, relate the additional work due to complexity of this nature to the first head, under which it will normally be possible to compensate for the additional complexity so created. If this were for any reason not possible, one might be forced to consider the matter as if it were so many different estates in order to arrive at a reasonable charge.

In general, however, when one comes to translate value into terms of the legal bill, the approach involves two ingrained habits of legal thought. There is nothing strictly logical about either, but they are so ingrained that all approaches have to take them into consideration. The first is that the correct method of charging is by means of a method of percentages, and the second is that the percentage is not a flat rate applied throughout the scale, but declines on a regressive scale as the value of the matters involved increases. In the *Property and Reversionary Corpn* case a strenuous effort was made to persuade the court, in the light of the fact that the 1972 Order (very similar in terms to the rules in the present case) did not prescribe any bands or percentages, that a flat rate ought to be taken over the whole. This was rejected by Donaldson J in accordance with the general feeling of the profession.

I am therefore left the twin problems of where the bands lie and what the percentages should be. In the *Property and Reversionary Corpn* case [[1975] 2 All ER 436 at 443, [1975] 1 WLR 1504 at 1511, **Costs LR (Core Vol) 54 at 60**], Donaldson J indicated that the divisions between the higher bands, when one is dealing with property approaching £2 million as a minimum in value, should fall at £¼ million, £1 million, £2 million, £5 million and £10 million. Although the value of money has changed considerably even since 1975, I would not quarrel with these divisions in any way. I do not, however, take it that the learned judge intended that the first band should be a simple band up to £¼ million at a low figure. It must, I think, "dovetail" into the charges for estates made up to £¼ million, and in this regard I refer, by way of illustration rather than strict guidance (since the figures have since been withdrawn) to the suggested Charges for Obtaining Grants and Administration set out in the Law Society's Gazette [March/April 1971, p 133].

I therefore think that in the case of an estate of the size of the present one, compounded of the large number of separate elements of which the present estate is compounded, the first band (to £¼ million) would be at 1½%; the next band (£¼ million to £1 million) at ½%; and the next band (£1 million to £2 million) at ⅙%. I must emphasise that these bands cannot be made to apply, and are certainly not intended to apply, to any other classes or work carried on by solicitors: they have no relevance whatsoever to ordinary straightforward conveyancing, for example, where there is only one asset to deal with at a time. They are intended to be confined solely to the work involved with a large number of assets. And they are solely confined to an estate of the present size: in the case of a smaller estate, the first rate would be too low.

I would therefore think that a realistic figure for the "value" heading ought to be rather more than that actually stated by Messrs Kitchens in their bill. However, and both sides agreed with this view of the matter, in view of the termination of instructions before the solicitors had completed their normal work, the sum under this heading falls to be reduced by 50%. It is obviously right that an allowance should be made for the premature termination of the work, and it is, I think, consistently with the heads of the rules, the only suitable head under which to effect such reduction, illogical though it may strictly be to utilise it in this manner. The more logical alternative would, of course, be to apply a suitable percentage reduction to the totality of heads (1), (2), (6) and (7). In view of the agreement of the parties, I do not pursue this alternative further in this case. The precise amount of the reduction must, in every case, be a matter of extreme difficulty, and it is complicated by the freely acknowledged fact that in the present case, by reason of his professional status, the first plaintiff was able to afford the solicitors a great deal of assistance in relation to values. As I have indicated, both sides agreed that a 50% reduction was a fair figure to take care of both these figures, and I entirely agree with their judgment.

I think that Messrs Kitchens have rightly not sought to charge any sums under heads (3), number and importance of the documents perused or (7), importance of the matter to the client. In the circumstances of this case head (3) is subsumed in the time expended, and though of course the matter was of great importance to the clients, it is not of any importance other than might be deduced from its general nature and size. A sum of £300 has been charged under head (4), the place where and circumstances in which the business or any part thereof was transacted but I see no justification for any such charge. The solicitors were not required to attend at any extraordinary place, or to act with any extraordinary degree of urgency, or any other matter of that nature.

Sums have also been charged under heads (1), complexity and (2), skill, labour, specialised knowledge and responsibility. I think that charges under both heads are justified, although it appears to me that the method of ascertaining such sums adopted by Messrs Kitchens, namely the taking of a percentage of head (6), is unsatisfactory. The two items together are charged at £5,100, and I am quite clear that this is too much. It is extremely difficult to say just how much ought to be charged under these two heads, but, having had my attention called to the correspondence, and to the documentation involved, not forgetting that as regards one or two matters the solicitors might, perhaps, have displayed even more skill than they did with advantage, a sum of a little more than half of the sum allowed would be justified.

Accordingly, at the end of the day I have reached the conclusion that the sum which ought to be charged is the sum of £8,500. This is, of course, in round figures: it is not possible to pretend to any greater accuracy. It will be seen that my figure agrees with that of the Law Society's certificate. I have no means of knowing precisely, or at all, how the Society's panel arrived at that figure, but it is at any rate satisfactory to me to find that the analysis which I have made above produces approximately the same result.

I therefore fix the amount of the bill in the sum of £8,500.

Order accordingly.

Nigel Hague for the plaintiffs.
James Goudie for the defendants.

Davidsons (a firm)
v
Jones-Fenleigh

Royal Courts of Justice,
Thursday, 6 March 1980

Before:
Roskill and Eveleigh LLJ

Headnote

The important question of whether a series of bills delivered by a solicitor to his client over a period of time should be treated as one bill or as a series of separate, individual statute bills was examined in this case. In this case four bills had been delivered and taxation under the Solicitors Act 1974 had been ordered of all the bills. If the bills were to be treated as separate bills in their own right, because of the time limits imposed by the Act, only one of the bills (the most recently delivered) would be subject to taxation. A review of the law, and in particular *Romer & Haslam* (1893) 2 QB 286, was carried out by the Court of Appeal and this case is of significant importance in Solicitors Act proceedings.

Judgment

(revised)

ROSKILL LJ: We need not trouble you further, Miss Hallon. This appeal from an Order of Mr Justice McNeill made on 15 January this year, at first sight seems to raise a simple issue under Order 14. But in truth it raises a point of general importance to solicitors. We have been told by Miss Hallon for the appellant solicitors, Messrs Davidsons who practice in North London, that not only is the point of general importance but that the Law Society is clearly interested in the outcome of this appeal.

It was, indeed, through this interest that Miss Hallon referred this morning to one previous decision of this court which to my mind is of great importance in resolving the matters in issue. We are grateful to those who drew Miss Hallon's attention to that authority which was not referred to before the learned judge.

As I say, the appellants are a firm of solicitors practising in North London. A former client of theirs, Mr Jones-Fenleigh, is the respondent. The appellants are the plaintiffs in these Order 14 proceedings and the respondent is the defendant. The appellants issued a writ against the defendant for £2,820.51, being the balance of what they claimed to be due under the last of four bills of costs which they had sent to the defendant for discharge by him.

The appellants had been retained by the defendant in connection with what were obviously complex matrimonial proceedings between the defendant and his wife. Those proceedings went on over a number of years; there were different aspects of those proceedings dealt with at different times, and the appellants, from time to time during those proceedings, sent three successive bills, all of which were paid without demur. Finally, after the defendant had withdrawn his instructions, they sent him the fourth and final bill out of which the present dispute arises.

The appellants sought judgment under Order 14 for the balance due under the fourth bill. The master gave the defendant conditional leave to defend provided that he paid that balance into the court and then, on the footing that that payment into court was duly made, he ordered all four bills to be taxed and made the appropriate order for reference to the taxing master. The appellants appealed to the Judge in Chambers, Mr Justice McNeill. That learned judge dismissed the appeal. The appellants now appeal further to this court.

At the outset of Miss Hallon's argument the question arose whether leave to appeal was necessary. It seems to us plain that leave is not necessary. If authority be required for that proposition, it is to be found in *Gordon* v *Cradock* (1964) 1 QB 503, a decision of this court. Mr Russell, for the respondents, did not contend otherwise.

The burden of Miss Hallon's argument has been this. These were, she says, four separate bills, and the learned judge and the master were wrong in treating them as one complete bill which could now be ordered to be taxed, as it were, in its totality. That was the first main ground of this appeal. The argument which found favour below was that these four bills were but one bill. The foundation for that argument was that the appellants were retained to conduct the entirety of the proceedings between the defendant and his wife, and that in legal theory at least, this being a single contract for the performance of that retainer in its entirety, the appellants were not entitled to any remuneration until the conclusion of those proceedings. Hence it was said that all four bills should be treated as one and that all should be the subject of a single taxation.

That argument has been attacked by Miss Hallon. She conceded that the fourth bill – which is the biggest – is liable to taxation under section 70 of the Solicitors Act because the application for taxation was made within the time limited by section 70(3). But it is said that as regards the other three bills, the time for taxation under the statute has long since passed, that if any taxation of them is to be ordered, it could only be under the inherent jurisdiction of the court, and that there is nothing to justify the exercise of that inherent jurisdiction since these three bills are not liable to taxation under section 70.

The first and, as it seems to me, the all important question, is whether these four bills should be regarded as four individual bills, or one single bill. If the latter be right, then plainly the order below should stand. But we have had the advantage of a much fuller argument than was available below, and in particular we have been referred to that decision of this court which I have already mentioned, *In Re Romer & Haslam* (1893) 2 QB 286. But before I refer to that case it is necessary to go back in legal history. There appears to be no doubt – and if authority for this is required it will be found in the judgment of Sir George Jessel, Master of the Rolls, *In Re Hall and Barker* (1878) 9 Ch 538 – that before the fusion of law and equity pursuant to the Judicature Acts of 1873 to 1875, in the old fashioned common law action a solicitor was not entitled to be paid until after he had completed his duties in that action.

The learned Master of the Rolls said, at 543:

> "Actions at common law did not, in former days, occupy a very long time, and were comparatively simple matters. Common Law Judges were perhaps not so familiar as they might have been with equitable proceedings, and there are instances where, to avoid, or to get rid of what was considered an unjust application of the Statute of Limitations, they extended that doctrine to a suit in equity."

But even at that date as the decision in *In Re Romer & Haslam* shows, equity applied more flexible principles, and after the fusion of law and equity it is plain that gradually, as common law cases became more complicated, the former rigid common law rule was mitigated on pragmatic grounds. Lip-service seems from time to time to have been paid to it, but by the time one reaches *In Re Romer & Haslam*, it is plain that the Court of Appeal, Lord Esher, Master of the Rolls, Lord Justice Bowen and Lord Justice Kay, recognised that in certain circumstances a solicitor might, in the course of a long drawn out common law action or arbitration, properly send in bills from time to time to his client, bills made out to a certain date or up to a certain point which is described in the judgments as a "natural break", intending them to be paid up to that date or point subject of course to the client's statutory right, as it then was, to have that bill taxed either after delivery or, in certain circumstances, even after payment.

But as the judgments in *In Re Romer & Haslam* show, for this entitlement to remuneration to arise a very clear intention had to be manifested by the solicitor when he sent in his bill to the client that it was intended to be a complete bill to date, which the solicitor wanted to have finally settled and that the solicitor was not, in sending in that bill, merely either telling his client how matters were going on or only seeking a payment on account towards whatever the final bill might be.

In *In Re Romer & Haslam*, the bill was submitted to Mr Justice Mathew as Judge in Chambers for taxation, and the learned judge made an order for taxation. There was an appeal from him to the Divisional Court, as was the practice in those days, and the Divisional Court reversed his decision. There was then a further appeal to this court, and this court reversed the Divisional Court and restored Mr Justice Mathew's order.

There are a number of passages in these judgments which I should cite, since the industry of counsel has not revealed any later decisions on this point since *In Re Romer & Haslam*. Lord Esher MR, at 293, said:

> "Now, with respect to the delivery of a solicitor's bill of costs, in cases where in fact several accounts have been delivered, two points may be, and generally are, raised – one of law and one of fact. If the solicitor insists that one of these accounts was a final bill of costs, the question of law arises whether at the time when he assumes so to deliver it, it could be delivered as a final bill. If a solicitor undertakes to carry through a legal transaction, the law is that he cannot send in a final bill of costs until that transaction is completed; the law on the point is the same in equity as at common law. But in equity the nature of many of the suits is such that they can be divided into stages, and the court may treat the legal transaction as finished although the suit has not been carried to its final conclusion; this is a most important feature of Chancery Proceedings. The ordinary procedure in equity is for the matter to go on to the stage of decree. In many suits there may be successive decrees; but the decision or decree has to be worked out – a process which may take years; and it becomes obvious that one part of the legal transaction undertaken by the solicitor may have been determined when the decree is made, and that the working out of the decree may form a new and distinct part of the legal transaction. In an ordinary common law action, the duties of the solicitor are completed when judgment is pronounced; the client gets nothing by the action until that time; though the circumstances of each action may differ, the law applicable to them is the same. That is the law in such a case as the present, and it is therefore necessary to consider whether, even although a solicitor may intend a bill to be final, he has power to send it in as a final bill."

The Master of the Rolls then turned to the facts of that case and reached the conclusion that the successive bills sent in were merely bills sent in on account, and that therefore the client was entitled to tax all those bills and Mr Justice Mathew's order was restored.

I turn to the judgment of Lord Justice Bowen which is of particular importance in its application to the facts of the present case. At 297 he said:

> "It seems to me extremely desirable that we should keep clearly in our minds what points are points of law and what are points of fact. When this is once done, it will be found that all the cases which have been cited to us fall naturally into their places. We have to consider whether the earlier bills of costs sent in were such bills of costs and so delivered as to make their delivery a delivery of bills of costs under the Solicitors Act. It is clear that they might have been such bills, had they been so treated by the parties. Were they divisions or chapters of one bill of costs delivered from time to time, or were the earlier ones delivered as bills of costs within the meaning of the statute? Whether they were delivered as bills of costs becomes a question of fact. To make up one's

mind on this part of the case one has incidentally to consider whether the solicitors had a right to deliver bills of costs, and, if not, whether the documents were taken by agreement of the parties as separate bills of costs, each standing, if I may so express it, by its own strength. In the first place, had the solicitors a right to insist that each document was independent of the others, and was a bill of costs within the statute? And this is a different question from the question whether the client had a right so to treat them. This draws us into a discussion as to whether at the time the bills were delivered there was such a natural break in the business as to justify the solicitors, if they wished, in sending in their bill and asking for payment. I need do no more than observe that the law as to common law actions, which is laid down by Lord Lyndhurst and Baron Parke, in *Harris* v *Osbourn* is, that *prima facie* a solicitor, when he is retained by the client, undertakes to finish his client's business. As to business which is not a common law action, but which may be a suit in equity, lengthy either by reason of the number of the parties or by reason of its comprehending a variety of really independent litigation, there may be natural breaks, and this is clearly laid down and explained by Lord Jessel, Master of the Rolls, in *In Re Hall and Barker*. It is not necessary in the present case to define the natural breaks which may occur in a Chancery suit. There has here been a protracted arbitration, and we need not and cannot define the breaks which may take place in such a proceeding; there may, however, be some breaks which must be recognised as such. When we have made up our minds that the solicitors had a right to treat any division of the proceedings as a natural break, we have to ask ourselves whether they exercised that right, for obviously they may have had the right and yet may not have intended to send in a bill of costs in exercise of that particular right. If, however, we determine that the solicitors had no such right, we must ask ourselves the further question of fact whether both parties agreed to treat the documents as bills delivered under the Act. Putting aside, therefore, the character of the breaks, we have to decide the question of fact whether there has been a delivery of a bill of costs under the Act by the delivery of a bill containing various items of costs. Payment on account by the client in respect of the separate bills is not conclusive to show that each of them was a separate bill of costs under the Act; it may be consistent with a clear understanding between the parties that the ultimate bill sent in should be the bill of costs, and that the payments were to be considered as made against that bill. It must always be a question of fact whether a document is a separate bill of costs or, so to speak, a chapter in a volume. In determining whether a document has been delivered as a bill of costs, it must not be forgotten that the onus of showing that it has been lies on the solicitor; he must make out as to each document of the series that there has been such a delivery of a bill of costs as to satisfy the law. In this particular case it is most material to observe that the delivery of the bills does not correspond, except perhaps in one case, with any natural break in the litigation."

Lord Justice Kay, at 301 and 302 said much the same thing. I will only read two or three short passages:

"If a solicitor is retained in a civil action (it is immaterial whether it be an action at law or in equity) *prima facie* his contract is entire; it is a contract to carry the matter through to a conclusion. The result of this is that he has no right under the statute to send in his bill and insist upon payment until the conclusion of the business to conduct which he was retained. But when we come to apply this rule to a complicated litigation, which may last a considerable time, it is difficult to apply literally, and say that the solicitor cannot send in his bill till there has been a final conclusion of the proceedings, and that the contract is an entire contract in such a sense that the solicitor has no remedy for his costs till that period has arrived."

The learned Lord Justice then stated the law in much the same terms as had Lord Justice Bowen.

There is now no doubt, I venture to think, what the law is. In a case such as the present, a solicitor is entitled to select a point of time which he regards an appropriate point of time at which to send in a bill. But before he is entitled to require that bill to be treated as a complete self-contained bill of costs to date, he must make it plain to the client either expressly or by necessary implication that that is his purpose of sending in that bill for that amount at that time. Then of course one looks to see what the client's reaction is. If the client's reaction is to pay the bill in its entirety without demur it is not difficult to infer an agreement that that bill is to be treated as a complete self-contained bill of costs to date.

Applying those principles to the present case it seems to me that there are, within the principles laid down in *In Re Romer & Haslam*, facts which lead irresistibly to the conclusion that each of these first three bills was intended to be and was accepted by the defendant as being, in relation to the period which it covered, a complete self-contained bill which the appellants expected and intended that the defendant should pay, as in fact he did.

Let me illustrate the position by reference to some of the bills. The first, for a comparatively small amount, is from April to September 1974; the total bill was £280.80, and there was £100 agreed as having been received on account. The balance due was £180.80. That was duly paid and receipted on 14 September. Then if one takes the next bill, that is from 2 October 1975 until 31 January 1977. That bill covers a longer period and totals £1,697. There were certain disbursements to counsel included in that bill. There was a payment on account of £1,000, and the balance was duly paid. The third bill was for the period 1 February 1977 to 21 February 1979, and that bill totalled £5,441.56. Again there were certain payments on account. The nett bill was £2,870, and that again was paid. All the payments were made without demur.

Then we come to the bill which is the cause of the present dispute. That bill totalled £10,936.39. £8,115.88 had been received on account. The balance was £2,820.51, which is the sum claimed in this action.

Looking at each of those first three bills, it seems to me, applying the principles laid down in *In Re Romer & Haslam*, that there was a clear intention on the part of the appellants, and indeed a plain agreement to be inferred from the conduct of the parties that those bills should be treated as completely self-contained bills covering the period down to the relevant date given.

It was argued that each bill only showed a regular pattern and that the payments ought to be treated only as payments on account of the sums ultimately due. I do not think that is right; they do not cover any consistent period of time. Each covers a different and irregular period of time.

Then it was said that those bills do not show on their face any "natural break", to use the phrase that is used in the judgments in *In Re Romer & Haslam*. If by "natural break" it is meant a "natural break" which can be identified as a particular point in the litigation that is so. But I do not see why there should not be a "natural break" ascertained by reference to one or more particular points of time. In the ultimate analysis it must always depend, as Lord Justice Bowen said, upon the right deduction to be drawn from the particular facts of each case. Neither Master Jacob nor Mr Justice McNeill had the benefit of being referred to *In Re Romer & Haslam*. If they had it may well be that each would have reached the same conclusion as I have done.

To my mind, and applying that decision to the facts of the present case, there are here not one but four bills. I therefore approach the remaining question on that basis.

It is conceded, as I have already said, that the fourth and last bill which is the biggest, is liable to taxation under the statute. No issue arises on that, but it was argued as regards the other three that notwithstanding the time had expired under the statute, we ought to order those other three to be taxed under the inherent jurisdiction of the court. Reference was made in this connection to the judgment of Mr Justice Cross (as he then was) in *In Re A Solicitor* (1961) 1 Ch 491.

We pressed Mr Russell to tell us what were the circumstances which would justify us ordering taxation under the inherent jurisdiction of the court. He argued that there was such disparity between the amount shown in this last bill – and indeed in the totality of these four bills – and the amount which was paid to the wife on account of her costs, as part of the overall settlement (the details of which I do not refer to) that there was, at any rate, a *prima facie* case for suggesting that the defendant had a grievance which the court ought to be ready to remedy. For my part, as I indicated during the argument, I do not think in the circumstances of this case one can possibly draw any inference from the difference between the various figures in the appellant's bills and the figure which was agreed to be paid by way of contribution towards the wife's costs. There may well be many different matters to be taken into account which could account for the differences. The defendant paid these first three bills without demur and I see no reason for allowing him to have second thoughts in relation to them at this late stage.

It was at one point argued by Mr Russell that there had here been an exercise of discretion by the Judge in Chambers in relation to inherent jurisdiction and therefore we ought not to interfere. With respect that is wrong, as Mr Russell ultimately accepted. There was no exercise of discretion by the Judge in Chambers. The Judge in Chambers, like the learned master, decided this case by reference to the fact that there was as each thought only a single bill and not four bills and but for that reason there was a right to taxation under the statute so that no question of discretion arose. We are in a position, therefore, to exercise our own discretion. On these facts I would not hesitate to refuse to order taxation of those first three bills under the inherent jurisdiction.

I ought to mention one other matter to which Lord Justice Eveleigh drew attention during the argument and which Mr Russell conceded to be well founded. When the summons under Order 14 was issued, the cross-summons taken out before the master was plainly limited to the fourth bill. The relief sought reads thus: "… the plaintiff's bill of costs delivered to the defendant for the recovery of which this action is brought be referred to the Taxing Master to be taxed and that the plaintiffs do upon the taxation give credit for all sums of money received from or on account of the defendant"; and then paragraph 3 says: "The plaintiffs be restrained from prosecuting this action touching the demand pending the reference … ". Lord Justice Eveleigh asked Mr Russell, that being the only matter which was before Master Jacob, how was it possible to defeat the plaintiff's present claim under Order 14 by a request for taxation of the first three bills, even assuming otherwise that taxation of them ought to be ordered. Mr Russell admitted he had no answer to the point because there ought to have been but was not a counterclaim. However, the learned judge seems to have proceeded in the court below on the basis that this defence was available and I would not wish to decide this appeal against the defendant on a technical point.

But, as I have said, ignoring this last point for present purposes I have no hesitation in refusing to exercise my discretion in favour of ordering taxation of these three bills under the inherent jurisdiction.

In the result, therefore, I would allow the appeal, I would set aside so much of the order below as ordered, all four bills to be referred for taxation, and I would order only the fourth bill to be taxed.

EVELEIGH LJ: I agree. In this case the solicitors were not retained for a single action or specific litigation where it may be that, *prima facie*, the contract is entire and one bill would be contemplated by the parties. In this case they were retained generally in relation to the defendant's matrimonial affairs, and it seems to me that it could not possibly be understood by the parties, nor indeed a workable rule, that the solicitors should not be paid until the relationship between the parties had ceased. That is what it would amount to, because seeing that the matter was so indefinite no specifically identifiable work could be envisaged during the relationship of solicitor and client.

The client in this case accepted the bills and he accepted them as final, and I think that the transaction here was the same as that envisaged by the Master of the Rolls, Sir George Jessel in *In Re Hall & Barker* (1878) 9 ChD 538, at 546 where he said:

> "The transaction amounts to this, in my opinion: 'We have done so much work; there is a convenient break in the business, up to which time we have made up our bill of costs; please to pay us up to that time, and when the outstanding matters are concluded, which we hope will be shortly, we will send in a further bill' ."

That was, in effect, the request being made to the defendant when the first bill and the subsequent bills were sent to him. That was the condition that he accepted. I agree with the order proposed by my Lord.

Order: Appeal allowed. Order below set aside. Taxation of fourth bill of costs only. Appellant's costs here and before Judge in Chambers.

Miss Gayle Hallon (instructed by Messrs Davidsons) appeared on behalf of the Appellants.

Mr Christopher Russell (instructed by Messrs Field, Fisher & Martineau, London Agents for Messrs Freer Bouskell & Company, Solicitors, Leicester) appeared on behalf of the Respondent.

Richards & Wallington (Plant Hire) Ltd
v
Monk & Co Ltd

In Chambers
1984

Headnote

This important 1984 case decides that where an employee is put forward by a company as an expert those putting him forward in that capacity must show that he has the appropriate knowledge to qualify. He can only be allowed a fee as an expert witness, rather than as a witness of fact, if he can demonstrate that the work done was "expert" in the sense that it was outside the ordinary functions of his work as an employee to enable an expert opinion to be given for the purposes of litigation. Whether or not an employee falls into that category must in each case be a question of fact for the taxing officer.

Judgment
(As approved by the Judge)

BINGHAM J: This is an application by Richards & Wallington (Plant Hire) Ltd to review a taxation of costs made by Master Martyn, the reasons being given by the master on 9 December 1983.

The action in which the taxation took place concerned the building of a by-pass at Cullompton in Devon. There were, in all, four parties directly or indirectly involved in the matter. The ultimate customer was the Ministry of Transport which, I think, at the time formed part of the Department of the Environment. As its management agent, it would appear, there acted the Devon County Council who were immediately involved as the customers so far as much of the history of this matter was concerned. The main contractor for building the by-pass was A Monk & Co, and the sub-contractor undertaking to carry out the earth moving part of the contract was Richards & Wallington (Plant Hire) Ltd, the Applicants on this review.

I have been supplied by the master with a helpful summary of the main dates relevant to this matter and that enables me to summarise the history fairly briefly. The works on the by-pass were apparently carried out between May 1967 and October 1969. The period of execution of the works was extended and the works were apparently made more expensive by large scale changes in the quantities, by a large increase in the quantity of bad ground which had to be removed and by the need to replace that bad ground with imported fill. From the early part of 1968 Mr Atkinson, whose fees feature largely in this review of taxation, was on the site and in August of 1969 Mr Kottler, whose fees also feature in this review, joined Richards & Wallington for the purpose of helping the management of that company with a number of different problems which were facing them, including a problem concerning this by-pass.

On 5 November 1970, Monk submitted their final account to the Devon County Council including claims by Richards & Wallington amounting to some £765,000. The response of the Devon County Council to that was to require submission of the claims in a different form and, after a good deal of additional work had been done by Monk, the claim was re-submitted in August 1971 in a slightly reduced sum of £752,000. This amounted to the sum being claimed by Richards & Wallington.

During the early months of 1972 Richards & Wallington pressed Monk for settlement and stressed the expense to which they were being put by being kept out of their money. But, in July 1972, the County Council informed Monk, and Richards & Wallington, that the Ministry did not accept the method of presentation and calculation of their claim. Accordingly, from July to December 1972 Richards & Wallington set about the preparation of a reformulated claim by representatives within the company, and it is relevant to point out that the claim for the fees of Mr Atkinson, which amount in total to some £47,000, are calculated beginning with the work that he did in July 1972 and the balance of fees is claimed from that time onwards. So far as Mr Kottler is concerned the fees are calculated from August 1972 onwards. Mr Kottler's position apparently is that in August 1972 he was due to leave the company but he stayed on and worked for the company on this claim and, perhaps, others.

From January to March 1973 there were negotiations between Monk and Richards & Wallington and the Devon County Council which came very close to agreement in that the Devon County Council evidently was willing to recommend a payment in the sum of £553,000 odd in settlement of Richards & Wallington's claim. At that stage it looked as if settlement was imminent but, unhappily, the settlement which was acceptable to the Devon County Council was unacceptable to the Ministry which, in January 1974, issued an extensive questionnaire on Richards' claim. This involved a very great deal of work to produce answers, not least, according to Richards & Wallington, because of the ill-directed nature of a number of the questions. That work occupied Richards & Wallington, including Mr Atkinson and Mr Kottler, from January 1974 until March 1975 when the claim was re-presented and rejected by the Devon County Council Surveyor. From March to June 1975 there were further negotiations. On 4 June 1975, the Engineer gave his decision, refusing the claim, and upon that decision being made Richards & Wallington decided to seek arbitration.

At that stage, in June 1975, they instructed solicitors. From July 1975 to June 1978 an arbitration of a tripartite nature – *Richards & Wallington* v *Monk* and *Monk* v *the Devon County Council* – wound its protracted course. Early in 1978 Richards & Wallington instructed Mr Quinlan, a well-known expert peculiarly versed in the preparation and presentation of claims of this kind. On 23 June 1978 there was a settlement of the proceedings between Richards & Wallington and Monk, the effect of which was to substitute Richards & Wallington in the arbitration against the County Council. A point was then raised as to the effect of this and a suggestion was made by the County Council that it gave rise to an estoppel. This matter was the subject of a Consultative Special Case which was adjudicated upon by Willis J and, subsequently, by the Court of Appeal, both of whom ruled against the Devon County Council. Accordingly, after the delay while those proceedings took place the arbitration then came back to life and almost immediately settled as between Richards & Wallington and the Devon County Council on 10 September 1979, there being then an agreed award by the arbitrator. A substantial sum was paid by the Devon County Council to Richards & Wallington taking account both of interest and of sums that had already been paid during the preceding months.

In the course of that brief narrative I have made reference to Mr Atkinson and Mr Kottler. They are the two gentlemen who were carrying out work, and the review of taxation is very largely concerned with the recoverability of their fees. Mr Atkinson was employed as a member of staff of Richards & Wallington, from the date that I have already mentioned, and was personally concerned with the work on the by-pass: he was paid on the same basis, so the taxing master has found, as any other similar employee and apparently was paid on a PAYE basis. Mr Kottler was appointed a non-executive director of Richards & Wallington and entered into a contract with Richards & Wallington under which he agreed to give his services as and when required at a daily fee. The fee that is now claimed in respect of his services is the total that has arisen as a result of the time undoubtedly spent.

That being the brief background it is submitted by Mr Butcher, for Richards & Wallington, that the recovery of the fees set out on page 22 of the original bill are recoverable by Richards & Wallington under this taxation, on a party and party basis, by a simple application of Order 62, rule 28(2), which, he says, leads inevitably to the conclusion that their fees should be recoverable. The work which they did, Richards & Wallington submit, went well beyond the ordinary work which would be necessary for presenting a claim to an engineer and in particular its reformulation went very well beyond the work necessary for preparation of a final account. This was not, Mr Butcher submitted, the ordinary work which one would expect to fall within the overhead commitment of a company presenting and pressing a claim in the ordinary course but was exceptional work directly done in order to formulate and present a claim and negotiate a settlement. The work was not done under the directions of a solicitor nor was it done by an expert, but it might have been, and it was argued that Richards & Wallington were not to be penalised because they did not go to solicitors or to an outside expert earlier, and this was work for which they could perfectly legitimately have claimed and recovered had the work been done by an outside expert.

Reliance was in particular placed on the decision of Lloyd-Jacob J in the case of *Re Nossen's Patent* [1969] 1 All ER 775, **Costs LR (Core Vol) 36**, and Mr Butcher laid stress on the principle contained in that case at 778 E–F which indeed represents, perhaps, the high-water mark so far as authority is concerned of his case.

The work which the two men did is not easy to categorise but can, I think, be fairly described in this way. Mr Kottler was concerned with the overall presentation and formulation of the claim. He was deciding how it should be put, how it should be presented and what information was needed in order to present the claim and formulate it in accordance with his decisions. Mr Atkinson was performing a subsidiary role, in effect, of digging out the information which was necessary in order to put flesh on the skeleton delineated by Mr Kottler: he was going into the papers and searching and excavating in order to find the factual material necessary to present the claim in accordance with Mr Kottler's decision.

The argument against allowance of these items, substantial as they are, has been very clearly and succinctly advanced by Mr Uff for the Devon County Council and he has advanced a considerable number of arguments as to why this work is not truly recoverable. He submits, first of all, that the court's power of review should be exercised only where an error of principle is shown and points out that, in this particular case, the taxing master had heard evidence, he had heard Mr Kottler give evidence and heard him cross-examined, and points out that the court is in no position to contradict the master's view on factual matters on which he has reached a decision. He further argues that a party cannot, in the ordinary way, recover his own costs of performing professional work and if he is to do so he must show that the work falls within a recognised category, for example, where a solicitor is acting for himself or in a case falling within an exception described by *Nossen*'s case. But in this case Mr Uff points out that the evidence which Mr Atkinson and Mr Kottler were to give in the action, on the assumption that they were to give evidence, was not in any way expert evidence but was characterised by the master in this way. The master said, in the course of his Reasons:

> "Both Mr Kottler and Mr Atkinson were concerned with the paperwork required to quantify the claim in cash terms. There was no dispute that a great deal of careful work would be necessary in going through the contemporaneous records and making the necessary calculations but the short point was whether these two gentlemen were expert witnesses whose proper fees would normally be allowed on a party and party basis or whether they were members of the staff of Richards with specialised knowledge and

experience who were employed by Richards to decide how much to claim. On the original taxation I had decided that the latter was the case."

He goes on to make clear that on reconsidering the matter he still considered that that was the case.

Mr Butcher has conceded in the course of his argument that the evidence which these gentlemen were to give was not strictly expert evidence and Mr Uff points out that no leave had been given to call them as experts, in accordance with the Rules of Court applicable to arbitrations, and the work that they did was of a purely factual and enquiring nature. It is suggested that the true expert in the case was Mr Quinlan and that if *Nossen*'s case were to be relied upon as allowing evidence of this kind to be treated analogously with expert evidence, and the cost of it to be recoverable, really there would be no dividing line between work of this kind and almost any other work which is done by a company's own expert employees in the course of preparing the claim itself. He further argues that much of this work was done before the Engineer's decision at a time when the claim was not justiciable at all and that the real difference between the claim that was put to the Engineer and the claim that went to arbitration was not in the substance of the two claims but in the need for proof. Mr Uff submits that what the two gentlemen were concerned with was not the providing of expert evidence relating to the claim but the provision of factual material with which to prove it.

The argument has been very clearly and helpfully presented on both sides and that enables me to present my decision rather more shortly. In substance I find myself in agreement with Mr Uff on the central submission which he makes. The dividing line between expert and factual evidence is never an easy one but it is relevant that the expert instructed on behalf of Richards & Wallington is Mr Quinlan and essentially what Mr Atkinson and Mr Kottler were doing, as I understand it and as I think the master understood it, was to dig out the basic factual material which was necessary to prove the claim and on which Mr Quinlan's expert evidence was to rest. I have no doubt that a great deal of work needed to be done, part of this perhaps being attributable to the difficulties of proof in which Richards & Wallington found themselves and various problems that they had to overcome. But essentially, I think, these two gentlemen were engaged on a factual exercise; they were certainly not independent experts; they were not, in truth, acting as experts at all and, in my judgment, these costs fall within the ordinary costs that a litigant must bear of digging out his own factual material, through his own employees, to prove his own case. Had outside experts been introduced to carry out this work then it by no means seems to me to follow that it would in any event have been recoverable as a cost of the litigation.

Accordingly, and on that main point, I conclude that the Devon County Council are entitled to succeed although I reach the decision with some slight regret since this is undoubtedly a very large cost to which Richards &

Wallington were put. But the matter is one that falls to be governed by principle and the principle itself is not, I think, in doubt. The paragraph in *Nossen*'s case that I have referred to does undoubtedly assist Mr Butcher to some extent but the facts of *Nossen*'s case were very special and the work that was being done was there work which the client was himself carrying out at the behest of an independent expert, saving the independent expert the cost of doing that work, and it was, I think, essentially work of an expert character. Accordingly, on the main issue, I conclude that the Devon County Council are right and that the challenge to the taxing master's decision must fail.

There is one minor point with which I can deal more briefly. In addition to this major point, on which the taxing master found for the Devon County Council, there were objections to other items in the bill. There were objections by Richards & Wallington and counter-objections by the Devon County Council. They were apparently heard separately and on these Richards & Wallington were very largely successful. It appears from the file that at one point the master's intention had been to disallow the costs of that hearing, or those hearings, so far as the Devon County Council was concerned but Richards & Wallington's solicitors failed to appear and in the event he did not disallow those costs. That was, I think, a wrong exercise of his discretion and, his discretion having been wrongly exercised, it is, I think, open to this court to hold that the discretion should have been exercised in such a way as to award the costs of those objections to Richards & Wallington. Ordinarily, the court sets its face against allocating the costs of different issues to different parties because of the extreme difficulty of taxing costs of issues but, in this case, it is, I think, relatively simple because the objections were themselves separate and the hearing was separate and it should therefore be reasonably straightforward to tax the costs of those objections in accordance with this decision.

Having said that, I very much hope that, the court having indicated that Richards & Wallington should have the costs of those objections and that there should, if necessary be a taxation, the matter can be the subject of agreement, because it seems in every way undesirable that further costs should be spent in this terrifyingly stale matter.

Mr Uff: I am much obliged. My Lord, I would ask for the costs of this appeal.

Mr Butcher: My Lord, I do not think there is very much I can say about that. I have, to a limited extent, succeeded on one issue; that might be something which could properly be taken into account when dealing with costs.

Bingham J: No. I am afraid that it has really occupied a very small part of the hearing today and it has not been the subject of a separate hearing as it was before the master. I think that the Devon County Council must have their costs of this review.

MR UFF: I am obliged, my Lord. My Lord, my learned junior has an application.

COUNSEL: Yes, my Lord. It is an application for a certificate for two Counsel for today. I do not know that I can add anything much to what your Lordship already knows in support of it.

BINGHAM J: No. Very well. There will be a certificate for two Counsel.

COUNSEL: I am much obliged, my Lord.

MR BUTCHER: My Lord, this is a fairly substantial matter and there is something which looks like a point of principle.

BINGHAM J: Yes. Well, what do you say about this, Mr Uff?

MR UFF: My Lord, we say that this is not a matter which comes that near to the boundaries of the principle as to merit –

BINGHAM J: Well, Mr Butcher has put the matter very plainly and he does not pretend really that this falls within the boundaries of existing decisions, but he does say that it raises an important question and it may be that the boundaries should be pushed a bit further out. That is essentially the sort of matter that the Court of Appeal ought to rule on, is it not?

MR UFF: If your Lordship so feels.

BINGHAM J: It is not a case where he is pursuing the matter in order to, as it were, keep you out of your money longer because it is he that is out of his money.

MR UFF: My Lord, the only two points that I could make are that this is, of course, an exceedingly stale claim – that is perhaps a matter on which both sides share some blame. My Lord, the other point is that your Lordship's decision has been entirely in accordance with existing principle and therefore it is not readily a matter which is going to extend the law, but I am in your Lordship's hands.

BINGHAM J: Well, no. There is a very large sum of money involved and if existing principle is not satisfactory, then it should be reviewed and it is in a way a striking thing that *Nossen*'s case is really the only authority that anybody can ever refer to.

MR BUTCHER: Your Lordship may be interested to know that this case has already given rise to a book which is being written on the subject by one of the parties in the case.

BINGHAM J: Yes. I think the master referred me to that.

MR BUTCHER: He did indeed.

BINGHAM J: Yes. Well, it will make it easier for him to write a further edition. I shall give you leave to appeal, Mr Butcher. Thank you.

Hart
v
Aga Khan Foundation (UK)

Court of Appeal, Civil Division
15, 16, 19 March 1984

Cumming-Bruce LJ and Bush J

Headnote

This is a valuable decision on the proper interpretation of the Litigants in Person (Costs and Expenses) Act 1975 and Order 62, rule 18; both the first instance and the Court of Appeal judgments repay study. Only the Court of Appeal decision is reproduced.

CUMMING-BRUCE LJ: The background of this appeal, in which the plaintiff appeals the order made by Lloyd J sitting with assessors ([1984] 1 All ER 239) on review of the taxation of her costs by the master, is as follows. The plaintiff is an actress of distinction who at all material times was actively pursuing her profession. She lives at 18 Thurloe Close, London. Immediately opposite her house there is now a building on an island site known as the Ismaili Centre. Contractors set about preparing the site for the building which now stands thereon. The course of that work, which involved pile-driving and, on the allegations of the plaintiff, who succeeded in the action, involved a great deal of noise and vibration, subjected her for a substantial period of time to nuisance. Having suffered the nuisance for as long as she could bear it she commenced an action on 21 November 1980 against the defendants claiming damages for nuisance arising out of the building activities on the site. She also claimed an injunction.

The chronology is as follows. On 21 November she issued her writ; on 13 January 1981 she applied for an interlocutory injunction (with success); there was an appeal against the judge's order on 12 February; the action came on for trial before Boreham J, beginning on 8 June, which lasted several days; judgment was delivered on 15 June when the judge awarded £750 damages and continued the injunction; on 24 June 1982 there was a taxation by the taxing master of the plaintiff's bill of costs; on 2 November the master heard and determined the plaintiff's objections to the taxation and on 2 December gave his reasons. The plaintiff sought review. On 23 June 1983 Lloyd J sat with two assessors and reviewed the taxation, and upheld it. Judgment was given on 7 July. The plaintiff appeals against the order of the judge upholding the taxation of the taxing master.

In the bill that the plaintiff submitted for taxation there are two items with which this court is now particularly concerned. The first was her claim for attendance at the hearing (item 8). She claimed for the first day of the hearing £1,520 based on two-thirds of the notional fee of leading counsel, junior counsel and solicitor attending the hearing and for subsequent days she claimed £520 on five different days, claims which were founded on the same notional approach to the taxation of her costs. The master taxed down those claims substantially, taking the view that he should tax on the basis only of two-thirds of the work that a solicitor would have had to do by way of attendance and rejecting her claim for two-thirds of the notional fees that a solicitor would have obtained on taxation with disbursements for counsel.

The other item of the bill which has been the subject of controversy is item 10 under the heading 'Preparation for the hearing', and her claim under item 10 alone is claimed at £4,474, which was taxed down by the master to £1,025.

It is quite clear that the plaintiff, for the purposes of preparing herself for the hearing of the interlocutory injunction and for the trial before the judge, did a great deal of work, extremely conscientiously, faced with formidable practical difficulties. By way of example of her difficulties, the defendants submitted expert reports which on perusal disclosed an attempt by the experts to apply a scientific analysis to problems of vibration and noise, a branch of the applied sciences which is still in an inchoate state, and, in order to understand the technical issues which the defendants wanted to raise at the trial, the plaintiff at first sought to instruct experts herself but was unable to obtain experts who would assist her. She is bitter about the response which she received from experts. She believes that they refused to act because it would not be personally in their interests to give evidence against a major building contractor. If she is right about that, it does not reflect well on the experts concerned, who, if those facts are well founded, had not got a proper understanding of their professional duty. In the result the plaintiff, with great determination, applied herself to trying to discover herself by reference to papers issued by authoritative bodies the material which would enable her to analyse and to take issue with experts relied on by the defendants.

It may well be, though as we have not seen the judgment of Boreham J we do not know, that the plaintiff was too apprehensive about the probable impact on the judge of expert evidence, because an experienced professional lawyer would know by experience that in nuisance cases judges pay far more attention to evidence that they find to be reliable about the actual effect of the building works than on theoretical opinions from experts. However that may be, there is no doubt, in my view, that over a period of nine months the plaintiff worked extremely hard. It was obviously a matter of very great difficulty for her, as it would be for anybody else, to put an accurate arithmetical figure on the hours that she actually worked. She thought that she was being moderate in asking the taxing master to accept the figure of some 250 hours as a perfectly reasonable figure without any element of exaggeration or greediness.

The taxing master appears to have formed the view that the time that she had necessarily and properly worked was something of the order of 86 hours, and when he came to consider the solution of the statutory problem with which he was faced he decided that a solicitor, in preparation for the trial, would probably have taken 40 hours of professional time. The plaintiff is deeply aggrieved both by the approach and by the result of the taxing master's decision.

One of the matters, as she candidly told us, which has led to her sense of genuine grievance is a consideration of the disparity between the figure allowed to her on taxation and the figure which the taxing master would probably have allowed had the defendants succeeded and asked the taxing master to tax their costs. They were represented by leading counsel, junior counsel and solicitors. They would have encumbered the case with a wealth of expertise which they thought might have affected the judge's mind and there would have been disbursements for the expenses of those experts, and experience shows that the fees charged by experts are very considerable. I learnt without surprise that the plaintiff has a deep sense of grievance having regard to that disparity. She knows that if she had lost the case she would have been faced with the most enormous bill of costs, for which indeed she had made financial provision by putting herself into a position in which she would have been able to sell real property if she was faced with that misfortune.

But, having said that, the time has come to remind myself that the problem is a statutory problem and that the question falls for resolution with reference to the provisions of the Litigants in Person (Costs and Expenses) Act 1975 and the rules made thereunder. The title of that Act is "An Act to make further provision as to the costs or expenses recoverable by litigants in person in civil proceedings". Section 1(1) provides:

> "Where, in any proceedings to which this subsection applies, any costs of a litigant in person are ordered to be paid by any other party to the proceedings or in any other way, there may, subject to rules of court, be allowed on the taxation or other determination of those costs sums in respect of any work done, and any expenses and losses incurred, by the litigant in or in connection with the proceedings to which the order relates."

So the Act does not describe the factors to be taken into account by the taxing master on the taxation of costs, but enacts that the taxation of the sums to which the party in person is entitled under section 1(1) shall be subject to rules of court. The relevant rule is RSC Order 62, rule 28A, which provides:

> "(1) On a taxation of the costs of a litigant in person there may, subject to the provisions of this rule, be allowed such costs as would have been allowed if the work and disbursements to which the costs relate had been done by or made by a solicitor on the litigant's behalf.

(2) The amount allowed in respect of any item shall be such sum as the taxing officer thinks fit not exceeding, except in the case of a disbursement, two-thirds of the sum which in the opinion of the taxing officer would have been allowed in respect of that item if the litigant had been represented by a solicitor.

(3) Where in the opinion of the taxing officer the litigant has not suffered any pecuniary loss in doing any work to which the costs relate, he shall not be allowed in respect of the time reasonably spent by him on the work more than £2 an hour.

(4) A litigant who is allowed costs in respect of attending court to conduct his own case shall not be entitled to a witness allowance in addition.

(5) Nothing in Order 6, rule 2(1)(*b*), or rule 32(4) of this Order or Appendix 3 shall apply to the costs of a litigant in person.

(6) For the purposes of this rule a litigant in person does not include a litigant who is a practising solicitor."

The question, therefore, which had to be determined by the taxing master was how to apply to the facts the provisions of the rule.

The first point taken by the plaintiff on this appeal is that, having regard to the terms of the rule, the taxing master should have allowed a notional figure, being two-thirds of what would have been taxed as disbursement to counsel under the item "attendance at the hearing".

When paragraph (1) is considered, it appears that the taxing master may allow such costs as would have been allowed if the work and disbursements to which the costs relate had been done by or made by a solicitor on the litigant's behalf. A solicitor has not got a right of audience in the High Court. The exercise is a notional exercise under paragraph (1). The taxing master has to say to himself, "She did not instruct a solicitor but I have to apply a statutory fiction for the purposes of taxation and decide what costs would have been allowed and what disbursements would have been allowed if the work had been done by a solicitor."

The plaintiff's submission is that the whole of that exercise was a statutory, imaginary exercise and there is nothing any more imaginary about imagining disbursements to counsel than about imagining the work which a solicitor would himself have done on the litigant's behalf; and as the solicitor would not have had a right of audience in the High Court the plaintiff submits that, in order to make sense of the notional exercise, the conclusion to which the court should arrive as a matter of construction is that, for purposes of attendance, the notional exercise should contemplate the solicitor himself charging a fee for the work that he has done and should also include the disbursements, themselves also notional, which the imaginary solicitor would necessarily have had to make when he instructed counsel to attend at the hearing, and, I would think, also such disbursements by way of retainer of experts as the solicitor would reasonably have made.

Having regard to the artificial nature of the exercise which has been imposed on the taxing master by paragraph (1), it is easy to see the force of the submission that the plaintiff unsuccessfully made to the judge, and has made to us. But paragraph (1), as a matter of construction, falls to be read with paragraph (2), and paragraph (2), which I have already recited, distinguishes between the amount to be allowed in respect of any item, being such sum as the taxing master thinks fit, not exceeding two-thirds of the sum which in his opinion would have been allowed in respect of the item if the litigant had been represented by a solicitor, as distinguished from the case of disbursements; because on a proper construction of paragraph (2) it is quite plain that, in the case of a disbursement, there is no deduction to be made of one-third of the amount of the disbursement. Disbursements are to be allowed at 100%. That, in my view (which is the same view as that taken by the master and the judge), points perfectly plainly to the inference that the draftsman of paragraph (2) was contemplating that disbursements would be actual disbursements as compared to notional disbursements. There is no other rational explanation for the distinction between the provision that the notional work of a solicitor should be taxed down to two-thirds in comparison with the 100% allowance to be made for disbursements.

There is another consideration which is relevant. The noun used by the Rule Committee in paragraphs (1) and (2) was "disbursements", which may be compared with the phrase in section 1 of the 1975 Act, which provides for allowing on taxation "sums in respect of work done, and any expenses and losses incurred". The word "disbursement" in the context of taxation was recognised as long ago as 1849 as having a particular meaning limiting the generality of the word. In *Re Remnant* (1849) 11 Beav 603 at 613, 50 ER 949 at 954 Lord Langdale MR expressed it as follows:

> "From this certificate, and from the inquiries which I have made [which he had made after seeking the collective opinion of taxing masters], it appears to me, that it is the practice of solicitors, who may have to pay or advance money on behalf of their clients, carefully to distinguish such professional disbursements as ought to be entered in their bills of costs, from such other advances or payments, as ought to be entered only in their cash accounts, as cash payments or advances. And it seems to me a very reasonable and proper rule, that those payments only, which are made in pursuance of the professional duty undertaken by the solicitor, and which he is bound to perform, or which are sanctioned as professional payments, by the general and established custom and practice of the profession, ought to be entered or allowed as professional disbursements in the bill of costs."

That description of the proper ambit of disbursements when used in the context of taxation of a solicitor's costs has undoubtedly prevailed ever since and there is to my mind no doubt at all that when the Rule Committee, for the purposes of drafting RSC Order 62, rule 28A, prescribed "On a taxation of the costs of a litigant in person there may ... be allowed such costs as would have been allowed if the work and disbursements ... had been done by or made by a solicitor ... ", they were using the noun "disbursements" in the sense in which ever since (and indeed before) 1849 it has been used in the context of taxation of costs. When paragraph (2) of rule 28A is read with paragraph (1) it is to my mind sufficiently clear as a matter of construction that the only disbursements that a litigant in person can claim on taxation are such disbursements as he has actually made and which, if made by a solicitor, would be regarded as necessarily and properly made for the purposes of the litigation. If, in fact, no disbursement has been made, then on a proper construction of rule 28A it would not be right for the taxing master to allow for a notional disbursement, such as, for example, a notional disbursement to counsel or a notional disbursement for any other purpose. There is no other meaning which can give a rational explanation of the distinction between the amounts to be allowed in respect of disbursements in paragraph (2) and the amounts to be allowed in the case of work done by a notional solicitor.

For those reasons I have no doubt that those grounds of appeal by which the plaintiff challenges the determination of the master and of the judge in respect of the disallowance of notional disbursements must fail, and I say no more about it.

The second item which arises on the grounds of appeal arises in respect of the amount that the taxing master allowed for work done. The way in which it was put in the sixth ground of appeal is as follows:

> "That the learned judge was wrong in his under-estimation of the hours of preparation. In the approximate 7 month duration of this action, there was a possibility of 28 weeks at 6 hours a day; a possible 840 hours. Acquiring the expert knowledge in order to counter the Defendants' expert witnesses and win the case, cannot even be estimated now. The learned judge misunderstood the Plaintiff in respect of hours worked and referred to her mistake when she had tried to submit earlier that if the notional counsel was not allowed, the hours for the solicitor would be greatly increased."

In order to consider that ground of appeal it is necessary to consider carefully the provisions of rule 28A(2): "The amount allowed in respect of any item shall be such sum as the taxing officer thinks fit ... "; so far so good. But the next words are of great importance: "... not exceeding ... two-thirds of the sum which in the opinion of the taxing officer would have been allowed in respect of that item if the litigant had been represented by a solicitor." The exercise which is therein imposed on the taxing master is to apply his mind to all the problems which the preparation for the action, including in this case the preparation for the interlocutory injunction, would have imposed on a conscientious solicitor who is notionally regarded as doing the work. The work actually done by the litigant in person, to a greater or lesser degree, may afford some guidance as to the work which a solicitor would have done. That would depend on the degree to which the litigant in person correctly appreciated the business involved. In many cases it is likely that the work actually done by a litigant in person will be of negligible assistance to the taxing master when considering what work a solicitor would have done on the case, but it is of course necessary for the taxing master to go carefully through the business involved in preparation for every stage of the trial; thus, in the case of discovery of documents (and in this case there was heavy discovery of documents), the master would ask himself how much work a solicitor would have had to do in order to prepare the list of documents, to inspect the documents of the other side and to take any decisions that might be necessary as to the need for further discovery; and, in relation to preparation for trial after discovery is concluded, the amount of work a nuisance case would involve, appreciation of all the relevant facts, noise, vibration and so on, and then consideration of the degree to which applied science was likely to be of any real assistance to the judge in deciding whether the work was such as to constitute a nuisance. Where, as in this case, the defendants submitted expert reports, the solicitor would have to peruse those reports to decide how far they were relevant, and to understand the reports, either by instructing experts on his own side (which the plaintiff in person unsuccessfully tried to do in this case) or, failing that, qualifying himself by reading published reports of what, if anything, the relevant applied sciences were likely to produce on their application to the facts of the particular nuisance case before him.

Those are all matters which the taxing master has to consider when considering the material before him on taxation. He then has to form his independent judgment, based on his experience as to the time that a solicitor would reasonably, necessarily and properly have taken to do that work. Having done that, the taxing master has to decide the fees that a solicitor would be allowed on a party and party taxation and then to allow to the litigant in person two-thirds of that sum. As the exercise which the rule requires imposes on the taxing master the duty to allow two-thirds of the sum which would have been allowed in respect of each item if the litigant had been represented by a solicitor, it is likely that the work actually done by a litigant in person will have very little relation to the work that a solicitor would have to do, but that will depend entirely on the nature of the litigation and the practical problems of preparation that the litigation throws up. The rule evidently contemplates that the taxing master, from his experience, would be able to analyse the material put before him and arrive at a reasonable (though inevitably not precise) figure that he would have taxed if a solicitor had done the work.

In the instant case the taxing master, having considered the material, decided, for item 10 of the bill, to proceed on the basis that a solicitor would have taken 40 hours to do all the necessary and proper work on preparation of the case. That is a question of quantum, which is particularly within the expertise of taxing masters.

On review, the judge sat with two assessors, one of whom, we are told, was a taxing master. They examined the taxing master's decision as to the notional 40 hours. They heard the submissions of the plaintiff and by the decision which is expressed in the judgment of Lloyd J they evidently accepted the 40 hours which the taxing master had allowed. That is to be collected from one sentence in the judgment. But the conciseness of the conclusion whereby the 40 hours was accepted by the judge, which must in the context mean the judge sitting with his assessors, who were there particularly for the purpose of assisting the judge on questions of quantum, must mean that the judge with his assessors, having applied their minds to the criticisms made to them by the plaintiff in person, decided that 40 hours was a figure which the taxing master could arrive at in the course of the exercise imposed on him by rule 28A(1) of forming his opinion about the amounts that would have been allowed to a solicitor. The relevant sentence of the judgment is ([1984] 1 All ER 239 at 243):

> "The master allowed £1,025. He took the view that a solicitor would have taken no more than 40 hours for the work in question, giving a total under item 10, including mark-up of £1,600 at the most. Two-thirds of that figure (which I accept) is the maximum which he could have allowed."

In my view there is no material before this court which could entitle this court to interfere with the decision of the judge sitting with assessors on the quantum of the notional time that a solicitor would have taken in respect of the item for preparation for trial. As a matter of construction rule 28A(2) proceeds on the basis that it is for the taxing master to form an opinion on what would have been allowed. On a review, where a judge is sitting with assessors, it is in my view clearly open to the court sitting with such assessors, on review of the opinion of the taxing master, to vary the opinion of the taxing master either as to the number of hours that a notional solicitor would have taken or as to the fee that a notional solicitor would have obtained on taxation. But it is clear from the terms of the judgment that there was in the opinion of the court, sitting with assessors, no sufficient ground shown for substituting a different opinion for the opinion of the taxing master. The approach, in my view, is the approach which is relevant whenever legislation confides to a court the determination of fact or opinion to a specified person or body. It is open to a court on review to reject the opinion of the taxing master only if it is shown on *Wednesbury* principles (see *Associated Provincial Picture Houses Ltd* v *Wednesbury Corp* [1947] 2 All ER 680, [1968] 1 KB 223) that the taxing master had regard to irrelevant considerations, or failed to take into account relevant considerations, or if the court is satisfied that the opinion of the taxing master on the facts was clearly wrong.

I am not satisfied that it has been shown to this court that Lloyd J, sitting with assessors, had material before him which should have led him to the view that the opinion of the taxing master was clearly wrong. For that reason, in relation to the figure of 40 hours (which, in the opinion of the taxing officer, he would have allowed if the litigant had been represented by a solicitor) no ground has been shown in this court for interfering with the opinion of the taxing master.

The next rule that falls for consideration is rule 28A(3):

"Where in the opinion of the taxing officer the litigant has not suffered any pecuniary loss in doing any work to which the costs relate, he shall not be allowed in respect of the time reasonably spent by him on the work more than £2 an hour."

The submission made to this court by the plaintiff is that, in the split of work between work done in working time and work done outside working time, the taxing officer was wrong and the court was wrong to uphold the taxing officer in the split of time which the taxing officer made between the time which he attributed to her as the time that she necessarily and properly spent on the work.

Before coming to an analysis of that submission made by the plaintiff, it is in my view sensible to look back to rule 28A(2). It is clear that that paragraph imposes an upper limit on the amount in respect of work done that the taxing master may allow. The matter was considered in this court in *Parikh v Midland Bank Ltd* [1982] CA Bound Transcript 101. This court then decided that, having regard to the provisions of paragraph (2), it provided an upper limit beyond which the taxing master might not go, so that, however many hours were reasonably spent by a litigant in person for the purposes of the exercise set out in paragraph (3), the upper limit that a litigant may recover cannot exceed two-thirds of the sum which, in the taxing master's opinion, would have been allowed in respect of an item if the litigant had been represented by a solicitor.

On the figures in the instant appeal the result is rather dramatic because the maximum that the taxing master could have allowed on the basis of a solicitor undertaking the work in 40 hours would be the sum of about £1,033. I say "about" because the variable is the difference between a mark up of 50% and a mark up of 60%, and the figure which I have just stated splits the difference between the two. That being the upper limit, as the order of the taxing master was £1,025, there can be no question of this court on a review varying the taxing master's order on the basis that it should have been £8 more than it actually was. The exercise is a notional exercise (there is not room for much precision) and this court would be quite wrong if it contemplated tinkering with the taxing master's order of £1,025 because it was £8 on the wrong side. The plaintiff, who has a very clear and informed judgment in this matter, accepts that she would have never dreamed of appealing to the judge, or to this court, if she had appreciated that the most that she could have got, if she did make out her case other than on 40 hours, was a few pounds more than the master in fact ordered. The gravamen of her case on item 10 is that it is the 40 hours which is completely wrong.

I have expressed my reasons for rejecting that submission and therefore, when one comes to the exercise of the split between working time and time spent on the case outside working time, it turns out that that exercise is irrelevant on the facts before this court because, if the whole of the amount had been allowed in working time, she could not have been allowed more than about £1,033. I have no doubt that the rule contemplates that the maximum amount under rule 28A(2) is the upper limit, and, if a litigant in person works reasonably for, say, 1,000 hours at £2 an hour outside working time, under this rule the unfortunate litigant is not allowed to recover more than the maximum under paragraph (2).

For that reason it is of no practical assistance for the purpose of determining this appeal to go into the whys and wherefores of the master's split when he split his figure of 86 hours as to 50% into hours done in working time and 50% done otherwise.

For myself I would hold that there is a great deal of force in the submission of the plaintiff that, given the nature of her work, it is quite wrong to take a narrow view about the period for which she was working in what would have been working time if she had got the contract referred to in the bundle. I would have thought that it might have been perfectly reasonable to say that the whole of the work that she did, on a sensible basis having regard to an actress's professional commitments, should have been regarded as having been done in working time, because I recognise the force of her case that, if she is disqualified by the business of the litigation from accepting work in a play which is going to take something like 15 weeks, the effect of this dislocation is likely to continue after the determination of that particular contract. However, having said that, and recognising that I have formed that view although the taxing master took a different view, it can have no practical result by reason of the impact of the upper limit prescribed by rule 28A(2).

In my view this is a case in which the plaintiff, honest and conscientious, is a victim of the terms of the rule. It has to be recognised that the Rule Committee had to devise a rule that would apply to vast numbers of taxations of costs of litigants in person. Sometimes, as the judge said, the effect of the rule may be to give a litigant in person rather more than an actual loss; in other cases (of which I regard this as one) the rule only enables the litigant in person to recover on taxation a sum substantially less than the sum that she actually lost. That follows from the words of the 1975 Act, and it may well be that in this unsatisfactory world it is impracticable for the Rule Committee to devise anything which is likely to work more fairly than the present rule, which is liable to work, in theory, upwards or downwards in any given case.

The plaintiff invites this court, irrespective of the outcome of the appeal, to make an observation, if it thinks it right, for the consideration of the Rule Committee on the figure of £2 an hour, which is the figure which is allowed for time when the litigant has not suffered any pecuniary loss. That figure was prescribed in 1976 and has remained unchanged ever since. It is, of course, a wholly artificial figure: it does not purport to be linked to any particular calculus; it is not expressed as being related to the average remuneration of any class of work person; it is plucked out of the air. The plaintiff has submitted that it is a ludicrous figure today and that it is wrong that work that she has reasonably done out of working time should qualify her for a payment of about £1 less than she would pay a cleaner doing the simple menial work which she may employ a cleaning lady to do.

One has to bear in mind that, when the Rule Committee determined to allow £2 an hour, they appreciated that that was a figure that would not be revised year by year by reference to changes in the average working remuneration of any class of citizens; they expected their rule to last for some time. I would go so far as to say that it would be useful for the Rule Committee to look at the figure in rule 28A in the year 1984 and decide whether, in their view, it is still the appropriate figure. It is for them then to decide whether to seek a statutory rule varying the amount of £2 an hour.

As I thought it unnecessary to deal with the detail canvassed under rule 28A(3), I would only say that, as a matter of construction, I have no doubt that the view taken by the judge as to the meaning of any pecuniary loss in doing any work was clearly right. It cannot have been the intention of the draftsman or the Rule Committee that, if any pecuniary loss was sustained, thereafter the approach of the taxing master to the work done should continue to be on the basis of that pecuniary loss as compared to the taxing master looking at the period when the work was done in the course of what would otherwise have been remunerative work which the litigant would have been undertaking.

I have one other observation. The plaintiff rightly has drawn attention to the difficulty of the notional exercise which the taxing master had to undertake, and the judge has observed that, at any rate in relation to disbursements, taxing masters and judges have differed in their approach. As far as disbursement goes there will be no difficulty now because the matter has been determined as a matter of construction, but, in relation to the work done by the notional solicitor, that does not present an easy problem to a taxing master, however experienced he is, for this reason: for work in the High Court, a solicitor has not got a right of audience; had a solicitor been instructed he would have briefed counsel and would also have made disbursements on experts in order to qualify counsel to deal with any expert problem that arose in the case. What work does the rule contemplate as the work which the notional solicitor has undertaken and done? Had the solicitor been retained for county court proceedings in which he had a right of audience which he was going on instructions to exercise, then the solicitor would have had to do all the work himself which was necessary to qualify himself to argue the case, to make his submissions on the law, to make his submissions on the facts and to qualify himself where the opposite party is calling experts or relying on expert reports, to analyse those reports and to cross-examine the experts in order to demonstrate to the court the frailty of their reasoning and of the fallibility of the belief that their science could usefully aid the judge in the practical problem that he had to decide. However, as these were High Court proceedings and not county court proceedings, there is no set of rules which, by rule of thumb, enables the taxing master to decide exactly what a solicitor would have been allowed on taxation. He has to form his own view about it.

I certainly do not have any intention of tying taxing masters to an obligation to condescend in their reasoning or in published reasons to a degree of detail which is otiose or unnecessary. To do so will only add greatly to the expense of taxations and the time taken on them. But I would venture to suggest, recognising that I speak without any experience of taxation, that, having regard to the terms of rule 28A(2), the exercise, necessarily imaginary, which the taxing master has to undertake is to postulate in relation to preparation for trial a solicitor doing all the work necessary and proper for the purpose of preparing a full brief to counsel with a concise review of the relevant facts, an identification of the issues of law and fact, an identification of issues on which expert evidence would be relevant and, where, as in this case, the litigant has not obtained any expert opinion so that she had to do all the work, learning the quasi science, herself, the solicitor would have had to do the same thing and would have had to qualify himself by obtaining published information of the kind that the litigant in person in this case succeeded in obtaining. I would think that, in order to undertake successfully the difficult exercise imposed on the taxing master under paragraph (2), that is the kind of approach which would be sensible and reasonable in a case similar to the present, because how the taxing master sets about identifying the notional solicitor's work will vary in the case of the business concerned. I am speaking, having in my mind the kind of problems that were likely to arise in a case of nuisance such as the present, in which the defendants had sent expert reports for agreement and consideration. It would, I think, when the taxing master is asked to give reasons for his decision, be helpful for him to give such detail as is reasonable, indicating the heads of work which a solicitor would have had to undertake and the time which, in his opinion, a solicitor would have taken under each head of work. I make these observations with some diffidence, recognising that I am wholly ignorant of the expertise which is enjoyed by taxing masters.

For the reasons I have stated, I would dismiss the appeal.

BUSH J: I agree with what Cumming-Bruce LJ has said. For the reasons expressed by him, I, too, would dismiss the appeal.

Appeal dismissed. Leave to appeal to the House of Lords refused.

The plaintiff appeared in person.
John Marrin for the defendants.

Goldman

v

Hesper

Court of Appeal, Civil Division
26 July 1988

Lord Donaldson of Lymington MR, Woolf and Taylor LJJ

Headnote

This case considered the circumstances under which documents that are privileged could be ordered to be produced for inspection in connection with taxation proceedings. Once a party puts forward privileged documents as part of his case, some measure of that privilege is temporarily relaxed. The taxing officer has the duty of being fair to both parties. He must not disclose the contents of a privileged document to the paying party unnecessarily; and he must see that the paying party is treated fairly and given a proper opportunity to raise a bona fide challenge. Disclosure of part or the whole of privileged documents occurs very rarely and the taxing officer no doubt uses all his expertise and tact in seeking to avoid that situation wherever he can.

TAYLOR LJ (giving the first judgment at the invitation of Lord Donaldson of Lymington MR).   This case raises a question of principle about taxation of costs on which there have been conflicting decisions. The question is whether on a taxation the paying party is entitled to see all the documents relied on by the claimant, including those which are privileged. The plaintiff is a solicitor. He and the defendant lived together for some time at 73 Wood Vale, Highgate, London N10, and he had two children by her. The parties fell out and the plaintiff brought proceedings to determine the property rights in the house. In the ensuing litigation the plaintiff acted and appeared at all stages on his own behalf, whilst the defendant was represented by solicitors and counsel. Before this court, however, both parties have been represented by counsel.

On 6 February 1985 the matter came before Mrs Barbara Calvert QC, sitting as a deputy judge of the High Court. She declared the house to be held in equal shares, ordered a sale and ordered the plaintiff to pay half the defendant's costs, to be taxed in accordance with the Legal Aid Act 1974. The case went back before Mrs Calvert on 5 August 1985 at the plaintiff's instance, but his application then was dismissed and he was ordered to pay all the defendant's costs on a common fund basis.

On 27 February 1986 the defendant delivered her bill of costs. The plaintiff wrote to the defendant's solicitors seeking permission to inspect all the papers lodged in support of the taxation. They refused, but the plaintiff had also written direct to the defendant. He enclosed a form of consent for her to sign, which she did, in the following terms:

> "Dear Sirs ...
>
> I understand that my bill of costs in the above matter is to be taxed at 2.30 pm on Tuesday the 13th May 1986 ... at the Divorce Registry. I understand also that [the plaintiff] wishes to inspect the papers lodged in support of the bill and requires about 2 hours for such inspection. I agree to his said inspection and waive any privilege that I may have for any papers or documents contained in the said papers."

On 7 May 1986, however, the defendant withdrew that waiver in a letter which was in the following terms:

> "It has been made clear to me, after consultation with The Law Society and yourself that it is *not* in my financial interest to grant [the plaintiff] the privilege of inspecting the papers lodged. In that case, I *withdraw* my privilege." (Her emphasis.)

It is convenient at this stage to break off from the chronology to deal with the point which was taken briefly by counsel for the plaintiff, namely that once a waiver of privilege has been made by the defendant she could not go back on it. Counsel for the plaintiff did not advance any authority for that proposition and did not develop it more than simply to state it. He was wise in my judgment to make no more of it than that because it has little merit. In my judgment it cannot succeed. In this instance no action had been taken on the letter of waiver, and the situation is not the same as it might have been if there had been some documents already dispatched to be inspected by the plaintiff. Here nothing had been done and nothing was spoiled. The pass had not been sold, and in my judgment the defendant was perfectly entitled, on taking advice, to withdraw the waiver and her withdrawal was effective.

On 29 April 1986 there was an application by the plaintiff for leave to inspect the papers in advance of taxation. That was dismissed by the senior registrar, Mr Registrar Tickle. The plaintiff appealed from that, but Anthony Lincoln J on 9 May dismissed his appeal with costs.

Between 13 May and 20 June the senior registrar conducted a taxation. When he concluded it, the plaintiff lodged an objection. The defendant filed answers, and on 1 August the senior registrar gave his reserved decision whereby he adhered to his original order. The plaintiff then sought a review of the taxation by a judge, and it was thus that the matter came before Eastham J, sitting with two assessors, on 6 February 1987 (see [1987] 2 FLR 352). The plaintiff argued, as he had before the registrar, the point of principle raised on this appeal. He sought also to challenge a number of individual items on the taxation. The judge rejected his argument on the principal point, but made two minor adjustments on two items. This resulted in a reduction of £29.25 from a total bill approximating to £4,000. Eastham J ordered the plaintiff to pay 75% of the defendant's costs of the review.

On 24 February 1987 the plaintiff went back before Eastham J, who granted him leave to appeal to this court. By his notice of appeal the plaintiff challenges the judge's ruling that he cannot inspect the documents. The defendant has put in a counter-notice challenging the judge's award to her of only three-quarters instead of all her costs of the review. The plaintiff has throughout based his main argument on the proposition that a party should, as a matter of natural justice, be entitled to see any document which his opponent seeks to use. He maintains that only by seeing the documents in this case can he be in a position to know whether, and in what way, to challenge any item of costs claimed. It is wrong for the registrar to see and act on his opponent's documents whilst he is denied sight of them. He has relied at each stage on the decision of Hobhouse J in *Pamplin* v *Express Newspapers Ltd* [1985] 2 All ER 185, [1985] 1 WLR 689. In that case the judge considered the conflict between two legal principles: first, the natural justice or fairness point, as raised by the plaintiff here; second, the right of a party to confidentiality in respect of privileged documents. He concluded that in the last resort the first principle must prevail. He said ([1985] 2 All ER 185 at 190, [1985] 1 WLR 689 at 695):

> "The answer is that, ultimately, the principle that each party must have the right to see any relevant material which his opponent is placing before the tribunal, and which that tribunal is taking into account in arriving at its decision, must prevail. In the final resort, the claimant must be put to his election whether he wishes to waive his privilege and use the material or to assert his privilege and retain the confidentiality of the document which the respondent is asking to see."

The judge went on to say that the need for election would rarely arise, either because the parties would be content to trust the expertise and experience of the taxing officer, or because the claimant might waive his privilege, or because, as in the case before him, sight of the documents was not necessary and the application for it was a mere fishing expedition. He held that no question of election arose at the time the claimant's documents were lodged, but if a factual issue arose on the taxation which was bona fide, not a sham or fanciful dispute, then the master or taxing officer might have to put the claimant to his election whether to waive the privilege or not rely on the document. The judge said ([1985] 2 All ER 185 at 190, [1985] 1 WLR 689 at 696):

> "The respondent may then take the stand that, if the claimant wishes to adduce evidence, he (the respondent) wishes to see it and comment on or contradict it. This will mean that the claimant will then have to elect whether he wants to use the evidence and waive his privilege or seek to prove what he needs in some

other way. The type of situation which this visualises is where, in the ordinary course, the claimant would seek to prove his allegation by simply producing a document. If, however, the respondent objects to the claimant using the document without his seeing it as well, the claimant may prove the allegation in another way; for example, if it is the solicitor who conducted the litigation who is attending the taxation, by that solicitor formally or informally giving oral evidence. The respondent could then formally or informally cross-examine the solicitor. The master would then decide, having taken into account any counter-evidence relied on by the respondent, whether he accepted the claimant's allegation. I do not visualise that this would happen, at least not often, but it does serve to illustrate the essentials of the situation."

The senior registrar in the present case declined to allow inspection or put the defendant to her election. In the course of his judgment he said:

"Throughout the proceedings the plaintiff claimed the privilege of inspecting the defendant's file of papers lodged for the purpose of the taxation and the hearing of his objections. He quotes as authority the case of *Pamplin* v *Express Newspapers Ltd* ... Having failed on appeal to see the papers before taxation he repeated his request time after time during the taxation and he does so in his objections. In effect he wished to see every letter, attendance note and instruction to counsel. In the judgment in the *Pamplin* case [1985] 2 All ER 185 at 189–190, [1985] 1 WLR 689 at 695–696 Hobhouse J said: 'Taxation, although adversarial, is not subject to all the incidents of ordinary litigation. Order 62 is, for present purposes, a self-contained code. The provisions of other orders for discovery and inspection of documents etc, do not apply ... It is the duty of the master to conduct the taxation as efficiently and economically as is consistent with doing justice on both sides. It is his duty to prevent the respondent from misusing or abusing the taxation proceedings.' It could be said, with some justification, by the defendant's solicitor that I did not prevent the respondent from misusing the taxation proceedings and that I allowed the plaintiff, for example, to question every attendance. The difficulty with which I was faced was, first, that the defendant had raised matters during the proceedings which were not chargeable as between party and party because they were not 'necessary either for disposing fairly of the cause or matter or for the saving of costs' and the decision as to apportionment between party and party costs and common fund costs was a delicate one, and, second, the plaintiff, who is a solicitor, questioned the need for attendances on the dates given and these have to be investigated in detail. Where the plaintiff challenged an attendance I required the defendant's solicitors to give an explanation of the circumstances justifying it. I checked the attendance note and gave the plaintiff the opportunity to reply. I considered it unnecessary and impracticable in this case to have the defendant's solicitor give evidence on oath and to allow the plaintiff to cross-examine her. The same procedure was adopted in respect of instructions to counsel. Most of the correspondence allowed in the party and party column was in the plaintiff's possession; the remainder was minimal. If taxations are to be conducted expeditiously the party attacking the bill cannot expect an inquiry into every single letter in a large bundle of correspondence."

Before the judge the plaintiff again relied on *Pamplin*'s case. However, the court was also referred to an earlier decision of Stevenson J in *Hobbs* v *Hobbs and Cousens* [1959] 3 All ER 827, [1960] P 112. That was a divorce case in which the co-respondent was ordered to pay costs. On the taxation the co-respondent objected to two items on the husband's bill. One was "instructions for brief", and the co-respondent applied to inspect the brief and its contents. Stevenson J held that he could not inspect them. He stressed the importance of privilege, and went on as follows ([1959] 3 All ER 827 at 829, [1960] P 112 at 116):

> "That is the principle with which the co-respondent in the present case finds himself faced when he says that he ought, as a matter of justice and common sense, to be allowed to inspect and closely examine the contents of the brief which has been delivered to counsel on behalf of his adversary. I am satisfied that he is not entitled to inspect that brief or its contents and I so determine the question that has been submitted to me on this reference."

The judge went on later in his judgment to say ([1959] 3 All ER 827 at 830, [1960] P 112 at 117):

> "Even if there were any doubt as to the view which I have expressed about the area covered by legal professional privilege, it is plain that in litigation in this Division it would have the most intolerable consequences if someone in the position of the present co-respondent were permitted to see the inside of the brief which was delivered on behalf of the petitioner."

Eastham J decided to follow the decision of Stevenson J rather than that of Hobhouse J. He took the view that the latter's attempt to find a way of reconciling privilege and natural justice was impracticable because it would be almost impossible to have the claimant's solicitor cross-examined, whether formally or informally, without referring to the privileged documents.

Before this court counsel for the plaintiff, in a most attractively presented argument, has accepted that there are here two conflicting legal principles, as identified by Hobhouse J. His submission is that openness of justice should prevail so that the paying party should see such documents as are necessary to enable him to challenge the bill if appropriate. "Can't see, won't pay" is the terse expression of that argument. He suggests that waiver of privilege should be partial only in the sense that it would be for the purposes of taxation only and not in regard to any subsequent or continuing substantive proceedings. Alternatively, he submits that the taxing officer should so conduct the taxation as to indicate to the paying party or his lawyer the time, relevance and expense framework of any privileged documents relied on, but not the content. His last fall-back position is an adoption of Hobhouse J's suggested procedure despite its difficulties.

The starting point in considering how far privilege extends in this context is in my judgment to look at the procedure for lodging documents on taxation. This is now laid down in RSC Order 62, which dates from April 1986 and is therefore later in time than the cases cited. Previously procedure was governed by a practice direction only (see *Practice Direction* [1979] 1 All ER 958). Order 62, rule 29(7), so far as is relevant, reads as follows:

> "A party who begins proceedings for taxation must, at the same time, lodge in the appropriate office ... (c) unless the taxing officer otherwise orders, a bill of costs ... and (d) unless the taxing officer otherwise orders, the papers and vouchers specified below in the order mentioned ... (iii) a bundle comprising fee notes of counsel and accounts for other disbursements ... (v) cases to counsel to advise with his advice and opinions, and instructions to counsel to settle documents and briefs to counsel with enclosures, arranged in chronological order ... (vii) the solicitor's correspondence and attendance notes ..."

It is therefore clear that there is now a statutory requirement on a claimant for costs to disclose privileged documents to the court. Normally, where prejudice exists it applies to protect disclosure not only to the opposing party, but also to the court. So the rule clearly makes inroads into that general protection. It follows that once a party puts forward privileged documents as part of his case for costs some measure of their privilege is temporarily and pro hac vice relaxed. In most cases, as Hobhouse J observed, no problem would arise on taxation about privilege. However, when the problem does arise the taxing officer has the duty of being fair to both parties: on the one hand, to maintain privilege so far as possible and not disclose the contents of a privileged document to the paying party unnecessarily; on the other hand, he has to see that that party is treated fairly and given a proper opportunity to raise a bona fide challenge. The contents of documents will almost always be irrelevant to considerations of taxation, which are more concerned with time taken, the length of documents, the frequency of correspondence and other aspects reflecting on costs. In my judgment, the approach adopted by Stevenson J in *Hobbs* v *Hobbs and Cousens* [1959] 3 All ER 827, [1960] P 112 was too rigid and uncompromising. There may be instances in which taxing officers may need to disclose part, if not all, of the contents of a privileged document in striking the appropriate balance. He will no doubt use all his expertise and tact in seeking to avoid that situation wherever he can. I do not envisage it occurring, except very rarely. Of course it is always open to the claimant not to rely on privileged documents which he regards as peculiarly sensitive.

It would not be practicable or helpful for this court to seek to lay down any firm criteria as to the circumstances in which such an extreme course may be necessary. All will depend on the facts of the individual case. One factor which may affect the course taken by the taxing officer may be whether the party is represented by a lawyer or costs clerk, or whether he appears in person. Clearly, in the former case there would be more opportunity for flexibility in the approach adopted by the taxing officer. He might, for example, think it appropriate to allow disclosure of privileged documents to the paying party's lawyer, but not to be divulged to his client. Although the approach suggested by Hobhouse J may only rarely be practicable, it too may in a proper case be a useful resort. Any disclosure of privileged documents which does have to be made in the exercise of the taxing officer's discretion would in my judgment be only for purposes of the taxation. That it is possible to waive privilege for a specific purpose and in a specific context only is well-illustrated by the decision of this court in *British Coal Corp* v *Dennis Rye Ltd (No 2)* [1988] 1 WLR 1113, (1988) *The Times*, 7 March. In that case documents which had been created for the purpose of civil proceedings were disclosed to the police for the purposes of criminal investigation. The question arose whether the waiver of privilege in favour of the police amounted to a waiver in favour of the defendant for the purposes of the civil proceedings. Neill LJ, giving the first judgment, said ([1988] 1 WLR 1113 at 1121):

> "The documents had been disclosed for the limited purpose of a criminal investigation and a criminal trial, in accordance with the plaintiff's duty to assist with criminal proceedings, and objectively that could not be construed as either an express or implied waiver of privilege in relation to the civil action."

By the same token voluntary waiver or disclosure by a taxing officer on a taxation would not in my view prevent the owner of the document from reasserting his privilege in any subsequent context. Applying this pragmatic approach to the present case, it seems to me that the course adopted by the registrar here was fair and reasonable. I can see no ground for considering that the fresh taxation which counsel for the plaintiff seeks would be justified, and accordingly I would dismiss this appeal.

So far the cross-appeal is concerned, counsel for the defendant has not addressed any argument to this court on it. It concerns only the order for costs made by the judge when he awarded three-quarters of the costs, whereas the cross-notice suggests he ought to have ordered total costs in favour of the respondent. Costs in that context were of course essentially a matter of discretion. The judge did give reasons as to why he adopted this course, and I for my part would see no basis for taking a different view on what was a matter of discretion.

Accordingly, I would dismiss the cross-appeal.

WOOLF LJ: I agree.

LORD DONALDSON OF LYMINGTON MR: I also agree.

Appeal dismissed; cross-appeal dismissed.

Nigel Pleming for the plaintiff.
Kay Jones for the defendant.

Finley
v
Glaxo Laboratories Ltd

Queen's Bench Division
9 October 1989

Hobhouse J
sitting with assessors

Headnote

This case (unreported but decided in 1989) is perhaps somewhat under-rated these days since it held that a taxing officer is not restricted to deciding an hourly rate on the basis of the information put before him by the parties to the particular taxation, but is entitled to have regard to other information, not least that of his own experience from taxing other bills.

HOBHOUSE J: This is a review of taxation under Order 62, rule 35. I bear in mind that it is, in effect, a re-hearing of the relevant aspects of the taxation and amounts to a review by this court of the taxation conducted by the district registrar.

In my judgment, this is not a case where I should direct that additional evidence should be admitted under the provisions of rule 35, and I do not so direct. Certain material was placed before us with the invitation that we should so direct, but I have decided that that evidence does not amount in truth to fresh evidence that ought to be placed before this court. The relevant passages amount, in effect, to matters that were already within the judicial knowledge of the court or within the capacity of my assessors to advise me. If I had thought that there was something in that evidence which it was necessary for the solicitor concerned to refer to, then of course I might well have taken a different view.

This was a taxation between a solicitor and the Legal Aid Fund. Upon this review, only the solicitor has been represented; the Lord Chancellor's Department has not been represented. I do not consider that it raises a point of principle which justifies a decision being given in open court, and I certainly would be reluctant to do so without hearing argument on both sides on relevant questions; but I have directed that a tape recording of my decision be made and that the parties, and any other persons with a legitimate interest, shall be at liberty to bespeak a transcript of my reasons.

Under Order 62, rule 12, the task of the district registrar and of this court is to consider what was "a reasonable amount in respect of all costs reasonably incurred". The fact that the Legal Aid Fund is the paying party is irrelevant, absence of means is irrelevant. I must assume that the client has adequate means to pay whatever are the reasonable and appropriate costs that have been incurred.

The nature of the case from which this matter arose was that there was an infant plaintiff, who was born in 1963. She was vaccinated against whooping-cough in the way that was normal at that date. But then she suffered catastrophic brain damage. The solicitor handled a tribunal claim successfully on her behalf, and later on, in 1984, he was instructed with a view to commencing proceedings against the various medical authorities. Limited Legal Aid certificates were granted, which were extended so as to allow the obtaining of expert advice and the opinion of counsel, which included the authority to obtain and consider the evidence of a Professor Stewart which had been given in 1986 in the case of *Kinnear*.

Professor Stewart was the leading authority on the matter of vaccine cases and the leading proponent of the possibility that negligence claims could be brought against the relevant medical authorities or, even, aspects of government. He had been the main witness for the plaintiff in the *Kinnear* case and had suffered a damaging cross-examination. The case had had to be abandoned a little later on, during the plaintiff's mother's evidence. It was clearly reasonable that the effect of his evidence in that case should be considered before advice to the plaintiff in the present case was given whether to continue with her case or to drop it. She was, of course, being represented by her next friends, her parents.

The solicitor, in due course, on 27 November 1986, advised the parents that the plaintiff's case should be dropped. That advice was accepted. No proceedings were in fact issued beyond what had been necessary to obtain the medical records from the hospital authorities.

The work which is the subject of the bill was done for the main part in the year 1986, and it is accepted that from the point of view of arriving at charging rates the court should treat it as having been done in 1986. The bill that was put in by the solicitor totalled over £19,000. The district registrar, upon original taxation, reduced it extensively – indeed, to a figure below £10,000. There were objections by the solicitor, the matter was reconsidered, and there were some increases in the bill but not enough to satisfy the solicitor.

The solicitor has brought the matter to this court, and he asks that the figure should be increased to something approaching his original claim.

There were complicating factors in the original bill. First (and I must say this, although it will be unsatisfactory to the solicitor), there was clearly one extravagant item included in the bill: that was, the amount of hours that were charged for in perusing the evidence that Professor Stewart had given and writing a very extensive note upon it. This is clearly one of the things that went wrong in the charging exercise and gave rise to some of the difficulties which followed.

The next point, for which the solicitor must also accept responsibility, is that he claimed a 125% uplift. That was not accepted by the registrar – in my judgment, correctly.

The third point, which was also of importance to the solicitor and he had been a leading party in the discussion of the matter, was a dispute between the Newcastle solicitors and the Newcastle District Registrar about the rates that it was proper to allow to solicitors upon taxation of their bills, whether on an inter partes basis or a solicitor and own client basis. This had been a dispute which had been going on for some time and there is general dissatisfaction among solicitors in the North East with the rates that have been allowed. That is a further and important aspect of the history of this case.

There are three matters which are directly raised by the appeal and which were the main matters the subject of discussion before the registrar. The first is the hourly rates to be allowed for a partner. The registrar allowed £35 per hour. The solicitor says it should be £45 per hour.

Next is the question of uplift. As I have said, the solicitor claimed 125%. The registrar allowed 85% so as to give a composite figure per hour in conjunction with the £35 per hour rate.

Finally, there is the question of the work done on perusing the Stewart transcript. The difference there was the 96 hours or thereabouts claimed and the 36 hours allowed.

The solicitor was, at the material times, effectively a sole practitioner. He had another solicitor with him for part of the time but that is not material to the present case. He had a special experience and knowledge of vaccine and similar matters. He brought to the consideration of the plaintiff's case a familiarity with the subject matter and a measure of expertise appropriate to a lawyer dealing with that class of case. It must also be borne in mind that he had acted for the plaintiff previously in the tribunal matter, so that he was aware of the background through that source. He is a practitioner in Newcastle and therefore fell within the jurisdiction of the Newcastle District Registry.

I will take first the Stewart transcript point. The evidence that Professor Stewart had given covered many days during the trial, and there can be no doubt that it involved technical matters relating to the effects of vaccination and the issues of negligence that can arise from that situation. It was necessary that that transcript should be assessed, and it was a heavy job to do it. It also required, and received, the expertise and familiarity with the subject that the solicitor had. It is not as if the solicitor were somebody who was coming to this sort of matter entirely for the first time. He holds himself out as being a person especially experienced in this field, and it must be borne in mind that although medical negligence matters involve technicalities, they are not necessarily of a different order from the technicalities involved in a whole range of other cases. The stage of the case which had been reached at the time that he was perusing the transcript was that it was in its earlier stages. What was having to be considered was whether or not litigation should be started on behalf of the plaintiff. There were many serious hurdles to be overcome before advice favourable to the plaintiff could be given. Furthermore, the *Kinnear* case was one which the solicitor already knew had collapsed and had not given rise to any finding in favour of a claimant in a similar position to that of the plaintiff. So, what he needed to do was to see whether, in Professor Stewart's evidence, there was enough left to justify the commencement of proceedings by the plaintiff. Professor Stewart had published previous papers and expressed previous views about these matters with which the solicitor was already familiar, and the solicitor needed to consider what was left of those views after they had been subjected to cross-examination in the *Kinnear* case.

In the view of the registrar, 36 chargeable hours was enough to allow for this exercise to be done. I have considered the matter also, I have taken the advice of the assessors, and I am of the same opinion. Ninety-six hours, which on the solicitor's basis of charging represents well over two weeks of chargeable work, is over-elaborate and excessive, and by a large margin is, in my judgment, excessive. One of the things that went wrong is that an elaborate type-written document was constructed, running in itself to very many pages, and that must have involved the solicitor in a lot of work; but my conclusion is that he lost his sense of proportion at that time, he was ceasing to act in the proper interests of his client, and the amount of time that he spent on it was not reasonable.

In arriving at this conclusion, I have disregarded the suggestion that the solicitor ought to have referred the whole matter to counsel. I accept the argument that he had the expertise himself and that if he had referred it to counsel he might well have been increasing costs rather than reducing them. But, the fact remains that he is charging for his own time and he should only be allowed a reasonable period of time. In my view, the district registrar, who clearly considered the matter closely also, arrived at the right conclusion.

The next point – and it is the one which formed the main part of the argument before me – is the rate per hour which should be allowed. It is clear that the rate which should be allowed is the actual cost, assessed on an objective basis. In other words, it is not answered merely by reference to what has been the cost to the solicitor in question of doing the relevant work on an hourly basis. It has to be assessed on an objective basis having regard to what is reasonable. Therefore, one must consider the position of other solicitors in the relevant area, not merely the position of the solicitor in question. One has to consider whether it is the appropriate level of fee earner that is claimed for. In the present matter it has been accepted, and I accept, that the appropriate level of fee earner for a case of this character was a senior litigation partner; and the solicitor concerned matched that description.

So, what one is considering is the appropriate hourly rate to allow for such a person. In the cases that have had to consider this matter, and indeed in the practice that has been established, one approaches this in two parts. One part is the "A" element, which is the actual cost; the second is the "B" element, which is the uplift. They inter-relate and cannot be considered wholly in isolation from each other. But the starting point undoubtedly is the assessment of the actual rate that ought to be allowed as a cost rate. At the relevant times, and indeed at the time of the taxation, the practice in the North East was to allow no more than £35 per hour as the "A" rate, and it appears that that was also treated as the rate even for a senior partner in that area at that time.

It is suggested, in the reasons of the district registrar, that he should assess matters as at the present day, and it is even suggested by him that he has given the solicitor credit for any inflation that has taken place as between 1986 and the present day. I am satisfied that it is obvious that he has not given the solicitor any credit for the intervening years; but in any event it is inappropriate that he should do so. The costs must be assessed as at the time that they were incurred or the work was done. That, in the present case, is the year 1986.

Viewing the matter objectively, and taking into account the evidence which was before the district registrar, I am satisfied that £35 per hour for a senior litigation partner is out of line. I have also had the advice of my assessors, which confirms the same conclusion.

I will not elaborate the evidence which has been placed before the district registrar and again before this court. It does and did include letters which were written to the district registrars at the relevant times, which formed a consensus of opinion from solicitors in the area and directed itself to the question of what was the true cost of solicitors' time in the area at that time. Before the district registrar, the solicitor himself put in an affidavit which supported that conclusion. He put in an affidavit from another solicitor which, in my judgment, was unfairly criticised and rejected by the district registrar. Furthermore, the solicitor put in material which was a "cost-of-time" exercise. I have looked at that afresh today, and I have taken advice upon it, and it has been discussed during the course of the oral argument before me. It appears that that cost-of-time exercise is not to be criticised as being unrealistic. It was, of course, only a cost-of-time exercise of this particular solicitor, but the basis and parameters do not seem to be open to substantial criticism. Therefore, on the material that is before me and on the advice that I have received, I consider that the £35 per hour is not adequate.

I take into account also the extensive experience of the registrar in taxing bills and his experience in dealing with arguments presented before him and the bills that he sees. But the position in the North East is that the £35 figure has achieved a measure of establishment, which has meant that it has been virtually impossible to displace it, as the experience of the solicitor in the present case indicates. It is not correct to draw any firm conclusion that it is a satisfactory level from the mere fact that many solicitors do not bother to challenge it. Both this court and the district registrar had evidence of the challenge that had been made, with substantial backing, to it at an earlier date.

On the evidence that I have received, I consider that the submission of the solicitor is correct and that the appropriate rate to allow as an actual cost of a senior litigation partner's time in a Newcastle city firm was £45 per hour. I stress the way in which I have expressed that, because there are many other individuals who may be involved. They may be junior partners, they may be employed solicitors, or they may be legal executives. Furthermore, there may be country firms to which those conclusions do not apply. So, the figure I have stated is the figure that I consider to be the fair assessment of the rate, on the evidence in this case, for the solicitor involved in this case at the date when he did the work.

That takes me to the second half of the calculation, which is the question of uplift and the "B" factor. One of the matters on which the district registrar was criticised in relation to the "A" factor, in my judgment correctly, was that he got too much involved, in considering the cost assessment, with questions of profit and with the question of the uplift that he was later going to apply. The simplest way to illustrate this point is by referring to the concluding passage in his reasons, where he said:

> "I cannot see, on the evidence before me, any compelling reasons why I should on this evidence increase the current allowed hourly rate. The allowed rate is £35 per hour. This plus an 85% mark-up gives a remuneration of £65 per hour, which I consider to be both fair and reasonable having regard to the weight of the case and Mr Deas's seniority."

The district registrar is quite right that at the end of any assessment of this kind he should stand back for a moment and consider the implications and the overall picture presented by his decision on the detail. That is what he is doing there. But it also shows that there is a relationship between the percentage that he chose to allow and the hourly rate. There are many other passages in his reasons where he allows the overall profit assessment to colour his views about the hourly rate.

I consider – and counsel has not sought to argue to the contrary – that, having substantially altered the hourly rate, it is appropriate and proper for me to reconsider the uplift that has been allowed.

The uplift factor was a subject that was referred to Kerr J in the *Leopold Lazarus* case at page 4 of the transcript [**Costs LR (Core Vol) 62**]. In view of the hour I will not read out what he says. He refers to appendix II to Order 62 in the earlier version, which is now a slightly different version in the current appendix. That requires the court, and indeed the taxing officer, in assessing the costs, to take into account, among other things, the complexity of the item or of the cause or matter in which it arises; the difficulty or novelty of the questions involved; the skills, specialised knowledge and responsibility required; the time and labour expended by the solicitor; the number and importance of documents; the importance of the cause or matter to the client; the amount of money involved, and so on.

This present case did involve matters of responsibility for the solicitor, because he was taking upon himself the responsibility of assessing the evidence that was available on a preliminary basis and advising the client. He advised against the continuation of proceedings and, far from his deserving to be marked down for that, he deserves credit for taking upon himself that responsibility and also being prepared to say, of his own judgment, that the proceedings should not continue as to do so would not be in the interests of the client and would, indeed, be a waste of time and money. It was an important case for the client. It potentially involved a very large sum of money. But the medical issues were ones which, although complicated and technical, were not outside the expertise of the solicitor; and it is because of this expertise that the matter was being dealt with by a senior partner.

One must also bear in mind that this case was a very early stage: it was at a stage of, essentially, perusal and advice. The solicitor was not involved in the preparation of complicated documents, nor was he involved in the conduct of any negotiations. Still less was he actually involved in the conduct of any litigation. All those factors might have put this case in a different light.

I have to consider what is the appropriate uplift for a senior partner in the conduct of a case of this character at the stage which it had reached. The starting point for this exercise is 50%; that is the advice I received, and it is also the practice in the North East. If one is concerned with a High Court or potential High Court action, that is the appropriate starting point for the uplift. Likewise I am satisfied that 125% was far too high for a case of this kind. One of the reasons, I suspect, why 125% was even being considered by the solicitor is the too low figure that he might have feared he was going to be allowed as an hourly rate. As I have already made clear, I would not lend support to the adoption of an unduly low hourly rate and then seeking to put it right by applying a higher uplift percentage. The right approach is that which I have emphasised, namely to adopt a realistic approach to the hourly rate to reflect the actual cost of the fee earner involved, and then to apply an appropriate but not excessive uplift.

The advice that I have had from my assessors in this matter is that no more than 75% is the maximum justifiable uplift in a case of this character, at the stage that it was at, and involving the work which it did involve at that stage. I am advised, and I have also formed the view, that 85% is too high and cannot be supported.

It must be borne in mind that 75% is half as much again as the 50% uplift that would be allowed in an ordinary case. Applying a 50 or 75% uplift to the actual rates that are allowable to a senior litigation partner still produces figures – if that be relevant – which represent a reasonable level of remuneration for a solicitor. In other words, they do satisfy the test of the standard basis: a reasonable amount in respect of the work reasonably done.

I would also, in this context, say with regard to the evidence that was placed before us as to the alleged exceptional character of this type of case, that it must be recognised that a lot of cases involve technical issues of difficulty, they involve the instructing of experts and the assessing of expert advice. In this respect, medical negligence cases are not different in kind from a number of other classes of litigation. In assessing the uplift, a sense of proportion must be observed, provided the first step is taken of assessing the actual appropriate hourly cost.

Accordingly, my decision is that the hourly rates should be based upon £45 per hour and that the uplift that should be applied is 75%, not the 85% that the Registrar took.

The outcome will be that the solicitor has done considerably better than he did before the district registrar.

Law Society
v
Persaud

Queen's Bench Division
May 1990

Hobhouse J
sitting with assessors

Headnote

In this 1990 case the court held that whilst a litigant in person is restricted in respect of profit costs, as laid down in Order 62, rule 15 and the cases decided thereunder, so far as disbursements are concerned those restrictions do not apply and in this particular case it was held that he was entitled to reasonable expenses in attending court, even in this case flying in from South Africa.

HOBHOUSE J: The defendant was living in South Africa and there received notice of the issue of a writ by the Law Society for the recovery of money allegedly owed under a legal aid certificate.

The plaintiffs had obtained summary judgment and a charging order which the defendant had successfully contested in person.

There remained a dispute between the parties over the disallowance by the taxing master, Master Wright, of various travelling expenses incurred by the defendant.

Those fell into two categories: first, the cost, totalling £1,391.25 of travelling from South Africa to England to defend the action in person, and second, the cost of travelling between Birmingham and London, the reasonable element of which was £74.

The plaintiffs did not suggest that the defendant had been extravagant or acted in bad faith. They said the disbursements did not come within the terms of Order 62, rule 18(1).

They said no solicitor would ever have been allowed to charge as a disbursement the cost of travelling from South Africa to England since the solicitor would already be in England.

Similarly, the costs of travelling from Birmingham to London would not be allowed to a solicitor because if a solicitor had been instructed it clearly should have been a solicitor in London who would not incur the costs of travelling from Birmingham to London.

The taxing master had accepted the plaintiff's submissions on those points.

His Lordship accepted that a London solicitor would never be justified in including in his disbursements the cost of travelling from South Africa to England or from Birmingham to London for the purpose of attending hearings in London.

But, it was contended, that was not the relevant scenario. The defendant was conducting the litigation himself. He argued that the disbursements were reasonably made because he chose not to instruct a London solicitor.

A course of conduct which reduced the overall costs bill could not be described as unreasonable unless it had some other characteristic which created that unreasonableness; acting in person was not such a characteristic.

The defendant argued that the disbursements were reasonable since they were necessary to enable him to defend the action in person and they had not increased the costs bill which the plaintiffs had had to bear.

The essence of the defendant's submission was that the making of greater disbursements had led to a reduction in so-called "profit" costs which made the disbursements reasonable.

Master Wright had concluded that the defendant had spent a total of 36 hours in respect of hearings, documents, letters and other miscellaneous items and that 4 hours 30 minutes should be allowed for waiting time.

An appropriate rate, if included in a solicitor's bill, would have been £63 an hour and in respect of waiting time £42 an hour giving a total of £2,457.

Under Order 62, rule 18(2) that fell to be reduced by one-third, giving a figure after other minor adjustments of £1,643.

His Lordship had been told that the rationale behind that rule was that it represented a rule-of-thumb distinction between the expense rate for a solicitor and the profit rate on the assumption that the expense rate was given a 50% mark-up to give an appropriate level of profit for a professional firm.

Thus, as a result of acting as an amateur litigator, the defendant had saved the plaintiffs £821.

There was a strong and valid analogy with the situation where a country solicitor, already familiar with the case, chose to do a summons in London rather than employing a London agent and/or counsel to represent his client.

The criterion of reasonableness was more than sufficient to cover the very modest travelling expenses incurred between Birmingham and London.

The situation regarding travel from South Africa to England was not so straightforward. The defendant could justify £747 of that cost (that is, £821 less £74) on the same logic as the Birmingham to London trips. But he had to find other reasons to justify the remaining £644.25 of the travel costs.

He had to argue that if he had been legally represented, he would have had counsel as well as a solicitor. That raised a more difficult question because he did not have counsel and was not, following the Court of Appeal decision in *Hart* v *The Agha Khan Foundation* ([1984] 1 WLR 994; **Costs LR (Core Vol)** 87), to be treated as if he notionally had had counsel.

It would have been reasonable for him to have been represented by counsel, as were the plaintiffs. Would those disbursements have been allowed if made by a solicitor on the litigant's behalf? His Lordship held that those were disbursements capable of recognition as solicitor's disbursements.

There was nothing in the Court of Appeal decision in *Hart v The Agha Khan Foundation* which precluded the taxing master from allowing reasonable disbursements which had in fact been incurred.

Unlike the costs in dispute in *Hart*'s case the defendant's disbursements were not notional but were actual and, if reasonable and if a solicitor had been employed, could and would have been included in a solicitor's bill.

The fact that the Court of Appeal had said one should not allow the cost of counsel who were not employed did not mean that the taxing master was required to disallow a disbursement actually incurred so as to avoid the necessity of employing not only a solicitor but also counsel.

Here the taxing master had approached the matter in too literal a fashion. On the facts of the present case the costs sought to be recovered by the defendant did not exceed what would have been the actual costs and disbursements allowable to a London solicitor.

If one translated the situation to that of a litigant in person resident in, say, Manchester or Sheffield having to defend and represent himself in proceedings in London, to assert that he should not be allowed to include as a disbursement the actually incurred cost of travelling from his home town to London to attend hearings was to introduce an absurdity and manifest injustice.

There was still an overall saving to the other side as a result of the relevant party having chosen to represent himself.

Stubbs

v

Board of Governors of the Royal National Orthopaedic Hospital

Queen's Bench Division
21 December 1988

Hirst J
sitting with assessors

Headnote

In this case (unreported but decided in 1988) Hirst J (as he then was) reaffirmed the approach of the courts in the *Eastwood* and *Leopold Lazarus* cases (see **Costs LR (Core Vol) 50** and **Costs LR (Core Vol) 62** respectively) in the use of averages for assessing the hourly rates and emphasised the importance of the taxing master's experience in such matters.

HIRST J: This is a summons to review an interim certificate issued as part of a taxation by Master Wright. The remainder of the taxation is still outstanding.

The plaintiff in the action was a nurse employed at the defendants' hospital. While in such employment she contracted tuberculosis. Her claim was for damages for personal injuries, the nub of her case being that the defendants had failed to observe departmental guide-lines for regular chest X-rays of their staff, thus exposing their staff and especially the plaintiff to the risk of contracting tuberculosis of the bone marrow from patients. This was obviously a very serious allegation so far as the defendants were concerned, since it attacked their whole system of care for their own nursing staff. It thus deserved, and received, careful investigation by the defendants and their solicitors Messrs Slaughter and May. Eventually evidence was obtained that, far from having conducted X-rays with insufficient frequency, they had undertaken more frequent X-rays than the guide-lines advised, and so had reduced them to two a year, in accordance with those guide-lines. Moreover, the defendants' solicitors managed to unearth the Hospital Chest X-Ray Register for the relevant year, 1975, which showed that the plaintiff's chest had in fact been X-Rayed at the very juncture at which she complained of lack of attention. Six months later, shortly before the trial was due, she discontinued by a consent order and was ordered to pay the defendants' costs.

The sole issues which arise on this review are first, as to the hourly rates allowed by the master for the respective years during which the proceedings were conducted, and secondly whether it was appropriate to proceed by interim certificate. I leave the latter point over until the end of this judgment.

The master's decision and his grounds on hourly rates are conveniently taken from his reasons, as follows –

> "The defendant's solicitors used a legal executive to conduct the matter, and he conducted it efficiently. The hourly rates they ask are: £25 in 1979: £30 in 1980: £35 in 1981 and 1982: £40 in 1983: £45 in 1984 and 1985 and £50 in 1986.
>
> The level of charging that solicitors are able to secure depends not on any magic formula but upon the force of competition in the open market. There is remarkable unanimity among solicitors practising in industrial disease actions as to what the market will stand. The same is true of those practising in the medical negligence field.
>
> I keep a note of the rates asked and conceded in industrial injury and disease cases. The rates asked in the present bill are, throughout the years the action ran, approximately 32% higher than that average. For instance the solicitor here asks £50 per hour for work done in 1986. One expects the solicitor to ask for work in 1986 an hourly rate of about £35: one expects the solicitor to ask for comparable rates in earlier years after allowing for inflation.
>
> I have looked through my notebook to discover the rates asked in medical negligence cases over the last year. The average rate asked for work done in the year 1986 was a little below £35 per hour. The rates asked for earlier years were comparable after allowing for inflation. As only 5 medical negligence cases came before me in the last 12 months I looked also at the figures asked in the 10 other professional negligence actions (solicitors, accountants and surveyors negligence actions) I taxed in the last year. The rates asked were on average approximately £35 per hour with corresponding rates for earlier years.
>
> The paying party in the present case asked me to allow £36 for work done in the present action in the year 1986 with corresponding rates for earlier years (after allowing for inflation). I saw no reason not to do so. I remained of the same opinion on hearing Objections 1, 2 and 3."

This approach is attacked by Mr Desch on behalf of the defendants, on the footing that it is unduly mechanistic. The use of an average, he submits, is fundamentally erroneous, particularly since, as he contends, this was a serious case which merited a rate well above the average. In any event, he submits, this approach wrongly leaves out of account relevant factors, in particular sub-paras (2)(*b*) and (*e*), of the factors required to be taken into account under Part 1 of Appendix II to Order 62 (hereinafter called "the Rule"), which provides as follows –

> "Amount of costs
>
> 1. (1)   The amount of costs to be allowed shall (subject to rule 18 and to any order of the Court fixing the costs to be allowed) be in the discretion of the taxing officer.

(2)   In exercising his discretion the taxing officer shall have regard to all relevant circumstances, and in particular to –

(*a*)   the complexity of the item or of the cause or matter in which it arises and the difficulty or novelty of the questions involved;

(*b*)   the skill, specialised knowledge and responsibility required of, and the time and labour expended by, the solicitor or counsel;

(*c*)   the number and importance of the documents (however brief) prepared or perused;

(*d*)   the place and circumstances in which the business involved is transacted;

(*e*)   the importance of the cause or matter to the client;

(*f*)   where money or property is involved, its amount of value;

(*g*)   any other fees and allowances payable to the solicitor or counsel in respect of other items in the same cause or matter, but only where work done in relation to those items has reduced the work which would otherwise have been necessary in relation to the item in question."

Mr Desch submits that these sub-paragraphs are particularly applicable in the present case.

Mr Stowe on behalf of the plaintiff disputes that this was an above average case at all; he does not question the seriousness of the allegation, but submits that it was neither difficult to investigate nor complicated. More fundamentally, however, he contends that the defendants' submission is in principle unsound in the light of previous authority and well established practice as reflected in the leading text books. It is because this case raises this point of principle that I acceded to the joint request of counsel on both sides to give this judgment in open court. It is convenient first to quote the relevant passage from *Butterworths Costs Service* A[156]–[159] which states as follows:

"[156]

There are several interacting factors which determine how much solicitors will charge for the work they have done.

[157]

Fee Earners   In common with other professions solicitors use a system of charging in which a distinction is made between members of the firm and employees who are predominantly engaged in the more professional work of interviewing clients, and witnesses, having conferences with counsel, drawing up deeds and documents, from those who are predominantly occupied in support services such as secretarial, messengerial and book-keeping work. The members of the firm doing professional work, ie partners, solicitors, legal executives and, frequently, senior articled clerks are classified as fee earners.

[158]

Economic Factor   The solicitor works out the costs of running his firm, including the normal overheads of rent, rates, office equipment plus wages and salaries and notional salaries for partners. The costs of running a firm will of course vary in different parts of the country. These costs will be divided by the number of fee earners and the proportion of their time spent in fee earner work to obtain an hourly rate for different levels of fee earner. There are various methods of attributing costs to fee earners; The Law Society's booklet 'The Expense of Time' goes into this question very thoroughly.

[159]

A and B Elements   The practice has grown up, and become incorporated in Order 62 and in the various scales, in bills of contentious costs drawn for taxation, of charging and allowing work according to two elements, A and B. The A figure represents the direct cost of doing the work, ie the fee earners rate multiplied by his time spent in certain categories of work such as attendances and perusals, plus an amount per item for letter and telephones. These costs are totalled to reach the A figure. To this is added a percentage uplift for 'care and conduct' which is called the B figure. The amount charged and allowed for the B figure should reflect factors such as the degree of skill required, the complexity or novelty of the case, the degree of reliance on counsel."

In *Greenslade on Costs*, p 1.50, the practice is described as follows under the heading "The expense rate" –

"At the core of all solicitor's costing is the calculation of the hourly expense rate. An increase of £2 per hour in the expense rate for a fee earner can probably lead to an increase in the firm's profits of a sum approaching £2,500 per annum. It is therefore the draftsman's task to seek to recover the highest proper expense rate and he should approach this exercise by a consideration of the facts of the particular case, of the seniority of fee earner reasonably justified by those circumstances and the cost to the firm of that fee earner untrammelled by any 'basic' expense rate that may be utilised by any particular court.

The general approach to the calculation of the expense rate was described by the assessors sitting with Brightman J in *re Eastwood (dec'd) Re Lloyds Bank Ltd v Eastwood* [1975] Ch 112, [1974] 3 All ER 603 [**Costs LR (Core Vol) 50**] in the following terms – which were agreed by the parties to the taxation and cited by Brightman J in his judgment –

'the proper costs per hour of the time spent having regard to a reasonable estimate of the overhead expenses of the solicitor's firm including (if the time spent is that of an employee) the reasonable salary of that employee or (if the time spent is that of a partner) a notional salary'.

In *R v Wilkinson* [1980] 1 All ER 597 Goff J described the expense rate as an 'hourly rate' which represents the 'broad average direct cost' of undertaking the work.

In *Leopold Lazarus Ltd v Secretary of State for Trade and Industry* (1976) 120 Sol Jo 268 [**Costs LR (Core Vol) 62**] Kerr J placed the responsibility for assessing the expense rate on the taxing officer –

'the assessment of the appropriate rate per hour would be based on the taxing master's knowledge and experience of the average solicitor or executive employed by the average firm in the area concerned.'

The stress is placed on the average cost of the average solicitor or legal executive – in the particular area concerned. The assessment is to be made by the taxing officer who will only obtain his information from evidence produced on the taxation of bills – inevitably there is a risk of a circular process, solicitors charging what the taxing officer allows so that in turn he will treat this as a true reflection of the cost of employing a solicitor in that area.

...

How then, is the 'broad average direct cost' to be calculated? In theory what is required is the calculation of the cost per hour to the firm of solicitors (in the case of a salaried fee earner) of employing that fee earner. The overheads of the firm are to be calculated, the salaries of fee earners on any overheads directly attributable to them deducted, the residual overheads divided equally between the fee earners, the salary and other overheads directly attributable to that fee earner added back and the total divided by the number of chargeable hours worked by the fee earner in the year."

These expositions are substantially based on the decision of Kerr J (as he then was) in the case of *Leopold Lazarus Ltd* v *Secretary of State for Trade and Industry*, briefly reported at (1976) 20 Sol Jo 268, **Costs LR (Core Vol) 62**, but also available to me in a full transcript from which I quote the relevant passages.

"In his answer the master helpfully summarised the practice concerning the computation of Item 26 in cases such as this. Having considered the weight of the proceedings and the responsibility and skill involved, the practice is then to arrive at a total figure consisting of two elements which are referred to as A and B in the judgment of the Court of Appeal in *Eastwood*'s case. The computation of the A figure involves an assessment of the reasonable direct cost, that is to say the grade of person (senior solicitor, assistant solicitor, legal executive, etc) whom it was reasonable to employ at each stage; an approximation of the cost of employment of each individual by considering the number of hours for each of them to be reasonably engaged; and assessing a rate per hour sufficient to cover the salary and the appropriate share of the general overheads of each such person. The assessment of the appropriate rate per hour would be based on the taxing master's knowledge and experience of the average solicitor or executive employed by the average firm in the area concerned. The total of the hours of each person multiplied by an appropriate cost per hour, together with an allowance for letters, telephone calls and telex messages, then produces what the Court of Appeal referred to as the A figure.

The B figure is then conventionally assessed by adding a percentage to the A figure which is appropriate in all the circumstances to cover matters which cannot be calculated on an hourly basis, that is to say supervision and other indirect expenses, together with what the master referred to in his answer as 'imponderables' which reflect the degree of skill, responsibility and the other factors set out in Rules of the Supreme Court Order 62 Appendix 2 Part X as required by paragraph 1(2) of Part X. As mentioned above, the increase for the B figure claimed in the present case was just under 50%, which would be perfectly normal and certainly not excessive in cases of this type. This is the figure which, in the case of an independent firm of solicitors, is expected to make a contribution to the profits of the firm. The appropriateness of the total of A and B, arrived at in this way, is then considered against the background of the proceedings as a whole and rounded off to a convenient sum which appears right in all the circumstances."

Later in the judgment Kerr J re-emphasised the importance of the master's experience and discretion as follows –

"The master then helpfully explained in his answer what he did on this particular taxation in relation to item 26. However, I do not propose to quote the rate per hour nor the way in which he arrived at it for the purpose of computing the A figure, because one finds – as has happened on other reviews of taxations – that the figures used in one taxation are thereafter quoted in other cases as though they set a binding precedent. In my view these are matters which are much better left to the experience and discretion of the taxing masters, having regard to the circumstances of each individual case."

May I say in parenthesis that in the present case it seemed to me difficult to expound the essence of Master Wright's decision without quoting the figures, but I need hardly stress that these should in no way be treated as creating any sort of binding precedent.

In the light of these well-established principles, I consider that Mr Stowe is right in submitting that, in arriving as Master Wright did at the A figure, the essence of the exercise was an appropriate apportionment of the estimated overhead expenses of the solicitors' firm having regard to the position, status, and likely rate of remuneration of the persons (e.g., partner and/or legal executive) who were employed on the case under consideration.

This, as Kerr J pointed out in the *Lazarus* case, is of its very nature suitable for assessment by the taxing master in the light of his very wide experience; it is also a matter which, contrary to Mr Desch's argument, is properly approached by reference to averages since it is unlikely that there will be a very wide divergence between comparable firms of solicitors operating in similar fields of work in similar geographical areas.

Consistency in the application of hourly rates on inter partes taxations is highly desirable both in the interests of general fairness, and to assist parties to negotiate reasonable settlements of disputes on costs.

If in any given case the solicitor in question wishes to seek to demonstrate that in his particular case there are some special factors involved which affect a fair hourly rate, it is always open to him to produce evidence to this effect, but none was produced in the present case.

Furthermore in my judgment in arriving at an appropriate hourly rate, consideration such as the importance of the case and the weight of responsibility involved do not enter into the assessment; indeed they do not enter the computation of the A figure at all save in cases (unlike the present one) where a question arises as to the appropriateness of the grade of persons (eg, partner and/or legal executive) employed. On the other hand these factors, and indeed all the factors listed in the rule, are of course highly relevant to assessing the B figure, as the closing words of sub-paragraph (3) of the rule show.

It follows in my judgment that the master's approach in arriving at the proper hourly rate was fully in accordance with the established practice, and in no way to be faulted.

This conclusion, however, is only relevant to one part of the overall taxation exercise, which in the present case is not complete. Before it is concluded, full consideration requires to be given in all its aspects to the B figure, and, at the end of the day, the most important final exercise must be undertaken, namely consideration of the appropriateness of the total of A and B against the background of the proceedings as a whole, in order to arrive at a convenient sum which appears right in all the circumstances (see the concluding sentence in the first passage from Kerr J's judgment in the *Lazarus* case quoted above).

It is therefore very important that, both in assessing the B figure, and in the concluding exercise just referred to, the master gives full weight to the special factors of this case as reflected in the summary of the issues given at the beginning of this judgment. In this context I consider Mr Desch is right that this was indeed a case of great seriousness and importance so far as the defendants were concerned, and one in which their solicitors rightly regarded themselves as bearing a heavy responsibility, and I reject any suggestion that it was run of the mill. These aspects should be fully reflected by the taxing master in the remaining stages of this taxation.

The decision to issue an interim taxation certificate was within the master's discretion (Order 62, rule 22(1)(*d*)) and I would not wish in any way to criticise the master's exercise of his discretion in the present case to issue such a certificate; but it is very important that such a course of action should not in any way be allowed to impede or circumscribe the all important overall review of the case as a whole before the final figure is arrived at.

Harrison and others
v
Tew

House of Lords
30, 31 October 1989, 25 January 1990

Lord Bridge of Harwich, Lord Ackner, Lord Oliver of Aylmerton,
Lord Jauncey of Tullichettle and Lord Lowry

Headnote

This is the House of Lords authority for the principle that section
70 of the Solicitors Act 1970 is a self-contained code for deciding
when a client may successfully challenge his solicitor's bill by way
of taxation proceedings and emphasises that there is no inherent
jurisdiction to make such orders outside that section.

25 January. The following opinions were delivered.

LORD BRIDGE OF HARWICH: My Lords, I have had the advantage of reading
in draft the speech of my noble and learned friend Lord Lowry. I agree with
it and for the reasons he gives I would dismiss the appeal.

LORD ACKNER: My Lords, I have had the advantage of reading in draft the
speech of my noble and learned friend Lord Lowry. I agree with it and for
the reasons he gives I would dismiss the appeal.

LORD OLIVER OF AYLMERTON: My Lords, for the reasons contained in the
speech to be delivered by my noble and learned friend Lord Lowry, I agree
that this appeal should be dismissed.

LORD JAUNCEY OF TULLICHETTLE: My Lords, I have had the advantage of
reading in draft the speech of my noble and learned friend Lord Lowry. I
agree with it and for the reasons he gives I would dismiss the appeal.

LORD LOWRY: My Lords, this is an appeal by leave of the Court of Appeal
from an order of that court (Dillon LJ and Sir Frederick Lawton, Nicholls LJ
dissenting) ([1987] 3 All ER 865, [1989] QB 307) dated 6 July 1987
allowing an appeal by the defendant, Geoffrey Herbert Tew (the
respondent), from an order of Sir Neil Lawson sitting as a judge of the High
Court in the Queen's Bench Division dated 2 December 1986, whereby he

dismissed an appeal by the respondent from an order of Master Creightmore dated 15 March 1984 that ten bills of costs delivered by the respondent to the first appellant should be referred to a taxing master to be taxed.

The question for decision is whether section 70(4) of the Solicitors Act 1974 precludes an application for taxation of a solicitor's bill of costs by the party chargeable after the expiration of 12 months from the payment of the bill or whether, notwithstanding the wording of that subsection, the court has an inherent jurisdiction to order taxation.

Section 70 of the Act, so far as material, provides:

"(1) Where before the expiration of one month from the delivery of a solicitor's bill an application is made by the party chargeable with the bill, the High Court shall, without requiring any sum to be paid into court, order that the bill be taxed and that no action be commenced on the bill until the taxation is completed.

(2) Where no such application is made before the expiration of the period mentioned in subsection (1), then, on an application being made by the solicitor or, subject to subsections (3) and (4), by the party chargeable with the bill, the court may on such terms, if any, as it thinks fit (not being terms as to the costs of the taxation), order – (a) that the bill be taxed; and (b) that no action be commenced on the bill, and that any action already commenced be stayed, until the taxation is completed.

(3) Where an application under subsection (2) is made by the party chargeable with the bill – (a) after the expiration of 12 months from the delivery of the bill, or (b) after a judgment has been obtained for the recovery of the costs covered by the bill, or (c) after the bill has been paid, but before the expiration of 12 months from the payment of the bill, no order shall be made except in special circumstances and, if an order is made, it may contain such terms as regards the costs of the taxation as the court may think fit.

(4) The power to order taxation conferred by subsection (2) shall not be exercisable on an application made by the party chargeable with the bill after the expiration of 12 months from the payment of the bill ... "

The respondent submits that this section covers the entire field and comprehensively regulates all applications for taxation by the party chargeable, whereas the appellants contend that, as between a solicitor and his client, the court retains at common law an inherent jurisdiction to order taxation even though the period fixed by section 70(4) has expired.

The relevant facts, which are more fully set out by Dillon LJ in his judgment (see [1987] 3 All ER 865 at 868, [1989] QB 307 at 314–315), can for the purpose of this appeal be shortly stated. In the 1970s the first appellant engaged in a number of transactions mainly consisting of sales, purchases and mortgages of land, in some of which the other appellants appear to have had an interest. The respondent, who had known him for many years, delivered the ten bills of costs between October 1977 and May 1981 and payment was effected by means of deductions from sums of money representing the proceeds of various sales standing to the first appellant's credit in the clients' account of the respondent. The application for taxation of the bills was made on 17 November 1983, more than 12 months after the last such deduction. A preliminary argument for the appellants that those deductions did not constitute "payment" under section 70(4) (which was not needed before the master and the judge, since they were in favour of the appellants on the main point) was, for the reasons contained in the judgment of Dillon LJ, unanimously decided by the Court of Appeal in the respondent's favour and has not been revived before your Lordships.

My Lords, having regard to the subject of the appeal, the commencement of Sir Frederick Lawton's judgment in the Court of Appeal provides an appropriate introduction to the inquiry. He said ([1987] 3 All ER 865 at 884, [1989] QB 307 at 335–337):

> "Ever since the late Middle Ages the courts have exercised a disciplinary jurisdiction over attorneys and solicitors as officers of the court (see Holdsworth *A History of English Law* (3rd edn, 1923) vol 3, p. 392). By the beginning of the seventeenth century the behaviour of some attorneys and solicitors was such that Parliament decided to impose some degree of regulation of them. It did so by the Act 3 Jac 1 c 7 (attorneys (1605)). The mischief which Parliament wanted to regulate was identified as follows: 'For that through the abuse of sundry attornies and solicitors by charging their clients with excessive fees and other unnecessary demands, such as were not, nor ought by them to have been employed or demanded, whereby the subjects grow to be overmuch burthened ...' It was enacted that attorneys and solicitors should obtain a 'ticket' (ie a receipt) for any fees paid to specified third parties and render a true bill to their clients. This statute seems to be the origin of the modern practice of delivering bills of costs."

The first important provision in the legislative history of statutes relating to taxation of costs (which is admirably traced by Dillon LJ in his judgment) is a 1729 Act (2 Geo 2 c 23 (attorneys and solicitors)), the main provisions of which are helpfully described by Nicholls LJ (see [1987] 3 All ER 865 at 877, [1989] QB 307 at 326). Section 23 prohibited the commencement of an action by an attorney or solicitor for the recovery of certain fees until one month after the delivery of a bill. That section also provided for the reference of bills for taxation on the application of the party chargeable without the need for a payment into court and on an undertaking by that party to pay the sum found due on taxation. Section 23 applied only to "fees, charges or disbursements at law, or in equity", which was interpreted as applying only to costs in some proceeding in a court of law or equity or some proceeding with a view to such a suit. Moreover, it contained no time limit or cut-off date for taxation applications. Before the 1729 Act, the courts had exercised inherent jurisdiction over solicitors as officers of the court to direct taxation of their bills on the application of their clients, but the practice was to require the client seeking taxation to bring the amount of the disputed bill into court.

The Solicitors Act 1843 was a consolidated and amending Act which repealed the 1729 Act. The difficulties arising from the phrase "fees, charges or disbursements at law, or in equity" were got over by the use of the wider phrase "any Fees, Charges, or Disbursements for any Business done" in section 37, which also repeated the former provision that a solicitor could not sue for his costs until after the expiration of one month from the delivery of his bill. It gave the court power to order taxation but also provided that, on an application made after a verdict should have been obtained or a writ of inquiry executed in any action for the recovery by the solicitor of his demand for costs, or after the expiration of 12 months from the delivery of the bill, the court should only direct taxation of the bill if special circumstances were proved to the satisfaction of the court. Section 39 provided that, where a trustee, executor or administrator was chargeable with a solicitor's bill, taxation of the bill might be ordered on the application of a beneficiary interested in the trust property. Section 41 provided that the payment of the bill should not preclude the bill being referred by the court for taxation, if special circumstances should appear to the court to require the same, "provided the Application for such Reference be made within Twelve Calendar Months after Payment". This proviso to section 41 of the 1843 Act is the origin of the time limit imposed by section 70(4) of the 1974 Act, with which this appeal is concerned.

The 1843 Act was superseded by the Solicitors Act 1932, which in turn was replaced by the Solicitors Act 1957. The relevant provisions of the 1932 Act were sections 65, 66 and 67, and they do not differ materially from the relevant provisions in the 1957 Act, which are as follows:

"**68.** – (1) Subject to the provisions of this Act, no action shall be brought to recover any costs due to a solicitor until one month after a bill thereof has been delivered in accordance with the requirements set out in the next following subsection …

69. – (1) On the application, made within one month of the delivery of a solicitor's bill, of the party chargeable therewith, the High Court shall, without requiring any sum to be paid into court, order that the bill be taxed and that no action shall be commenced thereon until the taxation is completed.

(2) If no such application is made within the period mentioned in the last foregoing subsection, then, on the application either of the solicitor or of the party chargeable with the bill, the court may, upon such terms, if any, as they think fit (not being terms as to the costs of the taxation), order – (*a*) that the bill shall be taxed; (*b*) that, until the taxation is completed, no action shall be commenced on the bill, and any action already commenced be stayed: Provided that – (i) if twelve months have expired from the delivery of the bill, or if the bill has been paid, or if a verdict has been obtained or a writ of inquiry executed in an action for the recovery of the costs covered thereby, no order shall be made on the application of the party chargeable with the bill except in special circumstances and, if an order is made, it may contain such terms as regards the costs of the taxation as the court may think fit; (ii) in no event shall any such order be made after the expiration of twelve months from the payment of the bill …

70. – (1)   Where a person other than the person who is the party chargeable with the bill for the purposes of the last foregoing section has paid, or is or was liable to pay, the bill either to the solicitor or to the party chargeable with the bill, that person or his executors, administrators or assignees may apply to the court for an order for the taxation of the bill as if he were the party chargeable therewith, and the court may make thereon the same order, if any, as they might have made if the application had been made by that party: Provided that, in cases where the court have no power to make an order except in special circumstances, the court may, in considering whether there are special circumstances sufficient to justify them in making an order, take into account circumstances affecting the applicant but which do not affect the party chargeable with the bill.

(2)   If a trustee, executor or administrator has become liable to pay a bill of a solicitor, the High Court may, upon the application of any person interested in any property out of which the trustee, executor or administrator has paid, or is entitled to pay, the bill, and upon such terms, if any, as they think fit, order the bill to be taxed, and may order such payments, in respect of the amount found due to or by the solicitor and in respect of the cost of the taxation, to be made to or by the applicant, or to or by the solicitor, or to the executor, administrator or trustee, as they think fit: Provided that in considering any such application the court shall have regard to – (a) the provisions of the last foregoing section as to applications by the party chargeable with the taxation of a solicitor's bill so far as they are capable of being applied to an application made under this subsection; (b) the extent and nature of the interest of the applicant ... "

The 1957 Act was amended in some respects by the Solicitors (Amendment) Act 1974. This explains why the 1974 Act with which your Lordships are concerned, although itself a consolidating Act, differs in certain respects from the 1957 Act. For the moment, I shall be content to say that sections 69, 70 and 71 of the 1974 Act correspond to sections 68, 69 and 70 of the 1957 Act.

My Lords, I come now to the critical question and, since I have concluded that the majority in the Court of Appeal were right in their opinion, it will be convenient for me first to set out the respondent's basic contention, followed by the appellants' arguments (which are significant) on the other side (to which I shall add some comments), and finally by what I see as the refutation of those arguments.

The respondent submits simply that section 70(4) means what it says and imposes an unconditional ban on all applications for taxation which are made more than 12 months after the bill has been paid. He concedes that the courts have already had at common law an inherent jurisdiction over solicitors as officers of the court, which includes the power, at the instance of the client though not of a third party, to order taxation of a bill of costs, but contends that, like other aspects of the common law, that jurisdiction can be overridden by the will of Parliament in the shape of a statutory enactment. The respondent would also remind your Lordships that the statutory time limit originated in section 41 of the 1843 Act and has been carried through to the present day. He adds the further argument that section 70, like its immediate predecessors, and indeed like the more discursive provisions of the 1843 Act, provides, in conjunction with the other provisions in Part III of the 1974 Act, a comprehensive statutory code regulating applications for the taxation of costs and providing for various consequences according to a time-scale.

Counsel for the appellants, with the aid of a careful analysis of Part III of the 1974 Act, in the course of which he drew your Lordships' attention to sections 61(3), (4) and (5) and 64(3), was able to make the point that Parliament has not shown an intention that in no circumstances will a solicitor ever have to face an inquiry into his bill of costs more than 12 months after it has been paid. He also referred to the general principle and policy that a solicitor's remuneration should be fair and reasonable *and no more*. He also recalled that disciplinary proceedings against solicitors in the Supreme Court are dealt with in sections 50 to 55. Section 50(2) provides:

> "Subject to the provisions of this Act, the High Court, the Crown Court and the Court of Appeal respectively, or any division or judge of those courts, may exercise the same jurisdiction in respect of solicitors as any one of the superior courts of law or equity from which the Supreme Court was constituted might have exercised immediately before the passing of the Supreme Court of Judicature Act 1873 in respect of any solicitor, attorney or proctor admitted to practise there."

While not disregarding the opening words of the subsection, counsel pointed out that the inherent jurisdiction in respect of solicitors is expressly preserved and submitted that this was true not only with regard to discipline but with a view to the taxation, assessment and moderation of costs. He further submitted that, since the court would clearly have disciplinary jurisdiction over a solicitor who was guilty of gross overcharging, itself a form of professional misconduct, it would be absurd to attribute to section 70(4) the effect of excluding by a time limit (which did not apply where disciplinary proceedings were concerned) the inherent jurisdiction to refer a bill for taxation.

He then relied on *In re A Solicitor* [1961] 2 All ER 321, [1961] Ch 491, a decision of Cross J on section 69(1) of the 1957 Act, and the only case which is directly in point on either side. It was the decision followed by Sir Neil Lawson when affirming the master's order. A bill of costs had been delivered on 25 November 1959, agreed by the client and paid (by an authorised deduction from funds in the hands of the solicitor) on 22 December 1959. The client applied for taxation by summons issued on 12 May 1960, but this date was not relevant, as it had been under section 41 of the 1843 Act and was to be again under section 70(4) of the 1974 Act (the relevant provision having been reamended by section 15(1)(*a*) of the Solicitors (Amendment) Act 1974), since, whether by inadvertence or design, it was, by virtue of the second proviso to section 66(2) of the 1932 Act and subsequently of the

second proviso to section 69(2) of the 1957 Act, the *order* for taxation
which had to be made within 12 months from the date of payment.
Eventually, the summons came before the master on 8 November 1960, by
which time the plaintiff's solicitors had appreciated the possible danger of
allowing the matter to go beyond 22 December. An application was made to
Cross J on 9 December to fix a day for the hearing of the summons that
term, but the state of his list was such that he was unable to give a day nor
could the parties get a day from any other judge. On 21 December the
summons came again before the master, who adjourned it into court. It was
heard by the judge on 14, 15, 17 and 20 March and judgment was given in
the plaintiff's favour on 29 March 1961. The plaintiff had made his
application in good time, and the facts show just how unfortunate he was in
ending up out of time (see [1961] Ch 491 at 497–498).

Cross J recited the provisions of the 1843 Act and, having observed that
the 1932 Act was a consolidating Act in relation to which there was a
presumption that it did not change the law (although the presumption would
yield to plain words to the contrary), continued ([1961] 2 All ER 321 at 327,
[1961] Ch 491 at 502):

> "The presumption against any change is strengthened in this case by the
> character of the change which, it is said, has been made. So far as I can see, there
> is nothing whatever to be said in favour of making the relevant date the date of
> the order instead of the date of the application, and everything to be said against
> doing so. To make the date of the order the relevant date is to encourage an
> unscrupulous respondent to delay the proceedings and, as happened in this case,
> is liable to give rise to suspicions that the respondent is playing for time, even
> when he is not. Further, even if both sides have the point in mind and co-operate
> in pressing on with the case, they may both be defeated by the state of the list or
> the illness of a judge. It is altogether wrong that the rights of the parties should
> depend on accidents of this sort, but, however sure I may be that Parliament did
> not intend the change, my duty is simply to construe the language of the Act. I
> have no power to rectify it, and with the best will in the world I cannot escape
> the conclusion that proviso (ii) to section 66(2) of the Act of 1932, contained an
> unintentional change in the law."

Having found that he could not help the plaintiff under the Act, Cross J
turned to the question of the inherent jurisdiction and observed ([1961] 2 All
ER 321 at 327, [1961] Ch 491 at 502–503):

> "From the earliest times the various courts of law and equity exercised control
> over the attorneys or solicitors who practised in them. In time the profession of
> attorney and solicitor came to be regulated by statute, but the inherent
> jurisdiction of the court over its officers continued to exist as a supplement to
> the statutory regulation. Thus in 1806, in *Ex p Arrowsmith* (13 Ves 124, 33
> ER 241), Lord Erskine, LC, held that the court had a general jurisdiction to
> order taxation of a solicitor's bill independently of the Act of 1729 (2 Geo 2
> c 23), which was the predecessor of the Act of 1843, and in *Storer & Co v
> Johnson* ((1890) 15 App Cas 203), the House of Lords held that, though there

was no power under the Act of 1843 to order taxation of part of a solicitor's bill, such an order could be made under the inherent jurisdiction."

Cross J then took note of the defendant's argument that, though the court had power under its inherent jurisdiction to make orders for taxation which were not within the scope of the current provisions of the Solicitors Acts, section 41 of the 1843 Act (and by implication, any similar provision) prohibited the court from dealing in any way with a bill which had been paid 12 months before the application to tax was made. He continued ([1961] 2 All ER 321 at 327–328, [1961] Ch 491 at 503):

> "I cannot accept that submission. In *Storer & Co* v *Johnson* ((1890) 15 App Cas 203 at 206), Lord Halsbury, LC, said: '... I think it is quite clear that the Solicitors Act, [1843], did not deprive the court of the jurisdiction which they always possessed to do justice in the premises when dealing with one of their own officers, and that they might therefore order that the costs should be taxed, although not in terms of the Solicitors Act ...' It is true that the precise point was not before him, but I do not see why I should qualify his language and read section 41 of the Act of 1843 as impliedly curtailing the inherent jurisdiction in any way. The presumption should, I think, be against any such curtailment. Further, it is to be remembered that to deal with a solicitor's costs under the inherent jurisdiction is not at all the same thing as to order a taxation of them under the Solicitors Act."

Having dealt with the question of special circumstances, Cross J then ordered the bill to be referred for taxation.

With the support of *In re A Solicitor* and the liberal interpretation there given to the words of Lord Halsbury LC, the appellants contended that the 1974 Act should not be construed so as to oust the inherent jurisdiction unless in clear and unambiguous terms it provides that the inherent jurisdiction is no longer to be exercised. By that submission they recognised, as did the members of the Court of Appeal, that the question is ultimately one of statutory construction according to the principles governing the relation between a statutory provision and the common law which has hitherto applied. As counsel for the appellants neatly put it, no question arose as to Parliament's supremacy; the only question was what Parliament had said. As a matter of construction he pointed to the words in section 70(4), "The power to order taxation *conferred by subsection* (2)", contending by reference to the words which I have emphasised that a further power to order taxation exists independently of section 70(2) which is not subject to the 12-month time limit imposed by section 70(4).

The appellants further relied on *Re Park, Cole* v *Park* (1889) 41 ChD 326, *Electrical Trades Union* v *Tarlo* [1964] 2 All ER 1, [1964] Ch 720 and *Symbol Park Lane Ltd* v *Steggles Palmer (a firm)* [1985] 2 All ER 167, [1985] 1 WLR 668.

Re Park was a case where a solicitor presented his bill more than a year before his client died. He then claimed in the administration of the estate and

Stirling J, whose decision and order were approved by the Court of Appeal, ordered that certain disputed items "should be adjudicated upon by the Taxing Master acting simply as Chief Clerk for this particular purpose" (see 41 ChD 326 at 330). Thus the solicitor received payment on the basis of quantum meruit.

In *Electrical Trade Union* v *Tarlo* Wilberforce J referred to *In re A Solicitor*, as well as to other cases, as illustrating the existence of the inherent jurisdiction. Time limits were not in question and, notwithstanding the eminence of the judge who decided *Tarlo*'s case, it does not in the circumstances advance the appellant's cause.

Symbol Park Lane Ltd v *Steggles Palmer (a firm)* was a case in which counsel on both sides, and indeed the Court of Appeal, assumed *In re A Solicitor* to have been rightly decided. Both counsel and the court concentrated on whether taxation *should* in the court's discretion be ordered. The answer was in the negative and the question whether taxation *could* be ordered was simply not considered.

A further submission for the appellants was that the amendment introduced by section 15(1)(*a*) of the Solicitors (Amendment) Act 1974 (to make the 12 months run, as it had done before 1932, from the payment of the bill to the *application* for taxation) showed that the draftsman was mindful of *In re A Solicitor* and provided legislative endorsement of the decision in that case. Quite apart from the fact that the amendment was effecting a change in the law, I do not think that by adopting it Parliament could be thought to have given *In re A Solicitor* a special status, when one recalls the many cases, such as *Re Sutton & Elliott* (1883) 11 QBD 377, in which the time-bar provision was assumed without argument to be of full force.

Finally, counsel submitted that, if there were no inherent jurisdiction to refer a bill for taxation, scandalous cases would occur from time to time in which elderly and helpless persons could find themselves victims without a remedy; no doubt they could sue for an account, but only if the solicitor had received money on their behalf.

My Lords, with a view to putting the case on the other side, I could not improve on what has already been said by the majority in the Court of Appeal. I shall, however, try to put fairly shortly the points which have impressed me and to notice particularly those which were emphasised before your Lordships.

With regard to the inherent jurisdiction, it is fallacious to pose the alternative that it was either abolished by the 1974 Act (or strictly by the 1843 Act) or else remained in full force and effect. The doctrine of the sovereignty of Parliament (Dicey's term) or the legislative supremacy of Parliament, as it is called in Wade and Bradley *Constitutional and Administrative Law* (10th edn, 1985) p 65 –

> "consists essentially of a rule which governs the legal relationship between the courts and the legislature, namely that the courts are under a duty to apply the

legislation made by Parliament ... "

One must distinguish between affirmative and negative provisions: the common law can co-exist with a statutory provision with which it is not inconsistent. Counsel for the respondent, as well as introducing the quotation from *Wade and Bradley*, referred your Lordships to *Coke's Institutes of the Laws of England* (2 Co Inst (1817) 200):

> "... it is a maxime in the common law, that a statute made in the affirmative, without any negative expressed or implyed, doth not take away the common law ... "

Dillon LJ referred to Lord Wilberforce's statement in *Shiloh Spinners Ltd* v *Harding* [1973] 1 All ER 90 at 102, [1973] AC 691 at 724–725 (see [1987] 3 All ER 865 at 874–875, [1989] QB 307 at 323) and that case was applied in *Official Custodian for Charities* v *Parway Estates Developments Ltd* [1984] 3 All ER 679 at 686–687, [1985] Ch 151 at 165.

I might venture to remind your Lordships of the terms of section 41 of the 1843 Act:

> "And be it enacted. That the Payment of any such Bill as aforesaid shall in no Case preclude the Court or Judge to whom Application shall be made from referring such Bill for Taxation, if the special Circumstances of the Case shall in the Opinion of such Court or Judge appear to require the same, upon such Terms and Conditions and subject to such Directions as to such Court or Judge shall seem right, provided the Application for such Reference be made within Twelve Calendar Months after Payment."

That provision impliedly and section 70(4) of the 1974 Act expressly were negative enactments which in my clear opinion ousted the inherent jurisdiction to refer a bill for taxation in conflict with what they laid down.

The appellants relied on *Storer & Co* v *Johnson & Weatherall* (1890) 15 App Cas 203, which provides a classic example of the court's jurisdiction to fill a gap and thereby to supply a defect in affirmative provisions without coming into conflict with those provisions. They were not justified in giving a wide effect to the words used by Lord Halsbury LC, as Cross J (again wrongly, in my view) did in *In re A Solicitor*, because the result thereby produced is contrary to principle. Dillon LJ cited a longer extract than Cross J from Lord Halsbury LC's speech, where he said (at 206):

> "The moment it was taken out of the region of the Solicitors Act and brought within the general jurisdiction of the Court, then the Court could exercise its own jurisdiction in the way it might think fit ... "

The House affirmed the decision of the Court of Appeal sub nom *Re Johnson & Weatherall* (1888) 37 ChD 433 at 443, in which (there being no reference to section 41 of the 1843 Act) Lindley LJ said:

> "I am not disposed to construe sect. 37 as depriving the Court of its power to refer part of a bill for taxation or of any other power which it had before."

I agree entirely with the construction which Dillon LJ placed on Lord Halsbury LC's observations (see [1987] 3 All ER 865 at 874, [1989] QB 307 at 323).

In re A Solicitor was, as Nicholls LJ aptly put it, "an especially hard case" (see [1987] 3 All ER 865 at 882, [1989] QB 307 at 332). The plaintiff had applied to the court well within time and was deprived of his statutory remedy only because (1) Parliament had changed the law (no doubt by mistake) and (2) the court, although warned of the danger, had pushed him out of time by failing to list his case for hearing. Furthermore, the judge thought the solicitor's bill was redolent of overcharging. I respectfully consider that he fell into error by giving too wide an effect to Lord Halsbury LC's general statement.

Counsel for the respondent gave your Lordships a clear picture of the working of section 70, culminating in an absolute bar imposed by section 70(4) and logically asked why, from 1843 onwards, Parliament when framing a code should impose a time limit and not intend it to have effect. At this point, of course, I recall the reference of counsel for the appellants to "the power to order taxation conferred by subsection (2)" and his argument that section 70(4) does not affect any other power to order taxation. Assisted, however, by the exposition of counsel for the respondent, I am clear that section 70 covers *every* application for an order for taxation which can be made by a party chargeable more than one month after delivery of the bill and that accordingly (to that extent) section 70(4), like section 41 of the 1843 Act, has displaced the inherent jurisdiction with regard to all bills which have been paid more than 12 months before the application to the court was made. I appreciate, of course, that *orders* for taxation can be made under the 1974 Act independently of section 70: see, for example, section 61(2), (4) and (5). I would also point out that, as the appellants have rightly contended for other purposes, a consolidating Act is to be presumed not to alter the law. But the point which counsel for the appellant extracts from the reference to section 70(2) would not have been arguable in the context of section 41 of the 1843 Act, 66(2) of the 1932 Act or 69(2) of the 1957 Act because of a difference in wording which is due merely to a different architecture of the statutory provisions.

I turn now to the appellants' argument based on section 50(2), which preserves the jurisdiction over solicitors that the court possessed before the Supreme Court of Judicature Act 1873. In the first place, that jurisdiction must be considered as affected by, for example, section 41 of the 1843 Act and, second, it is "subject to the provisions of this Act", including section 70(4). The thrust of the argument of counsel for the appellants was that it would be absurd to have disciplinary jurisdiction over a solicitor who had overcharged a client without also having power to refer the offending bill for taxation. I think, with respect, that this argument confuses two different powers: one is the power under section 70 to refer a bill for taxation on the application of the party chargeable; the other is the power to refer a bill to the taxing master for "assessment" or "moderation" in aid of disciplinary proceedings when a prima facie case of overcharging has been made out by the party aggrieved.

As indicated when I reviewed the appellants' arguments, they would have had a more attractive looking case if it were made to appear that, in the absence of inherent jurisdiction, a client who had been grossly overcharged would have no remedy once he had been careless or unfortunate enough to fall foul of the 12-month time limit. But it has to be said that in some cases the solicitor will have deducted his costs from money received on the client's behalf, in which case the client could sue under the ordinary jurisdiction described in *Re Park, Cole v Park* (1889) 41 ChD 326. And in some others the client could by making a complaint set in motion disciplinary proceedings, as described by the members of the Court of Appeal and, in particular, by Sir Frederick Lawton. As a result, while the onus of proof would lie on the complainant, the bill could well be referred to the taxing master and in appropriate cases a refund could be ordered by the court.

In the course of a well-marshalled argument, which missed no point that could have helped the cause, counsel for the appellant relied also on the ordinary jurisdiction to which Stirling J referred in *Re Park*, but on the facts of this case, as narrated by Dillon LJ, the client's action for an account of moneys come to the hand of the solicitor would have been met by a plea of settled account.

Accordingly, I would dismiss the appeal and affirm the order of the Court of Appeal.

Appeal dismissed.

M G Tugendhat QC and *Gordon Bishop* for the appellants.
Alan Newman QC and *Antony White* for the respondent.

Hunt
Appellant
and
R M Douglas (Roofing) Ltd
Respondents

House of Lords
4, 5, 6 October; 3 November 1988

Lord Bridge of Harwich, Lord Brandon of Oakbrook, Lord Griffiths,
Lord Ackner and Lord Jauncey of Tullichettle

Headnote

This House of Lords decision laid down the principle that
interest on costs runs not from the date of taxation, but from the
date of the order entitling the party to costs. The taxing masters
have the power to deal with delays in taxation which otherwise
operate unfairly under the above rule under Order 62, rule 28.

---

3 November. LORD BRIDGE OF HARWICH: My Lords, I have had the
advantage of reading in draft the speech of my noble and learned friend Lord
Ackner. I agree with it and, for the reasons he gives, I would allow the
appeal.

LORD BRANDON OF OAKBROOK: My Lords, for the reasons given by my
noble and learned friend Lord Ackner I would allow the appeal.

LORD GRIFFITHS: My Lords, I agree that this appeal should be allowed for
the reasons given in the speech of my noble and learned friend, Lord Ackner,
and I agree with the order that he proposes.

LORD ACKNER: My Lords, this appeal raises an important issue with regard
to costs – namely whether a litigant who has been awarded costs, is entitled
to interest on the amount of the costs from the date upon which judgment is
pronounced (referred to hereafter as "the incipitur rule"), or from the date
upon which the taxation of costs is completed by the issue of the taxing
master's certificate (the "allocatur rule").

The facts
This issue has twice been considered in the past 12 years by the Court of
Appeal and accordingly this appeal has come before your Lordships' House

by what is known as the "leapfrog" procedure. Hence the material facts can be stated quite shortly. On 24 September 1982 the appellant suffered personal injuries in an accident in the course of his employment with the respondents. On 28 March 1983 he issued his writ claiming damages. This was followed on 26 May 1983 by the statement of claim and thereafter by further pleadings to which there is no need to make any reference. On 1 November 1984 the action was settled and by consent Master Prebble ordered that all further proceedings in the action by stayed, except for the purpose of carrying into effect the terms of the agreement, which terms included:

> "(4)   That the defendants do pay to the plaintiff his costs of this action, including the costs of this application, to be taxed as between party and party on the High Court scale, failing agreement."

It is common ground that the master's order is a judgment or an order which carries interest, as if it were a judgment.

On 12 July 1985 the appellant commenced proceedings for the taxation of his costs and on 14 August 1985 rendered his bill, the total claim being £24,471.08 inclusive of VAT. On 9 December 1985 the appellant's solicitors gave notice of intention to claim interest on the taxed costs, to run from the date of pronouncement of judgment. On 15 January 1986 taxation took place and the sum allowed was £17,788.67 (inclusive of VAT). On 28 January 1986 a review of taxation was sought by the appellant. On 18 March 1986 the taxing master overruled the appellant's objections and on 4 June 1986 his certificate ("the allocatur") for £17,788.67 including VAT was issued.

On 19 March 1986 the appellant applied to Master Turner for an order that, pursuant to section 17 of the Judgments Act 1838, interest on the taxed costs of the action should run from the date of pronouncement of judgment. The master dismissed this application, concluding that he was bound by the decisions of the Court of Appeal in *K* v *K (Divorce Costs: Interest)* [1977] Fam 39 and *Erven Warnink BV* v *J Townend & Son (Hull) Ltd (No 2)* [1982] 3 All ER 312. On 20 May 1986 the appellant's appeal against this decision was heard by Sir Neil Lawson, sitting in chambers as a Judge of the Queen's Bench Division. He dismissed the appeal on the ground that he too was bound by these decisions of the Court of Appeal, but he granted a certificate pursuant to section 12(1) of the Administration of Justice Act 1969 and subsequently your Lordships granted to the appellant leave to appeal to your Lordships' House.

The Judgment Act 1838 and its application to interest on costs, prior to 1976

Prior to the passing of the Judgments Act 1838 interest on costs could not be recovered. The material provisions of the Act are sections 17, 18 and 20 which are in the following terms:

"17. ... every judgment debt shall carry interest at the rate of £4 per centum per annum from the time of entering up the judgment ... until the same shall be satisfied, and such interest may be levied under a writ of execution on such judgment." The statutory rate of interest has been increased from time to time.

"18. ... all decrees and orders of courts of equity, and all rules of courts of common law ... whereby any sum of money, or any costs, charges, or expences, shall be payable to any person, shall have the effect of judgments in the superior courts of common law, and the persons to whom any such monies, or costs, charges, or expences, shall be payable, shall be deemed judgment creditors within the meaning of this Act; and all powers hereby given to the judges of the superior courts of common law with respect to matters depending in the same courts shall and may be exercised by courts of equity with respect to matters therein depending ... and all remedies hereby given to judgment creditors are in like manner given to persons to whom any monies, or costs, charges, or expences, are by such orders or rules respectively directed to be paid. ...

20. ... such new or altered writs shall be sued out of the courts of law, equity, and bankruptcy as may by such courts respectively be deemed necessary or expedient for giving effect to the provisions herein-before contained, and in such forms as the judges of such courts respectively shall from time to time think fit to order; ... "

Section 20 was repealed by the Civil Procedure Acts Repeal Act 1879, section 2 and the Schedule Part 1.

The Act nowhere defines the vital words in section 17 "entering up the judgment". A different view was taken by the common law courts as opposed to the Chancery courts as to when the judgment could be said to have been entered up and section 20 was apparently relied upon as giving a power to the courts to regulate their practice in accordance with the view they took. The Court of Common Pleas awarded interest on costs from the date of the incipitur: see *Fisher v Dudding* (1841) 9 Dowl 872. Tindal CJ said, at 874:

"The question is, what is the meaning of the words that interest shall be allowed from 'the time of entering up judgment?' And it appears to me, that the legal meaning of those words must be taken to be the time of signing judgment, or making the entry of the incipitur in the master's book."

Erskine J said, at 875–876:

"In putting an interpretation upon this clause of the statute, we must look at the practice of the court to see what is the 'entering up' of the judgment, and it appears to me that the entry of the incipitur in the master's book must be taken to be that entering up which is contemplated, and although the judgment may be afterwards more formally entered on the roll, yet that is not the entering of the judgment from which interest must be calculated."

Maule J said, at 876:

"I am also of the same opinion. In the contemplation of law, entering up of the judgment is the writing down something in a book which is kept by the master for that purpose. That is called the incipitur, and the entry is only so made for the convenience of the parties, but it guides what is drawn up afterwards in a more formal manner on the record. The record, it is to be observed, is not usually drawn up, unless it is necessary that it should be so for the use of the parties for any particular purpose, and the incipitur, at the same time, that it is generally alone sufficient for all ordinary purposes, affords the materials for drawing up that more minute form on parchment, which on account of the expense, is usually dispensed with. In criminal cases, the same course is commonly pursued, and the record is only filled up in instances where from some circumstances it is requisite that it should be so. The fact of this not being generally done then, affords a clue to the intentions of the legislature, and shews that the statute was not meant to refer to the entering up of the judgment on the roll, which would often produce more expense than the interest would amount to, but to the general entering up of judgment in the master's book in the form of an incipitur. With regard to the justice of the case, the court cannot look to particular cases in laying down a general rule of practice; but I confess that I do not see that any injustice will be worked by the decision at which the court has arrived."

That decision was approved in *Newton* v *Grand Junction Railway Co* (1846) 16 M & W 139, a decision of the Court of Exchequer. Alderson B observed in the course of argument, at 141:

"Then, as to the interest, there is an uncertain amount, which is in the wrong pocket, and is there bearing interest; I see no injustice in saying, that as soon as it is reduced to certainty, that interest should be paid. Whatever be the sum, it is fructifying in the wrong pocket."

However the Court of Chancery apparently took a different view, its practice being referred to in *Boswell* v *Coaks* (1887) 57 LJ Ch 101, 105, by Lindley LJ who said:

"The right to interest on costs depends on the statutory enactment 1 & 2 Vict c 110 sections 17 and 18, and by section 20 of that Act the court is empowered to make orders framing new rules, and under that section the Court of Chancery by consolidated orders issued a form of writ of fi fa according to which interest on costs was to run from the date of the taxing master's certificate. There was no similar practice at common law, where the interest ran always from the date of the judgment."

The Supreme Court of Judicature Acts 1873 and 1875 set up the High Court of Justice. Section 16 of the Act of 1875 is in the following terms:

"The Rules of Court in Schedule 1 to this Act shall come into operation at the commencement of this Act, and as to all matters to which they extend shall thenceforth regulate the proceedings in the High Court of Justice and Court of Appeal. ... "

Section 33 of the Act of 1875 repealed "Any other enactment inconsistent with this Act or the [Supreme Court of Judicature Act 1873]." In Schedule 1 to the Act of 1875 there appeared in Appendix F, Form 1. That form directed the sheriff to levy the amount of costs allowed on taxation "together with interest thereon at the rate of £4 per centum per annum from the   day of   ." There was then a reference to a footnote which stated: "The date of the certificate of taxation. The writ *must* be so moulded as to follow the substance of the judgment or order."

In *Schroeder* v *Cleugh* (1877) 35 LT 850 there was a motion to vary an order of the master which gave interest on costs only from the date of his certificate. The order was affirmed, it being held that the effect of the Act of 1875 was to apply the Chancery practice throughout the High Court.

Some five years after the decision in *Schroeder* v *Cleugh*, that is in 1883, there were enacted new Rules of the Supreme Court. Order 42, rule 14 provided, inter alia, that: "The Forms in Appendix H shall be used, with such variations as circumstances may require."

Form 1 in Appendix H was for a writ of fieri facias, where the party entitled elected to execute by one writ for both judgment debt and costs. This directed the sheriff to levy the judgment debt and costs in the same form as in Appendix F to the Rules of 1875 but the old footnote was replaced. The new footnote said: "Day of the judgment or order, or day on which money directed to be paid, or day from which interest is directed by the order to run, as the case may be."

Form 2, which related to an order for costs only, and which gave the sheriff the same direction as to interest, leaving the day from which it was to run blank, contained no footnote.

The following year there was an application before Field J to determine the effect of the alteration of the statutory footnote. In his judgment (see *Pyman & Co* v *Burt, Boulton* [1884] WN 100) he said:

> "By Order XLII, rule 14 the form of writ of execution given in Appendix H is ordered to be used. That form, therefore, may be taken to express what the judgment and execution are to be for. Then what is the form given in Appendix H? It must be read in conjunction with the note appended to it. It provides for execution for the amount of the debt and interest from a day to be inserted, and for the amount of the costs with interest from a day to be inserted. By the note, which applies both to the interest on the debt and to the interest on the costs, it is provided that the day to be inserted shall be the day of the judgment or order, or day on which money directed to be paid, or day from which interest is directed by the order to run, as the case may be. The meaning of that is that there may be a judgment simply, in which case the interest on the debt and on the costs will begin to run at once; or there may be a judgment directing money to be paid on a future day, in which case the interest will begin to run from that day; or there may be a judgment with a special direction as to the day from which interest on the debt or on the costs is to run. In any particular case I could order that the interest on the costs should not begin to run until after they have been taxed. In

the absence of any special order, no distinction is made between interest on the debt and interest on the costs. Both begin to run from the day of the judgment."

Some months later Pearson J in the Chancery Division in *Landowners' West of England and South Wales Land Drainage and Inclosure Co v Ashford* (1884) 33 WR 41, having been referred to the decisions in *Schroeder's* and *Pyman's* cases and having had the benefit of the submissions of Mr Farwell as an amicus curiae, followed the decision of Field J and held that interest must be paid from the date of judgment. Chitty J did likewise in the following year in *In re London Wharfing and Warehousing Co* (1885) 54 LJ Ch 1137 and in 1887 in *Boswell v Coaks*, 57 LJCh 101 the Court of Appeal upheld the decision of North J who had followed the decisions of Pearson and Chitty JJ. In his judgment Cotton LJ said, at 105:

> "The previous order altered the common law rule which gave interest as from the date of the judgment. The case of *Schroeder v Cleugh* shews that that order allowed the time at which the interest is to be calculated to be varied to the prejudice of a successful party by postponing the date from which the interest could be claimed. Therefore it is wrong to say that there is anything like a vested interest at the moment when the judgment is delivered, but it is only an interest to be worked out by the rules in existence at the time when the judgment is to be enforced. Whether it was right or wrong to vary the old rule I give no opinion, but we have this rule which applies here; and therefore, without entering into the question which is the better form and which would better satisfy the claim of justice, I will only say here is the rule which applies here, and by that we are bound. I am therefore of opinion that the decision of North J is right, and the appeal must be dismissed."

In his judgment Lindley LJ said, at 105, 106:

> "When the Rules of 1875 were settled, the Chancery rules were left alone, and the old practice remained untouched, and that accounts for the fact that the practice was not touched till 1883. Then came the Rules of 1883; they struck out the old rules and made one code applicable to all divisions of the court, and then we find the writ of fi fa varied, and the present form made applicable to all divisions under which interest is made to run from the date of the judgment, not the allocatur. ... I think that the Rules of 1883 apply, and that the proper form of the writ of fi fa is that given in Appendix H, under which interest on costs runs from the date of the judgment, and not from the date of the taxing master's certificate. ... "

There are two later reported decisions of the Chancery Division where interest has been awarded on costs from the incipitur: see *Taylor v Roe* [1894] 1 Ch 413 and *Ashworth v English Card Clothing Co Ltd (No 2)* [1904] 1 Ch 704.

K v K (Divorce Costs: Interest) [1977] Fam 39
From 1884 to 1965 the principle that interest on costs ran from the date of judgment became firmly established. Throughout this period the *Annual*

Practice contained a note to the effect that interest on costs ran from the date of judgment and not from the date of the taxing master's certificate.

In 1965 new writs of execution were introduced by the Rules of the Supreme Court (Revision) 1965 (SI No 1776): see RSC Order 45, rule 12 and Appendix A Forms 53 and 54, which replace the old Forms 1 and 2 respectively. The footnote to Form 1 was omitted altogether. The note in *The Annual Practice*, subsequently *The Supreme Court Practice*, continued in the same form until after the decision of the Court of Appeal in *K v K (Divorce Costs: Interest)* [1977] Fam 39, a case in the Family Division. Since the Court of Appeal were, understandably, much concerned with the merits of the wife's claim to interest on costs awarded to her, it is convenient to set out the summary of the facts given by Lord Denning MR, at 46:

> "The parties were married in 1962 and divorced in 1972. The first part of the divorce proceedings took place in the county court. That was up to decree absolute. The husband was ordered to pay the wife's costs of those proceedings. The second part of the divorce proceedings took place in the High Court. These were the ancillary proceedings about periodical payments or a lump sum for the wife. On 17 May 1974, the husband was ordered to pay the wife a lump sum of £50,000 on or before 1 September 1974; and also to pay her costs, including those of American advisers and accountants in connection with the application. The husband paid the £50,000 promptly on the due date, 1 September 1974. The wife's solicitors in October 1974 lodged a bill of costs (both for the county court and the High Court) amounting to over £34,000. On taxation in August 1975 the amount was knocked down to about one-half. The amount allowed was only £16,651.67. For example, the American lawyers' fees were claimed at £9,500 but only allowed at £3,500. The American accountants' fees were claimed at £6,750, and only allowed at £2,400. On 18 August 1975, the husband was ordered to pay within 28 days the sum of £16,651.67, the amount of the taxed costs. He paid it on 1 September 1975, well within the 28 days.
>
> Now the wife's solicitors claim interest on these costs. They do not claim any interest on the £50,000 lump sum. They claim it on the costs of £16,651.67. Although that sum was paid promptly, on the due date, they claim that the husband ought to pay interest on that amount for the previous 15 months. That is, interest on it for 15 months from 17 May 1974. That was the date when the order for costs was made, although the amount of those costs was not ascertained until August 1975. The wife's solicitors base their claim on a note in *The Supreme Court Practice* (1976), p. 997 (62/35/7), which, I have discovered, has appeared in every edition since 1884/1885: 'Interest [on costs] now runs from the date of the order or judgment in the absence of any order to the contrary ... and not, as formerly decided, from the date of the taxing master's certificate.' Sir George Baker P [1976] Fam 729 rejected the wife's claim for interest on the costs. The wife appeals to this court.
>
> Since the President's judgment, the husband's solicitors have asked for information as to the date on which the wife's solicitors paid the disbursement for the fees of counsel and the bills of the English and American lawyers and accountants. These were all paid after August 1975, when the bills were

taxed. This shows the extraordinary nature of the wife's claim. She is claiming interest on those disbursements from 17 May 1974, to 18 August 1975, although she did not pay them until afterwards. And she is claiming that interest for her own benefit. If she were to recover that interest, she could not hand it over to the counsel or lawyers or accountants. She would keep it herself and pay tax on it. It would be taxable in her hands as unearned income at the highest rates. The husband would not be able to deduct it from his gross income for tax purposes. So the real beneficiary would be the tax gatherer."

In order to decide whether the wife's claim was sustainable in law, Lord Denning MR considered in some detail the history of the legislation as set out above, observing, despite the views expressed by Maule J and Alderson B which I have quoted, that the common law rule was but an "old technical view", whereas in contrast courts of equity "took a sensible view". Having accepted that the consequence of the Rules of 1883 was that interest on costs ran from the date of the incipitur and not from the date of the allocatur, he then considered the effect of the new forms of writ of execution prescribed in 1965. He said, at 48–49:

"In 1965, however, the offending note of 1883 was removed: see RSC Order 45, rule 12(1), Appendix A, Forms Nos 53–63. The old rules were revised and a new set of rules enacted. The old 1883 note (on which *Pyman & Co v Burt, Boulton* [1884] WN 100 was decided) was omitted altogether. What is the result? I do not suppose that the framers of the 1965 Rules gave any thought to it. But the plain fact is that we are rid of the 1883 note; and with it we are rid of *Pyman & Co v Burt, Boulton*, which was founded on that note alone: and we are rid of the cases which followed *Pyman & Co v Burt, Boulton*. In those circumstances, I think we are entitled to go back to the time before 1883. We can go back to the note which appeared in the statute of 1875, which says that the date to be inserted is 'the date of the certificate of taxation'. Alternatively, we are entitled to say that the rule of equity should prevail. In the further alternative, we are entitled to apply a little common sense. Interest should be payable whenever money is 'wrongly withheld' from the one who is entitled to it: see *Jefford v Gee* [1970] 2 QB 130, 140–146. When the sum is unascertained, the debtor cannot be expected to pay it until it is quantified. He cannot make a tender until he knows how much it is. He cannot be said to be 'wrongfully withholding' the money until it is fixed. So in all fairness interest should only run from the date of quantification: see the instances given in *Jefford v Gee*, at p 145. If he is given time to pay, it should only run from the time when payment falls due. That is admittedly the case with the lump sum of £50,000 which was payable on 1 September 1974. It should also be the case with the costs of £16,651.67 which was payable on taxation."

Stephenson LJ having also considered the history said, at 53–56, in regard to the new forms substituted by the Rules of 1965:

"I can detect no change of substance in the new forms themselves; the period from which interest was to run was still left blank in both, but the footnote to the first form disappeared. There may be more than one explanation of that, although there is nothing in the explanatory note to the new rules to indicate the true explanation. Was it carelessness? Or economy? Or an intention to change the law and alter the practice, as Sir George Baker P [1976] Fam 279, 285–287 held? According to the note 62/35/7 in *The Supreme Court Practice* (1976), p. 997, the law is unchanged and interest on costs still runs from the date of the order or judgment in the absence of any order to the contrary; and I should have found it hard to infer so large an intention from so small a disappearance if the statutory footnote to a prescribed form of writ of fieri facias had not been given this very same effect by the Court of Common Pleas in *Schroeder* v *Cleugh*, 46 LJ CP 365, and the Court of Appeal in *Boswell* v *Coaks*, 57 LJ Ch 101. I cannot assume that when the statutory instrument of 1965 revoked all the previous rules and orders made since 1883 a footnote with such a history as this was accidentally dropped without regard to its origin and its judicially declared importance. But what was the unexplained reason for its disappearance? It was not replaced by the footnote which preceded it. Did the incipitur rule go with it? If it did, did the allocatur rule return to fill the blank left by its disappearance? Or was the blank left to be filled by the courts? With or without regard to the unrepealed sections 17 and 18 of the Act of 1838?

I am inclined to infer from the abolition of the footnote and the failure to replace it uncertainty as to what the practice in 1965 was and a recognition that it was no longer settled, perhaps because claims to interest on costs had fallen out of use and so the date from which it should be paid was no longer being considered. It may have been thought, on the other hand, that the Act of 1838 itself laid down the incipitur rule without the aid of the footnote, that the footnote had not been needed for Form No 2 and was superfluous for Form No 1, and that in the absence of a footnote there was nothing to prevail over the Act of 1838. But though the 1883 footnote was based upon the Act of 1838 (see particularly the judgment of Lindley LJ in *Boswell* v *Coaks*, 57 LJ Ch 101, 105), the Act had not been taken literally as laying down the incipitur rule for interest and binding the courts to enforce it either on judgment debts or on costs. For it was never considered that the 1875 rules and footnote laying down the allocatur rule were ultra vires or that when the incipitur rule replaced it in 1883 the new footnote was ultra vires in so far as it laid down that when a judgment directed payment of money on a future date, interest ran only from that date and not from the date of entering the judgment. It is curious that the same treatment was not applied to an order for costs, even apparently where a separate writ of fieri facias was taken out for them. ...

Are we then freed by the removal of the statutory footnote to depart from the incipitur rule? Can we consider where justice and convenience lie, and having considered them prefer, as Sir George Baker P did, the allocatur rule and dismiss this appeal? We cannot, in my opinion, declare the allocatur rule to be again the law because it was the law before 1883 and the abolition of the 1883 footnote restores the earlier law; for the 1875 footnote, which was the foundation of the earlier law, has not been put back. We have to go back to the pre-existing law before the 1875 footnote and that was, as I have shown, not uniform. ...

If we are free to choose the better rule, my choice would not be North J's. I would choose the allocatur. True the payer of costs can invest the sum required to pay them at a rate of interest more profitable than $7^1/_2$ per centum per annum; but the payee may not have paid out large parts of the costs as early as the incipitur, for instance the fees of the wife's English and American lawyers and accountants in the present case. I regard it as on the whole more just and convenient that the costs (to borrow the language of Aldersons B's interjection in *Newton v Grand Junction Railway Co*, 16 M & W 139, 141) should fructify in the pocket of the payer, where they still are through no fault of his, than in the pocket of the payee where they, or a part of them, may still be because he (or she) has not yet expended them.

We are, in my judgment, free to choose the better rule and are no longer bound by the prescribed form to the incipitur rule. Indeed we ought to apply the principle laid down by this court for interest generally to interest on costs, unless there is some statutory provision which prevents us; and applied to interest on costs that principle reintroduces the allocatur rule because costs are not wrongfully withheld until quantification. At first sight sections 17 and 18 of the Act of 1838 appear to bar the allocatur rule. But they did not prevent the courts from applying the allocatur rule both before and after 1875 and, if I am right in the reason I have given for that, I am of opinion that the court has power to make the allocatur rule a rule of its practice."

Orr LJ agreed with both judgments. It will thus be seen that the Court of Appeal were unable to detect any change of substance in the new forms except the removal of the footnote from Form 53 which replaced the old Form 1. Accordingly, they concluded that the principle which had been established for some 80 years had thus been removed and they were accordingly able to reach the decision which they considered met the justice of the particular case. As Mr Jeffrey Burke for the appellant correctly points out the Court of Appeal overlooked that in the previous fi fa forms there were two separate blanks, one which related to the date from which interest on the damages or debt, the subject matter of the judgment was to run and the other which related to the date from which interest on costs was to run. In such circumstances it was necessary to provide a footnote as to how those blanks were to be filled in. In the new form there is only one blank for the date from which interest is to run and this has therefore to be calculated on the aggregate of the damages or debt together with the costs allowed on taxation. The possibility of differentiation between the two having been removed the form was thus a simplified version of its predecessor and the simplification removed the necessity for the note. Accordingly there was no warrant for the Court of Appeal to depart from the previous decision of the Court of Appeal in *Boswell v Coaks*, which was accepted to have been a correct decision when made and consistently applied for nearly a century thereafter.

Erven Warnink BV v J Townend & Sons (Hull) Ltd [1982] 3 All ER 312
Nearly six years later, the contest between the incipitur rule and the allocatur rule fell to be considered again by the Court of Appeal in a case where the

merits this time strongly favoured the incipitur rule. The plaintiffs brought a passing-off action in which after 25 days before Goulding J they succeeded. They lost in the Court of Appeal but succeeded in the House of Lords. The judgment of Goulding J was given on 29 July 1977, when he made an order granting the plaintiffs an injunction, an inquiry as to damages and their taxed costs of the action. In accordance with the usual practice, because an appeal to the Court of Appeal was pending, the plaintiffs did not proceed to tax their costs. After the decision of the House of Lords the plaintiffs proceeded to taxation and certificates were granted as follows. (i) On 25 February 1980 a certificate in the sum of £53,937.16 was granted pursuant to the order of Goulding J. (ii) On 25 February 1980 a certificate in the sum of £25,953.22 was granted pursuant to the order of 18 July 1979 in respect of costs of the appeal to the Court of Appeal. (iii) On 25 February 1980 a certificate was granted in the sum of £15,181.31 in respect of the costs of the appeal to the House of Lords – the total of the three certificates was thus £95,071.69. The defendants paid that sum on 28 March 1980, together with the sum of £982.26 in respect of interest on the taxed costs (other than costs in the House of Lords) from the date of the relevant certificates to payment. The plaintiffs had themselves made various payments to their solicitors on account of costs during the course of the proceedings – namely between 15 July 1976 and 8 October 1979, totalling £146,810.57. They had thus lost interest, not only on sums paid on account of costs prior to the judgment of Goulding J, and no-one suggested that they could claim interest on such costs, but also interest which could have been earned on the substantial sum, well in excess of the costs allowed on taxation, which they had paid well before the certificates of taxation. The plaintiffs appealed against the order of Slade J refusing their application for an order that the defendants pay to them interest at the statutory rate on the taxed costs from the date of the order for costs. Fox LJ, in giving the judgment of the Court of Appeal, again went through the history as recited earlier in this speech, and repeated the same error as was made by the Court of Appeal in *K* v *K* [1982] 3 All ER 312, 317 when he said that the new forms introduced in 1965 were unchanged except that the footnote to Form 1 had gone. The court having concluded that it was bound by the decision in *K* v *K* and that it had no discretion in the matter, set out its own views on the basis that it was free to consider the matter generally and gave leave to appeal to your Lordships' House, a facility of which advantage was not taken. Fox LJ said, at 319–320:

> "We do not think that either rule is satisfactory as to costs in all circumstances. We can see no sensible reason why the appellant wife in *K* v *K* should have succeeded (as she would have done if the incipitur rule had been applied) or why the present plaintiffs should wholly fail (as they must if the allocatur rule is applied). Nor does it seem to us that either rule is satisfactory in relation to interest generally. The incipitur rule cannot be satisfactorily applied to a judgment for payment at a future date (such as the order for the payment of the

£50,000 in *K v K*). Nor can the 'quantification' rule be satisfactorily applied to a judgment for unliquidated damages. It is not a useful approach in such a case to say that a person cannot be expected to pay until the liability has been quantified. The litigant who obtains a judgment for damages to be assessed has already suffered damage at the date when the judgment is pronounced. That he should have to wait for the damages until after they are quantified is necessary, but there is no reason why he should not have interest when, in the end, they are paid. In *Borthwick v Elderslie Steamship Co Ltd (No 2)* [1905] 2 KB 516, the Court of Appeal held that, in the case of a judgment for damages to be assessed, interest was payable from the date of the judgment. Romer LJ, after saying that the plaintiff was held entitled to recover damages the amount of which remained to be ascertained, continued, at p. 522: 'The amount has since been ascertained, and must be treated as if it had been mentioned in the judgment of the court; and the result is that the plaintiff has a judgment for an ascertained sum, dated on the day on which it is pronounced.' Whichever rule is adopted, therefore, some violence will have to be done to the general principle in order to secure a just result in certain cases. ...

The purpose of an order for costs is to give an indemnity, or partial indemnity, to the successful litigant in respect of his expenses of the litigation. If, therefore, he has made payments to his lawyers in respect of costs prior to taxation (and it is likely nowadays that he will) it is difficult to see why he should be denied interest as from the judgment or later payment on the amounts from time to time paid (up to the aggregate ultimately allowed on taxation). On the other hand, interest cannot be allowed in the *K v K* situation. It seems to us that the court is entitled to consider the purpose of the statute and to construe it as not permitting interest in such circumstances. If the date of judgment is accepted as the general principle, such a construction would merely be a limitation on the general principal in order to avoid absurd results, just as in the case of interest on a judgment on a fixed sum to be paid at a future date. ... The only alternative, we think, is to apply the allocatur rule rigidly in the case of costs."

Conclusion

The Court of Appeal in *K v K (Divorce Costs: Interest)* [1977] Fam 39 misapprehended the nature of the amendment made to the new form by the Rules of the Supreme Court (Revision) 1965, for the reasons already stated. The decision in *Pyman's* case [1884] WN 100 as to the effect of the Rules of 1883, as approved by the Court of Appeal in *Boswell's* case, 57 LJCh 101 was correct. Accordingly the incipitur rule prevails. I respectfully agree with the observations of the Court of Appeal that a satisfactory result cannot be achieved in every case, but in my judgment the balance of justice favours the incipitur rule for the following reasons.   1. It is the unsuccessful party to the litigation who, ex hypothesi, has caused the costs unnecessarily to be incurred. Hence the order made against him. Since interest is not awarded on costs incurred and paid by the successful party before judgment, why should he suffer the added loss of interest on costs incurred and paid after judgment but before the taxing master gives his certificate?   2. Since, as the Court of

Appeal rightly said in the *Erven Warnink* case [1982] 3 All ER 312 payments of costs are likely nowadays to be made to lawyers prior to taxation, then the application of the allocatur rule would generally speaking do greater injustice than the operation of the incipitur rule. Moreover, the incipitur rule provides a further necessary stimulus for payments to be made on account of costs and disbursements prior to taxation, for costs to be more readily agreed, and for taxation, when necessary, to be expedited, all of which are desirable developments. Barristers, solicitors and expert witnesses should not be expected to finance their clients' litigation until it is completed and the taxing master's certificate obtained. If interest is not payable on costs between judgment and the completion of taxation, then there is an incentive to delay payment, delay disbursements and taxation.   3. It is common ground between the parties that the unsatisfactory situation illustrated in *K v K* can be simply dealt with by an express agreement between the solicitor and his client that any interest recovered on costs and disbursements after judgment is pronounced but before the taxing master's certificate is obtained, which costs and disbursements have not in fact been paid prior to taxation shall as to the interest on the costs belong to the solicitor, and as to the interest on disbursements be held by him for and on behalf of the person or persons to whom the disbursements are ultimately paid.

For the sake of completeness I should add that Mr Goldblatt strongly argued that an order for payment of costs to be taxed cannot be a judgment debt within section 17 of the Act of 1838 because until taxation has been completed, there is no sum for which execution can be levied. This point appears to have been raised in the *Erven Warnink* case and disposed of at the end of the judgment on the basis that the courts have accepted since its enactment, that section 17 does apply to such a judgment and accordingly the law has gone too far for that argument. I agree. This acceptance is because a judgment for costs to be taxed is to be treated in the same way as a judgment for damages to be assessed, where the amount ultimately ascertained is treated as if it was mentioned in the judgment – no further order being required. A judgment debt can therefore in my judgment be construed for the purpose of section 17, as covering an order for the payment of costs to be taxed.

I accordingly would allow this appeal with costs, both in your Lordships' House and in the courts below, and would order that interest on the costs of this action should be payable by the respondent at the appropriate rates from 1 November 1984.

LORD JAUNCEY OF TULLICHETTLE: My Lords, I have had the advantage of reading in draft the speech prepared by my noble and learned friend Lord Ackner. I agree with it, and for the reasons that he has given I too would allow the appeal with costs, both in your Lordship's House and in the courts below, and would order that interest on the costs of this action should be payable by the respondent at the appropriate rates from 1 November 1984.

Appeal allowed with costs.

J Borke QC and *John Foy* for the plaintiff.
S Goldblatt and *Colin Edelman* for the defendant.

Chrulew and others
v
Borm-Reid & Co (a firm)

Queen's Bench Division
10 April, 16 May 1991

Waller J
sitting with
Master Berkeley and Mr R J Winstanley as assessors

Headnote

Where a *Calderbank* offer has been made under RSC Order 62, rule 27(3) there is no obligation on the offeror to show a breakdown of how the offer has been constructed. A global figure offered in settlement of the costs claimed in the bill will suffice.

In this case an offer of £8,750 had been made. The bill was taxed at £8,609. The defendants (the paying party) revealed at the end of the taxation that a *Calderbank* offer had been made. They sought disallowance of the plaintiff's costs of taxation. On review they sought an order that their own costs should be paid by the plaintiff. Waller J held that the defendants were not entitled to have their costs of taxation paid but that there should be no order as to costs of the taxation including the taxing fee, which would therefore be the responsibility of the plaintiff. The fact that an offer had not been accepted did not give the automatic right to recovery of the costs of taxation of the offering party. RSC Order 62, rule 27(4) states that a taxing officer *may* take an offer into account when exercising his discretion as to costs under the rule.

---

16 May 1991. The following judgment was delivered.

WALLER J: This is an application to review the decision of the chief clerk of the Supreme Court Taxing Office, Mr Burroughs, and Master P Hurst, and raises for consideration the exercise of the discretion of the taxing master in the light of what is termed a "*Calderbank* offer" made pursuant to RSC Order 26, rule 27(3) (see *Calderbank v Calderbank* [1975] 3 All ER 333, [1976] Fam 93). There is, I am told, no previous authority considering this matter, and it is for that reason that I have given leave for this judgment to be reported. I have sat on this matter with Master Berkeley and Mr Winstanley and am very grateful for the assistance that I have received from them.

The proceedings to which this matter relates arose out of an action in negligence against a firm of solicitors for failure to apply for a new lease under the Landlord and Tenant Act 1954. The plaintiffs were in effect successful in the action in that by an order made on 14 May 1990 the defendants were ordered to pay in addition to a sum of £19,500 paid into court on 19 April 1990 a further sum of £15,500 and were further ordered to pay the costs of the plaintiffs, including the costs of the application of 14 May to be taxed on the standard basis if not agreed. The costs were not agreed and a reference to tax was taken out on 31 May 1990. The matter came before Mr Burroughs, the chief clerk of the Supreme Court Taxing Office, who taxed the bill on 10 July 1990. At the end of the taxation the defendants revealed that a *Calderbank* offer had been made. The bill of costs excluding item 5 and the taxation fee had been taxed at £8,609.00. The *Calderbank* offer had been made on 20 June 1990 in the sum of £8,750 plus value added tax as applicable. In the event no value added tax was payable. The taxing officer was then asked by the defendants to disallow the costs of taxation, that is the taxation item and the taxing fee of £442.05. They did not, as I understand it, make any request to Mr Burroughs for an order in relation to their own costs.

Mr Burroughs looked at the *Calderbank* offer and the ensuing correspondence. The terms of the *Calderbank* offer by letter dated 20 June 1990 were as follows:

> "We, Ince & Co, Solicitors for the Defendants, are authorised to offer to you the sum of £8,750, plus VAT as applicable, without prejudice, save as to the costs of taxation, in full and final settlement of your clients' costs of the action pursuant to the Order dated 14th May 1990. In the event that this offer is not accepted we reserve the right to draw the Taxing Master's notice to this offer pursuant to Order 62 Rule 27(3)."

The response to that letter by letter dated 21 June 1990 was as follows:

> "We thank you for your letter dated the 20th June 1990 the contents of which we have noted. We calculate that our costs as drawn amount to £7,474 and that our disbursements as set out in our bill amount to £3,707.50 making a total of £11,181.50. It would appear that you are offering us £8,750 in settlement of this claim. We find it very difficult to consider your offer without a further breakdown as to how the sum is calculated. Our bill includes Counsel's fees of £2,070. We have paid our expert £1,087.50. Are these sums admitted by you? We would be grateful if you could break down your offer of £8,750 into profit costs, Counsel's fees, expert's fees and other disbursements and we will then be able to consider the position further. We would also be grateful to receive confirmation that your clients will pay VAT on the whole of our profit costs. We await to hear from you."

In their reply dated 26 June 1990 Ince & Co refused to give a breakdown, stating that they had "no wish to enter into a taxation by correspondence", but set out two matters of concern to them in relation to the assessment of the plaintiffs' costs.

According to Master Hurst in his reasons, it was common ground before him between the parties that the reason why Mr Burroughs refused to disallow the costs of taxation was that the defendants when requested by the plaintiffs had not broken down their *Calderbank* offer between profit costs and disbursement. This was challenged before me by Mrs Simon, who appeared for the plaintiffs. She asserted there were other reasons why Mr Burroughs refused to disallow the costs and I will return to that below. But, so far as Master Hurst was concerned, the sole consideration as to why Mr Burroughs refused to disallow the costs was that the defendants had refused the breakdown.

In Master Hurst's reasons in which he upheld Mr Burroughs's exercise of his discretion, he put the matter in the following way:

> "In reaching my decision on these objections I formed the view that the defendants had acted in accordance with Order 62, rule 27 and had acted reasonably in not providing further details of their *Calderbank* offer to the plaintiffs' solicitors. I was not persuaded that the plaintiffs' solicitors were entitled to the information which they sought, since it is part of the nature of litigation that opposing sides make offers in the hope of settling disputes and will do so both in order to disguise weaknesses in their own case as well to point up weaknesses in the opponents' case. Thus, whilst it would have been useful for the plaintiffs to know the information which they sought, I formed the view that they were not entitled to it. It was at one point suggested that it was necessary to go to taxation in any event to resolve the value added tax position but this did not appear to me to do so, since the value added tax position was conceded at the outset of the taxation. It was argued by Mr Boyd for the defendants that Mr Burroughs did not have all the correspondence before him and therefore was not in a position to make a proper decision. In my view Mr Burroughs was fully apprised of the situation and the fact that he did not have sight of all the correspondence did not in fact impair his ability to reach a decision. No evidence was put before me that Mr Burroughs had exercised his discretion otherwise than judicially and in those circumstances, although had the original taxation taken place before me I might have come to the opposite view, I saw no reason to overturn Mr Burroughs's perfectly proper exercise of his discretion."

I have to say that I, on any view, do not find this process of reasoning very satisfactory. Having demolished, as it seems to me rightly, the main plank of Mr Burroughs's reasoning for exercising his discretion in the way he did, it seems to me difficult to state in the same breath that there was no evidence before Master Hurst that Mr Burroughs had exercised his discretion otherwise than judicially. On any view, having taken away the main plank of Mr Burroughs's reasoning, there was called for a fresh exercise of the discretion.

The two competing submissions before us can be summarised as follows. Mr Moor, on behalf of the defendants, submitted that a *Calderbank* offer under Order 62, rule 27(3) should be treated by a taxing master just like a payment in in ordinary litigation. He submitted that, if a defendant beats a payment in, then, in the absence of special circumstances, he should not be ordered to pay the costs following the payment in and indeed should obtain his costs since that time.

Mrs Simon, on behalf of the plaintiffs, on the other hand, submitted that in taxation proceedings the procedure is different. She submitted that, on a proper construction of the rules, a *Calderbank* offer is simply one factor that a taxing master *may* take into account and that he has an unfettered discretion. She submitted that Mr Burroughs had all the files and the details of the underlying case before him and that all those matters plus the factor that the defendants had refused to give a breakdown of their *Calderbank* offer were taken into account by Mr Burroughs, and that thus Master Hurst was right not to interfere with Mr Burroughs' order.

Before considering Order 62, rule 27(3) in the taxation context, it is right to consider the correct approach to a *Calderbank* offer generally. A number of authorities relating to *Calderbank* offers and/or their equivalent were cited. My view is that the authorities are helpful as a matter of background to the construction of the rules which now expressly deal with such offers. But there is no need to go further than the Court of Appeal decision in *Cutts v Head* [1984] 1 All ER 597, [1984] Ch 290, where a full review of all authorities is carried out and where there are full citations from those passages in the authorities to which Mr Moor directed our attention. He for example placed great reliance on the passage quoted by Oliver LJ in *Cutts v Head* [1984] 1 All ER 597 at 601–602, [1984] Ch 290 at 300–301 from Cairns LJ's judgment in *Calderbank v Calderbank* [1975] 3 All ER 333 at 342, [1976] Fam 93 at 105, particularly the passage where Cairns LJ said:

> "Another example is in the Admiralty Division where there is commonly a dispute between the owners of two vessels that have been in collision as to the apportionment of blame between them. It is common practice for an offer to be made by one party to another of a certain apportionment. If that is not accepted no reference is made to that offer in the course of the hearing until it comes to costs, and then if the court's apportionment is as favourable to the party who made the offer as what was offered, or more favourable to him, then costs will be awarded on the same basis as if there had been a payment in."

Mr Moor also referred to a passage in the judgment of Megarry V-C in *Computer Machinery Co Ltd v Drescher* [1983] 3 All ER 153 at 156, [1983] 1 WLR 1379 at 1382–1383 quoted by Oliver LJ in *Cutts v Head* [1984] 1 All ER 597 at 608–609, [1984] Ch 290 at 310–311 emphasising the following passage:

> "In my view, the principle in question is one of perfectly general application which is in no way confined to matrimonial cases. Whether an offer is made

'without prejudice' or 'without prejudice save as to costs', the courts ought to enforce the terms on which the offer was made as tending to encourage compromises and shorten litigation; and the latter form of offer has the added advantage of preventing the offer from being inadmissible on costs, thereby assisting the court towards justice in making the order as to costs."

Cutts v *Head* [1984] 1 All ER 597 at 610, [1984] Ch 290 at 312 thus laid down, in the words of Oliver LJ –

"that it must now be taken to be established that the *Calderbank* formula suggested by Cairns LJ is not restricted to matrimonial proceedings but is available in all cases where what is in issue is something more than a simple money claim in respect of which a payment into court would be the appropriate way of proceeding."

At the end of his judgment Oliver LJ sounded what he termed as "one word of caution". He said ([1984] 1 All ER 597 at 610, [1984] Ch 290 at 312):

"The qualification imposed on the without prejudice nature of the *Calderbank* letter is, as I have held, sufficient to enable it to be taken into account on the question of costs; but it should not be thought that this involves the consequence that such a letter can now be used as a substitute for a payment into court, where a payment into court is appropriate. In the case of the simple money claim, a defendant who wishes to avail himself of the protection afforded by an offer must, in the ordinary way, back his offer with cash by making a payment in and, speaking for myself, I should not, as at present advised, be disposed in such a case to treat a *Calderbank* offer as carrying the same consequences as payment in."

With those observations Fox LJ also agreed (see [1984] 1 All ER 597 at 613, [1984] Ch 290 at 317).

The decision in *Cutts* v *Head* is now reflected in the provisions of the Rules of the Supreme Court. By Order 22, rule 14 it is expressly provided that a party may make a written offer without prejudice save as to costs, and it is further expressly provided that the court should not take such an offer into account if, at the time it is made, the party could have protected his position as to costs by means of a payment into court. Order 22, rule 14(2) refers to Order 62, rule 9(1). Order 62, rule 9(1) provides:

"The Court in exercising its discretion as to costs *shall* take into account ... (*b*) any payment of money into court and the amount of such payment ... (*d*) any written offer made under Order 22, rule 14, provided that the Court shall not take such an offer into account if, at the time it is made, the party making it could have protected his position as to costs by means of a payment into court under Order 22."

Mr Moor submitted that under Order 62, rule 9 it was in effect mandatory to award a party his costs if either there had been a payment of money into court which equalled or exceeded the money awarded at the end of the trial or if what had been achieved at the trial was equal to or more than had been offered by virtue of a *Calderbank* offer.

In relation to payment in he relied on *Findlay* v *Railway Executive* [1950] 2 All ER 969 at 971. There Somervell LJ referred to the principle adumbrated by Viscount Cave LC in *Donald Campbell & Co Ltd* v *Pollak* [1927] AC 732 at 811–812 in the following terms:

> "A successful defendant in a non-jury case has no doubt, in the absence of special circumstances, a reasonable expectation of obtaining an order for the payment of his costs by the plaintiff; but he has no right to costs unless and until the Court awards them to him, and the Court has an absolute and unfettered discretion to award or not to award them. This discretion, like any other discretion, must of course be exercised judicially, and the judge ought not to exercise it against the successful party except for some reason connected with the case."

The judgment of Somervell LJ then continued:

> "The first point to be decided here is whether a defendant who has paid money into court which has not been taken out and exceeds the sum awarded to the plaintiff is a successful litigant or a successful party within those two statements of the law. I hold that he is, and that the principles there laid down apply. The main purpose of the rules for payment into court is the hope that further litigation will be avoided, the plaintiff being encouraged to take out the sum paid in, if it be a reasonable sum, whereas, if he goes on and gets a smaller sum, he will be penalised wholly or to some extent in costs. Once, therefore, the money has been paid in, the *lis* between the parties simply is: Is that sum sufficient to cover the damage which has been suffered. *Prima facie*, therefore, the defendants in the present case are entitled to be paid their costs as from the date of payment in, but, of course, as in other cases, there may be circumstances connected with the case which entitled the judge to make some order other than that of giving the successful litigant his costs, and counsel for the plaintiff submitted that there were such circumstances in this case."

The facts were then gone into and it was decided that there were no circumstances entitling the judge to deprive the successful defendants of their costs in that particular case.

The above principle is applied even if the payment in precisely equals the sum ultimately awarded at the trial: see *King* v *Weston-Howell* [1989] 2 All ER 375, [1989] 1 WLR 579. This authority was not referred to by Mr Moor, but it demonstrates the fact that in relation to a payment-in situation the real issue between the parties after payment in is whether or not that is the right sum.

In relation to a *Calderbank* offer Mr Moor relies on the language of Cairns LJ quoted with approval by Oliver LJ, where he says in the Admiralty context that a party "will" be awarded his costs (see the passage quoted above). I think Mr Moor recognised that the position was not an absolute one in relation to a *Calderbank* offer any more than it is in relation to a payment into court. There may be circumstances where the court in its discretion will not order costs, but the reasons for not so doing will have to be special ones. In relation to a *Calderbank* offer it furthermore seems to me there must be in any event further room for flexibility. If the case is suitable for a payment into court then the payment-in provisions will apply. A *Calderbank* offer will only be made where the payment-in provisions do not apply. A *Calderbank* offer may be capable of being reasonably black or white, as for instance it is in the Admiralty context to which Cairns LJ was referring. A *Calderbank* offer may also however be utilised in a situation where one is not dealing with a monetary sum or an apportionment and in those circumstances a further degree of flexibility will be necessary. The right test in relation to a *Calderbank* offer is probably best expressed in the words of Ormrod LJ in *McDonnell* v *McDonnell* [1977] 1 All ER 766 at 770, [1977] 1 WLR 34 at 38 quoted by Oliver LJ in *Cutts* v *Head* [1984] 1 All ER 597 at 602, [1984] Ch 290 at 302 in the following words:

> "Clearly this is a very important consideration in exercising the court's discretion with regard to costs. It would be wrong, in my judgment, to equate an offer of compromise in proceedings such as these precisely to a payment into court. I see no advantage in the court surrendering its discretion in these matters as it has to all intents and purposes done where a payment into court has been made. A *Calderbank* v *Calderbank* offer should influence but not govern the exercise of the discretion. The question to my mind is whether, on the basis of the facts known to the wife and her advisers and without the advantage of hindsight, she ought reasonably to have accepted the proposals in the letter of 16th December, bearing always in mind the difficulty of making accurate forecasts in cases such as this. On the other hand, parties who are exposed to the full impact of costs need some protection against those who can continue to litigate with impunity under a civil aid certificate."

Obviously he is there referring to matrimonial proceedings but it will almost invariably, as it seems to me, be the correct test to consider in relation to a *Calderbank* offer whether the party "ought reasonably to have accepted the proposals in the letter". If the answer to that question is Yes, then as it seems to me, taking the fact that a *Calderbank* offer is now placed in the same position as a payment in under Order 62, rule 9, the party who has not reasonably accepted a *Calderbank* offer will be liable to pay the costs from the date at which that acceptance should have been made.

Thus I can summarise the position as it seems to me in the normal litigation context as follows.

(1) Where a payment in has been made and accepted under Order 22, rules 1 and 3, a party is absolutely entitled to its costs (see Order 62, rule 5(4)).

(2) Where there has been a payment in not accepted, then, if that payment in is equal to or beaten by the defendants, the defendants are entitled to their costs as the successful party unless there are special reasons for depriving the defendants thereof.

(3) A *Calderbank* offer can only be used where the payment-in provisions

are inapplicable, but where it is properly deployed, if the party to whom the offer is made has unreasonably failed to accept that offer, then the offering party will be entitled to costs post the time at which that offer should have been accepted unless there are special reasons for depriving the defendants thereof.

The basis for the above approach is that the successful party in litigation is entitled to have his costs unless there are special reasons.

I must now turn to Order 62, rule 27. The note to Order 62, rule 27(3) and (4) in *The Supreme Court Practice 1991* para 62/27/1 states that the rule has been extended "to Calderbank letters" (see also para 62/9/1) in taxation proceedings and the procedure is explained in Note 21 of the Masters' Practice Notes 1986, para 62/A2/32. That note reads as follows:

> "A party liable to pay costs to a party other than an assisted person may make a 'Calderbank' offer under the provisions of Order 62 Rule 27(3) at any time after the order for costs is made. If no offer has been made before the reference is taken, the party taking the reference should comply strictly with Order 62 Rule 30(3) and deliver a copy of the bill to the paying party within 7 days of taking the reference. If such an offer is made the party whose bill it is should at once inform the Chief Clerk who will thereupon stay the progress of the taxation for a period of 7 days from the date upon which the offer was made. If the offer is accepted within that time, the party whose bill it is may apply for the bill to be withdrawn and for the taxing fee to be abated in whole or in part. The existence of a 'Calderbank offer' must not be made known personally to the taxing officer to whom the taxation has been referred."

The above procedures were complied with in the instant case.

It is now important to set out the provisions of Order 62, rule 27 in extenso:

> "(1)   Subject to the provisions of any Act and this Order, the party whose bill is being taxed shall be entitled to his costs of the taxation proceedings.
>
> (2)   Where it appears to the taxing officer that in the circumstances of the case some other order should be made as to the whole or any part of the costs, the taxing officer shall have, in relation to the costs of taxation proceedings, the same powers as the Court has in relation to the costs of proceedings.
>
> (3)   Subject to paragraph (5), the party liable to pay the costs of the proceedings which gave rise to the taxation proceedings may make a written offer to pay a specific sum in satisfaction of those costs which is expressed to be 'without prejudice save as to the costs of taxation' at any time before the expiration of 14 days after the delivery to him of a copy of the bill of costs under rule 30(3) and, where such an offer is made, the fact that it has been made shall not be communicated to the taxing officer until the question of the costs of the taxation proceedings falls to be decided.
>
> (4)   The taxing officer may take into account any offer made under paragraph (3) which has been brought to his attention.
>
> (5)   No offer to pay a specific sum in satisfaction of costs may be made in a case where the person entitled to recover his costs is an assisted person within the meaning of the statutory provisions relating to legal aid.
>
> (6)   In this rule any reference to the costs of taxation proceedings shall be

construed as including a reference to any fee which is prescribed by the Orders as to Court fees for the taxation of a bill of costs."

There are, as it seems to me, two matters of distinction in relation to these rules as compared to ordinary litigation. First, and the matter primarily relied on by Mrs Simon, the language of Order 62, rule 27(4). There the word "may" is used in contrast to the language of Order 62, rule 9. Secondly, the starting point in relation to taxation seems not to be the same starting point as in litigation generally. Under Order 62, rule 27(1) the party whose bill is being taxed shall be entitled to his costs of the taxation proceedings in all normal circumstances. In other words there is not the expectation at the conclusion of taxation proceedings that the "winner" will obtain an order for costs and that the "loser" will obtain no order. By the time costs are being taxed under Order 62, rule 27, the "winner" is the person claiming the costs having to go through the taxation process and is prima facie entitled to the costs of so doing. In order for that party to be deprived of his costs, never mind having to pay the costs of the other party, it has to appear to the taxing officer, pursuant to Order 62, rule 27(2), that in the circumstances of the case some other order should be made as to the whole or any part of the costs. It is in that context that the taxing officer "may" take into account an offer made described as a *Calderbank* offer. I should say that at one time I felt that the word "may" was purely permissive in the sense of allowing a without prejudice offer to be referred to. But, on reflection, it seems to me that the contrast between the language of Order 62, rule 27(4) and Order 62, rule 9 is clear, as is the fact that the starting point will be that the party having his bill taxed should be entitled to his costs.

All that said, however, it must be clear that it was intended that a person who might otherwise have to pay costs should have a method by which he could put the other side on risk. In other words the policy considerations behind allowing a *Calderbank* offer in general litigation as described by Megarry V-C in *Computer Machinery Co Ltd* v *Drescher* [1983] 3 All ER 153 at 156, [1983] 1 WLR 1379 at 1382–1383 in the passage which I have cited, would seem equally applicable in the taxation context. It would thus seem to me that if the *Calderbank* offer is not to be taken into account there must be some circumstances relating to that offer or the taxation which make it one which should be ignored. It may for example have been too late. Alternatively, there may have been a failure by the paying party to give notice of some special objection which would enable the receiving party to be aware of a reason which he would not otherwise appreciate why his bill might be taxed down. This last sort of point again demonstrates the difference between taxation and ordinary litigation. Very often a paying party will have given no notice at all prior to the first taxation as to points that are going to be taken.

As I see it, it is difficult to improve on the test of whether "the offer should reasonably have been accepted" by the offeree party, but that has to be transferred to the taxation context. Indeed, I suspect that it was something like that test which was in fact applied by Mr Burroughs, and which he answered in the negative because he thought that the defendants should have broken down their offer.

As I have already indicated, it seems to me (and I have been assisted in coming to this view by the views of Master Berkeley and Mr Winstanley), where a *Calderbank* offer is made Master Hurst is right in saying that the offeror is not bound in ordinary circumstances to give details or the breakdown of how he reaches his offer. The whole purpose of an offer in effect of compromise is that it may reflect strengths and weaknesses in a variety of different areas. It may be different if there is a point which the paying party intends to take which would take the payee party by surprise. In this case I asked Mrs Simon whether she suggested there was any such factor, and she did not so suggest. I thus think that the decision of Master Hurst on this aspect was right. As already stated, it also seems to me that an essential plank of Mr Burroughs's reasoning is removed and that the discretion must thus be exercised afresh.

Exercising that discretion afresh, in my view the right question is: should the plaintiffs reasonably have accepted the offer? Putting the matter in a slightly different way: was there something that happened on the taxation which could not reasonably have been foreseen by the plaintiffs when considering the defendants' offer? As I have said, Mrs Simon did not suggest there was any matter which might have taken her by surprise. She did suggest that the matter was complex and that Mr Burroughs had the full details of the file, but that does not seem to us to amount to any special circumstance. She also relied on the fact that her bill had been miscalculated by her costs' draftsman. That again does not seem to be a circumstance on which the plaintiffs should be entitled to rely. Accordingly, since there was nothing on the taxation leading to a taxation at £8,609, other than simply a taxing down of various items, that demonstrates, as it seems to me, that the offer of £8,750 should reasonably have been accepted.

This brings me to the final aspect. On this review there is a claim not only to have the costs of the taxation disallowed including the taxation fee, but for the defendants to have their costs. From the reasons of Master Hurst, it does not seem that any application for costs was in fact ever made before Mr Burroughs. But certainly such an application was being made by virtue of the objections before Master Hurst. It is in this area that the distinction between taxation and ordinary litigation is once again important. The expectation at the conclusion of a taxation is that normally the party whose bill is being taxed will be entitled to his costs and there is not an expectation that the "winner" will receive an order for costs, i.e. that someone who succeeds in taxing the bill down will necessarily be entitled to his costs of attending the taxation. There may well be circumstances in which the failure to accept a *Calderbank* offer is so unreasonable that an order for costs will be made under Order 62, rule 27(2) in favour of the party who has successfully obtained a lowering of the bill as presented. But in circumstances such as the present, where the *Calderbank* offer has been beaten by only a very small amount, I do not think that the principle of *King* v *Weston-Howell* [1989] 2 All ER 375, [1989] 1 WLR 579, as applied in litigation generally, should apply to taxation proceedings.

In the circumstances of a case such as this, it seems to me that a proper exercise of the discretion would be to disentitle the plaintiffs from the costs of the taxation proceedings including the fee as from a date when they should reasonably have accepted the *Calderbank* offer, i.e. seven days after 20 July 1990. No point has been made that the taxation fee here would only have been abated. In those circumstances the appropriate exercise of the discretion would have been, and should be, to disallow the costs of the taxation proceedings including the taxation fee. No order is made that the plaintiffs should pay the defendants costs of the taxation.

Philip Moor (instructed by *Ince & Co*) for the defendants.
Sara Simon, solicitor (of *Burton Woolf & Turk*) for the plaintiffs.

Thomas
Respondent

and

Bunn
Appellant

Wilson
Respondent

and

Graham
Appellant

Lea
Respondent

and

British Aerospace plc
Appellant

House of Lords
24, 29, 30, 31 October, 1 November, 13 December 1990

Lord Keith of Kinkel, Lord Brandon of Oakbrook, Lord Brightman,
Lord Templeman and Lord Ackner

_____Headnote_____

This House of Lords case decided that, where judgment is given,
for damages to be assessed, interest on the damages runs from the
date of the decision on quantum, rather than the date of the
original judgment. There is a possible inconsistency between this
decision and that in *Hunt v R M Douglas (Roofing) Limited*.

13 December. LORD KEITH OF KINKEL: My Lords, I have had the
opportunity of considering in draft the speech to be delivered by my noble
and learned friend, Lord Ackner. I agree with it and for the reasons he gives
would allow each of these appeals. I would add that I agree also with the
supplementary observations of my noble and learned friend, Lord
Brightman.

LORD BRANDON OF OAKBROOK: My Lords, for the reasons given in the

speech of my noble and learned friend, Lord Ackner, I would allow the
appeal and make the orders proposed by him.

LORD BRIGHTMAN: My Lords, I have had the privilege of reading in
advance the speech to be delivered by my noble and learned friend, Lord
Ackner, and for the reasons given by him I would allow the appeals.

My Lords, I agree with my noble and learned friend that the precise
wording of the judgment or order in this type of case is not significant, *pace*
Eve J in *Ashover Fluor Spar Mines Ltd v Jackson* [1911] 2 Ch 355 to which
he refers. The order made by the registrar in *Thomas v Bunn* was that
"interlocutory judgment be entered for damages to be assessed", in contrast
to the orders in *Wilson v Graham* and *Lea v British Aerospace Plc* which
were in the form that "the defendant *do pay* ... damages to be assessed".
Thomas v Bunn accordingly falls within the first of the two alternative
forms of order described by Eve J at 359, while *Wilson v Graham* and *Lea
v British Aerospace Plc* fall within the second alternative. Eve J considered
that the latter form of order, which not only directs an inquiry but also itself
contains an express order to pay the amount found due, was within section
18 of the Judgments Act 1838. If the present appeals are allowed, it must
follow that Eve J's dichotomy is incorrect and that, where there is a split
trial, the precise form taken by the order is immaterial, and it does not
matter whether the liability judgment does or does not direct payment of
the damages to be assessed.

My only other observation is that the conclusion reached by this House, if
your Lordships allow the appeals, is entirely in accord with the decision in
Attorney-General v Lord Carrington (1843) 6 Beav 454. This case is of
respectable antiquity. It was decided only five years after the Judgments Act
1838 was passed, and therefore at a time when the pre-existing practice
against which the Act falls to be construed, must have been well present in
the minds of all concerned. In that case an information had been filed
seeking to recover two annuities from the estates of the second Lord
Carrington. By a decree made in December 1842 the lands were declared
chargeable with one of the annuities and the master was directed to take an
account of the arrears. It was also ordered in the same decree that the
amount so found due should be paid by the defendant into the bank. The
master made his report in April 1843. It was contended by the informant
that under sections 17 and 18 of the Act the defendant was liable to pay
interest on the sum certified calculated from the date of the decree down to
the date of the master's report. The defendant, however, argued, at 461:
"that there was no decree whereby any sum of money was payable, at least
until the amount had been ascertained by the master". Lord Langdale MR
found for the defendant and held that he was not chargeable with interest
during this period. This case has stood for 150 years without, so far as I am
aware, exciting any adverse comment, and I see no compelling reason for
departing from its principle today.

LORD TEMPLEMAN: My Lords, by section 35A of the Supreme Court Act 1981 (inserted by section 15 of and Schedule 1 to the Administration of Justice Act 1982), interest is payable at such rate as the court thinks fit or as Rules of Court may provide on all or part of the damages for personal injury between the date when the cause of action arose and the date of judgment. The interest currently awarded under the Act of 1981 is 2% per annum on general damages from the date of the writ and half the special investment account rate (half of 15%) on special damages from the date of the injury.

By section 17 of the Judgments Act 1838 every judgment debt carries interest from the date of the judgment until payment. For the reasons given by my noble and learned friend, Lord Ackner, I agree that in personal injury cases the interest runs from the date of the damages judgment.

In *Thomas v Bunn* the accident occurred on 22 October 1983. The defendant paid £15,000 on 2 August 1984, admitted liability on 23 May 1985 and made a further payment of £55,000 on 12 November 1985. On 5 December 1989 there was judgment by consent for £270,000 which sum took into account the £70,000 already paid and any interest payable pursuant to section 35A of the Act of 1981. No interest is payable under section 17 of the Act of 1838 for any period prior to 5 December 1989.

In *Wilson v Graham* the accident happened on 10 January 1986 and judgment for £196,970 was entered on 3 April 1990. No interest is payable under section 17 of the Act of 1838 for any period prior to 3 April 1990.

In *Lea v British Aerospace Plc* the accident happened on 18 February 1985, the defendant admitted liability in 1986, paid £10,000 in February 1988, a further £10,000 in February 1990 and paid £303,000 into court on 9 February 1990. The plaintiff and the defendant agreed damages at £450,000 and judgment for that sum was entered on 9 April 1990. No interest is payable under section 17 of the Act of 1838 for any period prior to 9 April 1990.

The incidence and rates of interest payable under the Act of 1838 and the Act of 1981 do not encourage early settlements of substantial claims for damages for personal injuries even when liability is admitted.

LORD ACKNER: My Lords, these three appeals by defendants in actions for damages for personal injuries reach your Lordships' House by virtue of leave given pursuant to section 12 of the Administration of Justice Act 1969. They arise in the following circumstances.

The respondent, Christine Thomas, was involved in a road accident on 22 October 1983. A writ was issued on 18 April 1984 and on 23 May 1985 a defence was served admitting liability. On 1 July 1986 interlocutory judgment was entered for damages to be assessed. On 12 October 1987 the district registrar in the Birmingham District Registry made an order by consent that the action proceed to trial before a judge as respects damages. The action was listed for trial on 5 December 1989 in Birmingham. The parties on that day agreed Miss Thomas's compensation at £340,000. By reason of two voluntary interim payments, £15,000 on 2 August 1984 and a further £55,000 on 12 November 1985, there fell to be deducted from this figure £70,000. Accordingly on 5 December 1989 Jowitt J ordered that judgment be entered for Miss Thomas in the sum of £270,000 with costs to be taxed if not agreed. He further ordered interest on this sum under the Judgments Act 1838 at the rate of 15% per annum backdated to 1 July 1986, the date of the interlocutory judgment referred to above. The entitlement to this interest was contested by the appellant, Mr Bunn.

On 10 January 1986 the respondent, Mr Neil Wilson, was involved in a road accident and he issued his writ on 14 April 1987. On 21 March 1989 Tucker J ordered that the issue of liability be tried as preliminary issue before the trial of the issue of damages. On 14 April 1989 Mr Steven Desch QC, sitting as a deputy judge of the Queen's Bench Division, heard the preliminary issue, found in favour of Mr Wilson and adjudged that the damages sustained by Mr Wilson be assessed by a judge of the Queen's Bench Division. On 3 April 1990 Drake J gave judgment in favour of Mr Wilson in the sum of £196,970. On Mr Wilson's application, resisted by the appellant Mr Graham, the judge awarded interest on a part of this sum at the rate of 15% per annum under the Judgments Act 1838 from the date of the judgment on liability, that is from 14 April 1989.

The respondent, Mr Lea, who at the material time was employed by the appellants, British Aerospace Plc, was seriously injured on 18 February 1985 when a boiler in his employers' premises suddenly exploded. On 22 January 1988 no defence having been served by the appellants, judgment was entered for Mr Lea with damages to be assessed. On 9 April 1990 the action having come before Jowitt J for the assessment of the damages, and the parties having agreed the damages at £450,000, judgment was entered in favour of Mr Lea for this figure. On his application, resisted by the appellants, it was ordered that the latter pay interest on the sum of £450,000 from the date of the interlocutory judgment given on 22 January 1988 up to the date of the interim payment of £20,000 and thereafter on the sum of £430,000 from the date of the interim payment until the date of the judgment 9 April 1990.

All three appeals raise the same question, namely whether interest on the damages awarded pursuant to section 17 of the Judgments Act 1838 should run from the date of the order or judgment made or given on liability (the liability judgment) or from the date when the damages were agreed or assessed and final judgment entered for the resultant figure (the damages judgment). It is no coincidence that these three appeals arise out of personal injury litigation. In recent times the following special rules have been established.

1.   Damages in personal injuries actions are assessed, not at the date when such damages were first sustained, but at the date of trial: see *Wright* v *British Railways Board* [1983] 2 AC 773. In the majority of other cases, except where there is some future or continuing loss, damages are assessed when the cause of action arose. In such cases the successful plaintiff in the

High Court is generally awarded, pursuant to section 35A of the Supreme Court Act 1981 (inserted by section 15 of and Schedule 1 to the Administration of Justice Act 1982), interest at the commercial rate from the date when his cause of action accrued to the date of judgment and this is unlikely to be less than the judgment rate under the Judgments Act 1838. (The position in the county court is governed by section 69 of the County Courts Act 1984.) In such cases the date from which the judgment interest runs should make little or no practical difference. It is common practice for the courts to order a split trial – liability being determined first and thereafter, if liability is established, the assessment of the damages to be paid. Frequently however liability is admitted and judgment is entered with an order that damages be assessed.

2.   Where personal injury (or wrongful death) is involved the court is required to award interest in the absence of special reasons for not doing so: see section 35A(2) of the Supreme Court Act 1981.

3.   In personal injury cases interest (referred to as the "conventional award" of interest) is awarded upon pain and suffering and loss of amenities at the rate of 2% per annum from the date of the service of the writ until judgment, and on the special damages at half the rate on special investment account from the date of the accident until judgment: see *Jefford* v *Gee* [1970] 2 QB 130 and *Birkett* v *Hayes* [1982] 1 WLR 816.

The issue which your Lordships have to determine is the true construction of section 17 of the Judgments Act 1838 which came into force long before rules were made to govern the award of interest in personal injury cases and indeed before negligence was established as a cause of action.

Section 17 is in the following terms:

"every judgment debt shall carry interest at the rate of £4 per centum per annum from the time of entering up the judgment … until the same shall be satisfied, and such interest may be levied under a writ of execution on such judgment." (The statutory rate of interest has been increased from time to time.)

If the words used in this section are considered in isolation, the problem would not appear to be a difficult one. It is accepted there cannot be a "judgment debt" until there is a judgment for a quantified sum, i.e. a final as contrasted with an interlocutory judgment. Such a final judgment is to carry interest from the time of entering up "the judgment", i.e. the judgment which creates the judgment debt, i.e. the final judgment. This is made doubly clear by the provision that the interest shall run "until the same shall be satisfied". Until there is a quantified sum which the judgment debtor is obliged by the terms of the judgment to pay, there is no judgment which he is able to satisfy. The final provision in the section that "such interest may be levied under a writ of execution on such judgment" must refer to the judgment which has created the judgment debt, that is the final judgment.

Accordingly the words of the section, taken on their own, visualise only a final judgment quantifying a sum of money – the damages judgment in this case, and not the liability judgment which may have been given some years earlier and which identifies no sum of money as being due and payable. How then has the present problem arisen?

Section 18 of the Judgment Act 1838 provides:

> "all decrees and order of courts of equity, and all rules of courts of common law … whereby any sum of money, or any costs, charges or expenses, shall be payable to any person, shall have the effect of judgments in the superior courts of common law, and the persons to whom any such monies, or costs, charges or expenses, shall be payable, shall be deemed judgment creditors within the meaning of this Act; and all powers hereby given to the judges of the superior courts of common law with respect to matters depending in the same courts shall and may be exercised by courts of equity with respect to matters therein depending … and all remedies hereby given to judgment creditors are in like manner given to persons to whom any moneys, or costs, charges, or expenses, are by such orders of rules respectively directed to be paid."

Section 18 thus elevates the decrees, orders and rules of court to which it refers to the status of a judgment giving rise to a judgment debt under section 17.

A long line of cases beginning with *Fisher* v *Dudding* (1841) 9 Dow 872 and continuing almost 140 years thereafter, most of which cases are referred to in the decision of your Lordships' House in *Hunt* v *R M Douglas (Roofing) Ltd* [1990] 1 AC 398; **Costs LR (Core Vol) 136**, established the principle that interest on awards of *costs* ran from the date upon which judgment was pronounced (the incipitur rule) and not from the date upon which the taxation of costs was thereafter completed by the issue of the taxing master's certificate (the allocatur rule). The attitude of the courts was encapsulated in the observation of Alderson B in *Newton* v *Grand Junction Railway Co* (1846) 16 M & W 139, when he said in the court of argument, at 141:

> "Then, as to interest, there is an uncertain amount, which is in the wrong pocket, and is there bearing interest; I see no injustice in saying, that as soon as it is reduced to certainty, that interest should be paid. Whatever be the sum, it is fructifying in the wrong pocket."

In *Hunt's* case, which concerned solely interest on costs, your Lordships overruled the decision of the Court of Appeal in *K* v *K (Divorce Costs: Interest)* [1977] Fam 39 and the subsequent case in the Court of Appeal which followed *K* v *K*, namely *Erven Warnink BV* v *J Townend & Sons (Hull) Ltd (No 2)* [1982] 2 All ER 312. In *K* v *K*, the Court of Appeal, wrongly basing itself upon the revision of the Rules of the Supreme Court 1965, considered itself entitled to depart from the previous decisions and in particular the decision of the Court of Appeal in *Boswell* v *Coaks* (1887) 57 LJ Ch 101, and decided that interest on costs should run from the date of the certificate of taxation.

In the *Erven Warnink* case, Fox LJ giving the judgment of the Court of Appeal, which concluded that it was bound by the decision in *K* v *K*, nevertheless set out the views of the court on the basis that is was free to consider the matter generally. I quoted those views in extenso in my speech in *Hunt's* case [1990] 1 AC 398, since they expressed the opinion, with which I respectfully concurred, that a satisfactory result cannot be achieved in every case whichever rule, the incipitur or the allocatur rule, was applied. In dealing with the submission that until the defendant's liability was quantified, there should be no liability to pay interest under the Act, the opinion of the Court of Appeal was expressed in these terms ([1982] 2 All ER 312, 319–320):

> "Nor can the 'quantification' rule be satisfactorily applied to a judgment for unliquidated damages. It is not a useful approach in such a case to say that a person cannot be expected to pay until the liability has been quantified. The litigant who obtains a judgment for damages to be assessed has already suffered damage at the date when the judgment is pronounced. That he should have to wait for the damages until after they are quantified is necessary, but there is no reason why he should not have interest when, in the end, they are paid. In *Borthwick* v *Elderslie Steamship Co Ltd (No 2)* [1905] 2 KB 516, the Court of Appeal held that, in the case of a judgment for damages to be assessed, interest was payable from the date of the judgment. Romer LJ after saying that the plaintiff was held entitled to recover damages the amount of which remained to be ascertained, continued, at p. 522: 'The amount has since been ascertained, and must be treated as if it had been mentioned in the judgment of the court; and the result is that the plaintiff has a judgment for an ascertained sum, dated on the day on which it is pronounced.' "

Borthwick's case had been cited in *Hunt's* case to your Lordships by Mr Goldblatt for the defendants, when submitting that in the case of a judgment for *damages* to be assessed there was no clear authority for the widely held view that damages, when quantified, fall to be treated as if written into the original order: see [1990] 1 AC 398, 403B. That case concerned the proper construction of a bill of lading and in particular an exception clause. Walton J held that although the ship was not in a fit condition for the carriage of meat, with the result that a cargo of frozen meat was found on its arrival at the port of destination to be damaged, the plaintiff Borthwick failed in his claim by reason of the terms of this exception clause. The trial judge did not make any assessment of the damages to which Borthwick would have been entitled, if he had found in his favour. An appeal to the Court of Appeal was allowed and the judgment (omitting formal parts) was drawn up in the following terms ([1905] 2 KB 516):

> "It is ordered that the plaintiff's appeal be allowed; that the above-mentioned judgment of ... Walton J on 9 March 1903 be wholly set aside, and instead thereof that judgment be entered in the action for the plaintiff against the defendants on all issues, for such sum as may be assessed by a referee to be agreed upon by the parties ... Liberty to apply."

Upon a further appeal to the House of Lords (*Elderslie Steamship Co Ltd* v *Borthwick* [1905] AC 93) the judgment of the Court of Appeal (*Borthwick* v *Elderslie Steamship Co Ltd* [1904] 1 KB 319) was affirmed. The assessment of damages was stood over by consent pending the appeal to the House of Lords. The amount for which judgment should be entered for the plaintiff was thereafter agreed between the parties. It was further agreed that interest should be paid, but no time was specified. A dispute arose as to the date from which interest ought to run, the defendants being willing to pay interest from the time when the amount of damages was determined until payment, and the plaintiff claiming interest from the date of the judgment given by the trial judge. The application was made to the Court of Appeal in pursuance of the liberty to apply.

In the Court of Appeal the defendants no longer disputed that where damages are ascertained, interest on the amount recovered runs from the date of judgment. Thus the question was – what was the date of the judgment under which the plaintiff recovered damages? The defendants contended that the first judgment that the plaintiff obtained was that given in the Court of Appeal and accordingly interest on the amount ultimately ascertained ran only from the date of that judgment. While the court had a power to antedate its judgment to the date of the judgment given by the trial judge, it was argued by the defendants that this was an exceptional power and there was no justification on the facts of the case for its exercise.

In his judgment Sir Richard Henn Collins MR said ([1905] 2 KB 516, 518–519):

> "The amount of damages to which the plaintiff is entitled has been agreed between the parties and is to be paid with interest. The sum due having been ascertained, the plaintiff claims interest upon it, not merely from the date when it was first decided he was entitled to recover judgment, but from the date of the trial, on the ground that *if his rights had been understood at the hearing he would have been entitled to an inquiry as to the amount of damages, and judgment would have been entered for a sum to be ascertained, carrying interest from the date of the judgment*. But at the trial he did not obtain judgment, and he had to come to this court, in which, for the first time, he was successful. If we apply to these circumstances the practice applicable under Order XL1, rule 3, to a judgment in a court of first instance, all to which he would be entitled would be to have judgment entered for him as of the date on which it was given, that is, the hearing in this court, with interest from the time when that judgment was pronounced." (Emphasis added.)

In that passage it appears to me that the Master of the Rolls was accepting the proposition which I have emphasised as stating what he, the Master of the Rolls, understood the law to be, which in no way differed from that so understood by Romer LJ in the passages to which I will shortly refer. The Master of the Rolls in his judgment rejected the plaintiff's application to antedate the judgment entered against him to the trial of the action, because he considered the court's power to antedate should only be exercised on good grounds shown, and this the plaintiff had failed to do.

In agreeing with the Master of the Rolls, Romer LJ said, at 521–522:

> "When a plaintiff has failed in the court below so that his action has been dismissed, if he succeeds on appeal it cannot, I think, be properly said that the judgment of the Court of Appeal must be regarded for all purposes as if it had been the judgment given by the judge in the court below. The judgment in favour of the plaintiff must be treated as of the date on which it was given in the Court of Appeal, subject to the right of that Court to antedate its judgment. That right should, in my opinion, be exercised with caution. In the present case the plaintiff failed at the trial; but this court took the view that he was entitled to recover damages, the amount of which remained to be ascertained. The amount has since been ascertained, and must be treated as if it had been mentioned in the judgment of this court; and the result is that the plaintiff has a judgment for an ascertained sum, dated on the day on which it was pronounced ... "

Romer LJ agreed with the Master of the Rolls that there was no sufficient ground for antedating the judgment. He also took the view that the parties, having agreed the amount of the damages and that this should bear interest, as a matter of construction of that agreement interest would run from the date on which the Court of Appeal gave the judgment which entitled the plaintiff to damages. He concluded by saying, at 522:

> "Therefore, as a matter of principle, and also on the construction of the agreement, I am of opinion that interest will only be payable from the date on which that judgment was given."

Borthwick's case was considered by Eve J in *Ashover Fluor Spar Mines Ltd* v *Jackson* [1911] 2 Ch 355 also cited to your Lordships in *Hunt's* case. In that case there was a consent order by virtue of which an action for an injunction to restrain a trespass on the plaintiffs' mines and for damages was compromised on terms that it should be referred to a special referee to ascertain the damages, the defendants to pay the amount so found. The referee reported that £1,515 was payable by the defendants to the plaintiffs. On the plaintiffs' motion that the referee's report might be adopted, the question was raised as to whether interest was payable on the damages and from what date.

The defendant's counsel in resisting the plaintiff's claim that interest on the amount ascertained by the official referee be backdated to the order of the judge, argued that the case was outside the Judgments Act 1838, as the judge's order was not an order whereby any sum of money was payable to the plaintiffs within section 18 of the Act, because a further order was necessary. On this basis he sought to distinguish *Borthwick's* case. Eve J accepted this submission, saying that the order of the Court of Appeal in *Borthwick's* case, which he recited, was in fact a judgment for the sum subsequently ascertained and on the sum being ascertained and a note of the amount being endorsed upon the judgment, execution would issue. It was thus an order whereby a sum of money was payable to the plaintiffs under section 18 of the Act.

Eve J dealt with two alternative forms in which orders in the Chancery Division were made. He said, at 359:

> "In the first of the two alternative forms the inquiry is directed, and liberty to apply, after the result has been certified, is given. In the second alternative the court, after directing the inquiry, goes on to order the defendant to pay the plaintiff the amount certified. The latter of these orders is, in my opinion, within, and the former outside, the provisions of section 18 of the Judgments Act 1838. An order which is so framed as to necessitate a further order being made before the obligation to pay arises cannot reasonably be regarded as 'an order whereby a sum of money' is payable, and in cases where the form adopted is that which gives the plaintiff liberty to apply, and nothing more, I do not see how any interest can run on the amount certified until the further order to pay has been made."

In the penultimate paragraph of my speech in *Hunt's* case I dealt with a specific point which had been pressed upon your Lordships by Mr Goldblatt. I said ([1990] 1 AC 398 at 416, **Costs LR (Core Vol) 136 at 148**):

> "For the sake of completeness I should add that Mr Goldblatt strongly argued that an order for payment of costs to be taxed cannot be a judgment debt within section 17 of the Act of 1838 because until taxation has been completed, there is no sum for which execution can be levied. This point appears to have been raised in the *Erven Warnink* case and disposed of at the end of the judgment on the basis that the courts have accepted since its enactment, that section 17 does apply to such a judgment and accordingly the law has gone too far for that argument. I agree. *This acceptance is because a judgment for costs to be taxed is to be treated in the same way as a judgment for damages to be assessed, where the amount ultimately ascertained is treated as if it was mentioned in the judgment – no further order being required.* A judgment debt can therefore in my judgment be construed for the purpose of section 17, as covering an order for the payment of costs to be taxed." (Emphasis added.)

It has been accepted throughout these appeals that a judgment debt is to be construed for the purpose of section 17 as including an order for the payment of costs to be taxed. The essential issue in this appeal is whether the observation in my speech contained in the words set out above which I have emphasised and which was clearly obiter, is correct.

In making that observation I was expressing my agreement with the obiter dicta of the Court of Appeal in the *Erven Warnink* case [1982] 3 All ER 312, 319–320 which I had quoted in my speech and which I have set out above. I was also concurring with the statement of Romer LJ in *Borthwick's* case [1905] 2 KB 516, as explained by Eve J in *Ashover's* case [1911] 2 Ch 355, again cited above. Before considering the validity of my dicta, I should interpose to make the point that it had no application to any of the cases before your Lordships' House, because as is apparent from the summary which I have given of the course of the litigation in all three appeals, the interlocutory judgment in the first appeal, the judgment on the preliminary issue in the second appeal and the interlocutory judgment in the third appeal, were each followed by a further judgment. Before any sum of money was payable to any of the appellants, *further orders were required*. Thus in none of the instant appeals was the interlocutory order, the interim judgment or interlocutory judgment capable of being classified as "an order whereby a sum of money" was payable following the approach of Romer LJ and Eve J. That however would be an unsatisfactory technical way of disposing of these appeals and would leave unanswered the essential question – does interest under the Judgments Act 1838 run before there is a judgment for a quantified sum?

Put shortly, the respondents argue that since it is accepted on all sides that *Hunt's* case establishes, and rightly establishes, that the liability to pay interest on costs does not have to await the quantification of those costs, but dates back to the date of the judgment awarding those costs, the same principle should apply to damages. If quantification is not necessary for the completion of the obligation to pay costs, the same principle should apply to damages. Sections 17 and 18 of the Judgments Act 1838 make no distinction between costs and damages, treating each as a judgment debt. Since interest *on costs* runs from the date the judgment was pronounced, then logically interest *on damages* awarded by that judgment should run from the same date. Further, the respondents contend that the decision in *Borthwick's* case [1905] 2 KB 516, as explained by Eve J in *Ashover's* case [1911] 2 Ch 355, even though its application is limited, has stood the test of time and is good law.

In answer to these contentions the appellants argue that there is no logical reason why the same rules should apply to damages as apply to costs, the assessment of damages being a different exercise from the taxation of costs. All that the taxing master is required to do is from his own experience to decide whether costs, *which have already been incurred*, have been reasonably incurred and then to put a reasonable figure on such costs as at the date of the incipitur or earlier. The costs having all been incurred by the date of the incipitur, the amount at which they will be taxed will be the same whenever the taxation takes place. In contra-distinction, a judge in assessing damages has to assess, not merely the damages suffered before the date of the interlocutory order or interim judgment, but also the damages suffered between then and the date of assessment and the further damages to be suffered in the future. There is no warrant for the fine distinctions arising out of the *Borthwick* and the *Ashover* decisions.

I accept that it is an anomaly that an order for payment of costs to be taxed is construed for the purpose of section 17 as a judgment debt, even though, before taxation has been completed, there is no sum for which execution can be levied. However the courts have accepted since its enactment that section 17 does apply to such an order and, for the reasons set out in my speech in *Hunt's* case, the balance of justice favours continuing so to treat such an order. The short question is – was I right in concluding that this acceptance is because "a judgment for costs to be taxed is to be treated in the same way as a judgment for damages to be assessed, where the amount ultimately ascertained is treated as if it was mentioned in the judgment – no further order being required". The answer is in the negative.

The wording of section 17 clearly envisages a single judgment which constitutes the "judgment debt". This "judgment debt" can only arise where the judgment itself quantifies the sum which the judgment debtor owes to his judgment creditor. The language of the section does not envisage an interlocutory judgment, but only a final judgment. This was clearly the view of Kindersley V-C in *Garner* v *Briggs* (1858) 27 LJ Ch 483, which was not cited in the *Borthwick* case or the *Ashover* case. In that case it was contended that a decree was not final because it was not a conclusive direction to anyone to pay a particular sum of money and that therefore the plaintiff could not be deemed a judgment creditor and thus able to rely on section 18 of the Judgments Act 1938.

Kindersley V-C said, at 485–486:

> "The principle of the decisions, subject to exceptional cases with respect to judgments at law is this: – to constitute a judgment debt, the judgment must not be interlocutory but final, for the payment of a specific sum of money, upon which there is nothing left to be done except to compute interest, and the party must also have an actual right to receive the money. ... Interlocutory directions are not final to determine the question of debt, and do not exist at law. Now, if the decree of May 1855 had directed that the £2,500, the amount of the policy, with interest, after deducting the premiums, should be paid by Dr Moore to the plaintiff, that would, upon the authority of *Duke of Beaufort* v *Phillips* (1847) 1 De G & Sm 321 have been final, and would have constituted a judgment debt, for although the accounts were involved, still the order would have been final, and there would have been an actual direction to pay the money to a particular person. In this case, however, instead of a decree for payment of the money, there was a direction that Dr Moore was liable to make good the money – not to the plaintiff, but to the estate of Messrs Houlditch, and that in the accounts which were then to be taken, he should be charged with that balance as an item of account. It was contended that this decree was final, and in one sense, no doubt, it was so, there being no reservation of further directions, but it was not final in the sense of there being a final direction to pay a particular sum of money to a particular person, and consequently that decree could not create a judgment debt. It is remarkable that not a single instance can be produced by the industry of counsel, in which a decree or order has been held to constitute a judgment debt, except where it has been a final decree, with an actual direction to pay the money ... The decree, therefore, is only final so far as it determines that, in taking the account, Dr Moore is to be charged with a certain balance, but it is not final as to directing him to pay the particular amount. I think, under these circumstances, that it does not constitute a judgment debt."

I accordingly take the view the judgment referred to in section 17 of the Judgments Act 1838 does not relate to an interlocutory or interim order or judgment establishing only the defendant's liability. The judgment contemplated by that section is the judgment which quantifies the defendant's liability, the judgment which has been referred to in the course of these appeals as "the damages judgment". The artificial distinction drawn in the *Borthwick* case [1905] 2 KB 516 based on the precise terms in which damages are ordered to be assessed can no longer stand.

As stated earlier in this speech, the issue which your Lordships have to determine is the true construction of a section in a statute over 150 years old. Rival submissions as to the hardship which would or would not arise if the Judgments Act interest was made to run in personal injury actions from interlocutory orders or judgments, as opposed to running from the final judgments, seem to me to be of no forensic value. They did however emphasise the obvious, viz that every reasonable effort shall be made to achieve with the minimum delay the final determination of all the issues in such litigation, if plaintiffs were not to lose substantial sums by way of interest which could be earned on the fruits of such litigation. In cases where liability is not seriously in issue, as indeed was the case in all these three appeals, then if for one reason or another finality cannot be achieved expeditiously, there should be greater resort to interim payments.

I would accordingly allow all three appeals, order that in each case the award of interest under section 17 of the Judgments Act 1838 should run from the date of the judgment which assessed or recorded the damages payable to each of the plaintiffs, with such consequential amendments as may be necessary in relation to the agreed so-called "conventional award" of interest. In *Thomas* v *Bunn*, the appellant did not seek an order for costs in your Lordships' House and accordingly none will be made. In *Wilson* v *Graham* and *Lea* v *British Aerospace*, the usual order was sought by the appellants, and accordingly in each of those appeals the respondent will pay the appellant's costs in your Lordships' House.

Appeals allowed with costs, save that no order for costs in Thomas v Bunn.

Hunt
v
East Dorset Health Authority

Queen's Bench Division
2 March 1992

Hobhouse J
sitting with
Chief Master Hurst and Mr John Webber as assessors

Headnote

This case shows that where under legal aid regulations authority for junior counsel only has been granted, the court has no residuary discretion to allow the fees of leading counsel. It also makes clear that leading counsel should always ensure that he is covered by a certificate or authority prior to undertaking work thereunder.

HOBHOUSE J: This is a review of a legal aid taxation by Master Devonshire. Following the hearing of objections, he gave his reasons on 14 October 1991. He disallowed the whole of the fees that had been incurred in instructing a silk, Mr Rodger Bell QC, to represent the plaintiff. The solicitors who instructed Mr Bell are Messrs J Tickle & Co. The period covered by his instructions was between November 1988 and the completion of the trial in the action in May 1989. The sum involved is £14,425 plus value added tax.

It was a personal injury action. The plaintiff was Robyn Hayley Hunt, a minor, suing by her mother and next friend, Eve Marie Hunt. The defendants were the East Dorset Health Authority. It was a heavy and relatively complex case. If the action had been successful, damages of the order of £400,000 would have been recovered. Instructing a silk was justifiable. The master accepted that it would have been a suitable case for the instruction of a silk at the trial. He put it this way: "Having regard to the complications and complexity of the case, it was one which was entirely suited for the instruction of both leading and junior counsel."

However, the legal aid certificate which had been granted did not give authority to instruct more than one counsel on behalf of the plaintiff. It was originally issued on 10 August 1982 in a form which stated:

"Description of legal aid offered: To take proceedings by her Mother and Next

Friend, Eve Marie Hunt, against the East Dorset Area Health Authority, for damages for medical negligence."

As initially issued, it was subject to certain conditions, which were later varied. During the relevant period, it was subject to only one condition, expressed in the words:

> "All offers of settlement and/or payments into Court not accepted within the prescribed period to be reported to the Law Society."

The trial of the action took place in May 1989 before French J. It resulted in judgment for the defendants with costs (which was entered on 17 May 1989). It will be appreciated from this that there was no party and party taxation of the costs incurred on behalf of the plaintiff.

The relevant regulations which applied at the time of the certificate and at the time that the costs were incurred were the Legal Aid (General) Regulations 1980, SI No 1894. Those regulations have since been replaced by the Civil Legal Aid (General) Regulations 1989, SI No 339, and the only differences between the relevant regulations in 1980 and those in 1989 are differences of numbering and small differences of wording. In the interests of accuracy I will refer to the 1980 Regulations, but the decision which I give is equally applicable to a similar situation under the 1989 Regulations and to the construction of the 1989 Regulations.

The 1980 Regulations include "Part VIII: Authority to Incur Costs". Regulation 60 provides:

> "*Instructing counsel*
>
> 60. – (1) Where it appears to an assisted person's solicitor that the proper conduct of the proceedings so requires, counsel may be instructed; but unless authority has been given in the certificate or by the secretary (*a*) counsel shall not be instructed in authorised summary proceedings; and (*b*) a Queen's Counsel or more than one counsel shall not be instructed.
>
> (2) Every set of papers delivered to counsel instructed by virtue of paragraph (1) shall include a copy of the certificate, any amendments to it and any authority to incur costs under this Part of the Regulations, and shall be endorsed with the legal aid reference number and in the case of authorised summary proceedings shall show the authority for counsel to be instructed, as appropriate; and no fees shall be marked thereon."

Regulation 61 deals with the power of the Law Society to give a general authority in respect of certain itemised matters, that is:

> "(*a*) obtaining a report or opinion of one or more expects or tendering expert evidence; (*b*) employing a person to provide a report or opinion (other than as an expert); or (*c*) bespeaking transcripts of shorthand notes or tape recordings of any proceedings."

Under that regulation the authority can limit the maximum fee payable for any such work.

Then under regulation 62 there is a specific authority which may be applied for in respect of matters which are either the same as or similar to the general matters covered by regulation 61.

Under regulation 64, which is headed "Effect of obtaining and failing to obtain authority", it is provided in paragraphs (2) and (3) that no question shall be raised –

> "as to the propriety of any step or act in relation to which prior authority has been obtained under regulation 60 ... "

And there are similar provisions in respect of regulations 61 and 62.

Coming to paragraphs (4) and (5), they provide:

> "(4)   Where costs are incurred in instructing a Queen's Counsel or more than one counsel, without authority to do so having been given in the certificate or under regulation 60(1), as the case may be, no payment in respect of those costs shall be allowed on any taxation, unless it is also allowed on a party and party taxation.
>
> (5)   Where costs are incurred in instructing counsel or in taking any step or doing any act for which authority may be given under regulation 61 or 62, without authority to do so having been given in the certificate or under regulation 60, 61 or 62, as the case may be, payment in respect of those costs may still be allowed on a taxation."

It is common ground that the present case does not come within regulation 60(1)(*b*) in the sense that it is accepted that there was never any certificate or other document which authorised the instruction of Queen's Counsel or more than one counsel. Similarly it is recognised that it does not come within paragraph (4) of regulation 64 because there never was any party and party taxation of the plaintiff's costs and therefore there never came a situation where the costs of instructing Queen's Counsel might have been authorised or allowed on a party and party taxation.

What is said on the present review, and was said to the taxing master, was that this case comes within paragraph (5) of regulation 64. Master Devonshire rejected that argument and I agree with his decision and would have been content to adopt his reasons.

In my judgment the scheme of the Regulations is clear. With regard to the instructing of Queen's Counsel, regulation 60(1) expressly states that, unless authority is given in the certificate or in some other specified way, "a Queen's Counsel or more than one counsel shall not be instructed".

That is a provision that expresses that an actual authority is required if more than one counsel, and specifically a Queen's Counsel, is to be instructed and specifies the way in which that authority has to be given.

Further, there is a provision which is a safeguard for any counsel who may be instructed. In regulation 60(2) it is required that every set of papers delivered to counsel shall include the relevant certificate. It is incumbent on counsel to check whether the appropriate certificate and authority exists: if the Regulations are being complied with he will be supplied with that document together with his instructions. If he does not find that document with the instructions that are tendered to him then it is incumbent upon him, if he seeks to look to the legal aid fund thereafter for remuneration, to see that the appropriate authority and certificate is obtained and supplied to him. If he does not take the simple and elementary course that is expressly spelt out in the Regulations, then he may find that he is acting without remuneration: the situation is in his hands and it is for him to require it to be remedied if anything has been overlooked.

There is also in the scheme an express exception in regulation 64(4), which opens with the words: "Where costs are incurred in instructing a Queen's Counsel or more than one counsel ..." So it is expressly addressing that specific situation. It then goes on to say that in the absence of the appropriate certificate or other authority "no payment in respect of those costs shall be allowed on any taxation, unless it is also allowed on a party and party taxation". One would think that nothing could be clearer than that. That is an express, mandatory, negative statement which is subject to only one, expressly stated, qualification. The appellants before me seek to displace that provision and, indeed, it has been accepted in the helpful argument by Mr Havers before me that, if he is to succeed, there must be some implicit qualification imposed on paragraph (4).

The effect of those provisions is as stated by Lloyd J in *Din* v *Wandsworth London BC (No 3)* [1983] 2 All ER 841 at 843, [1983] 1 WLR 1171 at 1174:

"... the whole purpose of Pt VIII of the 1980 Regulations is to enable local legal aid committees to exercise control over costs. This can only be done if solicitors keep strictly within the authority they have been granted. If there had been any doubt about the extent of their authority, which I do not think there was, the plaintiffs' solicitors could have gone back for amendment of the certificate, or for clarification. But they did not do so. As for counsel, a copy of the certificate should have been included in his papers: see regulation 60(2)."

With regard to the reliance on regulation 64(4) Lloyd J said that there was an alternative argument before him ([1983] 2 All ER 841 at 843, [1983] 1 WLR 1171 at 1174–1175):

"... the master had the discretion to allow these items under regulation 64(4), if they would have been allowed on a party and party taxation. But there was no party and party taxation in the present case. That being so, there was no discretion to allow the items."

These quotations from Lloyd J confirm that the general policy of the regulation is that in respect of the instructing of leading counsel, which is what he was concerned with in that case (but not quite in the same context as I am), there is a manifest policy of the Regulations that the authority to instruct leading counsel must be provided by the legal aid board and is not a matter of the discretion for the master. It is a question of authority and not a question of discretion for the master.

Contrary to that view, it has been submitted before me that the provisions of paragraph (5) produce a different result. On the question of construction the relevant words of paragraph (5) are:

> "Where costs are incurred in instructing counsel ... without authority to do so having been given in the certificate or under regulation 60 ... as the case may be, payment in respect of those costs may still be allowed on a taxation."

The opening words of paragraph (5) are in contrast to the opening words of paragraph (4). They are simply referring to costs incurred in instructing counsel in the same way as is described in regulation 60 and, in the context of the references to regulations 61 and 62, one can see that they are not concerned with matters of principle but with the extent of the authority that has been given to the solicitor in the conduct of the litigation and the incurring of costs.

In relation to instructing counsel, Mr Havers submits that a point under paragraph (5) might arise in relation to regulation 60(1)(*a*) and summary proceedings. But, whether that is correct or not, it may certainly arise in relation to any conditions or limitations that have been imposed in a certificate. There is no need to construe regulation 64(5) as having to apply to the instructing of a Queen's Counsel or two counsel. It has more than sufficient subject matter to be read literally and in accordance with its own terms and in its own context.

I have been invited to construe regulation 64(5) together with the remainder of the regulations in that part and specifically paragraph (4) of regulaton 64. This argument does not advance the appellants' argument before me because when one construes those two paragraphs together it is clear that a distinction is drawn between the situation where a Queen's Counsel or two counsel are instructed and where merely a single counsel is instructed. Where it is a question of two counsel being instructed then paragraph (4) is the governing paragraph. Where it is a matter of a single counsel or perhaps the ambit of the instructions to counsel as opposed to the number of counsel that have been instructed, then paragraph (5) is the governing paragraph. Reading the two paragraphs together, it is even more clear that the taxing master was correct in his conclusion.

It is argued that there is a need to redraft or to qualify to some extent paragraph (5) in order to make it consistent with the taxing master's decision. I do not agree. I consider that rejection of the appellants' argument does not involve any need to amend or reword paragraph (5). But, if their argument is to succeed, there would be a clear need to reword or qualify the express provisions of paragraph (4). That is not the function of the court. The legislature has made its intention clear in paragraph (4).

It was then argued that the decision of the master produced absurd results because experts' fees, which may be very substantial and may in some cases exceed the fees that are incurred in respect of counsel, can be the subject of a discretionary power under paragraph (5) whereas there is no discretionary power in respect of the cost of instructing two as opposed to one counsel under paragraph (4). That may be a result which has financial consequences but it is not an unreasonable result. It is perfectly comprehensible for the legislature to have decided that, in respect of the costs of instructing Queen's Counsel or more than one counsel, a specific authority must be obtained and, in respect of other matters, although they may involve a considerable expenditure of money, that a different procedure may be followed. There is nothing absurd or unreasonable about that conclusion. Nor does it lead to hardship, because the situation is covered by regulation 60(2) so that the counsel instructed knows where he stands. The solicitor has a clear duty to perform in obtaining express authority from the legal aid authority before he instructs leading counsel on the basis that he is to be remunerated out of the legal aid fund. No hardship results from implementing the mechanism that is provided by regulation 60 and if the solicitor and counsel between them do not follow that mechanism then they may find that counsel is unable to recover remuneration, as has happened in the present case.

This appeal, which I stress would be decided in exactly the same way under the 1989 Regulations as it has been under the 1980 Regulations, must be dismissed.

Appeal dismissed.

Philip Havers (instructed by *J Tickle & Co*) for the plaintiff.
Robert Jay (instructed by the *Treasury Solicitor*) for the Lord Chancellor.

Johnson and others
v
Reed Corrugated Cases Ltd

Queen's Bench Division
19, 21 March, 11 April 1990

Evans J
sitting with
Master Wright and Mr Philip Sycamore as assessors

Headnote

Although there were a number of issues the main point in this case was the judge's decision on mark-up. The judge accepted that in a "run-of-the-mill" case the mark-up should be 50% and cases more complicated would attract a higher uplift, but that the case would need to be very exceptional to approach 100% uplift.

The expense rate in each case should be determined by reference to the taxing officer's knowledge and experience of the average cost of the average solicitor in the relevant area at the relevant time. *The Expense of Time* booklet published by the Law Society was also examined. The individual expense of time calculations for a particular firm should not be used in the calculation of the expense rate for inter partes costs, although such information should not be entirely disregarded.

11 April 1990. The following judgment was delivered.

EVANS J: The taxation of costs recovered by the successful party in civil litigation and ordered to be paid to him by the losing party is regulated by RSC Order 62. These rules set out the new system introduced in 1986. The basis of taxation is given in Order 62, rule 12:

> "(1) On a taxation of costs on the standard basis there shall be allowed a reasonable amount in respect of all costs reasonably incurred and any doubts which the taxing officer may have ... shall be resolved in favour of the paying party ... "

The standard basis so described was new in 1986. I do not think that ultimately it is profitable to consider what relationship it may bear to the previous bases for "party and party" and "common fund" taxation. The criterion now is a reasonable amount for all costs reasonably incurred.

When a party is dissatisfied with the decision of a taxing officer, he may apply to that officer for a review under Order 62, rule 33 and he must deliver with the application a list of his objections (see rule 33(3)). The next stage in the proceedings, if either party is dissatisfied with the taxing officer's decision on review, is for that party to apply to a judge "for an order to review that decision either in whole or in part", and the taxing officer must be requested to state his reasons in writing (see rule 35(1)).

The judge is limited to the same evidence and the same grounds of objection as were before the taxing officer "unless the judge otherwise directs" (see rule 35(4)), and he may make "such order as the circumstances may require" (see rule 35(6)).

When the amount of costs is in question, Appendix 2 to Order 62 provides by paragraph 1(1) of Part I that the amount to be allowed is discretionary. Paragraph 2(2) provides:

> "In exercising his discretion the taxing officer shall have regard to all the relevant circumstances, and in particular to – (*a*) the complexity of the item or of the cause or matter in which it arises and the difficulty or novelty of the questions involved; (*b*) the skill, specialised knowledge, and responsibility required of, and the time and labour expended by, the solicitor or counsel; (*c*) the number and importance of the documents (however brief) prepared or perused; (*d*) the place and circumstances in which the business involved is transacted; (*e*) the importance of the cause or matter to the client; (*f*) where money or property is involved, its amount or value; (*g*) any other fees and allowances payable to the solicitor or counsel in respect of other items in the same cause or matter, but only where work done in relation to those items has reduced the work which would otherwise have been necessary in relation to the item in question."

These rules are supplemented by the Masters' Practice Notes 1986 printed in *The Supreme Court Practice 1988* vol 1, para 62/A2/31, p 1009. I quote the following extracts from them:

> 3.   The new Appendix 2 Part II is designed further to simplify the process of drawing, reading and taxing a bill of costs and thereby to reduce both time and expense. The principle provision is that items which are properly part of a solicitor's normal overhead costs, and as such provided for in his expense rates, are wholly to be excluded. Each chargeable item will be the subject of a discretionary allowance which should be shown in two parts, the first representing the direct costs of the work properly itemised and the second the appropriate allowance for care and conduct.
>
> 4.   The allowance for care and conduct is intended to reflect all the relevant circumstances of the case and in particular the matters set out in paragraph 1(2) of Part I of the new Appendix. It is also intended to reflect those imponderable factors, for example general supervision of subordinate staff, for which no direct time charge can be substantiated, and the element of commercial profit. Accordingly the allowances to be made for different items may, in the discretion of the taxing officer, be allowed at different rates. In

particular it is anticipated that, save in unusual circumstances, the rate appropriate to items 1, 2, 3 and 5 for care and conduct will be less than the rate appropriate for item 4 for general care and conduct."

(Paragraphs 17 and 19 are also relevant to subsidiary issues raised in these proceedings; I will refer to them separately below.)

The present application
This is for review of Mr Registrar Gee's decision dated 20 September 1989 answering objections taken to his original decision dated 29 September 1988 (certificate dated 23 January 1989). There were eleven actions begun by separate writs issued on behalf of individual plaintiffs in 1980 and 1981, all against the defendants as their employer. The claims were for personal injuries described collectively as tenosynovitis:

> "A complicated set of repetitive strain injury claims involving 11 plaintiffs who developed various hand, arm, wrist and elbow symptoms from working on different processes ... Apart from individual investigation of various aspects of each plaintiff's claim, more general investigated had to be carried out in respect of liability, causation and foreseeability ... "

The actions were consolidated in 1983 and the same firm of solicitors acted on behalf of all plaintiffs throughout. The solicitors are Brian Thompson & Partners, in this case their Manchester office, and I understand that establishing liability in this type of case was regarded, understandably and no doubt rightly, as a considerable professional success.

All the cases were settled, and apart from Johnson, who accepted £40,500 paid into court up to 11 November 1987, the other plaintiffs accepted relatively small sums, all between £750 and £5,000, the average of those ten being £2,800. The defendants' total liability therefore was about £68,000. The trial date was fixed for November 1987 but the last six cases were settled about one week before that date.

The plaintiffs' taxed costs were certified at £66,418.16 inclusive of disbursement and value added tax. The relevant objections were all disallowed.

The review before me raised five matters, one of which was treated as a matter of principle and is certainly of considerable importance to the solicitors concerned, and maybe to all solicitors practising in the Manchester area. That is the hourly rate allowed on taxation for work done by the successful party's solicitor. This includes both the basic "Part A" element and "Part B", commonly described as "uplift" or "mark up" and expressed as a percentage of the Part A figure. Parts A and B are now defined in RSC Order 62, Appendix 2, Part II, item 4 (see *The Supreme Court Practice 1988* vol 1, para 62/A2/22, p 1007) but they have their origin in the judgment of Brightman J in *Re Eastwood (decd), Lloyds Bank Ltd v Eastwood* [1973] 3 All ER 1079 at 1082, [1975] Ch 112 at 120, quoting the advice which he received from assessors in that case:

"... the taxation [of solicitors' costs] invariably proceeds on the following basis. The firm informs the taxing master of the period of time that has been spent by any partner or employee of the firm on any 'relevant' aspect of the case ... The firm submits (a) what is the proper cost per hour of the time so spent having regard to a reasonable estimate of the overhead expenses of the solicitor's firm including (if the time spent is that of an employee) the reasonable salary of the employee or (if the time spent is that of a partner) a notional salary. The firm will also submit ... what is a proper additional sum to be allowed over and above (a) by way of further profit costs."

The present wording is:

"4. Preparation

Part A: The doing of any work which was reasonably done arising out of or incidental to the proceedings, including – [numbered sub-paras (i) to (xiii)]

Part B: The general care and conduct of the proceedings ... "

This is supplemented by the Masters' Practice Notes 1986, which I have already quoted.

At issue in the present application are both the hourly rate and the mark-up claimed by the plaintiffs' solicitors. The claim was for £50 per hour for work done after 1 June 1979 until settlement in November 1987 with a Part B rate of 150%. The registrar allowed £48 per hour with a mark-up of 90% (the latter being a general figure to which there were some special exceptions, one of which gives rise to a subsidiary issue which I shall consider below). The defendants say that the figures should be £34 and 60%, respectively.

Although the hourly rate and the mark-up figure were treated during the argument before me as giving rise to separate issues, they must also be considered in the light of their combined effect. So long as the Part B allowance consists of a percentage uplift of the Part A hourly figure, the result will be an increased hourly rate, and it is the total figure which will represent the solicitor's actual or notional remuneration for the work done. But, having said this, both the rules and the Masters' Practice Notes 1986 which I have quoted mean that the two items represent different elements in the calculation, and separate consideration must be given to each.

(A) The background

The hourly rate
In *Leopold Lazarus Ltd* v *Secretary of State for Trade and Industry* (1976) SJ 268, **Costs LR (Core Vol) 62** Kerr J described the computation of the Part A figure as –

"assessing a rate per hour sufficient to cover the salary and the appropriate share of the general overheads of each such person (i.e. person employed on the case). The assessment of the appropriate rate per hour would be based on the Taxing Master's knowledge and experience of the average solicitor or executive employed by the average firm in the area concerned."

This reference to the average solicitor and the average firm in question has been repeated and emphasised in all the later judgments and reviews to which I have been referred. I have no reason to doubt that it represents the current practice throughout the whole country, nor that it is the proper basis in principle for the assessment of an hourly rate. If an individual solicitor or an individual firm charges more than the average figure, that may be for any number of reasons and they do not concern the paying party. The party is liable to pay no more than a reasonable amount for costs reasonably incurred, and, what is more, any doubts must be resolved in his favour, because Order 62, rule 12 expressly so provides. The same principle applies if the individual solicitor has done work which was not reasonably necessary, so that those costs were not reasonably incurred, or has spent an unreasonably long time on work which it was reasonable to do.

The later judgments and reviews to which I was referred include those of Hirst J in *Stubbs v Royal National Orthopaedic Hospital* (21 December 1988, **Cost LR (Core Vol) 117**) and Hobhouse J in *Finlay v Glaxo Laboratories Ltd* (9 October 1989, **Cost LR (Core Vol) 106**), as well as the registrars whose decisions in other cases I shall refer to below. A leading authority, however, is the judgment of Robert Goff J in *R v Wilkinson* [1980] 1 All ER 597, [1980] 1 WLR 396. This affirmed the general principle of taxation adopted in the *Leopold Lazarus Ltd* case as follows (at 601):

"... a solicitor's remuneration should consist of two elements: first, a sum computed on the basis of an hourly rate which represents the 'broad average direct cost' of undertaking the work; and second, a sum, usually expressed as a percentage mark-up of the broad average direct cost, for care and conduct."

The judgment was primarily concerned with claims made in the course of legal aid taxation in criminal cases which were based upon the Law Society publication entitled *The Expense of Time*. The first edition was published in 1972 and Robert Goff J was concerned with the second edition published in 1976 (see [1980] 1 All ER 597 at 600). There is now a fourth edition dating from 1986. Robert Goff J paid tribute to the work being done by the Law Society, which was and is aimed at assisting solicitors to calculate the actual and budgeted costs to them of work being done for clients, but he concluded as follows (at 608):

"For all these reasons, I have come to the conclusion that The Expense of Time, laudable though it is in many ways, does not in its present form provide a reliable basis for the taxation of costs; and I also conclude that it will be difficult in practice for any such system to form such a basis without some prior monitoring by an appropriate body."

The form of monitoring which he had in mind would involve not only the Law Society but also the Lord Chancellor's Department, professional accountants, and possibly the chief taxing master. It would also require machinery to keep the figures up to date (see [1980] 1 All ER 597 at 608).

The reasons why the second edition was held not to be an appropriate basis for taxation were these. It assumed that each fee-earning solicitor or employee worked 1,000 chargeable hours each year; the taxing master had taken 1,100 hours, which the judge could not disturb (see [1980] 1 All ER 597 at 606). It based the partner's notional salary on Civil Service scales for salaried lawyers; this could not be a useful guide (see [1980] 1 All ER 597 at 606). There were further criticisms of the method of calculation to which I need not refer, save to say that one of them – the need for separate figures for different types of work (see [1980] 1 All ER 597 at 608) – does not apply in the present case, because the firm of solicitors concerned does exclusively personal injury work and it acts either wholly or in the great majority of cases for trade unions representing individual plaintiffs.

From the court's point of view, Robert Goff J identified a "fundamental objection" consisting of the need for the taxing officer, if *The Expense of Time* calculation is taken as the basis for allowances, first, to check the relevant accounts submitted by the individual firm, and secondly, to consider the costs of other firms in the neighbourhood, if he is to assess an average figure (see [1980] 1 All ER 597 at 608).

The present situation
The fourth edition of *The Expense of Time* shows that many of the judge's comments and criticisms have been taken into account, and the text has been changed. Of the two major objections, the notional salary for equity partners is now based on the salary "which would be paid to an assistant solicitor whose experience would enable him or her to do the more straightforward work done by the principal", together with rates published monthly by the Law Society. The number of chargeable hours is dealt with as follows (*The Expense of Time* (4th edn, 1986) 12–13):

> "Your first step should be to install a time recording system which will record the time spent by a fee earner on any particular matter ... Until you have established the annual chargeable hours of each fee earner you will have to use an estimate but, unless it is realistic, an hourly expense rate based on an estimate will not produce information likely to be of any help in determining the expense of a particular matter to the firm; therefore, the early adoption of a time record is essential ... an estimate ... is not satisfactory, but it is better than not making a calculation at all. Such information as is available to The Law Society, from surveys and other sources, indicates that a reasonable estimate is 1100 chargeable hours per fee earner. However, this is an average: some fee earners will not achieve it; others will exceed it."

The introduction states that the objective "is to show you how to calculate the expense of running your practice ... and to relate that to individual fee earners ... it is NOT a means to calculating the charge to be made to the client" (p 14).

The present case

At the taxation hearing, the plaintiffs' solicitors relied upon the first affidavit of Pauline Anne Chandler, a partner who from the end of 1987 had as one of her responsibilities "to monitor all aspects of costs recovery", and who produced detailed *Expense of Time* calculations for Manchester and others of the firm's offices, together with a summary for Manchester alone. Relevant features of that calculation were that the chargeable hours for partners was estimated at 850 per annum and at 1,100 per annum for all employees, the number of employees being adjusted for any less than full time fee earners, e.g. articled clerks; and, secondly, the notional salary according to partners was the average of the top three salaried employees, to allow for the fact that individual highly experienced employed solicitors were paid commensurately high salaries. Alternative calculations allowed for salaries at the Law Society's published rates, for the years 1984–85 to 1987–88.

Mr Registrar Gee thought that the correct figure for chargeable hours, for all fee earners, was 1,000, that this produced average figures of roughly £45 to £58 per hour for the period 1984 to 1988, that some, though an unspecified, allowance should be made to reflect the effects of inflation between the date when the work was done and the date when costs would be paid ("today's pound for yesterday's work") and that the correct rate to award overall was £48 per hour, this being the figure for work which required a partner's attention.

The defendants objected; their reasons and the plaintiffs' observations were set out in some detail. The essential issue was whether the allowed figure should be in line with those previously allowed in the Manchester registry, or whether it should be based on *The Expense of Time* calculation put before him by the plaintiffs' solicitors. I should quote paragraph (a)(ii) of the plaintiffs' observations:

> "(a)(ii)   It is contended that The Expense of Time calculation presently before the Court and relating specifically to Brian Thompson & Partners is a reliable basis on which to assess the cost of personal injury litigation. It is based on the actual rather than the fictional cost of such litigation. The rates allowed previously almost as a matter of course by Registrars have been based partly on ignorance of the real cost of litigation because Solicitors themselves have not, by and large made any proper assessment of the cost upon which Registrars could reach more informed conclusions. Relying on rates previously awarded simply because it has always been done that way is not a justification for perpetuating such an unscientific system."

At the hearing of the objections further inquiries were made into the plaintiffs' calculations, and as a result several pages of computer print-out were produced by the defendants' solicitors, who had access to the necessary hardware. The allocation of overheads to individual fee earners was adjusted, so that a greater proportion was borne by the more highly remunerated, and different assumptions were made as to notional salaries and chargeable hours. The hourly figures produced ranged from £27 to £70 for 1984–85 and from £36 to £92 for 1987–88.

Miss Chandler's second affidavit produced revised, more detailed calculations which showed, inter alia, the hourly expense for individual fee earners, varying naturally with their individual salaries (or notional salaries for partners) and the proportion of overheads allocated to them.

Mr Registrar Gee took the calculations as his starting point, whilst recognising that the figures for any individual firm did not have to be taken in every case and that other firms' calculations would be required for an average to arise. He maintained his view that some allowance should be made for the depreciating effects of inflation ("today's pounds"). He held that all fee earners should have attributed to them 1,100 hours per annum of chargeable work and that the notional salary for partners should be assessed at £20,000 per annum, which he regarded as a fair compromise. The figures showed, he said, about £60 per hour for 1987–88 and that without going into details for previous years the overall figure would be £48, his previous taxation figure. This figure was confirmed by a rough estimate starting with £15 per hour in 1974 and adding for inflation year by year; this produced either £64 or £71 per hour, the former being exceedingly close to £60 for current work by a partner.

He then referred to an argument by the defendants' solicitors, to the effect that £40 per hour was the most which those doing defence (insurance) work could charge their clients in similar cases. His reasons for rejecting this imply, I think, either that defence work is undertaken at a loss, or that it justifies a lower rate than the "going rate as between solicitor and client for the average firm doing this sort of work in this area". I do not, with respect, find this part of the reasons easy to follow.

The parties' contentions
These appear sufficiently from the summary which I have already given of the history of these proceedings. Certain other matters emerged in the course of argument which I can usefully mention here. The plaintiffs' solicitors act regularly for individual plaintiffs in personal injury actions, on the instructions of trade unions to whom they look for payment of their fees. These are set at not less than the amount recovered or recoverable on taxation in cases where the plaintiff succeeds, that being a substantial majority of the total number of cases in which proceedings are issued. During the period from 1984 to 1988 there were three and later five equity partners, the two new ones having been solicitor employees. Individual cases tend to be handled by individual fee earners, so that even a partner will delegate little of the work, even routine work, in cases which he or she is handling. In the present case, for example, Miss Chandler, a partner, did all the work herself except where an "outside" agent was employed (and allowed at £32 per hour).

I was also told that other firms of solicitors in Manchester have prepared or are preparing *Expense of Time* calculations, although (with apparently one exception to which I shall refer below) none have been placed before registrars, and that discussions are in progress with or through local law societies so that other firms' or average figures can be made available to registrars.

Other reviews

The two recent judgments already mentioned, and transcripts of the registrar's reasons in other recent cases, were referred to in argument; they included *McCamley* v *Cammell Laird Shipbuilders Ltd* (6 February 1990, unreported), in which the plaintiff applied for review and which I heard at the same time as the present case, although I shall give a separate judgment in due course.

The general observation which I make is that running through all these judgments and reasons is a common thread, that is the principle that the rules require the registrar to assess the broad average direct cost of the work done by an average firm in the relevant area at the relevant time (see *R* v *Wilkinson* [1980] 1 All ER 597 at 604, [1980] 1 WLR 396 at 403–404).

Individual cases were as follows.

Stubbs v *Royal National Orthopaedic Hospital* (21 December 1988, **Costs LR (Core Vol) 117**). The defendants instructed a leading firm of City solicitors; the work was done by a legal executive. The claims were (hourly rates) 1979 £25, 1980 £30, 1981–82 £35, 1983 £40, 1984–85 £45, 1986 £50. The plaintiffs said that the rate should be £36 for 1986 and less, allowing pro rata for inflation, in previous years. The master referred to notes which he kept of the rates claimed in other cases. Hirst J held that it was proper to approach the assessment by reference to averages, and he upheld the master's allowance.

Finlay v *Glaxo Laboratories Ltd* (9 October 1989, **Costs LR (Core Vol) 106**). The infant plaintiff suffered catastrophic brain damage after an whooping cough vaccination. The claim was for work done by a solicitor who had special knowledge and experience of such cases, and who undertook exceptional personal responsibility by advising the plaintiff not to pursue a claim for damages in the light of a High Court judgment in a similar case. The work was treated as done in 1986. The solicitor practised in Newcastle. The registrar awarded £35, apparently on the basis that that was the going rate. Evidence included letters from local solicitors which together formed a consensus of opinion as to what was the true cost of time in the area at that time. There was also an *Expense of Time* calculation from the solicitor concerned. Hobhouse J increased the figure to £45 for a senior litigation partner, but he reduced the mark-up from 85% to 75%.

The registrars' decision in date order were as follows.

Mr Registrar Gee (Manchester) in *Gregory* v *William Kenyon & Sons Ltd* (23 March 1988, unreported) (asbestos). Work done by present plaintiffs' solicitors who produced figures for 1984 to 1987. Allowance £30 based on existing practice, increased to £34 when certain *Expense of Time* calculations were introduced.

Mr Registrar Evans (Manchester) in *Leah Jones v Crewe Health Authority* (1 July 1988, unreported). Work done 1984. Allowance £40. Calculations were produced for period from April 1986 (only) showing £57–62. Work done 1984 to 1987 – allowance £52.50 (average).

Mr Registrar Freeman (Manchester) in *Carter v Shell (UK) Ltd* (17 October 1989, unreported). Work done 1979 to 1987 by a senior partner. Allowance £33 (average) increased to £37 (average), including an assessment of "the current rate" to £50 (£32 allowed for a legal executive).

Mr Registrar Lambert (Sheffield) reported on 11 May 1989 that local solicitors were invited to supply information and that based on that information the registrars accepted £50 per hour for current (1989) work by an experienced solicitor.

Mr Registrar Evans in *McCamley v Cammell Laird Shipbuilders Ltd* (6 February 1990, unreported). Work done (by the present plaintiffs' solicitor) 1984 to 1988. The current Manchester rate was assessed at £45. Allowance of £40 confirmed, plus 100%.

I have summarised the details of these cases for reasons which appear below, and not because I wish to give any encouragement to the citation of individual decisions as authority for any other case. The decision in any particular case must always depend upon the circumstances of that case and upon the knowledge and experience of the registrar. It is also important that there shall be consistency of decisions between registrars and in similar types of case, "both in the interests of general fairness, and to assist parties to negotiate reasonable settlements of disputes on costs" (per Hirst J in *Stubb's* case). But this means consistency arising from the registrars' accumulated knowledge of local conditions and their experience of the figures being claimed in taxations which they conduct regularly in the course of their work. This is a factor which counts against, rather than for, reference being made to the details of other cases, just as it is, in my view, a reason for not placing exclusive or undue reliance upon figures showing the costs of the particular firm or solicitor in any individual case.

"Today's pounds"
An almost invariable feature of taxation is that the costs in question were incurred before, sometimes long before, the year in which they have to be assessed. Payment comes even longer after the event. During any period of inflation, therefore, the amount of costs awarded and paid to the successful party will be worth less in real terms than the historical costs which were incurred.

This is essentially a dispute about interest. The solicitor who wishes to guard against the effects of inflation in this way can request interim payments at least sufficient to cover the costs which he incurs. So the solicitor can safeguard himself. But the result of this, as the plaintiffs' solicitors pointed out to the registrar, is to shift the burden of inflation to the client. He paid the amount of costs when they were incurred; he recovers some years later that same amount, but no more, in depreciated pounds. Hence the slogan, today's pounds for yesterday's work.

The client would be indemnified against this loss of purchasing power if the award of costs included interest from the date when they were incurred, or partly indemnified, depending on the rate of interest. If the rate was equivalent to the borrowing rate and the money was borrowed, then the indemnity would be complete.

The House of Lords recently held that interest on the amount of costs awarded runs from the date of the judgment or order under which they are paid: see *Hunt v R M Douglas (Roofing) Ltd* [1988] 3 All ER 823, [1990] 1 AC 398, **Costs LR (Core Vol) 136**. The Court of Appeal held in a related case that interest cannot be recovered from any earlier date.

The judgments of Hirst and Hobhouse JJ to which I have referred both state in terms that the reasonable amount of costs is to be assessed at the respective dates when they were incurred. So did Robert Goff J in *R v Wilkinson* [1980] 1 All ER 597, [1980] 1 WLR 396. I am not aware of any judicial authority to the opposite effect.

The learned registrar in the reasons for his original taxation in the present case said:

> "... there is a danger of taxation becoming too much of an exact science. The fact that costs have been paid later in the day is one of the factors one takes into account in arriving at a fair rate and I propose to follow the earlier practice and look at rates (or in this case calculations) for earlier years. There will be an element of averaging tempered by the knowledge that it is today's pounds that is going to pay for yesterday's work. Without fudging the issue, I do not propose to decide one way or the other on this issue."

This is, if I may say so, a realistic approach which owes much to the desire to prevent taxation from becoming "too much of an exact science". But I am bound to say that it is wrong in law to make an allowance in favour of the receiving party on this ground, or to allow this factor to have any influence on the assessment of a reasonable rate for work that was done in earlier years. The wish to make some allowance rests upon a feeling that amounts awarded as costs should carry interest from the date the costs were incurred, and this as the authorities make clear they do not do. In fact, since the amount recovered does carry interest from the date of judgment (here the settlement in November 1987), there is a double compensation for the receiving party if any allowance is made for depreciation in the "real" value of the pound during the period, here 1987 to 1989, in respect of which interest will be recovered.

In his further reasons, the registrar adopted "with a certain amount of refinement" what he said in his original decision; he calculated that "one should allow something between the hypothetical average and today's rate", but he also said that "in principle it is not right to allow average or escalating rates".

In my judgment, no allowance should be made for the consequences of inflation, for the reasons which have already been given. The reasonable amount for costs reasonably incurred must be assessed by reference to the average cost of the average solicitor "in the relevant area *at the relevant time*" (*R v Wilkinson* [1980] 1 All ER 597 at 604, [1980] 1 WLR 396 at 403–404; my emphasis). The registrar realised, however, in the passage which I have quoted, that this overlaps another question, which he also addressed. When the costs were incurred over a number of years, does there have to be a calculation of actual costs year by year, or can one figure be taken as an average for the whole period? This, in my view, is not a question of principle, nor is it strictly a matter for calculation. The amount to be allowed is a matter for assessment by the registrar, taking into account such factors, including historical costs figures and calculations, as are relevant and which he finds helpful – see further below. Whether he takes an average figure covering a number of years or an annual figure which he applies to the work done in each particular year is a matter of convenience and entirely a question for him, in the particular circumstances of the individual case. (Cf Hirst J's judgment in *Stubbs v Royal National Orthopaedic Hospital* (21 December 1988, **Costs LR (Core Vol) 117**).)

Because the registrar has made some allowance, though unquantified, for the effects of depreciation since 1980–81 when the present cases began, and also because any such allowance in respect of the period after November 1987 represents "double counting" in terms of interest for the receiving party, I must hold that on this ground alone the registrar's decision was based on an error of law.

The correct approach
This application is treated by both parties as giving rise to a question of principle, not because a dispute whether £48 or some lower figure should be allowed in the present case is such a question, but because the plaintiffs' solicitors produced detailed *Expense of Time* calculations for their own firm's overheads and their partners' notional salaries and they invited the registrar to base his assessment on those figures. The registrar went part but not all of the way with this submission. He adopted as a statement of general principle what he had said in a previous case, *Gregory v William Kenyon & Sons Ltd* (23 March 1988, unreported), and he made the calculations his "starting point" in the present case.

His detailed reasons in both cases make it clear that he was conscious of two things. First, the figures for one firm can never of themselves establish or be evidence of an average. He expected other Manchester firms to follow suit in due course, so that an average might begin to emerge. This he regarded as the beginning of a process whereby a new figure might become established as a "going rate" for the Manchester area, which would be subject to increase from time to time, "not by some arbitrary guess work, but perhaps in line with inflation". Secondly, he was aware of the need to assess an appropriate figure under the new rules for standard costs, regardless of whether that was or might have been the correct figure on a "common fund" taxation under the former rules.

In my judgment, the registrar was in error in placing this amount of emphasis on the figures produced by one firm, and in basing his assessment on those figures when, as was inevitable, he could only confirm or check them as "reasonable" or average figures against his own knowledge and experience of other firms. (In *Gregory's* case he said: "I am sure that they are well within the range of figures which would be produced by other large firms in this town." This belief must rest in part upon his knowledge of what figures those other firms have claimed, and upon his general knowledge and experience of the economics of conducting a solicitor's practice in the area.) The registrar's approach is exemplified by his remarks about the proper way to regard future inflation, which I have quoted above. The choice is not between "arbitrary guess work" on the one hand and the calculated effects of inflation on the other hand. The registrar's assessment is neither guess work nor a precise accounting exercise (which can never be an exact science in any event). Rather, his judicial assessment of the proper figure, based upon his general knowledge and experience, is what the rules require.

This is not to say that the figures produced by an individual firm must be disregarded. Rather the reverse; it is the registrar's responsibility to have a general awareness of the level of costs incurred by the average firm from time to time. How best he can acquire this knowledge is a separate matter, about which I will say something more below. What I should emphasise here is that, as the history of the present application shows, a detailed examination of individual accounts is likely to increase the costs and delay of taxation proceedings beyond acceptable limits. (The tail must not wag the dog. The costs of litigation are heavy enough on their own account.) The ease, though not the cheapness, of obtaining computer print-outs and photocopies makes the risk a substantial one, which in my view the courts should guard against, both in the interests of litigants and of protecting their own procedures.

My general conclusion is that the registrar placed a wrong amount of emphasis on the figures produced in the present case, and upon the computer-aided analyses of those figures which were then made. I therefore echo the judgment in *R v Wilkinson* that, whilst *The Expense of Time* represents a policy of encouraging solicitors to estimate their actual and budgeted overhead costs in the interests of efficient financial accounting, the calculations so made should not be regarded as forming the basis (or even the starting point) for assessing the average solicitor's average costs. The basis, and the starting point, is the registrar's *general* – I emphasise the word "general" – knowledge and experience of the relevant matters.

There remains the question, however, of what weight, if any, the registrar should give to *Expense of Time* calculations, if they are produced in a particular case. The answer, in my judgment, is that, if the figures for an individual solicitor, or firm, are produced for the purposes of the assessment in that case, then they should be given very little weight. This is for the following reason, which is one of principle. There is some talk of the registrar being required to establish a "market" rate, but this requires some caution. The "market" is for charges, not for costs, and not only is the assessment of costs unconnected with charges, but "Part A" costs are specifically limited to the cost of providing fee-earning services. There is no market in such costs, because the consumer or purchaser pays charges which include both the profit element and those items of overheads which are not included with Part A. Of course, the level of charges is some evidence of costs, but at best the relationship is indirect and it may vary greatly from case to case. It is difficult to think of any better evidence of different solicitors' costs, as opposed to charges, than the amounts which they claim on taxation, case by case, year in, year out. A second reservation about market levels is that a market price, by definition, is distinct from the price at which any particular bargain is struck. The individual price at best is evidence of the state of the market at the time. No bargain is ever struck with regard to a solicitor's costs, except indirectly when charges are agreed.

If these objections to *Expense of Time*-type calculations are borne in mind, and the calculations are not wholly irrelevant to the assessment of costs, then it becomes necessary to consider the actual figures which were put in evidence in the present case. Although a comprehensive list of overheads, they are subject to two major assumptions, these being the level of notional salaries attributed to partners and the apportionment of total overheads between individual fee earners, who might range, though not in this case, from senior partners to articled clerks, depending on the kind of work which was done. The problem of apportionment remains even when, as here, the firm's internal arrangements are such that the whole of the chargeable (fee-earning) work was done by one person, who is one of the comparatively small number of partners. That cannot but mean that some of the work, which might have been done by a junior employee or articled clerk, is charged for at an higher rate than would otherwise be justified for that work. I appreciate that the problem is alleviated by averaging, and that some cases are handled by highly paid employees, which might justify higher charges in those cases; the calculated charges range from £33 to £87 per hour (1987–88 figures) depending on the assumptions made. The point I make is that these assumptions are important, and they may vary from firm to firm; I am not sure whether there can be such a thing as an "average" method of distributing the work, as distinct from an average cost for work actually done.

More fundamental, however, is the figure which is taken as average number of chargeable hours worked by fee earners in the course of the year.

The Expense of Time booklet, which I have quoted above, stresses the importance of establishing the firm's actual figures, and the poor substitute which estimated figures can provide, even the Law Society's figure of 1,100 hours. The plaintiffs here cannot produce any actual figures, though I understand that they are in the process of recording current procedures. They first took 850 hours for partners and 1,100 hours for employees; the registrar on review has taken 1,100 hours overall. I should stress that low figures do not imply any reduction in working hours. A partner especially may spend much of his or her time on administration, training and other necessary or worthwhile occupation for the benefit of the firm. The relevant inquiry is how many chargeable hours the average fee earner works in the course of the year, with due allowance for those whose employment is less than full time.

Naturally enough, hourly cost is highly sensitive to variations in the "hours worked" figure. The following should be borne in mind. Allowing for a 44-week year, i.e. eight weeks for holidays, training, sickness and other absences, a five-day week and a seven-hour day, i.e. 9 am until 5 pm, less one hour for lunch, the theoretical total is 1,540 hours. 1,100 hours represents a five-hour day. The "lost" two hours per day represents time which cannot be or is not charged to individual clients. The plaintiffs here explained this on the basis that the average employee would spend two hours per day in opening the post, in legal research and discussion, and in other breaks, including tea and non-chargeable time taken by telephone calls.

It seems to me that the resulting estimate of five hours' chargeable work each day, for the average and, it must be assumed, fully occupied employee, might do less than justice to that person, for two reasons at least. The low amount of chargeable work done might suggest either a lack of diligence or of employment, with which the client or cost-paying party is not concerned. Secondly, it seems likely to me that many if not all solicitors employees in the average firm work much longer hours than this. The question of overtime presents a real difficulty, which was noticed by the registrar in the present case. Hours worked in overtime do reduce the overhead cost per chargeable hour; on the other hand, there is force in the observation that enthusiasm and the willingness to work longer hours should not be penalised, but should be rewarded with additional costs. The problem, however, only arises if no extra payment is made for overtime; if it is, then the overheads are increased and the hourly rate is less affected by it.

I do not need and do not propose to attempt an answer to this difficult and ancillary question. It is a useful example of the way in which undue reliance upon any accounts, whether for one solicitor or for a number of firms, tends to widen the area of inquiry and multiply the number of issues, without a correspondingly greater chance of arriving at a precise figure, even when the accounts are of the highest standard and they are interpreted with a qualified accountant's expertise. This seems to me a major disadvantage of permitting any such accountancy exercise to play a major part in the assessment of costs upon taxation between two parties to any particular piece of litigation. And the figures are highly sensitive to the assumptions made regarding the number of chargeable hours, as one example will suffice to show. Mrs Smith QC for the plaintiffs referred me to the computer figures covering the period from 1984–85 to 1987–88 – the first and last relevant years for which they are available – and suggested that these the registrar should take into account, as he appears to have done. If the notional salary recommended by the Law Society was taken for each of those years, the calculated cost per hour was between £40.34 and £53.12. Taking a notional salary of £20,000, as the registrar did, the figures are £53.97 and £59.44 respectively. These figures all assume 1,100 chargeable hours. If 1,500 hours is assumed, the figures are as follows:

	Recommended	*£20,000*
1984–85	1,500 hours £29.58	1,500 hours £39.58
	(1,100 hours £40.34)	(1,100 hours £53.97)
1987–88	1,500 hours £38.95	1,500 hours £43.58
	(1,100 hours £53.12)	(1,100 hours £59.44)

For 1,500 hours, therefore the range is from £29/£39 to £38/£43, depending on the notional salary awarded to partners. Assuming 1,100 hours and a £20,000 salary, the registrar took £60 (£69.44) for 1987–88.

The accounts were explained to me and my assessors in detail, as they were to the registrar, and I must express my appreciation for the help which counsel was able to give us. I hope that it will not seem ungrateful if I say, as I must, that in my view presenting such figures, requiring non-expert analysis, i.e. by persons who are not accountants, is misconceived as a means of assisting the court in a particular case. Assessing costs is not an exact science; neither is accountancy. Treating the latter as if it were, so that the results of an accountancy exercise can be used as a basis for the former, seems to me to achieve the worst of both worlds. The registrar's general knowledge and experience of local conditions and circumstances remains the only firm basis for reliable and consistent taxation.

Does it follow, then, that the information contained in such accounts must be disregarded, and that registrars should remain in ignorance of it? In my judgment, the answer to this is a vehement No. It is part of each registrar's stock-in-trade that he has a *general* – again, I stress the word "general" – knowledge of these matters and that if necessary he has some knowledge of the figures for local firms. It appears from the reasons given by registrars in other cities – Newcastle and Sheffield, perhaps Birmingham also – that there have been communications between local firms, acting individually or collectively through local law societies, and registrars. I was told that similar discussions are taking place or are proposed between the Manchester Law Society and local registrars, all with the aim of informing registrars what the current level of overheads is and what the likely consequences of inflation are. I can see no objection to these consultations taking place and I for one would encourage them. They are the most practicable way of equipping the registrar directly with the local knowledge which he needs for the discharge of his function, and they are the only practicable way of informing him, not of the figures for one or a small number of firms, but of a range of figures which enable him to form a view about the average.

There remains, however, the fact that the registrar's daily experience of the sums being claimed by local firms is an efficient way of giving him the same information, although indirectly. The reasons given in other cases, to which I have been referred, emphasise more than once the importance of this factor for individual registrars. In my judgment, that is the true starting point for assessing the hourly rate. The figure may require adjustment in the particular case. If locally a certain figure becomes the going rate for routine cases, i.e. ones of a particular kind with no unusual features, and that rate is unrealistically low, then local solicitors are justified, in my view, in making approaches to registrars of the kind that already take place, these being for the purpose of providing general information and being unconnected with any particular case. I suppose that a situation might arise where registrars might seem impervious to all such representations and might persist in awarding an hourly rate which was unreasonably low; in those but not in any other circumstances I can envisage that an individual party might be justified in requiring the registrar to hear evidence, not only of the party's solicitor's own costs but of other solicitors' costs for similar work also. That, however, would be an extreme case, and except in such unusual circumstances the registrar should not be required, in my view, to hear detailed accountancy evidence of solicitors' overhead costs in the course of inter-party taxation.

I wish to add, for the avoidance of doubt, that I do not support any idea that part of the court's functions on an inter-party taxation is to discipline solicitors into charging less than they have done, or to regulate the amount of their charges to their clients. The court is not concerned with charges, only with costs; it is not concerned with any market, except indirectly, certainly not to influence any market. Its function, as Order 62, rule 12 requires, is to assess the reasonable amount of costs for work reasonably done; that, and nothing else.

(B) Mark-up

General
The issue is whether this should be 150%, which the plaintiffs claimed at the original taxation, or 60%, as the defendants contend, the registrar having allowed 90%.

In support of the claim, the plaintiffs point to the pioneering nature of the allegations of strain injuries caused by a wide variety of processes, involving much research into the medical aspects, and to the need to investigate the nature of each individual plaintiff's employment, including the advice of expert witnesses (engineers). Against this, the defendants rely principally on the amounts accepted as damages, all except one being within or close to the limits of country court jurisdiction.

The registrar decided that the case merits more than a "run-of-the-mill" 50%, and that the correct figure is somewhere between the norm and the exceptional. He awarded 90% because it "falls just short of the cases I have awarded 100% in".

I have had the benefit of my assessors' views, and it confirms my own judgment that this litigation is not above mid-scale in its degree of complexity and difficulty, being neither straightforward, on the one hand, nor as burdensome as many cases, particularly heavy "test" cases, sometimes are. What the submissions and the reviews to which I was referred (mostly in the context of Part A charges) make clear is that there has been a tendency, at least in the Manchester registry, for percentage mark-ups to be allowed which are significantly higher than in other centres, certainly than in London.

For example, the Newcastle registrar allowed 85% for a solicitor who was highly experienced in a particularly difficult case (whooping cough litigation), which Hobhouse J reduced to 75%. I am advised that a taxing master in London would allow at most 75% in the present case. Yet the plaintiffs claim 150% and the registrar allowed 90%. I surmise that there may have been a period when the Part A figures allowed in Manchester was unreasonably low, but a reasonable total was achieved by increasing the mark-up accordingly.

I approach the assessment on the following basis. I am advised that the range for normal, i.e. non-exceptional, cases starts at 50%, which the registrar regarded, rightly in my view, as an appropriate figure for "run-of-the-mill" cases. The figure increases above 50% so as to reflect a number of possible factors – including the complexity of the case, any particular need for special attention to be paid to it and any additional responsibilities which the solicitor may have undertaken towards the client, and others, depending on the circumstances – but only a small percentage of accident cases results in an allowance over 70%. To justify a figure of 100% or even one closely approaching 100% there must be some factor or combination of factors which mean that the case approaches the exceptional. A figure above 100% would seem to be appropriate only when the individual case, or cases of the particular kind, can properly be regarded as exceptional, and such cases will be rare. I am aware that the figures cannot be precise, but equally in my view the need for consistency and fairness means that some limits, however elastic, should be recognised.

On this basis, the claim for 150% is clearly inappropriate, and the registrar's allowance of 90% places this case in or close to the category of exceptional.

My conclusions are that 90% is certainly too high, and that the appropriate figure is 75%. This is consistent with the likely London allowance, but I reach it independently and in the light of the advice which I have received from my assessors.

(C) **The overall cost figure**

I have considered carefully whether the case should be remitted to the registrar so that he can assess a proper figure in the light of this judgment. In the result, I have decided that this will not be necessary. There is a great deal of evidence, not only about the plaintiffs' solicitors' actual costs, but also about figures which have been awarded during recent years by registrars in Manchester and other districts. I have had the benefit of considered advice from my two assessors, one of whom is familiar with practice in Northern England. (I emphasise that the decision is my own.)

The work was carried out during the period from 1979 to November 1987. I was told that about 40% was during 1987, about 30% during the period from 1984 to 1987 and about 30% before 1984.

A relevant factor in my view is that all of the work charged for was done by the same solicitor, who is skilled and experienced in work at partner level. That is the way in which the particular firm organises itself, and it may well be beneficial and efficient for all concerned. But it does mean that a senior solicitor spent some time on tasks which could be performed by a junior employee. This factor must tend to reduce the figure which represents a reasonable overall figure for all the work done, though the unchallenged figure of £32 allowed for outside clerks must also be borne in mind.

The correct overall figure in my judgment is £40 per hour. If this is uplifted by 75%, the total allowance, or charge, is £70 per hour, an average figure for the years 1979 to 1987. This is also, in my view, a reasonable total, and I so order. The award will carry interest from November 1987.

Mark-up – joint conference

A specific question arises with regard to the mark-up allowed for one item of the plaintiffs' solicitors costs, that is attending the joint conference in November 1987 at which both parties were represented by leading counsel and final settlement was reached. I was told that the negotiations were conducted by counsel and that rooms were made available in the same building for the supporting teams, including of course the plaintiffs' solicitor. It is clear from this account that she was actively engaged in the process of negotiation, although not face to face with the defendants' representatives, and that her knowledge of the issues and of the different plaintiffs enabled her to play a vital part. The registrar allowed 75%. The defendants say that this should be reduced to 30%, that being the normal figure for work of a supportive nature. The plaintiffs claimed 100%. In my judgment the registrar's approach is correct, in that he allowed a figure approaching though lower than the overall mark-up figure. Having reduced that figure to 75%, the appropriate figure for this item in my judgment is 65%.

Copying charges

Paragraph 17 of the Masters' Practice Notes 1986 (see *The Supreme Court Practice 1988* vol 1, para 62/A2/31, pp 1010–1011) reads as follows:

> "There is no longer any provision for copy documents since the making of copies of documents is in general to be considered as part of a solicitor's normal overhead expense. The taxing officer may in his discretion make an allowance for copying in unusual circumstances or when the documents copied are unusually numerous in relation to the nature of the case: for example, they will, in general, be allowed in proceedings in the Court of Appeal. Where this discretion is invoked the number of copies made, their purpose, and the charge claimed must be set out in the bill. If the copies have been made out of the office the cost should be shown as a disbursement. If made in the office, a profit cost equivalent to the commercial cost should be claimed. A charge based on the time expended by a member of the solicitor's staff will not be allowed."

The plaintiffs claimed £1,045 as the cost of copying 10,450 pages at 10p each page:

> "149.   Copy documents to accompany briefs to Leading Counsel 3,445 pages; Junior Counsel 3,445 pages. Copy documents to accompany instructions to [three experts, total 3,560 pages] Total pages 10,450."

The registrar allowed this item and the defendants objected. Among their observations the plaintiffs said that the commercial rate was 18p "so that claiming 10 pence per page ... is therefore eminently reasonable". The registrar disallowed the defendants' objections because in his view "the number of copies was sufficiently exceptional as to justify a charge".

I do not see the relevance of claiming that the commercial cost was 18p when no disbursement is claimed. The claim is for 10p per page, and the sole question is whether this is a proper case for the taxing officer to exercise his discretion, because of "unusual circumstances or where the documents copied are unusually numerous in relation to the nature of the case". Otherwise, the cost of copying is part of the solicitors' normal overhead charges.

There was some uncertainty at the hearing as to what constituted the 3,445 pages which were copied for both leading and junior counsel. They included the pleadings of eleven actions, experts' reports (medical and general) which were partly dealing with individual cases and partly concerned with general issues, and what may be called general medical literature. Since the hearing, my assessors have examined the documents in question.

Mrs Smith submitted that the maximum number of pages which might require copying in a personal injury case of a normal kind would be 1,000, and that therefore this case did involve an unusual number. I sympathise with this submission, but I am troubled that neither the plaintiffs nor the registrar have made an allowance for the number which in the normal case would form part of the solicitor's general overheads. Moreover, there were here not one, but a total of eleven cases, at least six of which remained active when briefs were delivered. I have received clear and firm advice from my assessors that in these circumstances the documents were not unusually numerous for the type of case. It is also relevant, in my judgment, to take into account that the case merits a high though not an exceptional mark-up figure covering the whole of the hourly costs claim. I have concluded that the objection should be upheld, and this item disallowed.

Perusals
Item 5t of the bill reads as follows:

> "5t)   Perusals from time to time over 8 years at say 30 mins per year each plaintiff (9 of them) 36 hours."

The claim for 36 hours was reduced to 18 hours, leaving an allowance of 15 minutes per case per year.

The registrar allowed this item and dismissed the defendants' objection. He said:

> "This is a common item and of course in an ideal world every item of time spent would be properly recorded ... I am not so far from practice, however, that I cannot recall the reality of the situation, namely that ... no matter how carefully a bill is prepared or records are kept not all time is going to be fully recorded."

The submission for the plaintiffs put the claim on a rather different basis. There are numerous occasions, it is said, in the course of a year when time is taken up, e.g. in reading and filing reports or in answering telephone calls, in respect of which no separate charge is made. Therefore, a total of 15 minutes per case per year is not an unreasonable estimate of the time spent on these unrecorded items. The plaintiffs' written observations were that "no matter how carefully a bill is prepared, it is impossible to cover or properly record every minute spent ... "

In fact, I note from the bill that frequent claims are made for periods as short as five minutes, for telephone calls and for reviewing the position in individual cases.

In my judgment, the submission that there were unrecorded occasions when chargeable time was spent on these cases must be rejected. This leaves the registrar's decision that in practice, as I readily accept, not all time will be fully recorded, even for those items of work in respect of which a claim is made. But I do not see why there should always be an under-recording. The claims invariably are for "global" figures, mostly to the nearest five minutes, below half an hour, or to the nearest quarter of an hour above that. No doubt there were some occasions when the period spent was slightly more, others when it was slightly less. There is no evidence that any substantial item was not recorded at all. In my judgment, therefore, this item must be disallowed.

Taxation

Paragraph 5(*a*) of Part II of Appendix 2 and paragraph 19(i) of the Masters' Practice Notes 1988 (see *The Supreme Court 1988* vol 1, para 62/A2/31, p 1011) refer to this item:

> "5.   *Taxation*
>   (*a*)   Taxation of Costs (i) Preparing the bill (where allowable) and preparing for and attending the taxation; (ii) Care and conduct; (iii) Travelling and waiting.
>   (*b*)   Review (i) Preparing and delivering objections to decision of taxing officers on taxation or answers to objections, and considering opponent's answers or objections, as the case may be; attending hearing of review. (ii) Care and conduct. (iii) Travelling and waiting."

> "19.   (i)   No details of the work done need be provided for item 5(*a*) but on taxation the party entitled to the costs must justify the amount claimed. In general the drawing of a bill of costs is not fee-earner's work and, save in exceptional circumstances, no charge should be sought for such work. Charges paid to an agent will not be allowed."

The plaintiffs claimed a total of 67 hours 45 minutes for:

> "TAXATION
>
> 318)   (a)   collating papers and preparing bill for taxation ...
>   Preparation of Bill
>   (57 hrs 05 mins over 7 days)
>   Checking typed bill
>   all recorded time
>   (10 hrs 40 mins over 4 days)"

In addition, there was a claim "Preparing for taxation and attending same estimated at 15 hrs".

The registrar gave reasons in detail for his original decision that a fee should be allowed for preparation of the bill. He adopted these reasons in his later decision after objections, and so I will quote them here:

> "The bill is well drawn and I pay tribute to the way it has been drawn but that in itself is not an exceptional circumstance. Miss Chandler submits that I have discretion which I undoubtedly have ... that this is one of those exceptional [cases] where she would not have used an in- or out-of-house cost draftsman because, putting it bluntly, they would not have known where to start. And it is submitted that if, anyone else had done it, checking the bill would not have taken much less time. I think that I have to ask: was it reasonable for a senior partner to prepare this bill rather than use a notional in-house cost draftsman or an out-of-house cost draftsman. Miss Chandler actually prepares a lot of her bills because, probably rightly, she thinks she would make a better job of it. Let me assume that there is an experienced in-house cost draftsman at Brian Thompson & Partners [BT & P] who knows how BT & P want their bills presented. Were there such an animal at BT & P, ought I to have expected Miss Chandler to send this bill to him? I conclude that this is one of those

extremely exceptional cases where it was proper for Miss Chandler to do the work herself and charge it out. I therefore allow a fee for preparation of the bill."

This involves a number of matters, one of which was non-controversial. The bill was very well drawn, and it is a credit to Miss Chandler's drafting. I was told that in fact she draws only a small number of bills in the course of a year. It appears from the figures for overheads that the firm make little use of "outside" costs draftsmen. The cost of time spent in drafting bills therefore is included either in the salaries paid to employees or in the notional salaries attributed to equity partners.

For these costs to be chargeable as a fee earner's time, the Practice Notes require that "exceptional circumstances" must be shown (paragraph 19(i)). This is not the same as asking whether it was reasonable for a senior partner to prepare the bill, which is the question which the registrar posed. But the relevant factors are broadly the same, however the question is framed. It is said that a cost draftsmen "would not have known where to start", but, assuming a competent draftsman and reasonable records, I do not know why not. Then it is submitted that checking the bill would not have taken much less time – than the 67 hours 45 minutes claimed. This too I am unable to accept. The time claimed for checking (10 hours 40 minutes) seems to me ample, even if the bill was prepared by a draftsman other than Miss Chandler herself. These views take account of my assessors' advice.

On review, the registrar confirmed his original allowance of this item, at £48 per hour plus 60% mark-up. He treated it as a matter of principle and asked that some guidance be given as to whether his approach was right. As already stated, the correct approach is to ask, in accordance with the Practice Note, whether there were exceptional circumstances which justify charging for the fee earner's time in this case. There is a strong presumption, in my view, against charging the client, or the paying party, for time spent preparing the bill. The circumstances must be exceptional for this to be done. The present case, in my view, was not so complicated, even with consolidation, that a costs draftsman could not reasonably be required to draw the bill, nor were there any special circumstances such as confidentiality, delicacy or any other feature of the case which required a partner to do the work; a possible example given in argument is when the costs were incurred by another firm. The registrar concluded:

"It will be a rare case where I consider it proper to allow for a solicitor's time for preparing a bill and indeed this is the first case in which I have done so."

With respect, I cannot share his view that there were exceptional circumstances here. This is not to say that the plaintiffs' solicitors should not continue to operate on the basis that partners and solicitor employees do prepare the bills in cases in which they have been engaged – that is entirely a matter for them, and it may be administratively and financially efficient for them to do so. But this does not mean that, save in exceptional circumstances, the cost of time so spent by a fee earner can be charged to the paying party on taxation, and in my judgment no such circumstances exist here.

Taxing officer's certificate to be amended following recalculation of allowable costs. Leave to appeal to the Court of Appeal granted.

Janet Smith QC (instructed by *Brian Thompson & Partners*, Manchester) for the plaintiffs.
G Chambers (instructed by *James Chapman & Co*, Manchester) for the defendants.

Loveday
v
Renton and another (No 2)

Queen's Bench Division
25 November, 12 December 1991

Hobhouse J
sitting with
Master Martyn and Mr Phillip Sycamore as assessors

Headnote

This is perhaps the most important of the recent costs cases deciding a number of different matters, but in particular deploring the use of artificially inflated uplift figures as a way of trying to compensate for artificially depressed hourly rates. There is also much material in this important decision relating to counsel's fees and in particular that counsel can only be paid for doing what he is instructed to do. The judge (Hobhouse J as he then was) also held that where a case was truly exceptional in terms of weight, complexity and responsibility a 125% profit costs mark-up was justified.

12 December 1991. The following judgment was delivered.

HOBHOUSE J: This is an appeal by way of further review of the taxation by Master Prince of the bills of the solicitors and counsel who acted for the plaintiff under legal aid certificates. The relevant action was started in 1982 and was effectively concluded by the judgment of Stuart-Smith LJ sitting as an additional judge in the Queen's Bench Division on 30 March 1988 (see *Loveday* v *Renton* [1990] 1 MLR 117). The effect of his judgment was that the plaintiff could not succeed in the action. Since the plaintiff was legally aided, he ordered a legal aid taxation of the plaintiff's costs. It is that taxation with which I am now concerned.

The action was one of a number which arose out of injuries to young children which were alleged to have been suffered by reason of the administration to them of whooping cough vaccine. The sums of money involved in the litigation as a whole were very substantial. There were some 200 cases and each, subject to liability, could be expected to give rise to an award of damages of the order of £¼m. On the defendants' side there were health authorities and doctors. The Wellcome Foundation, although only joined in some of the actions, successfully applied to be joined in the present action since, as a major manufacturer of the vaccine, it had an important interest in the question whether the vaccine was unsafe and liable to cause the alleged injuries; but they were joined on terms that they would in any event bear their own costs. The subject matter of the litigation was one of considerable public concern and interest.

The *Loveday* action was not originally intended to be taken as the lead case. However when another case, the *Kinnear* case (see *Dept of Health and Social Security* v *Kinnear* (1984) 134 NLJ 886), collapsed without producing a decision which would be decisive of the general body of cases, the *Loveday* case was brought forward, effectively as the test case, and Stuart-Smith J (as he then was) in June 1986 ordered a preliminary question of fact to be tried, whether or not the proper administration of the vaccine to young children was capable of causing permanent brain damage. This issue was deliberately formulated so as to exclude any peculiarities that might exist in any individual case.

The trial of that issue started on 5 October 1987 and lasted for some 65 working days. On 18 December 1987 the trial was adjourned prior to the Christmas break. On 11 and 12 January 1988 the taking of evidence was completed. The evidence adduced during the trial had consisted almost entirely of expert evidence of a highly technical character concerning the potential effect of the vaccine upon the human body and in particular upon the neurological system and the assessment of statistical evidence. The documentation was very heavy and ran to some 100 lever arch files, the Wellcome Foundation having prepared and produced a "library" of some 50 files containing the literature on the subject. The learned judge's judgment took two days to read and with its appendices extends to just under 300 pages of transcript.

Before the court rose on 18 December the judge indicated that he would expect the parties to produce written submissions and he suggested a scheme which they should follow. Accordingly, those representing the active parties, that is to say the plaintiff and the Wellcome Foundation, set to work to prepare such documents and this was done prior to the end of January 1988. On 1 February the court sat to hear the final submissions and these took a further three weeks, ending on 23 February, when judgment was reserved. One of the points which I have to consider is the work which was done between 18 December 1987 and 31 January 1988 in connection with the preparation of the written submissions put in by the plaintiff.

Upon the legal aid taxation the plaintiff's solicitors put in bills which ran to about 200 pages and incorporated the disbursements which represented the fees for which counsel had submitted fee notes. Owing to the fact that the Law Society had commendably been making payments on account and the long history of the matter there was and still remains some confusion about some of the items. It is not useful however now to rehearse those difficulties. Following the initial taxation of the bill, objections were raised by the solicitors and the relevant counsel. Master Prince heard those objections, including submissions by counsel, and, having allowed some and disallowed others, gave his reasons on 23 May 1991. The solicitors and counsel are dissatisfied with certain of his answers to their objections and have appealed to this court by way of further review asking that certain items that had been disallowed should be allowed either as claimed or at a higher sum than allowed by Master Prince.

The Legal Aid Board granted authority under regulations 114 and 116 of the Civil Legal Aid (General) Regulations 1989, SI No 339, to apply to a judge to review the taxation and the aggrieved parties have been represented before me by counsel. The Lord Chancellor's Department have not elected to be represented on this hearing. In the usual manner the court has been assisted by assessors.

The basis of taxation is that laid down in RSC Order 62, rule 12(1): "... there shall be allowed a reasonable amount in respect of all costs reasonably incurred ... "

The solicitors

I will take the appeal of the solicitors first. Their appeal relates to the uplift to be applied to the profit costs for care and conduct. As set out in Part II of Appendix 2 to RSC Order 62 a solicitor's bill should be broken down so as to deal respectively with (1) interlocutory attendances, (2) conferences with counsel, (3) attendance at trial or hearing and (4) preparation. No question arises in respect of the allowance for care and conduct under headings (1) to (3). Under heading (4), preparation, the ingredients are:

> "*Part A*: The doing of any work which was reasonably done arising out of or incidental to the proceedings including [and then 13 items are listed].
>
> *Part B*: The general care and conduct of the proceedings.
>
> *Part C*: The travelling and waiting time in connection with the above matters."

The outstanding question relates to "The general care and conduct of the proceedings". The solicitors originally claimed 200%. On the taxation the master reduced it to 125% and also reduced the hourly rates claimed. On the review after having heard the objections, the master increased the hourly rates but reduced the care and conduct further to 100%. The solicitors say that he should not have done so, that he certainly should not have reduced the 125% further and that in any event the rate of 125% is too low.

The master's decision can legitimately be criticised since, if he had previously considered that 125% was the appropriate uplift, he was not justified, on the hearing of the objections, in reducing it. The reason that he gave was that, having increased the hourly rates, he should stand back and consider the overall rate that resulted and therefore could properly reduce the uplift. In doing so he considered that such an approach was sanctioned by what had been said by this court in *Finlay v Glaxo Laboratories Ltd* (9 October 1989, **Costs LR (Core Vol) 106**).

In that case it was stressed that the first step in assessing the proper sum to allow for profit costs was to assess the appropriate hourly rates. The court deplored any artificial depression of those rates; it considered that they should be the actual rates which represented the actual cost to the solicitor at the relevant time of doing the relevant work (assuming always that the solicitor has acted reasonably and that the costs are incurred at the appropriate level). In the same connection the court deplored the use of artificially inflated uplift figures as a method of compensating for artificially depressed hourly rates. The situation which gave rise to the *Finlay* case was a practice which had grown up in the North East of England which had precisely those characteristics: the hourly rates were too low and an excessive uplift was used to mitigate the consequences of those rates. On appeal by way of review to this court, the court had adjusted both the rate (upwards) and the uplift (downwards) so as to approach the matter in a proper fashion and give to the solicitor the appropriate allowance on taxation for his profit costs. Master Prince was not faced with that situation. The hourly rates were intended to be realistic rates and the uplift was intended to be the uplift that was appropriate to take account of the general care and conduct of the proceedings.

The matter with which the court is concerned in the present case is what is the appropriate figure (or figures) for uplift having regard to the criteria which are set out in paragraph 1(2) of Part I of Appendix 2. In this context it is accepted that it is legitimate to look at the different sections of the solicitors' bill. The principal part, A, related to the litigation which led up to and included the trial before Stuart-Smith J. But there were also two lesser bills, B and C, which related to interlocutory appeals to the Court of Appeal in the latter part of 1985 and the early part of 1987. Master Prince drew no distinction between the main bill and these further bills. In respect of each he allowed an uplift of 100%. I see no ground whatever for interfering with his allowance of 100% in respect of bills B and C. There was nothing to take those parts of the proceedings, which were the subject of separate costs orders, out of the ordinary category so as to place them in some exceptional category. It will be appreciated that I do not have to consider whether the 100% allowance is not still too high for those bills and I will say no more about it. But I must not be taken as having approved an allowance of an uplift of 100% on the preparation work for those appeals.

With regard to bill A one has to take into account that the preparation work applies to the case as a whole throughout its history. It is the "general" care and conduct of the proceedings that is relevant. Part of the proceedings correspond very closely to the work which was the subject of the *Finlay* case and in respect of which the court allowed an uplift of 75%. However, the *Finlay* case only concerned the early stages of a case and work done in relation to advising whether or not the action should continue. The present case involved work which included the preparation for an actual trial.

In my judgment it is clear that an uplift of at least 100% is justified. The question of causation which was tried was complex and difficult and could fairly be described as including elements of novelty even though there had been a previous similar action (the *Kinnear* action). The solicitor was required to show an understanding of technical evidence which differed in degree, though not in kind, from that experienced in other cases involving scientific or medical disputes. The volume of the documentation was very large indeed and required detailed consideration. The matter was important to the client, but not exceptionally so. As regards the solicitors' actual client, Mrs Loveday, there was nothing to take the case out of the ordinary run of a substantial personal injuries action. The damages claimed in the action were no greater than in many other similar actions.

However, the action was in effect being fought as a test action and therefore there were many other prospective claimants who were depending upon the solicitors' conduct of this action and upon a decision in favour of the plaintiff upon the trial of the preliminary issue. It would therefore, in my judgment, be wrong to approach this litigation having regard solely to the actual plaintiff on the record and ignoring the existence of the other claimants and the very large sums at issue overall. Further, I consider that I should have in mind that the Legal Aid Board was also treating this case as a test case being fought for the benefit of a large number of legally aided claimants. This is illustrated by the fact that the Legal Aid Board authorised the employment of four counsel including two leading counsel. The Legal Aid Board were expecting the solicitors to conduct it as a test case and in the assessment of the solicitors' reasonable charges that factor should be taken into account. It is also relevant that the case was being fought as a test case by the Wellcome Foundation. They were concerned to establish, as they ultimately did, the fact that it could not be proved that the vaccine caused brain damage. This litigation and this individual case therefore had the same character on both sides and the care and conduct called for was similar on both sides. The litigation was also being conducted against a background of legitimate public interest and concern. The solicitor having the conduct of this matter further deserves credit for the uninterrupted personal attention which he gave to it.

I have rehearsed these matters, not because I consider that the taxing master was unaware of them, but to show that there is a basis for putting this case into an exceptional category. To justify an uplift in excess of 100% it is necessary, as has recently been restated by Evans J in *Johnson v Reed Corrugated Cases Ltd* [1992] 1 All ER 169 at 184 [**Costs LR (Core Vol) 180**], to demonstrate that the case is exceptional. There has been a tendency among some firms of solicitors to put forward grossly inflated percentages by way of uplift and a failure to appreciate that to justify an uplift even as high as 100% requires the demonstration that the case is exceptional.

In the present case, having regard to the features to which I have referred, I am satisfied (not without some hesitation) that the taxing master was wrong to alter his own original assessment on bill A of an uplift of 125%. I consider that 125% is at the top end of the bracket of uplift which would be proper for this case overall and I would not have interfered with a figure which lay somewhere between 125% and 100%. But I do accept the solicitors' submission before me that 100% was too low for bill A and I shall therefore reinstate the original allowance of 125%. To that extent the solicitors' appeal succeeds.

Counsel

The other aspects of this review concerned the renewal of certain of the objections of counsel to the fees which had been disallowed in respect of the work which they had done. There were four counsel involved; originally there had only been two. The original team of one leader and one junior was supplemented in 1986 with an additional junior pursuant to an authority dated 4 September 1986. On 19 March 1987 the Legal Aid Board authorised the solicitors to brief two leading counsel and two junior counsel on the trial of the action, making a team of four in all. In the taxation, the leader who joined the team in 1987 was called the "second" leader even though he was considerably senior to the "first" leader and had been instructed specifically because of his expertise and experience in handling the heaviest types of civil litigation.

The outstanding disputes on counsel's fees primarily relate to the brief fees to be allowed. Each of the two leaders had claimed a brief fee of £130,000, which the taxing master originally reduced to £50,000 but after hearing the objections raised to £95,000 each. For the two junior counsel the first had claimed a brief fee of £117,500, which after reduction to £25,000 was increased to £47,500, and the second junior had claimed £65,000, which after reduction to £23,000 was increased to £45,000. There was no issue about the refresher rate; after hearing the objections the master allowed the rates claimed, £1,000 per day for each leader, £500 per day for each junior.

In assessing a brief fee it is always relevant to take into account what work that fee, together with the refreshers, has to cover. The brief fee covers all the work done by way of preparation for representation at the trial and attendance on the first day of the trial. But in heavy litigation, particularly where there is a team of barristers and experts, additional work is involved in ensuring that the client is properly represented and his case fully developed beyond simply appearing in court. In this litigation counsel had to meet together to consider their strategy and tactics and prepare material. They also had to have meetings with their experts, including meetings with exerts from abroad, prior to their going into the witness box to give their evidence. Some of these meetings were lengthy and took place at weekends. Then there was the work involved in the preparation of final submissions. Each counsel has said that between the time the court rose on 18 December 1987 and the start of the final submissions on 1 February 1988 he expended a very substantial number of hours working on this case and preparing the written submissions for which the judge had asked.

Substantial sums of money are involved and the counsel have claimed the right to be compensated for having meetings with experts and each other and for preparing the final submissions in addition to the remuneration they are to receive by way of brief fee and refreshers. For example, the first leading counsel has claimed an additional £20,650 and the second leading counsel an additional £24,500 for work done preparing their final submissions. The master allowed these claims in the figure of £3,000 for each leader. The calculation of the claim was in each case based upon the actual number of hours and the application, pro rata, of the refresher rate. The master rejected this calculation as wholly unreasonable but was persuaded to allow to counsel an "enhanced" fee for having to prepare the final submissions in the way that was requested by the judge.

I consider that in principle the approach of the taxing master was correct. Counsel are only entitled to charge for work which they have been instructed to do and, where the work is done on legal aid, which has been authorised by a legal aid certificate (see *Din* v *Wandsworth London BC (No 3)* [1983] 2 All ER 841, [1983] 1 WLR 1171). Instructing counsel on legal aid is governed by the legal aid regulations (currently regulation 59 of the Civil Legal Aid (General) Regulations 1989), which, among other things, require that any instructions delivered to counsel shall include a copy of the certificate or other authority to instruct counsel; there is no need for counsel to be unaware of the extent to which work is or is not authorised. In the present context the authorisation was for representation at the trial and the relevant instructions were the delivery of the brief. It follows that the counsel have to base their claim to remuneration upon the delivery of the brief and what was required for the representation of the assisted party in court. The remuneration should therefore be the brief fee and the daily refreshers. The daily refreshers are calculated by reference to the time during which the trial is proceeding and certainly cannot be charged for days the court is not sitting (see *Lawson* v *Tiger* [1953] 1 All ER 698, [1953] 1 WLR 503 and RSC Order 62, Appendix 2, Part I, paragraph 2(2)(*b*)). This conclusion does not mean that counsel should not be remunerated for necessary work which is an incident of the proper representation of their client. It means that in a privately funded case a barrister must negotiate a brief fee that is sufficient to cover such work (or make some other special agreement for the delivery of supplementary instructions and/or the agreement of an additional fee: see Order 62, rule 15) and in legal aid work the barrister may on the legal aid taxation require that the brief fee (and the refresher rate) properly reflect the amount of work that actually had to be done.

In the present case I consider that the brief fee should be assessed and allowed having regard to the full history of the trial as now known. It thus should take into account the need for counsel to have meetings with each other and with experts out of court hours and to prepare final submissions. But it should also take account of the fact that all heavy trials include such a need to a greater or lesser extent. The preparation by counsel of his examinations-in-chief and cross-examinations and of his final submissions are an ordinary part of his conduct of a trial on behalf of his client. It is all part of the work which he accepts an obligation to perform by accepting the brief and for which he is remunerated by the brief fee and the agreed refreshers.

Written submissions are now a commonplace feature of heavy civil litigation and are no longer exceptional. (For example, in the Commercial Court they are specifically expected and provided for in the *Guide to Commercial Court Practice* (see *The Supreme Court Practice 1991* vol 1, paras 72/A1—72/A31).) Skeleton arguments, dramatis personae, chronologies etc are now required for a wide range of proceedings in court and in chambers. To some extent it has always been an incident of advocacy that forensic documents may have to be produced. Unless some different agreement is made, the brief fee must take all this into account. The difference between the present case and other cases is only a difference in degree.

Having regard to what I have said and to the general principle which is conveniently stated in Appendix 2, Part I, paragraph 1(2)(g) that in allowing fees the taxing officer should have regard to any other fees and allowances payable to counsel in respect of other items in the same case where the work done in relation to those items has reduced the work which would have otherwise been necessary in relation to the item in question, I should as the first step identify what items of work are to be treated as covered by the brief fee and refreshers and to what extent fees already allowed overlap with the brief fee.

On this review the counsel (except the second junior counsel) have maintained their claim to be remunerated for other items of work done during the period between delivery of the brief and the completion of the trial and some fees have been allowed by the taxing master in respect of such items. The relevant items are conveniently listed in the schedule (which appears as a table to this judgment) prepared by Mr Birts QC, who appeared on this review for the four counsel as well as for the solicitors.

First leading counsel
Item 4: preparation 30 June 1986 to 13 July 1987   In so far as this item relates to the period before the delivery of the brief in April 1987, the hours worked cannot *as such* be remunerated as they do not relate to work covered by a certificate or by actual instructions. In so far as it relates to later work it is work which clearly must be remunerated by the fee paid on the delivery of the brief. Accordingly the taxing master was right wholly to disallow this item as a *separate* item. The brief was delivered in April 1987 and the total volume of work reasonably done by counsel by way of preparation for the purposes of the representation of the plaintiff at the trial and its conduct on her behalf must be taken into account in assessing the reasonable brief fee and it is immaterial that he actually did some of the work in anticipation of

the delivery of the brief. The work had to be done some time by the counsel instructed to represent the plaintiff at the trial and he should be remunerated for it in his brief fee (and not, in the absence of separate authorised instructions, in any other way). It is not uncommon (although not in this case, and it is not to be encouraged) that the actual brief is delivered late and the barrister has to start his preparation for his appearance at the trial on the faith of the solicitor's statement that he will deliver a brief; this does not prejudice the assessment of the proper brief fee when the brief is later delivered.

Items 5 and 6: consultations with the second leader on 30 July and 21 and 24 September 1987 These consultations were to form part of the preparation for representation at the trial. Meetings between members of the team of counsel are a necessary incident of that preparation. The taxing master was right to disallow those items as separate items. They are to be taken into account in assessing the brief fee.

Item 8: preparation (1 day) 13 November 1987 It appears that on this day the court did not sit but that counsel understandably took the opportunity to work in chambers as part of their continuing task of keeping themselves prepared to represent the plaintiff in court. The taxing master pointed out that refreshers were only payable whilst the trial was actually proceeding and referred to Order 62, Appendix 2, Part I, paragraph 2(2)(*b*)(i). Accordingly such work must be taken into account in assessing the brief fee and the refresher rate and cannot be separately charged for. It is not done pursuant to any separate instructions delivered by the solicitor or authorised by a certificate. The taxing master correctly said: "Such time must be subsumed either in his basic fee or his refreshers." He correctly disallowed the item.

Item 13: preparation of final submissions 3 to 31 January 1988 This is the item to which I have referred earlier. It was claimed at £20,650 and the taxing master has allowed £3,000. Here again the work must, in my judgment, be remunerated by the brief fee and refreshers and should not in principle be separately remunerated. It is part of the representation of the plaintiff at the trial. What was required was that the counsel involved in that representation should prepare the final submissions. They had to do that work in any event. The fact that those submissions are reduced or partly reduced into the form of a written document is beside the point. The work is essentially the same. It is not done pursuant to separate instructions given by the solicitor or authorised by any certificate. Therefore, if the decision of the master is to be criticised at all, it is for allowing a sum of £3,000 as opposed to disallowing this item altogether. The work done should be taken into account in assessing the brief fee. I have at my own request been shown the written final submissions that were put in on behalf of the plaintiff and it must be commented that the quality and extent of the written submissions (particularly having regard to the fact that they represent the product of a team of counsel) demonstrate that the great bulk of the hours worked cannot have been attributable to the need to prepare that document but rather to the normal type of work done in the preparation of conventional final submissions. The document is unimpressive and on the face of it does not begin to justify the fees apparently being charged for its preparation. In my judgment, even if it were legitimate to charge for the preparation of that document as a separate item of work, the fees claimed would be unreasonable and should not be allowed and the appropriate fee would only be a fraction of that claimed. The master allowed counsel the sum of £3,000; in my view no separate sum should have been allowed. But, as it has been, I will take the fact that that sum has already been allowed into account in my decision on the proper sum to be allowed for the brief fee.

Item 14: evening preparation February 1988   This item has been withdrawn and is clearly covered by the refreshers charged.

Second leading counsel
Item 1: perusing and advising 8 July 1987   This item has been bedevilled by inaccurate information which was given to the taxing master and, initially, to this court. It now appears that, following the authorisation given in March, a brief was delivered to the second leader, and entered by his clerk, on 6 April 1987. At that stage the brief consisted only of a backsheet. The second leader did not himself accept the brief at that stage; he wanted to know more about what was involved before he did so. The solicitors started to deliver the papers in the case to him in June and he started to work on them. By 8 July he reckons that he had already worked the equivalent of seven days on them. At the beginning of July pursuant to a certificate dated 7 July 1987 the second leader was instructed to advise on 8 July in consultation with the other three counsel and they did so. The second leader has claimed to be paid £9,800 for this work and the master allowed £500. In so far as the work amounted to preparation, it was the same work as was required for preparation for the representation of the plaintiff and therefore falls to be remunerated by the brief fee. If it were to be separately remunerated, then the sum allowed would have to be taken into account when assessing the brief fee so as to avoid remunerating the same work twice. The second leader has said that part of the preparatory work was concerned with satisfying himself that he should accept the brief. This does not alter the position: he did accept the brief and will receive the brief fee. If he had declined the brief he would not have been entitled to any remuneration. The approach of the taxing master was correct and the relevant question on this item therefore is what the second leader should be allowed for advising in consultation. The consultation lasted 1½ hours and involved a review of the plaintiff's preparations for the trial. With some hesitation, I consider that the second leader's fee for this consultation, having regard to the importance and scope of the advice that he was being asked to give, should be increased to £1,000.

Items 3 and 4: advising (sic) with experts on two Sundays in

October   These items are examples of the work which has to be done during the course of a heavy trial and fall to be remunerated by the brief fee and refreshers. The master in fact allowed £1,050 for these two items. I do not consider that any higher fee should be allowed.

Items 5, 6, 7 and 10: preparations and perusals   These items are covered by what I have said earlier and were properly disallowed as separate items by the taxing master.

Items 8 and 9: perusal and the preparation of the final submissions   These items are the equivalent of item 13 for the first leader. Here the taxing master has again allowed an "enhanced" fee of £3,000. For the same reasons as I have given earlier, I do not consider that this figure should be increased.

First junior counsel
The only items which the first junior claims which concern the trial period are 60A and 61. Both were correctly disallowed by the taxing master, item 61 because it was never in the bill and item 60A because it was an example of counsel conferring with an expert without separate instructions and could not therefore support any separate fee. The first junior has also drawn attention to the work that he did during January 1988 in preparation for the final submissions and asks that this be taken into account in assessing his brief fee. The amount of time that he devoted to the case during that month appears to be significantly less than that of the leaders.

Second junior counsel
She did not ask for reasons and has not sought to raise any point before me except the parity of her brief fee with that of the first junior. They have each been allowed refreshers at £500 per day and she originally put in her brief fee at £65,000 against the first junior's £117,500. The master clearly recognised that such a distinction between them was not justified and, although he reduced the first junior's fee to £47,500, he only reduced her fee to £45,000. I have no particulars beyond what appears in the solicitors' bill and the objections regarding her individual contribution to the case.

The brief fees
Approaching the matter in the way that I have indicated, I consider that all the brief fees should be the subject of further revision even though the original claims of counsel overall were clearly excessive. It must be remembered that these fees relate back to 1987 and that, although this was a heavy case, it was in no way unique and ought to have imposed upon counsel no greater a burden of work and expertise than a number of other heavy civil cases. Counsel already command a high level of remuneration and it should not be further increased save for good reason. The first leader and the first junior have correctly pointed out that they were retained from an early date and were originally expecting a trial in 1986 or early 1987 and

consequently suffered as a result of the successive adjournments. But the brief fee can only remunerate counsel for the work done on the brief delivered and lost opportunities can only be taken into account as a general background fact to the level of barristers' fees overall in the same way as their overhead expenses and lost time. It is however legitimate for counsel, once his brief has been delivered and accepted, to point to the commitment of time that it involves both for preparation and in the reservation of time for the trial. In assessing the brief fee one also has to take into account what will be earned by way of refreshers and what will be the totality of the work that will be required from counsel in the proper discharge of their obligations to protect the interests of their client and the extent to which that work will not be separately remunerated.

Having regard to these matters and the factors listed in paragraph 1(2) of Part I of Appendix 2 to Order 62, I consider that the proper brief fees to be allowed to counsel for the plaintiff in this action are:

First leading counsel	£125,000
Second leading counsel	£125,000
First junior counsel	£70,000
Second junior counsel	£50,000.

I have not been asked to make any distinction between the two leaders and have not done so; their positions were slightly different but in the result the differences broadly cancelled out. As regards the juniors, since they are both receiving the same refreshers, I consider that there should be a difference in favour of the first junior to reflect his seniority and the greater responsibility that he had for the conduct of the case.

I appreciate that I am differing from the assessment of an experienced taxing master and have only done so after consulting my assessors and because I consider that additional factors should be taken into account.

Remaining items

I will go through these in the order in which they occur in Mr Birts's schedule.

Item 4   Disallowed, covered by the brief fee.

Items 5 and 6   Disallowed, covered by the brief fee; no separate instructions.

Item 8   Disallowed, covered by the brief fee and refreshers.

Item 13   Allowed at £3,000 in accordance with Master Prince's decision; see above.

Item (1)   Allowed at £1,000; see above.

Items (3) and (4)   Allowed by the master at £450 and £600 respectively; see above.

Items (5) to (8)   Disallowed, covered by the brief fee and refreshers.

Item (9)   Allowed at £3,000 in accordance with Master Prince's decision; see above.

Item (10)   Disallowed, covered by the brief fee and refreshers.

Item (11)   Appeal withdrawn, allowed at £16,000.

Item 12   This item does not appear on any bill and was correctly disallowed.

Item 16   This item does not appear in the bill and was correctly disallowed.

Item 17   Allowed at £65.

Item 18   Allowed at £2,000; this item related to perusing the documents in the *Kinnear* action which was additional work necessary for the conduct of the plaintiff's case in the present action; it has not been separately remunerated and was authorised by the Legal Aid Board; the claim for £5,000 has not been substantiated and, on the evidence available, no more than £2,000 can be justified. In my judgment the taxing master was wrong wholly to disallow it.

Item 20   Allowed at £250: the taxing master's assessment cannot be said to be outside the appropriate range for 1986 (see *Simpsons Motor Sales (London) Ltd* v *Hendon Corp* [1964] 3 All ER 833, [1965] 1 WLR 112).

Items 60A and 61   Disallowed, covered by the brief fee and refreshers; besides, item 61 was not in the bill.

Order accordingly.

Peter Birts QC and *Simon Browne* (instructed by *Teacher Stern Selby*) for the plaintiff.

TABLE OF ITEMS

	Objection no	Nature of item and date work done	Amount claimed in bill	Amount allowed (before review)	Judge
Solicitors	1	Uplift: Bill A		100%	
		8 November 1982–15 June 1988	200%	(125%)	125%
	2	Uplift: Bill B		100%	
		22 October 1985–14 November 1985	200%	(125%)	100%
	3	Uplift: Bill C		100%	
		December 1986–February 1987	200%	(125%)	100%
First leading counsel	4	Preparation			
		30 June 1986–13 July 1987	£56,000	nil	nil
	5	Consultation (with second leading counsel) 30 July 1987	£525	nil	nil
	6	Consultation (with second leading counsel) 21 September 1987	£600	nil	nil
		Consultation (with second leading counsel) 24 September 1987	£225	nil	nil
	7	Brief fee on trial		£95,000	
		5 October 1987	£130,000	(£50,000)	£125,000

	Objection no	Nature of item and date work done	Amount claimed in bill	Amount allowed (before review)	Judge
	8	Preparation (one day) 13 November 1987	£1,000	nil	nil
	13	Preparation of final submissions 3–31 January 1988	£20,650	£3,000 (nil)	£3,000
	14	Preparation (evening) 2 February 1988 3 February 1988 4 February 1988	£250 £250 £250	nil	nil
Second leading counsel	(1) 8 July 1987	Perusing and advising (seven days)	£9,800	£500	£1,000
	(2)	Brief fee on trial 5 October 1987	£130,000	£95,000 (£50,000)	£125,000
	(3)	Advising (with Professor Menkes) 11 October 1987	£1,050	£450	£450
	(4)	Advising (with Dr Barrie) 25 October 1987	£1,200	£600	£600
	(5)	Preparation 12 November 1987	£450	nil	nil
	(6)	Preparation 13 November 1987	£1,000	nil	nil
	(7)	Perusal (one day) 16 December 1987	£1,000	nil	nil
	(8)	Perusal (five days) 27 December 1987	£5,000	nil	nil
	(9)	Preparation of final submissions 5–31 January 1988	£24,500	£3,000	£3,000
	(10)	Perusing/preparation (one day) 21 February 1988	£1,750	nil	nil
	(11)	Joint opinion (one month) 24 May 1988	£20,000	£16,000 (£5,000)	£16,000
First junior counsel	12	Junior counsel's fee 30 July 1985	£500	nil	nil
	16	Consultation (with Mrs Loveday) 9 August 1985	£235	nil	nil
	17	Drafting affidavit 10 October 1985	£100	£65	£65
	18	Perusing papers 1 June 1986	£5,000	nil	£2,000
	20	Brief on application 9 June 1986	£750	£250	£250
	46	Brief fee on trial	£117,500	£47,500 (£25,000)	£70,000
	60A	Conference (with Professor Miller) 4 December 1987	£200	nil	nil
	61	Conference (with Dr Newton) 14 December 1987	£175	nil	nil
Second junior counsel	12	Brief fee on trial	£65,000	£45,000 (£23,000)	£50,000

Pauls Agriculture Ltd
v
Smith and others

Queen's Bench Division
17 January 1992

Judge Peter Crawford QC
sitting as
a Judge of the High Court

Headnote

One of the line of "delay" cases in the early 1990s. The taxing master had directed that "interest on the Defendant's bill should not be chargeable" during a defined period. The entitlement to interest is a statutory entitlement under section 17 of the Judgments Act 1838 and a taxing master cannot deprive a party of his entitlement to that interest. It is permissible under Order 62, rule 28(4) for a taxing master to disallow part of the costs calculated by reference to some or all of the interest that was payable. It was further held that before expressing an opinion framed in terms of a period of interest, it is essential to know the amount of the principal sum upon which interest is accruing.

JUDGE PETER CRAWFORD QC: In this case the successful defendants in an action brought against them by the plaintiffs appeal from a judgment of the chief taxing master, Master Hurst, in relation to a determination made by him to disallow part of the costs of the action pursuant to his powers under RSC Order 62, rule 28(4).

The circumstances are that the defendants were initially unsuccessful after a trial which lasted some 50 days and occupied a great many witnesses. There was then an appeal. In the appeal the defendants were successful. Accordingly, they obtained an order for costs against the plaintiffs of the trial and of the appeal. There was then a delay of 10½ months before the bill was lodged for taxation.

Upon taxation the taxing master purported to exercise his power under Order 62, rule 28(4)(b)(ii) to disallow part of the successful defendants' costs. The form in which he did so was to direct that interest on the defendants' bill should not be chargeable for the period from 29 March 1990 until 11 January 1991. The bill was a substantial one. The effect of that finding was to disallow £12,147.71.

From that finding the defendants appeal. They appeal on two grounds, the first relating to jurisdiction and the second relating to merits. As to jurisdiction, it is said the master had no power to frame his order in those terms. In order to determine that point it is necessary to look at the terms of the rule. This provides (omitting irrelevant matter):

> "Where a party entitled to costs ... (b) delays lodging a bill of costs for taxation, the taxing office may ... (ii) after taking into account all the circumstances (including any prejudice suffered by any other party as a result of such ... delay ... and any additional interest payable under section 17 of the Judgments Act 1838 because of the ... delay), allow the party so entitled less than the amount he would otherwise have allowed on taxation of the bill or wholly disallow the costs."

The point is made on behalf of the defendants that the entitlement to interest under section 17 of the 1838 Act is a statutory entitlement, and that the rule as drafted does not permit the taxing master to deprive a successful party of that interest. What it does do is to permit the taxing master, having taken additional interest payable into account, to allow the party entitled to costs less than the amount that it would otherwise have been allowed.

Strictly, the objection taken is a good one in my judgment. What the master has power to do is to disallow part of the costs or disallow the whole amount of the costs. What he may not do in terms is to disallow part of the interest. Nevertheless the distinction is a highly technical one, because what the master may do is to disallow part of the costs calculated by reference to some or all the interest that was payable. Further, the master in this case was alive to the technicality because, at the conclusion of his judgment, he said:

> "If that [i.e. the disallowance of interest] gives rise to difficulty I will disallow a figure. I do not propose to make any alteration to the taxing fee or to the costs of taxation. By adjusting the interest in this way I consider that the Plaintiffs can be no worse off than they would have been had there been no delay."

I think that, if correctly noted, is a slightly unfortunate way of putting it because in fact the master did not state the precise figure that he was disallowing. The intention is, however, clear enough, and if that were the only objection taken to his finding the appeal would fail.

The appeal is, however, advanced on another basis as well, namely as to the merits. It is said in summary that the decision of the master amounted to an excessive and unjustifiable penalty.

It is true, as I have been reminded, that it is incumbent on parties to litigation in the courts at all stages to comply with the rules. The master himself referred to the decision of Anthony Lincoln J in the decision of *Re K (a minor)* (1988) 138 NLJ 262 where he said that it is the duty of the court to ensure that civil proceedings must proceed at a sensible pace and the court must ensure that the parties uphold time limits.

It is also true that some latitude is allowed by the court from time to time in cases of difficulty or complexity so as to permit the reasonable conduct of litigation. In this context I was referred to the decision of Walton J in *Papathanassiou v Dutch Communication Co Ltd* (9 May 1985, unreported) where he made the point (admittedly in connection with rules the terms of which have since been altered) that the stated period of three months from beginning proceedings for the taxation of costs was one which of necessity fell to be treated with a certain amount of elasticity. In making that observation, he observed that he had the authority of his assessors, namely one of the masters of the taxing office, and a solicitor who was sitting as an assessor with him.

In this case it is submitted on behalf of the successful party that, first, "all the circumstances [to take the phrase from rule 28(4)(b)(ii)] do not justify any or any substantial penalty". Second, that the master himself did not have in mind the full or all relevant circumstances. First, I take the latter point. At the date of the master's determination of this issue the proceedings had reached the stage where submissions had been addressed to the master on various points of principle arising on the bill, and the master had given his decision thereon. The application of those points of principle to the figures in the bill had not been done. That was done later by the parties in the usual way, and figures were put before the master again on a subsequent occasion. It is submitted on behalf of the defendants that therefore at the time when the master made his decision he was unaware of the final figures involved in the bill and could not therefore have been aware of the precise implications of the order in the terms in which he made it.

In my judgment that is a sound submission, and it seems to me that before expressing an opinion framed in terms of a period of interest, it is essential for the court to be aware of the principal sum upon which that interest is accruing, otherwise the final result cannot be known and the final sum may be excessive or, on the other hand, insufficient. It seems to me that if it is not possible to determine the sum in some other way decisions framed by reference to periods of interest or amounts of interest would better await the determination of the capital sum.

I now proceed to what is perhaps the most substantial issue in this case, and that is the merits. This was, as I have indicated, a heavy action. Obviously some time was required to prepare and lodge a bill. There was correspondence very soon after the judgment. By a letter dated 25 April 1988, i.e. shortly after the judgment at first instance, the plaintiffs' solicitors, then the successful party, wrote to the defendants' solicitors in these terms:

> "Subject to the outstanding issue of the appeal, we are arranging for a bill of costs to be drawn up and lodged for taxation. Due to the volume of papers in this matter we anticipate that we will require more than the time allowed under the rules for lodging the bill, and we will be grateful if we may therefore have your confirmation that time for our client to lodge a bill may be extended to the end of the summer vacation",

a period of four or five months. This was accepted without comment by the defendants' solicitors, who replied on 3 May 1988 that they had no objection to lodgement of the bill being extended to the end of the summer vacation.

In an affidavit filed on behalf of the plaintiffs, it is said that their letter of 25 April was written by reference to the outstanding appeal; but the terms of the letter suggest otherwise. That tends to show that the lodging of the bill of costs was not regarded by the plaintiffs, at that stage of the proceedings the successful party, to be a matter of urgency. Subsequently, of course, the tables have turned and on appeal the defendants became the successful party. In their case no formal application for an extension was made, but I have been reminded of *Practice Direction* [1986] 3 All ER 724, [1986] 1 WLR 1054, which permits the parties to proceed without any formal application and permits the point to be raised on the subsequent hearing for taxation, which was in fact done in this case. In his decision the master observed that the delay in this case bordered on the inordinate but was not inexcusable. The observation that the delay "bordered on" the inordinate constituted, in my judgment, a finding that it was not inordinate. It may have become close to it, but it was not. The phrase "inordinate and inexcusable delay" used by the master is, of course, one which has been borrowed from other jurisdictions of the court and is in common use. The master held that it is necessary to show inordinate or inexcusable delay before disallowing part of a successful party's costs.

A submission was advanced to me by counsel for the plaintiffs that in so holding the master was wrong. It seems to me, however, that that observation of his went to matters of taxation practice which it would ill behove me sitting in this jurisdiction to disagree with. It seems to me consistent with practice in other divisions of the court, and it does not surprise me in the least that it should be the practice in the taxing office. If it is the practice in the taxing office that there should be inordinate or inexcusable delay before a party is deprived of costs then none was found in this case. Nor was this a case in which any prejudice was shown on the part of the plaintiffs. Indeed none was asserted.

It follows that this is a case where the plaintiffs were not prejudiced and the defendants were not guilty of inordinate or inexcusable delay. What the defendants were guilty of was a breach of the rules; but a breach of the rules which the master found in terms to be excusable. In those circumstances it appears to me to be an inappropriate exercise of the jurisdiction under Order 62, rule 28(4)(b)(ii) to deprive the successful party of any significant measure of his costs. The jurisdiction, as it were, to fine may be appropriate where the delay has been inordinate or inexcusable. Indeed the jurisdiction permits the taxing master to deprive a successful party of the whole of his costs if the circumstances justify it; or, alternatively, a party may be deprived of part or all of his costs if the delay has been shown to be prejudicial to the unsuccessful party in the action. Where neither of those conditions is fulfilled it seems to me inappropriate for the court to exercise a punitive power. Accordingly, in my judgment, this appeal succeeds.

Appeal allowed.

Amanda Grant (instructed by *Russell Jones & Walker*) for the plaintiffs.
M Bacon, costs draftsman, of *Guillaume & Sons*, Weybridge, for the first defendants.
The second defendants were not represented.

Brush and another
v
Bower Cotton & Bower (a firm)
and other applications

Queen's Bench Division
24, 25, 26 November 1992

Brooke J
sitting with
Chief Master Hurst and Mr Anthony Girling as assessors

Headnote

Probably the most quoted case on taxations at the present time. The case decided a number of important matters, perhaps the most important of which is that time is allowed for recording and preserving of information for the proper conduct of client's affairs, but that unrecorded time will only be allowed in any substantial amounts in a most unusual case. The case also held that communications between counsel and solicitors and between solicitors and the court can be remunerated. In the former case simply because counsel does not choose to make a charge does not mean that the solicitor is not entitled to charge for the communication. The case is a refreshing reminder that the courts can and do keep up with changing practice. The danger with the case however is that of simply quoting it as "the *Brush* case" without looking at what it actually decided.

BROOKE J: I have been hearing summonses in relation to taxation of costs in chambers for the last two and a half days. In view of the fact that the points I have to consider raise issues of general interest and importance in relation to the taxation of costs, I am giving this judgment with the consent of the applicant in open court. At the end of the part of my judgment in which I will be dealing with matters of principle, I will revert into chambers simply to apply these principles to individual items in the case.

There are before the court six summonses in six different actions seeking orders pursuant to RSC Order 62, rule 35 that the taxation and review of Mr Alan Brush's legal aid costs in those actions, which was conducted by Master Prince, should be reviewed and Mr Brush's objections to Master Prince's original taxation of costs allowed, and that I should make appropriate orders in relation to the amendment of the taxing master's certificate.

The six actions have been called for convenience "BMT", "BCB", "Racecourse", "Pit No 1", "Pit No 2" and "Bankruptcy". They were all interlinked in the sense that they all form part of the efforts which were made by Mr Brush in the mid-1980s, acting through his solicitor, Mr Kemp, who was the principal litigation partner in Stunt & Son, a five-man firm of solicitors practising in Chelmsford, to stave off personal bankruptcy and to restore his financial fortunes.

In four of the actions, BMT, Racecourse, Pit No 1 and Pit No 2, the plaintiffs were variously Business Mortgages Trust plc or its associated company, Business Mortgages (Midland) Ltd. Mr Brush was a defendant in the first two of these actions. In the other two he was joined as an intervenor, since the actions were brought against one of his companies, Trimvale Ltd, which was in liquidation. Mr Brush was a guarantor of Trimvale's liabilities under the relevant mortgage deed.

In each of these actions the plaintiffs were seeking possession of lands charged under mortgage deeds and recovery of the sum secured by the relevant mortgages. Their claims exceeded £1m. The defendant contended that the plaintiffs were estopped from asserting that they were entitled to possession, and counterclaimed damages for breach of contract and negligence in the region of £2,750,000. The BMT action was treated as the lead action. The Bankruptcy action was an appeal against a bankruptcy order made against Mr Brush in the Chelmsford County Court on 8 June 1987. Finally, the BCB action was a solicitor's negligence action brought jointly by Mr Brush, a Mr Carter and Trimvale Ltd in 1980 against a firm of solicitors who had acted for them in connection with an earlier part of the history, which led to Mr Brush's ultimate bankruptcy. No steps at all had been taken in relation to the prosecution of this action between December 1980, by which time the defence had been served and unconditional leave to defend had been given, and March 1986 when Mr Kemp was first instructed. As soon as the action was revived by notice of intention to proceed, the defendants sought to have it struck out for want of prosecution. They failed before the master but succeeded before the judge on appeal, and Mr Brush was advised by leading counsel in the autumn of 1986 that he had no reasonable prospects of a successful appeal against the judge's order.

The work done by Mr Kemp as Mr Brush's solicitor under a series of legal aid certificates spanned the period of about 20 months between the end of March 1986 and November 1987, and it was an important part of Mr Farber's submissions to me on behalf of the applicant that, at any rate until the autumn of 1986, Mr Kemp was heavily involved at one and the same time in the carriage of difficult issues both in the BMT and also in the BCB litigation, trying to keep a number of balls in the air at the same time.

The six bills his firm presented for legal aid taxation showed total solicitors' fees claimed of about £184,000. About 75% was taxed off, leaving about £46,000 from which the mandatory legal aid reduction of 5% was then made. After written objections had been submitted, about £10,000 was restored across the whole range of objections on review by the taxing master and Mr Brush now seeks a further review pursuant to RSC Order 62, rule 35. On this review I sat with two assessors pursuant to RSC Order 62, rule 35(5) and I remind myself of the provisions of rule 35(6):

> "On an application under this rule the judge may make such order as the circumstances may require and in particular may order the taxing officer's certificate to be amended or, except where the dispute as to the item under review is as to amount only, order the item to be remitted to the same or another taxing officer for taxation."

I will now turn at a little greater length to the facts of the case. I consider that the most convenient way of dealing with this is to quote from the reasons given by the taxing master. He describes the position like this:

> "From perusal of the papers before me, it was evident that Mr Brush has had a remarkable career. It seems that he has had little education but that he was a millionaire before he was 30, penniless at 35, and a millionaire again at 36. He had a remarkable aptitude for discovering land rich in sand and gravel and, by dint of hard work and application, built up a business in recovering these minerals from various sites and selling them. When he instructed Mr Kemp, the senior partner of Stunt & Sons, solicitors, of Chelmsford in Essex, in connection with these proceedings in early 1986, he had encountered financial difficulties, his companies had failed, and he was bereft of funds. In 1980 he was left with three properties, Leez Priory, Woodhall Mortimer racecourse (the racecourse) and the Heybridge Hall gravel pit (the gravel pit). The gravel pit was bordered on two sides by a river, on the third side by a canal, and on its remaining side by land (the chalet site) retained by the Williams family who had sold the gravel pit to Mr Brush. Mr Brush and the senior member of the Williams family, Mr Cecil Williams, were in conflict for various reasons and Mr Williams would not sell the chalet site to Mr Brush, and the gravel pit was therefore valueless. It was exhausted of gravel and waterlogged. In 1979 and 1980 together with a colleague, a Mr Carter, Mr Brush almost succeeded in secretly purchasing the chalet site from the Williams family by negotiating a purchase through a nominee chain of purchasers. Mr Brush's then solicitors, by mistake, revealed Mr Brush's involvement and the Williams family withdrew from the sale. The market value of the land at the time was £100,000. This was the basis of the negligence action against the solicitors who were acting for Mr Brush in the purchase. In 1981 Mr Brush succeeded in negotiating with another member of the Williams family to purchase the chalet site but the price had then jumped to £300,000. By Autumn 1983 the price had again risen, by agreement to £350,000. Mr Brush, however, considered that the land together with the gravel pit could realise a very handsome profit. In order to raise the funds to purchase the chalet site, Mr Brush negotiated with Business Mortgages (Midland) Ltd to loan him or Trimvale Ltd, his company, sums totalling £438,500, on the security of Leez Priory, the racecourse, the gravel pit and the chalet site. Mortgages were granted, sums were advanced, prior mortgages were redeemed

and Mr Brush believed that the interest on the sums advanced was to be rolled up until the chalet site was acquired and then sold with the gravel pit and the racecourse, when all the liabilities under the mortgages would be discharged. Part of the advances were used to pump the water out of the gravel pit and other advances were applied to repaying the arrears of interest and life insurance premiums on policies arranged with the loans. The mortgage offer to finance the purchase of the chalet site was made in October 1982 with a completion date, by when the advance was to be taken up. This date was extended on several occasions by Business Mortgages (Midland) Ltd and arrears of interest accumulated. The last extension to the take-up time expired at the end of November 1983. The delays were due to the difficulties which arose in coming to an agreement on the terms of the contract for the purchase of the chalet site between Mr Brush and the Williams family. These appeared to have been resolved and a letter was written by Mr Brush's solicitors to the Williams' family solicitors on 24 November 1983 and the funds requested from Business Mortgages to complete the purchase. Business Mortgages, however, withdrew their offer, Mr Brush's plans collapsed and litigation, including the claims for possession of Leez Priory, the gravel pit, and the racecourse commenced. Creditors, including Business Mortgages (Midland) Ltd, took proceedings against Trimvale Ltd and against Mr Brush. A legal aid certificate was issued to Mr Brush on 25 October 1985 to defend proceedings in the High Court brought by Business Mortgages (Midland) Ltd for possession of Leez Priory under the mortgage which Mr Brush had executed, and to counterclaim. The certificate was limited 'up to and including close of pleadings, pre-trial review or summons for directions and discovery, and the counsel's opinion thereafter'. The nominated solicitors were a different firm of solicitors whom Mr Brush was at the time instructing, but little action was taken by that firm under the certificate and they have submitted no bill. Mr Brush consulted Messrs Stunt & Son, solicitors of Chelmsford, Essex, in about March 1986 and instructed Mr Kemp, the senior partner of that firm to take control of all of his affairs. The legal aid certificate (together with others) was amended to nominate Mr Kemp as the solicitor handling the various actions on 2 April 1986. On that day Mr Kemp wrote a letter of 35 pages, including appendices, to Mr Brush in order, as Mr Kemp said in the letter, 'to have a synopsis of your situation as I understand it from you at present'. It is clear from it that Mr Kemp had become seised of all Mr Brush's affairs at that date, including his personal circumstances, marriages and divorces, the history of his banking activities, his other financiers, his business affairs and property interests, and his creditors secured and unsecured. The letter also covered details of the various firms of solicitors whom he had instructed and details of his accountants past and present. It included details of the legal aid certificates that had been granted to him and were still current. Mr Kemp asked for £10,000 on account of costs for pre-legal aid and non-legal aid work, but I did not come across any indication that such sum was ever received. Mr Brush instructed Mr Kemp to act for him and Mr Kemp assumed responsibility for the conduct of the litigation thereafter. The scope of the costs due to Messrs Stunt & Sons therefore under the civil aid certificate commences on 2 April 1986 and ends on 6 October 1987. With the end of the action for possession of Leez Priory, the three other actions involving the racecourse and the gravel pit also came to an end."

I will now set out the history. First the BCB action and then the BMT action. In the BCB action the alleged act of negligence took place on 25 March 1980. The statement of claim was served on 2 June. Leave to defend pursuant to RSC Order 14 was granted on 17 December and the defence was served on 23 December 1980. Between 1981 and 1986 the plaintiffs endeavoured to obtain separate representation, which was refused. They changed solicitors but no steps were taken in the action. After Mr Kemp was instructed in March 1986, on 25 March the plaintiffs served notice of their intention to proceed. This was the day when the relevant limitation period expired. On 22 April the defendants issued the summons to strike out the action for want of prosecution. This summons was eventually returnable on 3 July 1986. On 10 June their affidavit supporting their summons was served. On 1 and 2 July junior counsel was briefed and the plaintiffs' affidavit was filed. On 1 July counsel was briefed on behalf of the plaintiffs and the following day the plaintiffs' affidavit was filed. On 3 July the master refused the application to strike out the proceedings but made an unless order, directing the plaintiffs to serve their list of documents by 31 July.

Four days later the defendants served their notice of appeal to the judge in chambers. The plaintiffs' list of documents was served on 31 July. In August instructions were given to counsel to advise and instructions were given to a valuer in relation to the valuation of the land. The defendant's list of documents was served and the defendants inspected the plaintiffs' documents.

On 3 October the defendants filed a further affidavit and also applied to the judge in chambers to strike out the proceedings as frivolous and vexatious. On 9 October different junior counsel was briefed to attend the appeal. The following day a further affidavit by Mr Brush was filed and Mr Piers Ashworth QC, sitting as a deputy judge, allowed the defendants' appeal and struck the action out for want of prosecution.

In October instructions were given to leading counsel but on 7 November leading counsel advised that it was not reasonable to prosecute an appeal to the Court of Appeal. That was the end of that matter and the legal aid certificate was discharged on 20 November.

Turning to the chronology of the BMT action, the action to enforce the security under the mortgage deed was started by originating summons on 22 October 1984. On 2 February 1986 the plaintiff served notice of intention to proceed and on 2 April legal aid was transferred to Mr Kemp's firm, who served notice of change of solicitor. Later in April the plaintiffs served two affidavits, one of them a long one in support of the originating summons. Mr Kemp received notice of a first hearing date at the beginning of May and instructed junior counsel three weeks later. The first hearing of the originating summons was on 5 June. Shortly after that junior counsel, who was pessimistic about the merits of Mr Brush's position, wrote two notes relating to the merits.

On 9 July a long affidavit by Mr Brush was served. On 24 July there was the second hearing of the originating summons, when directions were given for the service of the defence and counterclaim. On 7 October instructions were sent to leading counsel and on 22 October Mr Kemp went with his client to a consultation with leading counsel.

On 4 November there was the third hearing of the originating summons. The master then made an unless order in relation to the defence and counterclaim and further affidavits to be served by the defendant, directing that unless these were served by 25 November 1986, he would be debarred from defending. Discovery was also ordered.

On 20 November leading counsel wrote an opinion advising that it was reasonable to continue with the defence of the proceedings but that the matter should be reviewed after the discovery and inspection was complete. The defence and counterclaim was served on 25 November. This was a very substantial document on which leading counsel had advised. After setting out the history of the matter over the first three pages, there were then pleas of a number of alleged oral assurances given to the defendant by different representatives of the plaintiffs through 1982 into 1983. The events of November 1983 were pleaded, and then a plea that the defendant relied on the assurances which gave rise either to estoppels or to collateral contracts. An allegation followed that the plaintiffs had failed to provide finance for the purchase of the Chalet site in breach of the agreements and assurances and the collateral contracts which had been arranged.

In the counterclaim, following a plea of estoppel, a very complex counterclaim was served, relying not only on breaches of contracts but also on alleged negligence and breach of an alleged duty of care. The counterclaim fell into two parts: part A was a claim for loss of profit from exploitation of the joint site under six different items which totalled just over £1,750,000; part B of the counterclaim involved other consequential losses under 11 different heads, which would total about £1m more. The conduct of the defence up to this stage involved substantial legal and factual analysis which was certainly out of the ordinary.

On 25 November the other affidavits were also served on behalf of the defendants. The reply and defence to the counterclaim was served in January and the action was set down for trial with what appeared to me to be the hopelessly optimistic estimate of five days with a trial date of 19 October 1987. At the end of January the plaintiffs served their first list of documents, which was later to be supplemented by two supplemental lists. They also requested further and better particulars of the defence and counterclaim.

At the beginning of March the defendant served his first list of documents, which the plaintiffs inspected at the end of that month. On 16 April the plaintiffs issued a summons seeking an order for further and better particulars of the defence and counterclaim. That summons was heard on an occasion when Mr Kemp himself appeared on 29 April and an unless order was made directing these particulars to be served by 10 June.

The defendant inspected the plaintiffs' documents on 6 May. On 8 June a bankruptcy order was made against Mr Brush in the Chelmsford County Court. On 10 June the further and better particulars of the defence and counterclaim were served, just beating the deadline ordered by the master. On 24 June the plaintiffs issued a summons to strike out the defence and counterclaim because these further and better particulars were inadequate. On 6 July notice of appeal was issued against the bankruptcy order. The legal aid authorities told Mr Kemp to jog along under the legal aid certificate for the time being. On 24 July he was banned from acting further under legal aid except to oppose the application to strike out the defence and counterclaim and to obtain leading counsel's opinion on the merits of the counterclaim.

On 31 July the master struck out paragraph 35(b) of the defence and counterclaim but otherwise allowed the counterclaim to stand. Instructions were delivered to new leading counsel on 4 August. On 14 August the plaintiffs issued a further summons to strike out the defence and counterclaim for failure to make discovery in accordance with the master's order the previous November. This was returnable on 26 August. On that day legal aid authority came through to oppose the application to strike out. Mr Kemp appeared on the application before the master but was unsuccessful in resisting it and the defence and counterclaim were struck out.

The first creditors' meeting took place on 1 September when a trustee in bankruptcy was appointed. On 8 September notice of appeal was issued against the striking-out order and a very long affidavit was drafted to support the appeal. However on 10 September leading counsel advised in pessimistic terms in relation to the merits of the counterclaim now that discovery had been, for all practical purposes, completed. This led to the discharge of legal aid certificate on 6 October. The original trial date was vacated by agreement. Hoffmann J heard the appeal on 20 October but refused the appeal. So that was the end of the BMT action and also the other four matters to which I have referred, apart from some post-legal aid skirmishes which do not affect this review.

So far as taxation was concerned, when the BMT action was struck out there was an order for taxation of costs in that action. The BCB bill was lodged in May 1988 and the BMT bill in September 1988. There was a taxation hearing in May 1989. Objections were lodged in July 1989, the taxing master conducted his review of the objections at the end of November 1989 and gave his written reasons in September 1991. There followed on 1 November 1991 the issuing of the summons before me.

I now turn to the principles which guide the court in relation to matters of costs. They are of course covered by RSC Order 62. Rule 12(1) provides:

"On a taxation of costs on the standard basis there shall be allowed a reasonable amount in respect of all costs reasonably incurred and any doubts which the taxing officer may have as to whether the costs were reasonably incurred or were reasonable in amount shall be resolved in favour of the paying party; and in these rules the term 'the standard basis' in relation to the taxation of costs shall be construed accordingly."

Rule 17(1) provides:

"Subject to the following provisions of this rule, the provisions contained in Appendix 2 to this Order for ascertaining the amount of costs to be allowed on a taxation of costs shall apply to the taxation of all costs with respect to contentious business."

Paragraph 1 of Part I of Appendix 2 reads:

"(1)   The amount of costs to be allowed shall (subject to rule 18 and to any order of the Court fixing the costs to be allowed) be in the discretion of the taxing officer.

(2)   In exercising his discretion the taxing officer shall have regard to all the relevant circumstances, and in particular to – (a) the complexity of the item or of the cause or matter in which it arises and the difficulty or novelty of the questions involved; (b) the skill, specialised knowledge and responsibility required of, and the time and labour expended by, the solicitor or counsel; (c) the number and importance of the documents (however brief) prepared or perused ... (e) the importance of the cause or matter to the client; (f) where money or property is involved, its amount or value; (g) any other fees and allowances payable to the solicitor or counsel in respect of other items in the same cause or matter, but only where work done in relation to those items has reduced the work which would otherwise have been necessary in relation to the item in question.

(3)   The bill of costs shall consist of such items specified in Part II as may be appropriate, set out, except for item 4, in chronological order: each such item (other than an item relating only to time spent in travelling and waiting) may include an allowance for general care and conduct having regard to such of the circumstances referred to in paragraph (2) above as may be relevant to that item."

The Supreme Court Practice 1993 vol 1, para 62/A2/2 explains:

"The scales which formerly appeared in Appendix 2 are no longer to be applied and the amount of all costs is now discretionary. For assistance in the interpretation and application of the Appendix reference should be made to the Masters' Practice Notes 1986 which were settled and published as a Practice Direction (No 1. of 1986) dated April 9, 1986, see para. 62/A5/6, by agreement between the Law Society and the taxing masters and are applicable to all taxations in the Supreme Court Taxing Office. A Practice Direction issued in the Supreme Court Taxing Office technically has no binding force on taxing officers outside that office, but it is in the general interests of the profession that taxing practice should so far as is possible be standard throughout the court system."

Part II of Appendix 2 recites three initial items, first interlocutory attendances, then conferences with counsel and then attendance at trial or hearing. Item 4 is entitled "Preparation". This is split up into three parts.

Part A is: "The doing of any work which was reasonably done arising out of or incidental to the proceedings, including ... " and then 13 items are set out. I should stress, in relation to what will appear later in this judgment, that those 13 items are illustrative of what is meant under Part A. The fact that any particular item of work is not expressly set out there does not mean ipso facto that it was not reasonably done arising out of or incidental to the proceedings within the meaning of Part A.

Part B relates to the general care and conduct of the proceedings and Part C relates to travelling and waiting time in connection with the above matters.

Finally, I turn to the Masters' Practice Notes 1986. Paragraph 3 explains that the principle provision of the new Appendix 2, Part II is that items which are properly part of a solicitor's normal overhead costs and as such are provided for in his expense rate are wholly to be excluded. Paragraph 4 relates to what is called the factor B allowance under care and conduct, to which I will later return. Paragraph 9 says:

> "... Travelling time will be allowed in respect of each item at the full amount of the appropriate expense rate. Waiting time will be similarly allowed but neither travelling time nor waiting time will attract any allowance for care and conduct."

Paragraph 10 relates to the charging of letters and telephone calls and paragraph 13 relates to properly kept and detailed time records, to which I will also return.

One judgment of the court should be mentioned at this stage. This is the judgment of Sachs J in *Francis v Francis and Dickerson* [1955] 3 All ER 836, [1956] P 87. There are three passages which are, in my judgment, as relevant today in relation to legal aid taxation as they were relevant in 1955. The first is when Sachs J said ([1955] 3 All ER 836 at 839, [1956] P 87 at 94):

> "First, the primary and, so long as the case is conducted reasonably within the ambit of the civil aid certificate, the only duty of a solicitor in conducting an assisted case is to his client. Not only is that the general intent of the Legal Aid and Advice Act, 1949, but s. 1(7)(a) specifically states that saving only certain express exceptions the solicitor's 'relationship' with (which naturally includes 'his duties to') his client remain unaffected by the fact that the client is an assisted person. Indeed one of the fundamental principles on which the legal aid system is based is that the assisted person, his solicitor and his counsel, have the same freedom in the conduct of an assisted case, and are entitled to the benefit of the same relationships, as in a similar matter where the lay client is not an assisted person. Solicitor and counsel have thus to approach the consideration of any problem as to incurring reasonable expense to attain justice in an assisted case in the same way as if the lay client were a person whose means enabled him to fight that particular case in a reasonable manner."

I interpose here to say that, although the events with which I am concerned occurred before the enactment of the Legal Aid Act 1988, the same principle is carried on under section 31 of the Legal Aid Act 1988.

The second passage in Sachs J's judgment to which I need to refer is when he said ([1955] 3 All ER 836 at 840, [1956] P 87 at 95):

> "When considering whether or not an item in a bill is 'proper' the correct viewpoint to be adopted by a taxing officer is that of a sensible solicitor sitting in his chair and considering what in the light of his then knowledge is reasonable in the interests of his lay client. That is, of course, a very different angle to that called to mind by the observation. It is wrong for a taxing officer to adopt an attitude akin to a revenue official called on to apply rigorously one of those Income Tax Act rules as to expenses which have been judicially described as 'jealously restricted' and 'notoriously rigid and narrow in their operation'. I should add that, as previously indicated, the lay client in question should be deemed a man of means adequate to bear the expense of the litigation out of his own pocket – and by 'adequate' I mean neither 'barely adequate' nor 'super-abundant'."

Finally Sachs J said ([1955] 3 All ER 836 at 841, [1956] P 87 at 96):

> "Where a solicitor bona fide acting in what he considers the best interests of his client has incurred expenditure which, unless allowed on legal aid taxation, will fall on him personally, it would be wrong for the court to be astute in seeking reasons to disallow the items, and in particular care must be taken not to be affected by what is colloquially termed 'hindsight'. Indeed, there is authority for saying that as regards such honestly incurred expenditure (assuming there is nothing that can fairly be termed unwarrantable or excessive about it) the taxing officer on a 'common fund' taxation should take a 'liberal view' (per Horridge J, in *Re Lavey, ex p Cohen & Cohen* ([1921] 1 KB 344 at 354). In no matter is this more important than when dealing with expenditure on inquiries, for otherwise a tendency towards 'payments by results' might creep in, which would indeed be contrary to the best interests of justice."

Mr Farber also drew my attention to the judgment of Walton J in *Maltby* v *D J Freeman & Co* [1978] 2 All ER 913 at 916, [1978] 1 WLR 431 at 435, **Costs LR (Core Vol) 64 at 66**:

> "When dealing with the various matters mentioned, the easiest to deal with, because, assuming, as indeed ought always to be the case, proper records have been kept, there should be little room for argument, is of course the fifth, the time expended by the solicitor or his employees. In a good many cases, although by no means all, it is also the logical starting point in that it gives in itself a good indication of the weight of the matter as a whole. I would, however, make one gloss; however meticulously time records are kept, this will always, save in the plainest of all possible cases, represent an undercharge. No professional man, or senior employee of a professional man, stops thinking about the day's problems the minute he lifts his coat and umbrella from the stand and sets on the journey home. Ideas, often very valuable ideas, occur in the train or car home, or in the bath, or even whilst watching television. Yet

nothing is ever put down on a time sheet, or can be put down on a time sheet, adequately to reflect this out of hours devotion of time. Thus it will be a rare bill which can be simply compounded of time and value; there must always be a third element, usually under the second head."

I referred just now to paragraph 13 of the Masters' Practice Notes 1986, which says:

"Properly kept and detailed time records are helpful in support of a bill provided they explain the nature of the work as well as recording the time involved. The absence of such records may result in the disallowance or diminution of the charges claimed. They cannot be accepted as conclusive evidence that the time recorded either has been spent or if spent, is 'reasonably' chargeable."

In *Re Frascati* (2 December 1981, unreported), a judgment in chambers which is cited in the current edition of *Cook on Costs* (1991) p 23, Parker J said:

"The right to charge cannot depend upon the question whether discussions are recorded or unrecorded. It must depend, initially, upon whether they in fact took place and occupied the time claimed. If they are recorded in attendance notes this will no doubt ordinarily be accepted as sufficient evidence of those facts. If they are not so recorded it may well be that the claimant is unable to satisfy the taxing officer or master as to the facts. But neither the presence nor the absence of an attendance note is conclusive. It may well be for example that it is wholly impractical in some instances to keep such notes. In an exceptionally complex case, such as this which is occupying two fee earners there may be short but important discussions in respect of which it would be wholly unreasonable to expect attendance notes to be kept. In such cases an estimate of the time involved is inevitable. The question which then arises for decision is whether the estimate given is reasonable. This is a matter wholly for the taxing authorities. In general, however, all such discussions involving any substantial period of time should be recorded and an estimated addition should only be allowed for short discussions which it would be impracticable to record."

Moving forward another 11 years, in his judgment in *Johnson* v *Reed Corrugated Cases Ltd* [1992] 1 All ER 169 at 187, **Costs LR (Core Vol) 180 at 200** Evans J totally rejected a claim for unrecorded time. He said after reciting the facts:

"In my judgment, the submission that there were unrecorded occasions when chargeable time was spent on these cases must be rejected. This leaves the registrar's decision that in practice, as I readily accept, not all time will be fully recorded, even for those items of work in respect of which a claim is made. But I do not see why there should always be an under-recording. The claims invariably are for 'global' figures, mostly to the nearest five minutes, below half an hour, or to the nearest quarter of an hour above that. No doubt there were some occasions when the period spent was slightly more, others when it was slightly less. There is no evidence that any substantial item was not recorded at all. In my judgment, therefore, this item must be disallowed."

Mr Farber sought to rely on the judgment of Walton J in *Maltby* v *DJ Freeman & Co (a firm)* [1978] 2 All ER 913, [1978] 1 WLR 431 to justify a very substantial claim for unrecorded time. In my judgment, in the light of the approach of Parker and Evans JJ in more recent cases, claims such as this are likely to be viewed with very considerable care and it would only be in an unusual case that any substantial allowance would be made for unrecorded time.

There were four principal issues which arose for decision on these reviews. These were respectively the hourly rate (the A factor), the percentage uplift for general care and conduct (the B factor), the amount allowed for the item "Documents" under the heading "Preparation" and, fourthly, a sub-item of the last, whether dictation time in relation to attendance notes and file notes should be allowed. There were then a number of more general, smaller issues to which I will refer in due course.

I can dispose of the first of these issues fairly quickly. In BCB, the 1986 action, the hourly rate was claimed at £47.50. The taxing master allowed £40.00 and, on review, £43.50. In BMT where the events went on into 1987, the claim was £50.00; £40.00 was allowed and £43.50 was allowed on review.

In *Johnson* v *Reed Corrugated Cases Ltd* [1992] 1 All ER 169, **Costs LR (Core Vol)** 180 the headnote, which conveniently summarises the judgment of Evans J, says:

> "When assessing the amount of solicitor's costs reasonably incurred in a particular case for the purpose of a taxation on the standard basis pursuant to RSC Order 62, rule 12, a taxing officer is required to calculate the allowable costs by reference to the average cost of an average solicitor in the relevant area at the relevant time on the basis of his general knowledge and experience of the economics of conducting a solicitors' practice in that area and without making any allowance for the consequences of inflation in respect of work completed in earlier years."

In his reasons, the taxing master showed that he was guided by *Johnson* v *Reed Corrugated Cases Ltd* which had recently been decided, and he adopted a figure which was based on his experience as representing the broad average direct cost in 1986–87 for solicitors practising in the counties surrounding London. His reasons conclude with the words: "£43.50 is, in my judgment, a fair figure in the circumstances of this case."

On this review, I have had the greatest possible assistance from Master Hurst, the chief taxing master, and Mr Girling, a solicitor of great experience and similar experience in litigation practice in a country area outside London to that of Mr Kemp in this case. Both of them advised me unequivocally that the hourly rates claimed by Mr Kemp were appropriate on the principles set out in the *Johnson* case. The chief taxing master has advised me that it took some time for the effect of Evans J's judgment to be appreciated in so far as it affected the practice of taxing masters and I in no way criticise Master Prince for the assessment that he made. However, I have no hesitation in accepting the advice from my assessors and accordingly I restore the amount claimed for hourly rates.

The second principal matter to be considered is the uplift for general care and conduct, generally known as the B factor. Paragraph 4 of the Masters' Practice Notes 1986 reads:

> "The allowance for care and conduct is intended to reflect all the relevant circumstances of the case and in particular the matters set out in paragraph 1(2) of Part I of the new Appendix. It is also intended to reflect those imponderable factors, for example general supervision of subordinate staff, for which no direct time charge can be substantiated, and the element of commercial profit. Accordingly the allowances to be made for different items may, in the discretion of the taxing officer, be allowed at different rates. In particular it is anticipated that, save in unusual circumstances, the rate appropriate to items 1, 2, 3 and 5 for care and conduct will be less than the rate appropriate to item 4 for general care and conduct."

Item 4, of course relates to preparation. In the present case a claim for 100% was made in both BMT and BCB. The taxing master allowed 75% in each case and that amount stayed the same on his review.

In *Johnson v Reed Corrugated Cases Ltd* [1992] 1 All ER 169 at 184, **Costs LR (Core Vol) 180 at 197** Evans J dealt with the factor B uplift in the following terms:

> "I am advised that the range for normal, i.e. non-exceptional, cases starts at 50%, which the registrar regarded, rightly in my view, as an appropriate figure for 'run-of-the-mill' cases. The figure increases above 50% so as to reflect a number of possible factors – including the complexity of the case, any particular need for special attention to be paid to it and any additional responsibilities which the solicitor may have undertaken towards the client, and others, depending on the circumstances – but only a small percentage of accident cases results in an allowance over 70%. To justify a figure of 100% or even one closely approaching 100% there must be some factor or combination of factors which mean that the case approaches the exceptional. A figure above 100% would seem to be appropriate only when the individual case, or cases of the particular kind, can properly be regarded as exceptional, and such cases will be rare. I am aware that the figures cannot be precise, but equally in my view the need for consistency and fairness means that some limits, however elastic, should be recognised."

Mr Farber pressed for the 100% uplift claims in both the BMT and BCB actions and he referred me to points of similarity and points of difference with the uplifts which have been allowed in three recent cases: in *Johnson* itself, where an uplift of 75% was allowed; in *Loveday v Renton (No 2)* [1992] 3 All ER 184, **Costs LR (Core Vol) 204**, where an uplift of 125% was allowed; and in *Finlay v Glaxo Laboratories Ltd* (9 October 1989, **Costs LR**

(Core Vol) 106) a decision of Hobhouse J, in which an uplift of 75% was given.

Mr Farber referred to these last two cases as weighty and substantial commercial-Chancery cases involving leading counsel and senior juniors. Two particular points he called in aid were, first, that so much was happening on so many fronts with so many deadlines that there was a particular need for special attention to be paid to the litigation. Mr Kemp could never relax, so many balls were in the air at one time. Secondly, having regard to the importance of this case to Mr Brush, the reluctance of Mr Carter, the second plaintiff in the BCB action, to be involved with Mr Brush in litigation, the ever-threatening bankruptcy with its consequent effect on legal aid and Mr Brush's personal family circumstances, the case called for special attention and also required the solicitor to undertake additional responsibility towards the client in that it was necessary to try to shield him from the worry and strain of litigation.

Before I consider Mr Farber's further submissions, there is a helpful passage in the judgment of Hobhouse J in *Loveday v Renton (No 2)* [1992] 3 All ER 184 at 187–188, **Costs LR (Core Vol) 204 at 206** to which I should refer:

> "The outstanding question relates to 'The general care and conduct of the proceedings'. The solicitors originally claimed 200%. On the taxation the master reduced it to 125% and also reduced the hourly rates claimed. On the review after having heard the objections, the master increased the hourly rates but reduced the care and conduct further to 100%. The solicitors say that he should not have done so, that he certainly should not have reduced the 125% further and that in any event the rate of 125% is too low. The master's decision can legitimately be criticised since, if he had previously considered that 125% was the appropriate uplift, he was not justified, on hearing of the objections, in reducing it. The reason that he gave was that, having increased the hourly rates, he should stand back and consider the overall rate that resulted and therefore could properly reduce the uplift. In doing so he considered that such an approach was sanctioned by what had been said by this court in *Finlay v Glaxo Laboratories Ltd* (9 October 1989, [**Costs LR (Core Vol) 106**]). In that case it was stressed that the first step in assessing the proper sum to allow for profit costs was to assess the appropriate hourly rates. The court deplored any artificial depression of those rates; it considered that they should be the actual rates which represented the actual cost to the solicitor at the relevant time of doing the relevant work (assuming always that the solicitor has acted reasonably and that the costs are incurred at the appropriate level). In the same connection the court deplored the use of artificially inflated uplift figures as a method of compensating for artificially depressed hourly rates. The situation which gave rise to the *Finlay* case was a practice which had grown up in the North East of England which had precisely those characteristics: the hourly rates were too low and an excessive uplift was used to mitigate the consequences of those rates. On appeal by way of review to this court, the court had adjusted both the rate (upwards) and the uplift (downwards) so as to

approach the matter in a proper fashion and give to the solicitor the appropriate allowance on taxation for his profit costs. Master Prince was not faced with that situation. The hourly rates were intended to be realistic rates and the uplift was intended to be the uplift that was appropriate to take account of the general care and conduct of the proceedings."

In my judgment, that passage correctly sets out the approach which the court should have to an issue like this in what I might call the post-1986 taxation practice era.

In *Loveday* v *Renton (No 2)* Hobhouse J went on to consider various attributes of that case to see whether it fell into the exceptional category, and Mr Farber drew attention to these by way of illustration of the way in which comparable features were, he said, to be found in the BCB and BMT litigation. First, Hobhouse J said (at 188), that in contrast to *Finlay* v *Glaxo Laboratories Ltd*, "The present case involved work which included the preparation for an actual trial" and Mr Farber submitted that this was the case in BMT. He suggested that a similar situation arose in BCB, where the solicitors were endeavouring to show that they were more or less ready for trial in the interlocutory proceedings. Hobhouse J said: "The volume of documentation was very large indeed and required detailed consideration."

Mr Farber has pointed out that in *Loveday* v *Renton (No 2)* the documentation before the court ran to 100 files. In the BMT/BCB litigation the total case papers, not necessarily those that would have eventually come to the court trial, had comprised 330 files and required detailed consideration.

In *Loveday* v *Renton (No 2)* Hobhouse J continued: "The matter was important to the client, but not exceptionally so." In the BMT/BCB litigation, Mr Farber submitted with considerable justification that the litigation was of exceptional importance to the client. Hobhouse J also said:

"There was nothing to take the case out of the ordinary run of a substantial personal injuries action. The damages claimed [£250,000] in the action were no greater than in many other similar actions."

Mr Farber submitted that BMT and BCB were out of the ordinary run of cases of their type, at least during the period during which Mr Kemp's firm were involved. He submitted that a case can be out of the ordinary not only because of the nature and substance of the matters in dispute, but also because of the intensity of the litigation, and that the damages in BMT and BCB were substantial and greater than in average civil litigation.

Mr Farber was also critical of the taxing master in the present case for two remarks which he made. The first was when he said that: "100% is the level of uplift that I would allow in a case which was exceptionally complex in its content." Secondly: "I must tax the bill on the standard basis and I am in no doubt that the appropriate uplift in this matter is 75%."

So far as the second comment is concerned, in my judgment the fact that the taxation was on the standard basis, as opposed to the indemnity basis, could have no proper bearing on what the appropriate uplift should be for the factor B percentage.

So far as the first matter is concerned, it is true that in *Johnson v Reed Corrugated Cases Ltd* [1992] 1 All ER 169, **Costs LR (Core Vol) 180** it could be said that Evans J was seeking to distinguish a category of cases as approaching the exceptional at 100% and a category of cases which could be described as exceptional, which were over 100%. While not in any way wishing to differ from Evans J, who has greater experience in this field, I do not consider that at this very far end of the range much profit is to be gained by quibbling over the use of words. I certainly accept that, as one gets higher and higher above 75%, more and more it should be said that a case should be approaching the exceptional.

Mr Farber then relied on a number of matters, particularly referring me to those seven principles, which have sometimes been called the "seven pillars", which are described in paragraph 1(2) of Order 62, Appendix 2, Part I. He submitted that this litigation approached the exceptional and justify the factor B uplift of 100%.

My assessors have considered these submissions with great care and have given me their advice. I have, without the benefit of their great experience of taxation, also formed my view of what the appropriate uplift should be and, for all practical purposes, I had independently reached the same views as my assessors. So far as BMT was concerned, there was a very large amount at stake in the claim and counterclaim, although the claim itself presented no particular difficulties. The counterclaim was for a very substantial amount. Litigation was of crucial importance to Mr Brush. It was a difficult case to argue and prepare and to plead. It was based on oral assurances, giving rise to allegations of estoppel or collateral contracts or the existence of a duty of care. It would be a difficult case to argue and prepare not only on issues of liability but also on issues of quantum. It involved, as I have indicated, the perusal of a very large number of documents and it needed intense application over periods of time and very considerable command of the relevant facts by the solicitor who was responsible not only for the tactics in individual aspects of the whole of the work that he was doing trying to stave off his client's personal bankruptcy (and on tactics he would be acting on the advice of counsel), but also in relation to the strategy which should be adopted. The view that I have formed and the judgment that I have formed with the assistance of my assessors is that the appropriate uplift in that case is not the 100% claimed, this case is not in that category, but it should be 90%.

In the BCB case this was a rather different matter. On the face of it this was not a particularly unusual piece of civil litigation. The job of the solicitor was to do his level best for his client, inheriting a situation in which a great deal of time had slipped by and the limitation period was past, and endeavouring to salvage a substantial claim for his client from being struck out. The work would involve the preparation of the affidavit evidence needed to satisfy the master or the judge on appeal at an interlocutory stage that notwithstanding an inordinate and inexcusable delay, the defendants would not be able to show that the delay had given rise to substantial risk that it was no longer possible to have a fair trial of the issues in the action or were such as were likely to have caused serious prejudice to them. This would involve very careful consideration of the issues as to which it could be said that, although oral evidence would be needed of events which had taken place six or seven years ago, there was sufficient documentation available to show that a fair trial was still possible and the defendants would not be prejudiced to an extent which was more than de minimis.

Added to that task which, as I have said, is a task which confronts solicitors fairly often in this type of litigation, was the additional problem that this was running side by side with the BMT litigation. If one fits the chronology in side by side, important events were happening in both and Mr Kemp was having to keep a number of balls in the air at once and also to liaise with counsel and, very importantly, to keep the client in his confidence. In all those circumstances, although initially I was of the view and my assessors were also, I think, of the view that the claimed uplift was grossly excessive, we have taken the view in the last resort that the approach of the master was correct and that this was a case which warranted, so far as factor B on preparation was concerned, a 75% uplift. I would not disturb the master's view of it. I will refer to the uplift on other items in Part II of Appendix 2 in due course.

I now turn to the third principal issue which relates to the time spent in preparation in connection with documents. In BMT there was a claim in relation to partner's time for 742 hr 45 min of recorded time and 158 hr of unrecorded time, making a total of 900 hr 45 min. The taxing master allowed 325 hr of recorded time and no unrecorded time and on the review, although he increased the hourly rate, he made no change to his allowance of 325 hr. In BCB under the same heading, there was a claim for 293 hr 30 min. The taxing master allowed 52 hr and did not change his view on the review.

In connection with BMT, the taxing master had some observations to make about the attendance notes and I will refer in a moment to a specific issue which relates to those. In connection with BCB the taxing master said: "I have already referred to the way the hours said to have been recorded are computed, which in my view are wildly extravagant."

Mr Farber has submitted in each case that the taxing master's value judgment as to what to allow for the perusal of documents and time spent with documents was coloured by his views about the attendance notes and that he gave too much weight to matters in the attendance notes which manifestly were not being put forward as part of the claim under "documents". The master, he contended, failed to consider whether the work undertaken was useful to the client and necessary for the conduct of the case. Mr Farber submitted that examination of the attendance notes or samples of them would show that the time spent was reasonable, the work was useful to the client and was necessary for the conduct of the case and he referred me, in relation to unrecorded time, to the authority which I have already mentioned and, in general, to the judgment of Sachs J in *Francis v Francis and Dickerson* [1955] 3 All ER 836, [1956] P 87.

Before I come to decide what allowance ought to be made for time spent with documents generally, I will turn to the question of the time spent on dictating attendance notes. I should say that in this case (and I have had the opportunity of reading a fairly significant sample of the attendance notes, and my assessors have read very many more) there are a great number of these notes. Master Prince in his reasons dismissed time spent on dictating them as an allowable charge. He said:

> "The time spent in preparing attendance notes is not a charge which solicitors can make as a fee-earner in dealing with a matter under any basis of taxation. The cost of the time must be subsumed in the solicitor's overheads. The authority for this is *Jackson v Parker & Gurney-Champion (a firm)* [1985] CA Transcript 678."

All the Court of Appeal did in that case, however, was to record without approval or disapproval the existing practice. It set out the arguments for and against altering the practice but it declined to express a view even as an obiter dictum, because the issue did not require to be decided and because the point had not been argued before the judge, who was sitting with assessors, and the Court of Appeal did not have the benefit of assessors sitting with them when the point was argued before them.

In *Jackson v Parker & Gurney-Champion (a firm)* one of the specific grounds of appeal was that the taxing master had wrongly disallowed in its entirety time spent by the defendants on the preparation of attendance notes. I need to read in some detail from this unreported judgment, because this point is of general importance to solicitors. Oliver LJ said:

> "Thus we have had the assistance of argument from Mr Cooke on behalf of the Law Society on the point of principle said to be raised by this case whether what appears to be the well-established practice of disallowing the cost of preparation of attendance notes regardless of their purpose or content is or is not justified. How far we can do more than express an obiter view on the point and whether we should do so remains to be considered ... The third point taken and the one on which the Law Society has been ably represented by Mr Cooke, is that, as appears from his written answers, the master, in making the arithmetical calculation, took no account of the time taken in dictating attendance notes. Master Clews had some substantial (and, from what I have seen, fully justifiable) criticisms of the attendance notes in this particular case but, in addition to that, he gave as a reason for excluding them the following: 'Attendance notes are brought into being so that the solicitor may properly carry out the work which he has been retained to do, and like time spent on looking up the law, the time spent in making them is not chargeable against the client. I have not found any authority on the point and I accept that the plaintiff's test – does the client have a right to them or not – is not a conclusive

test of the chargeability of a document ... but I followed what I believe to be the correct principle in the well-established practice.' That it is a well-established practice is not in dispute. It is so stated in *Cordery on Solicitors* (7th edn, 1981) p 99ff and appeared as long ago as 1961 in the fifth edition. We have been referred to various authorities, but none of them is of any real help on the point. What no one has been able to give us any real guidance upon is the extent or history of the practice, the reason why it was adopted in the first instance and why it is adhered to, and the consequences of a change of practice on taxations. Had this point been argued before the judge, who had the benefit of assessors sitting with him (one of whom was the chief taxing master) we should have had the benefit of his judgment and their views. As matters stand the question is, in my view, academic to the result of the instant case. The defendants claim to have spent a staggering total of 243 hr dictating attendance notes – having seen specimens, my surprise at the size of the total is tempered by wonder at the industry – but in comments on an itemised bill which the defendants at a late stage sought to introduce before the master, the number of *chargeable* hours allocated to this head was just under ten and I cannot conceive that, even if any allowance had been made by the master, it could possibly have affected the result, having regard to the fact that the figures were being used only as a cross-check. Mr Cooke, however, in a helpful argument, has urged us to express a view on the matter for the benefit of the profession. 'Attendance note', he argues, is merely a label. It may cover the mere note that an attendance took place with a note of the time taken, the sort of document normally included in any solicitor's file in order to enable his costing clerk or department to make up the bill to the client. It is, he suggests, in relation to that sort of note that the practice originated and to which it should properly be confined. It is something devised by the solicitor entirely for his own benefit and to assist in the running of his office. On the other hand there may be much more elaborate notes – for instance notes of conferences with counsel or telephone conversations relating to offers of settlement and so on, which are either wholly for the client's benefit or which can be said to be of a hybrid type, that is, partly for the benefit of the client and partly for the benefit of the solicitor – for instance, a note which not only records information for transmission to the client but enables any other person in the office who takes over the conduct of the case, either temporarily or permanently, to understand what has happened up to date. The time taken in dictating such note should not, he submits, be excluded as a matter of principle. Each case must depend on its own facts but he suggests that there ought in principle to be allowed time taken in recording and preserving information necessary to be recorded and preserved for the proper conduct of the client's business. He draws attention to the wording of RSC Order 62, rule 25: 'All costs shall be allowed except in so far as they are of an unreasonable amount or have been unreasonably incurred.' Mr Scott Baker QC on the other hand argues that there being, as it appears that there is, a settled practice in the Taxation Office of the Supreme Court, this court should be very reluctant to upset it and particularly should not do so without knowing precisely the ambit of the present practice and having the benefit of the views of the taxing masters. We were at one stage invited to consider whether we should adjourn for the purpose of appointing assessors but, having regard to the time already wasted and the vast expense of this litigation, we declined to do so. In any event, Mr Scott Baker argues, time taken by a solicitor in recording information is, as it were, part of the carrying on of his practice. It is something he would be expected to do in the ordinary pursuit of his calling and is covered by and embraced in the remuneration represented by the profit element or B figure in his costs. He also urges upon us, if any alteration in practice is to be made, to confine chargeability to the time taken in making notes which are strictly and solely for the client's benefit. I confess that, speaking for myself, I find an attractive logic in Mr Cooke's submissions that a document should not be excluded from chargeability merely because someone has dignified it by the title of an 'attendance note'. Having said that, however, I do not for my part think that the public interest would be well served by the pronouncement of obiter views about the correctness of a practice which has stood now unchallenged for a quarter of a century or more, in the absence of a full investigation into the origins and reasons for the practice and the likely consequences of any change. I have in mind particularly the trend of modern taxation practice to simplify the procedure and reduce the expense of taxations and the possible consequences of a change of practice which might have the effect of casting on the taxing masters the burden of considering and dissecting a vast number of miscellaneous file entries in order to assess for whose benefit they were brought into being. The point is, in my view, one of no practical importance to the instant case and, with deference to Mr Cooke and to the Law Society, I feel that I must decline to express any concluded view and leave the matter to be properly and fully investigated, as a matter of law and fact and of practice, in a case where it is of direct significance." (Oliver LJ's emphasis.)

In the present case, the issue is one of direct significance and I have the very great benefit of the advice and assistance I have received from my two assessors, who include the chief taxing master.

Mr Farber has argued before me that dictation time should be allowed in principle in pursuance of the general principles for the recovery of costs, which I have already set out in this judgment. He adopted the submissions which were made on behalf of the Law Society in *Jackson v Parker & Gurney-Champion (a firm)*. The effect of his submissions were these. Each case turns on its own facts but, in principle, the time taken in recording and preserving information necessary to be recorded and preserved for the proper conduct of a client's affairs should be allowed. The phrase "attendance note" is merely a label and notes which are wholly or partly for the client's benefit should be chargeable to the extent that they are for the client's benefit. He submitted that attendance notes such as those in the present litigation which cover conferences, attendances on counsel and client in person and on the telephone, gathering evidence and so on, were for the benefit of the client and they would enable others to take over the case, temporarily or permanently, smoothly and with full information as to what had occurred. He described Mr Kemp's way of working which was to take a jotting of interviews with the benefit of such shorthand he possessed and then to dictate a full note later. This would save time for everybody, and to write up the note during the interview would simply prolong the length of the interview and increase the cost claim. He drew my attention to a longer description of the justification for the chargeability of attendance notes, which is set out in the objections.

Having taken the advice of my assessors, which coincides with the view which I had independently formed, I have no difficulty at all in accepting the principle urged on me by Mr Farber that work properly and reasonably done in furthering the client's interests may reasonably include the preparation of attendance and file notes recording what work has been done. The time spent in preparation of these notes should be recorded. The emphasis must always be on the question whether this work is reasonable. In the present case, I have no hesitation in saying that the work was excessive. The chief taxing master, who has very great experience in these matters, had never seen anything like the amount of detail recorded by Mr Kemp. That, however, only goes to quantum of recovery of costs, it does not go to the question whether there should be recovery in principle under this item. In my judgment, having had the benefit of full argument and having received the benefit of the advice of my assessors, it appears to me wholly consistent with the taxation regime which has succeeded the 1986 changes that the cost of work done in preparation of these notes should be recoverable in principle in accordance with the principles which I have set out.

Having considered that issue, I now go back to the main issue relating to the time spent on documents. My assessors have examined the relevant attendance notes with meticulous care. They have not of course examined all of them but they have examined many, many of them. For my part, I have examined a large file of the notes which has given me a very good idea of Mr Kemp's practice and I have also examined a substantial number of others of them. In my judgment, the claim for unrecorded time should be disallowed. I can see no warrant for that. In relation to recorded time, the taxing master taxed down the claim for over 742 hr to 325 hr. In my judgment he made an underestimate of the time which was reasonably and properly spent in connection with documents and taking into account the principles which I have set out in relation to the time spent in preparing attendance and file notes, I consider that a total allowance of 490 hr should be allowed under this head.

In the BCB action the claim under the same item was for 264 hr 30 min recorded time and 20 hr 30 min unrecorded time. The master disallowed the unrecorded time and I disallow the unrecorded time. In relation to the recorded time, the master, both on taxation and on review, allowed only 52 hr. In my judgment, having taken the advice of my assessors, an allowance of 170 hr is appropriate. I bear in mind what I have said about the scale of the work which would be needed in order to prepare the appropriate defence against the application that the proceedings should be struck out.

I now turn to a number of other points of principle of less immediate importance The first relates to the mark-up in relation to items other than item 4 (preparation) in Part II. The master allowed a mark-up of 33$\frac{1}{3}$% for interlocutory work, except for one situation when Mr Kemp was appearing on his own without counsel in which he allowed 75%. One should start with a norm of 35%. Bearing in mind the view I have formed of the weight of this litigation, in my judgment in general a mark-up of 50% is appropriate in relation to interlocutory work which Mr Kemp attended where counsel had been instructed. Mr Farber has shown us attendance notes where Mr Kemp was doing very much more substantial than simply sitting behind counsel keeping silent. He had an encyclopaedic grasp of all the issues and was able to assist to quite a significant degree in the discussions which took place before and after interlocutory appointments.

In relation to interlocutory work which Mr Kemp did on his own without counsel in BMT, in my judgment a mark-up of 90% would be appropriate. I will come to individual points of detail in relation to BMT in due course but there was one occasion when Mr Kemp took his client to attend leading counsel for the first time in consultation. It was a very important moment in the litigation because junior counsel had, up to that stage, taken a generally pessimistic view of the litigation. The master allowed a 33$\frac{1}{3}$% mark-up. In my judgment a 75% mark-up would be appropriate for that item of work.

I now turn to two matters which again are of some contemporary importance. They relate to the time spent by the solicitors in discussing the matter with counsel outside formal attendances and the time spent in communicating with the court. In his reasons Master Prince dealt with the court first and then counsel. He said:

> "Objection No 23, court – letters out 8, telephone calls 4.   I disallowed these because I did not consider them to be fee-earner's work and therefore chargeable under preparation. This item is intended to cover the preparation of the case for hearing. Such matters as attending court, issuing process or arranging dates and times of hearings are not considered to be fee-earners work. I refer to Order 62, Appendix 2, Part II, paragraph 4, which sets out in 13 paragraphs the work which is chargeable under the heading 'Preparation'. I cannot accept that any of the letters or telephone calls under this paragraph related to preparation as described."

I should say at once that the learned master misdirected himself on the proper construction of that paragraph. As I have already pointed out, the 13 examples are simply illustrative of the matters which may be covered under the heading "Preparation". They do not set out to be all-inclusive. The master continued:

> "Objection No 24 Counsel.   Under this paragraph 25 minutes of time was charged, 25 letters out and 25 unit telephone calls were charged and 10 hr 35 mins on timed telephone attendances. The solicitors set out at great length why they considered these letters and telephone calls ought to be allowed. I reply quite shortly that again in Order 62, Appendix 2, Part II, paragraph 4

correspondence with counsel does not appear in any of the paragraphs. From their appearance in the bill and from the reasons for the objections which the solicitors have put forward, they are quite clearly instructions to counsel for conferences or advices of counsel. In my view, counsel is an expert instructed by the solicitors who have the conduct of litigation to assist in advising on certain matters such as quantum, evidence, documents, directions and merits in a case, and in order to do so he must be instructed properly in writing in full and be supplied with the necessary documents to enable counsel properly to do any work which he is instructed to do. I refer again to the *Code of Conduct for the Bar of England and Wales* (3rd edn, 1985), the same paragraph as that to which I referred earlier: '120. A barrister should be separately instructed and remunerated by a separate fee for each item of work which he undertakes ... ' I accept that there may be occasions when counsel is required to carry out certain work urgently because of a deadline or, for example, in connection with the negotiations to settle. In such cases his instructions should be clearly set out in the body of the bill and not under 'Preparation' and should be contained in either a letter or on customary size paper, to enable counsel to see exactly what he is being asked to advise on. There are many other times, from my experience of taxing bills, and indeed in practice when corrections, clarifications or minor discussions on points which are before counsel can be carried out on the telephone. These, in my view, are not separate instructions and conferences and can only be subsumed in counsel's fees and the solicitor's fees generally in the matter. Counsel has made no charge in respect of any of the matters which were referred to me in this paragraph and, in my view, they are improperly included. I have allowed him 25 letters and 25 telephone calls as a sensible approximation of correspondence with counsel, advising him of the hearings, arranging appointments for conferences and similar matters. In my view, it should only be such matters that are properly included under the heading 'Preparation'. I am exercising my discretion in allowing such items, particularly since they are not included in the appendix to Order 62."

So far as that passage in the learned master's judgment is concerned, it appears to me that he has misdirected himself as to the appropriate approach. Again, I deal with this matter after taking careful advice from my assessors, with which I agree. There may be occasions in the course of the modern conduct of litigation after a set of instructions has been delivered to counsel to perform a particular piece of work, for example to settle affidavits or to settle a defence and counterclaim, that counsel may have discussions over the telephone with his instructing solicitors which may be initiated by either side.

In relation to the charging of these discussions, which are part and parcel of the work which counsel is doing in accordance with his original set of instructions, different counsel may have different ways of dealing with this. In some sets of chambers, counsel may make a note of the time spent on a set of papers, including time spent on discussions of this kind, which he will give to his clerk for his use when he is valuing the total amount of time that counsel has spent on the instruction.

In other sets of chambers I am told counsel's clerk may make a separate charge for telephone attendances of this kind. Whatever may be the practice in counsel's chambers, I can see no reason at all, and no reason which could be properly based on the passage of the previous *Code of Conduct* on which the taxing master relied, why counsel should not be paid for this work without the need for a separate set of instructions to attend a telephone conference. Nor do I see any reason why the solicitor should not be paid if the time is spent in the interests of the client in progressing his case and the work is reasonably and properly done by him and accordingly fits into the principles for the recovery of costs on taxation which I have already set out. I see no reason why the solicitor should not be paid, even if there are no separate instructions in relation to these attendances, even if he receives no separate fee note from counsel in respect of the cost of the attendance and even if it is not apparent from the fee note received by the solicitor that counsel has made any charge at all.

Accordingly, as a matter of principle, there is in my judgment no reason to treat the recovery of costs for time spent in this way in any way differently from the ways in which a solicitor can be remunerated for other work done in properly advancing his client's case. Of course, it may be that some other matter may arise after instructions have been delivered which take the cost of attendances of this kind outside the four corners of the instructions being delivered and will necessitate the delivery of a new set of instructions. For instance, it sometimes happens that events move rather fast after counsel is instructed and there may be a need to instruct counsel to obtain an injunction quickly. Alternatively, it may be that after counsel has discussed the matter with the solicitors, he may point out that he ought to be instructed to do an additional piece of work which is not covered within the four corners of his present instructions. On that sort of occasion, he will need separate instructions. So far as this case is concerned, where junior counsel was being instructed to carry out blocks of work quite properly, and from time to time had discussions with his instructing solicitor which are a familiar feature of the way in which work is now carried on in the process of litigation, I do not see any reason for the restrictive type of rule which Master Prince indicated was the appropriate basis on which taxation should be approached.

When I turn to time spent communicating with the court, I am advised that before 1986, when there was an intricate scale of fees recoverable for different items of work in the appropriate appendix to Order 62, the cost of communication with the court would be subsumed in the separate scale fees. The scale fees have gone and, in my judgment, there is no reason in principle why solicitors should not be able to recover for time appropriately and reasonably spent in communicating with the court, on the same basis as they can recover for time appropriately and reasonably spent in other respects in furthering their client's interests. As I have already said, the lists set out under Part A of paragraph 4 of Appendix 2, Part II is not intended to be all inclusive and I can see no reason in principle why remuneration should not be recovered on the usual appropriate basis.

In this context counsel helpfully drew my attention to a decision of the county court in *Foot* v *Wandsworth London Borough* [1987] CLY 3106. I should make it clear that I have considered the short note of the decision of the county court judge but, in my judgment, the governing principles are those which I have set out in this judgment and I drew no assistance from this case.

I turn to a quite different matter. Mr Kemp was a litigation partner in a small firm of solicitors with a small number of staff and it is reasonable to say from what I have read that his firm was, to a great extent, overwhelmed by the scale of this litigation. On occasion, instead of hiring courier services, either Mr Kemp or a legal executive or somebody else from the office would act as a courier to take papers either up to London or, on one occasion, down to the plaintiff's solicitors in Bristol, because of an emergency. The master totally disallowed these claims which were based on the time spent by the relevant member of Mr Kemp's firm. In my judgment, he was correct to disallow them but he was not correct to allow nothing at all. In my judgment against these headings a notional charge for a courier service ought to be allowed.

Next I turn to an occasion when a secretary in the office carried out work which was appropriate for a fee-earner. What the master said against objection no 29, where recorded time of 79 hr 20 min was spent by Mr Kemp's secretary and personal assistant, was:

"To justify the work of [Mrs H], the solicitors have referred to an Appendix A to their objections, paragraph (xi). Mr Kemp refers to [Mrs H] as his secretary and personal assistant who is very responsible and experienced and could properly be seconded to the temporary category of a fee-earner in collating documents. Mr Kemp described to me the work which [Mrs H] did which this item covered. It was in large part searching through the 45 feet of shelf space of files which the case generated to find documents as and when required, for which [Mrs H] from her extensive knowledge of the case knew where to look, photocopying and placing the copies into ringbinders and paginating them. This, in my view, is exactly the work of secretaries and clerks, whose expenses are covered by the firm's fee-earners' expense rates. Mr Kemp in his objections refers to Appendix F para (xvii) at p F3, but I cannot see anything in that appendix which justifies allowing [Mrs H's] costs as a fee-earner. [Mrs H] is, as Mr Kemp has said, his secretary and personal assistant and as such the expenses for employing her are included in the overhead expenses of the firm covered by Mr Kemp's hourly expense rate of £43.50. If the expenses in employing [Mrs H] are then allowed again as a fee-earner, the firm is receiving those expenses twice over, once in Mr Kemp's hourly rate, which covers them, and once in an expense rate for the number of hours worked by [Mrs H] on this litigation. This cannot be right and I disallowed the objection."

My assessors have looked very carefully at the time spent in relation to this claim. To a large part, the work can properly be described as clerical work and, to that extent, I do not allow the claim. On the other hand, there were features of the work which has been done which would be properly charged by a fee-earner at an appropriate rate. To the extent that the work was fee-earner's work, in my judgment it ought to be allowed. When I come to the schedule, I will set out the appropriate allowance there.

Next there was a claim for £1,500 being the premium for additional professional indemnity insurance. Because of the scale of this litigation, Mr Kemp's firm's previous insurance cover was inadequate in the event that things went wrong and there was a claim for damages for professional negligence. This item of expenditure was incurred to ensure that the firm was adequately covered. The taxing master disallowed this claim. I am satisfied that he was correct to disallow it. In my judgment, if solicitors hold themselves out as competent and qualified to attract work at particular levels, they have got to be equipped with appropriate overheads, including appropriate indemnity insurance, in order to enable them to deal with it. I do not exclude the possibility that in a particular case the solicitor may come to an agreement with a private client who wishes to have his services to cover an item like this, and I do not exclude the possibility that in an appropriate case the legal aid authorities might grant authority. In the absence of any special authority, I am of the very clear view that the taxing master was correct to disallow this claim.

Next, the costs of the objections. The master assessed the costs at £500. As I have said, I have power under Order 62, rule 35(6) to make such order as the circumstances require. I do not consider the allowance of £500 adequate. Accordingly, I set aside the master's assessment in this case and direct that this issue of the costs of the objections be remitted to the chief taxing master for taxation. He is willing to accept this reference. I also direct that the costs of this review be taxed by the chief taxing master and I direct expedition in each case.

I now come finally to a point which arose in relation to the extent of the legal aid certificate in the BCB case. The original legal aid certificate, which was an emergency certificate, was granted permitting Mr Brush to continue as first plaintiff to take proceedings for damages for negligence against BCB, limited to service of notice of change of solicitors, service of notice of intention to proceed and thereafter further inquiries at a cost not to exceed £250 plus value added tax. Soon after that, that limitation was extended to £750 on 8 April.

Having considered Mr Kemp's relevant file notes of his discussions with the legal aid authorities, I am completely satisfied that what was intended in this certificate was that the further inquiries themselves could be pursued at a cost not exceeding £250 or £750, as the case might be, and that the cost of the two notices could be in addition to that.

On 6 May the conditional limitation of legal aid was extended to representation on an application to dismiss for want of prosecution, limited to representation at the appropriate hearings. At one stage of the discussion in this court, there appeared to be considerable doubt as to whether what Mr Kemp was doing was properly covered by the certificates which he received. In *Din v Wandsworth London BC (No 3)* [1983] 2 All ER 841 at 843, [1983] 1 WLR 1171 at 1174 Lloyd J explained the reasons why certificates have got to be strictly construed. He said:

> "I would therefore uphold the master's disallowance of these items. If the result seems harsh, I would only comment that the whole purpose of Part VIII of the 1980 Regulations is to enable local legal aid committees to exercise control over costs. This can only be done if solicitors keep strictly within the authority they have been granted. If there had been any doubt about the extent of their authority, which I do not think there was, the plaintiff's solicitors could have gone back for amendment of the certificate, or for clarification. But they did not do so. As for counsel, a copy of the certificate should have been included with his papers: see regulation 60(2). The construction which I have put upon the certificate is not new."

He explains how it has already been set out in the *Legal Aid Handbook 1976* p 185. Mr Farber suggested that the limitation should only relate to the hourly rates and that the uplift should somehow or other be in addition to the sums listed on the certificate. In my judgment, this is quite wrong. The legal aid authorities were limiting the amount which would be appropriately recoverable to the amount set out in the certificate, whether it was £250 or £750, or whatever it might be for the time being. Expenditure sanctioned in part 1 of the bill (which related to the work for which remuneration was recoverable until the extension was granted in early May) was strictly limited to the costs of the two notices and £750 worth of work. There is no way in which the extended certificate granted later could have retrospective effect to permit the recovery of fees for work which had been done before the extension to the certificate was granted.

Order accordingly.

Martin Farber (instructed by *Stunt & Son*, Chelmsford) for the applicant.

Platt
v
GKN Kwikform Ltd

Queen's Bench Division
24 October 1991

Before:
Waller J
sitting with
Master Prince and Mr McKeown

Headnote

Calderbank offers in respect of bills of costs may be made under RSC Order 62, rule 27(3) but nothing in that rule precludes the making of a valid offer before a bill has been lodged or taxation proceedings have been commenced. The rule sets a time limit of 14 days from the delivery of a bill of costs after commencement of taxation before which a *Calderbank* offer had to be made. It is not necessary to renew an offer made prior to commencement of taxation proceedings once taxation proceedings have been commenced.

---

24 October. The following judgment was handed down.

WALLER J: I was assisted in this review by Master Prince and by Mr McKeown and I am grateful for their assistance. The review relates to an important point of practice if the decision of Master Martyn, the subject of the review, be correct. What Master Martyn decided was that having regard to the change in the Rules of the Supreme Court in 1986, if a party makes a *Calderbank* offer (*Calderbank* v *Calderbank* [1976] Fam 93) prior to the commencement of the taxation, then unless that *Calderbank* offer were repeated during the currency of the taxation proceedings, it is ineffective and something that cannot be taken into account by the taxation officer or the taxing master.

What happened in this case was that judgment, together with an order for costs, was obtained in favour of the plaintiff on 8 July 1988. On 14 December 1988 the plaintiff's solicitors sent a bill to the defendants' solicitors which they received on 16 December 1988. By letter dated 12 January 1989, the defendants' solicitors wrote a letter marked "Without prejudice save as to the costs of taxation" and saying "We hereby offer under [*Calderbank v Calderbank*] £19,115 in full settlement of your inclusive costs and disbursements and VAT". By letter dated 16 January 1989 that offer was rejected. On 15 March 1989 the plaintiff's solicitors informed the defendants' solicitors that the papers had been lodged with the court on 8 March and that they had been allocated to Master Martyn's chambers. On 10 October 1989 the taxation came before Master Martyn at the conclusion of which the defendants indicated to the master that an offer had been made and that on the basis of their calculations, the costs as taxed were below such offer. The defendants on that basis sought an order for the plaintiff's costs of taxation, including the taxing fee, to be disallowed and for the defendants to be awarded their costs of the preparation for, and their attendance on, taxation. The plaintiff's solicitors indicated that they wished to check the calculations, which the master agreed they could do, indicating, as is common ground, that the cost of taxation would follow the event.

It is now common ground that the costs as taxed by the master came out at a figure lower than the offer made in the defendants' letter dated 12 January 1989, but, by letter dated 19 February 1990, the plaintiff's solicitors contended that the offer of 12 January 1989 was ineffective, the bill having been served on 14 December 1988 and the offer not being made until 12 January 1989.

The matter had to be restored to Master Martyn and on 19 June 1990 he found that no offer had been made which imposed a financial penalty upon the plaintiff. The defendants lodged objections to the order of Master Martyn and the plaintiff made answer to those objections. There was a hearing before Master Martyn on 10 October 1990 and the master delivered reasons in February 1991.

RSC Order 62, rule 27 provides:

"(1) Subject to the provisions of any Act and the Order, the party whose bill is being taxed shall be entitled to his costs of the taxation proceedings. (2) Where it appears to the taxing officer that in the circumstances of the case some other order should be made as to the whole or any part of the costs, the taxing officer shall have, in relation to the costs of taxation proceedings, the same powers as the court has in relation to the costs of proceedings. (3) Subject to paragraph (5), the party liable to pay the costs of the proceedings which gave rise to the taxation proceedings may make a written offer to pay a specific sum in satisfaction of those costs which is expressed to be 'without prejudice save as to the costs of taxation' at any time before the expiration of 14 days after the delivery to him of a copy of the bill of costs under rule 30(3) and, where such an offer is made, the fact that it has been made shall not be communicated to the taxing officer until the question of the costs of the taxation proceedings falls to be decided. (4) The taxing officer may take into account any offer made under paragraph (3) which has been brought to his attention. (5) No offer to pay a specific sum in satisfaction of costs may be made in a case where the person entitled to recover his costs is an assisted person within the meaning of the statutory provisions relating to legal aid. ..."

What the master said about that rule was as follows:

> "Regrettably, in my view, the rule did not take account of the common and
> sensible practice whereby, as happened here, a copy of the bill is sent, as soon
> as it is ready, to the paying party in the hope of agreement. No information is
> available, but as the practice was common before 1986, there is every reason to
> suppose that in many cases the costs are negotiated and agreed and no
> reference for taxation is ever needed. Rule 30(3) requires a copy of the bill to
> be sent 'within seven days after beginning the proceedings for taxation' to
> 'every other person entitled to be heard on the taxation'. In turn, rule 27 allows
> the paying party to 'make a written offer to pay a specific sum ... ' expressed to
> be 'without prejudice save as to the costs of taxation' at any time before the
> expiration of 14 days after the delivery to him of a copy of the bill of costs
> *under rule 30(3).*
>
> It is very clear to me that, whatever may have been intended, this new and
> specific provision imposes two conditions: (a) delivery of a copy bill within the
> specified time; and (b) the offer being made within 14 days thereafter. If a copy
> bill has been served earlier, I would accept a letter sent within seven days of
> taking the reference saying that the copy is deemed to have been served. The
> rule makes no provision for informal offers or negotiations followed by a
> formal offer under rule 27(3) later than 14 days nor does it provide for the
> possibility that the paying party may decide to make a later and higher formal
> offer. I was referred to paragraph 21 of the Masters' Practice Notes 1986 (*The
> Supreme Court Practice 1991*, note 62/A2/32). Although I was one of the
> masters who approved that document, I now think it is misleading and reflects
> what was intended and, I believe, stated in an earlier draft prepared by the
> Horne Committee before the parliamentary draftsman redrafted Order 62 in
> his conventional manner. A draft of the revised paragraph 21 is in the schedule
> to these reasons.
>
> In my judgment there was no rule 27 offer and indeed the plaintiff's
> solicitors ignored rule 29(1) which requires a reference to be taken within three
> months of judgment, and also rule 30(3) and, in turn, the defendants' solicitors
> thought they were complying with rule 27 but failed to read it carefully. It
> remains to consider whether the offer in the letter dated 12 January 1989 was
> still open ... " (My emphasis.)

The master then continued to consider whether the offer was still open or
whether it had been rejected by the commencement of the taxation
proceedings. Before us that was conceded not to be a necessary exercise in
the sense that there was clearly a rejection of the offer by letter dated 16
January 1989. Paragraph 21 of the Masters' Practice Notes 1986, to which
the master refers, provides:

> "A party liable to pay costs to a party other than an assisted person may make
> a *Calderbank* offer under the provisions of RSC, Order 62, rule 27(3) at any
> time after the order for costs is made. If no offer has been made before the
> reference is taken, the party taking the reference should comply strictly with
> RSC, Order 62, rule 30(3) and deliver a copy of the bill to the paying party
> within seven days of taking the reference. If such an offer is made the party
> whose bill it is should at once inform the chief clerk who will thereupon stay the

progress of the taxation for a period of seven days from the date upon which the offer was made. If the offer is accepted within that time, the party whose bill it is may apply for the bill to be withdrawn and for the taxing fee to be abated in whole or in part. The existence of a *Calderbank* offer must not be made known personally to the taxing officer to whom the taxation has been referred."

It will be seen from paragraph 21 quoted above, that those who drafted the practice notes contemplated a *Calderbank* offer being able to be made at any time "after the order for costs is made". The effect of the decision of Master Martyn is however that RSC Order 62, rule 27 lays down a strict code under which a *Calderbank* offer can only be made and taken into consideration by the taxing master if (a) a taxation has commenced under Order 62, rule 29; (b) a bill has been sent after commencement of that taxation under Order 62, rule 30(3); and (c) the *Calderbank* offer has been made within 14 days of delivery of the bill.

What Order 62 contemplates in relation to taxation proceedings is the following timetable. First, under Order 62, rule 29 a party is required to begin proceedings for taxation of costs within three months after the judgment or order. Thus in this case, judgment having been on 8 July 1988, taxation proceedings should have been commenced in or about October 1988. No point was taken in relation to the fact that the taxation proceedings were commenced more than three months from the date of judgment. In the light of the taxing master's powers to extend time under Order 62, rule 21 and his powers under Order 62, rule 29(4) and (5), there was no point that could have been taken particularly by the plaintiff who himself commenced and proceeded with the taxation from 15 March 1989.

Second, it is contemplated under Order 62, rule 30(3) that a party whose costs are to be taxed should, within seven days after beginning the proceedings for taxation, send a copy of his bill of costs to every other party entitled to be heard on the taxation, and notify the proper officer that he has done so. Thus, to comply with that timescale, a bill should have been sent following commencement of the taxation proceedings. If those proceedings had commenced in October 1988 as they should have been, such a bill should have been sent in October 1988. If the taxation proceedings were only commenced by the plaintiff's letter dated 15 March 1989, then the bill should have been sent within seven days of that letter. It was common ground before us that the taxation proceedings did not commence prior to 15 March 1989 and it was further common ground that it would have been otiose for the plaintiff's solicitors to have sent a further bill post 15 March 1989 having sent their bill by letter dated 14 December 1988.

What the plaintiff submits as held by the master is that Order 62, rule 27(3) lays down a strict period during which a *Calderbank* offer must be sent if it is to be effective. The plaintiff submits that the period commences with the day upon which a copy of the bill of costs under Order 62 rule 30(3) is delivered at the commencement of the taxation proceedings and ends with a day 14 days after delivery of that bill. If that is a proper construction of the rule, it means, as the master has held, that paragraph 21 of the Masters' Practice Notes 1986 is inaccurate and that any *Calderbank* offer made prior to the commencement of the taxation proceedings and not repeated after commencement of the taxation proceedings is ineffective. Indeed, it seems to be suggested that if there is no delivery of a bill under Order 62 rule 30(3), no effective *Calderbank* offer can be made.

In the master's reasons, he suggests that at the very least there must be a sending of a letter stating that the previous bill is deemed to have been served.

The defendants submit that there are two answers to the plaintiff's contentions. First, they submit that there is nothing in Order 62, rule 27(3) which states that a *Calderbank* offer must be made in order to be effective after the commencement of taxation proceedings. They say, on a proper construction of rule 27(3), all that the words do is place a time by which a *Calderbank* offer must be sent. Their submission is either that the period of 14 days after delivery of a bill under Order 62, rule 30(3) never expired in this case because the plaintiff never sent a bill under rule 30(3), or, if the plaintiffs are entitled to say that it was otiose for them to deliver a bill under rule 30(3) it must be deemed that such a bill was sent once the taxation proceedings went ahead on the basis of a bill already sent. On the basis of these submissions the plaintiffs say that the *Calderbank* offer was thus made before the expiration of 14 days as required by rule 27(3).

Second, and in the alternative, the plaintiff submits that under Order 62, rule 27(2) the taxing officer has a general discretion and the same powers as the court has in relation to the costs of the proceedings. They say that in those circumstances even if Order 62, rule 27(3) has not been strictly complied with, there is nothing to prevent the taxing master taking account of a *Calderbank* offer delivered prior to the commencement of such proceedings within the general discretion under Order 62, rule 27(2).

We have had great sympathy with Master Martyn in relation to tackling the construction of this rule. He recognised how inconvenient it was if the rule had changed the previous practice. The difficulty is that there is force in the argument that the rule lays down its own code because why make specific provision in rule 27 at all if it is not so intended? There is also some difference in language between rule 27(3) and the provisions applicable to ordinary proceedings. The offer only "may" be taken into account under rule 27(4) whereas in ordinary proceedings in relation to a *Calderbank* offer the position is different. Under RSC Order 22, rule 14(2) read together with Order 62, rule 9(*d*) where a *Calderbank* offer is made, the offer "shall" be taken into account. Furthermore, under Order 62, rule 27(5) it is specifically providing that a *Calderbank* offer cannot be made in relation to an assisted person within the meaning of the statutory provisions relating to legal aid.

However, it equally seems a strange and unfortunate construction of the rule that if a party due costs has delivered a bill prior to taxation, but decides not to redeliver the bill once taxation has commenced because it is otiose so to do, he should thereby be able to prevent an effective *Calderbank* offer being made. Even if physical delivery of a bill or the sending of a letter, as contemplated by the master, is not a prerequisite, because it is possible to deem or treat one as having been delivered in situations like the present case, it would still be harsh to expect a party to re-send a *Calderbank* offer in order for that to be effective, rather than be entitled to treat the previous offer as such an offer. In our judgment, properly read, RSC Order 62, rule 27(3) does only produce a time by which a *Calderbank* offer must have been made. There is in fact nothing in the rule which states that it can only be made during taxation proceedings and nothing which says it can only be made once a bill has been delivered during such proceedings. The rule simply lays down the time by which an offer must be made. In any event, even if that were wrong, it seems to us that the very wide powers given under RSC Order 62, rule 27(2), must entitle a taxing master to take account of such an offer when made prior to the commencement of the proceedings.

We thus take the view that the taxing master was not constrained to rule that the *Calderbank* offer made in this case was ineffective and one of which he could take no notice. It furthermore seems to us that there was no necessity to consider whether the offer had been rejected. He should simply have asked himself whether the sending of a bill and the making of a *Calderbank* offer prior to the commencement of the taxation proceedings were circumstances in which he should make some other order than that which should normally have followed in relation to the costs of the taxation proceedings. As we understand the view he formed, he would have disallowed the plaintiff's costs of taxation, their taxation fee, and ordered the plaintiff to pay the defendants' costs of taxation if he had felt entitled to take account of the offer. That being his view, and one with which we concur, we allow the appeal to the extent of making an order as envisaged above and we further order the plaintiff to pay the costs of this appeal.

Colin Nixon for the defendants.
John Cherry QC and *Neil Garnham* for the plaintiff.

Piper Double Glazing Ltd
v
DC Contracts (1992)

Queen's Bench Division
13 November, 23 December 1992

Potter J

Headnote

The taxation in this case arose out of arbitration proceedings in which claims consultants acted on behalf of the claimant to whom costs had been awarded. On taxation the claims consultants appeared on behalf of the claimant. The review considered the position of the claims consultant – whether they were acting as solicitors and the extent to which their costs should be allowed. It also considered the powers of taxing masters to tax such costs.

---

23 December 1992. The following judgment was delivered.

POTTER J: This is an application pursuant to RSC Order 62, rule 15 for review of a taxation carried out by Mr Peter Rogers sitting as a deputy master in respect of the costs of Piper Double Glazing Ltd (the claimant) incurred in an arbitration against DC Contracts (the respondent) in which F Mastrandrea Esq (the arbitrator), appointed by the president of the Royal Institution of Chartered Surveyors in respect of a dispute between the parties arising out of sub-contracts for the supply and fixing of replacement windows, doors, screens and infill panels at Kingsward House, Chicksand Estate, London, made an award in favour of the claimant and, inter alia, ordered that the respondent should pay the claimant's costs.

Preliminary issues in the review raise an interesting question as to the position of claims consultants employed to act for the claimant in its conduct of the arbitration, and, in particular, the powers (if any) of taxing masters in connection with the taxation of the costs of such consultants pursuant to Order 62. Accordingly, this judgment is given in open court.

The claims consultants in this case, James R Knowles Ltd, trading as James R Knowles (Knowles), are a company holding themselves out as offering a complete range of professional services to, inter alia, the construction industry including claims appraisal and resolution of disputes up to and including their resolution by arbitration. To this end they employ a multi-disciplinary staff qualified in various specialities. These include qualified surveyors, non-practising barristers and arbitrators, some of whom have dual qualifications. Any or all of these may exercise their various roles and functions in the course of providing arbitration services including the giving of legal advice, settling pleadings, the provision of expert testimony and advocacy services at interlocutory and substantive hearings before arbitrators, all as part of the package provided. However, in that the services of these individuals are rendered through, and under the umbrella of, their employer, Knowles, and in that their range of services is rendered without any express division of function of the kind encountered by a client who separately employs solicitor, barrister and expert witness, the services provided by Knowles are not identifiably or exclusively the services of any of those disciplines.

The brief history and background of the matter is as follows. There were two sub-contracts concerned, one for the supply and one for the fixing of replacement windows and other fittings on a council housing estate. Both incorporated English proper law provisions and agreements for the resolution of disputes by arbitration, applying the provisions of the Arbitration Act 1950. Disputes arose between the claimant and the respondent, the claimant alleging that the respondent had wrongfully determined the sub-contracts. In spring 1987 the claimant consulted Knowles in connection with the dispute. From that time, until the conclusion of the subsequent arbitration, Knowles acted on the claimant's behalf, to the knowledge of the respondent and later of their legal advisers.

Following the reference of the disputes to arbitration and the appointment of the arbitrator, the arbitration proceedings were finally concluded in July 1990 after hearings lasting for a total of 18 days. The claimant was successful and awards were made in its favour for sums in excess of £118,000. A final award was made in respect of the fixing contract by consent on 2 July 1990 and a final award was made in respect of the supply contract on 4 June 1990. The claimant's costs of the arbitration were dealt with in the final awards both of which were made by consent.

Paragraph 0.3(a) of the final award dated 4 June 1990 provided:

> "By consent ... the respondents shall bear the claimants' costs of these proceedings to be taxed, if not agreed, by a Taxing Master of the Supreme Court, as provided for and where appropriate in Order 62 RSC."

Paragraph 0.2(b) of the final award dated 2 July 1990 provided:

> "By consent ... the respondents shall pay the claimants' costs upon the standard basis to be taxed if not agreed."

By virtue of section 18(2) of the Arbitration Act 1950, those costs fell to be taxed in the High Court.

The total of the costs sought to be recovered by the claimant on taxation was just over £98,000. On 3 December 1990 Knowles lodged with the

Supreme Court Taxing Office an itemised bill of costs on behalf of the claimant which ran to 76 pages. On 13 November 1991 two representatives of Knowles appeared for the claimant and Mr Brown, a solicitor of Messrs Freedmans, the respondent's solicitors, together with a costs draftsman, appeared on the taxation before the deputy master.

On that occasion Mr Brown took the preliminary point that, as the claimant had not been represented by solicitors, the bill of costs which had been submitted by Knowles was not capable of being taxed by a Supreme Court master and that the bill ought to be dismissed as it stood. The deputy master rejected the submissions made by Mr Brown on that point and proceeded with the consent of the parties to tax the claimant's bill. In doing so, he based himself on a fully reasoned written decision of Master Hurst made on 18 April 1989 on a taxation of costs in *William Tarr & Co Ltd* v *Royal Insurance plc* (8 April 1989, unreported) in which a similar point was taken and rejected. That decision has been followed on a number of occasions since in taxations of arbitration costs carried out by taxing masters.

Dissatisfied with the decision of the deputy master in a number of respects, on 2 December 1991 the respondent lodged objections in writing in respect of six matters, which objections were answered by the claimant on 20 December 1991. At the hearing of the objections on 10 February 1992, the costs draftsman appearing for the respondent reargued the preliminary point taken by Mr Brown, submitting that on the proper interpretation of Order 62, the taxing master had authority to tax only solicitors' and counsel's fees or the costs of a litigant in person and there was no scope for taking bills submitted in respect of the costs of any other category of person. Again, the deputy master rejected that submission, dismissing the first preliminary objection of the respondents which embodied it. I need not concern myself with the other objections taken, because the preliminary issues before me are concerned only with the substance of the first objection.

The first agreed preliminary issue is as follows:

> "1.   Where in an arbitration conducted in England or Wales in accordance with English law: (i) a party is represented by a person who is neither a qualified solicitor nor a barrister ('the unqualified person'), but who provides services and performs functions similar to those provided or performed by a solicitor or barrister; and (ii) an award is made by the arbitrator in favour of that party, which includes a direction that another party should pay the first party's costs of the arbitration; and (iii) the award provides for such costs to be taxed in the High Court, if not agreed, as provided for in Order 62 of the Rules of the Supreme Court; and (iv) the arbitration agreement or reference to arbitration contains no provision excluding the recovery of such costs; in proceedings for the taxation of costs pursuant to the award, does the court, on a proper construction of Order 62 and/or Sections 20 to 25 of the Solicitors Act 1974, have power to allow any amount for the costs incurred by the unqualified person in relation to the conduct of the arbitration?"

A second preliminary issue has been stated as follows:

> "2.   If the court does have power to allow amounts for the costs so incurred by the unqualified person in relation to the conduct of the arbitration, are those costs to be allowed or to be assessed on the basis set out by Master Hurst in *William Tarr & Co Ltd* v *Royal Insurance PLC* (8 April 1989, unreported), that being that the costs recovered cannot, by virtue of rule 28(1) of Order 62, be more than the amount recoverable had the arbitration been conducted by solicitor and counsel and, if not, upon what basis should they be assessed or allowed?"

In relation to the second preliminary issue, that was not a matter argued before the deputy taxing master. However, the parties have informed me that it would assist them if the issue were to be dealt with on this review. I have, therefore, heard argument upon it.

The relevant provisions of statute and the Rules of the Supreme Court appear to be as follows. So far as the powers of an arbitrator to award costs are concerned, section 18 of the 1950 Act provides:

> "(1)   Unless a contrary intention is expressed therein, every arbitration agreement shall be deemed to include a provision that the costs of the reference and the award shall be in the discretion of the arbitrator of umpire, who may direct to and by whom and in what manner those costs or any part thereof shall be paid, and may tax or settle the amount of costs to be so paid or any part thereof, and may award costs to be paid as between solicitor and client.
>
> (2)   Any costs directed by an award to be paid shall, unless the award otherwise directs, be taxable in the High Court."

As to taxation of such costs in the High Court, RSC Order 62, rule 2(2), provides:

> "This Order shall have effect, with such modifications as may be necessary, where by virtue by any Act the costs of any proceedings before an arbitrator or umpire or before a tribunal or other body constituted by or under any Act, not being proceedings in the Supreme Court, are taxable in the High Court."

Order 62, rule 19, provides:

> "(1)   Subject to paragraphs (2) and (3), a taxing master and a registrar (other than a district registrar) shall have power to tax ... (b) the costs ordered by an award made on reference to arbitration under any Act or payable pursuant to an arbitration agreement ..."

Order 62, rule 29, provides as follows:

> "(1)   Subject to paragraph (2), where a party is entitled to recover taxed costs or to require any costs to be taxed by a taxing officer by virtue of ... (c) an award made on an arbitration under any Act or pursuant to an arbitration agreement; or (d) an order, award or other determination of a tribunal or other body constituted by or under any Act, he must begin proceedings for the taxation of those costs either within three months after the judgment,

direction, order, award or other determination was entered, signed or otherwise perfected ...

(5)   Proceedings for the taxation of costs shall be begun by producing the requisite document at the appropriate office.

(6)   For the purpose of this rule – (a) the requisite document shall be ascertained by reference to Appendix A1 to this Order ...

(7)   A party who begins proceedings for taxation must at the same time lodge in the appropriate office – (a) a copy of the requisite document produced under paragraph (5) ...”

The requisite document is specified in Order 62, Appendix 1, paragraph 3, which provides:

“Where a party is entitled to require taxation by a taxing officer of the costs directed to be paid by an award made on the arbitration under any Act or pursuant to an arbitration agreement and no order of the Court for the enforcement of the award has been made, the requisite document for the purposes of rule 29 is the award.”

The basis upon which the deputy master (following Master Hurst) rejected the preliminary point taken and embarked upon the taxation, and the grounds upon which the claimant has relied before me, can be summarised as follows.

(1)   Apart from any express or implied limitations or powers conferred by the agreement of the parties to an arbitration, the powers of arbitrators with regard to costs are governed principally by the provisions of section 18 of the 1950 Act (see also section 28). In this case the powers of the arbitrator with regard to costs have not been restricted or enlarged by the agreement of the parties.

(2)   As already set out above, section 18(1) of the 1950 Act provides that “the costs of the reference and award shall be in the discretion of the arbitrator”. This provision empowers the arbitrator: (a) to direct to and by whom such costs shall be paid; (b) to tax or settle the amount of costs to be so paid; (c) to award costs to be paid as between solicitor and client (see generally Mustill and Boyd *Commercial Arbitration* (2nd edn, 1989) 663).

(3)   The “costs of the reference” include all expenses properly and reasonably incurred in the course of the arbitration (see 2 *Halsbury's Laws* (4th edn) para 608 and *Re Autothreptic Steam Boiler Co Ltd and Townsend Hook & Co* (1888) 21 QBD 182).

(4)   An arbitrator must exercise judicially the discretion conferred upon him by section 18(1). That means that, in the absence of special circumstances, an arbitrator cannot properly exercise his discretion as to the award of costs so as to deprive a successful party of its costs of the reference (see *Lewis v Haverfordwest RDC* [1953] 2 All ER 1599, [1953] 1 WLR 1486). Logically, the same principle must apply equally to the other powers conferred upon an arbitrator by section 18(1), including the power he enjoys himself to tax or settle the costs to be paid.

(5) There are no statutory or other restrictions upon the right of a party to be represented in an arbitration by the advocate of his choice, or, indeed, to employ a lay, qualified or unqualified person to represent him in the arbitration and to progress it generally.

(6)   The unqualified terms of section 18(1) of the 1950 Act are wide enough to cover an award of costs in respect of sums which a party is liable to pay for any professional services rendered in the conduct of the arbitration, whether by practising barristers, solicitors, surveyors or other experts, or by unqualified persons who, for reward, perform services of the kind commonly rendered by those persons.

(7)   In this case no restriction was imposed upon the arbitrator by the relevant arbitration agreements or any other agreement between the parties in respect of any of the above matters, nor was any limitation on the nature or amount of the costs to be recoverable imposed by the terms of the consent order made by the arbitrator.

(8)   Section 18(2) of the 1950 Act provides that, unless the award otherwise directs, any costs directed by an award to be paid, are taxable in the High Court. Thus the combined effect of section 18(1) and (2) is as follows: (a) an arbitrator is given power himself to tax or settle the amount of any costs directed to be paid; (b) in the event of an arbitrator declining himself to tax or settle the amount of such costs and giving no direction that such costs should be taxed otherwise than in the High Court, the costs are taxable in the High Court.

(9)   In this case the costs were so taxable, in the case of the final award dated 4 June 1990, by virtue of the order to that effect and, in the case of the final award dated 2 July 1990, by virtue of the statutory provision in section 18(2).

(10)   In carrying out a taxation of costs awarded by an arbitrator in cases of this kind, the taxing master acts as the delegate of the arbitrator (see *HG Perkins Ltd* v *Best-Shaw* [1973] 2 All ER 924 at 930, [1973] 1 WLR 975 at 982 and authorities there cited). As such, the taxing master has no power to refuse to carry out an order for taxation, or to "go behind" the order or award because he considers it to be wrong or "ultra vires" (see *Cope* v *United Dairies (London) Ltd* [1963] 2 All ER 194 at 195–196, [1963] 2 QB 33 at 38, **Costs LR (Core Vol)** 23 per Megaw J).

(11)   That being so, save in so far as constrained by statute or the terms of Order 62, it follows that, on taxation, a taxing master has the same powers to tax and award costs incurred in respect of the services of third parties in the progress of the arbitration as the arbitrator would have if he personally exercised his powers to tax.

(12)   Whereas the detailed provisions of Order 62 reflect the fact that the primary function of that order is to regulate the award and assessment of the costs of proceedings in the High Court, and that the right to conduct proceedings in the High Court is confined to litigants in person and persons acting by a solicitor (see RSC Order 5, rule 6(1)), the powers of a taxing

master are not confined to the costs of such persons when exercising his powers as the delegate of an arbitrator pursuant to section 18 of the 1950 Act. That is because of the express provision made in Order 62, rule 2(2), that the order –

> "shall have effect, *with such modifications as may be necessary*, where by virtue of any Act the costs of any proceedings before an arbitrator ... are taxable in the High Court."

Thus, whereas the taxing master might otherwise be constrained by the terms of various rules and the provisions of the appendices in relation to particular aspects of taxation, he is not prevented from adapting or extending the concept and application of "standard costs" or "indemnity costs" (if awarded) to cover costs incurred in respect of the conduct of the case by claims consultants, such as Knowles.

(13)   By acting as claims consultants in the arbitration, Knowles neither acted as a solicitor nor purported to act as a solicitor within the letter or spirit of section 20(1) or section 25(1) of the Solicitors Act 1974. An unqualified person does not "act as a solicitor" within the meaning of section 25(1) merely by doing acts of a kind commonly done by solicitors. To fall within that phrase, the act in question must be an act which it is lawful only for a qualified solicitor to do and/or any other act in relation to which the unqualified person purports to act as a solicitor (cf *Re Ainsworth* [1905] 2 KB 103). Equally, where section 25(1) provides that –

> "No costs in respect of anything done by any unqualified person acting as a solicitor shall be recoverable by him, or by any other person, in any action, suit or matter",

that sanction applies only to acts which may only be done by a solicitor or acts purportedly done in that capacity. There is no suggestion in this case that, in acting in the arbitration, Knowles were doing an act which only a solicitor might do, nor that they purported so to act. Accordingly, the taxing master was not precluded by any provision of the 1974 Act from taxing and awarding Knowles their costs upon the standard basis, as ordered by the arbitrator.

On behalf of the respondent, Mr Bowdery does not take substantial issue with any of the propositions above enumerated from (1) to (10) inclusive. However, in relation to proposition (11), he does not accept that the taxing master has the same powers to tax and award costs as the arbitrator would have if he exercised his powers personally. He submits that the terms of Order 62, which is intended to be a complete code as to costs in relation to High Court proceedings, anticipate that the taxing master will engage only in the award and assessment of solicitors' costs and disbursements (including experts' fees and the fees of counsel) and "litigant in person" costs and disbursements, and that his powers of taxation do not extend to costs incurred by non-solicitor representatives acting as if they were solicitors. He further submits that the intention and proper construction of the words of

Order 62, rule 2(2), that "This Order shall have effect, with such modifications as may be necessary" are not such as to import the major change in the basis or methods of taxation which he submits would be required to accommodate the assessment and award of such costs. He says that those words are included in the text of the rule simply to enable the machinery set out in Order 62 to be applied to the taxation of costs in respect of proceedings before an arbitrator or other tribunal with the minimum necessary changes mutatis mutandis in the subsequent wording of the order, rather than to make any changes of substance in the method of taxation. By way of example he argues that a modification is obviously required to the words of Order 62, rule 12 (in which the "standard" basis and the "indemnity" basis of taxation are provided for) in relation to the provision at paragraph (3) that:

> "Where the Court makes an order for costs without indicating the basis of taxation ... the costs shall be taxed on the standard basis."

There, says Mr Bowdery, the word "court" should be read as "arbitrator" or "umpire". He submits that, in the absence of express language, the court should be reluctant to adopt any construction of Order 62, rule 2(2), the result of which would be to alter the customary methods of taxation, in the sense that the taxing master would be obliged to engage in the unaccustomed exercise of reviewing the reasonableness of charges incurred by non-lawyers acting as lawyers and persons exercising multi-disciplinary functions. He makes the point that the authority of *HG Perkins Ltd* v *Best-Shaw* [1973] 2 All ER 924, while making clear that the taxing master acts as the delegate of the arbitrator, also held that an order by an arbitrator directing taxation in the High Court meant that the taxing master must carry out the taxation pursuant to Order 62 and did not have any discretion to tax in any other way. I pause to observe that, that being so, it is an authority which begs the question posed in this preliminary issue, rather than answering it.

Mr Bowdery does not resile from his acceptance that a claimant in an arbitration who employs a non-qualified representative is entitled to be awarded the costs thereby incurred, but he submits that, where such award is sought, the proper mode of obtaining it is to seek an order for taxation *by the arbitrator himself*, or by some other competent delegate whose jurisdiction or powers are not circumscribed by the terms of Order 62. However, he argues, if the arbitrator orders a High Court taxation, or makes no special provision, then an award of such costs is outside the purview of Order 62.

In sum, Mr Bowdery submits that in a taxation pursuant to Order 62, rule 19(1)(b), the proper interpretation of Order 62, rule 2(2) does not allow for the creation of a third category of recoverable costs, namely the costs of a non-solicitor representative and submits that such fees are only recoverable to the extent that they may be properly awarded as the disbursements of a litigant in person as provided for in Order 62, rule 18(1) and (2).

Finally, Mr Bowdery submits that to hold otherwise, and to interpret the powers of the taxing master as extending to an award and taxation of costs on the standard basis in respect of the costs of a claims consultant, would be to adopt an interpretation which is in breach of the Solicitors Act 1974 and, in particular, in breach of section 25(1), which provides that no costs in respect of anything done by any unqualified person acting as a solicitor shall be recoverable by him or any other person in any action, suit or matter.

I do not consider that Mr Bowdery's submissions are correct. So far as Order 62, rule 2(2) is concerned, I see no reason to place the narrow construction for which he contends on the words "with such modifications as may be necessary". In my opinion, to adopt such a construction would be to negate in an important respect and in an unjust manner the intention of section 18(2) of the 1950 Act that any costs directed to be paid by the award of an arbitrator should be taxable in the High Court. Given the freedom of any party to an arbitration to employ a lay or non-qualified representative to conduct his case, given the power of the arbitrator to make an order in respect of the costs of such a representative and given that the taxing master, in effecting the taxation, is the delegate of the arbitrator in that task, it seems to me that there are no compelling reasons for adopting the construction contended for by Mr Bowdery. Indeed, quite the reverse.

Further, in so far as Mr Bowdery's submission depends upon an assumption that taxing masters are on unfamiliar ground when considering the charges of persons other than solicitors, as I understand the position that is not so. Taxing masters frequently consider the charges of all kinds of professional and non-professional people as well as those of lawyers in other jurisdictions, and they are becoming increasingly experienced in that kind of exercise.

I would add that, if the court were driven to adopt Mr Bowdery's approach, it would effect a considerable injustice in this case. It is quite apparent that the respondent was aware throughout this case of costs being incurred by the claimant in employing Knowles as its representative and it is also clear that, at the time the final awards were drawn up by consent, including the provisions as to costs, no reservation was made as to the point later taken. One cannot but conclude that to adopt Mr Bowdery's arguments would be to achieve an effect quite contrary to the arbitrator's intention and understanding in making his award as well as that of the claimant. However, whether or not that is so, I have no hesitation in upholding the decision of the deputy master on this aspect on the basis of principle and construction.

Whereas the code contained in Order 62 is primarily a code for the taxation of costs in the High Court, Order 62, rule 2 plainly comprehends the process of taxation applying to quite other proceedings, whether before an arbitrator, a tribunal or other body constituted by or under any Act in relation to which the rights of audience and rules of procedure may be substantially different from High Court proceedings. In providing for such modifications "as may be necessary", the necessity referred to, in my view, anticipates such modification to the rules as may be necessary to give full and proper effect to any costs order made by the arbitrator or other tribunal and to the presumed intention of such order to make a real and effective award of costs to the party in whose favour such order has been made. After all, in principle it is the purpose of a costs order to effect reimbursement to the successful party of all costs properly and reasonably incurred in the proceedings.

Order 62, rule 12, which sets out two bases of taxation (the standard basis and the indemnity basis) by which such purpose is to be achieved, does so, not by reference to the identity or profession of the person in respect of whose services the costs have been incurred, but simply by reference (in the case of an order for costs on the standard basis) to "a reasonable amount in respect of all costs reasonably incurred". Later references in the rules and appendices to solicitors and counsel are no more than the product of the de facto position as to rights of audience and the right to appear on the record in the High Court. They should not, in my view, be regarded as limiting the scope of the words in Order 62, rule 2(2), which provide for such modifications as are necessary. Where, in proceedings in other forums, reasonable costs may reasonably have been incurred, there seems to me no reason in policy or logic why the power of the taxing master should be limited in the way contended for by Mr Bowdery.

I also reject the submission that so to hold would be, in effect, to adopt an interpretation which is in breach of the 1974 Act. While I do not doubt that costs incurred in an arbitration are indeed costs incurred "in any action, suit or matter", and while it also appears to be the position that acts done by representatives of Knowles in this context were acts by "unqualified persons" so far as the Solicitors Act is concerned, it does not appear to me that they were "anything done by [such persons] *acting as a solicitor*".

So far as I am aware, Knowles have not at any stage held themselves out as solicitors, but have at all times acted specifically as "claims consultants" in relation to their representation of the claimant. Section 25 of the 1974 Act is linked and, in my view, falls to be construed with the sections which precede it. Those sections are penal in nature and relate to unqualified persons acting as solicitors (section 20), pretending to be solicitors (section 21), drawing or preparing instruments of transfer of charge etc., the drawing of which is limited to solicitors and certain other exempted professions (section 22), and preparing papers for probate etc (section 23). By section 24 those penal provisions are applied to bodies corporate. In these circumstances, it seems clear to me that the words "acting as a solicitor" are limited to the doing of acts which only a solicitor may perform and/or the doing of acts by a person pretending or holding himself out to be a solicitor. Such acts are not to be confused with the doing of acts of a kind commonly done by solicitors, but which involve no representation that the actor is acting as such. On that basis, it seems plain to me that Knowles did not "act as a solicitor" in conducting the arbitration on behalf of the claimant.

Accordingly, on the basis of the facts existing in this case, I answer the first preliminary issue in the affirmative.

So far as the second preliminary issue is concerned, after careful thought, I consider that the first part is stated in a matter too general to be susceptible of a "Yes" or "No" answer and that the second part is, similarly, too generally phrased to be susceptible of a clear cut answer, divorced from the context of particular items claimed and/or challenged in the bill of costs.

The taxation of a bill is not dealt with, or indeed reviewed, on a global basis. The sum eventually certified is the build-up of a number of items conventionally set out in the bill on the lines provided for in Order 62, Appendix 2, paragraph 1(3), Part 2. Whether the taxation is conducted on the standard basis or the indemnity basis, each item is discretionary and assessed as a reasonable amount to be allowed for the item of work done or the disbursement made, assessed on the basis of a competent solicitor (whether partner or assistant), counsel or expert, acting within the scope of his own expertise and taking into account the generally accepted level of charges appropriate for the services rendered at the relevant time.

In so far as the taxing master may, in the case of a claims consultant, be considering a new and/or unconventional breed of litigator, it may be that the taxing master will consider that some difference of approach will be called for, not least to accommodate the extent to which, in relation to various items of work, it might be the case that the fee earner concerned has acted in a multi-disciplinary capacity. It might be, at least in theory, that in performing a particular task, the fee earner has in effect done two jobs at the same time and saved money for the client. On that basis, it might be, again at least in theory, that the taxing master would consider it appropriate to allow a charging rate for the single fee earner higher than the rate which might have been allowed in respect of two individual fee earners jointly rendering the same service. On the other hand, it may well be that a lower charging rate or fee will be considered appropriate in the case of an employee of a claims consultant who the master considers lacks the expertise of a conventional qualified fee earner or otherwise provides a less valuable service. If the employment of claims consultants becomes widespread in the arbitration field, it may be that the taxation of their bills will become a developing science, in relation to which taxing masters will consider that particular scales or methods of charge, different from those developed in relation to solicitors, are appropriate.

Whether or not that is so, I have no doubt that taxing masters will and should be reluctant to develop or apply scales of charges, or indeed any approach to the taxation of the costs of claims consultants, which might lead to any overall increase in the costs of arbitration.

Plainly, Order 62, rule 18(1) envisages that a litigant in person cannot recover more than it would have cost if the services of a solicitor had been employed; paragraph (2), which limits the amount allowed in respect of any item (save for any disbursement) to two-thirds of a solicitor's proper charge, is a rule-of-thumb measure aimed at deducting the profit element in the solicitor's bill. By analogy, it may be thought inappropriate that the fees of a claims consultant, whether charged on a fixed fee basis, or by the hour, or as a basic fee plus a percentage, should be taxed so as to produce a result which removes the de facto protection hitherto afforded to a paying party by the unspoken assumption in Order 62 that a solicitor's reasonable charges (subject to taxation) represent the maximum amount of costs recoverable. Equally, it would appear anomalous to sanction as reasonable a bill which in total exceeds the reasonable charges allowable to a solicitor for his services, not least because those services are provided subject to valuable regulatory controls and professional obligations of a kind which are unlikely to be applicable to an incorporated company of claims consultants.

Having said that, it does not seem to me that it is appropriate for the court to come to any decision, or to give any direction in general terms, about the "ceiling" of the sums to be assessed on such taxations, beyond reiterating that the definition of the scales of standard and indemnity costs contained in Order 62, rule 12(1) and (2), should continue to be applied by taxing masters in relation to the taxation of costs under Order 62, rule 2, notwithstanding that the costs may be wholly or principally the costs of employing claims consultants such as Knowles. For the reasons I have indicated, I do not doubt that, on any such taxation, a critical approach will be properly adopted in any case where a taxing master is faced with an itemised bill which appears to him to have been drawn on a basis more costly than the reasonable cost of conducting an arbitration through a solicitor. More than that it does not seem to me appropriate to say, outside the confines of a review relating to specific items claimed or challenged on taxation.

Accordingly, beyond the guidance to be derived from the observations above, the court declines to answer the question posed in the second preliminary issue.

Order accordingly.

Martin Bowdery (instructed by *Freedmans*) for the respondent.
Derrick Turriff (instructed by *Alexander Tatham & Co*, Manchester) for the claimant.

Ridehalgh
v
Horsefield and another and other appeals

Court of Appeal, Civil Division
14–17, 20, 21 December 1993, 26 January 1994

Sir Thomas Bingham MR, Rose and Waite LJJ

Headnote

This is the leading case on the principles to be applied in deciding whether to make a "wasted costs" order under Order 62, rules 10(1) and 28(1). The judgment of Sir Thomas Bingham MR has particular value in defining the circumstances in which such orders should, or should not, be made.

26 January 1994. The following judgment of the court was delivered.

SIR THOMAS BINGHAM MR: This is the judgment of the court. Different sections of the judgment have been written by different members. Each of us concurs fully in all sections.

There are six appeals before the court. All of them (save one, in which this issue has been compromised) raise the same question: in what circumstances should the court make a wasted costs order in favour of one party to litigation against the legal representative (counsel or solicitor) of the other? It is a question of great and growing significance. It is desirable that this court should give such guidance as it can.

Two of the cases before us come on appeal from the county court. Three come on appeal from the High Court, one from each division. In all of these cases wasted costs orders were made and the legal representatives who were the subject of the orders appeal. In the remaining case, the issue first arose in this court: on allowing an appeal against the decision of a county court, the court invited the solicitors who had acted for the parties in the court below to show cause why they should not be ordered personally to pay the costs thrown away. The solicitors have appeared by counsel in this court in response to that invitation.

Since the question raised by these appeals is of general concern to their members, both the Law Society and the General Council of the Bar sought and were granted leave to make submissions to the court. Since the question is also of concern to the public, we offered the Attorney General a similar opportunity, of which he took advantage, and counsel were accordingly instructed to represent the wider public interest. All the parties to the six appeals were also represented, save for one party in the compromised appeal. We gratefully acknowledge the help we have had from all solicitors and counsel involved in mounting and presenting these cases.

Our legal system, developed over many centuries, rests on the principle that the interests of justice are on the whole best served if parties in dispute, each represented by solicitors and counsel, take cases incapable of compromise to court for decision by an independent and neutral judge, before whom their relationship is essentially antagonistic: each is determined to win, and prepares and presents his case so as to defeat his opponent and achieve a favourable result. By the clash of competing evidence and argument, it is believed, the judge is best enabled to decide what happened, to formulate the relevant principles of law and to apply those principles to the facts of the case before him as he has found them.

Experience has shown that certain safeguards are needed if this system is to function fairly and effectively in the interests of parties to litigation and of the public at large. None of these safeguards is entirely straightforward, and only some of them need be mentioned here.

(1)   Parties must be free to unburden themselves to their legal advisers without fearing that what they say may provide ammunition for their opponent. To this end a cloak of confidence is thrown over communications between client and lawyer, usually removable only with the consent of the client.

(2)   The party who substantially loses the case is ordinarily obliged to pay the legal costs necessarily incurred by the winner. Thus hopeless claims and defences are discouraged, a willingness to compromise is induced and the winner keeps most of the fruits of victory. But the position is different where one or both parties to the case are legally aided: section 17 of the Legal Aid Act 1988 and Part XIII of the Civil Legal Aid (General) Regulations 1989, SI No 339, restrict the liability of legally assisted parties to pay costs if they lose. And sometimes the losing party is impoverished and cannot pay.

(3)   The law imposes a duty on lawyers to exercise reasonable care and skill in conducting their clients' affairs. This is a duty owed to and enforceable by the client, to protect him against loss caused by his lawyer's default. But it is not an absolute duty. Considerations of public policy have been held to require, and statute now confirms, that in relation to proceedings in court and work closely related to proceedings in court advocates should be accorded immunity from claims for negligence by their clients: *Rondel* v *Worsley* [1967] 3 All ER 993, [1969] 1 AC 191; *Saif Ali* v *Sydney Mitchell & Co (a firm) (P, third party)* [1978] 3 All ER 1033, [1980] AC 198; section 62 of the Courts and Legal Services Act 1990.

(4)   If solicitors or barristers fail to observe the standards of conduct required by the Law Society or the General Council of the Bar (as the case may be) they become liable to disciplinary proceedings at the suit of their

professional body and to a range of penalties which include fines, suspension from practice and expulsion from their profession. Procedures have changed over the years. The role of the courts (in the case of solicitors) and the Inns of Court (in the case of barristers) has in large measure been assumed by the professional bodies themselves. But the sanctions remain, not to compensate those who have suffered loss but to compel observance of prescribed standards of professional conduct. Additional powers exist to order barristers, solicitors and those in receipt of legal aid to forgo fees or remuneration otherwise earned.

(5)   Solicitors and barristers may in certain circumstances be ordered to compensate a party to litigation other than the client for whom they act for costs incurred by that party as a result of acts done or omitted by the solicitors or barristers in their conduct of the litigation.

It is the scope and effect of this last safeguard, and its relation with the others briefly mentioned, which are in issue in these appeals. We shall hereafter refer to this jurisdiction, not quite accurately, as "the wasted costs jurisdiction" and to orders made under it as "wasted costs orders". These appeals are not concerned with the jurisdiction to order legal representatives to compensate their own client. The questions raised are by no means academic. Material has been placed before the court which shows that the number and value of wasted costs orders applied for, and the costs of litigating them, have risen sharply. We were told of one case in which the original hearing had lasted five days; the wasted costs application had (when we were told of it) lasted seven days; it was estimated to be about half way through; at that stage one side had incurred costs of over £40,000. It almost appears that a new branch of legal activity is emerging, calling to mind Dickens's searing observation in *Bleak House*:

> "The one great principle of English law is, to make business for itself ...
> Viewed by this light it becomes a coherent scheme, and not the monstrous
> maze the laity are apt to think it."

The argument we have heard discloses a tension between two important public interests. One is that lawyers should not be deterred from pursuing their clients' interests by fear of incurring a personal liability to their clients' opponents; that they should not be penalised by orders to pay costs without a fair opportunity to defend themselves; that wasted costs orders should not become a back-door means of recovering costs not otherwise recoverable against a legally aided or impoverished litigant; and that the remedy should not grow unchecked to become more damaging than the disease. The other public interest, recently and clearly affirmed by Act of Parliament, is that litigants should not be financially prejudiced by the unjustifiable conduct of litigation by their or their opponents' lawyers. The reconciliation of these public interests is our task in these appeals. Full weight must be given to the first of these public interests, but the wasted costs jurisdiction must not be emasculated.

The wasted costs jurisdiction

The wasted costs jurisdiction of the court as applied to solicitors is of long standing, but discussion of it can conveniently begin with the important and relatively recent case of *Myers v Elman* [1939] 4 All ER 484, [1940] AC 282. At the end of a five-day hearing before a jury the plaintiff obtained judgment for damages for fraudulent conspiracy against five defendants, with costs. Nothing could be recovered from any of the defendants. Nor, perhaps, was any recovery expected, for at the end of the trial the plaintiff's counsel applied for an order that the costs of the action should be paid by the solicitors who had acted for the defendants.

Notice was duly given to the solicitors and a further five-day hearing followed to decide whether the solicitors or any of them should make payment. In the case of one solicitor, Mr Elman, the trial judge (Singleton J) considered two complaints: that he had filed defences which he knew to be false; and that he had permitted the filing of an inadequate affidavit verifying his clients' list of documents. In considering these complaints the judge had before him a considerable correspondence between Mr Elman and his clients which the plaintiff's advisers had (naturally) not seen before; the reports of the case do not disclose how it came about that the clients' privilege in that correspondence was waived.

Singleton J rejected the complaint relating to the defences but upheld that based on the defective affidavit of documents. Nothing, held the judge, should be said which might prevent, or tend to prevent, either solicitor or counsel from doing his best for his client so long as the duty to the court was borne in mind, but if he were asked or required by the client to do something which was inconsistent with the duty to the court it was for him to point out that he could not do it and, if necessary, cease to act (see *Myers v Rothfield* [1939] 1 KB 109 at 115, 117). The judge ordered Mr Elman to pay one-third of the taxed costs of the action and two-thirds of the costs of the application. Mr Elman appealed, and the Court of Appeal by a majority reversed the decision of the judge. It appeared that the work in question had been very largely delegated to a well-qualified managing clerk and the conduct complained of had been his, not Mr Elman's. The majority held that to make a wasted costs order the court must find professional misconduct established against the solicitor, and such a finding could not be made where the solicitor was not personally at fault.

On further appeal to the House of Lords, Lord Russell of Killowen dissented on the facts but the House was unanimous in rejecting the Court of Appeal's majority view. While their Lordships used different language, and may to some extent have seen the issues somewhat differently, the case is authority for five fundamental propositions.

(1)   The court's jurisdiction to make a wasted costs order against a solicitor is quite distinct from the disciplinary jurisdiction exercised over solicitors.

(2)   Whereas a disciplinary order against a solicitor requires a finding

that he has been personally guilty of serious professional misconduct, the making of a wasted costs order does not.

(3)   The court's jurisdiction to make a wasted costs order against a solicitor is founded on breach of the duty owed by the solicitor to the court to perform his duty as an officer of the court in promoting within his own sphere the cause of justice.

(4)   To show a breach of that duty it is not necessary to establish dishonesty, criminal conduct, personal obliquity or behaviour such as would warrant striking a solicitor off the roll. While mere mistake or error of judgment would not justify an order, misconduct, default or even negligence is enough if the negligence is serious or gross.

(5)   The jurisdiction is compensatory and not merely punitive.

When *Myers* v *Elman* [1939] 4 All ER 484, [1940] AC 282 was decided, the court's wasted costs jurisdiction was not regulated by the Rules of the Supreme Court, although RSC Order 65, rule 11 did provide for costs to be disallowed as between solicitor and client or paid by a solicitor to his client where such costs had been "improperly or without any reasonable cause incurred" or where "by reason of any undue delay in proceeding under any judgment or order, or of any misconduct or default of the solicitor, any costs properly incurred have nevertheless proved fruitless to the person incurring the same". There was also provision in Order 65, rule 5 for a solicitor to pay costs to any or all parties if his failure to attend or deliver a document caused a delay in proceedings. But the rules reflected no general wasted costs jurisdiction. Following the decision the rules were not amended to regulate the court's inherent wasted costs jurisdiction, but the jurisdiction itself was preserved by section 50(2) of the Solicitors Act 1957. In 1960 a new rule (which later became Order 62, rule 8(1)) was introduced which did regulate, although not enlarge, this inherent jurisdiction. The new rule provided:

> "Subject to the following provisions of this rule, where in any proceedings costs are incurred improperly or without reasonable cause or are wasted by undue delay or any other misconduct or default, the Court may make against any solicitor whom it considers to be responsible (whether personally or through a servant or agent) an order – (a) disallowing the costs as between the solicitor and his client; and (b) directing the solicitor to repay to his client costs which the client has been ordered to pay to other parties to the proceedings; or (c) directing the solicitor personally to indemnify such other parties against costs payable by them."

In paragraphs (a) and (b) the effect of the old rule was reproduced. In paragraph (c) the effect of *Myers* v *Elman* was recognised. It is plain that expressions such as "improperly", "without reasonable cause" and "misconduct" are to be understood in the sense given to them by their Lordships in that case.

Both before and after introduction of the new rule, contested applications for wasted costs orders against solicitors did come before the courts. *Edwards* v *Edwards* [1958] 2 All ER 179, [1958] P 235, *Wilkinson* v

Wilkinson [1962] 1 All ER 922, [1963] P 1, *Mauroux* v *Sociedade Comercial Abel Pereira da Fonseca SARL* [1972] 2 All ER 1085, [1972] 1 WLR 962, *Currie & Co* v *Law Society* [1976] 3 All ER 832, [1977] QB 990 and *R & T Thew Ltd* v *Reeves* (*No 2*) [1982] 3 All ER 1086, [1982] QB 1283 are examples. But we believe such applications to have been infrequent. In the course of their practices the three members of this court were personally involved in only one such application.

During the 1980s the tempo quickened. In *Davy-Chiesman* v *Davy-Chiesman* [1984] 1 All ER 321, [1984] Fam 48 a legally aided husband made an application for ancillary relief against his wife. The judge who heard the application dismissed it, observing that it was without any merit, should not have been made and most certainly should not have been pursued to the end. The wife obtained the usual costs order against the husband, not to be enforced without leave of the court. She then sought costs against the legal aid fund. The Law Society, as administrator of the legal aid fund, applied that the husband's solicitor personally pay the costs of both husband and wife. The judge rejected that application and the Law Society appealed. The judgment of the Court of Appeal is authority for two propositions. (1) Subject to any express provision of the Legal Aid Act 1988 or regulations to the contrary, the interrelationship of lay client, solicitor and counsel and the incidents of that relationship, for instance relating to privilege, are no different when the client is legally aided from when he is not. (2) Although a solicitor is in general entitled to rely on the advice of counsel properly instructed, he is not entitled to follow such advice blindly but is in the ordinary way obliged to apply his own expert professional mind to the substance of the advice received.

On the facts, the Court of Appeal held that the solicitor should have appreciated the obvious unsoundness of the advice given by counsel after a certain date, and should have communicated his view to the Law Society. The court therefore allowed the appeal in part. The court plainly regarded counsel as substantially responsible, but there was at the time no jurisdiction to make an order against a barrister.

In *Orchard* v *South Eastern Electricity Board* [1987] 1 All ER 95, [1987] QB 565 the plaintiff was again legally aided with a nil contribution. His claim failed. The usual order, not to be enforced without leave, was made in the defendants' favour. An application was made against the plaintiff's solicitors personally and this was dismissed both by the trial judge and on appeal. In the course of his judgment on appeal, Donaldson MR made certain observations about the position of the Bar, but it would seem that these were obiter since no claim was or could have been made against counsel for the plaintiff. The case is notable first for Donaldson MR's ruling on the exercise of the jurisdiction under Order 62, rule 8 as it then stood. He said ([1987] 1 All ER 95 at 100, [1987] QB 565 at 572):

> "That said, this is a jurisdiction which falls to be exercised with care and
> discretion and only in clear cases. In the context of a complaint that litigation

was initiated or continued in circumstances in which to do so constituted serious misconduct, it must never be forgotten that it is not for solicitors or counsel to impose a pre-trial screen through which a litigant must pass before he can put his complaint or defence before the court. On the other hand, no solicitor or counsel should lend his assistance to a litigant if he is satisfied that the initiation or further prosecution of a claim is mala fide or for an ulterior purpose or, to put it more broadly, if the proceedings would be, or have become, an abuse of the process of the court or unjustifiably oppressive."

Secondly, the decision re-affirms that a solicitor against whom a claim is made must have a full opportunity of rebutting the complaint, but recognises that he may be hampered in doing so by his duty of confidentiality to the client "from which he can only be released by his client or by overriding authority" (see [1987] 1 All ER 95 at 100, [1987] QB 565 at 572). Thirdly, the judgments highlight the extreme undesirability of claims for wasted costs orders being used as a means of browbeating, bludgeoning or threatening the other side during the progress of the case (see [1987] 1 All ER 95 at 104, 106, [1987] QB 565 at 577, 580). Such a practice, it was pointed out, could gravely undermine the ability of a solicitor, particularly a solicitor working for a legally aided client, to do so with the required objectivity and independence.

In 1986 the relevant Rules of the Supreme Court were amended. Order 62, rule 8 became Order 62, rule 11, but with some rewording. It now reads:

"(1)   Subject to the following provisions of this rule, where it appears to the Court that costs have been incurred unreasonably or improperly in any proceedings or have been wasted by failure to conduct proceedings with reasonable competence and expedition, the Court may – (a) order – (i) the solicitor whom it considers to be responsible (whether personally or through a servant or agent) to repay to his client costs which the client has been ordered to pay to any other party to the proceedings; or (ii) the solicitor personally to indemnify such other parties against costs payable by them; and (iii) the costs as between the solicitor and his client to be disallowed; or (b) direct a taxing officer to inquire into the matter and report to the Court, and upon receiving such a report the Court may make such order under sub-paragraph (a) as it thinks fit."

It is noteworthy that the reference to "misconduct" is omitted, as is the implication that any conduct must amount to misconduct if it is to found a wasted costs order. More importantly, reference to "reasonable competence" is introduced, suggesting the ordinary standard of negligence and not a higher standard requiring proof of gross neglect or serious dereliction of duty.

The Court of Appeal had occasion to construe the new rule in *Sinclair-Jones v Kay* [1988] 2 All ER 611 at 615–616, [1989] 1 WLR 114 at 121–122. In his judgment May LJ read the new rule as substantially different from the old and as intended to widen the court's powers. It was no longer necessary to apply the test of gross misconduct laid down in the older authorities. "The court regarded the new power as salutary, particularly as a means of penalising unreasonable delay." ([1989] 1 WLR 114 at 121A.)

In *Holden & Co (a firm) v CPS* [1990] 1 All ER 368, [1990] 2 QB 261, the court's decision in *Sinclair-Jones v Kay* was criticised and not followed, but the correctness of that judgment was affirmed in *Gupta v Comer* [1991] 1 All ER 289, [1991] 1 QB 629, where Order 62, rule 11 as it then stood was again considered. Part of the court's reasoning in upholding the earlier decision cannot, it would seem, survive later authority, but there is no ground to question its conclusion that the new rule was intended to cut down limitations hitherto thought to restrict the court's jurisdiction to make wasted costs orders.

In his judgment in *Gupta v Comer*, Lord Donaldson of Lymington MR referred to legislative amendments to section 51 of the Supreme Court Act 1981 which would enable new rules to be made "imposing an even stricter standard than that which Order 62, rule 11 has been held to impose" (see [1991] 1 All ER 289 at 293, [1991] 1 QB 629 at 635). This was a reference to what became the Courts and Legal Services Act 1990. Section 4 of that Act substituted a new section 51 in the Supreme Court Act 1981. Relevant for present purposes are the following subsections of the new section:

"(1) Subject to the provisions of this or any other enactment and to rules of court, the costs of and incidental to all proceedings in – (a) the civil division of the Court of Appeal; (b) the High Court; and (c) any county court, shall be in the discretion of the court ...

(6) In any proceedings mentioned in subsection (1), the court may disallow, or (as the case may be) order the legal or other representative concerned to meet, the whole of any wasted costs or such part of them as may be determined in accordance with rules of court.

(7) In subsection (6), 'wasted costs' means any costs incurred by a party – (a) as a result of any improper, unreasonable or negligent act or omission on the part of any legal or other representative or any employee of such a representative; or (b) which, in the light of any such act or omission occurring after they were incurred, the court considers it is unreasonable to expect that party to pay ...

(13) In this section 'legal or other representative', in relation to a party to proceedings, means any person exercising a right of audience or right to conduct litigation on his behalf."

The new section 51(6) was extended to civil proceedings in the Crown Court. Section 111 made a similar amendment to the Prosecution of Offences Act 1985, applicable to criminal proceedings in the Court of Appeal, the Crown Court and the magistrates' court. Section 112 of the Act amended the Magistrates' Courts Act 1980 to similar effect. We should also draw attention to section 62 of the 1990 Act, which was in these terms:

"(1) A person – (a) who is not a barrister; but (b) who lawfully provides any legal services in relation to any proceedings, shall have the same immunity from liability for negligence in respect of his acts or omissions as he would have if he were a barrister lawfully providing those services.

(2)   No act or omission on the part of any barrister or other person which is accorded immunity from liability for negligence shall give rise to an action for breach of any contract relating to the provision by him of the legal services in question."

With effect from 1 October 1991, Order 62, rule 11 was amended to supplement the new section 51 of the 1981 Act. It is enough to summarise the effect of the rule without reciting its full terms. Where the court makes a wasted costs order, it must specify in its order the costs which are to be paid. As under previous versions of the rule, the court may direct a taxing officer to inquire into the matter and report back or it may refer the matter to a taxing officer. The court may not make an order under section 51(6) unless it has given the legal representative a reasonable opportunity to appear and show cause why an order should not be made, although this obligation is qualified where the progress of proceedings is obstructed by a legal representative's failure to attend or deliver a document or proceed. The court may direct the Official Solicitor to attend and take such part in any proceedings or inquiry under the rule as the court may direct.

Some aspects of this new wasted costs regime must be considered in more detail below. It should, however, be noted that the jurisdiction is for the first time extended to barristers. There can in our view be no room for doubt about the mischief against which these new provisions were aimed: this was the causing of loss and expense to litigants by the unjustifiable conduct of litigation by their or the other side's lawyers. Where such conduct is shown, Parliament clearly intended to arm the courts with an effective remedy for the protection of those injured.

Since the Act there have been two cases which deserve mention. The first is *Re a Barrister* (*wasted costs order*) (*No 1 of 1991*) [1992] 3 All ER 429, [1993] QB 293. This arose out of an unhappy difference between counsel and a judge sitting in the Crown Court in a criminal case. It was held on appeal, in our view quite rightly, that courts should apply a three-stage test when a wasted costs order is contemplated.   (1) Has the legal representative of whom complaint is made acted improperly, unreasonably or negligently?   (2) If so, did such conduct cause the applicant to incur unnecessary costs?   (3) If so, is it in all the circumstances just to order the legal representative to compensate the applicant for the whole or any part of the relevant costs? (If so, the costs to be met must be specified and, in a criminal case, the amount of the costs.) We have somewhat altered the wording of the court's ruling but not, we think, its effect.

The second case, *Symphony Group plc* v *Hodgson* [1993] 4 All ER 143, [1994] QB 179, **Costs LR (Core Vol) 319**, arose out of an application for costs against a non-party and not out of a wasted costs order. An observation of Balcombe LJ is however pertinent in this context also ([1993] 4 All ER 143 at 154, [1994] QB 179 at 194, **Costs LR (Core Vol) 319 at 328**):

"The judge should be alert to the possibility that an application against a non-party is motivated by resentment of an inability to obtain an effective order for costs against a legally aided litigant. The courts are well aware of the financial difficulties faced by parties who are facing legally aided litigants at first instance, where the opportunity of a claim against the Legal Aid Board under section 18 of the Legal Aid Act 1988 is very limited. Nevertheless the Civil Legal Aid (General) Regulations 1989, SI No 339, and in particular regulations 67, 69 and 70, lay down conditions designed to ensure that there is no abuse of legal aid by a legally assisted person and these are designed to protect the other party to the litigation as well as the legal aid fund. The court will be very reluctant to infer that solicitors to a legally aided party have failed to discharge their duties under the regulations – see *Orchard* v *South Eastern Electricity Board* [1987] 1 All ER 95, [1987] QB 565 – and in my judgment, this principle extends to a reluctance to infer that any maintenance by a non-party has occurred."

Improper, unreasonable or negligent

A number of different submissions were made on the correct construction of these crucial words in the new section 51(7) of the Supreme Court Act 1981. In our view the meaning of these expressions is not open to serious doubt.

"Improper" means what it has been understood to mean in this context for at least half a century. The adjective covers, but is not confined to, conduct which would ordinarily be held to justify disbarment, striking off, suspension from practice or other serious professional penalty. It covers any significant breach of a substantial duty imposed by a relevant code of professional conduct. But it is not in our judgment limited to that. Conduct which would be regarded as improper according to the consensus of professional (including judicial) opinion can be fairly stigmatised as such whether or not it violates the letter of a professional code.

"Unreasonable" also means what it has been understood to mean in this context for at least half a century. The expression aptly describes conduct which is vexatious, designed to harass the other side rather than advance the resolution of the case, and it makes no difference that the conduct is the product of excessive zeal and not improper motive. But conduct cannot be described as unreasonable simply because it leads in the event to an unsuccessful result or because other more cautious legal representatives would have acted differently. The acid test is whether the conduct permits of a reasonable explanation. If so, the course adopted may be regarded as optimistic and as reflecting on a practitioner's judgment, but it is not unreasonable.

The term "negligent" was the most controversial of the three. It was argued that the 1990 Act, in this context as in others, used "negligent" as a term of art involving the well-known ingredients of duty, breach, causation and damage. Therefore, it was said, conduct cannot be regarded as negligent unless it involves an actionable breach of the legal representative's duty to his own client, to whom alone a duty is owed. We reject this approach (1) As already noted, the predecessor of the present Order 62, rule 11 made reference to "reasonable competence". That expression does not invoke technical concepts of the law of negligence. It seems to us inconceivable that by changing the language Parliament intended to make it harder, rather than easier, for courts to make orders.   (2) Since the applicant's right to a wasted costs order against a legal representative depends on showing that the latter is in breach of his duty to the court it makes no sense to superimpose a requirement under this head (but not in the case of impropriety or unreasonableness) that he is also in breach of his duty to his client.

We cannot regard this as, in practical terms, a very live issue, since it requires some ingenuity to postulate a situation in which a legal representative causes the other side to incur unnecessary costs without at the same time running up unnecessary costs for his own side and so breaching the ordinary duty owed by a legal representative to his client. But for whatever importance it may have, we are clear that "negligent" should be understood in an untechnical way to denote failure to act with the competence reasonably to be expected of ordinary members of the profession.

In adopting an untechnical approach to the meaning of negligence in this context, we would however wish firmly to discountenance any suggestion that an applicant for a wasted costs order under this head need prove anything less than he would have to prove in an action for negligence –

> "advice, acts or omissions in the course of their professional work which no member of the profession who was reasonably well-informed and competent would have given or done or omitted to do ... [an error of judgment] such as no reasonably well informed and competent member of that profession could have made." (See *Saif Ali* v *Sydney Mitchell & Co* [1978] 3 All ER 1033 at 1041, 1043, [1980] AC 198 at 218, 220 per Lord Diplock.

We were invited to give the three adjectives (improper, unreasonable and negligent) specific, self-contained meanings, so as to avoid overlap between the three. We do not read these very familiar expressions in that way. Conduct which is unreasonable may also be improper, and conduct which is negligent will very frequently be (if it is not by definition) unreasonable. We do not think any sharp differentiation between these expressions is useful or necessary or intended.

Pursuing a hopeless case

A legal representative is not to be held to have acted improperly, unreasonably or negligently simply because he acts for a party who pursues a claim or a defence which is plainly doomed to fail. As Lord Pearce observed in *Rondel* v *Worsley* [1967] 3 All ER 993 at 1029, [1969] 1 AC 191 at 275:

> "It is easier, pleasanter and more advantageous professionally for barristers to advise, represent or defend those who are decent and reasonable and likely to

succeed in their action or their defence than those who are unpleasant, unreasonable, disreputable, and have an apparently hopeless case. Yet it would be tragic if our legal system came to provide no reputable defenders, representatives or advisers for the latter."

As is well known, barristers in independent practice are not permitted to pick and choose their clients. Paragraph 209 of the Code of Conduct of the Bar of England and Wales provides:

"A barrister in independent practice must comply with the 'Cab-rank rule' and accordingly except only as otherwise provided in paragraphs 501, 502 and 503 he must in any field in which he professes to practise in relation to work appropriate to his experience and seniority and irrespective of whether his client is paying privately or is legally aided or otherwise publicly funded: (a) accept any brief to appear before a court in which he professes to practise; (b) accept any instructions; (c) act for any person on whose behalf he is briefed or instructed; and do so irrespective of (i) the party on whose behalf he is briefed or instructed (ii) the nature of the case and (iii) any belief or opinion which he may have formed as to the character reputation cause conduct guilt or innocence of that person."

As is also well known, solicitors are not subject to an equivalent cab-rank rule, but many solicitors would and do respect the public policy underlying it by affording representation to the unpopular and the unmeritorious. Legal representatives will, of course, whether barristers or solicitors, advise clients of the perceived weakness of their case and of the risk of failure. But clients are free to reject advice and insist that cases be litigated. It is rarely if ever safe for a court to assume that a hopeless case is being litigated on the advice of the lawyers involved. They are there to present the case; it is (as Samuel Johnson unforgettably pointed out) for the judge and not the lawyers to judge it.

It is, however, one thing for a legal representative to present, on instructions, a case which he regards as bound to fail; it is quite another to lend his assistance to proceedings which are an abuse of the process of the court. Whether instructed or not, a legal representative is not entitled to use litigious procedures for purposes for which they were not intended, as by issuing or pursuing proceedings for reasons unconnected with success in the litigation or pursuing a case known to be dishonest, nor is he entitled to evade rules intended to safeguard the interests of justice, as by knowingly failing to make full disclosure on ex parte application or knowingly conniving at incomplete disclosure of documents. It is not entirely easy to distinguish by definition between the hopeless case and the case which amounts to an abuse of the process, but in practice it is not hard to say which is which and if there is doubt the legal representative is entitled to the benefit of it.

Legal aid
Section 31(1) of the Legal Aid Act 1988 provides that receipt of legal aid shall not (save as expressly provided) affect the relationship between or

rights of a legal representative and client or any privilege arising out of the relationship nor the rights or liabilities of other parties to the proceedings or the principles on which any discretion is exercised. (The protection given to a legally assisted party in relation to payment of costs is, of course, an obvious express exception.) This important principle has been recognised in the authorities. It is incumbent on courts to which applications for wasted costs orders are made to bear prominently in mind the peculiar vulnerability of legal representatives acting for assisted persons, to which Balcombe LJ adverted in *Symphony Group plc* v *Hodgson* and which recent experience abundantly confirms. It would subvert the benevolent purposes of this legislation if such representatives were subject to any unusual personal risk. They for their part must bear prominently in mind that their advice and their conduct should not be tempered by the knowledge that their client is not their paymaster and so not, in all probability, liable for the costs of the other side.

Immunity

In *Rondel* v *Worsley* [1967] 3 All ER 993, [1969] 1 AC 191 the House of Lords held that a barrister was immune from an action for negligence at the suit of a client in respect of his conduct and management of a case in court and the preliminary work in connection with it. A majority of the House held that this immunity extended to a solicitor while acting as an advocate. In *Saif Ali* v *Sydney Mitchell & Co* [1978] 3 All ER 1033, [1980] AC 198 a majority of the House further held that the immunity only covered pre-trial work intimately connected with the conduct of the case in court. These decisions were based on powerfully argued considerations of public policy, which included: the requirement that advocates should be free to conduct cases in court fearlessly, independently and without looking over their shoulders; the need for finality, so that cases are not endlessly re-litigated with the risk of inconsistent decisions; the advocate's duty to the court and to the administration of justice; the barrister's duty to act for a client, however unsavoury; the general immunity accorded to those taking part in court proceedings; the unique role of the advocate; and the subjection of advocates to the discipline of their professional bodies.

We were reminded of these matters when considering submissions on the interaction of sections 4, 111 and 112 of the Courts and Legal Services Act 1990 and section 62 of the same Act. On one submission, section 62 must be read subject to the other sections. On that view, if an advocate's conduct in court is improper, unreasonable or negligent he is liable to a wasted costs order. On a second submission, sections 4, 111 and 112 must be read subject to section 62. On that view, a wasted costs order can only be based on improper, unreasonable or negligent conduct which does not take place in court and is not intimately connected with conduct of the case in court. On yet a third submission, sections 4, 111 and 112 should be read subject to section 62 but in a more limited sense: improper or unreasonable conduct would found an order whether in court or out of it, but negligent conduct would not found an order unless it fell outside the ambit of the recognised immunity for work at the trial and before it.

In our judgment (and subject to the important qualification noted below) the first of these submissions is correct, and for a number of reasons. (1) There is nothing in sections 4, 111 and 112 to suggest that they take effect subject to the provisions of section 62. (2) Part II of the 1990 Act, in which section 62 (but not the other sections) appears, is directed to widening the categories of those by whom legal services are provided. It was therefore natural to enact that those providing services also or formerly provided by lawyers should enjoy the same immunity as lawyers. To the same end, section 63 enacts that such persons should enjoy the same professional privilege as a solicitor. There is nothing in section 62 to suggest that it is intended to qualify the apparently unqualified effect of the other sections, to which (in the scheme of the Act) it is in no way related. (3) Nothing in the 1990 Act warrants the drawing of any distinction between improper and unreasonable conduct on the one hand and negligent conduct on the other. Such a distinction is in any event unworkable if, as we have suggested, there is considerable overlap between these expressions. (4) If the conduct of cases in court, or work intimately connected with the conduct of cases in court, entitles a legal representative to immunity from the making of wasted costs orders, it is not obvious why sections 111 and 112 were applied to magistrates' courts, where no work would ordinarily be done which would not be covered by the immunity. (5) It was very odd draughtsmanship to define a legal representative in section 51(13) as a person exercising a right of audience if it was intended that anyone exercising a right of audience should be immune from the liability imposed by section 51(6). (6) It would be anomalous to interpret an Act which extended the wasted costs jurisdiction over barristers for the first time as exempting them from liability in respect of their most characteristic activity, namely conducting cases in court and advising in relation to such cases. It would be scarcely less anomalous to interpret an Act making express reference to negligence for the first time as exempting advocates from liability for negligence. (7) It is one thing to say that an advocate shall be immune from claims in negligence by an aggrieved and unsuccessful client. It is quite another for the court to take steps to rectify, at the expense of the advocate, breaches by the advocate of the duty he owed to the court to further the ends of justice. (8) It is our belief, which we cannot substantiate, that part of the reason underlying the changes effected by the new section 51 was judicial concern at the wholly unacceptable manner in which a very small minority of barristers conducted cases in court.

We referred above to an important qualification. It is this. Although we are satisfied that the intention of this legislation is to encroach on the traditional immunity of the advocate by subjecting him to the wasted costs jurisdiction if he causes a waste of costs by improper, unreasonable or negligent conduct, it does not follow that we regard the public interest considerations on which the immunity is founded as being irrelevant or lacking weight in this context. Far from it. Any judge who is invited to make or contemplates making an order arising out of an advocate's conduct of court proceedings must make full allowance for the fact that an advocate in court, like a commander in battle, often has to make decisions quickly and under pressure, in the fog of war and ignorant of developments on the other side of the hill. Mistakes will inevitably be made, things done which the outcome shows to have been unwise. But advocacy is more an art than a science. It cannot be conducted according to formulae. Individuals differ in their style and approach. It is only when, with all allowances made, an advocate's conduct of court proceedings is quite plainly unjustifiable that it can be appropriate to make a wasted costs order against him.

Privilege

Where an applicant seeks a wasted costs order against the lawyers on the other side, legal professional privilege may be relevant both as between the applicant and his lawyers and as between the respondent lawyers and their client. In either case it is the client's privilege, which he alone can waive.

The first of these situations can cause little difficulty. If the applicant's privileged communications are germane to an issue in the application, to show what he would or would not have done had the other side not acted in the manner complained of, he can waive his privilege; if he declines to do so, adverse inferences can be drawn.

The respondent lawyers are in a different position. The privilege is not theirs to waive. In the usual case where a waiver would not benefit their client they will be slow to advise the client to waive his privilege, and they may well feel bound to advise that the client should take independent advice before doing so. The client may be unwilling to do that, and may be unwilling to waive if he does. So the respondent lawyers may find themselves at a grave disadvantage in defending their conduct of proceedings, unable to reveal what advice and warnings they gave, what instructions they received. In some cases this potential source of injustice may be mitigated by reference to the taxing master, where different rules apply, but only in a small minority of cases can this procedure be appropriate. Judges who are invited to make or contemplate making a wasted costs order must make full allowance for the inability of respondent lawyers to tell the whole story. Where there is room for doubt, the respondent lawyers are entitled to the benefit of it. It is again only when, with all allowances made, a lawyer's conduct of proceedings is quite plainly unjustifiable that it can be appropriate to make a wasted costs order.

Causation

As emphasised in *Re a Barrister (wasted costs order) (No 1 of 1991)* [1992] 3 All ER 429, [1993] QB 293, the court has jurisdiction to make a wasted costs order only where the improper, unreasonable or negligent conduct complained of has caused a waste of costs and only to the extent of such wasted costs. Demonstration of a causal link is essential. Where the conduct is proved but no waste of costs is shown to have resulted, the case may be one to be referred to the appropriate disciplinary body or the legal aid authorities, but it is not one for exercise of the wasted costs jurisdiction.

Reliance on counsel
We indorse the guidance given on this subject in *Locke* v *Camberwell Health Authority* [1991] 2 Med LR 249. A solicitor does not abdicate his professional responsibility when he seeks the advice of counsel. He must apply his mind to the advice received. But the more specialist the nature of the advice, the more reasonable is it likely to be for a solicitor to accept it and act on it.

Threats to apply for wasted costs orders
We entirely agree with the view expressed by this court in *Orchard* v *South Eastern Electricity Board* [1987] 1 All ER 95, [1987] QB 565, that the threat of proposed applications should not be used as a means of intimidation. On the other hand, if one side considers that the conduct of the other is improper, unreasonable or negligent and likely to cause a waste of costs we do not consider it objectionable to alert the other side to that view; the other side can then consider its position and perhaps mend its ways. Drawing the distinction between unacceptable intimidation and acceptable notice must depend on the professional judgment of those involved.

The timing of the application
In *Filmlab Systems International Ltd* v *Pennington* (1993) *The Times*, 9 July, Aldous J expressed the opinion that wasted costs orders should not, save in exceptional circumstances, be sought until after trial. He highlighted a number of dangers if applications were made at an interlocutory stage, among them the risk that a party's advisers might feel they could no longer act, so that the party would in effect be deprived of the advisers of his choice. It is impossible to lay down rules of universal application, and sometimes an interlocutory battle resolves the real dispute between the parties. But speaking generally we agree that in the ordinary way applications for wasted costs are best left until after the end of the trial.

The applicant
Under the rules, the court itself may initiate the inquiry whether a wasted costs order should be made. In straightforward cases (such as failure to appear, lateness, negligence leading to an otherwise avoidable adjournment, gross repetition or extreme slowness) there is no reason why it should not do so. But save in the most obvious case, courts should in our view be slow to initiate the inquiry. If they do so in cases where the inquiry becomes complex

and time-consuming, difficult and embarrassing issues on costs can arise: if a wasted costs order is not made, the costs of the inquiry will have to be borne by someone and it will not be the court; even if an order is made, the costs ordered to be paid may be small compared with the costs of the inquiry. In such cases courts will usually be well-advised to leave an aggrieved party to make the application if so advised; the costs will then, in the ordinary way, follow the event between the parties.

Procedure

The procedure to be followed in determining applications for wasted costs must be laid down by courts so as to meet the requirements of the individual case before them. The overriding requirements are that any procedure must be fair and that it must be as simple and summary as fairness permits. Fairness requires that any respondent lawyer should be very clearly told what he is said to have done wrong and what is claimed. But the requirement of simplicity and summariness means that elaborate pleadings should in general be avoided. No formal process of discovery will be appropriate. We cannot imagine circumstances in which the applicant should be permitted to interrogate the respondent lawyer, or vice versa. Hearings should be measured in hours, and not in days or weeks. Judges must not reject a weapon which Parliament has intended to be used for the protection of those injured by the unjustifiable conduct of the other side's lawyers, but they must be astute to control what threatens to become a new and costly form of satellite litigation.

"Show cause"

Although Order 62, rule 11(4) in its present form requires that in the ordinary way the court should not make a wasted costs order without giving the legal representative "a reasonable opportunity to appear and show cause why an order should not be made", this should not be understood to mean that the burden is on the legal representative to exculpate himself. A wasted costs order should not be made unless the applicant satisfies the court, or the court itself is satisfied, that an order should be made. The representative is not obliged to prove that it should not. But the rule clearly envisages that the representative will not be called on to reply unless an apparently strong prima facie case has been made against him and the language of the rule recognises a shift in the evidential burden.

Discretion

It was submitted, in our view correctly, that the jurisdiction to make a wasted costs order is dependent at two stages on the discretion of the court. The first is at the stage of initial application, when the court is invited to give the legal representative an opportunity to show cause. This is not something to be done automatically or without careful appraisal of the relevant circumstances. The costs of the inquiry as compared with the costs claimed will always be one relevant consideration. This is a discretion, like any other, to be exercised judicially, but judges may not infrequently decide that further proceedings are not likely to be justified. The second discretion arises at the final stage. Even if the court is satisfied that a legal representative has acted improperly, unreasonably or negligently and that such conduct has caused the other side to incur an identifiable sum of wasted costs, it is not bound to make an order, but in that situation it would of course have to give sustainable reasons for exercising its discretion against making an order.

Crime

Since the six cases before the court are all civil cases, our attention has naturally been directed towards the exercise of the wasted costs jurisdiction in the civil field. Attention has, however, been drawn in authorities such as *Holden & Co (a firm)* v *CPS* [1990] 1 All ER 368, [1990] 2 QB 261 and *Gupta* v *Comer* [1991] 1 All ER 289, [1991] 1 QB 629, to the undesirability of any divergence in the practice of the civil and criminal courts in this field, and Parliament has acted so as substantially (but not completely) to assimilate the practice in the two. We therefore hope that this judgment may give guidance which will be of value to criminal courts as to civil, but we fully appreciate that the conduct of criminal cases will often raise different questions and depend on different circumstances. The relevant discretions are vested in, and only in, the court conducting the relevant hearing. Our purpose is to guide, but not restrict, the exercise of these discretions.

Ridehalgh v *Horsefield and anor*

Mr Ridehalgh (the landlord) owned a house in Blackpool. In the middle of July 1985 he let it for 12 months to Mr Horsefield and Miss Isherwood (the tenants). When the 12 months came to an end the landlord re-let the house to the tenants for a further 12 months. When that 12 months came to an end he again re-let the house to the tenants, this time for 2 months. In October 1987 he let the house to them for a fourth time, again for 12 months. In October 1988 he let the house to the tenants for the fifth and last time, for 12 months expiring in October 1989.

When the letting came to an end the landlord consulted solicitors. They issued county court proceedings seeking possession and alleging various breaches of covenant. The tenants launched a cross-action claiming damages for breach of covenant. These actions were fully pleaded, and were eventually consolidated. The consolidated action remains alive and has not yet been heard. It was not alleged by the landlord in those actions that the tenants' original tenancy had been a protected shorthold tenancy. The landlord's solicitor had not been able to obtain a copy of the original tenancy agreement and was therefore unable to establish the nature of that tenancy.

Later he was able to obtain a copy of the original tenancy agreement from the rent officer (although not of the protected shorthold tenancy notice which the landlord instructed him had also been served). Under cover of a letter dated 4 July 1990 he accordingly served on the tenants a notice dated 5 July 1990 under Case 19 of Schedule 15 to the Rent Act 1977, which had been added to that Act by section 55(1) of the Housing Act 1980. The notice was expressed to expire on 5 October 1990.

On 17 January 1991 the landlord's solicitor issued proceedings claiming possession of the house under Case 19. He pleaded (as was necessary if he was to rely on that case) that before the original agreement had been made in July 1985 the landlord had given the tenants written notice that the tenancy was to be a protected shorthold tenancy within the meaning of the Rent Act 1977 and the Housing Act 1980.

In their defences the tenants advanced a number of pleas. Relevantly for present purposes, both tenants denied receipt of a protected shorthold tenancy notice.

In the spring of 1991 when this action was proceeding towards trial the solicitors for the landlord and the tenants independently consulted textbook authority. The landlord was a man of limited means. The tenants were legally aided. It is understandable, and it was the case, that neither solicitor undertook profound research and neither consulted counsel (which, indeed, the tenants' solicitor had no authority to do). The tenants' solicitor, however, concluded that the parties' respective cases stood or fell on whether or not (as the landlord contended and the tenants denied) a protected shorthold tenancy notice had been served before the original tenancy had been granted. His analysis was this.   (1) If the notice had been duly served, the subsequent tenancies in 1986, 1987 and 1988 were protected tenancies vulnerable to a claim for possession under Case 19.   (2) The periodic tenancy which arose on expiry of the last fixed term tenancy in October 1989 was accordingly an assured shorthold tenancy pursuant to section 34 of the Housing Act 1988.   (3) The notice given under Case 19, although inappropriate in form, was effective to determine the assured shorthold tenancy pursuant to section 21(4) of the 1988 Act and to entitle the landlord to possession.   (4) If, however, the notice had not been duly served, the tenants were statutory tenants and the landlord was not entitled to possession.

The tenants' solicitor accordingly telephoned the landlord's solicitor, in a commendable attempt to shorten the forthcoming hearing and avoid unnecessary costs, and suggested that the hearing should be confined to the single, conclusive, factual issue whether the notice had been duly served or not. The landlord's solicitor agreed.

In truth this analysis, and the conclusion drawn from it, were fundamentally unsound. If the notice had been duly served, the original tenancy was indeed a protected shorthold tenancy. But the succeeding tenancies in 1986, 1987 and 1988 were not protected shorthold tenancies but protected tenancies, by virtue of section 52(2) of the Housing Act 1980. It remained open to the landlord to seek possession under Case 19. When the last fixed term tenancy expired in October 1989 the tenants became statutory tenants under sections 2 and 3 of the 1977 Act. Section 34 of the

1988 Act had no application because no new tenancy had been granted after the section came into force in January 1989 and no tenancy had been entered into on or after that date. As statutory tenants the tenants were vulnerable to a claim by the landlord under Case 19. But that case requires that proceedings for possession should be commenced not later than three months after the expiry of the Case 19 notice, and here the landlord's proceedings were commenced 12 days after the expiry of the three-month period.

The landlord's solicitor appreciated (after commencement of proceedings) that they had been commenced more than three months after expiry of the Case 19 notice, but he did not regard that as a matter of any significance since the solicitors had agreed that that notice was properly to be regarded as a notice under section 21 of the 1988 Act, and section 21 contained no special time limit for bringing proceedings.

The case came on for hearing before Judge Holt in the Blackpool County Court on 17 October 1991. The landlord's solicitor opened his case along the lines which the solicitors had agreed. The tenants' solicitor confirmed his agreement on the issue for the court to decide. The judge expressed some bewilderment about the legislation, but did not question the solicitors' agreed analysis even though section 34 was read in detail. The landlord's solicitor acknowledged that his pleaded case was based on Case 19 and not section 21, but neither the tenants' solicitor nor the judge queries that and it was tacitly agreed that the claim should be treated as if made under section 21.

The factual issue whether the protected shorthold tenancy notice had been served or not was vigorously contested before the judge over two days. At the end of the hearing the judge gave an extempore judgment which runs to nearly 30 pages of transcript. She found that the notice had been duly served, thus accepting the evidence of the landlord and rejecting the evidence of the tenants. She accordingly made a possession order in favour of the landlord.

The tenants then consulted new solicitors (whose conduct of the matter is open to no possible criticism) and gave notice of appeal. But the new solicitors were at a disadvantage because they did not have all the papers and did not know the basis of the judge's decision. The notice of appeal, as originally drafted by counsel (who had not of course appeared below), took the point that the Case 19 proceedings were out of time; neither he nor the tenants' new solicitors appreciated that judgment had in fact been given under section 21 of the 1988 Act.

The landlord consulted counsel, who correctly advised that the case had proceeded on a wrong basis in the court below. In a skeleton argument and in a respondent's notice he sought to uphold the judge's order on the basis that the landlord was entitled to possession under Case 19. He sought to overcome the problem that the action had been commenced after expiry of the three-month time limit by contending that this was a directly provision, for the benefit of the tenant, which the tenants had waived.

The tenants' counsel had by this time learned of the basis on which judgment had been given below. He accordingly settled an amended notice of appeal and a skeleton argument in which he abandoned reliance on the Case 19 time point. Instead, he contended that the Case 19 notice which had been given was not an effective notice under section 21. But a few days later, when he had seen the landlord's skeleton argument and respondent's notice, he settled a supplemental skeleton argument. In this he revived his argument that, if this was a claim under Case 19, the proceedings were out of time. He met the waiver argument by contending that the time limitation went to jurisdiction and the parties could not confer jurisdiction on the court by consent.

The tenants' appeal against Judge Holt's decision was fixed for hearing on 10 or 11 March 1992. A week before, on 3 March, on the advice of counsel, the landlord's solicitor wrote to the tenants' new solicitors an open letter proposing terms on which the appeal could be compromised. This letter did not in terms concede that judgment had been given below on a false basis nor that the possession order could not stand, and it sought to maintain Judge Holt's costs order. The tenants had very little time to respond to the letter, and most of the costs of the appeal had by then been incurred anyway.

The Court of Appeal (Purchas and Mann LJJ) heard the tenants' appeal over two days. They held that the agreed basis upon which the case had been fought in the court below was fundamentally unsound for the reasons summarised above. In a reserved judgment handed down on 26 March 1992 Mann LJ held that section 34 of the 1988 Act (which he described as of "a complexity which does not admit of paraphrase") did not apply because no tenancy had been entered into after the commencement of the Act. In October 1989 the tenants became and therefore remained statutory tenants. They did not become assured shorthold tenants and accordingly section 21 of the 1988 Act was of no materiality. But they were vulnerable to a claim properly made under Case 19. Unfortunately for the landlord, however, the proceedings under Case 19 had not been commenced within the three-month time limit. The court held that the time limit went to jurisdiction. It accordingly concluded that the judge's decision could not be supported either on the ground on which it had been given or on the ground argued by the landlord on appeal. It allowed the appeal with an expression of sympathy for the landlord "because if his summons had been issued 12 days earlier and his case then been conducted on the correct basis, his claim for possession ... would on the judge's findings seem to have been unanswerable".

When the Court of Appeal's judgment was handed down there was a discussion of costs. The court made no order in relation to costs save for legal aid taxation of the tenants' (new) solicitors' costs of the appeal. The court indicated that it was "minded to make an order and will make an order that the solicitors concerned in the court below shall be personally and severally and jointly liable to reimburse the legal aid fund on an indemnity basis for any costs incurred not already met by charges in favour of that fund on the legally assisted parties". Purchas LJ had indicated that the court was concerned to protect the legal aid fund so far as was proper. The solicitors were given time to show cause why an order should not be made against them.

After the Court of Appeal's decision, the landlord served a further notice seeking possession under Case 19. The tenants did not give up possession. After expiry of the notice (and within the statutory time limit) he issued further proceedings claiming possession under that case. The tenants served a defence denying that the landlord had served a protected shorthold tenancy notice before the 1985 tenancy agreement had been made and denying that Judge Holt's judgment concluded that issue. At a hearing before Judge Proctor in October 1992 the tenants sought to re-litigate that issue, contending that it was not res judicata. The judge rejected the argument and made a possession order under Case 19. The tenants appealed against Judge Proctor's order. In July 1993 their appeal was dismissed.

The solicitors who acted for the landlord and the tenants in the action heard by Judge Holt appeared by counsel in this court and sought to show cause why the proposed wasted costs order should not be made against them. The landlord himself is to be indemnified by the Solicitors' Indemnity Fund in relation to all costs orders made against him in that action. At issue now are the costs incurred in the action by the legal aid fund.

It has never been suggested that either the landlord's or the tenants' solicitor acted improperly or unreasonably. The question was whether they had acted negligently. In his additional skeleton argument for the solicitors, Mr Hytner QC did not dispute that the landlord's solicitor had been negligent in failing to bring Case 19 proceedings in time and that the tenants' solicitor had been negligent (though not, it was said, actionably so) in failing to take the point. But plainly this negligence, assuming it to be such, did not cause the action to proceed as it did in the county court: that was the result of the solicitors' agreement that if the protected shorthold tenancy notice had been served the landlord was entitled to possession because section 34 converted the tenants' holding into an assured shorthold tenancy which the notice under Case 19 was effective to determine under section 34. It is now plain that the solicitors' agreement was based on a misunderstanding of the law. Were they negligent in failing to understand the law correctly?

Dismay that a straightforward dispute between landlord and tenant should have led to four county court actions (one still undecided), two appeals to this court and the passing of three years (so far) since the litigation began might well prompt an answer unfavourable to the solicitors. We can well understand why Purchas and Mann LJJ reacted as they did. But we do not in all the circumstances think it right to stigmatise the solicitors' error as negligent, for these reasons.

(1)   This legislation is very far from straightforward. Mann LJ commented on the complexity of section 34 of the 1988 Act. Judge Holt commented that she couldn't make head or tail of it. We sympathise with her. It is unfortunate that legislation directly affecting the lives of so many citizens should not be more readily intelligible.

(2)   The solicitors do not appear to have approached the case in a careless way. There is nothing to contradict their statements that the textbooks they consulted did not give a clear answer to their problem. They could not be expected to bring the expertise of specialist counsel to the case. Nor could they reasonably expect to be remunerated for prolonged research. We do not think their error was one which no reasonably competent solicitor in general practice could have made.

(3)   It is significant that a most experienced county court judge saw no reason to cavil at the basis upon which it had been agreed to conduct the case. Had the error been egregious, it is hard to think the judge would not have corrected it.

(4)   Counsel appearing for the tenants on appeal from Judge Holt did not regard the basis on which the case had been argued below as unsustainable. On the contrary, he argued (among other things) that the statutory tenancy which began in October 1989 was an assured shorthold tenancy by virtue of section 34 of the 1988 Act, which was the basis of the solicitors' agreement criticised by the Court of Appeal. We think it significant that experienced counsel did not discard the argument as obviously wrong.

After two days of argument by counsel, and having reserved judgment, this court was able to take a clear view of the legal point at issue. This view was directly contrary to the solicitors', and is plainly right. But it does not follow that the solicitors were negligent in forming the opinion they did. We do not think they were.

There is a further consideration. Had the landlord stuck to his Case 19 claim before Judge Holt, and had the tenants relied on the time point, the landlord would have failed. There might or might not have been an appeal. But it seems clear that the parties would at some stage have wished to litigate the issue whether the protected shorthold tenancy notice had been served before the first letting. This might have been decided on the first, or on a later, occasion. It seems likely, given the history of this litigation, that the tenants would have sought to appeal against an adverse finding on this issue whenever it was made. Thus although the solicitors' mistaken agreement to fight the case on the basis they did must have led to some waste of costs, it would be wrong to regard all the costs incurred before Judge Holt and in the Court of Appeal as wasted.

Allen v Unigate Dairies Ltd

The plaintiff's solicitors appeal against the third part of a wasted costs order made at Liverpool County Court on 10 May 1993 by Judge Lachs. Their appeal against parts one and two of his order has been compromised by agreement between the parties.

The plaintiff, who was legally aided, claimed damages for noise-induced hearing loss said to have been caused by exposure to a decrater machine at his place of work. On the day of trial in March 1993, before opening, the claim was dismissed by consent, it being then accepted that the plaintiff's workplace was not dangerously noisy. The judge held that the appellants had been negligent in failing to discover this at an earlier stage and ordered, so far as is presently material, that there should be no legal aid taxation of their costs after 1 November 1992.

The case for the appellants is that they had relied on the instructions of their client to themselves and to their expert, on the reports of their expert and on counsel and had acted as reasonably competent solicitors.

Before examining the relevant material, a preliminary point arises under the Legal Aid Regulations as to the form of the judge's order.

It is apparent from regulation 107 of the Civil Legal Aid (General) Regulations 1989, SI No 339, that a judge has no power to forbid legal aid taxation. Regulation 107(1) states that costs "shall be taxed in accordance with any direction or order given" and regulation 107(3)(b) states that a final judgment decree or order "shall include a direction ... that the costs ... be taxed on the standard basis". By virtue of regulation 107(4) if such a direction is not given "costs ... shall be taxed on the standard basis". It follows that taxation of a legally assisted person's costs is mandatory and must take place after final judgment whether or not the judge orders it.

However, a judge does have power, under section 51(6) of the Supreme Court Act 1981 and regulation 109(1), to order that, on taxation, wasted costs shall be disallowed or reduced after notice has been given by the taxing officer to the solicitor or counsel enabling him to be heard.

In the present case no criticism was made of counsel. But if no taxation took place he could not be paid by the Legal Aid Board.

Accordingly the appropriate procedure in a legally aided case, if a judge properly concludes that a wasted costs order is appropriate, is for him to order legal aid taxation, to send, if he wishes, a copy of his judgment to the taxing officer and to direct under section 51(6) that wasted solicitors' costs after a particular date be disallowed and consideration be given to whether counsel's fees be disallowed or paid by the Legal Aid Board.

The central question in the present appeal is whether there was before the judge material justifying his conclusion that the appellants had been negligent.

He reached this conclusion having regard to the following matters.   (1) The "extremely skimpy statement" taken from the plaintiff in September 1988;   (2) the plaintiff's advisers' failure to make appropriate inquiries about the plaintiff's place of work;   (3) the fact that there was no dangerous level of noise at the plaintiff's place of work;   (4) the lack of explanation as to why matters were not clear until the morning of the trial;   (5) the failure to obtain counsel's opinion and a full report;   (6) the failure to inquire as to the significance of a line on a plan, provided by the defendants, which depicted a wall; (7) the failure to recognise the confusion between "decrater", "recrater" and "flyer" which was apparent on sight of the defendants' expert's report; (viii) the failure to take any steps properly to identify the plaintiff's place of work and the effect of noise there.

For the appellants, Mr Mansfield submitted that, on a true analysis of the evidence, there was no substance in any of these criticisms.

In addition to the skimpy statement, the schedule to the questionnaire annexed to the particulars of claim gave details about the plaintiff's place of work. The plaintiff's instructions to the appellants and their expert described working in the back bay bottle reception area and used the words "flyer" and "decrater" when referring to the noisy machine. The plaintiff's expert had interviewed the plaintiff in July 1992 and marked the site plan provided by the defendants on his instructions: it was not then suggested that the line to which the judge referred denoted a wall. The plaintiff's expert referred to the bottle reception area as the back bay where the plaintiff worked, to the machine as a decrater, also known as "the flyer", and to the defendants' disclosed noise level tests as showing in 1986 dangerously excessive levels from the decrater, which the expert assumed was in the bottle reception area. The defendants' expert's report served in September 1992, far from suggesting any error in this approach, also referred to the decrating machine known as "the flyer" in the back bay. The plaintiff's expert, to whom the appellants again referred in early 1993, did not suggest that an inspection of the site was necessary: in any event the layout had changed since the plaintiff worked there. There was nothing in the defence or the correspondence from the defendants' solicitors to alert the appellants to the fact that, as was demonstrated on the morning of the trial, there was a de-stacker but no decrater in the back bay and there was a solid wall between the decrater and the plaintiff's place of work. At pre-trial conferences with two different counsel, neither had suggested that such a fundamental error had been made. It was not until 6 May 1993, a few days before the hearing on the costs application, that the defendants' solicitors conceded in an affidavit that their expert was wrong.

In the light of this material this experienced judge in our judgment fell into error. The appellants acted throughout on the plaintiff's instructions and obtained appropriate legal and expert advice on which they were entitled to rely. With the benefit of hindsight it is clear that the plaintiff was unlikely to have been exposed to excessive noise if there was a wall between him and the decrater. But, in our judgment, there was nothing prior to the date of trial which ought reasonably to have put the appellants on inquiry either as to the significance of the line on the plan or as to the possibility that the plaintiff was not exposed to noise from the decrater. It is, indeed, regrettable, having regard to the present climate favouring a cards-on-the-table approach to litigation, that the defendants' solicitors, if they were aware of it, did not, in correspondence, expressly point out to the appellants the error which they were making. Accordingly, the appellants did not act improperly, unreasonably or negligently.

We are conscious that it is particularly necessary in relation to the many thousands of industrial deafness claims which are being pursued in Liverpool and elsewhere that firm judicial control should be exercised over the parties to such litigation and their legal advisors. We have no doubt that in an appropriate case a wasted costs order or a direction that on legal aid taxation the taxing officer shall disallow or reduce costs, is a useful means for exercising such control. But in the present case, for the reasons given, this was not an appropriate case for such an order. Accordingly, we set aside the judge's order disallowing legal aid taxation and to that extent this appeal is allowed.

Roberts v *Coverite (Asphalters) Ltd*

The plaintiff's solicitor appeals against an order made by Judge Tibber at Edmonton County Court on 14 April 1993 that he should pay the defendants' costs of the action.

The plaintiff, legally aided with a nil contribution since September 1987, claimed the price of work done by proceedings instituted in the county court on 10 November 1988. The appellant, in accordance with the practice of London practitioners, sent to the court with the particulars of claim, notice of issue of legal aid and the original legal aid certificate. It was the court's practice to serve a copy of the notice of issue with the summons. The appellant asked in his accompanying letter that one copy of the notice (which he sent in duplicate) be sealed and returned to him. The court did not serve a copy of the notice of issue on the defendant nor return a sealed copy to the appellant and it was accepted that this was the court's fault. The appellant assumed that the court had served the notice on the defendant, for the claim was served and a defence was filed.

Initially the claim was for a little over £3,000 plus interest. By amendment in September 1989 this became £4,677 and a claim was added on a dishonoured cheque in the sum of £531. No amended defence was served. In February 1990 the defendant admitted that a sum of £232 was due. In March 1990 the plaintiff sought summary judgment for that sum plus the amount of the cheque, i.e. £763, but that application was adjourned and further particulars were twice supplied by the plaintiff. On 25 February 1992, the appellant "reminded" the defendants' solicitors of the plaintiff's legal aid and expressed surprise that no offer had been made, drawing attention to the sum of £763 apparently due. On 26 February the defendants' solicitors replied, acknowledging that £232 was due but saying that this would not of itself result in an order as to costs. They said they would amend to deny the claim on the cheque if necessary and stated that the failure to give notice of issue of the legal aid certificate would entitle them to an order against the appellant personally for their costs to date. The appellant did not reply. There were no further negotiations and no payment into court There was no application to amend the defence. In September 1992 the appellant filed a certificate of readiness with a time estimate of one and a half days and in October 1992 the case was set down for trial on 15 March 1993. On 17 February 1993 the defendants' solicitors wrote to the appellant saying that five days would be necessary and seeking a rearranged date for trial. On 1 March the appellant refused this request. On 3 March the defendants offered £2,500 including costs in settlement, referring again to the failure to notify the issue of legal aid and to the possibility of an order against the appellant personally for costs under Order 62, rule 11. The appellant replied that the plaintiff would accept £2,500 plus costs which he estimated at £4,500 plus VAT. On 11 March the defendants offered £5,000 inclusive of costs. On 15 March at the door of the court the case settled for £2,500 plus costs on scale 1 without prejudice to the defendants' application for costs against the appellant.

In November 1988 the relevant regulations were the Legal Aid (General) Regulations 1980, SI No 1894. Regulation 51 provided:

"(1)   Whenever an assisted person becomes a party to proceedings, or a party to proceedings becomes an assisted person, his solicitor shall forthwith – (a) serve all other parties to the proceedings with notice of the issue of a certificate; and (b) if at any time thereafter any other person becomes a party to the proceedings, forthwith serve similar notice on that party.

(2)   Copies of the notices referred to in paragraph (1) shall form part of the papers for the use of the court in the proceedings.

(3)   Where an assisted person's solicitor – (a) commences any proceedings for the assisted person in the county court; or (b) … and at the same time files a copy of the notice to be served in accordance with paragraph (1), the registrar shall annex a copy of the notice to the originating process for service."

For the appellant, Mr Mansfield submitted that paragraph (1) to the regulation must be read with paragraph (3), so that where proceedings are commenced in the county court by someone who is already legally aided, compliance with regulation 51(3) is a complete performance of the solicitor's obligation. On this basis the appellant was not in breach of regulation 51. In any event, even if he was in breach of that obligation by not serving the notice personally and direct, he was acting in accordance with the practice of other solicitors in the London area. As the appellant in due course received a defence, there was no reason for him to suspect that only part of the documents which should have been served had been served, save that a sealed notice of issue of the legal aid certificate was not returned to him, as he had asked. The learned judge, submitted Mr Mansfield, placed too much weight on this and failed to give any weight to the fact that the court itself had failed to serve the notice. The appellant's failure to realise that this had not been returned to him does not, submitted Mr Mansfield, amount to culpable behaviour within *Saif Ali* v *Sydney Mitchell & Co* [1978] 3 All ER 1033, [1980] AC 198 because other solicitors had adopted the practice.

In any event, submitted Mr Mansfield, even if the appellant's conduct was properly categorised as negligent, the judge failed to give any proper consideration to the question of causation. A wasted costs order can only be made if costs have been wasted by reason of the culpable conduct. Here, the costs were incurred by defending the claim. It was not sufficient for the judge to be satisfied that the defendants would have sought to settle at the outset if they had known that the plaintiff was legally aided; it also had to be established on the balance of probability that, with that knowledge, they would either have made an acceptable offer or paid into court a sufficient sum to win on costs at the end of the day. In February 1992, when the defendants' solicitors knew that the plaintiff was legally aided, no payment was made into court nor was any attempt at settlement made by the defendants' solicitors. It was not until one week before the hearing that they made their first offer of settlement and although, in February 1992, the defendants' solicitors acknowledged that £252 was due, that sum was not paid into court.

For the defendants, Mr Weddell submitted first that regulation 51(1)(a) imposes an absolute duty on a solicitor to serve a notice of issue of a legal aid certificate personally and that regulation 51(3) is, as the judge found, a belt and braces provision. He points out that (3) refers to "a copy of the notice" whereas (1) refers to the notice. Regulation 8, which relates to service of notices under the legal aid regulations, refers only to notices, not copies of notices.

In our judgment, so far as notification of issue of a legal aid certificate is concerned, there is no significant difference between a notice and a copy of a notice. The solicitor for the legally assisted person receives from the Law Society a legal aid certificate. He prepares a notice of its issue and he must serve notice of its issue on the other party: whether he does so by a document properly described as an original or a copy is in our judgment entirely immaterial.

Mr Weddell further submitted that the appellant did not send the notice to the court for service but sent it for return to himself. This in our view overlooks the fact that, as is apparent from the accompanying letter, he sent two copies of the notice, only one of which was to be returned to him.

We are unable to accept Mr Weddell's submission that the appellant's conduct here amounted not to mere negligence but to recklessness. Clearly the appellant was in error in failing to observe that the sealed copy of the notice had not been returned to him and in assuming that the court would have effected service of the notice. But we are wholly unpersuaded that this amounted to improper, unreasonable or negligent conduct.

In any event, we are unable to accept Mr Weddell's submissions on causation. He said that the judge, having accepted the evidence of the defendants' director, Mr Speroni, and the defendants' solicitor that advice to settle would have been followed, was entitled to conclude that settlement would have been made at an early stage. Mr Weddell also pointed out that settlement was ultimately achieved at a figure in the region of a third of the value of the claim including interest. But in our judgment the conclusion is inescapable that the judge did not properly address the question of causation. We accept Mr Mansfield's submission that the history of events between February 1992 and March 1993 which we have earlier set out makes it impossible to conclude on the balance of probabilities that with knowledge that the plaintiff was legally aided in November 1988 the defendants would have made either a successful payment into court or an acceptable offer earlier than they did.

Accordingly, we take the view that there was no proper basis here for the judge to make a wasted costs order against the appellant. We add only this. When a solicitor opts for the court to serve process he should expressly inform the court that he wishes notice of issue of legal aid to be served by the court.

In the light of this conclusion, it is unnecessary to determine the difficult question as to whether the judge had any jurisdiction to make the order he did, having regard to the fact that the act or omission relied on occurred prior to October 1991 when the Courts and Legal Services Act 1990 came into force, but complaint was not made until March 1993. This court held in *Fozal v Gofur* (1993) *The Times*, 9 July, that the Act is not retrospective, so section 51(6) would not provide jurisdiction. Order 62, rule 11, under the old form of which the county court had jurisdiction (see *Sinclair-Jones v Kay* [1988] 2 All ER 611, [1989] 1 WLR 114), was amended from 1 October 1991 to refer to section 51(6). But there are no transitional provisions in the Act or the rule. The answer depends on whether, on the proper construction of section 16 of the Interpretation Act 1978, there was, on 1 October 1991, an accrued right capable of enforcement by legal proceedings. Having regard to the view which we have formed on the merits of this matter, it is unnecessary for us to embark on answering that question.

This appeal will accordingly be allowed and the judge's order set aside.

Philex plc v Golban

The appellants in *Philex plc v Golban* are solicitors against whose firm a wasted costs order was made in the Companies Court. Their client had claimed to be a creditor of the company, which was solvent. The debt was disputed. The client had nevertheless made use of the statutory demand procedure as a means of pressure to force payment. The company applied for and obtained an injunction to restrain the issue of a winding-up petition, and an order for their costs of that application against the client on an indemnity basis. Having reason to doubt the solvency of the client, the company applied further that their costs should be made the subject of a wasted costs order against his solicitors. The judge made such an order, not upon the ground that the solicitors were open to any criticism for issuing the statutory demand in the first place, but because at a later stage (when the payment time allowed by the statutory demand had expired) they were parties to a negotiating offer which made unreasonable or improper use of the implied threat of a winding-up petition as an inducement to the company to compromise the claim.

The facts, which are helpfully set out in the full and careful judgment of Knox J, were these. On or about 18 December 1992 the alleged debtor company Philex plc completed the purchase of a property in north-west London (the property) for a price in the region of £370,000. The alleged creditor, Mr S Golban, claimed to be entitled to an introduction fee or commission on the purchase, in respect of which he invoiced Philex as follows on 22 December 1992:

> "For introduction of the above property purchased from L & S Properties at purchase price of £370,000 and completion taken place on 21st Dec 1992. Agreed commission of 3% £11,100."

The claim was promptly denied on behalf of Philex, whose finance director, Mr Torbati, replied on 24 December:

> "We are in receipt of your invoice ... which we do not understand. So far as we are aware we have no liabilities outstanding to yourselves."

On that same day (24 December) the appellant firm (acting as solicitors for Mr Golban through a partner to whom it will be convenient to refer as "the solicitor") served on Philex a statutory demand in the approved Form 4.1. That form has indorsed upon it in heavy black type the warning "REMEMBER! The company has only 21 days after the date of service on it of this document before the creditor may present a winding-up petition".

It was signed by Mr Golban, who designated the solicitor as the person to whom any communications were to be addressed. The demand re-asserted the commission claim in the sum of £11,100 and alleged that Philex had refused to pay it. The letter from the solicitor's firm covering service of the statutory demand included a note that their offices would be closed from 1.30 pm that day (24 December) to 9.30 am on Monday 4 January 1993.

On 31 December 1992 Iliffes, solicitors acting for Philex, wrote to the solicitor's firm in response to the statutory demand. They disputed that Mr Golban had at any time acted for or been engaged for any purpose by Philex, which did not deny that he had been concerned in discussions with it about the purchase but contended that the company had been given to understand that he was acting exclusively on behalf of the vendors. The letter continued:

> "Our client is a solvent company. The reason that our client refuses to pay your client the sum claimed or any other sum is that your client has no entitlement to be paid. The alleged debt is disputed by our client and your client's statutory demand is an abuse of the process of the Companies Court. Unless we receive your client's undertaking by 4 pm on Monday 4th January 1993 [which was the first working day after the date of that letter and was also the day on which the solicitor's office was due to re-open] that he will take no further steps in relation to the statutory demand and that he will not issue a winding-up petition in respect of it our client will make an immediate application to the

Companies Court to restrain your client from presenting a petition and will apply for its costs on the indemnity basis in accordance with the principles laid down in *Re a Company* [a reference to Hoffmann J's re-affirmation in *Re a Company (No 0012209 of 1991)* [1992] 2 All ER 797 at 800, [1992] 1 WLR 351 at 354 of the principle that it is an abuse of the process of the Companies Court to present a winding-up petition to secure payment of a debt concerning which there is a genuine dispute] ... "

The solicitor duly found that letter of 31 December waiting for him when he returned to his office on 4 January, and sent a copy of it (together with a copy of the law report of *Re a Company*) to his client Mr Golban, whom he knew to be abroad and not due to return until 5 or 6 January. He did not feel that he could give the required undertaking without instructions from his client. The 4 pm deadline allowed by Iliffes' letter of 31 December accordingly passed, and on 5 January Iliffes issued an originating application in the Companies Court, returnable on 25 January, and seeking an order for an injunction restraining Mr Golban from presenting any petition to wind up Philex based upon the statutory demand. That application was served on the solicitor's firm the same day (5 January) under cover of a letter which stated that the affidavit in support would be served shortly.

This supporting affidavit was in fact served on the solicitor's firm on Friday 8 January. It was sworn by Mr Torbati, who stated Philex's general case as follows. Mr Golban had indeed introduced the property to Philex's managing director (Mr Sabourian) and had acted as an intermediary to convey to the vendors certain offers that were initially made for it by Philex. Those offers did not, however, bear fruit. Philex thereafter entered into direct negotiations with the vendors which led eventually to an agreement for sale in which Mr Golban had played no part. Mr Torbati went on to describe Mr Sabourian as having expressed the wish, nevertheless, to make some ex gratia payment to Mr Golban for his introduction. He had suggested a figure of £2,000, which Mr Golban had rejected as wholly inadequate.

The solicitor did not read this evidence on the Friday on which it was served, but considered it on Monday 11 January (having in the meantime sent a copy of it without comment to Mr Golban). It should be noted that the judge had no criticism to make, down to that point, of the solicitor's conduct in any respect whatsoever.

On that same day (11 January) the solicitor wrote a letter to Iliffes which contained no more than a simple acknowledgement of receipt of the affidavit. His client's comments on that affidavit were received on 13 January: it may safely be assumed (although privilege has not been waived) that those comments dissented strongly from Mr Torbati's version of events.

The expiry date of the 21-day period allowed by the statutory demand was 14 January. On that day the solicitor was telephoned by Mr Evered of Iliffes, who asked him whether Mr Golban was intending to resist the pending application for an injunction against presentation of a petition (due to be heard on 25 January), pointing out at the same time that it was now

crystal clear that there was a genuine dispute about the claim and that Mr
Golban was at risk of having to pay costs on an indemnity basis if he
invoked the winding-up procedure. The solicitor replied that he had
explained this to his client, who was nevertheless adamant that he was owed
the money and wanted to go ahead. When Mr Evered asked him whether he
intended to issue a petition, because if he did Philex would apply
immediately for an ex parte injunction to restrain its advertisement, the
solicitor replied that he would have to take instructions and would get back
to him on that point. After that conversation, the solicitor had to leave
immediately to attend a court engagement, and when he returned to his
office he found a fax copy of an ex parte injunction which had been obtained
by Iliffes that day prohibiting the issue by Mr Golban of any petition to wind
up Philex until the conclusion of the hearing due to take place on 25 January.

On Friday 15 January at the latest (it was possible, according to the
finding of the judge, that the relevant advice had been given two days earlier,
on 13 January) the solicitor advised Mr Golban specifically that in the
current state of the evidence a genuine dispute existed as to the subject
matter of the statutory demand, and that it would be an abuse of the process
of the court to present any petition founded upon it. Mr Golban accepted
that advice, but at the same time gave the solicitor certain instructions, as to
which there has, again, been no waiver of privilege, but it may safely be
assumed from what followed that they included a request to see if something
in the nature of a compromise could be salvaged from the existing situation.
The solicitor accordingly that same day drafted a letter to Iliffes, to which
reference will be made shortly, but did not post it that day because he wanted
to have it approved by counsel to whom he submitted the draft for
consideration over the weekend.

On 18 January Iliffes faxed a letter to the solicitor seeking to substantiate
a suggestion previously made that Mr Golban had become the subject of
bankruptcy proceedings, and giving him notice:

> "unless terms can be agreed for the relief sought and payment of our client's
> costs prior to the hearing of the application on 25 January we shall ask that an
> Order be made against your firm personally to pay our client's costs on the
> indemnity basis."

On 19 January the solicitor sent to Iliffes the letter which had been
submitted in draft to counsel. It included the following passages:

> "It appears from your client's affidavit that he has offered payment of £2,000 to
> our client in satisfaction of the claim. Whilst our client wishes to reserve his rights
> to pursue the full claim he is nevertheless prepared to accept payment of £2,000
> together with our reasonable costs if this can be agreed before 25 January. If not,
> our client intends to issue proceedings for the full amount of his claim and seeks
> your confirmation that the sum of £2,000 will be paid into court in such
> proceedings. In spite of his reservations arising from the discrepancy between
> what you have stated on behalf of your client and what your client states in his

affidavit our client accepts that the evidence contained in the affidavit establishes, prima facie, a dispute rendering inappropriate the continuation of the winding-up procedure and confirms that he does not intend to present a winding-up petition. We note your comments regarding our position and the alleged bankruptcy of our client. He has, as you know, denied to us that he is bankrupt and in view of your persistence in asserting this we have made a search against our client which has disclosed that there are no subsisting entries. We are therefore unable to agree with your contention that we should be personally liable for costs and will certainly oppose any such application."

The proposal in that letter for settlement of Mr Golban's claim for £2,000 and his costs was rejected by Iliffes on 21 January. No agreement was reached as to how matters should proceed at the hearing on 25 January. The upshot was that counsel attended that hearing, on the instructions of the solicitor on behalf of Mr Golban, and offered no resistance to an order for an injunction in the terms prayed by the originating application. An order was made that Mr Golban should pay Philex's costs of the application on an indemnity basis. An application intimated at that hearing for such costs to be paid by the solicitor's firm personally was adjourned to a later date, and was dealt with by Knox J on 30 June 1993 when he made the wasted costs order now under appeal. This was an order that the solicitor's firm –

"do pay the wasted costs incurred by [Philex] after 13 January 1993 to be taxed if not agreed but credit should be given for such costs as would have been incurred in disposing of the [application] by consent."

The judge's reasons for treating the costs incurred by Philex from and after 14 January 1993 as "wasted" for the purposes of section 51(6) and (7) were expressed in these terms:

"I have come to the conclusion that it was unreasonable and indeed improper to use proceedings which by 11 January 1993 [the solicitor] should have realised and did realise amounted to an abuse of the process of the court as a vehicle to secure a compromise on the basis of the £2,000 claim which at one stage was offered. [The solicitor] did indeed, on his own evidence, advise his client Mr Golban not to proceed with the statutory demand on 15 January. He should, and indeed may, have done so, when Mr Golban gave [the solicitor], on or about 13 January, his comments on Mr Torbati's affidavit. The fact that Mr Golban continued to believe in the merits of his case for commission is not any justification for not accepting that the winding-up procedure was inappropriate and should not be followed."

This passage makes it clear that the conduct of the solicitor which the judge regarded as unreasonable or improper for the purposes of section 51(7) consisted of his adoption on Mr Golban's behalf from and after 14 January 1993 of the tactic of threatening the use of a winding-up petition, presented in abuse of the process of the court, as a bargaining counter to improve his client's prospects of persuading Philex to accept a compromise of the claim at the suggested figure of £2,000 plus costs.

The appellant firm submits that this finding of misconduct was not open to the judge on the evidence and can only have been founded on a misreading of the correspondence. It points out: (1) that the relevant compromise was proposed in the letter of 19 January, in which it was quite clearly and unconditionally stated that Mr Golban accepted that the evidence established a bona fide dispute making the continuance of the winding-up procedure inappropriate, and confirmed that he did not intend to present a winding-up petition. There was therefore no question of the solicitor using potentially abusive proceedings as "a vehicle to secure a compromise".   (2) That the compromise proposal was in any event contained in a letter whose text had been approved by counsel on whose advice the solicitor was entitled to rely.

With every respect to the views of a judge with wide experience in this field of the law who had obviously given the case detailed and careful attention, these submissions are, in our judgment, well-founded. We do not suggest that there could never be circumstances in which a solicitor who advised his client to make use of a threat of proceedings that would (if brought) amount to an abuse of the process might be found to have been guilty of improper or unreasonable conduct. It is simply that we are unable to find any evidential basis for the judge's conclusion that misconduct of that sort had occurred in the present case. The solicitor was, moreover, entitled to rely upon the fact that from 15 January onwards he was acting on the advice of counsel, both generally in regard to the prosecution of Mr Golban's claim to commission and specifically in regard to the compromise proposal, the terms of which (as proposed in the letter of 19 January) had been approved by counsel.

Mr Otty, arguing in support of the notice to affirm which has been served in the appeal by Philex, suggested that there was an alternative ground on which the judge could (and in his submission should) have based a wasted costs order. From 14 January onwards the solicitor had a client who was eligible in law (the 21 days of the statutory demand having expired) to present a winding-up petition, and who – although willing to acknowledge that the debt demanded was a disputed debt, and willing even to accept that to present a petition would involve abuse of the court process – was nevertheless not prepared to take the crucial step of instructing his solicitor to give a formal undertaking to the court that no petition would be presented. From that point, therefore, so Mr Otty argued, it became the solicitor's duty to stop acting altogether, and to tell Mr Golban that he must either take different advice or act in person. Had the solicitor ceased to act from 14 January onwards, the wasted costs would, it is asserted, have been saved.

We are unable to accept that argument. The solicitor was not criticised by the judge for anything he did (or omitted to do) down to and including 13 January. It would involve setting an over-scrupulous standard for the solicitor, as well as running some risk of unfairness to the client, if the solicitor were to be expected to terminate his retainer abruptly on 14 January, with the hearing only 11 days away, solely upon the ground that the client, although willing to give appropriate assurances, was unwilling to authorise the formal undertaking which would make any contest at that hearing unnecessary. Nor does it appear to us that the costs of a contested hearing on 25 January would necessarily have been saved by his ceasing to act. It is by no means unlikely that Mr Golban, deprived of his solicitor, would have insisted upon maintaining his opposition and would have resisted the application thereafter as a litigant in person. The same objection applies to Mr Otty's alternative submission (to which it is unnecessary to refer in detail) that costs could have been avoided if advice that presentation of a petition would be abusive of the process had been given to Mr Golban by the solicitor on 13 January instead of 15 January 1993.

For these reasons the appeal will be allowed and the wasted costs order discharged.

Watson v *Watson*

The appeal in *Watson* v *Watson* lies against a wasted costs order made in financial proceedings between a former husband and wife. The wife, on legal advice, had persisted in maintaining a technical point of law which, when litigated at a contested hearing, was found to be wholly without merit. The specific default on the part of her solicitor which gave rise to the order had been his failure to answer adequately a letter from the husband's solicitors in which his attention had been drawn to a point which the court was later to find wholly conclusive against the wife's objections. The judge considered that a full and proper answer to that letter would greatly have improved the prospects of the matter proceeding by consent, and would thus have saved the expense of a contested hearing to debate what turned out in the end to be an unarguable point. She therefore made a wasted costs order against the wife's solicitor in respect of part of the costs of the contested hearing at which the wife's objections had been overruled.

A brief reference needs first to be made to the legal background against which the proceedings had arisen. In the Family Division – unlike other areas of the law where parties sui juris can obtain an order by consent disposing of the action on terms which involve no consideration by the court of their fairness – the court retains a supervisory jurisdiction to approve proposed financial compromises between spouses on their merits (see *Livesey* (*formerly Jenkins*) v *Livesey* [1985] 1 All ER 106, [1985] AC 424). Where a "clean break" compromise is to be effected on the basis of a payment of capital in extinguishment of future rights of maintenance, the terms for which the court's approval is sought may provide for the capital to be transferred to the maintained spouse outright, or for it to be settled on trust for that spouse for a life interest only, with remainder to the children of the family. If the capital is to be settled, the court will either approve a trust deed already tendered to it in draft, or else (if no draft has yet been agreed) approve the proposed trust provisions in principle, leaving the parties to agree the details between themselves. In the latter case, the court retains a residual jurisdiction to approve the terms of the trust deed in default of agreement between the parties.

In cases where the capital is to be settled, the best practice (as the judge observed in the present case) is undoubtedly to follow the course of having a draft trust deed ready for court approval at the time when the consent order is made: there can then be no scope for argument about trusts which are already defined at the point of compromise in a definitive instrument which itself forms part of the terms of settlement expressly approved by the court. There may however be circumstances in which that proves impracticable, and agreement has to be obtained in principle for trusts which are to be worked out in detail later. Though that is a sensible procedure, and may in some circumstances be the only possible one, it is a course fraught with risk of future dispute. Opposing views are liable to arise, for example, as to when the primary trusts declared on the face of the court order take effect: do they vest an immediate interest in the beneficiaries from the moment that the order is perfected, or do they remain inchoate until incorporated in the proposed trust deed?

It was the emergence of difficulties such as these which underlay the proceedings in the present case. Mr and Mrs Watson's marriage had taken place in November 1974. Their only child Robert was born in April 1976. By July 1977 the parties had separated, and they never again lived together, despite attempts at reconciliation. The husband was a man of some wealth. The wife suffered (and still suffers) from a drug dependency problem which was a principal cause of the failure of the marriage and was sufficiently acute to require Robert to be brought up by his father from the age of three. In July 1977 the parties had signed a deed of separation which contemplated arrangements under which the wife would become entitled to have properties purchased for her occupation during her life by trustees who would hold the reversion for Robert if he attained the age of 25, and subject to that upon such trusts as the husband should appoint.

Divorce proceedings were started by the husband in 1988 on the ground of their long-term separation. In October of that year the wife claimed financial relief in the same proceedings. She was slow in pursuing her claim, and no hearing date was fixed before 2 March 1992 (one month before Robert's sixteenth birthday). On 21 February 1992 the husband's solicitors wrote to the wife's solicitors with proposals for a clean break settlement of all the wife's outstanding claims for maintenance from the husband (or his estate) upon terms that the wife's current home (a London flat) should be settled, together with a fund of £150,000, upon trust for her for life. It was proposed that "the ultimate beneficiary of the Trust" should be Robert "who will be entitled, providing he has attained the age of 25 years, to the capital fund on the earlier of your client's remarriage or her death".

That proposal was not accepted, and the parties came to court prepared for a contested hearing on 2 March 1992. Their professional advisers began to talk. Door-of-the-court discussions, always by nature urgent, had in this case a particular immediacy because no one had been able to predict with any confidence that the wife would attend the hearing at all: she had nevertheless come to court on this occasion, and if the matter was to be compromised on her instructions it would be necessary to take advantage of her presence by concluding a firm agreement there and then.

The discussions bore fruit. A compromise was agreed, very much on the lines of the letter that had been written by the husband's solicitors, in that it provided for a fund of realty and investments to be settled on the wife for life. Because this had been expected to be a contested hearing, there was as yet no draft trust deed in being. Provision would therefore have to be made in the order for such a deed to be drawn up later. In the course of the negotiations the wife's advisers had pressed hard for the agreement of the husband to pay her future costs of approving the ultimate form of the trust deed. This was refused, and the wife submitted to a direction that each party should (in this as in all other respects) bear their own costs.

A draft order was written out in counsel's handwriting, and the parties then went before Judge Wilcox (sitting as a deputy High Court judge), where the nature and effect of the order were explained to him and he approved it. That consent order of 2 March 1992 (perfected on 4 March) reads (so far as relevant) as follows:

> "By consent IT IS ORDERED:
>
> (1)   that the Petitioner [husband] do as soon as is practicable effect two settlements upon and for the benefit of the Respondent [wife] as follows:– (a) the flat at 8, Stafford Mansions, London SW11 shall be held by trustees who shall hold the property upon terms that: (i) the Respondent may occupy the property during her lifetime and following her death the property shall pass to the child of the family Robert Watson absolutely, and, (ii) the Trustees shall have power upon request being made to them by the Respondent [to invest in an alternative property] and (b) the sum of £150,000.00 shall be settled upon the trustees upon terms that the whole of the income arising therefrom shall be payable to the Respondent during her lifetime, with reversion, following her death to the child of the family Robert Watson absolutely ...
>
> (2)   that both of the two trusts described in the preceding paragraph shall be subject to the following additional terms: (a) the trusts shall be established in the Cayman Islands, (b) the Trustees shall be Ansbacher Ltd or a similar trust company established there, at the nomination of the Petitioner, (c) the cost of establishing the two trusts shall be borne by the Petitioner, and (d) in the event that the Respondent dies before the child of the family, Robert, attains the age of 25 years, then his reversionary interests shall be accumulated (subject to a power in the trustees to advance capital in their discretion) until he shall attain the age of 25, whereupon he shall be entitled to the capital of both trusts absolutely."

The order further provided for payment by the husband to the wife of a lump sum of £2,500, and that each party should bear his or her own costs.

There had been one oversight in the drafting of the consent order, in that it omitted a provision (which had been common ground in the negotiations) that her life interest should subsist only until remarriage. The order was amended by consent under the slip rule on 6 April 1992 to make good this omission.

Later that month the husband's solicitors sent to the wife's solicitors a first draft, and in June a second draft, of a trust deed which contained two provisions that were to prove controversial. These were that Robert's reversionary interest should not be vested in him absolutely, but should be made contingent: (a) upon his attaining the age of 25 (we shall refer to this as "the age contingency"); and (b) upon his being alive at the date of the falling in of the prior income interest given to his mother – i.e. at the date of her death or remarriage (we shall refer to this as "the survivorship contingency"); with an ultimate gift over to the husband in the event that Robert failed to fulfil either contingency.

The wife's solicitor referred the drafts to the wife's matrimonial counsel, who advised that they should be submitted to specialist trust counsel in the same chambers.

On 7 July 1992 the wife's solicitor wrote to the husband's solicitors objecting, on counsel's advice, both to the age contingency and to the survivorship contingency (and consequently to the gift over to the husband) upon the ground that they represented a cutting down of the interests provided for Robert under the original consent order – interests which (as they contended) were vested and indefeasible. In their reply of 16 July 1992 the husband's solicitors maintained a contrary view of the construction of the order, asserting that both contingencies were already implicit in its terms. This was referred by the wife's solicitor to counsel, on whose advice he wrote to the husband's solicitors on 6 September asserting that the interests to be taken by Robert under clause 1 of the consent order were "immediately vested remainder interests" unaffected by the subsequent trust for accumulation of income up to the age of 25, and citing authority of some antiquity for that proposition.

The husband's solicitors then, for their part, consulted counsel, on whose advice they wrote to the wife's solicitor on 16 October 1992. In their first paragraph they stated that they were willing to delete the age contingency. In the remainder of the letter they concentrated upon the survivorship contingency. It was pointed out that if Robert was treated as taking an immediate and indefeasible reversionary interest, then in the unfortunate event that he should predecease his mother – dying either under the age of 18 or over that age unmarried and intestate – the reversion would pass to his next of kin under his intestacy. One of his next of kin would be the wife, whose life interest would become enlarged pro tanto into an interest in capital. The whole basis (it was pointed out) of the negotiations which had resulted in the wife being given an income interest only in the relevant trust property was that she ought not to be given access to any substantial sums of capital because of the risks to which capital would be subject in her hands as a result of her addiction.

The letter therefore proposed that the consent order should be further amended by introducing the words "if then living" into the relevant provisions of paragraph (1), so as to put it beyond doubt that Robert's interests were to be subject to the survivorship contingency. The relevant passages of the letter ended by saying:

"If we cannot agree it will be necessary to issue a summons before a High Court Judge for directions to be given as to the appropriate construction, implementation or amendment of the Order of the 2nd March 1992. We understood ... that you would be making an application. If we do not hear from you within 14 days with your confirmation that we have reached agreement on the outstanding issues, we shall issue a summons ourselves."

On 14 December 1992 the wife's solicitor replied:

"We have had an opportunity of speaking with Counsel concerning this matter who has advised that it must be brought back to Court under the liberty to apply provision. We are accordingly obtaining a date as speedily as possible as our client has been substantially prejudiced by the inaccurate drawing up of the trust and your client does not seem prepared in any way to be of any assistance in the interim."

After the husband's solicitors had replied on 17 December refuting the suggestion of prejudice to the wife's interests and stating that they had hoped that the matter could have been dealt with by consent and a "substantive response" received to their letter of 16 October, the wife's solicitor responded on 23 December by saying:

"Your hope that this matter could have been dealt with by consent has been prevented by your intransigence in respect of the question of costs. We do not see why our client should have a further charge in respect of her costs hanging over her head by virtue of your mistake, not the first in this case in relation to this settlement. If your client is prepared to undertake our costs in relation to these matters, our Counsel may take a different view in relation to the way that this matter can be dealt with. We take the view that we are entitled to an Order for costs and returning the matter to court is the only way in which this can be dealt with."

The correspondence was brought to an end by the husband's solicitors who wrote on 6 January 1993:

"Our client is not prepared to pay your client's costs in relation to our unnecessarily extensive correspondence over this issue. You could have limited your client's costs by accepting long ago the proposals which we put forward. We are not prepared to engage in any further correspondence with you regarding this matter."

The wife's solicitor accordingly took out a summons claiming the court's approval of a form of trust deed which would give Robert an absolute and indefeasible interest in reversion. It was supported by an affidavit exhibiting the correspondence from which we have quoted. The summons came before Booth J on 10 March 1993 and was dismissed by the judge, who made an order authorising the settlement to proceed in the form proposed by the husband's solicitors. The judge made it plain that she regarded the objections taken by the wife's advisers to any provision making Robert's reversionary interest contingent upon surviving his mother's death or remarriage as wholly without merit. Firstly it was quite wrong, she said, to subject a consent order negotiated outside the court door to the very strict rules of construction that would be appropriate to a most carefully drafted deed or other legal document. Secondly, on construing any consent order in matrimonial proceedings it was essential to look behind the words of the order to see what the parties desired to achieve, and the possibility of the wife becoming entitled to a capital interest in any circumstances lay wholly outside the contemplation of both parties at the time.

The wife was at all material times legally aided. After Booth J had delivered judgment, Mr Pointer, counsel for the husband, asked for a wasted costs order against the wife's solicitor in respect of the husband's costs of the application. He made no corresponding application against either of the counsel who had advised the wife. There was some discussion with the judge as to the basis on which a wasted costs order might be made. Mr Pointer said that he relied firstly on the fact that the wife's solicitor had sought a form of trust deed which was unsupportable on any proper interpretation of the consent order, and secondly on his failure at any time "properly to address the substance" of the letter of 16 October 1992. The judge expressed some doubts about the first ground, but described herself as "appalled" by the lack of response to the letter of 16 October. She acceded however to the objection by the wife's counsel that a wasted costs order should not be made without giving the wife's solicitor a proper opportunity of answering the complaint on which it was founded, and she adjourned the application to be restored in the near future, with leave to the wife's solicitor to file an affidavit in the meantime if so advised. According to the note of the judge's remarks made by the husband's solicitor, counsel for the wife asked the judge at that point –

> "whether she could advise that the charges against those instructing her were for a contribution to the husband's costs because of the failure to [answer sensibly the letter of 16 October 1992 and] negotiate upon the terms of the letter dated 16 October 1992. Mrs Justice Booth confirmed this."

Pending the adjourned hearing of the application for a wasted costs order, the wife's solicitor swore an affidavit in which he expressed his understanding that Booth J had accepted at the main hearing that her rejection of the substantive arguments raised on behalf of the wife was not a ground on which she would make a wasted costs order: he therefore concentrated on the criticism of his failure to answer specifically the points raised in the letter of 16 October. He confirmed that he had at all times acted, in connection with the approval of the terms of the draft deed, on the advice of matrimonial and trust counsel. He had referred the letter of 16 October to counsel and received advice which made it clear to him that there was no question of any agreement or compromise in relation to the construction of the trust deeds. He said:

> "The reason for rejecting any proposals in the letter of 16 October were the same as before and the same as advanced at the Hearing namely that [the husband's solicitors] were introducing into the trust deed a contingency not provided for in the Court Order."

He added that even if his answers to the 16 October letter were thought to have been inadequate, no costs had been wasted in consequence: the only answer he could have given was the one advised by his counsel – namely a repetition of the contention that the consent order had created vested rights in his client and her son to the removal of which he could not agree unless the court were so to direct.

The hearing of the wasted costs order application took place on 7 April 1993. Mr Pointer relied upon the two grounds he had already indicated at the main hearing, namely: (a) the intransigent pursuit by the wife's solicitor of a case that he knew, or ought reasonably to have known, was hopeless; and (b) the failure by the wife's solicitor to deal in specific detail with the terms of the letter of 16 October.

The judge expressed strong sympathy, in the course of her judgment, with ground (a), but in the end she refrained from basing any wasted costs order upon it. Her forbearance in this respect was in our opinion fully justified for the following reasons.

(1)   The practice of stating trusts in principle on the face of a consent order, the details of which are to be set out in a formal trust instrument for subsequent agreement and execution is one which (as we have observed at the start of our judgment on this particular appeal) opens up hazardous territory in which there is wide scope for dispute and misunderstanding. The absence of any authority cited to us as to how the court acts in such circumstances suggests, moreover, that it is territory uncharted by any guidance as to principle. The wife's solicitor had every justification, therefore, for taking a strict and cautious view of his client's rights (and those of Robert). The fact that the judge in the upshot was prepared to view the case robustly and to brush his scruples aside as pedantic does not mean that the solicitor was wrong to prepare himself for the possible doubts of a more cautious and less confident tribunal by insisting that his client's apparent vested rights should be defended at a contested hearing.

(2)   The wife's solicitor did not maintain his stance independently. He was at all material times advised by both matrimonial and trust counsel, neither of whom was sought to be made a respondent to the wasted costs order application. If the judge intended, by her references to *Davy-Chiesman v Davy-Chiesman* [1984] 1 All ER 321, [1984] Fam 48, to suggest that there were analogies between that case and this, we would respectfully disagree. Counsel's views may not in the end have prevailed before the judge, but they were cogent and clear, and it was entirely reasonable for the wife's solicitor to have acted on them.

(3)   The judge had already committed herself, by her remarks at the end of the main hearing, to absolving the wife's solicitor from liability to a wasted costs order on this ground.

We therefore hold, despite Mr Pointer's able argument in support of the respondent's notice which has been served by the husband, that the judge was right not to base any wasted costs order on ground (a).

We turn to ground (b), on which the husband was successful. The judge repeated her earlier strictures on the failure of the wife's solicitor to deal more fully with the letter of 16 October. The fact that it had always been common ground between the parties that the wife would take no interest (vested or contingent) in the capital to be settled under the "clean break" agreement was (as she had held at the substantive hearing) the crucial factor in the case. It was nevertheless not a factor to which either side had previously referred in correspondence. When, therefore, the husband's solicitors raised it for the first time in their letter of 16 October, it became the duty of the wife's solicitor to take it up, bring a fresh mind to bear on it, and make use of it to give a new turn to the negotiations. Had he followed that course, there would have been an improved chance that common sense would have prevailed on both sides and a basis reached for an unopposed application to the court to have a draft trust deed incorporating the survivorship contingency formally approved. Those views were summarised by the judge in the following terms:

> "In my judgment the matter that was raised by [the husband's solicitors] was a matter of importance which had not been addressed before, as [the husband's solicitors] point out, by the court order, by the parties or indeed by their advisers. It was a matter which was relevant and should have been resolved. I accept the submission of Mr Pointer that it was inadequate for [the wife's solicitor] on behalf of the wife once the matter was raised merely to say that the question should be placed before the court without more ado. It is a very different matter to place an application, if there had to be an application, before the court on a consent basis, which could have been done by one solicitor without representation by the other side but with a letter indicating consent, from the matter being raised in court where the issue is in conflict and where both parties have to be represented by counsel and solicitors, thereby incurring very substantial costs indeed. If this matter had been discussed in the way that the first matter in issue between the parties had been (that is, deferring Robert's interests until the age of 25), agreement might have been reached. If not, at least the husband and his advisers would have known the practical objections raised by the wife to their very sensible suggestion of how that matter should have been resolved. As it was, the wife's case was not clear until the hearing or shortly before it. There is a responsibility upon all legal practitioners to take every step possible to avoid a contested court hearing, thereby incurring additional costs. As I said during discussion of these matters following upon my judgment of 10 March, I was, and continue to be, appalled by the fact that that letter of 16 October 1992 was not answered and was not dealt with. That seems to me to be a very serious omission which comes within

the guidelines given in the criminal case of *Re a Barrister (wasted costs order) (No 1 of 1991)* [1992] 3 All ER 429, [1993] QB 293, and referred to in *The Supreme Court Practice 1993* Supplement. I think that that was an unreasonable omission. It amounted to a failure properly to negotiate a clearly relevant matter which could then have been dealt with without incurring the substantial costs that ultimately followed."

Those conclusions, reached by a judge with unrivalled experience in the field of matrimonial finance, are entitled to the fullest respect. Nevertheless the reasoning which they incorporate was in our judgment unsound in two respects.

Firstly, the conduct of the wife's solicitor in regard to the 16 October letter was not conduct which could in our judgment be properly described (whatever criticisms may be made of it in other respects) as unreasonable. The original agreed intention to ensure that the wife had no capital under the proposed settlement was not a surprise factor in the case: indeed the very fact that this intention had been fundamental to the negotiations which led up to the consent order provided the chief reason for the court's conclusion at the main hearing. The only effect, therefore, of the letter of 16 October was to give this factor a specific emphasis which it had not so far received in correspondence. Such emphasis certainly required the wife's solicitor to give it renewed and serious consideration. It is difficult, however, to think of any way in which he could have done that more effectively than by taking the step (which he did) of passing the letter on to counsel for his further specific advice. Once counsel had advised that his views were unchanged – i.e. that the terms of the original consent order were nevertheless still to be regarded as creating an interest in capital which (although reversionary) was free of the survivorship or any other contingency and was immediately and immutably vested in Robert or his estate – the wife's solicitor was entitled to construe his duty to his client as leaving him with no alternative but to continue his opposition to any proposal that Robert's vested rights should be cut down by agreement. This does not mean that he was entitled to escape criticism altogether. The judge had ample justification for finding the wife's solicitor's replies to the letter of 16 October too grudging, perfunctory, and generally unhelpful to be acceptable when judged according to the highest standards of the profession. But those are not the standards which the court has to apply when considering whether a solicitor's conduct has been sufficiently unreasonable to merit the making of a wasted costs order against him. When the criterion which we have described in our statement of general principles as the acid test is applied to the conduct of the wife's solicitor in regard to the answering of the letter, we regard it as conduct which, although undeserving of praise, does nevertheless permit of a reasonable explanation.

Secondly, on the question of causation, the judge's remarks appear to us to go no further than to say that a fuller response to the letter would have improved the prospects of an uncontested hearing. They fall substantially short of any finding sufficient to establish that causal link (which we have described in our statements of principle as essential) between the conduct complained of and the costs alleged to have been wasted. Nor would there have been scope, in our judgment, for any such finding to have been made. It could not be assumed that if the factor introduced into the correspondence by the letter of 16 October had been specifically addressed, there would have been no need for a contested hearing. A specific response could only have proceeded, in the light of counsel's latest advice, on the lines of "We are sorry: we have carefully considered the factor you mention and taken advice about it, but we are advised that we have no option in our client's best interests but to persist in our objections". The matter would still have had to come back to court on a contested basis.

For these reasons the appeal in *Watson* v *Watson* will be allowed and the wasted costs order made against the wife's solicitor will be discharged.

Antonelli and others v *Wade Gery Farr (a firm)*
In the summer of 1987 Mr Antonelli, a property developer of somewhat unsavoury reputation, and two of his companies (we shall refer to them compendiously as "Mr Antonelli") wished to buy a property called Ermine Court in Huntingdon. The property consisted of a number of flats, a shop and some space used for car parking. Mr Antonelli wished to intensify the development of the site, in particular by building on the car parking space. His offer was accepted and he instructed the defendant, a local firm of solicitors, to handle the conveyancing of the transaction. Although Mr Antonelli paid the vendor the balance of the purchase price in March 1988 the sale was not completed until July 1990.

By then Mr Antonelli and the defendant solicitors had long fallen out. On 12 June 1990 he issued a writ against them, accompanied by a statement of claim settled by counsel. It had become plain that the property could not be developed, partly because the car parking bays had been let to the owners of the flats, and also that the date for serving a rent review notice on the shop had passed. A number of complaints were accordingly pleaded against the defendant solicitors, including failure to complete on time and failure to make proper inquiries, and a very large claim was made. The statement of claim was amended in September 1990 by different counsel.

The trial was fixed to begin on Monday 6 April 1992. On 16 March 1992 a third member of the Bar, whom we shall call "C", became involved on Mr Antonelli's side. She was instructed to resist an application for security for costs. In the event the application was never heard, but C kept the pleadings in the action.

On Wednesday 1 April 1992 C was asked if she would represent Mr Antonelli at the trial due to begin in five days' time. She said she would. On that day, and on the following days, she pressed for a conference to be arranged with her client, even going to the length of telephoning the solicitor in charge of the case at his home. But no conference was, as we understand, arranged. On Friday 3 April Mr Antonelli, who had received legal aid up to but not including the trial, was refused legal aid for the trial. By Friday evening, with the case due to begin first thing on Monday, C had received no brief and no witness statements. She had seen a copy of her expert's report, but this had been taken away again and she had no copy. She had that day received a bundle of documents prepared by the other side; those acting for Mr Antonelli had not prepared a bundle. Thus all C had to prepare over the weekend for her opening of the case on Monday morning was the pleadings and the defendant solicitors' bundle of documents.

When C arrived at court on Monday morning she received from Mr Antonelli a copy of a bundle of documents which he had himself prepared. Its contents differed from the defendant solicitors' bundle; many of the pages were illegible; and C had no time to familiarise herself with it before the court sat. C was expressly instructed by Mr Antonelli not to seek an adjournment, because he was under financial pressure and wanted a result. But, appreciating that her claim for damages was quite inadequately particularised, C did ask the trial judge (Turner J) if he would agree to determine liability first and then quantum if it arose. This course was resisted by the defendant solicitors and the judge did not agree. He did however direct the defendant solicitors to serve a request for further and better particulars at once and C to reply to it by 10.30 am the next day. This was done.

It is unnecessary to rehearse the full history of the trial. It became clear that the basis on which part of Mr Antonelli's damages had been claimed was still unsatisfactory. Further pleading was needed. At 10.30 am on the morning of Wednesday, 8 April the judge accordingly indicated that he would dismiss that damages claim "unless full and proper particulars setting out precisely how the claims are made up are served by 10.30 on Monday morning". Counsel originally instructed for Mr Antonelli and the defendant solicitors (neither of whom appeared at the trial) had estimated the length of the trial at five and seven days respectively, and it seems clear that at this stage the hearing was expected to last until Monday, 13 April. C was also seeking to re-amend her statement of claim to plead a new head of damage, as a result of answers given by Mr Antonelli which made it hard to sustain the original basis of claim; the judge did not refuse leave finally, but he made clear that he would not grant leave unless the claim was more fully particularised.

In a commendable endeavour to complete the case expeditiously, the judge announced on Wednesday, 8 April that the court would sit at 10.00 am on Thursday, Friday and Monday. With the same end no doubt in view, he indicated when the court sat on Thursday morning that he would be assisted by counsel putting their submissions in writing. He added that he would not prevent oral submissions but would not encourage them. Counsel for the defendant solicitors agreed. C did not demur. When the court adjourned on Thursday, it was expected that the evidence would be completed by mid-morning the next day. The judge indicated that when the evidence had finished he would adjourn until 2.00 pm before receiving submissions. Both parties agreed. The judge observed that on that basis "we will just about finish this case, the oral part of it, tomorrow".

As hoped, the oral evidence finished by about 11.30 on the morning of Friday, 10 April. Counsel for the defendant solicitors handed up to the judge a copy of his closing submissions in manuscript. He also gave C a copy, but the copy was neither complete nor legible. C, who indicated some unfamiliarity with this procedure, said she was still working on her submissions. The judge handed down to the parties a note he had prepared entitled "Principal Issues of Fact", intended to indicate to counsel the areas in which he would welcome submissions. The first of these was directed to the development potential of the site. The judge then adjourned until 2.00 pm.

When the court sat again at 2.00 pm, C had still not received a full and legible copy of the written submissions of counsel for the defendant solicitors. He then made relatively brief oral submissions. When he had finished C handed up her own written submissions, to the extent she had completed them. She made some oral submissions. She then indicated that she wished to have the opportunity to make further submissions on Monday morning. At 3.17 pm on Friday afternoon the court adjourned until 10.00 am on Monday.

On Monday, 13 April the hearing opened with discussion of the re-amendment C was seeking to make to the statement of claim. The judge deferred ruling on this until liability had been determined. C gave the judge her further written submissions prepared over the weekend, and addressed the court on the issues. At 11.15 the judge reserved judgment and adjourned.

On Friday, 22 May 1992 the judge gave his reserved judgment. In this he made various comments critical of the defendant solicitors' handling of the case, but dismissed the action. He rejected Mr Antonelli's evidence and held that the defendant solicitors' defaults had not caused him damage. On behalf of the defendant solicitors an application for a wasted costs order was then made against Mr Antonelli's solicitors and C, his counsel. The judge directed that the claim and the answer to it should be properly pleaded, and this was duly done.

The application came on for hearing by the same judge on 3 August 1992. After an hour's adjournment, the claim against the solicitors was compromised on the solicitors' undertaking to pay a sum equal to the excess payable by them under their policy of insurance. Those underwriting the defence of the defendant solicitors accepted this settlement because they were also underwriting the claim against Mr Antonelli's solicitors and would, by continuing, have been claiming against themselves. But, as the judge later observed –

> "it is in the highest degree improbable that the sum offered and accepted is other than a small fraction of what was likely to have been the effect of an order (if any) made at the end of the current proceedings."

So the application went on against C alone. At the end of a full day's hearing the judge again reserved judgment, which because of other commitments he was not able to deliver until 27 November 1992.

The defendant solicitors based their application against C on six grounds. Two of these the judge in his judgment rejected and no more need be said about them. Of the four grounds the judge upheld, counsel for the defendant solicitors has in this court found it impossible, having heard the argument for C, to maintain his reliance on one. This related to the rent review of the shop. We consider that this concession was rightly made, since the argument advanced by C in the court below, although unlikely to succeed, could not properly be abandoned without Mr Antonelli's consent. There remain three grounds upon which the judge found against C. These were   (1) C's failure to complete her written submissions on Friday, 10 April, obliging the court to sit again on Monday, 13 April.   (2) C's pursuit of the claim relating to the development potential of Ermine Court.   (3) C's unreasonable slowness in the conduct of the proceedings. We shall return to these three grounds below.

But the judge also held against C on a more fundamental, far-reaching ground. Earlier in his judgment he had referred to the following parts of paragraphs 501 and 601 of the Bar's Code of Conduct:

> "501.   A practising barrister must not accept any brief or instructions if to do so would cause him to be professionally embarrassed ... (b) if having regard to his other professional commitments he will be unable to do or will not have adequate time and opportunity to prepare that which he is required to do ...
>
> 601.   A practising barrister (a) must in all his professional activities ... act ... with reasonable competence and take all reasonable and practicable steps to avoid unnecessary expense or waste of the Court's time ... (b) must not undertake any task which: (i) he knows or ought to know he is not competent to handle; (ii) he does not have adequate time and opportunity to prepare for or perform ... "

Then, having dealt with the various complaints one by one, the judge said:

> "In summary then, a number of areas have been identified in which, due to the conduct of counsel, the time of the court and thus of the defendants was expended unnecessarily. Before that can justify an award of costs being made against counsel personally on the application of the opposing party, I would have to be satisfied that the conduct giving rise to the complaint fell in one or more of the categories (a) negligent, (b) unreasonable or (c) improper. Having regard to the nature of the action and the volume of potentially relevant evidence, both oral and documentary, for counsel to have accepted an 'unseen' brief at the time and in the circumstances already described, despite the submissions made to me this afternoon, was 'unreasonable' and was likely to and did give rise to 'improper' conduct on her part. The unreasonableness stems from the manifest improbability of counsel being able to achieve an adequate grasp of the broad issues involved in the case, quite apart from the absolute necessity of having a full and adequate grasp of the details of the

evidence. In my judgment, for counsel to have accepted such a 'brief' at such short notice was, on any showing, both improper as well as being unreasonable. All the matters identified above as being open to substantial criticism were the direct consequence of those faults."

In the result, the judge held that the several failures of C which had been discussed in his judgment had unnecessarily prolonged the proceedings to the extent of at least one full court day. He accordingly ordered that the costs of one full day of the trial be paid by C personally to the defendant solicitors to the extent that such costs were not recovered from the plaintiffs or their solicitors. The order made plain that the sums recovered from the plaintiffs' solicitors under the settlement of the wasted costs application against them were to be treated as discharging the order against C to the extent that those sums exceeded the taxed costs of the preparation and delivery of trial bundles. The judge also ordered that the costs of the application for a costs order against C be paid by her to the defendant solicitors save to the extent that such costs had been increased by the adjournment of one hour of the hearing of the application. In practical terms, the principal sum which C (or, in truth, her insurer) is at risk of having to pay under the wasted costs order is about £1,100. The costs of the application for both sides (increased on C's side by changes of solicitor) are estimated to exceed £40,000.

Counsel for the defendant solicitors expressly abandoned on appeal the fundamental, far-reaching ground on which the judge had found against C, which indeed had not been advanced on their behalf before the judge. The extract from paragraph 501 of the Bar Code which the judge cited, presumably because he regarded it as relevant, is in truth irrelevant. The cited extract prohibits barristers accepting work which, because of other professional commitments, they are too busy to handle properly. That was not C's position and it was never suggested that it was. Paragraph 601 does, it is true, require barristers to show reasonable competence and avoid unnecessary expense and waste of court time, and also requires barristers not to undertake work beyond their competence or which they have inadequate time to prepare. But the judge omitted all reference to the cab-rank rule, paragraph 209 of the Bar Code, which we have cited above. When C was asked on Wednesday, 1 April to conduct this case on the following Monday she was not in our judgment entitled to refuse. She did not then know how inadequate her instructions would be (and she tried to procure reasonable instructions), but even if she had known she would not have been entitled to refuse. By Friday the inadequacy of her instructions was only too plain, but she would not even then have been entitled to refuse to act, unappetising though the prospect was. Paragraph 506 of the Bar Code provides:

"A practising barrister must not ... (d) except as provided in paragraph 504 return any brief or instructions or withdraw from a case in such a way or in such circumstances that his client may be unable to find other legal assistance in time to prevent prejudice being suffered by the client."

In short, C could not properly let Mr Antonelli down at the eleventh hour. There was no reason to think that anyone else would be better placed to conduct the case than she. She was professionally obliged to soldier on and do the best she could. The judge's failure to appreciate this vitiates not only his fundamental criticism, but also the three specific criticisms, since he held these to be the direct consequence of C's improper and unreasonable conduct in accepting instructions at all at such short notice.

That conclusion enables us to deal briefly with the judge's three specific criticisms. But we must consider those criticisms, since the defendant solicitors served (with leave) a respondent's notice contending that even if C did not act improperly or unreasonably in accepting the trial brief at short notice the judge's specific grounds of criticism remained independently valid and were not the result of late delivery of the brief.

(1)   We do not share the judge's conclusion that C is to be blamed for the court's sitting on Monday 13 April. The judge's earlier order had plainly contemplated a sitting on that day. The timetable had altered, but the order had never been varied or revoked. That apart, the judge (probably because he blamed C for accepting the brief at all) made inadequate allowance for the difficulties under which C laboured throughout, having during the hearing to settle further and better particulars, re-amend her statement of claim, familiarise herself with a new bundle, collect the evidence from her witnesses, try and make good the effect of damaging answers by her witnesses in evidence and, as the week wore on, prepare to cross-examine the opposing witnesses during a lengthened hearing day. It is unnecessary to consider whether the judge had power to direct that closing submissions should be in writing, since neither counsel objected. But C was fully entitled, indeed bound, to ensure that adoption of that procedure did not put her client in a worse position than if the conventional procedure had been followed. Before answering submissions on behalf of the defendant solicitors she was entitled either to hear them or, if they were in writing, study them. When counsel for the defendant solicitors sat down on the afternoon of Friday 10 April, she had not had the chance to study the written submissions. Nor, in fact, had she been able to complete her own written submissions. Had her submissions been oral she would not have completed them that afternoon. Justice plainly demanded that the hearing be adjourned until Monday 13 April.

(2)   We cannot, again, share the judge's view that C acted unreasonably in pursuing the claim for loss of development potential. In his judgment the claim rested on the assertion of Mr Antonelli and never had an outside chance of success. He noted that in C's closing submissions no substantive argument was advanced. It is certainly true that this was a most unpromising head of claim. But Mr Antonelli was himself a property developer, He was entitled to seek the court's ruling on the issue, with such little support as his expert gave him. The judge treated Mr Antonelli's knowledge on this aspect as a principal issue of fact. In the absence of any waiver by Mr Antonelli, we

do not know what (if any) advice C gave on pursuit of this claim or what instructions he gave. We do not, however, think that this was one of those situations in which C was entitled simply to decline to pursue the claim if her instructions were to do so. In our judgment she should not be held liable under this head.

(3)   In upholding the complaint that C's conduct of the proceedings had been unreasonably slow, the judge said:

> "Point (iii) is made good by a reading of the transcripts. On many occasions it was quite unclear to what issues either individual questions or sections of examination or cross-examination were directed. Moreover, there were a number of instances where questions were long, rambling and inchoate. There were no less than seven occasions upon which there were embarrassing pauses while counsel appeared not to know what the next question should be or topic to be investigated. Counsel's uncomprehending reply to this point merely serves to underline its validity."

The transcript certainly shows that the judge was on occasion tried by C's conduct of the proceedings; he was on occasion critical of her opponent also. But this is the sort of question on which very great weight must be given to the judgment of the trial judge. From his vantage point he can observe signs of unfamiliarity, lack of preparedness, laziness, incompetence and confusion with much greater perspicacity than an appellate court with only a transcript to work on. Very rarely could an appellate court be justified in interfering. But with some hesitation we feel we should do so here: first, because it might well be unfair to leave this criticism standing when the judge's fundamental criticism has been rebutted; and secondly, because (as indicated above) we think the judge made insufficient allowance for the great difficulties under which C laboured in presenting this ill-prepared and anyway very difficult case.

We would set aside the judge's order, quash the order against C personally and order that the defendant solicitors pay C the costs of the application against her.

No wasted costs order against solicitors in Ridehalgh v Horsefield. Appeals in the other actions allowed.

Benet Hytner QC (instructed by *Weightman Rutherfords*, Liverpool) for the former solicitors in the first action.
F P Nance (instructed by *Rawsthorn Edelstons*, Preston) for the tenants in the first action.
Duncan Matheson QC and *Guy Mansfield* (instructed by *Barlow Lyde & Gilbert*) for the solicitors in the second action.
The defendants in the second action did not appear.
Duncan Matheson QC and *Guy Mansfield* (instructed by *Barlow Lyde & Gilbert*) for the solicitors in the third action.
Geoffrey Weddell (instructed by *Colin Bishop & Co*) for the defendants in the third action.

Duncan Matheson QC and *Guy Mansfield* (instructed by *Barlow Lyde & Gilbert*) for the solicitors in the fourth action.

Timothy Otty (instructed by *Iliffes*) for the applicant in the fourth action.

Duncan Matheson QC and *Guy Mansfield* (instructed by *Barlow Lyde & Gilbert*) for the solicitors in the fifth action.

Martin Pointer (instructed by *Penningtons*) for the petitioner in the fifth action.

Rupert Jackson QC and *David Hodge* (instructed by *Richards Butler*) for counsel in the sixth action.

Gregory Chambers (instructed by *Mills & Reeve*, Norwich) for the defendants in the sixth action.

Ian Burnett and *James Laughland* (instructed by the *Treasury Solicitor*) appeared as amici curiae.

Duncan Matheson QC and *Guy Mansfield* (instructed by *Barlow Lyde & Gilbert*) for the Law Society.

Rupert Jackson QC and *David Hodge* (instructed by *Janice Bye*) for the General Council of the Bar.

Symphony Group plc
v
Hodgson

Court of Appeal, Civil Division
24, 25 March, 28 April 1993

Balcombe, Staughton and Waite LJJ

Headnote

This is an important Court of Appeal decision in the expanding line of authorities, which lays down the circumstances in which the court will, in its discretion, order a non-party to pay the costs of any proceedings.

---

28 April 1993. The following judgments were delivered.

BALCOMBE LJ: These appeals, from an order made by Robin Stewart QC sitting as a deputy judge of the High Court on 3 August 1992, raise important questions on the exercise by the court of its jurisdiction under section 51 of the Supreme Court Act 1981 to order that the costs of proceedings be paid by some person other than a party to those proceedings.

The plaintiff, Symphony Group plc (Symphony), carries on business as a manufacturer and supplier of kitchen units. The defendant, Lawrence Colin Hodgson, aged 25, was employed by Symphony as an estimating supervisor at a salary of £9,900 pa, with overtime his earnings were of the order of £12,500 pa. Mr Hodgson's contract of employment with Symphony contained restrictive covenants which provided, inter alia, that for one year after the termination of his employment he should not be engaged or interested in the manufacture or sale of kitchen furniture and that during the same period he should not work for certain listed companies engaged in the business of the supply and/or manufacture of kitchen furniture. On 29 May 1992 Symphony added, as they were entitled to do under the terms of the contract, the name of Halvanto Kitchens Ltd (Halvanto) to this list. Halvanto is a competitor of Symphony and is also engaged in the manufacture and supply of kitchen units.

In early January 1992 Mr Hodgson was exploring the job market. In March he saw Ellis Fairbank Associates, a recruitment agency, by whom he was introduced to Halvanto and on 16 March he had an interview with Mr Andrew Bramley, the managing director of Halvanto. Mr Hodgson was asked to come for a second interview and to bring with him his contract of employment with Symphony. On 14 April he had a second interview with a representative of Halvanto and shortly afterwards he was offered a job by Halvanto – a formal written offer and acceptance was dated 30 April, but the judge found that the actual offer was made and accepted on 14 April. On 1 May Mr Hodgson gave to Symphony, who at that time knew nothing of what he had been doing, written notice to terminate his employment. There were meetings in the following week between Mr Hodgson and representatives of Symphony and Mr Hodgson steadfastly refused to say who were his new employers. Symphony assumed that he was going to a competitor but did not know who. Mr Hodgson left Symphony's employment on 8 May 1992 and on the same day went to the offices of Messrs Walker Morris, solicitors who acted for Halvanto, and there drafted a letter to Symphony claiming that Symphony had repudiated his contract of employment by certain actions taken between 1 and 8 May 1992.

On 11 May Symphony issued a writ in the Queen's Bench Division of the High Court, to which Mr Hodgson was the sole defendant, claiming damages and injunctive relief against him and on the same day obtained an ex parte injunction from Schiemann J. The statement of claim was served on 12 May and on the same day Mr Hodgson was granted an emergency legal aid certificate. Accordingly the maximum period during which Halvanto could have financed Mr Hodgson's case was the four days between 8 and 12 May. Since that latter date Mr Hodgson has been in receipt of legal aid and Walker Morris and counsel instructed by them have acted for him under the terms of a legal aid certificate or certificates. Symphony's solicitors were notified of the grant of legal aid to Mr Hodgson on the following day, 13 May, and were in due course duly served with notice of the issue of his full legal aid certificate. Symphony's application for interlocutory relief came on inter partes on 15 May before Sir Gervase Sheldon, sitting as a judge of the High Court, when he continued the interlocutory injunction until trial or further order and directed a speedy trial. It was at that hearing on 15 May that Symphony first learned that Halvanto was Mr Hodgson's new employer. On 27 May Symphony's solicitors wrote to Halvanto a letter, addressed for the attention of Mr Bramley, which contained the following passages:

> "Our client has clearly notified you that its employees are under post-employment obligations restraining them from working for competitors. Despite this however, you have offered employment to one of Symphony's existing employees, Mr Lawrence Hodgson. That offer of employment has been accepted and since you have clearly induced Mr Hodgson to breach his contract of employment, Symphony now holds you liable to it in damages. Symphony intends to issue proceedings against you to recover such damages and we would be grateful if you would let us know whether any solicitors are instructed to accept service of those proceedings."

On 1 June Walker Morris, as solicitors for Halvanto, confirmed that they had instructions to accept service of any proceedings that Symphony might issue. At no time has Symphony sought to join Halvanto as a defendant to the action against Mr Hodgson, nor to initiate separate proceedings against Halvanto. At no time before the hearing of the action against Mr Hodgson did Symphony tell Halvanto that it might seek to make Halvanto liable for payment of the costs of that action.

The full trial of the action started on 22 June; by then pleadings had been closed, discovery completed and witness statements exchanged. This reflects considerable credit on everyone concerned: the parties, their solicitors and the court. The hearing lasted over eight days, the main issues being the validity of the restrictive covenants and whether Symphony had repudiated Mr Hodgson's contract of employment. In the course of the hearing Mr Bramley gave evidence for Mr Hodgson. On 6 July Robin Stewart QC sitting as a deputy judge delivered a written judgment which ran to 31 closely typed pages. He found for Symphony on every issue and granted substantial injunctive relief against Mr Hodgson, the claim for damages not being pursued by Symphony. He also made an order for costs against Mr Hodgson but, as Mr Hodgson was legally aided, directed that that order should not be enforced without the leave of the court. Realistically there is no prospect of Mr Hodgson being able to pay those costs which we were told could run into six figures.

In the course of his judgment the deputy judge expressed severe criticism of the actions of Halvanto and Mr Bramley. I cite the following passages by way of example:

> "When the defendant left the employment of the plaintiffs, his intention was to take up employment as a trainee sales representative, covering the Lancashire area with Halvanto Kitchens Ltd. They are direct competitors of the plaintiffs. On the face of the covenants in his contract of employment, this was in direct breach of those covenants. The evidence establishes, in my judgment, beyond any doubt, that both the defendant and Mr Andrew Bramley, the managing director of Halvanto Kitchens Ltd, knew that this was, on its face, a breach of the terms of the covenants, and intended by their conduct to take the plaintiffs on. Mr Bramley has in the preceding months twice considered taking on salesmen from the plaintiffs. Twice, on his admission, he had been advised by his solicitors against it, because of restrictive covenants in the contracts of employment of the respective salesmen ... Contrary to what Mr Andrew Bramley said in his statement ... the first interview of the defendant on 16 March 1992 was not for any specific job, but a general interview of a candidate who might possibly fit in somewhere. I find it difficult to give any description to that paragraph of Mr Bramley's statement other than that it was deliberately misleading ... In evidence, the defendant and Mr Bramley told me that the offer of 14 April was conditional on Halvanto being satisfied about the non-enforceability of the restrictive covenants. Had that really been the case, one would have expected that Mr Bramley would have referred the matter to his solicitors for their advice. But on his own evidence, he did not. He said that he and his chairman, Mr Curtis Wright, discussed the covenants,

and by themselves decided that they were too wide and unenforceable. I find this evidence unsatisfactory and incredible."

At the end of the judgment counsel for Symphony applied for an order that Halvanto should pay its costs of the action. The deputy judge could of course have dismissed the application then and there if he thought it had no substance. He did not do so, and in those circumstances very properly directed that the application be adjourned to a date to be fixed to enable Halvanto to be represented and that prior to any such hearing Symphony should serve upon Halvanto a notice setting forth the basis upon which the costs application was made.

By a summons dated 14 July 1992 Symphony gave notice of its application to Halvanto, the grounds of the application being contained in a schedule to the summons. The schedule is lengthy, extending to six and a half pages of typescript, but the matters on which Symphony relies to support its claim against Halvanto can be grouped under two main heads. (1) Paragraphs 2(1) to (10) inclusive relate to the employment of Mr Hodgson by Halvanto with knowledge of the restrictive covenants by which he was bound, and are all issues which could have been raised by Symphony against Halvanto if the latter had been joined as a party to the action. (2) Paragraphs 2(11) to (13) relate to the conduct of Mr Hodgson's defence to Symphony's action. I cite below selected portions of the schedule to illustrate the nature of the detailed allegations made against Halvanto:

"2 ... The plaintiffs rely upon the following facts and matters, which are either taken from the judgment delivered on Monday, 5th July 1992 or from the evidence given by Mr Andrew Bramley, the Managing Director of Halvanto, as a witness. – (1) Both the defendant and Mr Bramley on behalf of Halvanto knew that the proposed employment of the defendant by Halvanto was, on its face, a clear breach of the terms of the covenants contained in the defendant's contract of employment with the plaintiffs; (2) Each of them by their conduct intended 'to take the plaintiffs on.' ... (5) Mr Bramley so valued the defendant, that he was prepared to flout the restrictive covenants, and to take on the defendant as a trainee sales representative; a job for which he had no relevant experience and background; and at a salary package worth, with a car, some £17,000 pa.; (6) Contrary to what Mr Bramley said in his statement ... the first interview of the defendant on 16th March 1992 was not for any specific job, but a general interview of a candidate who might possibly fit in somewhere ... (9) *The Terms of the Offer* Halvanto was prepared to pay 'over the odds' to gain the services of the defendant, an unproven trainee because of his particular knowledge of the plaintiff's business, knowledge of a type that would not otherwise be available to the competition ... (11) At some point during the week of 4th May 1992, Mr Bramley referred the defendant to Messrs Walker Morris, solicitors to Halvanto ... rather than continue to use the sole principal firm he had already instructed in relation to his contract of employment, Nichols & Co. This large commercial firm is not in the habit of conducting litigation on Legal Aid. The defendant stated that he had not received a bill in respect of the pre-Legal Aid work. Mr Bramley said he did not know who was paying for this and said 'You will have to ask the Chairman, Mr Wright.' There is a clear inference to be drawn that the defendant's advice was being financed by his new employers at this stage and prior to the grant of Legal Aid ...

3. By reason of the above facts, Halvanto should pay the plaintiff's costs of this action. Halvanto sought to 'take the plaintiff on' and it should pay the costs of having failed in its attempt. It has been the driving force behind the defendant's defence in this action. Through Mr Bramley it steered the defendant towards its solicitors. It appears it has financed the defendant and has maintained his defence prior to the grant of Legal Aid. The plaintiffs' further rely on the fact that Mr Bramley was in regular attendance throughout the trial, almost on a daily basis, and played an active part in the proceedings, both in and out of the witness box. In pursuit of his company's objectives Mr Bramley has not hesitated to deceive the Court. His evidence is described in the judgment as 'incredible', 'unsatisfactory' and intended 'deliberately to mislead'. In such circumstances it is entirely appropriate that Halvanto, which had so much to gain from such underhand conduct, should bear the plaintiff's costs."

Symphony's summons came before the deputy judge on 31 July 1992, when both Symphony and Halvanto were represented by counsel. Halvanto's solicitors had previously indicated that Halvanto would take as a preliminary point that Symphony's application was an abuse of the process of the court. At the hearing before the deputy judge, Mr Gibbons, counsel for Halvanto, did not proceed with that submission, although he denies that he withdrew any application to that effect, and the order as approved by the deputy judge and drawn up contains no record of any such withdrawal as Mr Hochhauser, counsel for Symphony, had contended it should. The two preliminary points which were raised by Halvanto at this hearing were. (1) that the deputy judge should discharge himself on the grounds of apparent bias; and (2) that there was no case to answer on the basis that Symphony adduced no further evidence than that contained in the testimony of Mr Andrew Bramley, Halvanto's managing director, and the findings of fact contained in the judgment delivered on 6 July 1992.

The deputy judge ruled against Halvanto on both these points but gave leave to appeal. He then went on to give directions in preparation for the resumed hearing of Symphony's application against Halvanto, of which the only one necessary to mention here is the first:

"... the Plaintiff be entitled at the hearing of this application to rely upon the transcript of the evidence of Mr Andrew Bramley, Halvanto's Managing Director, and the findings of fact in the judgment delivered on 6th July 1992 as provisional findings of fact against Halvanto ... "

He then directed that, should Halvanto file a notice of appeal against his dismissal of its preliminary points, all further compliance with his directions should be stayed pending the outcome of the appeal. He then gave Symphony leave to appeal against the stay, and directed that the costs of that day's hearing be reserved to the resumed hearing.

Halvanto gave notice of appeal on 1 September 1992 and on 3 September 1992 Symphony cross-appealed against the order reserving costs of the hearing of 31 July, asking instead that Halvanto should pay the costs of that hearing in any event. On the same day Symphony also appealed against the stay of the directions.

Halvanto's appeal came before this court (Nourse and Steyn LJJ) on 21 January 1993, when the appeal was adjourned to a full three-judge court and Halvanto was given leave to amend its notice of appeal and Symphony was given leave to lodge an amended respondent's notice.

By its amended notice of appeal Halvanto asserts that the circumstances of the case were not such as to permit an order for costs being made against Halvanto by exercise of a judicial discretion in accordance with reason and justice as stated by Lord Goff of Chieveley in his speech in *Aiden Shipping Co Ltd v Interbulk Ltd, The Vimeira* [1986] 2 All ER 409, [1986] AC 965. It then elaborates that assertion by reference largely to the grounds set out in the schedule to Symphony's summons against Halvanto, although also by asserting that Symphony, having decided not to join Halvanto as second defendant to the action, was not entitled (having thereby deprived Halvanto of the chance of winning such an action) to seek an order for costs against Halvanto without the necessity of the attendant risks of litigation that such an action would have brought. Halvanto also maintains its contentions that the evidence of Mr Bramley, and the findings of fact contained in the judgment of 6 July 1992, could not in law be admissible against Halvanto and that the deputy judge should have discharged himself from hearing the application on the grounds of apparent bias. Symphony then served a respondent's notice seeking to affirm the judge's decision on 17 listed grounds. Those being the relevant facts, I turn to the issues which arise on this appeal.

Until the decision of the House of Lords in the *Aiden Shipping* case, it had not been appreciated that the wording of section 51 of the Supreme Court Act 1981, or of its statutory predecessors, empowered the court to order a non-party to proceedings to pay costs. It was thought that some limitation must be put upon the generality of the words – see *Forbes-Smith v Forbes-Smith and Chadwick* [1901] P 258 at 271, *John Fairfax & Sons Pty Ltd v E C de Witt & Co (Australia) Pty Ltd* [1957] 3 All ER 410, [1958] 1 QB 323 and the *Aiden Shipping* case [1985] 3 All ER 641, [1985] 1 WLR 1222 in this court – and that limitation was that the court could only order the costs to be paid by any of the parties. To that limitation there was one apparent exception, namely the ability to order a solicitor to a party to pay costs occasioned by his misconduct, but this was understood to be an exercise by the court of its inherent jurisdiction over solicitors as officers of the court, and was in any event regulated by the provisions of the Rules of the Supreme Court (now Order 62, rule 11). In the *Aiden Shipping* case the House of Lords held that section 51 should not be interpreted as being subject to the implied limitation, and that the *jurisdiction* to award costs was without limit. However in the course of his leading speech in that case Lord Goff made it clear that the *exercise* of the jurisdiction should be limited in accordance with the requirements of reason and justice. He said ([1986] 2 All ER 409 at 413, [1986] AC 965 at 975):

> "… it is not surprising to find the jurisdiction conferred under section 51(1), like its predecessors, to be expressed in wide terms. The subsection simply provides that 'the court shall have full power to determine *by whom* … the costs are to be paid'. Such a provision is consistent with a policy under which jurisdiction to exercise the relevant discretionary power is expressed in wide terms, thus ensuring that the court has, so far as possible, freedom of action, leaving it to the rule-making authority to control the exercise of discretion (if it thinks it right to do so) by the making of rules of court, and to the appellate courts to establish principles upon which the discretionary power may, within the framework of the statute and the applicable rules of court, be exercised." (Lord Goff's emphasis.)

And later ([1986] 2 All ER 409 at 416–417, [1986] AC 965 at 980–981):

> "In the vast majority of cases, it would no doubt be unjust to make an award of costs against a person who is not a party to the relevant proceedings … I do not, for my part, foresee any injustice flowing from the abandonment of that implied limitation. Courts of first instance are, I believe, well capable of exercising their discretion under the statute in accordance with reason and justice. I cannot imagine any case arising in which some order for costs is made, in the exercise of the court's discretion, against some person who has no connection with the proceedings in question. If any problem arises, the Court of Appeal can lay down principles for the guidance of judges of first instance; or the Supreme Court Rule Committee can propose amendments to the Rules of the Supreme Court for the purpose of controlling the exercise of the statutory power vested in judges subject to rules of court."

The facts of the *Aiden Shipping* case indicated the kind of close connection with the proceedings that Lord Goff had in mind. Following damage to a ship, the owners had made a claim against the charterers under a charterparty. The charterers in turn claimed against the sub-charterers under a sub-charter. Both claims went to arbitration and there were two awards. Both awards were ultimately remitted for further consideration and disputes then arose as to the scope of the remissions. The owners in the head charter arbitration and the charterers in the sub-charter arbitration issued originating notices of motion seeking a wider remission. Both remissions were by agreement heard together. As Donaldson MR pointed out in his judgment in the Court of Appeal if the claims had started by action rather than by arbitration, this would have been the classic "third party" situation and a court would have had power under the rules to make the owners pay the charterers' costs of the action, such costs to include any costs paid by the charterers to the sub-charterers in the third party proceedings (see [1985] 3

All ER 641 at 646, [1985] 1 WLR 1222 at 1228). Because these were arbitrations and not actions, the Court of Appeal held, regretfully, that Hirst J, the judge at first instance, did not have the power to make such an order as to costs; the House of Lords held that he did and restored his order to that effect.

Since the *Aiden Shipping* case there has been a number of reported decisions where the court has been prepared to order a non-party to pay the costs of proceedings. These decisions may be conveniently summarised under the following heads.

(1) Where a person had some *management* of the action, e.g. a director of an insolvent company who causes the company improperly to prosecute or defend proceedings: see *Re Land and Property Trust Co plc* [1991] 3 All ER 409, [1991] 1 WLR 601, *Re Land and Property Trust Co plc (No 2)* (1993) *The Times*, 16 February, *Re Land and Property Trust Co plc (No 3)* [1991] BCLC 856, *Taylor v Pace Developments Ltd* [1991] BCC 406, *Re A Company (No 004055 of 1991)*, *ex p Doe Sport Ltd* [1991] BCLC 865, [1991] 1 WLR 1003 and *Framework Exhibitions Ltd v Matchroom Boxing Ltd* [1992] CA Transcript 873. It is of interest to note that, while it was not suggested in any of these cases that it would never be a proper exercise of the jurisdiction to order the director to pay the costs, in none of them was it the ultimate result that the director was so ordered.

(2) Where a person has maintained or financed the action. This was undoubtedly considered to be a proper case for the exercise of the discretion by Macpherson J in *Singh v Observer Ltd* [1989] 2 All ER 751, where it was alleged that a non-party was maintaining the plaintiff's libel action. However, on appeal the evidence showed that the non-party had not been maintaining the action and the appeal was allowed without going into the legal issues raised by the judge's decision: see *Singh v Observer Ltd* [1989] 3 All ER 777.

(3) In *Gupta v Comer* [1991] 1 All ER 289, [1991] 1 QB 629 this court approached the power of the court to order a solicitor to pay costs under Order 62, rule 11 as an example of the exercise of the jurisdiction under section 51 of the 1981 Act.

(4) Where the person has *caused* the action. In *Pritchard v J H Cobden Ltd* [1988] Fam 22 the plaintiff had suffered brain damage through the defendant's negligence. That resulted in a personality change which precipitated a divorce. This court held that the defendant's agreement to pay the costs of the divorce proceedings could be justified as an application of the *Aiden Shipping* principle (see [1988] Fam 22 at 51).

(5) Where the person is a party to a closely related action which has been heard at the same time but not consolidated – as was the case in *Aiden Shipping* itself.

(6) Group litigation where one or two actions are selected as test actions: see *Davies (Joseph Owen) v Eli Lilly & Co* [1987] 3 All ER 94, [1987] 1 WLR 1136.

I accept that these categories are neither rigid nor closed. They indicate the sorts of connection which have so far led the courts to entertain a claim for costs against a non-party. However, it seems to me that the particular circumstances in this case require this court to accept the invitation of Lord Goff in the *Aiden Shipping* case and to lay down some principles for the guidance of judges of first instance when they are asked to make an order for costs against a non-party and in doing so I am well aware of what Lloyd LJ said in *Taylor* v *Pace Developments Ltd* [1991] BCC 406 at 408:

> "There is only one immutable rule in relation to costs, and that is that there are no immutable rules."

I am also aware of the observations warning against laying down rules for the exercise of a discretion in relation to costs generally by Bowen LJ in *Jones* v *Curling* (1884) 13 QBD 262 at 271 and by Brett MR in *The Friedeberg* (1885) 10 PD 112 at 113. nevertheless I am fortified by the fact that Lord Goff considered that such guidance might well become necessary and I believe that the circumstances of this case indicate the present necessity for guidance. In my judgment, the following are material considerations to be taken into account, although I do not suggest that there may not be others which are relevant.

(1)   An order for the payment of costs by a non-party will always be exceptional: see the *Aiden Shipping* case [1986] 2 All ER 409 at 416, [1986] AC 965 at 980 per Lord Goff. The judge should treat any application for such an order with considerable caution.

(2)   It will be even more exceptional for an order for the payment of costs to be made against a non-party, where the applicant has a cause of action against the non-party and could have joined him as a party to the original proceedings. Joinder as a party to the proceedings gives the person concerned all the protection conferred by the rules, e.g. the framing of the issues by pleadings, discovery of documents, the opportunity to pay into court or to make a *Calderbank* offer (see *Calderbank* v *Calderbank* [1975] 3 All ER 333, [1976] Fam 93), and the knowledge of what the issues are before giving evidence.

(3)   Even if the applicant can provide a good reason for not joining the non-party against whom he has a valid cause of action, he should warn the non-party at the earliest opportunity of the possibility that he may seek to apply for costs against him. At the very least this will give the non-party an opportunity to apply to be joined as a party to the action under Order 15, rule 6(2)(b)(i) or (ii).

Principles (2) and (3) require no further justification on my part; they are an obvious application of the basic principles of natural justice.

(4)   An application for payment of costs by a non-party should normally be determined by the trial judge: see *Bahai* v *Rashidian* [1985] 3 All ER 385, [1985] 1 WLR 1337.

(5)   The fact that the trial judge may in the course of his judgment in the

action have expressed views on the conduct of the non-party neither constitutes bias nor the appearance of bias. Bias is the antithesis of the proper exercise of a judicial function: see *Bahai v Rashidian* [1985] 3 All ER 385 at 388, 391, [1985] 1 WLR 1337 at 1342, 1346.

(6) The procedure for the determination of costs is a summary procedure, not necessarily subject to all the rules that would apply in an action. Thus, subject to any relevant statutory exceptions, judicial findings are inadmissible as evidence of the facts upon which they were based in proceedings between one of the parties to the original proceedings and a stranger: see *Hollington v F Hewthorn & Co Ltd* [1943] 2 All ER 35, [1943] KB 587 and *Cross on Evidence* (7th edn, 1990) 100–101. Yet in the summary procedure for the determination of the liability of a solicitor to pay the costs of an action to which he was not a party, the judge's findings of fact may be admissible: see *Brendon v Spiro* [1937] 2 All ER 496 at 503, [1938] 1 KB 176 at 192 per Scott LJ, cited with approval by this court in *Bahai v Rashidian* [1985] 3 All ER 385 at 389, 391, [1985] 1 WLR 1337 at 1343, 1345. This departure from basic principles can only be justified if the connection of the non-party with the original proceedings was so close that he will not suffer any injustice by allowing this exception to the general rule.

(7) Again the normal rule is that witnesses in either civil or criminal proceedings enjoy immunity from any form of civil action in respect of evidence given during those proceedings. One reason for this immunity is so that witnesses may give their evidence fearlessly: see *Palmer v Durnford Ford* (*a firm*) [1992] 2 All ER 122 at 125, [1992] QB 483 at 487. In so far as the evidence of a witness in proceedings may lead to an application for the costs of those proceedings against him or his company, it introduces yet another exception to a valuable general principle.

(8) The fact that an employee, or even a director or the managing director, of a company gives evidence in an action does not normally mean that the company is taking part in that action, in so far as that is an allegation relied upon by the party who applies for an order for costs against a non-party company: see *Gleeson v J Wippell & Co Ltd* [1977] 3 All ER 54 at 58, [1977] 1 WLR 510 at 513.

(9) The judge should be alert to the possibility that an application against a non-party is motivated by resentment of an inability to obtain an effective order for costs against a legally aided litigant. The courts are well aware of the financial difficulties faced by parties who are facing legally aided litigants at first instance, where the opportunity of a claim against the Legal Aid Board under section 18 of the Legal Aid Act 1988 is very limited. Nevertheless the Civil Legal Aid (General) Regulations 1989, SI No 339, and in particular regulations 67, 69 and 70, lay down conditions designed to ensure that there is no abuse of legal aid by a legally assisted person and these are designed to protect the other party to the litigation as well as the legal aid fund. The court will be very reluctant to infer that solicitors to a legally aided party have failed to discharge their duties under the Regulations

– see *Orchard v South Eastern Electricity Board* [1987] 1 All ER 95, [1987] QB 565 – and, in my judgment, this principle extends to a reluctance to infer that any maintenance by a non-party has occurred.

I now consider these principles in relation to the facts of the present case.

(1) Speaks for itself.

(2) It is clear that Symphony has at all material times had a cause of action in tort against Halvanto. "It is established that, where a third person with knowledge of a contract 'has dealings with the contract breaker which the third party knows to be inconsistent with the contract, he has committed an actionable interference' ": see *Clerk and Lindsell on Torts* (16th edn, 1989) 815, paragraph 15–08 and cases there cited. Symphony knew of Halvanto's identity by 15 May 1992 and was threatening proceedings on 27 May 1992. We were told by Mr Hochhauser that the reason why Symphony decided not to join Halvanto as a party to the action was that so long as it had an injunction against Mr Hodgson it did not need one against Halvanto, and that having immediately obtained an immediate interlocutory injunction against Mr Hodgson it had suffered, and would suffer, no damage. I accept that these may have seemed good reasons at the time but I do not find them a sufficient justification for a departure from this basic principle. Sub-paragraphs (1) to (10) inclusive of paragraph 2 of the schedule to Symphony's summons of 14 July 1992 all relate to issues which could have been raised by Symphony against Halvanto if Halvanto had been joined as a party to the action. I do not seek to justify Halvanto's actions to which the judge took such exception, but it would be unjust to Halvanto to allow these issues to be raised now in this summary procedure where Halvanto has been deprived of any legal right to control the action (e.g. by an offer of settlement or payment into court) and of all the procedural protection to which it would have been entitled if the claims had been brought against it by action in the normal and proper way.

(3) It is not suggested by Symphony that it ever warned Halvanto of the possibility that it might seek to make Halvanto liable for the costs of its action against Mr Hodgson before 6 July 1992 when the judge delivered his judgment in that action. The result is that Halvanto was neither made a party to the action by Symphony, nor did it have the opportunity to protect itself by applying to be made a party. When Mr Bramley gave his evidence he did so in ignorance of what lay in store for Halvanto, and with the benefit of hindsight it now appears that at least some part of his cross-examination – e.g. that directed to the position of Walker Morris and their acting for Mr Hodgson – was with a view to this application being made. In my judgment, Mr Gibbons was justified in comparing the procedure here of evidence (Mr Bramley's) first, and pleadings (the schedule to Symphony's summons of 14 July 1992) later, to what the Queen said at the trial of the knave in Lewis Carroll's *Alice's Adventures in Wonderland*: " 'No, no!' said the Queen. 'Sentence first – verdict afterwards.' " – even though Mr Gibbons wrongly attributed this quotation to the King.

(4) and (5)   The fact that Halvanto applied for the deputy judge to discharge himself is not surprising given the strength of the judge's remarks which I have quoted above. Yet as all members of the court (including Parker LJ, who dissented) recognised in *Bahai v Rashidian*, a hearing of the application by anyone other than the trial judge is going to present very considerable practical difficulties. If the judge does hear Symphony's application and finds against Halvanto, it seems to me to be inevitable that Halvanto will be left with a feeling that justice has, at the very least, not been seen to be done. If the application is heard by some other judge, the costs implications are horrendous. These problems suggest to me that this is not a suitable case for the exercise of a discretion which, under the principles of *Aiden Shipping*, the court undoubtedly has.

(6)   If Symphony's claim against Halvanto were the subject of an action proper, the judge's findings of fact made in his judgment in Symphony's action against Mr Hodgson would not be admissible as evidence of those facts against Halvanto. In my judgment, the connection of Halvanto with the original proceedings is by no means close enough to ensure that Halvanto will not suffer injustice by allowing this evidence to be admitted by way of exception to the general rule.

(7) and (8)   Again I can see no valid reason in the circumstances of the present case to justify the exceptions to these two principles which would be required if Mr Bramley's evidence in the Hodgson action is to be allowed to justify the present claim against Halvanto.

(9)   Sub-paragraphs (11) to (13) of paragraph 2 of the schedule to the summons of 14 July 1992 raise an allegation that Walker Morris were not representing Mr Hodgson in the action, but were in fact representing Halvanto. This carries by inference the allegation that they were in breach of their duty to the legal aid fund. I am not prepared to make that inference on the basis of the findings of fact by the judge in his judgment of 6 July 1992, and the transcript of the evidence of Mr Bramley, on which Symphony has elected to rely as the sole evidence to support its application for costs against Halvanto.

In my judgment therefore Halvanto has made out its primary claim that the grounds set out in Symphony's summons are not such as could justify the exercise of discretion in making an order for costs against Halvanto in the Hodgson action to which Halvanto was not a party. I do not find it necessary to deal with Halvanto's appeals against the specific directions made by the judge on 3 August 1992 since these directions are merely symptoms of the error into which the deputy judge fell when he indicated he was prepared to entertain Symphony's application for costs against Halvanto. In my judgment, he should have dismissed it summarily as soon as it had been made.

I would allow Halvanto's appeal, dismiss Symphony's appeal and cross-appeal, and dismiss Symphony's summons of 14 July 1992.

STAUGHTON LJ: I entirely agree with the judgment of Balcombe LJ and with the orders proposed by him. After the deputy judge had given judgment in the action on 6 July 1992, it could not in my opinion be just for him to entertain an application that Halvanto should pay the costs of Symphony. It follows that for the deputy judge to make such an order would be a wrong exercise of the discretion conferred by section 51 of the Supreme Court Act 1981.

I reach that conclusion for two reasons. First, like Balcombe LJ I take the view that at least part of the cross-examination of Mr Bramley was directed, objectively speaking, not at the pleaded issues in the trial but at securing admissions which would justify an order under section 51. That is not to say that the questions should never have been asked, or should have been disallowed by the deputy judge if objection had been taken; they may well have also been relevant to Mr Bramley's credibility. But objectively speaking, as I say, their main function now appears to have been to establish a case under section 51.

Neither Mr Bramley nor Halvanto had any warning that questions which would tend to make out such a case would be asked. Neither had reason to obtain professional advice on the topic before Mr Bramley gave evidence. Neither was represented by counsel at the trial, who might (for example) have asked further questions in re-examination. The main purpose of pleadings is to inform one party of the case which the other will seek to make against him. That is an essential feature of justice, and was entirely absent here.

Nevertheless there are cases, as Balcombe LJ has shown, where a person may be ordered to pay costs on the basis of evidence given and facts found at a trial to which he was not a party. Before such an order is made, it must be just and fair that the stranger should be bound by that evidence and those findings. In my judgment that is not the case here.

My second reason is that the deputy judge's findings were reached without the assistance of submissions from counsel representing Halvanto, or of any further evidence that Halvanto might have called. It is true that by his direction they were to be regarded only as provisional findings of fact against Halvanto. No doubt in further proceedings he would consider with care whether they were shown to be wrong. But human nature suggests that he might be slow to reach that conclusion. And in any event there will, in my opinion, be a legitimate feeling of grievance if he does not do so.

Once again, that may not be an insuperable objection in every case; but it is in this case. The only fair and just method of judging Symphony's application would be to start again with a clean sheet, new evidence and a new judge. But even if Symphony wished to pursue that course, I do not think that it should be allowed to do so under section 51. The section was not designed for procedure of that kind. If Symphony wish to sue Halvanto for procuring a breach of contract, and if the costs in this action would be part of the damages (as to which I express no opinion), that must be the subject of a separate action.

WAITE LJ: For the reasons given by Balcombe and Staughton LJJ, with which I agree entirely and to which I do not wish to add anything, I agree that Halvanto's appeal should be allowed and the appeal and cross-appeal of Symphony should be dismissed together with Symphony's summons of 14 July 1992.

Appeal of Halvanto allowed. Appeal and cross-appeal of Symphony dismissed. Symphony's summons of 14 July 1992 dismissed. Leave to appeal to the House of Lords refused.

James F Gibbons (instructed by *Booth & Co*, Leeds) for Halvanto.
Andrew Hochhauser (instructed by *Eversheds Hepworth & Chadwick*, Leeds) for Symphony.

Skuse
v
Granada Television Ltd

Queen's Bench Division
6, 7, 8 October 1993

Headnote

This important decision of Drake J decided two separate points. First, it was the first reported case which allowed an interlocutory appeal direct to the judge in chambers from a decision of a taxing master rather than under the review procedure laid down under Order 62, rule 35. The judge held that where a taxing master makes a decision during the course of hearing a rule 28 application an appeal from that decision lies direct to the judge in chambers at that stage. The second point which the case decides is that where, in support of rule 28, the applicant alleges that the respondent is being maintained by a third party, discovery of privileged documents should only be ordered in clear cases on the principle applicable where fraud is alleged, namely that very strong evidence thereof is required.

---

7 October. DRAKE J: This is the plaintiff's appeal against an order made by Master Rogers on 13 August 1993. He ordered disclosure by the plaintiff's solicitors to the defendants' solicitors of a bundle of privileged documents, the disclosure to be limited to the defendant's legal advisers. He also ordered that, should the plaintiff appeal against that order, then the order would be suspended pending the final determination of the appeal.

This appeal has given rise to a number of issues, some of a very technical procedural nature, with each side seeking to argue points of jurisdiction and estoppel. The plaintiff says that the taxing master had no jurisdiction to make the order. The defendants say that he did have that jurisdiction but that I have no jurisdiction to hear an appeal against the order.

I will give a brief outline of the history of the matter. It arises in an action for libel though no libel law is involved on this appeal. The plaintiff, Dr Skuse, was the forensic scientist who gave evidence for the prosecution in the trial of the Birmingham Six. They were convicted in 1975. The convictions were eventually, many years later, quashed on appeal. In 1985 the defendants broadcast a programme in which it was alleged that the plaintiff, as a Home Office forensic scientist investigating the Birmingham bombings and giving evidence for the Crown at the trial, had failed to show the skill, knowledge, care and thoroughness to be expected of him in that role. The plaintiff sued the defendants for libel. The defence pleaded, inter alia, that the words were not defamatory of the plaintiff, alternatively that they did not bear the meaning complained of by the plaintiff. The parties agreed that the trial should be by judge alone.

In October 1991 Otton J ordered the determination of a preliminary issue to determine whether the words are defamatory of the plaintiff and, if so, what is their meaning. Later Brooke J held that the words are defamatory but bore a meaning less defamatory than that contended by the plaintiff. Both parties appealed. The Court of Appeal on 30 March 1993 held in favour of the plaintiff. Counsel for the plaintiff asked for costs, both in the Court of Appeal and before Brooke J, who had ordered costs in cause. It is what happened then at the appeal, at the end of that appeal, and later, with regard to costs which gives rise to the issues I now have to decide.

After the plaintiff had asked for costs of the appeal and in the court below, and after a fair amount of argument before the court, the Court of Appeal ordered the defendants to pay the plaintiff's costs both of the appeal and below. They also ordered, having said that they found the matter a difficult one to decide, that the costs should be taxed and paid forthwith. They observed that without such an order, the plaintiff would run the risk that he might be unable through lack of funds to pursue the action. It is a matter of history that at a much earlier date the plaintiff had been maintained or partly maintained by Sir James Goldsmith, but he had ceased to finance the plaintiff at some time in 1991. No suggestion was made to the Court of Appeal in March 1993 that the plaintiff was at that time maintained by anyone, nor that his solicitors, Peter Carter-Ruck & Partners, had in any way acted improperly by acting on any form of speculative or contingency basis, but that is the allegation which the defendants have since and do still make.

The taxation procedure then commenced. On 18 June 1993 the defendants gave a notice of objections as to costs and on 2 July they issued a summons before the taxing master. The notice made allegations which I will condense to describe as allegations that the plaintiff has been and is being maintained in the action and that his solicitors are acting on an improper basis of a speculative or contingency nature.

On 12 July Master Rogers ordered the parties to file affidavits dealing with the issues raised on the defendants' summons of 2 July and for further directions to be given by him on 13 August. On 13 August he made the order, part of which is subject to the present appeal. He ordered that the taxation should be heard by him on 4 and 5 October, but he also made the orders the subject of the present appeal, that the plaintiff's solicitors should give disclosure of a bundle of privileged documents which they had lodged with the court. Interestingly, he also ordered that the order for disclosure should be suspended if the plaintiff gave notice of appeal against it. That appeal, which is to be contrasted with a review of the taxation, would be to a judge under the provisions of RSC Order 62, rule 28(5). It is the procedure which the plaintiff has followed in making this appeal. The defendants have taken the preliminary point that I have no jurisdiction to entertain such an appeal. If they are right, it means, as they recognise and say is the fact, that the master erred in making the order that his disclosure order should be subject to an appeal.

Mr Downey, who clearly has a very considerable knowledge and experience of matters relating to the powers of taxing masters and in particular to Order 62, has submitted as follows.   (1) Order 62 is a self-contained code which governs taxation proceedings.   (2) Apart from the provisions of Order 62, rule 28(5), any party who is dissatisfied with a decision of a taxing master must apply for a review by the taxing master under Order 62, rule 33, and if he remains dissatisfied after the review he may then apply under rule 35 for a review by a judge, who may, and I believe usually does, appoint assessors to sit with him on the review. Accordingly, save as is provided under rule 28(5), there is no direct appeal from a taxing master. Order 58, rule 1, which provides for appeals from a master to a judge in chambers, does not apply because the effect of Order 1, rule 4 is to exclude a taxing master from the provisions of Order 58.   (3) Order 62, rule 28(5) does provide for an appeal from a taxing master to a judge but such appeals are restricted to (and I quote, in part): "an appeal ... from the exercise by a taxing officer of the powers conferred by this rule" – that is to say, rule 28.   (4) The defendants' case is that the taxing master has not yet exercised any power under rule 28. That power will only have been exercised when he gives a decision under rule 28(2) and section 51(6) of the Supreme Court Act 1981, disallowing all or part of the plaintiff's costs on the grounds that the plaintiff's solicitors have acted improperly, that is to say by acting on a contingency basis and/or that the plaintiff is being maintained. Therefore, says, Mr Downey, any order that the defendants must pay the plaintiff's costs would offend against what has been called the indemnity principle, that is to say that a plaintiff should not recover costs when he personally would not have to pay costs had he lost the issue in respect of which the costs were ordered. I merely observe here that in the present case, I am not dealing with speculation as to whether or not the plaintiff might lose the issue in respect of which costs have been ordered because the plaintiff has already won that issue.   (5) The plaintiff says that the taxing master has already exercised powers under rule 28 by ordering the plaintiff to give discovery of the privileged correspondence. That correspondence is relevant to the alleged maintenance of the plaintiff or the improper conduct of his solicitors. The defendants say that in ordering that discovery the taxing master was exercising his powers under rule 20(*d*) but not under rule 28.

In my judgment, the master was certainly exercising his powers under rule 20(*d*), but under what powers did he make an order for discovery of those particular documents? In my judgment the answer is clearly that he was in the process of exercising his powers under rule 28. So it really comes to this: are the words in rule 28(5), "The exercise ... of the powers conferred by this rule", limited to the final decision made by the taxing master or do they apply to the process of inquiring into the alleged improper conduct? It seems to me that, as a matter of construction of the rule and also as a matter of ordinary language, the taxing master was exercising his powers under rule 28. The heading to that rule, and indeed also to the connected Order 62, rule 10, is: "Powers of taxing officers in relation to misconduct, neglect etc". I think he was exercising those powers when he ordered discovery of documents which related solely to alleged "misconduct etc". It seems to me that, if Mr Downey were right, there would either be no appeal at all against the taxing master's order for discovery of privileged documents, or at least no appeal until after they had already been disclosed and the master had given his final decision on the alleged maintenance and misconduct of the plaintiff's solicitors. A possible alternative suggestion is that an appeal against the order for disclosure would lie by way of review under rule 33 with a subsequent appeal to a judge under rule 35 at a later stage.

I cannot believe that the rules provide for such a tortuous procedure. In my judgment it boils down to this. On all aspects of what I would call ordinary taxation, the procedure is by way of review ultimately to the judge, who normally sits with assessors; but, where some form of serious misconduct is in issue, an appeal lies under rule 28(5) to the judge in chambers. As I have already observed, it is clear from paragraph 6 of the taxing master's order of 13 August 1993 that he considered that the plaintiff has the right of appeal against the order for discovery. In my judgment the taxing master was right in that view, so I rule that I do have jurisdiction to entertain the plaintiff's appeal.

I understand, however, that Mr Downey next wishes to submit that even if I have the jurisdiction to hear the appeal, I should not permit this plaintiff to pursue this appeal on the ground that the taxing master had no jurisdiction to make the order for disclosure. If I have understood correctly, the defendants' submission will be that the plaintiff has left it too late to make any challenge to the master's jurisdiction to inquire into and make any order consequent upon the alleged misconduct of the plaintiff and/or his solicitors, but I must now proceed to hear submissions as to the precise arguments along those lines.

The court heard submissions on the appeal.

8 October. DRAKE J: Having previously ruled that I have jurisdiction to hear this appeal, I now deal with the appeal itself. The plaintiff appeals against an order of the taxing master made on 13 August 1993. The original notice of appeal was only against the order that the plaintiff's solicitors should disclose a bundle of privileged documents but, by the amended notice of appeal (I have given leave to amend), the plaintiff appeals against the

whole order. The grounds are, firstly, that in the circumstances of this case the master has no jurisdiction to hear an application by the defendants that the plaintiff's costs should be disallowed on the grounds of what I call improper conduct on the part of the plaintiff or his solicitors, i.e. that the plaintiff has either been secretly maintained or that his solicitors improperly financed his appeal. Secondly, and by way of an alternative, that the master is estopped per rem judicatam because of the decision of the Court of Appeal when they made the order for the defendants to pay the plaintiff's costs. The order of the Court of Appeal on 30 March 1993 was that the defendants pay the costs of the appeal and before the judge below, such costs to be taxed and paid forthwith.

The plaintiff starts with the submission that at least by inference or by making the order for disclosure of certain documents the master has assumed jurisdiction to determine the defendants' objection. The defendants say that there can be no appeal on this ground until the master has given a final decision on the defendants' objection. I reject this argument. The master has assumed jurisdiction by giving directions in particular by ordering disclosure of documents, which documents are relevant only to the objection of the defendants to the plaintiff recovering any costs.

So that brings me to the substance of the plaintiff's grounds of appeal. Firstly, that the master has no jurisdiction to determine an issue already determined by the Court of Appeal. Now, the difficulty with that argument is that the Court of Appeal have not determined the issue raised by the defendants' allegation of improper conduct on the part of the plaintiff or his solicitors. That is because the issue was never raised before the Court of Appeal; they were wholly unaware it existed. Mr Suttle for the plaintiff is right in submitting that, if the master upheld the defendants' objection, the result would be directly contrary to the result of the order of the Court of Appeal. Their order was for the defendants to pay the plaintiff's costs of the appeal and below, such costs to be taxed and paid forthwith, and they ordered that latter payment forthwith because they thought it would be right in the circumstances for the plaintiff to have the costs in order to assist, or at any rate not hinder, him in continuing with the action. Nevertheless, I find it impossible to say that the Court of Appeal have already determined the issue raised by the defendants' objection since they have never been seised of that issue.

However, next the plaintiff says that if the defendants wish to pursue this objection it should have been raised before the Court of Appeal. Mr Suttle cited from the judgment of Sir James Wigram V-C in *Henderson v Henderson* (1843) 3 Hare 100, 115, approved in *Yat Tung Investment Co Ltd v Dao Heng Bank Ltd* [1975] AC 581, 590:

> "In trying this question I believe I state the rule of the court correctly, when I say, that where a given matter becomes the subject of jurisdiction in, and of adjudication by, a court of competent jurisdiction, the court requires the

parties to that litigation to bring forward their whole case, and will not (except under special circumstances) permit the same parties to open the same subject of litigation in respect of matter which might have been brought forward as part of the subject in contest, but which was not brought forward, only because they have, from negligence, inadvertence, or even accident, omitted part of their case. The plea of res judicata applies, except in special cases, not only to points upon which the court was actually required by the parties to form an opinion and pronounce a judgment, but to every point which properly belonged to the subject of litigation, and which the parties, exercising reasonable diligence, might have brought forward at the time."

It is a matter of fact that the defendants did not make or mention their objection to the Court of Appeal. The defendants have not by affidavit evidence explained why the matter was not raised in the Court of Appeal. Mr Downey in his submissions to me and at my request gave me two explanations, although he was anxious to say that they were imperfect and that he would not do full justice to them without the opportunity to have them set out fully by way of affidavit evidence. But the substance of his two explanations seemed to me to be clear. It was, firstly, that the hearing of this appeal was originally fixed for 28 October 1993 but was brought forward by the court so that in fact it began on 6 October. Mr Downey says that had the hearing remained on 28 October the defendants would before then have given an explanation on affidavit and that explanation would have been very detailed. But the imperfect précis of the reasons why the matter was not raised in court is that at that time the defendants did not feel they had any sufficient information on which to put forward that objection. I do observe that the notice of objection when it was made was made not very long afterwards, but is dated 18 June 1993 and is so detailed that a good deal of the material must, I think, have been in the possession of the defendants well before 18 June.

But the second ground on which Mr Downey says the matter was not raised in the Court of Appeal is that, as a matter of procedure, it was not necessary or proper to raise it at that stage because the correct procedure is to follow the Rules of the Supreme Court, which lay down a procedure for raising such an objection under Order 62, rule 28 before a taxing master. Therefore the proper time to raise it is after reference to him and not at the time when the court orders taxation. So, by way of an example, in any ordinary action decided at first instance where a party is successful and asks for and is given an order for costs to be taxed if not agreed, it is on the taxation that the objection should be made, not at the time when the judge is asked to make the order. Well, I can see force in this argument.

However, it is also right to say that there is nothing in the rules which would have prevented the defendants from raising the matter before the Court of Appeal. Had they done so, I think that (but for one matter to which I will turn shortly) the Court of Appeal would have been strongly inclined to have referred the objection to the taxing master. Mr Suttle says they would not necessarily have done so because the plaintiff could have made short submissions in law which would have shown that the defendants' objection was misconceived. At the very least, he submits, the Court of Appeal would have expressly referred the matter to be decided by the master probably with expedition and that would have avoided the need for the present appeal.

In my judgment, the defendants should have raised the matter before the Court of Appeal and it is principally for these reasons that I say that. There was argument before the Court of Appeal about the merits of making an order for immediate taxation of the plaintiff's costs of the appeal and in the court below. When the court made the order, they made it clear that they had considered it with care and they gave the reasons for making the order that, on balance, such an order would be likely to contribute to the interests of justice. That is because without such an order the plaintiff might be unable to continue with his action. As the defendants' objection is that the plaintiff was being financed in some way, it follows that that objection would completely have removed the basis on which the Court of Appeal made the order for immediate taxation. Because of this concern of the Court of Appeal to see that no injustice was done to the plaintiff by keeping him out of such costs as he was entitled to, I think they would have been very anxious, if at all possible to do so and without any prolonged argument, to dispose of any objection raised to the plaintiff's right to recover the costs. If the matter could not have been decided summarily by the court without further evidence or without more than brief argument, I think the Court of Appeal would have referred the matter to the taxing master to be dealt with under Order 62, rule 28 although they would almost certainly have made sure that the matter was dealt with with special expedition.

Mr Suttle says they might have adjourned the issue for evidence to be filed and then after an adjournment have themselves decided the matter. I think that is very unlikely. However, I think it is possible that they would have been persuaded to hear short submissions in law, that the defendants' objection was misconceived, fundamentally flawed and had no prospect of success for the reasons which Mr Suttle has argued before me fully on this appeal.

But for the one matter to which I have already briefly alluded, I think that, although possible, it is still unlikely that the court would have entertained arguments along that line. But the one matter which makes it much more likely that they would have entertained such submissions is the fact that Dr Skuse had offered security for the costs of the appeal. The security was by way of a charge on a house owned by him. The security was clearly good. In principle it had been agreed on by the defendants' solicitors. It had been offered as early as some time before 18 June 1992, on which date the defendants' solicitors sent to the plaintiff's solicitors a draft legal charge. On 16 July 1992 the plaintiff's solicitors returned it to the defendants' solicitors with two amendments ready for engrossment. The defendants' solicitors appear to have taken no further action until nearly eight months later, by which time the appeal was almost due to be heard. On 4 March 1993 they returned the charge to the plaintiff's solicitors proposing very substantial amendments. Then, after further correspondence, the defendants' solicitors on 18 March sent the engrossed document to the plaintiff's solicitors to be sent to the plaintiff for execution. The plaintiff's solicitors sent it to the plaintiff for execution but the appeal was heard on 23 March before the document had been executed.

In my judgment, had the Court of Appeal heard of those facts, they would have dismissed summarily any attempt by the defendants to defer the immediate taxation of the costs of the appeal by reason of an objection of the type now made by them. The fact that Dr Skuse was willing and able to provide that security, and indeed incurred substantial costs in having the charge prepared, appears to me to render hopeless the defendants' prospects of proving an agreement of the type necessary to sustain their objection by the sort of evidence by which they propose to attempt to prove that objection. But, be that as it may, what I find is that in all these circumstances the failure of the defendants even to mention their objection to the Court of Appeal is such as to render it unjust to permit them to do so at a later date. On this first ground I would allow this appeal.

The plaintiff next submits that the master lacks jurisdiction because the defendants' objections show no case, i.e. their notice of objection shows on its face that there are no prospects whatsoever of the objection being made out. Mr Suttle submits that if this is not a ground for holding that the taxing master lacks jurisdiction, I should nevertheless hold that the defendants' objection is an abuse of process and should be struck out or stopped, in the exercise of the inherent jurisdiction of the court. I made it plain during argument that I would not inquire into and rule on the merits of the defendants' objections by hearing detailed evidence upon it. I said, and I repeat now, that on the information I do have about the nature of the defendants' objections, it appears to me that their case is weak and they will have great difficulty in establishing it. They allege that the plaintiff is being secretly maintained or that his solicitors improperly financed him by giving him credit on a speculative or contingency basis to prosecute his appeal, i.e. that they had an agreement that they would in no circumstances seek to recover their costs unless the plaintiff wins.

The defendants cannot suggest the identity of any maintainer and the nature of their case is simply this. They believe that the plaintiff is of limited means and that those were not enough to pay for the costs of his appeal had he lost. Therefore, they say, it must follow either that some third party had agreed to pay those costs, or that his solicitors were giving him credit on an improper basis. I doubt whether they have good evidence to support this case but, I repeat, I have not enquired fully into the evidence or heard substantial argument upon it. But Mr Suttle's submission is that the very grounds for the defendants' objection shown in their notice of objection are not enough to provide any basis for an order depriving the plaintiff of his costs of the appeal. This is because Dr Skuse is the plaintiff in the action and his solicitors, Peter Carter-Ruck & Partners, are the solicitors on the record. There is therefore a presumption that Dr Skuse is personally liable for their costs. This can only be displaced by proving that there was an express or implied agreement binding on the solicitors that Dr Skuse would not have to pay the costs of the appeal *in any circumstances* – to which I give emphasis: see *per* Lloyd J in *Reg* v *Miller (Raymond)* [1983] 1 WLR 1056, 1061. Furthermore, unless there was such an agreement, the plaintiff remained personally liable to his solicitors even if he were maintained by some third party. In order to establish grounds for depriving the plaintiff of the costs awarded in his favour in the Court of Appeal, it would be necessary for the plaintiff to show "that there was a bargain, either between [some third party] and the solicitors, or between the plaintiff and the solicitors, that under no circumstances was the plaintiff to be liable for costs," *per* Bankes LJ in *Adams* v *London Improved Motor Coach Builders Ltd* [1921] 1 KB 495, 501, cited in *Reg* v *Miller* [1983] 1 WLR 1056.

In the present case, the defendants' notice of objection does not go that far. I have looked carefully through that notice of objection and I can find nothing which suggests any agreement between a third party maintainer or the plaintiff's solicitors and the plaintiff which would satisfy the test I have cited from *Reg* v *Miller*.

What I do find is reference to the very large costs likely to be incurred in the full trial of this libel action estimated by the defendants at between £600,000 and £700,000. But the objection is in fact limited to an alleged improper agreement covering the costs of the issue decided on the appeal. So the notice of objection, in my judgment, clearly includes some irrelevant or almost completely irrelevant material. Nowhere does it even allege an agreement of a nature which would deprive the plaintiff of his right to the costs. In my judgment, therefore, the taxing master has no grounds on which to pursue his inquiry into the defendants' notice of objection. His order for disclosure of documents was therefore made on a false basis, as would be any continuation of the proceedings before him. He has completed what I would call his ordinary taxation of the plaintiff's costs and there is nothing further left for him to inquire into. Therefore, on that ground also I would allow this appeal.

Another ground on which the plaintiff submits that the defendants' notice of objection is misconceived is that the defendants, even if they could show an agreement sufficient to amount to misconduct, cannot show that the costs ordered by the Court of Appeal to be paid by the defendants were wasted within the meaning of Order 62, rules 10 and 11, Order 62, rule 28, and section 51(6) and (7) of the Supreme Court Act 1981. Section 51(7) provides that costs are "wasted" if they are "incurred by a party – (*a*) as a result of any improper, unreasonable or negligent act or omission on the part of any legal representative … " Mr Suttle submits that the costs awarded by the Court of Appeal cannot be said to have arisen as a result of any improper agreement between the plaintiff and his solicitors or some third party even if, which is strongly denied, any such agreement existed. Mr Downey responds that the costs were the result of such an improper agreement, if it exists, because without such an agreement the plaintiff would have been unable to pursue his successful appeal.

I accept that the defendants need not show that the improper agreement was the sole cause of the costs; a partial cause will suffice: see *Mainwaring* v *Goldtech Investments Ltd* (1991) *The Times*, 19 February; Court of Appeal (Civil Division) Transcript No 48 of 1991. But the defendants must show that the costs in question were, to quote from the transcript of Sir Christopher Slade's judgment in that case, "thrown away as a result of the unreasonable or improper conduct of the proceedings by the solicitors". In my judgment, none of the costs of the appeal in which the plaintiff with the help of his legal advisers was entirely successful can be said to have been "thrown away" as the result of the conduct of his solicitors. Therefore on this ground too I hold that the defendants have no grounds on which to pursue their objection.

Finally, looking at the substance of this appeal in the round and taking into account all the circumstances, including the history of the proceedings, the failure of the defendants to mention their grounds of objection to the Court of Appeal and what I find to be their lack of any prospects of succeeding on their objection because it is fundamentally misconceived or flawed, I find that the objection is an abuse of the process of the court and under the inherent jurisdiction of the court I would strike it out or order it to be dismissed.

Having allowed the appeal on those grounds, it is unnecessary for me to decide the plaintiff's appeal with regard to the order for disclosure of the privileged bundle. However, I heard quite a lot of argument and, lest I be held wrong on having allowed the appeal against the jurisdiction of the master or on the grounds to which I have referred, I will, albeit somewhat briefly, give my judgment on this matter.

I will start back to front by stating that, if I thought that any order for disclosure were warranted, I would certainly order it to be limited to those parts of the documents which are relevant to the issue before the master. The documents do contain references to costs. These are of some relevance to the defendants' objection even if, as may be the case – for I will not reveal the contents of the documents – that may not assist the objection but instead favour the plaintiff. However, the documents contain other material which, in my judgment, is clearly irrelevant to the defendants' objection. Disclosure of that material could prejudice the plaintiff's case in the libel action. Since the documents are privileged documents, I can see no justification for having that material disclosed and very good reasons for the contrary. Had I ordered disclosure therefore of any part of the bundle, I would have ordered that the document should be edited so as to remove irrelevant material. What I would have done would have been to ask the plaintiff to submit a draft edited bundle and I would have approved the editing or amended it in order that justice might be done.

But, as I said, that is starting back to front and, to go to the front: should the master have made an order for discovery? The plaintiff submits that as the documents are privileged he should have been given the chance of being put to election, either to rely on the documents or withdraw them: see *Pamplin* v *Express Newspapers Ltd* [1985] 1 WLR 689, referred to in *Goldman* v *Hesper* [1988] 1 WLR 1238, **Costs LR (Core Vol) 99**. In my judgment, that situation applies when a party lodges a privileged document for taxation in order to claim the costs of it. If the other party wishes to see it to dispute that claim for costs, the plaintiff must be given the right to elect to withdraw it and not claim costs or he must disclose it. I think the more relevant authority to the position in this case is *Derby & Co Ltd* v *Weldon (No 7)* [1990] 1 WLR 1156. That shows that discovery of privileged documents should only be ordered in clear cases, and where fraud is alleged there must be strong evidence of fraud. In the present case it is not fraud which is alleged but a form of improper conduct and, in my judgment, the same principle applies. Further, in my judgment, there is no strong evidence of the improper conduct; on the contrary. So I find therefore that it would be wrong in this case to order disclosure of the privileged documents.

If I am wrong on that, then the decision whether or not to order disclosure was a matter for the taxing master in the exercise of his discretion. But now on an appeal it is for me to decide in the exercise of my discretion, and, in all the circumstances of this case, I would exercise my discretion so as not to order disclosure. I would add simply this: if the documents contained anything which contradicted or appeared to contradict the plaintiff's solicitors' affidavit evidence denying the existence of the sort of agreement alleged by the defendants, I would not hesitate to exercise my discretion to order disclosure. All I need say is in this case I would not exercise my discretion to order disclosure. For all those reasons, this appeal is allowed.

Appeal allowed. Summons of 2 July 1993 dismissed with costs on indemnity basis. Leave to appeal refused.

Stephen Suttle for the plaintiff.
Raoul Downey for the defendants.

Royal Bank of Scotland

v

Allianz International Insurance Co and others

(unrevised judgment)

In the High Court of Justice
Judge in Chambers
Tuesday, 7 June 1994

Garland J
(Judgment in open court)

Headnote

This so far unreported 1994 decision of Garland J is an extremely important case in relation to Order 62, rule 28 delay applications. The judge reviewed earlier decisions and held that:
(1)   the words "inordinate or inexcusable" were an unwarranted gloss on the word "delay" which does not admit of qualification;
(2)   "prejudice" was not a necessary ingredient for the application to succeed; and
(3)   even where, as in that case, the parties went back to the trial judge for clarification of his original order, that was not a sufficient justification to defeat a rule 28 application.

GARLAND J: Two principal matters of concern in civil litigation are delay and costs. These proceedings are an unhappy example of the combination of both and an example also of the common experience that when matters start to go wrong, they usually continue to do so.

This is an appeal from an Order of Chief Taxing Master Hurst made on 30 March 1994 in taxation proceedings on the plaintiffs' Bill of Costs lodged on 1 May 1992 when he dismissed the defendants' application under Order 62, rule 28(4). Behind this simple statement there lies a long and complex history.

In 1982 Williams & Glynn's Bank wished to construct a new central administration building on a site in Islington. They engaged Trollope & Colls Management Ltd to plan and manage the project. The actual contractors were Sindall Construction Ltd ("Sindalls"). By a policy of insurance dated 16 February 1983, the defendants agreed to indemnify

Williams & Glynns' Bank and Sindalls against loss and damage in respect of physical loss or damage to permanent and temporary works, plant and temporary buildings. Sindalls engaged subcontractors to install, test and commission the fire mains. Williams & Glynn's Bank became part of the plaintiffs. By September 1985 construction was well advanced and it was expected that the building would be ready for occupation early in December. On the evening of 24 September 1985 a fire main burst causing a very serious flood in the basement. Much electrical heating and air conditioning plant and other equipment was badly damaged. Making good the damage delayed completion by at least 6 months and caused serious disruption to many finishing trades.

In 1987 by Action R 2496 the plaintiffs claimed against Sindalls both insured and uninsured loss quantified at £5.3 million. By a second action commenced on 5 March 1988 (R No 794) the plaintiffs claimed against the defendants the insured loss which had originally formed part of the Sindalls claim. On 12 May 1988 the actions were consolidated and proceeded in the Queen's Bench Division. Mr Justice Brooke was assigned to the case and conducted pre-trial hearings in order to define the issues and to identify those common to both Sindalls and the defendants on the one hand, and those involving only Sindalls or the defendants on the other. The date fixed for trial was 4 June 1990. On 31 May the plaintiffs settled their claim against Sindalls for £1,050,000 inclusive of interest and costs. The plaintiffs paid Sindalls £100,000 in respect of their costs of defending the claim for insured losses.

The trial of Action R No 794 began on 4 June but on 6 June leading Counsel agreed terms on which the matter could be compromised subject to the approval of the defendants. This approval was forthcoming and on 8 June their solicitors, Messrs Davies Arnold Cooper ("DAC") wrote to the plaintiffs' solicitors, Messrs Norton Rose ("NR") confirming that this was the case and agreeing the proposed order for costs.

> "The Defendants will pay the Plaintiffs their costs of Action 1988 R No 794 to be taxed if not agreed."

At the same time, they clearly saw the potential for the present dispute, namely that the Sindall action having been settled on a costs inclusive basis, consideration would have to be given to apportioning the common costs which would require to be separated from costs wholly incurred in Action R 794. The defendants (who had already paid £385,000 on account) paid a further £2.2 million to the plaintiffs and £100,000 to reimburse them in respect of the sum they had paid to Sindalls. On 11 June, NR wrote saying that they considered common costs a matter for taxation and that DAC could make whatever submissions they thought appropriate. A formal Tomlin Order was drawn up on 12 June but not perfected until the 29th. According to the Rules, the plaintiffs therefore had until 29 September to lodge their Bill of Costs.

They did not do so until 24 December. It was in the sum of £650,000. The defendants took exception to the form and contents of the Bill which they contended wholly failed to attempt any apportionment and did not clearly distinguish common costs and costs attributable to Action R 794 alone. Counsels' fees were claimed in full, no allowance being made for the Sindall action; so were experts' fees. They maintained that "costs of Action 1988 R 794" plainly indicated costs attributable to the claim against them as distinct from costs attributable to or shared with the claim against Sindalls.

By agreement, the dispute was brought back before Brooke J on 23 September 1991 for a ruling. The plaintiffs contended that he did not have jurisdiction to interpret the consent order he had made, but eventually agreed that he should. The plaintiffs' principal argument was that there should be no apportionment notwithstanding the form of the costs order. The general practice is that since after consolidation there are no longer two separate actions, a successful plaintiff who obtains an order for costs against only one defendant is in the same position as a plaintiff who has sued two or more defendants and succeeded only against one. He can take the whole of the general costs of the action but is not allowed the increased costs of the other defendants unless the Order specifically provides for them. The defendants, of course, contended that the Order in the present case did make a specific provision by being limited to the costs of Action R 794.

The plaintiffs relied on *Medway Oil & Storage Co Ltd* v *Continental Contractors Ltd* [1929] AC 88, **Costs LR (Core Vol)** 5 which deals with claim and counterclaim. In the absence of special directions where both claim and counterclaim either succeed or are dismissed with costs, there is no apportionment. The same principles are applied to appeal and cross-appeal (*Greaves* v *Nabarro* (1939–40) 56 TLR 339). The defendants submitted that these principles did not apply to consolidated actions against different defendants and referred to the converse situation of different plaintiffs suing the same defendant, not in consolidated actions but in separate actions where the evidence in the leading case was to be deemed to have been taken in the others (*Boguslawski* v *Gdynia Ameryka Line (No 2)* [1951] 2 KB 328). Brooke J thought it the clearest possible inference from the judgments of the Court of Appeal that had the actions been consolidated, there would have been apportionment.

Brooke J concluded that, because the Sindall case had been settled for a figure inclusive of costs and the defendants had been ordered to pay only the costs of R No 794, there should be a bill setting out the costs claimed exclusively against each defendant and identifying the common costs. The defendants therefore succeeded and were awarded their costs (a matter which assumed some significance later) but the plaintiffs were given leave to appeal, Brooke J saying,

"… not on the basis that I have any doubts but the Court of Appeal may very well want to have a look at the inter-relation argument, the Polish case and the general line of authority."

There was no appeal.

Unhappily, the parties could not agree a form of Order to reflect Brooke J's judgment and many months passed. On 6 February 1992, the defendants made a payment on account of £287,020. The costs, as subsequently taxed, plus interest at 15% pursuant to section 17 of the Judgements Act 1838, would then have stood at £322,517. On 2 March 1992 the parties went before Brooke J again and an Order was made, paragraphs (3), (4) and (5) of which provided:

> "(3)   it is hereby declared that the Plaintiffs' entitlement to 'their costs of Action 1988 R No 794' as set out in the said Order does not, upon the true meaning of the said Order and/or upon the true construction of the agreement which gave rise to the said Order, include in full those items of costs in the consolidated action which are properly attributed to issues common to both Action 1987 R No 2496 and Action 1988 R No 794 – that is to say the issue of the extent to which the completion of the Plaintiffs' building works at the Angel, Islington, London N1, was delayed by the flood on 24 September 1985.
>
>   (4)   it is hereby ordered that items of costs which are properly attributable to issues common to both Action 1987 R No 2496 and Action 1988 R No 794 as set out in (3) above should on taxation be divided or apportioned between Action 1987 R No 2496 and Action 1988 R No 794.
>
>   (5)   it is hereby ordered that the Plaintiffs do prepare a Bill of Costs showing the costs claimed against the Defendant Insurers in Action 1988 R No 794, and showing the common costs (as set out in (3) and (4) above) divided or apportioned between the Defendant Insurers and Sindalls with any reasons for an apportionment thereof other than an equal division being set out in the Bill or in such other form as may be agreed between the parties or as the Taxing Master may direct."

On 1 May 1992, the plaintiffs lodged their second Bill drawn in accordance with the Order of 2 March 1992 in the total sum of £587,000 apportioning the majority of items, including Counsels' fees 80/20. In the event the Bill was taxed at just under £260,000 (subject to minor uncertainties) and an apportionment of 50/50 made.

In correspondence before 2 March 1992 the defendants had raised the question of an application under Order 62, rule 28(4). Brooke J had expressed anxiety about the accrual of interest in September 1991 and on 2 March 1992 made some trenchant comments. The taxation was begun by Master Martyn in March 1993. The defendants served a Notice of Intention to seek an order under rule 28(4) but the master required a summons to be issued and served. This was not heard until 9 June when he declined to make an Order on the ground that the application should have been dealt with as a preliminary issue and did not consider the merits at all. The defendants appealed to Ognall J. The appeal was heard on 1 and 2 November 1993. Ognall J held that the master should have dealt with the application under rule 28(4) on its merits and remitted the matter for hearing by another master. He, too, expressed concern about delay and the accrual of interest. I take the view that I must approach the application of rule 28(4) *de novo* on the material before me.

On 1 March 1994 the application pursuant to Order 62, rule 28(4) was heard by Chief Taxing Master Hurst. By his judgment on 30 March 1994 he dismissed the application and it is from his Order of the same date that the defendants now appeal, four years after the making of the Order for costs and after three interventions by High Court judges.

There is a measure of agreement between the parties as to the relevant periods of delay. One alternative is that delay ran from 24 December 1990 when the first bill was lodged (the defendants conceding that six months would be a reasonable time for its preparation) to 29 March 1991 and then 2 March 1992 to 2 May 1992. The other is that there was delay from 29 September 1990 (the date when the bill should have been lodged according to the Rules) and 23 September 1991. The parties accepted that the period from 23 September 1991 to 2 March 1992 was neutral. The master considered the first alternative appropriate. It is a period of 333 days. In my view, that is correct.

Interest pursuant to section 17 of the Judgements Act 1838 runs from the date of the judgment and during the relevant periods accrued at 15%. From 6 February 1992 the capital sum was reduced by the payment on account so the total sum accruing during the relevant periods is £30,071 (see schedule for working).

I now turn to Order 62. Rule 10(1) under the heading "Misconduct or Neglect in the Conduct of any Proceedings" provides:

> "(1)   Where it appears to the Court in any proceedings that anything has been done, or that any omission has been made, unreasonably or improperly by or on behalf of any party, the Court may order that the costs of that party in respect of the act or omission ... shall not be allowed ...
>
> (2)   Instead of making an order under paragraph (1) the Court may refer the matter to a Taxing Officer, in which case the Taxing Officer shall deal with the matter under Rule 28(1)."

This rule, of course, applies to the costs of the proceedings. Rule 28 applies to both. Paragraph (1) provides, under the heading "Powers of Taxing Officer in Relation to Misconduct, Neglect etc":

> "(1)   Where, whether or not on a reference under Rule 10(2), it appears to the Taxing Officer that anything has been done, or that any omission has been made, unreasonably or improperly, by or on behalf of any party in the taxation proceedings or in the proceedings which gave rise to the taxation proceedings, he may exercise the powers conferred on the Court by Rule 10(1)."

Rule 4 is as follows:

> "(4)   Where a party entitled to costs –
>
> (a)   fails without good reason to commence or conduct proceedings for the taxation of those costs in accordance with this Order or any

direction, or
(b)   delays lodging a bill of costs for taxation, the Taxing Officer may –

   (i)   disallow all or part of the costs of taxation that he would otherwise have awarded that party; and

   (ii)   after taking into account all the circumstances (including any prejudice suffered by any other party as a result of such failure or delay, as the case may be, and any additional interest payable under S.17 of the Judgements Act 1838 because of the failure or delay) allow the party so entitled less than the amount he would otherwise have allowed on taxation of the bill or wholly disallow the costs."

These provisions replace the former Order 62, rule 7(5) which was in the following terms:

"(5)   Where a party entitled to costs fails to procure or fails to proceed with taxation, the Taxing Officer in order to prevent any other parties being prejudiced by the failure, may allow the party so entitled a nominal or other sum for costs or may certify the failure and the costs of the other parties."

Reference is made to this rule because cases decided while it was in force may not be applicable to the present rule, one feature of which is that sub-paragraph (b), delay in lodging a bill, is *prima facie* also a breach of (a), failure to commence or conduct the proceedings in accordance with Order 62. There was doubt, under the old rule 7(5) whether simple delay in lodging a bill fell within its terms (*Chapman* v *Chapman* [1985] 1 All ER 757). It was, however, necessary to show prejudice, but in *Jones* v *Roberts* (1986) *The Times*, 2 August it was held that prejudice could be inferred where the delay was "inordinate and inexcusable".

There was some difference between the parties as to the approach to rule 28; reference was made to *Regina* v *Legal Aid Board ex parte Bateman* [1992] 3 All ER 490 and *Pauls Agriculture* v *Smith & Ors* [1993] 3 All ER 122, **Costs LR (Core Vol) 218**. Sub-paragraphs (a) and (b) are conditions precedent or, in the words of Jowitt J in *ex parte Bateman*, "triggers", to the exercise of the taxing officer's power under (i) and (ii). The difference is that (a) requires the absence of "good reason" whereas (b) simply requires delay. The delay in (ii), "such delay", is the same as the delay in (b) and must be the cause of any prejudice or additional interest becoming payable, but these two matters are part of "all the circumstances" unlike "prejudice" in the former rule 7(5). Mr Marrin QC submitted the "delay" in the present rule should be "inordinate and inexcusable" not only because the rule applies penal sanctions (which can also be compensatory) but also because it would reflect the practice under the former rule – see, for example, *Jones* v *Roberts*, Lexis transcript pages 8 and 13, *Pamplin* v *Fraser* [1983] 1 WLR 1385 at 1391. *Pauls Agriculture Ltd* v *Smith* (HHJ Crawford QC sitting as a Deputy Judge of the Queen's Bench Division) was an appeal from an order of the Chief Taxing Master who had disallowed part of the receiving party's costs because of delay in lodging the bill. He held that it was necessary to find "inordinate and inexcusable" delay. HHJ Crawford QC declined to disagree with what he took to be settled practice in the Taxing Office. In the instant case, the Chief Taxing Master acknowledged the practice but in his judgment at pages 30 and 31 elected to follow Jowitt J in *ex parte Bateman*. In so doing, he was undoubtedly right. In my view "delay" in rule 28(4)(b) and (ii) does not admit of qualification. If there is delay the taxing officer can exercise his powers "after taking into account all the circumstances". Clearly the duration and culpability of the delay are relevant circumstances which have to be considered along with others.

Returning to the facts of the instant case, it is, of course, apparent that the plaintiffs lodged bills on 24 December 1990 and 1 May 1992. The defendants concede that lodging a bill on 24 December 1990 would not have been unreasonable, having regard to the weight and complexity of the case. Mr Slater QC puts his case in two principal ways:

(1)   The plaintiffs failed to "commence or conduct" proceedings under (a) by insisting, wrongly, that they were entitled to substantially all the costs of both actions without apportionment, having been warned at the outset what the defendants' contentions would be.

(2)   So far as the defendants rely on sub-paragraph (a) there was no "good reason" – indeed quite the contrary: the plaintiffs tied themselves to a wrong view of the law.

(3)   Alternatively, the bill which was lodged on 24 December 1990 was drawn on a wholly incorrect basis and had to be withdrawn and replaced by a quite differently prepared bill which enabled the defendants to see that they were not being asked to pay costs properly attributable to the Sindall action. Accordingly, there was no lodging of a bill until 1 May 1992. The rule contemplates a properly drawn bill capable of being taxed.

(4)   Even if it is necessary to qualify "delay" under sub-paragraph (b), it was, on the facts, both inordinate and inexcusable.

(5)   For the purposes of (ii), the defendants had suffered prejudice from the incidence of interest under the Judgements Act 1838.

Mr Marrin QC submitted:

(1)   There was no failure to comply with any requirement of Order 62. There was a *bona fide* dispute apparent before the Order was made on 12 June 1990 which was not resolved until after full legal argument before Brooke J.

(2)   Even if there was a failure to comply with sub-paragraph (a), there was "good reason". The plaintiffs advanced a *bona fide* arguable view of the law: rule 24 cannot be intended to penalise a party who takes a properly arguable point.

(3)   The defendants' case relies on a purposive construction of sub-paragraph (b): a bill must be "capable of being taxed" or "properly drawn". Since rule 28(4) is penal, this construction should not be adopted. In any event the bill as lodged could have been taxed, the taxing master could have

done his own apportionments.

(4) If there was delay, on authority it must be shown to be inordinate and inexcusable. The observations of Jowitt J are *obiter*. For the reasons advanced at 1, 2 and 3, the delay was neither inordinate nor inexcusable.

(5) If there is to be an exercise of discretion, it should not be against the plaintiffs who acted reasonably in taking a point open to them. The sanction for being found to be wrong was the order for costs made by Brooke J.

(6) *Prejudice.* The plaintiffs accept that the paying party does not have to prove prejudice, but it is a relevant consideration. None has been proved. So far as interest is concerned, the defendants have had the use of their money and have not adduced evidence as to the rate of interest they received on it. Any loss should be calculated using a figure of 15% minus a commercial rate.

I hope I do no injustice to leading Counsel by summarising their most helpful arguments relatively briefly. Mr Slater and Mr Marrin both invited my attention to passages in the Chief Taxing Master's judgment. This is, of course, a rehearing. However, it would appear that at page 34 the Chief Taxing Master regarded the delivery of the first bill to be an "extreme case" where the taxation would have been adjourned for the bill to be redrawn had the parties not elected to go direct to Brooke J. He observed that the plaintiffs would have been ordered to pay the costs thrown away in any event and that this had happened because Brooke J ordered the plaintiffs to pay the defendants' costs of and occasioned by the application.

At page 37, the Chief Taxing Master, having earlier accepted Jowitt J's view that "delay" means simple unqualified delay, said:

> "The purpose of Order 62, rule 28 is to give the taxing master powers in relation to misconduct, neglect etc in respect of acts or omissions made by or on behalf of any party to the proceedings. In this case there is no question of any misconduct or neglect on the part of the Plaintiffs or those representing them. I can find no failure such as is contemplated by rule 28(4)(a) or (b) nor anything which requires the Plaintiffs or those representing them to be penalised or disciplined, nor do I consider it appropriate to compensate the Defendants for the delay which did occur when they have already had an order from Mr Justice Brooke in respect of the costs … of the application."

With all due respect, I take the view that the Chief Taxing Master was incorrect in his approach. True, the plaintiffs had not done anything morally wrong: this the defendants conceded. The questions were whether they had failed to commence or conduct the proceedings in accordance with Order 62 without good reason or had delayed lodging a bill until 1 May 1992 and then whether, in his discretion, the powers given by (i) or (ii) should be exercised. The order for costs made by Brooke J was no compensation for interest accruing during a period of delay. The references to the heading to rule 28 and then to "acts or omissions" in paragraph (1) were inapposite to paragraph (4). In any event, the heading does not stop at Misconduct or

Neglect: the enigmatic "etc" can clearly include delay.

In my view, the Chief Taxing Master was wrong to dismiss the application. I accept both Mr Slater's main contentions. The plaintiffs took an obstinate and uncompromising stance, having received a sum which included costs from Sindalls and consented to an award of costs in Action 1988 R 974 only. This resulted in the lodging of a bill which was entirely inappropriate and had to be completely redrawn. There was, in my view, a delay of 333 days – a surprisingly small fraction of four years. I do not consider that taking an arguable but wrong stance in law is "good reason" in an adversarial system. In any event Mr Slater succeeds under sub-paragraph (b). There can, to my mind, be no doubt that the defendants were prejudiced by the accrual of interest as they were by inability to get on with the taxation until a properly drawn bill was lodged.

The Act of 1838 is an admirable incentive to the early payment of judgment debts but tends to be a disincentive to the early completion of taxation because the rate of interest exceeds commercial rates. The receiving party may have nothing to lose and something to gain by leisurely progress. Interest under the Statute cannot be disallowed or the rate reduced: a result has to be achieved by reducing the capital sum to such a figure that when interest is added back, the sum of the two, when subtracted from the original combined figure for costs plus interest, equals the deduction sought to be made.

There is, in my view, force in Mr Marrin's point that there should be a set off for interest that the defendants received while the money was in their hands. Since I have no evidence, I will assume it (as did Mr Marrin) to be 5%. The defendants' loss must be calculated using a figure of 10% for a period of 333 days. The appropriate factor for interest will be 8.36%, giving a reduction of £19,817.95 (see Schedule).

However, I regard this figure as provisional and will ask the parties to carry out their own calculations to check it.

Counsel for Plaintiff: *Mr J C N Slater QC* and *Mr S F Coles*.
Counsel for Defendant: *Mr J W Marrin QC*.

Thomas Joyce
(Plaintiff)
and
Kammac (1988) Ltd
(Defendants)

(unrevised judgment)

The Royal Courts of Justice
Queen's Bench Division

Before:
Morland J
(sitting with assessors)
The Chief Taxing Master (Master Hurst)
Mr A Cowan
Solicitor

Headnote

In this important 1995 case the judge held that where prior to the grant of legal aid a plaintiff is represented under the Green Form scheme, then his solicitors pre-legal aid inter-partes remuneration is limited to the amount they have recovered under the Green Form scheme and any extensions thereto, unless there is an express agreement which was spelt out to the client at the relevant time, fixing him with liability for any additional costs. Any such agreement will be scrutinized with great care to ensure that it is fair to the client.

Judgment

MORLAND J: This is an appeal to review taxation of the successful plaintiff's costs pursuant to Order 62, rule 35. It is in effect an appeal by his solicitors against the written decision of District Judge Kenneth Wilkinson, an expert in the field, given on 20 October 1993 in the Liverpool County Court.

District Judge Wilkinson disallowed the plaintiff's pre-Legal Aid Certificate costs claimed at £897.57p other than the "Green Form" costs. The appeal was confined to this disallowance. The appeal was out of time but I gave leave to appeal out of time, the defendants not objecting.

I dismissed the appeal on 28 April 1995 stating shortly that the contractual retainer entitled "General Authority", which purported to make the plaintiff potentially liable to his solicitors for their pre-certificate costs, was illegal, a sham and a device to circumvent the restrictions imposed by the Legal Aid legislation.

As I was told that there were a large number of solicitors who recover or seek to recover such costs in similar circumstance, but I hope not by means of a document similar to the "General Authority", and there is some uncertainty and no direct authority as to a plaintiff's entitlement to recover such costs from an unsuccessful defendant, I decided to defer giving a detailed and reasoned judgment. This I now do in open court.

I am very grateful for the help and comments of the Chief Taxing Master and of Mr Cowen, a very experienced litigating solicitor, both during the hearing and after receiving the first draft of this judgment. However I emphasise that I alone am responsible for the conclusions and reasoning of this judgment. I also learnt much from the written decision of District Judge Wilkinson. I was told that neither the Law Society nor the Legal Aid Board wished to appear on the appeal.

On 9 September 1988 the plaintiff, when employed by the defendants at their premises, sustained fractures to his collar bone and ribs and other injuries when he was trapped between a forklift truck and a lorry.

On 12 September 1988 the plaintiff consulted his solicitors, then John Callaghan and Co, now called Burke Edwards, then and now a sole partner firm.

The plaintiff received advice and assistance under the Green Form Scheme. He did not have to pay towards the cost of the Green Form because his income and capital were insufficient.

On 12 September 1988 the plaintiff saw his solicitors for one hour and five minutes. During that time he signed an application for a Legal Aid Certificate to cover bringing proceedings against his employers. A limited Legal Aid Certificate was not granted until 13 October 1989. At least in part the delay was due to the inadequacy of the plaintiff's replies to the Department of Social Security. The plaintiff's contribution was nil. Eventually a full certificate was granted. The defendants' payment into court was accepted on 9 March 1992. Thus prima facie the plaintiff was entitled to all the costs of the action.

Also during the consultation on 12 September 1988 the plaintiff signed the contractual retainer entitled "General Authority". This document was drafted by the plaintiff's solicitors, who, I was told to my surprise, sent it to the Law Society for approval and it was said approved by the Ethics and Guidance Committee.

Paragraph 1 of the "General Authority" states

"1.   I instruct John Callaghan & Company to act on my behalf at my own Solicitor and own client costs on the indemnity basis and I further instruct them to credit me with any green form costs or other costs recovered on my behalf save where the Legal Aid Regulations require receipt of those recovered costs in connection with the Statutory Charge, etc., which has been explained to me. Save as above, I understand that I am personally responsible for all the above described costs but notwithstanding instruct my Solicitor to commence proceedings as soon as possible and/or continue proceedings irrespective of any green form advice or application for legal aid and/or refusal of legal aid and I further instruct my Solicitor not to increase the possibility of my personal costs liability by making application for extension of the financial limit of the green form. I further understand that the Legal Aid Regulations might require my Solicitor to repay Green Form costs to the legal aid authority. If I withdraw my instructions, I agree to pay my Solicitor and own client costs on an indemnity basis, whether agreed between us or fixed by the Court, before I receive any papers released by my Solicitor at his absolute discretion."

Paragraph 3 states

"3.   I authorise my Solicitor to make any interlocutory application or appeal which my Solicitor considers appropriate in order to expedite the settlement of my claim or otherwise, and understand that the Court can make any Order it wishes in respect of costs, and I indemnify my Solicitor in respect of those costs, whether appropriate or not, and whether to be enforced or not by my Solicitor."

Paragraph 4 states

"4.   I acknowledge the entitlement of my Solicitor to receive adequate instructions and to be placed in funds periodically on demand by him to enable him to continue to act for me and, in the absence thereof, I consent to any appropriate and/or related application made by my Solicitor to remove himself from the Court Record as continuing to act for me, in which event, I agree to be personally liable and to pay all my Solicitor costs, whether agreed or fixed by the Court, on an Indemnity basis and I acknowledge the entitlement of my Solicitor to charge interest on any outstanding bill relating to any contentious or non contentious business and to retain my papers until payment of all his costs."

Part 1 of the plaintiff's solicitors' bill represents the pre-legal aid certificate costs which is the subject of this appeal details the work done between 12 September 1988 and 13 October 1989.

It should be noted that there were three personal attendances by the plaintiff on 12 September 1988 for 1 hour 5 minutes, on 6 December 1988 for 15 minutes and on 3 January 1989 for 25 minutes. I shall assume that in September and October 1988 letters were sent to potential witnesses, the police and the defendants. At the material time the Green Form Scheme financial limit allowed two hours work to be done subject to any extension by the Law Society.

In the plaintiff's solicitors' file are three copy letters. The first dated 20 September 1988 purports to enclose an "application for extension of green form financial limit in duplicate". There was no evidence before me as to the grounds of the application. Despite it is said of a search the Law Society have no record of its receipt or refusal nor has the plaintiff's solicitors. I was told that the Law Society do not keep such records. Refused applications need to be kept by the solicitor. Granted applications also need to be kept by the solicitor and submitted in due course with the costs claim to the Law Society. There was no evidence before me as to what had happened to this application and nothing on the solicitors' file was produced.

The second letter dated 28 September 1988 was to the plaintiff. It was a proforma letter which significantly made no reference to the "General Authority" of 12 September nor of the purported application on 20 September for extension of the Green Form Limit.

The letter said:

> "Dear Client,
>
> The Legal Aid Authority has acknowledged receipt of your application for legal aid and they should write to you soon ...
>   In the meantime, we should like to remind you of the following points –
>   1.   We confirm that we have not agreed a fee between us in respect of our costs which we expect largely to be met by your unsuccessful opponent. In this respect, we remind you of the possibility of personal liability in respect of those costs, estimated by the Legal Aid Authority at 10%, not ordered by the Court to be paid by your opponent, even if you are successful if (sic) your claim. Our decision to pursue our entitlement to those costs might be influenced by the nature of those costs, for example, whether or not incurred by any unnecessary attendance and/or work incurring unnecessary costs, etc. You should obtain confirmation of our advice from the Legal Aid Authority or from independent legal advice."

The third letter dated 14 November 1988, the date of the letter before action, purported to enclose another "application for extension of the green form financial limit in duplicate". Again there was no evidence before me as to the grounds of the application. Again despite it is said of a search the Law Society have no record of its receipt or refusal nor has the plaintiff's solicitors. Why this second application was sent is completely obscure.

I was shown by way of example an "application for Extension of Green Form financial limit GF3 – Legal Aid Board Legal Aid Act 1988" in another case. I do not know whether a similar form was in use under the relevant earlier legislation but I shall assume that it was. It contains the following:

Is the client currently applying for Legal aid?   ☐ Yes   ☐ No

If yes, state the reference number of the Legal aid application/certificate: _____

Please attach copies of all previous related extensions, granted or refused. All extensions granted must be submitted when claiming payment.

For official use

Granted to: £195.00

Refused:

Comments: To include applying for Legal

Aid (If Necessary) and obtaining Surveyors

Report

Authorised
signatory: [signed]

Legal Aid area no: 15

Date: 14/APR/1993

I am left with a suspicion that these three letters although apparently contemporaneous came into existence more for appearance's sake so that the plaintiff's costs would be recoverable from the defendants.

Common Law Principles

I shall begin by considering the principle upon which the unsuccessful party to litigation is liable to pay costs to the successful party when the court makes an order for costs in favour of the successful party. I shall consider that principle first without considering the impact of the Legal Aid Act 1988 or earlier Legal Aid Acts upon that principle.

The general principle is that the party in whose favour the order for costs was made, the receiving party, is entitled to be indemnified in respect of such costs that he was primarily and potentially legally obliged to pay to his solicitors. It matters not whether the receiving party was able or not to discharge that legal obligation so long as the primary potential legal obligation to his solicitors existed. It matters not whether the receiving party was able to discharge that legal obligation from funds of his own or funds provided by friends, family, trade union, employer, insurer or otherwise so long as the obligation was primarily his (see *Davies* v *Taylor (No 2)* [1973] WLR 610 per Lord Cross of Chelsea at page 616H).

The receiving party's obligation to his solicitor may be the result of an express or implied contract. In many cases there will be a contract between solicitor and client in the form of a written retainer spelling out the client's obligation to pay his solicitor's costs. In other cases the obligation of the client to pay his solicitor's costs will be implied from the circumstances in which the solicitor is retained by the client asking the solicitor to act for him in a claim or piece of litigation and the solicitor agreeing to act.

The fact that a solicitor may subsequently waive in whole or in part his claim for costs against his own client is immaterial so long as the client had that primary potential obligation to pay his own solicitor's costs.

So far as the party, against whom the order for costs is made, the paying party, is concerned his obligation to pay the costs ordered is limited to indemnifying the receiving party. That is he is only obliged to pay such costs that the receiving party was primarily and potentially legally obliged to pay to his solicitor.

The leading authority for this indemnity principle is the decision of the Court of Appeal in *Gundry* v *Sainsbury* [1910] 1 KB 645, **Costs LR (Core Vol) 1** where Sir H H Cozens Hardy MR said at [1910] 1 KB 645 at 648, **Costs LR (Core Vol) 1 at 1**

> "'The question in this case was whether the successful plaintiff was entitled to the costs of the action, he having stated in his cross-examination that he had verbally agreed with his solicitor that he (the plaintiff) should not pay him any costs', and a little further on, 'In this case the agreement between client and solicitor was that the client should pay the solicitor nothing in respect of costs'."

at [1910] 1 KB 645 at 649, **Costs LR (Core Vol) 1 at 1**

> "What are party and party costs? They are not a complete indemnity, but they are only given in the character of an indemnity. I cannot do better than read the opinion expressed by Bramwell B in *Harold* v *Smith*: 'Costs as between party and party are given by the law as an indemnity to the person entitled to them; they are not imposed as a punishment on the party who pays them, nor given as a bonus to the party who receives them. Therefore, if the extent of the damnification can be found out, the extent to which costs ought to be allowed is also ascertained'. Now in the face of the evidence which the learned county court judge has accepted, and which he was perfectly justified in accepting, if he had ordered the defendant to pay these costs he would have been giving a bonus to the party receiving them. That is contrary to justice and to common sense and also to the law as laid down in *Harold* v *Smith* (5 H&N 381). That is a decision which has remained undisturbed for fifty years, and I am not prepared to depart from it.

and where Fletcher Moulton LJ said at [1910] 1 KB 645 at 651, **Costs LR (Core Vol) 1 at 3**

> "Supposing the costs payable by the client to his solicitor under the agreement are less than those which the taxation shews to be the normal costs, what then? The latter part of the section provides for such a case. The principle that party and party costs are only an indemnity – an imperfect indemnity, it is true, but never more than an indemnity – is so deeply rooted in our law that the proviso is put in for the purpose of preventing the earlier part of section 5 'Attorney and Solicitors Act 1870' from ever giving rise to a case in which costs could be made a profit. By this proviso it is enacted that the client who has entered into such an agreement shall not recover from the person liable to pay to him the costs a greater sum than he himself is under the agreement liable to pay to the solicitor. This proviso is only declaratory in a special instance of what is the

general law as to awarding costs throughout our legal system."

Gundry v *Sainsbury* was applied in a criminal case by the Divisional Court
in *British Waterways Board* v *Rose Norman* (26 October 1993) (McCowan
LJ and Tuckey J). I was referred to the transcript of McCowan LJ's judgment
where he said at page 14 giving the conclusion of the court

> "There must have been an understanding between them (that is Rose Norman
> and her solicitors) amounting in law to a contract that they would not look to
> her for any costs if she lost."

Legal Aid Legislation
The Legal Aid Act 1988 received the Royal Assent on 29 July 1988 but Parts
III ("Advice and Assistance") and IV ("Civil Legal Aid") did not come into
force until 1 April 1989 (SI 1989/288). Until that date the earlier Legal Aid
Acts of 1974, 1979 and 1982 remained in force. Section 31 of the 1988 Act
also did not come into force until 1 April 1989.

The relevant Acts and Regulations together with notes for guidance are
conveniently set out in the Legal Aid Handbook 1986 prepared by the Law
Society (7th Edition). The 1988 Act and 1989 Regulations are set out in the
8th Edition.

In considering the Green Form Scheme the starting point is Part I of the
1974 Act.

The relevant words of section 3(1)(b) are:

> "Where a person seeks or receives any advice or assistance, then if at any time
> (whether before or after the advice or assistance has begun to be given) it
> appears to the Solicitor ... that the cost of giving it is likely to exceed the limit
> applicable ... the Solicitor ... shall not give it so as to exceed that limit except
> with the approval of the appropriate authority."

The relevant words of section 4(1) are:

> "In respect of advice or assistance given to any person ... the client shall not,
> except in accordance with the following provisions of this section (ie the
> client's contribution) be required to pay any charge or fee."

Regulation 65 of the Legal Aid (General) Regulations 1980 should also be
noted although it only applies where a certificate has been issued:

> "Where a certificate has been issued in connection with any proceedings the
> assisted person's Solicitor or Counsel shall not receive or be party to any
> payment for work done in those proceedings during the currency of that
> certificate (whether in the scope of the certificate or otherwise) except such
> payments as may be made out of the fund."

Of importance is regulation 15 of the Legal Advice and Assistance
Regulations (No 2) 1980 which reads:

> "... where it appears to the Solicitor that the cost of giving advice and

assistance is likely to exceed the limit applicable ... he shall apply ... for an extension ..."

The Notes for Guidance read (page 209):

> "Once a legal aid certificate or legal aid order has been issued, no more advice or assistance under the Green Form Scheme will be paid out of the legal aid fund. As a general rule no extension is likely to be granted once an application for a legal aid certificate or a legal aid order has been lodged.
>
> A Solicitor who exceeds the prescribed financial limit cannot obtain payment of the balance from the legal aid fund, nor can he obtain payment unless there has first been an application to the Secretary for an extension which has been refused and the client, having been informed of such refusal, elects to instruct the Solicitor on a private basis."

In argument section 31(3) of the 1988 Act was much stressed it reads:

> "A person who provides advice assistance or representation under this Act shall not take any payment in respect of the advice assistance or representation except such payment as is made by the Board or authorised by, or by regulation under this Act."

Although this section did not come into force until 1 April 1989, the earlier statutory framework in my judgment had the same effect.

I have been informed that the Rules of Court and Regulations Division of the Lord Chancellor's Department have sent out a consultation paper on "Green Form Costs" together with Draft Rule Amendments to

> Order 62, rule 18(1) of the Supreme Court Rules 1965
> Order 38, rule 17(1) of the County Court Rules 1981
> Rule 11(1) of the Matrimonial Causes (Costs) Rules 1988.

I have also been told that District Judge Wilkinson's decision and this consequent appeal to review "has generated intense interest throughout the profession".

In my judgment it is inappropriate that a Puisne Judge albeit advised by assessors of great experience and expertise should lay down guidelines or make pronouncements of general application especially as neither the Law Society nor the Legal Aid Board were represented before me.

On pages 24 and 25 of his judgment District Judge Wilkinson states that six conditions must be satisfied before a client can become subject to a private retainer after the statutory retainer under the Green Form Scheme has been terminated. While not dissenting from the views of the District Judge again I do not consider it appropriate for myself to pronounce upon the six conditions in the absence of considered submissions by the Law Society and the Legal Aid Board.

Furthermore in the present case the statutory requirements of the Green Form Scheme had not been exhausted and there was a legal aid certificate application pending.

I emphasise that this judgment is given within the factual context of this particular case subject to the law applicable at the time as I hold it to be.

In my judgment the following principles of law emerge from the common law and statutory provisions set out above.

(1)   Once a person becomes a client under the Green Form Scheme in relation to a claim receiving advice and assistance the solicitor has a mandatory obligation to comply with the relevant regulations.

See *Drummond v Lamb* [1992] 1 All ER 449 per Lord Keith of Kinkel when the 1988 Act was being considered where he said at 452

> "It is to be observed that his regulation contemplates that there may be successive applications by a solicitor for further increases in the statutory limit if it appears to him that the limit authorised upon earlier application is likely to be exceeded. This is entirely consistent with section 10, which leaves it to the board to determine the final extent to which the statutory limit may be exceeded, such determination obviously being capable of being achieved on any number of successive applications ...
>
> These arguments cannot, however in my opinion prevail against what seem to me to be the plain terms of section 10(1) and (2) of the Act. Subsection (2) states the limit of £50. The reference in sub-s (1)(a) to the solicitor, where it appears to him that the cost of giving advice and assistance is likely to exceed that limit, determining to what extent it can be provided without exceeding the limit can only have in contemplation that the solicitor is to perform that exercise before the limit has been exceeded. The purpose no doubt is to encourage the solicitor to keep the cost of the advice and assistance, if possible, within the limit. The provision in sub-s (1)(b) that the solicitor shall not give advice and assistance so as to exceed the limit, except with the approval of the board, must be mandatory since otherwise it would be deprived of all practical effect. If something is not allowed to be done except with the approval of the board that thing cannot consistently with the Act be done at all unless the approval of the board exists at the time of doing it."

(2)   Breach of the solicitor's statutory obligation under regulation 15 of the Legal Advice and Assistance Regulations (No 2) 1980 to apply for extensions for increases in the statutory limit to the Green Form Scheme, being mandatory, or any device including any purported agreement with the client having the purpose of evading the statutory restrictions is unlawful. Once the Green Form with extensions is exhausted, a client, if he chooses, may in my judgment enter into an agreement with a solicitor on a private retainer basis.

(3)   It follows that the plaintiff's solicitors' "General Authority" is unlawful. In particular the sentence in paragraph 1 clearly flouts the Regulations and is illegal which states

> "I understand that I am personally responsible for all the above described costs but notwithstanding instruct my Solicitor to commence proceedings as soon as possible and/or continue proceedings irrespective of any green form advice or application for legal aid and I further instruct my Solicitor not to increase the

possibility of my personal costs liability by making application for extension of the financial limit of the green form."

It breaches section 4(1) of the 1974 Act.

(4)   In practice, Mr Simpson conceded, no client had ever been asked to pay his solicitor's costs under the purported obligation in the "General Authority". I have no doubt that from the outset no client was ever expected to pay. It was a sham to enable the solicitor to recover costs incurred outwith the Green Form Scheme from the defendant if he was unsuccessful. It was a device to surmount what would otherwise be a contingency agreement. It purported to create a potential primary liability upon the client for his solicitor's costs thus enabling the costs to be recoverable from the unsuccessful defendant on the indemnity principle.

(5)   Mr Simpson submitted that on grounds of public policy a client should be allowed to be subject to a private retainer during the currency of the statutory Green Form Retainer and while a Legal Aid certificate application is being processed which normally takes about three months. He submitted that otherwise investigation into a claim and the taking of witness statements would be delayed to the prejudice of the client.

In most cases sufficient preliminary investigations can be undertaken under the Green Form Scheme especially if extended. If there are problems of great urgency, there is in practice no difficulty in obtaining emergency legal aid certificates to cover urgent work.

I agree with District Judge Wilkinson that a client cannot at the same time be subject to both a statutory retainer and a private retainer in relation to the same matter. In effect that was what the plaintiff's solicitors' "General Authority" sought to achieve

Therefore this appeal is dismissed.

Waterson Hicks
v
Eliopoulos and others

Court of Appeal
14 November 1995

Const:
Neill LJ
Evans LJ
Millett LJ

Headnote

The submissions in this case involved inter alia the extent of the ostensible or actual authority of a costs draftsman instructed in taxation proceedings by his professional client and, although the court did not reach a final decision on the point since in their Lordships' view the circumstances of the case did not require a decision in this regard, both Neill LJ and Evans LJ gave their views on the matter. A costs draftsman may appear only as the duly authorised representative of the solicitor instructing him but in the view of Neill LJ, other parties to the litigation are entitled to assume, in the absence of any information to the contrary, that the costs draftsman has the same authority as the solicitor would have had to consent to orders which were not plainly collateral to the matters before the taxing officer.

Draft Judgment

NEILL LJ:

Introduction
This is an appeal from the order dated 28 July 1993 of Mr Simon Goldblatt QC sitting as a Deputy Judge of the High Court whereby it was declared that a taxing certificate dated 6 October 1992 was null and void as against the first and second defendants in the action and it was ordered that the judgment obtained by the plaintiffs dated 3 December 1992 be set aside in respect of the first and second defendants. The appeal is brought by leave of Lord Justice Mann dated 15 November 1993.

The plaintiffs Waterson Hicks are a firm of solicitors. In 1990 they carried out professional work in connection with arbitration proceedings in London.

The defendants became dissatisfied with the plaintiffs' services and they consulted new solicitors. They also declined to pay the plaintiffs' fees.

By a writ issued on 24 May 1991 the plaintiffs commenced proceedings to recover their fees. Leave to serve the proceedings out of the jurisdiction was obtained in respect of the second and third defendants, Ilios Shipping Co SA (Ilios) and Spacetop Navigation Limited (Spacetop). Spacetop are shipowners. Ilios are an agency company. The companies are controlled by Captain Eliopoulos, the first defendant.

The plaintiffs issued a summons under Order 14. The summons was fixed for hearing on 25 October 1991. On 22 October 1991, that is, shortly before the hearing, the defendants issued an application under Order 12, rule 8 seeking (a) to set aside the issue and service of the writ and (b) an order that the writ had not been duly served upon the third defendant. In addition a declaration was sought that the court had no jurisdiction over the defendants.

The hearing took place before Evans J on 25 October 1991. The third defendant's application to set aside service was dismissed with costs and the plaintiffs' application for summary judgment succeeded against the third defendant. The plaintiffs were awarded the sum of £16,598 inclusive of interest against the third defendant together with their costs.

The remaining applications, being the applications by the first and second defendants under Order 12, rule 8 and the plaintiffs' application against the first and second defendants under Order 14 were not dealt with on that day but were adjourned generally with liberty to apply. Costs as between the plaintiffs and the first and second defendants were reserved.

The two outstanding applications were re-listed for hearing on 17 January 1992. On 16 January payment was made of the principal sum due under the judgment which had been entered following Evans J's order. By 17 January only a few hundred pounds of interest remained outstanding. This sum of interest was paid at a later date.

It seems that at the hearing on 17 January 1992 the first and second defendants did not pursue their application under Order 12, rule 8: see paragraph 7 of Mr Brunton's affidavit sworn on 26 May 1993. Accordingly, Gatehouse J made an order that the plaintiffs' costs of and occasioned by the summons as against the first and second defendants should be paid by them in any event. On the Order 14 summons the first and second defendants were given leave to defend. Gatehouse J ordered that the issue to be tried was:

> "Whether the first and/or second defendant is liable in respect of the plaintiffs' bills of costs."

The order gave directions as to discovery and provided that the costs should be costs in cause.

The plaintiffs then prepared a bill of costs setting out the costs which they had incurred in obtaining judgment against Spacetop. An appointment for the taxation of this bill of costs was made to take place before Mr Hemming, a taxing officer of the Supreme Court, on 13 August 1992.

The bill which was sent to the defendants' then solicitors, Vincent, French and Brown, was described in these terms:

> "Bill of costs of the plaintiff to be taxed on the standard basis and paid by the third defendant pursuant to the order of Mr Justice Evans dated the 25th day of October 1991."

At the taxation before Mr Hemming on 13 August the plaintiffs were represented by Mr Geoffrey Brunton, who was then a partner in Waterson Hicks, and he was assisted by Mr Neil McMeekin, a costs draftsman. Mr French of Vincent French and Brown did not attend himself at the taxation but instructed an independent cost draftsman, Mr Bennett of Crouch Law Costs Service.

Mr Bennett had been instructed only shortly before the hearing. On 11 August Mr French sent him a fax. It was in these terms:

> "*TIMIOS STAVROS*
> Dare we ask you about this one, which is due to be heard at 1115, 13.8.92.
>
> You may recollect attending at Waterson Hicks' offices to look at their files in connection with the above.
>
> The clients were unable to settle and the matter went to litigation, which is still going on. The bills themselves were not really put in issue and it was admitted that the third defendant was a liable party on those bills.
>
> The matter went to an Order 14 hearing, at which judgment was given against the third defendant.
>
> Summary judgment hearing against the first and second defendants was adjourned with no order as to costs against them and eventually at the subsequent hearing they were given leave to defend.
>
> The bill attached is for the costs of the Order 14 hearing against the third defendant and also the costs of an application made just before the hearing contesting jurisdiction.
>
> We do not quarrel with the disbursements, except that only one third of the costs of service should be included in this bill, being applicable to the third defendant.
>
> However, we would appreciate your input regarding the rates and hours particularly because in the hands of the third party solicitors this would have been looked at as a routine piece of debt collecting litigation. The critical Order 14 affidavit was settled by counsel for £75 and the voluminous exhibit was in fact only correspondence. ...."

Mr Bennett replied on the following day, complaining that the matter had been left to the last minute. On the same day, 12 August, he sent a fax to Waterson Hicks. It was in these terms:

> "Re *TIMIOS STAVROS*
> ...
>
> We have just been instructed by the third defendant's solicitors, Messrs Vincent French & Brown and apologise on their behalf for the lateness and

the brevity of our observations upon your bill of costs, which we set out below.

1. Entitlement to costs.

The Order dated 25th October 1991 provides for the plaintiff's costs to be paid by the third defendants in respect of their application under Order 12 rule 8. The third defendants were also ordered to pay the plaintiff's costs for obtaining judgment against them.

Costs as between the plaintiffs and the first and second defendants have been reserved for a further Order.

It is the third defendant's submission that the plaintiff's bill has been incorrectly drawn, as the bill ought to have been split between the three defendants in view of Order 62/3/16 and the fact that the plaintiffs are able to return to court to obtain an order on costs against the first and second defendants. ...

We reserve the third defendants rights to challenge any further item of your bill not covered by these observations."

In his affidavit sworn on 26 May 1993 Mr Brunton explained what happened at the hearing before Mr Hemming. Mr Brunton referred to Order 62, rule 8(9) and submitted that, as there was no likelihood of any further order being made in the action because by that date both the principal and the interest claimed had been paid, Mr Hemming ought to tax forthwith the costs of the interlocutory proceedings against all three defendants. In paragraph 8 of his affidavit Mr Brunton continued:

"I can clearly recall that Mr Hemming explained to Mr Bennett the application and asked him whether he consented to it. After argument, Mr Bennett consented to the application and agreed to the taxation proceeding on that basis."

Later that day, 13 August 1992, Mr Brunton sent a fax to Mr French to tell him what had happened. The fax was in these terms:

"We refer to the taxation this morning. As you will be aware, the court taxed our costs against all three defendants on a joint and several liability basis, in the sum of £7048.90p. This was pursuant to your representative's agreement that the taxation should proceed against all three defendants as if the order of 17 January 1992 had been a final order. Interest runs on the sum of £7048.90 at judgment interest rate, that is to say 15% per annum.

... As at today, the interest stands at £603.20, so that the total amount payable is £7652.10. You will appreciate that interest runs at £2.90 per day henceforth up until the date of payment.

We look forward to receipt of your clients' remittance grossed up to the date of payment within the next seven days. In default, not only will enforcement proceedings be taken, but we shall ensure that the matter attracts the maximum possible publicity in the shipping press and elsewhere."

On the same day Mr Bennett sent a report by fax to Mr French:

"Just a brief report upon the taxation this morning. As you are aware the bill was drawn in the total sum of £10,033.20. I am pleased to say that I have been able to reduce the bill to £6713.20, taxing fee therefore amounts to £335.70 giving a grand total of £7048.90. Interest thereon is running at £2.90 per day from 17 January 1992 as Waterson Hicks had managed to obtain a further order against the first and second defendants making all three defendants jointly and severally liable for their costs."

It is clear that when Mr French received these two faxes he took no immediate action. In his affidavit sworn on 22 July 1993 Mr French gave this explanation:

"I realise now that I should have been aware that the bill had been taxed against all three defendants notwithstanding the fact that no order had been made by the court obliging the first and second defendants to pay those costs at that stage. However, I did see that the bill had been taxed down and due to the fact that I was heavily engaged in other matters I did not focus my mind on the significance of this point. In all honesty and with the benefit of hindsight I can see that this was a mistake on my part and that I failed to take the appropriate steps to protect the interests of my clients and particularly the interests of the first and second defendants."

In the next paragraph of the affidavit Mr French confirmed that neither the first nor the second defendants had any information about the outcome of the taxation until they had received a letter from Waterson Hicks in December 1992.

On 5 October 1992 Waterson Hicks sent a further fax to Mr French pointing out that they had received no reply to the fax of 13 August. The fax set out the sum due at that date and continued:

"We trust that enforcement proceedings will not be necessary although naturally would appreciate receiving your client's remittance by return in order to avoid the same. We look forward to hearing from you."

On 6 October Mr French replied:

"We did not respond to your fax because we were unhappy at the threat contained in it. The more conciliatory tone in your fax is appreciated. We are taking instructions and will revert as soon as possible."

A week later on 12 October Waterson Hicks sent Mr French a copy of the taxation certificate. The taxation certificate was dated 6 October 1992 and stated:

"In pursuance of the orders herein dated 25 October 1991 and dated 17 January 1992 I certify that I have taxed the costs of the plaintiff at the sum of £7048.90.

The certificate was signed by Mr Hemming as Taxing Officer.

On 19 October 1992 Waterson Hicks sent a further fax:

"I refer to our recent telephone conversation and my fax last week. You assured me that you would be taking instructions but I regret to note that I have not yet heard from you. Kindly advise promptly of your client's intentions regarding settlement of the order dated 6 October failing which we will have no option but to seek to enforce directly in Greece with all incumbent costs."

There was no reply from Mr French.

On 10 November Waterson Hicks sent a further fax:

"Our fax of 13 August demanding payment of the costs ordered against your client Captain Eliopoulos and his companies did not elicit a response from you. You subsequently advised us on 6 October that you were taking instructions and would revert as soon as possible. Another month has passed and nothing has happened. It is now almost three months from the date of the order against Captain Eliopoulos. ... Please advise us by return when we will receive payment."

On the following day Waterson Hicks received a fax stating that Mr French was abroad and that their fax would be drawn to his attention as soon as he returned.

Waterson Hicks sent a further fax on 19 November and on 23 November they wrote as follows:

"We have now received the sealed order of the taxation office. A copy is attached for your reference.

Kindly confirm that we will now receive payment of the amount due by return. We have not received proper response to our fax of 10 November nor have we received a response to our fax on 19 November. We propose to correspond directly with your client unless we hear from you promptly."

Again there was no reply from Mr French and on 8 December 1992 Waterson Hicks sent a fax direct to Captain Eliopoulos and to Ilios to tell them that judgment had been entered against all three defendants. The fax concluded:

"Please confirm by close of business on Friday 11 December that remittance has been effected and by what route.

We have corresponded with you directly since we have not received any response from your solicitors Messrs Vincent French & Brown."

Captain Eliopoulos' reaction was to instruct fresh solicitors.

Correspondence then followed between Waterson Hicks and William A Crump, the new solicitors instructed by Captain Eliopoulos.

By this time a sealed judgment dated 3 December 1992 had been drawn up. It was in these terms:

"Pursuant to the order of Mr Justice Evans dated 25 October 1991.

It is this day adjudged that the third defendant do pay the plaintiff the sum of £16,598 inclusive of interest up to 25 October 1991.

The costs of and occasioned by this application by the third defendant to be paid by the third defendant.

And pursuant to the order of Mr Justice Gatehouse dated the 17th Day of January 1992 it is ordered that the plaintiff's costs of and occasioned by the

Order 12 rule 8 summons as against the first and second defendants be paid by
the first and second defendants in any event.

The above costs have been taxed and allowed in the sum of £7048.90 as
appears by the taxing officer's certificate dated the 6th day of October 1992.

On 9 February 1993 William A Crump wrote to Waterson Hicks drawing
attention to the final paragraph of the judgment dated 3 December 1992.
They wrote:

"The final paragraph thereof is clearly in error and does not reflect the court's
intention. The costs which have been taxed and allowed pursuant to the taxing
officer's certificate of 6 October 1992 are those costs of and occasioned by the
application against the third defendant to be paid by the third defendant. The
only costs order as against our clients is in relation to the Order 12 rule 8
summons. Those costs have not been taxed."

William A Crump enclosed a draft amended judgment.

Further correspondence then ensued. Waterson Hicks maintained that the
defendants' representative at the taxation had consented to the application
that the taxation should proceed against all three defendants. In addition
they pointed out that if the defendants had wished to appeal against the costs
as taxed they should have lodged objections within the 21 day time limit
provided in Order 62, rule 33(2).

For their part William A Crump drew attention to the fact that the bill of
costs had been drafted in relation to the costs against the third defendants
only and that Mr Bennett had no authority to consent to the inclusion of any
costs against the first and second defendants.

The hearing before the master

No agreement could be reached, however, and on 17 May 1993 William A
Crump, acting on behalf of Captain Eliopoulos and Ilios, issued a summons
seeking an order that the taxing certificate dated 6 October 1992 should be
set aside and the time for carrying in objections should be extended pursuant
to Order 62, rule 22(1)(e). This summons was heard by Master Martyn in
chambers on 26 May 1993 and was dismissed. Master Martyn gave a
judgment of which we have a note. He concluded that at the hearing on 13
August 1992 before Mr Hemming, Mr Bennett could have said that he had
instructions only on behalf of the third defendant, or could have accepted
the offer of an adjournment which Mr Hemmings had proposed. Master
Martyn further decided that it was not a proper case to extend time for the
objections.

The hearing before the judge

There was then an appeal to the judge in chambers. The appeal came before
Mr Simon Goldblatt QC, sitting as a Deputy Judge of the High Court, on 28
July 1993. He made an order setting aside the judgment dated 3 December
1992 and declaring that the taxing certificate dated 6 October 1992 as

against the first and second defendants was null and void. He further ordered that the proceedings should be transferred to the Mayors and City of London County Court and refused leave to appeal.

It is clear that the judge set aside the judgment and the taxing master's certificate with considerable regret. Furthermore, he made it plain that had he been dealing with the case as a matter of discretion he would have rejected the appeal unhesitatingly. He came to the conclusion, however, that the certificate was null and void. Put shortly, his reasons were:

(a)   That Mr Bennett had no authority to make the concession he did.

(b)   That the taxing officer had no jurisdiction to issue the certificate because the first and second defendants had had no notice of the application to tax.

(c)   That the taxing officer had no jurisdiction to issue the certificate because there was no order of the court pursuant to which a taxation could take place against the first and second defendants.

Leave to appeal from the judge's order was given by Lord Justice Mann on 15 November 1993.

The appeal

On 26 May 1993 Master Martyn described the case before him as "a confused and messy problem". The judge deprecated the mess into which the case had got. It is difficult to disagree with these assessments.

Before turning to the issues raised on the hearing of the appeal it will be convenient to set out certain salient facts.

(1)   Before the hearing on 13 August 1992 the following relevant orders for costs had been made:

    (a) that the application by Spacetop under Order 12, rule 8 be dismissed with costs.

    (b) that there should be judgment against Spacetop for £16,598 with costs.

    (c) that the costs of the hearing on 25 October 1991 between the plaintiffs and the first and second defendants should be reserved.

    (d) that the first and second defendants should pay the costs of and occasioned by the Order 12, rule 8 summons.

    (e) that the costs of the summons under Order 14 against the first and second defendants should be costs in cause.

(2)   The bill of costs which was drawn up by Waterson Hicks was a bill directed to Spacetop alone, though it would appear that it included items which related partly or wholly to the other two defendants.

(3)   Mr Bennett's instructions were limited to attending before Mr Hemming to raise objections to the bill on behalf of Spacetop. He was successful in reducing the bill by almost a third.

(4)   At the outset of the hearing before Mr Hemming Mr Brunton drew attention to Order 62, rule 8(9). This paragraph provides:

"Where it appears to a taxing officer on application that there is no likelihood of any further order being made in a cause or matter, he may tax forthwith the costs of any interlocutory proceedings which have taken place."

(5)   Pursuant to Order 62, rule 8(9) Mr Hemmings would have had power to tax forthwith the "in any event" order made on 17 January 1992 against the first and second defendants by Gatehouse J. He was not asked to do this, however, because the bill before him did not purport to include any costs relating to the hearing on 17 January 1992 or indeed any costs after 28 October 1991.

(6)   According to Mr Bennett's statement, he agreed that the taxation should be against all three defendants, though it seems clear that he agreed reluctantly.

I come therefore to the issues raised on this appeal.

Much of the argument before us on the hearing of the appeal was directed to two issues:

(a) The authority, if any, of Mr Bennett to agree that the taxation should be against all three defendants.

(b) The jurisdiction of the taxing officer.

I have come to the conclusion, however, that the crucian question is whether the first and second defendants can now contest the validity of the judgment dated 3 December 1992.

The powers of taxing officers are set out in Part IV of Order 62. Order 62 was made under powers conferred by section 84 of the Supreme Court Act 1981. It seems clear from Order 62, rule 19(1) that an order for the payment of costs has to be made before the power to tax can be exercised. In the present case, as I have explained, the bill of costs did not contain any costs relating to the hearing on 17 January 1992 and there was therefore no relevant order for costs against the first and second defendants. Technically therefore the taxing officer could not have included any reference to the first and second defendants in the certificate.

I am satisfied, however, that had Mr French himself attended the taxation on 13 August 1992 he would have had ostensible authority to have agreed that the taxation should proceed not only against Spacetop but also against the other two defendants. It may well be that Mr French would have had the implied authority of the first and second defendants as well, but it is not necessary to decide this point.

The nature and extent of a solicitor's ostensible authority was considered in detail by the Court of Appeal in *Waugh v H B Clifford & Sons* [1982] Ch 374. It is convenient to refer to the headnote at 375 which accurately reflects passages in the judgment of Brightman LJ at 387. The material part of the headnote reads:

"The solicitor retained in an action had ostensible authority as between himself and the opposing litigant to compromise the suit provided that the compromise did not involve matters collateral to the action; the matter was not collateral to the action unless it involved extraneous subject matter, and that a compromise did not involve colateral matter merely because it contained terms which the court could not have ordered by way of judgment in the action. ..."

It is to be remembered that one third of the bill had been taxed off and that by 13 August 1992 all the sums due under the judgment including interest had been paid. The question whether Captain Eliopoulos and Ilios were liable for the fees remained outstanding, but Waterson Hicks were not seeking any costs in relation to the 17 January 1992 hearing nor indeed any costs after the last date (28 October 1991) referred to in the bill relating to Spacetop. In these circumstances Mr French could have agreed on behalf of the first and second defendants that the judgment insofar as it related to costs could be made against all three defendants. The first and second defendants might have had a claim against Mr French for making such an agreement, but I am satisfied that to do so would have been within his *ostensible* authority, even if not his implied authority.

In fact, however, Mr French did not attend the taxation. Mr Bennett attended with limited instructions. He had no actual authority to act on behalf of the first and second defendants, nor in my view had he any implied authority to do so.

There is clearly a strong argument that if a solicitor sends to a taxation an independent costs draftsman he represents to the opposing party that the costs draftsman has the same authority to deal with the costs of the proceedings generally as he would have had himself. On the other hand it could be said that a costs draftsman in the position of Mr Bennett was clearly attending only to deal with the taxation of the Spacetop bill and that neither Mr Hemming nor Mr Brunton could have reasonably assumed that he had been given any wider authority.

On the facts of the present case, however, I do not find it necessary to reach a final decision as to the ostensible authority of an independent costs draftsman, though I am inclined to the view that where a solicitor sends a costs draftsman to a taxation the other parties to the litigation are entitled to assume, in the absence of any information to the contrary or unless the sums involved are very large, that the costs draftsman has the same authority as the solicitor would have had to consent to orders which are not plainly collateral to the matters before the taxation officer.

In the present case, however, any unauthorised action taken or consent given by Mr Bennett was in my view ratified by Mr French in the next three months or so. It was argued on behalf of the first and second defendants that ratification requires some positive step and that Mr French had indicated in October 1992 that he was awaiting instructions. In the context, however, the "instructions" would have been understood to relate to the method of payment and not to the question whether the taxation against all three defendants was going to be challenged. Furthermore, Order 62, rule 33(2) provided that an application to the taxing officer for a review had to be made within 21 days. Mr French was notified on 13 August 1992 both by Mr Brunton and by Mr Bennett that the taxation had been against all three defendants. He took no steps to challenge what had happened either then or at any time before the judgment was entered on 3 December 1992.

It is true that the judgment dated 3 December 1992 was in a confusing form and that the reference to the order dated 17 January 1992 was inapposite. Nevertheless, I am satisfied that by his inaction in the period between 13 August 1992 and 3 December 1992 Mr French plainly ratified the consent which Mr Bennett had given on 13 August.

In my view it is now too late for the first and second defendants to challenge the judgment of 3 December 1992 or to seek a review of the taxing master's certificate. I would allow the appeal.

LORD JUSTICE EVANS: I entirely agree and would add only the following in relation to the hearing before Mr Hemming, the taxing officer, when an independent costs draftsman appeared on behalf of the third defendant. In the course of the hearing, he was asked to and did agree that the costs in question should be taxed against the first and second defendants also. He might have objected, but did not, that there was no order against those defendants which permitted taxation "forthwith" and that the proceedings against them had not been finally resolved. On the other hand, the apparent good sense of dealing with the taxation of the same costs in question on that one occasion, rather than incurring the costs of an adjournment so that further formal orders could be obtained, influenced him to agree with what was proposed. He may not have appreciated that a judgment for costs against the third defendants probably could not be enforced, whereas a judgment against the first or second defendants probably could.

As regards the authority, actual or apparent, of an independent costs draftsman who attends before the taxing officer, it should be remembered that he can appear on behalf of the party only as the duly authorised representative of the solicitor who has instructed him to be there. The scope of his apparent authority would be the same, in my judgment, as that of any costs draftsman employed by the firm. It is unnecessary to decide in these proceedings whether his authority would be co-extensive with that of the firm or of the solicitor himself.

MILLETT LJ: I agree.

London Borough of "A"

v

M and SF

Family Division
October 1994

Cazalet J
sitting with assessors

Headnote

This Family Division case considered the nature of exceptional circumstances and the interpretation of "a larger amount" in the context of the Legal Aid in Family Proceedings (Remuneration) Regulations 1991 and in particular regulation 3(4)(c). The interpretation of "a larger amount" contrasts with that placed upon it by Eastham J in *Freeman* v *Freeman* (21 February 1992, unreported). Cazalet J held that the "larger amount" was specifically referable to the specified sums prescribed by the Regulations and that these prescribed figures should be the starting point of any calculation. "Guidelines" for the preparation of family division bills under the 1991 Regulations were also given.

CAZALET J: The taxation gave rise to three points which the district judge described as "difficult and important" –

(1) What is the meaning of "other exceptional circumstances of the case" in regulation 3(4)(*c*)(iii) of the 1991 Regulations?

(2) If there are other exceptional circumstances of the case or exceptional competence or exceptional expedition within the meaning of regulation 3(4)(*c*) of the 1991 Regulations may the taxing officer have any, and if so what, regard to the rates prescribed by the 1991 Regulations in arriving at the "larger amount" specified in that regulation?

(3) Where in a bill of costs exceptional competence, exceptional expedition or other exceptional circumstance is claimed how should such be set out in the bill and be dealt with by the district judge or taxing officer?

The background to the review
On 4 May 1993 His Honour Judge Coningsby WC, upon the making of an

interim care order, ordered that the costs of the second respondent, for whom Messrs Bond Solon acted, be taxed in accordance with the provisions of the Legal Aid Act 1988. On 18 May 1993 the solicitors' bill of costs was lodged and on 9 June 1993 it was provisionally taxed by District Judge Segal. On 28 June 1993 the solicitors gave notice that they did not accept the outcome of the provisional taxation and sought an appointment for reconsideration. That appointment was fixed on 9 August 1993 and proceeded as a taxation in the presence of the solicitors and their costs draftsman. The district judge had before him at the taxation a letter dated 28 June 1993 from the solicitors, a copy of which has been supplied to us, setting out the solicitors' arguments to justify the exceptional circumstances which they invited District Judge Segal to find present as well as the hourly rates and other remuneration sought in their bill. It is unnecessary at this stage to refer to that letter since we have had the benefit of full argument from Mr Farber, counsel on their behalf. Remaining dissatisfied with the result of the taxation the solicitors sought and obtained on 17 September 1993 authority from the Legal Aid Board to carry in objections to the taxation. Such objections were duly lodged and on 11 January 1994 District Judge Segal reviewed the taxation. On 17 January 1994 District Judge Segal delivered his written reasons upon the objections to the taxation, such document running to 19 pages. Both I and my assessors are of the view that this is a most helpful document setting out concisely the difficulties faced by a taxing officer in construing and applying the 1991 Regulations.

In his judgment the district judge drew attention to the fact that solicitors and costs draftsmen are finding it very difficult to identify and isolate those circumstances of a case which are likely to qualify as exceptional. He referred to a succession of bills of costs containing no specific particulars and making vague general assertions followed by a request that the taxing officer allow throughout the bill a charging rate well in the excess of the prescribed rate, or a mark-up or both with no attempt to distinguish those items of work which were exceptional from those which were not. The district judge pointed out that this makes it almost impossible for the taxing officer on the one hand to ensure that the solicitor is remunerated reasonably for those items of work which were genuinely exceptional and on the other hand to protect the legal aid fund. On 11 March 1994 the solicitors applied for a review of taxation before the judge. Because of the importance of this case two assessors were appointed to sit with me and we heard argument on behalf of the solicitors over two days.

The case
The local authority was the applicant in a case concerning a young child. The first respondent was the mother, and the solicitors concerned acted for the second respondent, the stepfather. Whilst the mother and stepfather were living in homeless persons' accommodation a hostel worker had noticed marks of injuries on the child. Subsequently further injuries were reported

and the child's mother stated that the stepfather had punched the child on the side of the head. The mother then withdrew that statement, but the police surgeon reported injuries to the child consistent with such a blow. Later the mother attended a child protection conference with marks of injury upon her face. She said that she was frightened of her husband. The child went to live with grandparents. A series of decisions by the local authority ended with the child moving back to live with the mother and stepfather so as to be part of a family assessment at the local authority's assessment centre. Further bruising and injury to the child were observed on various occasions over a period of three months. The stepfather was then sentenced to nine months' imprisonment for violent disorder associated with poll tax demonstrations. A new family assessment began but the mother failed to co-operate. The stepfather, following a successful appeal, was released from prison some months later. Although it was clear to the local authority that he posed a danger to the child the mother refused to sever her relationship with him. Care proceedings were taken. Those proceedings culminated in a six day hearing beginning on 26 April 1993 and ending on 4 May 1993 when, after strenuously contesting the care applications for six days, the mother and stepfather withdrew their opposition. An interim care order was then made.

Evidence was given at the hearing by six social workers, one child care co-ordinator, one health visitor, two general practitioners, two police officers and one chartered psychologist. These witnesses were all called on behalf of the local authority with the hearing ending before the respondents' cases had started. The length of hearing had been estimated at ten days. The matter proceeded at country court level throughout and was heard by His Honour Judge Coningsby QC at the Royal Courts of Justice.

The evidence of the local authority witnesses was challenged both factually and as to objectivity by Mr Solon, who appeared as solicitor/advocate on behalf of the second respondent. The local authority was represented by leading counsel. As well as the mother other parties in the case were the maternal grandparents, the paternal grandmother, the local authority and the child, represented by a guardian ad litem. There were five respondents in all to the application. Six incidents of physical abuse to the child were alleged over a two year period. A consultant educational psychologist prepared a six page report in respect of the stepfather. The written evidence included an 18 page assessment report, 18 pages of police interviews, a 36 page guardian ad litem report, as well as evidence from the maternal grandparents and their witnesses running to 38 pages. The written evidence amounted in all to 294 pages.

The taxation

In their bill of costs the solicitors pointed to the fact that the judge had certified that there should be a "special allowance" for the conducting solicitor. The solicitor went on to say that –

"In view of the exceptional circumstances of the case we have claimed larger amounts than those specified in the schedule for some aspects of the work done as particularised in the body of the bill, but we have claimed routine correspondence, travelling and waiting at the relevant Schedule rates."

The fact that the judge certified that there should be a special allowance is not, in my view, of relevance to a taxation under Schedule 1 to the 1991 Regulations. If the taxing officer is to step outside the prescribed rates he must be satisfied that he is entitled to exercise his discretion under regulation 3(4). This regulation is not concerned with "special allowances" as such, and accordingly such a phrase is irrelevant to any taxation carried out in care proceedings.

In calculating the "larger amounts" the solicitors adopted what they described as "the broad average direct costs rate" at £70 per hour. They sought this rate for the main preparation item and for attending both the interim hearings and the final hearing. It is to be noted that the rate prescribed by Schedule 1 to the 1991 Regulations for preparation by a fee earner whose office is situated within legal aid area 1 is £60.25 per hour and for attendances an hourly rate of £63 per hour is specified. In addition to those sums, however, the solicitors sought a 75% mark-up for (i) general care and attention on the main preparation items, (ii) each day of the six day trial and (iii) an earlier interim hearing which lasted almost five hours. On a shorter interim directions appointment the solicitors sought a care and attention mark-up of 50%.

In taxing the bill District Judge Segal found that the only exceptional circumstance was the solicitor's membership of the Children Act Panel. He allowed £70 per hour as claimed in respect of the main preparation item (item 4 in Schedule 1 of the 1991 Regulations); he disallowed entirely the claim for a 75% care and attention mark-up in respect of that main preparation item. In respect of each attendance at a hearing he restricted the solicitors' hourly rate to £63, being the sum prescribed by Schedule 1 to the 1991 Regulations. He further disallowed completely the claims for a care and attention mark-up in respect of all hearings. His reasons for so doing are set out in full in his 19 page judgment.

The 1991 Regulations provide by regulation 3(2) that the amounts to be allowed on determination under this regulation shall be –

"(a) In accordance with Schedule 1 where the certificate was issued in relation to care proceedings."

Accordingly Schedule 1 to the Regulations applies to this taxation. Regulation 3(4)(c) provides that –

"On determination the relevant authority ...

(c) may allow a larger amount than that specified in column 2 or column 3, as the case may be, of Parts I, II, III, V or Schedule 1 and 2(a) where it appears to him reasonable to do so having regard to –

(i)   the exceptional competence with which the work was done, or
(ii) the exceptional expedition with which the work was done, or
(iii) any other exceptional circumstances of the case including, in the case
      of a care proceedings, the fact that the solicitor was a member of the
      Law Society's Children Act Panel."

The regulation goes on to provide that the relevant authority may allow a lower amount than that specified in respect of such matters where it appears reasonable to do so having regard to any failure on the part of the solicitor to provide timely preparation or advice or for any similar reason. Such question of a lower amount is not relevant to this application. In the instant review the court is concerned only with the circumstances in which a "larger amount" may be awarded, how it is to be sought and how it should be assessed by the district judge or taxing officer. Part I of Schedule 1 relates to preparation, and includes writing and receiving letters, making and receiving telephone calls, all other preparation work and travelling and waiting time in connection therewith. Part II of Schedule 1 relates to conferences with counsel and is not relevant to this matter. Part III relates to attendances at the trial or hearing of the matter or other application including travelling and waiting. Part V relates to the taxation and review of taxation of costs.

The nature of exceptional circumstances
The first question raised in this review is to determine the meaning of the words "any other exceptional circumstances" as such appear in regulation 3(4)(c)(iii) of the 1991 Regulations. We were asked to hold that where the work done by the lawyers on a case in a qualitative or quantitative sense is, for example, complex, novel, onerous in terms of responsibility, weight or the like then such may constitute an exceptional circumstance making it "reasonable" to allow a "larger amount" than the specified rate. In his reasons District Judge Segal pointed out that the fact that the magistrates may consider a case exceptionally grave, important or complex does not of itself amount to an exceptional circumstance of the case within the meaning of regulation 3(4)(c)(iii). If it did then the schedule itself would hardly ever apply to a case transferred to the county court, yet in fact the schedule is regularly applied to such cases. The district judge went on to say that he considered that when taxing a county court bill the taxing officer must consider whether by the standards of the type of case which is transferred up from the magistrates' court and is heard in the county court, there are any exceptional circumstances of the case which can be seen to be outside a typical county court case. In this case District Judge Segal found that the only exceptional circumstance was Mr Solon's membership of the Law Society's Children Act Panel.

It was argued by Mr Farber that "exceptional" means "out of the ordinary", "unusual", "special", that "circumstances" means "a condition of time, place etc that accompanies or influences an event or condition" or "that which surrounds materially, morally or logically".

We do not feel that a legal definition can be given to the words "exceptional circumstances" or is necessary. The courts are well used to dealing with these words and taxing officers are well able to recognise exceptional circumstances. We will later in this judgment indicate those matters which we consider may be amongst those that are capable of constituting exceptional circumstances but we emphasise that there is no basis for limiting a taxing officer's discretion by attempting to compile an exhaustive list of "exceptional circumstances". These will change as the law procedure, society and its problems change. What is exceptional today may not be exceptional tomorrow. For example the early cases of child sexual abuse may well then have been viewed as exceptional. However, such cases are now regularly before the courts.

It was further submitted to us that the correct test is to look at the circumstances of the particular case without emphasis on the level of court in which the case is heard. We should then ask the question –

> "Is there something unusual in the particular case whatever level of court in which it is heard which affects the work of the lawyers in a qualitative and/or quantitative sense making is reasonable to allow more than the specified rate?"

In our view the level of court is no more than an indicator of complexity and weight. For example, a case transferred to the High Court might turn into a run of the mill action for any number of unforeseen reasons; a party might abandon a claim or an expert might alter a view, circumstances might change so that it becomes manifestly plain that a party was not suitable to have care of a child. Similarly a case in the county court or even the magistrates' court which seemed relatively straightforward when set down might develop considerable complexity because, for example, further claims were made by interveners or because further facts came to light which made a party's claim weaker or stronger. We consider that "exceptional circumstances of the case" must mean the circumstances of the particular case at whatever level of court is heard. The fact that a case might be difficult for an experienced tribunal of whatever level is no more than an indicator of the potential presence of exceptional circumstances. It is only if the case affects the work done by the lawyers in a qualitative or quantitative sense that it becomes reasonable for the taxing authority to exercise the discretion.

Are there exceptional circumstances in the present case?
In this case District Judge Segal found that the only exceptional circumstance was the solicitor's membership of the Law Society's Children Act Panel. He therefore allowed an enhanced rate of £70 per hour on the preparation item rather than the rate specified in Schedule 1 of £60.25 per hour but came to the conclusion that there were no other exceptional circumstances. In particular he found that long hearings undertaken by solicitors without reliance on counsel did not of themselves constitute exceptional circumstances.

As has been pointed out District Judge Segal concluded that in care cases membership of the Children Act Panel in itself constitutes an exceptional circumstance of the case. He reached this decision notwithstanding a decision of the Legal Aid Board to the contrary. The Legal Aid Board reference is CLA8 at page 80 of the 1993 *Legal Aid Handbook* and states –

> "Membership of the Law Society's Children Panel is not in itself an exceptional circumstance justifying payment of an enhanced rate under regulation 3(4)(*c*) of the Legal Aid in Family Proceedings (Remuneration) Regulations 1991 but membership of the Panel may be a factor which contributes to a decision that enhanced rates are justified under regulation 3(4)(*c*)(iii) of those regulations."

I agree with the approach of the district judge and have reached the conclusion that the wording of regulation 3(4)(*c*)(iii) is only consistent with the construction that membership of the Law Society's Children Act Panel in care proceedings is in itself an exceptional circumstance which gives a discretion to the determining officer to allow a larger amount than that specified where it appears to him reasonable so to do. In other words membership of the Panel itself will be an exceptional circumstance and qualify for a larger amount although it will be in the discretion of the taxing officer as to whether that larger amount may be reasonably given in any particular part of the bill of costs in question.

In argument before District Judge Segal a decision of the Legal Aid Board Costs Appeal Committee (provisional reference CLA(9)) was cited. That decision states as follows –

> "Care proceedings; enhanced rates; possible exceptional circumstances; point of principle, when considering a claim for enhanced rates on the basis of regulation 3(4)(*c*)(iii) of the Legal Aid in Family Proceedings (Remuneration) Regulations 1991, consideration should, when deciding if there are 'any other exceptional circumstances' of the case, be given to whether any of the following existed –
>
> (1) The case fulfilled the complexity criteria requiring the transfer of the case to a care centre.
>
> (2) Innate difficulties of communication with the client, eg mental health problems, deafness, speech impairment or autistic clients.
>
> (3) A conflict of expert evidence as opposed to merely contested expert evidence and/or a proliferation of expert witnesses.
>
> (4) Serious contested allegations of abuse.
>
> (5) Long hearings (ie in excess of two days) undertaken by solicitors without reliance on counsel.
>
> (6) The involvement of a number of children with different needs."

The above list is non-exhaustive. The factors cited relate to the circumstances of the case itself and not to claims for enhanced rates based on regulation 3(4)(*c*)(i) and (ii) of the 1991 Regulations. Regard should be given to the manner in which the work was done and, so this decision states, the presence of one or more of the above factors may justify payment of an enhanced rate. District Judge Segal considered that (2) and (6) were certainly capable of being exceptional circumstances of the case. It is, however, our view that the presence of these factors in some cases will do no more than persuade the taxing officer to allow as reasonable more hours of work than would otherwise normally be remunerated. District Judge Segal found that (3) and (4) were frequently encountered by the district judges of the Principal Registry in the course of trying care cases and while such were capable of being exceptional circumstances of the case they would in practice seldom have this effect. He did not regard (5) as capable of amounting to an exceptional circumstance of the case in view of the fact that a solicitor advocate was remunerated as an advocate by the higher allowance under item 9 for attending without counsel at the trial.

We consider that, as a general rule, where a solicitor appears as an advocate this is not an exceptional circumstance of the case. Where a Panel solicitor appears as an advocate in care proceedings this is an exceptional circumstance of the case, but whether such an exceptional circumstance justifies of itself the allowance of a "larger amount" is a question for the exercise of discretion. For example, the attendance of a Panel solicitor upon an uncontested interim care order application with no contested directions or other features may well attract simply the rate provided in Part I.

This case was originally estimated to last ten days; it ran for six days. We do not consider that length necessarily of itself is exceptional, though of course it may well be a strong pointer. If exceptional circumstances are found in a particular case then we would expect the district judge to exercise his discretion to allow a larger amount to a solicitor advocate where, for example, the hearing lasted more than two days. We have had drawn to our attention the Law Society's code for advocacy published in their professional standards bulletin No 10. This was prepared in connection with the provision of advocacy services as defined by section 119 of the Courts and Legal Services Act 1990. In particular we refer to rule 4.3 of that code which states –

> "Advocates (whether or not they are also litigators and whether they are instructed on their own or with another advocate) must in the case of each brief consider whether consistently with the proper and efficient administration of justice and having regard to –
> (i)   the circumstances including the gravity, complexity and likely cost of the case,
> (ii)   the nature of their practice,
> (iii)   their ability, experience and seniority,
> (iv)   their relationship with the client,
> the best interests of the client would be served by instructing or continuing to instruct them in that matter."

It seems to us that this code properly applied is relevant for the purpose of establishing whether a solicitor advocate conducting a long case constitutes an exceptional circumstance. We have further had drawn to our attention the procedures for the Law Society's Children Act Panel membership, notes for the guidance of new applicants and a membership application form. These provide for general advocacy experience, specific training, interview, specific care case experience, payment of a fee and a five year qualification period. Knowledge of the law and procedure together with ethical issues and professional skills are required as well as references from clerks to the justices and guardians ad litem. Each solicitor appointed to the Panel is required to provide a written undertaking in rigorous terms when representing a child in proceedings covered by the Children Act. These matters emphasise the higher standard of knowledge and expertise in this field which are required of a Panel solicitor. In this case Mr Solon was a member of the Panel. He was not however representing a child and therefore his membership of the Panel was not mandatory. However, the fact that in these care proceedings he was representing a parent and not the child does not affect the existence of the exceptional circumstance.

In order to determine whether there are exceptional circumstances appertaining to a particular case it is necessary to look to its specific features. In the instant case the number of parties contesting the issues, the number of witnesses including expert witnesses and social workers, the number of counsel involved including leading counsel for the local authority (some indication of complexity with an added adrenalin factor for the other advocates, in particular a solicitor advocate), the estimated length of hearing of ten days, the nature and number of the allegations are all indicators of factual and/or legal complexity. The second respondent stepfather was a demanding client. He had a criminal record. He was not coherent in terms of instructions. He was volatile, aggressive and difficult. The judge had to rise on one occasion because of his extreme behaviour in court. There were allegations and counter-allegations between the mother, the client and the grandparents. This was a five way contest. Credibility was crucial to the client's claim and his behaviour and background made additional demands upon his advocate in handling his case in court.

This was a heavy case. It had no novel features but it had certain features which, in our view, constituted exceptional circumstances.

The exercise of the discretion in assessing the larger amount
Having established that this case does contain exceptional circumstances and that a discretion therefore arises pursuant to regulation 3(4)(*c*)(iii) of the 1991 Regulations the question then arises as to how that discretion should be exercised. Regulation 3(7) provides that –

> "In exercising his discretion under this Regulation or in relation to any provision of the Schedules where the amount of costs to be allowed is in his discretion, the relevant authority shall exercise his discretion in accordance with paragraph 1(2) of Part I of Schedule 1 to the Rules."

"The Rules" means the Matrimonial Causes (Costs) Rules 1988 ("The 1988 Rules") which provide under Schedule 1, Part I, paragraph 1(2) that –

> "In exercising his discretion the taxing officer shall have regard to all the relevant circumstances, and in particular to –
> (*a*)   the complexity of the item or of the cause or matter in which it arises and the difficulty or novelty of the questions involved;
> (*b*)   the skill, specialised knowledge and responsibility required of, and the time and labour expended by, the solicitor or counsel;
> (*c*)   the number and importance of the documents (however brief) prepared or perused;
> (*d*)   the place and circumstances in which the business involved is transacted;
> (*e*)   the importance of the cause or matter to the client;
> (*f*)   where money or property is involved its amount or value;
> (*g*)   any other fees and allowances payable to the solicitor or counsel in respect of other items in the same case or matter, but only where work done in relation to those items has reduced the work which would otherwise have been necessary in relation to the item in question."

These provisions are familiar to taxing officers as similar provisions appear in Order 62 of the Rules of the Supreme Court. They are usually referred to as the "Seven Pillars".

Our attention was drawn to rule 3(1) of the 1991 Regulations which expressly incorporates, inter alia, paragraph 1(4)(*a*) of Part I of Schedule 1 to the Matrimonial Causes (Costs) Rules 1988. Rule 1(4)(*a*) provides that –

> "An allowance for general care and conduct, having regard to such of the circumstances referred to in sub-paragraph (2) as may be relevant, may be included (*a*) in respect of costs payable out of the legal aid fund in accordance with rule 10 only in items 1 to 4 of Schedule 2."

In considering the impact of this provision we were faced with some difficulty. First, paragraph 1(4)(*a*) of Part I of Schedule 1 to the 1988 Rules appears to be incorporated into the 1991 Regulations in a manner which is equally applicable to Schedule 1 (care proceedings) as to Schedule 2 (prescribed family proceedings). Second, paragraph 1(4)(*a*) of Schedule 1, Part I to the 1988 Rules only refers to "Schedule 2". This must, of course, be a reference to Schedule 2 to the 1988 Rules and not to either Schedule 1 or Schedule 2 to the 1991 Regulations. Third, paragraph 1(4)(*a*) of Schedule 1, Part I to the 1988 Rules refers to costs payable out of the legal aid fund "in accordance with rule 10". The 1988 Rules were made pursuant to powers contained in section 50 of the Matrimonial Causes Act 1973. This section was repealed by section 46(3) of and Schedule 3 to the Matrimonial and Family Proceedings Act 1984 with effect from 14 October 1991 by Commencement Order (No 5), SI No 1211. Revoking the power to make the 1988 Rules had the effect of revoking the 1988 Rules themselves. However the Family Proceedings (Costs) Rules 1991 (made in exercise of powers under section 40(1) of the Matrimonial Family Proceedings Act 1984) preserve the 1988 Rules (save for rule 10 and Schedule 2 which arises out of rule 10) by providing in rule 2(2) that the 1988 Rules shall have effect as if part of the 1991 Rules. There is therefore no longer a rule 10 of the 1988 Rules in existence. The 1991 Regulations accordingly purport to incorporate paragraph 1(4)(*a*) of Schedule 1, Part I to the 1988 Rules which rule relates to costs payable out of the legal aid fund in accordance with rule 10, that being a rule which no longer exists. It is difficult to see what the intention was of those who drafted the 1991 Regulations in endeavouring to incorporate this particular provision. It may simply have been an error. However, Mr Farber submitted that it is appropriate for us to incorporate this provision and to apply it to Schedule 1 to the 1991 Regulations as well as to Schedule 2; in which event there would be a broad discretion to provide a general uplift in respect of items 1 to 4 set out in Schedule 1, Part I to the 1991 Regulations.

For the reasons given I do not consider that Schedule 1, Part I, rule 1(4)(*a*) of the 1988 Rules applies to Schedule 1 to the 1991 Regulations. However, even if it did, I do not consider that its effect would be to limit the taxing officer's powers to provide a mark-up only for items 1 to 4 of Schedule 1. A "larger amount", pursuant to the provisions of regulation 3(4)(*c*), is expressly allowed for conferences with counsel (Part II) and attendances (Part III) of Schedule 1 to the 1991 Regulations. The rates in Schedule 1, Parts II and III to the 1991 Regulations are the same as the rates in Schedule 2(*a*) to the 1991 Regulations, save for attending court without counsel, and so do not appear to have any built in mark-up, contrary to what appears to be the position in regard to item 4 of Schedule 1, Part I. A comparison of this latter item 4 with items 4 and 5 of Part I of Schedule 2 to the 1991 Regulations shows the prescribed rate of the 1991 Regulations as £64.50 per hour with no expressly permitted mark-up, whereas the 1988 Rules show for items 4 and 5 the prescribed rate of £43 per hour plus 50% per hour to cover the general care and conduct of the proceedings. Yet if no mark-up were to be allowed for conferences and attendances, the discretion permitted under regulation 3(4)(*c*) would be limited to increasing only the hourly rate. Since the hourly rate is intended to reflect the direct cost of the work and not the complexity or other exceptional circumstances there would then appear to be no power to exercise a discretion to reflect a mark-up for exceptional circumstances in the particular case arising under any part other than Part I. Yet regulation 3(4)(*c*) expressly permits the discretion to allow a larger amount, when appropriate, to be exercised in respect, inter alia, of Parts I, II, III and V of Schedule 1.

Furthermore I note that the word "general" is used in reference to care and conduct in regulation 1(4)(*a*). Whilst a general care and conduct mark-up is applicable in considering preparation (item 4) I do not consider that a general care and conduct mark-up would be applicable for conferences and attendances. Thus rule 1(4)(*a*) should be seen as having no bearing, directly or indirectly, on any assessment either outside or within Part I of Schedule 1 to the 1991 Regulations since I do not consider it to apply here.

Having found that he had a discretion on the basis of the exceptional circumstance of Mr Solon being a member of the Children Act Panel District Judge Segal took the view that the taxing officer must in exercising his discretion have a starting point. He considered that starting point to be the amount or amounts fixed by Schedule 1 to the 1991 Regulations. He considered that the words "larger amount" in regulation 3(4)(c) of necessity entail a consideration of the amount fixed by the rules when the taxing officer is considering whether to exercise his discretion. If he is not to have regard to the amount fixed in the schedule how is he to ascertain what other amount would constitute a "larger" amount? I agree with this approach and I consider that the starting point is the taxing officer's consideration of the fixed rate. Once he has the fixed rate in mind the taxing officer must then go on and ascertain what "larger amount" may be appropriate.

Mr Farber's submissions as to how the "larger amount" is to be calculated
Mr Farber submitted that once exceptional circumstances were found and a discretion thereby established to allow a larger amount than that specified in Schedule 1, Part I then such discretion entitled the taxing master to adjust both the hourly rate and/or to allow a percentage mark-up in all or any of Parts I, II, III and V of Schedule 1 to the 1991 Regulations. He supported this argument with an analysis of paragraph 3(1) of the 1991 Regulations which requires the sums to be allowed to legal representatives in connection with family proceedings to be determined in accordance with, inter alia, Part XII of the Civil Legal Aid (General) Regulations 1989.

Contained within Part XII of those regulations is General Regulation 107(3)(b) which requires legal aid taxations to be carried out upon a standard basis. A standard basis of taxation is defined by RSC Order 62, rule 12 as follows –

> "On a taxation of costs on the standard basis there shall be allowed a reasonable amount in respect of all costs reasonably incurred and any doubts which the taxing officer may have as to whether the costs were reasonably incurred or were reasonable in amount shall be resolved in favour of the paying party: and in these rules the term 'The standard basis' in relation to the taxation of costs shall be construed accordingly."

Rule 38 of the County Court Rules incorporates RSC Order 62 into county court taxations.

Mr Farber submitted that as there was nothing in the 1988 Rules or the 1991 Regulations which prohibits adjustments to hourly rates then, in the absence of guidance as to how the "larger amount" is to be assessed, the district judge's discretion must be exercised in accordance with normal judicial taxing principles.

He argued, which I accept, that it is now well established that a solicitor's remuneration shall consist of two elements, first, a sum computed on the basis of the hourly rate which represents the broad average direct cost of undertaking the work, and second, a sum usually expressed as a percentage mark-up of the broad average direct cost for care and conduct (see *R v Wilkinson* [1980] 1 All ER 597 at 601, following *Lloyds Bank Ltd v Eastwood* [1975] Ch 112, **Costs LR (Core Vol) 50** and *Leopold Lazarus Ltd v Secretary of State for Trade and Industry* (1976) 120 Sol Jo 268, **Costs LR (Core Vol) 62**). The broad average direct cost refers to an hourly rate which reflects the broad average direct cost of doing work measured by reference to the cost of average firms of solicitors in the relevant area. The hourly rate does not reflect and must not be adjusted to reflect factors such as the complexity of work: complexity and similar items should be reflected in the mark-up for care and conduct. It is established that the hourly rate and the care and conduct mark-up are to be calculated independently of one another, the hourly rate simply on the broad average direct cost basis and the mark-up assessed taking into account established relevant factors, including the "Seven Pillars".

In view of the lack of assistance in the 1991 Regulations (or the earlier 1988 Rules) to guide a taxing officer in the exercise of his discretion Mr Farber further submitted that after a taxing officer has assessed the hourly rate and a percentage mark-up, following established principles, the figure arrived at would almost invariably be a larger figure than the specified rate. Mr Farber concluded that the taxing officer would then stand back and take a broad view of the matter effectively exercising his knowledge, experience and discretion in arriving at the "larger amount" that should be allowed.

In conducting this overview Mr Farber invited us to construe the absence of the words "higher rate" or "larger rate" from the 1991 Regulations and 1988 Rules as support for the proposition that the taxing officer in carrying out this exercise is freed from the specified "rate" and should fix a "larger amount", which allows for changes to hourly rates and/or the application of mark-ups, without paying any regard to the prescribed rates save for the initial starting check-point that the amount proposed exceeded the prescribed rate.

Mr Farber sought to derive support for his argument from the decision of Eastham J sitting with two assessors in the matter of *Freeman v Freeman* (21 February 1992, unreported). That was a case under the Matrimonial Causes (Costs) Rules 1988, rule 10 of which (now revoked) contained similar provision to the 1991 Regulations by permitting a taxing officer to allow a –

> "Larger amount than that specified in (the Schedule) where it appears to him reasonable to do so having regard to –
> (i)   the exceptional circumstances with which the work was done, or
> (ii)   the exceptional expedition with which the work was done, or
> (iii) any other exceptional circumstances of the case."

The learned judge in that case held that on its natural construction where a court or a taxing officer is satisfied that there are exceptional circumstances in the case then the taxing officer is "completely freed" from the fixed amounts specified in the second schedule and it is his duty thereafter to assess what in all the circumstances is a fair and reasonable fee both in regard to the hourly rate and also in relation to the mark-up. In that case Eastham J with the assistance of his assessors allowed an hourly rate of £40 per hour where the specified rate was £32 per hour, £45 per hour where the specified rate was £34 per hour and £50 per hour where the specified rate was £36.50 per hour. In addition he allowed a care and conduct mark-up.

Mr Farber cited two further cases, *R* v *Dunwoodie* [1978] 1 All ER 923 and *"B"* (21 March 1986) an unreported decision of Master Hurst. In *R* v *Dunwoodie*, at page 931, Slynn J (as he was then) in considering the Legal Aid in Criminal Proceedings (Fees and Expenses) Regulations 1968 held –

> "If it appears to the taxing authority having taken into account all the relevant circumstances referred to in regulation 7(1) that nevertheless owing to exceptional circumstances the sums payable by virtue of the 1968 Regulations would not provide fair remuneration for the work actually done and he so certifies any limitation contained in the regulations on the amount of any fee payable does not apply."

In the case of *"B"* (above cited) consideration was given to Criminal Remuneration Regulations which came into force in 1982. Since a point of principle was involved the Chief Taxing Master, Master Hurst, invited the Lord Chancellor to make representations with a view to ensuring that the public interest was taken into account. The representations on behalf of the Lord Chancellor were to the effect that the determining officer should not wholly disregard the regulations and should not proceed only on the principles which govern common fund taxations. In his judgment the Chief Taxing Master effectively allowed an enhanced rate representing the broad average direct cost of carrying out the work by the solicitors with a care and conduct uplift. Mr Farber relied upon this as support for the proposition that where "exceptional circumstances" or other reasons for stepping outside a scale arise then the correct approach is to go back to basic principles and assess the broad average direct cost of the work with an appropriate mark-up for care and conduct.

As to the mark-up for care and conduct Mr Farber submitted that *Brush* v *Bower Cotton and Bower (a firm)* [1993] 4 All ER 741, **Costs LR (Core Vol) 223** gives useful guidelines as to the amount of a mark-up, these being 35% on interlocutory items, including attending court, as a starting point and thereafter an uplift of about 50% to possibly as much as 90%, depending upon the particular circumstances of the case.

Mr Farber concluded his arguments with reference to the requirement that the taxing master should stand back and consider the overall effects of the amount allowed. He argued that if it seems that the larger amount to be allowed can be assessed in a sum which meets the justice of the case (*a*) by using a specified rate and a mark-up in accordance with principle, or (*b*) by adjusting the hourly rate in accordance with principle and applying a specified mark-up or no mark-up, where no mark-up is specified, then the taxing master can do so. Costs are to be assessed adopting a broad approach and if the larger amount which it is reasonable to allow in a particular case can be assessed by adjusting only one element in the cost equation while using specified elements in other parts of the equation then this can be done as long as the element which is varied is varied in accordance with principle and the consequence is that a "reasonable" larger amount is ascertained and allowed.

Proper approach to the exercise of the discretion
The importance of the exercise of the general discretion by the district judge or taxing officer was clearly explained by Evans J (as he then was) in *Johnson v Reed Corrugated Cases Ltd* [1992] 1 All ER 169, **Costs LR (Core Vol) 180** when he said at [1992] 1 All ER 169, 183F, **Costs LR (Core Vol) 180, 196** –

> "There remains however the fact that the registrar's (district judge's) daily experience of the sums being claimed by local firms is an efficient way of giving him the same information, although indirectly. The reasons given in other cases, to which I have been referred, emphasise more than once the importance of this factor for individual registrars. In my judgment, that is the starting point for assessing the hourly rate."

He had earlier said ([1992] 1 All ER 169 at 180F, **Costs LR (Core Vol) 180 at 192**) –

> "The registrar's (district judge's) assessment is neither guess work nor a precise accounting exercise (which can never be an exact science in any event). Rather his judicial assessment of the proper figure based upon his general knowledge and experience is what the rules require."

At [1992] 1 All ER 169, 183B, **Costs LR (Core Vol) 180, 195** Evans J continued –

> "Assessing costs is not an exact science; neither is accountancy. Treating the latter as if it were, so that the results of an accountancy exercise can be used as a basis for the former, seems to me to achieve the worst of both worlds. The registrar's (district judge's) general knowledge and experience of local conditions and circumstances remains the only firm basis for reliable and consistent taxation."

I think that it is important to emphasise the above observations as it is clearly established law that the district judge will call upon his own experience and knowledge. District judges and taxing officers may be reasonably expected to be able to recognise exceptional circumstances when they come across them. Once those exceptional circumstances are identified the exercise of their discretion is what is required rather than the application of a precise mathematical calculation.

Mr Farber submitted that such discretion entitled the taxing master, according to principle, to adjust the hourly rate and/or to allow a percentage mark-up. I agree that there is no prohibition in the 1991 Regulations against adopting either course. However what is required is a calculation of a reasonable "larger amount". To prescribe the method in which that "larger amount" shall be calculated is in my view unhelpful because at the end of the day it comes down to an exercise by the district judge or taxing officer of his discretion and, other than giving guidelines, it is not appropriate to seek to fetter such discretion. However in anticipation that it may be of some assistance to district judges or taxing officers we will endeavour to describe how we have exercised our discretion in the instant case.

It is well established, as contended by Mr Farber, that a solicitor's remuneration should in general consist of two elements, the first a sum representing the broad average direct cost of undertaking the work and the second a percentage mark-up for care and conduct. This is indeed the case in an Order 62 or similar taxation. However we are reviewing a taxation under the 1991 Regulations. Those Regulations, made under the powers conferred upon the Lord Chancellor by the Legal Aid Act 1988 as amended, specify a prescribed rate. The prescribed rate in this case for preparation work is £60.25 per hour and is a sum that is inclusive of any care and conduct mark-up. It is a global figure the constituents of which are not specified in the regulations.

As has been pointed out Mr Farber derives support from the unreported case of *Freeman* v *Freeman*. Having considered the transcript of the judgment in that case I consider that, in three areas, Eastham J did not go as far as Mr Farber contends –

(1)   In the course of his judgment Eastham J said as follows –

> "Looking at the rule again it seems to me that on its natural construction where a court is satisfied or a taxing officer is satisfied that there are exceptional circumstances in the case, then he the taxing officer is completely freed from the fixed amounts specified in the second Schedule and it is his duty thereafter to assess what in all the circumstances is a fair and reasonable fee both in relation to the hourly rate and also in relation to the mark-up."

I interpret the words "completely freed" as meaning "no longer bound by". I do not consider that the learned judge meant "can wholly disregard". In exercising his discretion the taxing officer must have a starting point, a point to depart from, and I consider that the starting point must be the amount specified by Schedule 1.

(2)   The learned judge cited with approval the comments of Evans J in *Johnson* v *Reed Corrugated Cases Ltd* (above cited) and referred approvingly to the practice of consultation between the local solicitors and local district judges in order to ascertain the "going rate" for expense rates of solicitors in any particular locality. Eastham J went on to say that whilst he did not have the benefit of such consultations he did have the benefit of assessors in determining what was a reasonable hourly rate. In arriving at

that hourly rate it is clear that Eastham J arrived at his figures by an exercise of judicial discretion based upon, in particular, the knowledge and experience of his assessors. He initially increased the hourly rate from £32 to £40. In other words he conducted an exercise in judicial discretion using the knowledge and experience of his assessors (as a taxing officer would in conducting a taxation) and arrived at the hourly rate by taking as a starting point the fixed amount under the schedule. He did not approach the assessment of costs simply by applying common fund taxation principles. He paid full regard to the views of his assessors which would have been based upon their knowledge and experience in this field, which should have reflected, as one of the relevant factors, the prescribed costs charged for work which did not involve any exceptional circumstances.

(3)   The learned judge was dealing with the 1988 Rules. These specified, as to Part I, an hourly rate and a separate care and conduct mark-up. The judge arrived at his hourly rate as above indicated and then considered a care and conduct mark-up remarking that "the court is freed from the 50% mark-up imposed by the rule". Again the learned judge was clearly conducting an exercise in discretion rather than applying a mathematical formula. The regulations with which we are dealing do not have provision for a separate care and conduct uplift. The 1991 Regulations only contain a figure for an hourly rate which must be presumed to be inclusive of case and conduct. The nub of Mr Justice Eastham's decision was that when exceptional circumstances arose pursuant to the 1988 Rules *both* the hourly rate and the care and conduct uplift could be altered.

As has been indicated Mr Farber also relied upon *R v Dunwoodie* (above cited) as support for the proposition that where exceptional circumstances were found one fell back on "broad average direct costs" and a "care and conduct mark-up" as the basis of assessment. This case concerned the taxation of fees in criminal cases pursuant to the Legal Aid in Criminal Proceedings (Fee and Expenses) Regulations 1968. Under those Regulations basic fees were provided with set minima and maxima for hearing and preparation for solicitors and counsel in the Court of Appeal and Crown Court and for solicitors in the magistrates' court. The regulations went on to provide –

> "If it appears to the taxing authority having taken into account all the relevant circumstances referred to in paragraph (1) of this regulation that nevertheless owing to exceptional circumstances the sums payable by virtue of these regulations or any of them would not provide fair remuneration for the work actually and reasonably done by the solicitor and counsel as the case may be, he shall certify accordingly and where he so certifies any limitation contained in these regulations on the amount of any fee payable shall not apply."

In his judgment Slynn J (as he then was) defined "exceptional circumstances" in this way –

> "In my judgment as a matter of construction 'exceptional circumstances'

referred to in regulation 7(6) are circumstances exceptional to the particular case. If a taxing authority finds a particular case involved exceptional difficulties of fact or law he can certify. The case may for example and purely by way of example have required exceptional investigations of the fact or the law and involved much greater time and anxiety than usual in analysing the evidence required and tracing witnesses and considering voluminous documents. In cases such as those the taxing authority has power to certify and the limitation goes."

It will therefore be seen that the decision of Slynn J was based upon particular regulations. In my view the words "he shall certify accordingly and where he shall so certify any limitation contained in these regulations on the amount of any fee payable shall not apply" are highly relevant for, given the express wording of the relevant regulation to the effect that the limitation is to be removed, it is clear pursuant to those Regulations that the fee to be allowed was at large. In other words it is expressly to be assessed without regard to the figures contained in the regulations.

We are faced with a different situation. The "larger amount" that we are required to assess is, in my view, linked and referable to the specified sums under the Regulations themselves.

Turning to the case of "B" (unreported) upon which Mr Farber also relied, the transcript of the decision of the Chief Taxing Master shows that his decision was based upon the wording of regulation 3(5) of the 1982 Regulations which dealt with the taxation of costs in criminal proceedings. Nowhere in those Regulations so far as I can see does any form of words similar to "larger amount" appear.

Accordingly in my view these latter two cases were decided upon materially different Regulations to those in the instant case and are of limited assistance.

We are called upon to review a decision made pursuant to the 1991 Regulations. We are bound by these Regulations and the wording of them. Clearly the starting point is the figure prescribed by the Regulations and that is not a figure which is analogous to a pure hourly rate as it is in these Regulations a figure that is presumably intended to reflect an hourly rate and care and conduct mark-up, both inclusive.

In a taxation under these provisions we must of course first look at the empowering regulations. We have already referred to the relevant provisions of regulation 3(4)(c).

The empowering words "may allow a larger amount" are specific and can only be referring to a sum which is assessed by reference to the prescribed rates.

These Regulations came into force in 1991. The present figures were revised in April 1992. Since the advent of care proceedings under the Children Act 1989 on 14 October 1991 numerous taxations have taken place up and down the country where sums have been claimed by solicitors and allowed by district judges at the precise rates specified in Schedule 1.

This, in our view, is a most significant factor which the district judge or taxing officer must bear in mind when exceptional circumstances arise and he is required to exercise his discretion.

The district judge's knowledge and experience of work carried out at the prescribed rate will provide him with a suitable yardstick by which to assess the larger amount of costs to be allowed when exceptional circumstances arise. That this yardstick should be one of the factors brought into account in the exercise of discretion is, in my view, further supported by the words of regulation 3(4)(c) and regulation 7 which do not seek (whether by inclusion or exclusion) to limit the exercise of discretion, save that it can only be based on circumstances which are relevant.

That is not to say that the taxing officer will not carry out the broad average direct costs and care and conduct uplift approach advocated by Mr Farber. His experience of rates in his locality should enable him to do this quite readily and he will no doubt have in mind the product of that calculation. Indeed such a calculation may well produce the highest limit of the bracket which commences at the level of the prescribed rate. The taxing officer must then however exercise the discretion in the manner so clearly stated by Evans J in *Johnson* v *Reed Corrugated Cases Ltd* (above cited). It seems to me in exercising that discretion that the district judge's general knowledge and experience as well as his particular knowledge of the numerous taxations carried out by him and/or others upon the basis of the prescribed rates is one of the beacons that will guide him in the exercise of his discretion in assessing the larger amount to be paid for exceptional work. As I have said I do not consider that the decision of Eastham J in *Freeman* (above cited) sought to indicate otherwise. However if I am wrong about this then whilst this decision must be of considerable persuasive authority I respectfully take the view that a district judge when standing back and formulating his overall assessment must keep in mind as a controlling yardstick for a larger amount the fact that numbers of solicitors are carrying out work, not within the exceptional circumstance range, at the prescribed rates.

Assessing the instant bill
With the benefit of my assessors' advice I consider that the following matters are relevant in determining the larger amount. (1) The starting point must be the prescribed rates in Schedule 1 to the 1991 Regulations. For advocacy this is £63 per hour and for non-routine preparation work £60.25 per hour. As I have already indicated these are not figures which are analogous to a pure hourly rate and are presumably intended to reflect an hourly remuneration inclusive of a care and conduct mark-up.

The broad average direct costs of solicitors is assessed in the light of the knowledge and experience of the district judges and taxing officers of the Principle Registry in the numerous cases taxed by them over the period in question. We also have regard to the guidelines on mark-up as set out both in

Brush v *Bower Cotton and Bower* (above cited) and *Johnson* v *Reed Corrugated Cases Ltd* (above cited). In the former an uplift of 35% on interlocutory items, including attending court, was allowed as a starting point and thereafter an uplift of about 50% or possibly as much as 90% depending upon the particular circumstances of the case. In the latter (which was a pioneering case of repetitive strain injury) Evans J concluded that the appropriate mark-up was 75%. I also considered the amount of an appropriate mark-up when sitting with assessors in the case of *Foroughi* v *Foroughi* (30 July 1993, unreported). In that matter a mark-up claimed at 150% was reduced to 100%. I stated that –

> "In my view to justify a percentage uplift of 150% a case would not have to be just exceptional but extraordinary. To achieve an uplift of 100% a case would indeed have to be exceptional."

All three of these cited cases were based on conventional "broad average direct cost" taxations. In none of them was the court required to determine a "larger amount" over and above a figure already inclusive of mark-up as expressed by the 1991 Regulations. They are not therefore of direct value as precedents, but rather form part of the fund of knowledge which the district judge employs when exercising his discretion. In assessing how to approach this bill we have identified eight areas of claim which require individual consideration –

(1) The hearing on 18 January 1993

This was an interim care application which lasted for about five hours. We consider that such hearing was properly dealt with a Panel member, such membership constituting the only exceptional circumstance. Although Panel membership constitutes an exceptional circumstance, nevertheless it will not of itself necessarily justify an increase above the prescribed rate. However, in the particular case we think that the exceptional circumstances justify the rate being fixed at £75 per hour with no mark-up. This represents an uplift for advocacy to reflect membership of the Children Panel at approximately 20%.

(2) The hearing on 11 March 1993

This was a 25 minute directions hearing. Normally there would be no need for an advocate with the skill of a Children Act Panel member to attend such hearing unless acting for the child. In this matter however Mr Solon took part in discussions and negotiations lasting for over three hours. We therefore find that it was reasonable for him to attend that directions hearing and exercise our discretion to remunerate him at the enhanced rate of £75 per hour as at the hearing of 18 January 1993.

(3) The final hearing

This lasted for six days until it collapsed as indicated above. We have already pointed out that the district judge might well exercise his discretion to allow the larger amount to a solicitor advocate where, for example, the hearing lasted more than two days. Here the trial was listed for ten days and actually ran for six. We have held that a figure of £75 per hour reflects the advocacy by the Panel member in the present case. Such figure in our view does not fully reflect the additional exceptional circumstances that exist in dealing with such a hearing when a solicitor advocate is involved. We assess the appropriate figure in this case for advocacy at the substantive hearing as £95 per hour. This is approximately 50% more than the hourly rate prescribed in the Regulations. It is intended to reflect both membership of the Children Panel and the other exceptional circumstances we have found to exist. In a case that may be considered as most exceptional a district judge is likely to arrive at a higher figure. In a case with its exceptional element lower down the scale than the present case, a figure lower than £95 per hour may be appropriate. In short we do not prescribe £95 per hour as a figure set in stone, but it may be a useful bench mark for practitioners and taxing officers.

(4)   Attendances upon the stepfather

As already stated, the stepfather was volatile, aggressive and difficult. We consider that his behaviour was extreme enough to constitute of itself an exceptional circumstance. The 1991 Regulations prescribe a rate for non-routine preparation of £60.25 per hour. Allowing for Panel membership we would allow £72 per hour and to reflect the difficulty of dealing with this demanding client we conclude that £84 per hour is a reasonable sum to allow for these attendances.

(5)   Attendances on client and others contemporaneously with the final hearing

For the reasons above stated and to reflect the exceptional circumstances of this case we feel that these should be remunerated at the rate of £90 per hour.

(6)   Consideration of documents/preparation for trial

We consider in this matter that this is appropriately remunerated by the rate of £90 per hour to reflect Panel membership.

(7)   All other non-routine items

These are in our view also appropriately remunerated by the rate of £72 per hour to reflect Panel membership.

(8)   Routine letters and telephone calls, waiting and travelling

By their very nature these items are routine and are not in any way exceptional. They will therefore be remunerated at the prescribed rate set out in the 1991 Regulations, namely £3.60 for letters written and telephone calls, £1.80 for receiving routine letters and £28.75 per hour for waiting and travelling.

Guidelines in submitting a bill of costs where exceptional circumstances arise

We have been invited to give some guidance by way of assistance to the profession, costs draftsmen, and taxing officers in dealing with bills of costs pursuant to the 1991 Regulations where it is claimed that exceptional circumstances have arisen. It is of course not appropriate to restrict a taxing officer's discretion. Suffice to say however that we would consider that an uplift in the hourly rate for membership of the Children Act Panel in cases properly lasting more than two days would normally be justified. In this case on the preparation rate the uplift given above the rate of £60.25 per hour was of the order of 20%. We have found that to be reasonable.

Likewise we would regard a similar uplift in hourly rates in respect of attendances without counsel at the hearing of cases properly lasting more than two days as being reasonable. We refer to the Law Society's code for advocacy and the need set out in paragraph 4.3.1 of the code for solicitors to consider the likely costs of the case. Paragraph 4.1 of the code requires them not to accept instructions to act as an advocate if –

"(a) They lack the necessary experience;
(b) They will have inadequate time to prepare;
(c) The instructions seek to limit their authority;
(d) They will be unable to maintain professional independence;
(e) They have been responsible for actions that are in dispute; or
(f) There is a risk of a conflict or breach of confidence."

We would expect taxing officers to be vigilant in ensuring that solicitors do not seek to manufacture exceptional circumstances by acting as advocates in matters where clearly it was unsuitable that they should act. However, where a Panel solicitor appears in private proceedings then because such proceedings are not care proceedings the solicitor's Panel membership will not of itself constitute an exceptional circumstance within the meaning of the regulations. However, it should be seen as a pointer towards an exceptional circumstance arising.

Length of a substantive hearing or indeed an interlocutory hearing may be relevant. It will be seen that in the instant matter the prescribed figure has been increased by a mark-up. We observe that Schedule 1 to the 1991 Regulations provides, at Part IV, fees for junior counsel. We note that those fees are specified for hearings lasting up to and including a full day but that for more than a full day's hearing the rates are discretionary. There are material distinctions, however, within the Regulations as to the assessment of barrister's fees as contrasted with those of solicitor advocates. First, the barrister's brief fee will reflect preparation, the solicitor will charge separately for this and his preparation fees will not be assessed as part of his attendance at court. Second, the fee for the barrister is fixed within a bracket for a hearing of up to one day. Thereafter it is discretionary. The solicitor advocate's prescribed rate for attending court is fixed. Third, the discretion exercisable in respect of the assessment of the barrister's fee is not conditional upon an exceptional circumstance arising.

Nevertheless bearing in mind the standards required of a solicitor advocate by the Law Society's code for advocacy and in particular the requirements and standing of the Law Society's Children Act Panel we consider that where a solicitor advocate is involved then if the case lasts more than two days that is an indicator that the prescribed rate may well need to be increased.

So far as attendances at trial with counsel are concerned we would normally expect these to be remunerated at the specified rate. When counsel conduct a matter it will be unusual for the attendance of a Children Act Panel member sitting behind counsel to justify remuneration at anything other than the specified rate.

Factors which may raise an exceptional circumstance

For the reasons which we have already given we do not attempt to set out an exhaustive list of exceptional circumstances or to restrict the discretion of the taxing officer. Suffice to say that we regard the following matters as worthy of note –

(1) Where a case is transferred upwards to a care centre or from a care centre to the High court we do not regard the fact of transfer as conclusive of "exceptional circumstances". It is no more than an indicator of complexity and weight.

(2) Innate difficulties of communication with the client (for example through mental health problems, deafness, speech impairment, the client being autistic or requiring an interpreter) may constitute exceptional circumstances, although consideration may first be given as to whether the matter has not in fact been covered by longer than the normal hours of attendance being claimed.

(3) A conflict of detailed expert evidence as opposed merely to contested expert evidence and/or a proliferation of expert witnesses is more likely to constitute an exceptional circumstances.

(4) Detailed contested allegations of sexual or other serious abuse may but will not necessarily constitute exceptional circumstances.

(5) Hearings in excess of two days undertaken by solicitors without reliance upon counsel may well raise an exceptional circumstance.

(6) A large number of parties with completing applications may but will not necessarily constitute an exceptional circumstance.

(7) A conflict between the guardian ad litem and the child in a case where the child proceeds to instruct his or her own solicitor could well constitute an exceptional circumstance both for the solicitor for the guardian and the solicitor for the child.

(8) The involvement of children with different needs may but will not necessarily constitute an exceptional circumstance.

We emphasise that in each case where "exceptional circumstances" are said to arise there must be a factor or combination of factors in the particular case being taxed which is/are exceptional/unusual in care proceedings. The category of circumstances which might qualify as "exceptional" must have an effect in a qualitative or quantitative sense on the work required of the lawyer seeking an exercise of the discretion.

Where such an exceptional circumstance is said to arise it is insufficient for the solicitor simply to claim in a narrative of the bill that "This was a complex and extremely arduous case with voluminous paper work and difficult issues", or that "This was a difficult and complex case in which instructions on the many complex and lengthy reports and statements were not always easy to obtain" or some other generalised phrase followed by a request that the taxing officer allow throughout the bill a charging rate in excess of the prescribed rate or mark-up or both. Taxing officers cannot be expected to sort the wheat from the chaff and unless bills of costs are drafted in a way which identifies and particularises those specific items of work in respect of which the taxing officer's discretion is sought, the taxing officer will have difficulty in identifying specific "exceptional circumstances" and will therefore be bound by the specified rates in Schedule 1 to the 1991 Regulations.

Where "exceptional circumstances" are sought to be established and solicitors seek remuneration on the basis of the exercise of the taxing officer's discretion pursuant to regulation 3(4)(c) then the exceptional circumstances must be specifically identified. The existence of an exceptional circumstance is unlikely normally to lead to an enhanced discretionary rate throughout the bill. Rather the taxing officer will apply a "larger amount" to such parts of the bill as may be appropriate. For example, if a solicitor needs the assistance of an interpreter in order to take instructions then this may justify a "larger amount" in respect of attendances upon the client and/or conferences and/or correspondence to and from the client and telephone calls. It would be unlikely to attract a "larger amount" in respect of dealing with witnesses and other parties, preparation and consideration of and dealing with documents, negotiations and notices, instruction of counsel, and any other matter where the inability to communicate direct with a client has not affected the particular class of work which that solicitor is conducting.

There will be many attendances and applications which will not be exceptional and which will attract the specified rate. Where an hourly rate is sought in excess of the specified amount this should be stated and an explanation of how it is calculated provided. The bill should also identify and justify the specific areas of activity where it is claimed that the larger amount should apply.

This will add to the burden of solicitors and costs draftsmen in preparing bills and of taxing officers in determining them but, as has already been pointed out, if the taxing officer is to protect the legal aid fund on the one hand and ensure on the other that the solicitor is properly remunerated for those items of work which are genuinely exceptional this procedure must, in our view, be adopted.

Finally I direct that no part of this judgment shall be reported which might lead to the identification of the child concerned in the substantive care proceedings.

Jonathan Alexander Ltd
v
Proctor

Court of Appeal, Civil Division
19, 21 December 1995

Hirst, Peter Gibson LJJ and Buxton J

Headnote

The right of a director of a company to represent that company in court proceedings was considered in this case. An award of costs under section 51 of the Supreme Court Act 1981 cannot be made in favour of a director of a company representing that company in court proceedings. There are no provisions in the County Court Rules and the director is not acting as a litigant in person under the Litigants in Person (Costs and Expenses) Act 1975.

---

21 December 1995. The following judgments were delivered.

HIRST LJ: This is an appeal brought with leave of the single judge by the appellants, Jonathan Alexander Ltd (the company), from the order of Deputy Circuit Judge Hunter, made on 3 June 1994 in the West London County Court, whereby he ordered that the appeal of the respondent, Amanda Proctor (the defendant), from the order for costs made against her by District Judge Trent on 7 April 1994, be allowed.

The company claimed against the respondent the sum of £1,702.63, being the balance of the cost of building work. To that claim, which was not disputed as to the unpaid balance, there was a defence and counterclaim, supported by an extensive Scott schedule, alleging that some of the work was not done properly and that some of the materials supplied were of poor quality. After a three-day trial the company succeeded, and the sum of no less than £14,300 counterclaimed was reduced to £1,672. Judge Medawar QC ordered that there be judgment for the company on the claim in the sum of £30.63 (the counterclaim being dismissed), and that the company's costs in the action, to include the claim and the counterclaim, were to be taxed on scale 2 "with leave to the defendant to argue costs as a preliminary point before the District Judge".

At the trial, the company had been represented by one of its directors with leave of the court, and the crucial question which Judge Medawar was in effect reserving to the district judge was whether, in the circumstances, it was in principle entitled to recover its costs. These total a sum of approximately £25,000, of which the lion's share is in respect of an hourly rate for the director's time, though they also include some £7,500 disbursed in respect of the fees of expert witnesses, on which we were not asked to make a separate ruling.

On 7 April 1994 the matter came before District Judge Trent. He dismissed the defendant's application for an order that the company was not entitled to its costs pursuant to Judge Medawar's order. However, District Judge Trent's decision was reversed on appeal on 3 June 1994 by Deputy Circuit Judge Hunter.

In his judgment, the judge relied on a passage in *The County Court Practice 1995* p 1595, which states under the heading "Meaning of 'costs' ":

> "In the present context the term 'costs' is used to connote the cost of conducting litigation but – save in the case of a litigant in person – includes solely the remuneration of solicitors (and occasionally lay representatives in small claims matters), including repayment of disbursements (including counsel's fees) incurred in the course of litigation."

The judge then identified the source of the court's power, cited below, to give leave for a director to appear on behalf of the company, but said that there was nothing to suggest that the exercise of this power "endows the company with the status of a litigant in person", and that this was supported by a further note in *The County Court Practice 1995* p 8639, which states:

> "A litigant in person is now entitled to recover costs: Litigants in Person (Costs and Expenses) Act 1975. There is no definition of a 'litigant in person' in either the Act or the Rules, nor is there a reported case on the point. It is suggested that a company which is allowed to appear by a director or other officer is not entitled to costs as a litigant in person as the company itself cannot appear personally but only by an agent."

On behalf of the appellant, Mr Dyer submitted that the correct starting point is section 51 of the Supreme Court Act 1981 (as substituted by section 4 of the Courts and Legal Services Act 1990), which provides so far as relevant as follows:

> "(1)   Subject to the provisions of this or any other enactment and to rules of court, the costs of and incidental to all proceedings in – (a) the civil division of the Court of Appeal; (b) the High Court; and (c) any county court, shall be in the discretion of the court.
>
> (2)   Without prejudice to any general power to make rules of court, such rules may make provision for regulating matters relating to the costs of those proceedings including, in particular, prescribing scales of costs to be paid to legal or other representatives.
>
> (3)   The court shall have full power to determine by whom and to what extent the costs are to be paid … "

This, he submitted, gave the court the widest possible discretion, and he drew particular attention in the present context to the words "legal *or other representatives*" at the end of section 51(2). This provision, he submitted, rendered inaccurate the notes quoted above from *The County Court Practice*, at all events since 1981. He suggested that the editors had not caught up with the present statutory position.

Mr Dyer pointed out that the power in the court to grant a right of audience on behalf of a company to a director is now based on section 27(2)(c) of the 1990 Act, which gives a right of audience before a court in relation to any proceedings to a person who "has a right of audience granted by that court in relation to those proceedings".

So far as the county court is concerned, however, this power extended back well over 100 years (see section 72 of the County Courts Act 1888, reproducing section 10 of the repealed County Courts Act 1852; see also *Charles P Kinnell & Co Ltd* v *Harding Wace & Co* [1918] 1 KB 405, [1918–19] All ER Rep 594).

In summary, he submitted that, the director having been granted a right of audience in this action as the company's representative, the trial judge had a completely unfettered discretion to award the company its costs pursuant to section 51 of the 1981 Act.

As a second string to his bow, Mr Dyer submitted that the company was a litigant in person within the scope of section 1(1) of the Litigants in Person (Costs and Expenses) Act 1975, which provides that, in proceedings inter alia in a county court:

"Where ... any costs of a litigant in person are ordered to be paid by any other party of the proceedings ... there may, subject to rules of court, be allowed on the taxation or other determination of those costs sums in respect of any work done, and any expenses and losses incurred, by the litigants in or in connection with the proceedings to which the order relates."

He submitted that the phase "in person" defines the status of the litigant, i.e. as being an unrepresented as opposed to a represented litigant; thus the term "litigant in person" is as apposite to a company as it is to an individual, seeing that the company remains the litigant throughout, and seeing that the Act, which gives no definition of a litigant in person, draws no distinction between an individual and a corporate person.

On behalf of the defendant, Mr Lord made it clear that the court's power to grant a right of audience to the director was not disputed, and so not the issue presented before this court.

On the first issue raised by Mr Dyer, Mr Lord submitted that the crucial question was to determine the meaning of the term "costs" in the relevant legislation and rules of court. Apart from two special exceptions referred to below, this term was, he submitted, restricted first to charges and disbursements incurred by solicitors, and secondly, since 1975, to sums in respect of any work done, and any expenses and losses incurred, by litigants in person.

The former was provided for by CCR Order 38, rule 3(1), which stipulated under the heading "Costs to be regulated by scales" that: "For the regulation of solicitors' charges and disbursements ... there shall be three scales of costs ..." The latter were provided for by Order 38, rule 17 under the heading "Litigant in person", which, in effect, reproduces section 1 of the 1975 Act.

The two special exceptions are: (1) a fee or reward charged by a lay representative in small claims proceedings, as laid down in Order 19, rule 4(1), which provides –

"In this rule, 'costs' means – (a) solicitors' charges, (b) sums allowed to a litigant in person pursuant to Order 38, rule 17, (c) a fee or reward charged by a lay representative for acting on behalf of a party in the proceedings";

and (2) in the High Court, a case falling within RSC Order 62, rule 2(2), which provides that Order 62 shall have effect –

"with such modifications as may be necessary, where by virtue of any Act the costs of any proceedings before an arbitrator ... are taxable in the High Court."

Thus, in *Piper Double Glazing Ltd v DC Contracts (1992) Ltd* [1994] 1 All ER 177, [1994] 1 WLR 777, **Costs LR (Core Vol) 256** Potter J held that arbitration costs fall within the scope of this rule, seeing that under section 18(1) of the Arbitration Act 1950, unless a contrary intention is expressed therein, every arbitration agreement is deemed to include a provision that the costs shall be in the discretion of the arbitrator, and that any costs directed by an award to be paid shall, unless the award otherwise directs, be taxable in the High Court. It follows, Mr Lord submitted, that the first note quoted above from *The County Court Practice 1995* is accurate.

I now proceed to consider these rival arguments.

The lynchpin of Mr Dyer's arguments is section 51 of the 1981 Act. It is, in my judgment, of paramount importance to observe that in sub-section (1) the general discretion is subject to the provisions of "this or any other enactment and to rules of court", and that sub-section (2) empowers (but does not require) the making of provision in the rules prescribing inter alia "scales of costs to be paid to legal or other representatives".

It follows that one must look to any other relevant enactment and to the relevant rules of court in order to determine the extent of the courts' jurisdiction. Only if and to the extent that such enactments or rules make provision in relation to costs to be paid to a company director, or other company representative, who has been granted a right of audience, can such a person fall within the scope of the words "other representatives" in section 51(2).

No such provisions appear in the rules, as Mr Lord rightly points out. Indeed, the only rule relating to other representatives is CCR Order 19, rule 4(1)(c), quoted above, dealing with lay representatives in small claims proceedings. The 1975 Act, of course, falls within the category of any other enactment in section 51(1). It follows that, in my judgment, section 51 does not avail Mr Dyer.

This conclusion is reinforced by a further point made by Mr Lord, which is to my mind valid, that, if Mr Dyer's argument were right, there would seem to be no need for the special provision relating to arbitration costs as identified in the *Piper Double Glazing* case, nor for Order 19, rule 4(1)(c).

It follows, in my judgment, that Mr Dyer can only succeed if he can bring his case within the 1975 Act. Ingenious though Mr Dyer's submission was, I found it very difficult to reconcile with the ordinary meaning, as I understand it, of the description "litigant in person", viz an unrepresented individual. To extend this description to a company would require clear words, yet there is nothing in the 1975 Act which enlarges the ordinary meaning.

I would therefore, as a matter of first impression, reject the submission that a company can constitute a litigant in person. This first impression is fully confirmed by the reasons advanced by Peter Gibson LJ in the judgment which he is about to deliver, with all of which I agree. I would therefore dismiss this appeal.

I do so with great regret, since it seems to me that this case reveals a serious lacuna in the law, and results in a considerable injustice to the company, which properly incurred very substantial costs in defeating a grossly inflated counterclaim. This may be an appropriate topic for consideration by the Rules Committee, since it would seem that a quite simple amendment to the rules could bring company directors within the scope of "other representatives" under section 51(2) of the 1981 Act. The judge's judgment makes it clear that leave for such representation is regularly granted in the county court.

PETER GIBSON LJ: There are two issues in this appeal. One is whether the costs on scale 2 awarded to the successful plaintiff company, which appeared and acted by its director at the trial in the county court proceedings, included costs incurred otherwise than in consequence of the employment of a solicitor. The other is whether the company, so acting and appearing, is a litigant in person for the purposes of the Litigants in Person (Costs and Expenses) Act 1975 and so able to recover costs pursuant to CCR Order 38, rule 17.

(1) Costs
The first issue turns on the meaning of the term "costs". On this issue Mr Dyer's argument for the company proceeded on the footing that the company was not a litigant in person. His submission was that under section 51 of the Supreme Court Act 1981 (now section 4(1) of the Courts and Legal Services Act 1990), which gave the court, including the county court, the widest discretion in relation to the costs of an incidental to all

proceedings, and enabled rules of court to be made prescribing scales to be paid to legal or other representatives, costs could not be limited to the costs of legal representatives, including their disbursements. He submitted that an unjustified fetter was placed on the court's discretion by the judge and by the passages in *The County Court Practice 1995* to which Hirst LJ has referred.

The discretion conferred on the court was by section 51(1) subject to the provisions of the 1981 Act or any other enactment (no such provision is suggested apart from the 1975 Act) and to the rules of court.

I turn first to the rules of court prescribing scales of costs to be paid to legal and other representatives.

In the County Court Rules 1981 the relevant rule is Order 38, rule 3. It is apparent from rule 3(1) that the scales of costs are for the regulation of solicitors' charges and disbursements. True it is that following the 1975 Act Order 38, rule 3(3D) was introduced and that allows a litigant in person, in the circumstances there specified, to receive a gross sum. But apart from the special provisions in Order 38, rule 17, which relate to litigants in person, and to the equally inapplicable provision in Order 19, rule 4 relating to costs in small claims cases (which specifically allow the costs of lay representatives of a party), there is nothing to suggest that the term "costs" can refer to other costs such as those actually or notionally incurred by a party, who is not a solicitor, spending time on the litigation instead of earning money elsewhere.

There is, therefore, no provision of the rules that would enable the plaintiff, who was not, and did not employ, a solicitor, to recover costs. That is consistent with the meaning traditionally attributed to "costs". In *London Scottish Benefit Society* v *Chorley* (1884) 13 QBD 872 at 876, [1881–5] All ER Rep 1111 at 1113 (a case in which it was held that a solicitor who was made a party to an action and defended it successfully, himself was entitled to the same costs as if he had employed a solicitor) Bowen LJ pointed out that costs are the creation of statute. He then went on to refer to the passage in 2 Co Inst 288, as affording a key to the true view of the law of costs:

> "Here is express mention made but of the costs of his writ, but it extendeth to all the legal cost of the suit, but not to the costs and expenses of his travel and loss of time, and therefore 'costages' cometh of the verb 'conster,' and that again of the verb 'constare,' for these 'costages' must 'constare' to the court to be legal costs and expenses."

Bowen LJ continued (13 QBD 872 at 877, [1881–5] All ER Rep 1111 at 1113):

> "What does Lord Coke mean by these words? His meaning seems to be that only legal costs which the Court can measure are to be allowed, and that such legal costs are to be treated as expenses necessarily arising from the litigation and necessarily caused by the course which it takes. Professional skill and labour are recognised and can be measured by the law; private expenditure of labour and trouble by a layman cannot be measured."

These remarks were approved and applied by this court in *Buckland* v *Watts* [1969] 2 All ER 985, [1970] 1 QB 27.

The enactment of the 1975 Act was intended to enable the court to provide that a litigant in person, who would otherwise not obtain an award of costs for his work, could recover. As was said by Lloyd J in *Hart* v *Aga Khan Foundation (UK)* [1984] 1 All ER 239 at 241:

> "The whole object of an award for costs is to indemnify the successful party to a greater or lesser extent against costs which he has in fact incurred. He cannot recover costs which he has not incurred. To this general principle Parliament has provided a limited exception in the case of a litigant in person. Provided he has suffered pecuniary loss, he can recover for work which he has himself done up to two-thirds of what would have been allowed if that work had been done by a solicitor."

As Lloyd J stated, prior to the 1975 Act, litigants in person were not allowed anything for their time and trouble, but only for their out-of-pocket expenses (see [1984] 1 All ER 239 at 240, 242, [1984] 1 WLR 994 at 996, 998). Although he was speaking in a High Court case, in my opinion, the same applies to the county court. If Mr Dyer were right, the 1975 Act operates to limit the discretion of the court to indemnify the litigant in person for his time and trouble. I cannot accept that. But for the 1975 Act the litigant in person could not recover "costs" at all.

The construction of "costs" which I favour is also in accord with the emphasis laid by Potter J in the arbitration case *Piper Double Glazing Ltd* v *DC Contracts (1992) Ltd* [1994] 1 All ER 177, [1994] 1 WLR 777, **Costs LR (Core Vol) 256** on the wording of RSC Order 62, rule 2(2) as to Order 62 having effect "with such modifications as may be necessary", which enabled him to allow the recovery of costs of non-qualified representatives.

Accordingly, there being no statutory provision or rule of court that assists the company, I am in no doubt but that Mr Dyer cannot succeed on the first issue.

(2) *Litigants in Person (Costs and Expenses) Act 1975*

A company is a persona ficta. As has been said of a company, "it does not have a soul to be damned or a body to be kicked". It is a consequence of the artificial nature of the company as a legal person that inevitably actions by it and decisions for it have to be taken by natural persons. The law of agency is at the root of company law (see Gower's *Principles of Modern Company Law* (5th edn, 1992) pp 139, 164). The acts of the authorised agent, acting within the scope of his authority, are under the ordinary principles of agency the acts of the company. When a company authorises a director to act and appear for it in court proceedings, and the court allows the director to act and appear, the company acts and appears by the director. The company is the litigant.

The crucial question is whether it can be said of the company so acting and appearing that it is a litigant in person for the purposes of the 1975 Act. My Dyer would answer that question in the affirmative. In agreement with Mr Lord, I would unhesitatingly answer that question in the negative. I do so for the following reasons.

(i)   A litigant in person in ordinary parlance is a party to litigation who represents himself by appearing in court himself. If someone other than himself represents him, then notwithstanding that that other person is his agent, that party is not a litigant in person. The statement which Hirst LJ has cited from *The County Court Practice 1995* p 1639 accords with how, in my opinion, the term "litigant in person", in relation to a company, would generally be understood. The company appears by a representative, its director, and hence it is not a litigant in person.

(ii)   It has repeatedly and authoritatively been stated that a company cannot appear in person (see Co Litt 66b, *Charles P Kinnell & Co Ltd v Harding Wace & Co* [1918] 1 KB 405 at 413, [1918–19] All ER Rep 594 at 598 per Swinfen Eady LJ, *Frinton and Walton UDC v Walton and District Sand and Mineral Co Ltd* [1938] 1 All ER 649 at 649 per Morton J and *Tritonia Ltd v Equity and Law Life Assurance Society* [1943] 2 All ER 401 at 402, [1943] AC 584 at 586 per Viscount Simon LC, with whom Lord Atkin, Lord Thankerton, Lord Macmillan and Lord Clauson agreed). It has also been said that a company is not in the same position as a litigant in person (see *Scriven v Jescott (Leeds) Ltd* (1908) 153 SJ 101 per Bray J). Against that background, it is to my mind highly improbable that without any indication that Parliament intended the term "litigant in person" to apply to a company, the 1975 Act applied to a company represented by a director.

I would, therefore, dismiss this appeal. But I would like to add two further comments. The first is that, although we have been told that of the claimed costs of £25,000, £7,500 consists of experts' fees, we have not been asked to rule on whether such disbursements made by the company can be recovered under an award of costs. The second is that, like Hirst LJ, it does seem to me to be unjust that a successful party is prevented from recovering any costs if it is a company choosing to act by its own director, whereas an individual in such circumstances can recover under the 1975 Act. I, too, hope that this can be looked at by the rule-makers, particularly as it would appear from the judge's judgment that in the county court companies regularly act and appear by lay representatives.

BUXTON J: I agree with Hirst and Peter Gibson LJJ that the first basis on which the appellant company put its case must fail. Counsel for the company relied heavily on section 51(2) of the Supreme Court Act 1981. That subsection, however, does no more than create a rule-making power in respect of scales of costs to be paid to "legal or other representatives"; the latter, by section 51(13), being "any person exercising a right of audience or right to conduct litigation on his behalf". It is argued that in this case the director, Mr Buchanan, was exercising a right of audience under section 27(2)(c) of the Courts and Legal Services Act 1990, as a person granted a right of audience by the court in relation to the proceedings in which he was permitted to represent the company. However, even granted that that is so, section 51(2) of the 1981 Act does no more than create vires to make rules in relation to the scales of costs, if any, to be paid to such a representative. It says nothing as to whether or not any particular category of representative is entitled to costs, or whether his client is entitled to have him feature on his bill of costs. It does not displace in any particular case the rule that allowable costs are, and are limited to, remuneration for the exercise of professional legal skill (see *Buckland* v *Watts* [1969] 2 All ER 985 at 987, [1970] 1 QB 27 at 37 per Sir Gordon Willmer, applying the judgment of Bowen LJ in *London Scottish Benefit Society* v *Chorley* (1884) 13 QBD 872 at 876, [1881–5] All ER Rep 1111 at 1113, a case already referred to by Peter Gibson LJ). It was that rule that required the passing of the Litigants in Person (Costs and Expenses) Act 1975 to make specific provision for the remuneration of litigants in person. However, this part of the company's argument does not rely on the 1975 Act, but on a general right to claim costs in respect of a (legally) unqualified representative. No such right exists.

The alternative and less preferred way in which the company puts its case is quite different. On this basis of claim, Mr Dyer says that Mr Buchanan, in arguing the case, was not a representative of the company, but was the company itself. It was the company that was in court. It was therefore a litigant in person and can claim remuneration as such, though now subject, as on the first basis of claim it would not have been, to the limits as to quantum prescribed by, in particular, CCR Order 38, rule 17(4).

This way of putting the claim is attacked in two ways by the defendant. First, it is said that it is not legally possible for the company to act "in person", or directly as itself at all. The company can only act by its agent; so Mr Buchanan could only have been an agent for the company, and could not be the company in person. Second, even if that is not right, the 1975 Act by its terms only applies to individuals and not to companies.

I am satisfied, as are Hirst and Peter Gibson LJJ, that the second of these arguments is correct, and therefore that this part of the appeal must also fail in any event. I do, however, consider also the first argument deployed by the defendant, because the view that I take of it is relevant also to the narrower question of the construction of the 1975 Act. I address this issue with considerable diffidence, not least because my approach to it differs somewhat from that of Peter Gibson LJ.

I start with the issue of principle argued by the defendant. Although a company can only act by an agent, because there is no such thing as "the company" as such, there are often situations where it is possible, and sometimes necessary, to say that "the company" has done something or has acted in a certain way. That fact, and the legal grounds on which that conclusion is reached, are described in the opinion of the Privy Council delivered by Lord Hoffmann in *Meridian Global Funds Management Asia Ltd v Securities Commission* [1995] 3 All ER 918 at 923–924, [1995] 2 AC 500 at 506–507. It is true that in that case, as in the cases which the court applied, namely *Tesco Supermarkets Ltd v Nattrass* [1971] 2 All ER 127, [1972] AC 153 and *Re Supply of Ready Mixed Concrete (No 2), Director General of Fair Trading v Pioneer Concrete (UK) Ltd* [1995] 1 All ER 135, [1995] 1 AC 456, the Board was speaking of "attribution" in the sense of culpability. I do not, however, see that that can make a difference to the way in which the court should approach the root question, "Was the act of individual A in law the act of company B?" Where, as in the present case, the managing director of the company undertakes a specific task for the company, I do not find difficulty in principle in contemplating that the rules governing the attribution of his acts to the company makes his acts those of the company itself, and not merely those of an agent of the company. The case would be different if the company employed someone who, in the case of an individual litigant, would be regarded as an agent: most conspicuously a solicitor, or a lay claims consultant or other representative.

That, however, is as to principle. As I will explain later in this judgment, in this particular case the circumstances in which, and the rules under which, Mr Buchanan was permitted to act for the company, prevented his acts being attributed to the company as its own. The company thus fails on this point in the event, even though I cannot accept the defendant's argument in the broad and general terms that it was advanced.

Even, however, if I am wrong about that, and it was indeed the company that was conducting the case in the person of Mr Buchanan, the question remains of whether the company was a litigant "in person" for the purposes of the 1975 Act. A series of cases, very conveniently summarised in the judgment of Scott J in *Arbuthnot Leasing International Ltd v Havelet Leasing Ltd* [1991] 1 All ER 591 at 595, [1992] 1 WLR 455 at 460, indicates that it was generally accepted before 1975 that the expression "litigant in person" was applicable only to an individual. This, I should emphasise, is a different proposition from the rule that applies in the High Court that a company must be represented by solicitors and counsel. The proposition concerns not a rule of representation, but the meaning of the term "in person". Judges of high authority who assumed that that term could only apply to an individual include Morton J in *Frinton and Walton UDC v Walton and District Sand and Mineral Co Ltd* [1938] 1 All ER 649 at 649 and Viscount Simon LC in *Tritonia Ltd v Equity and Law Life Assurance Society* [1943] 2 All ER 401 at 402, [1943] AC 584 at 586. Given that usage, it was in my view incumbent on the draftsman of the 1975 Act to employ specific language if he sought to extend the provisions of that Act to limited companies. By adopting the expression "in person" he did the reverse of that. And, quite apart from the language used in the Act, there is no reason to think that Parliament did intend to extend the relief granted by that Act beyond the case of individuals. Twenty years later, and with the experience of changing patterns of litigation and of representation, particularly in the county courts, it is possible that a different policy view would be taken if the issue was reconsidered. However, the extension of the provisions of the 1975 Act to limited companies would indeed be an extension of those provisions, and not an application of them.

There is a further reason why the 1975 Act cannot apply to limited companies in the absence of specific provisions to that effect. That the 1975 Act so applies only even starts to be arguable if the company itself can be said to be present in court. I have indicated how, in my view, it may be possible in general terms to approach that first hurdle. However, in the case before us an officer of the company can only act for the company with the leave of the court. That is clear from the provisions as to rights of audience already cited in this judgment, and from the long-standing practice in the county courts that is set out in the judgment of Swinfen Eady LJ in *Kinnell* v *Harding Wace & Co* [1918] 1 KB 405 at 413, [1918–19] All ER Rep 594 at 598. Mr Buchanan thus acted in court and could only have so acted with the leave of the judge. However, if (as the argument that the company was there in person demands) Mr Buchanan was the company, he would have been present as a litigant, and thus would have had a right to act and be present there whatever the judge's view of the matter. This consideration I think demonstrates that, even if it is theoretically possible to say that a company itself appears in court, it is not possible to advance that proposition when the person said to be the company is in court not by right but only with leave.

Those considerations lead me to conclude that, against the background of the rules of the court as to representation, it is not in fact possible in this case to say that the company itself acted. This difficulty is a further reason for thinking that the terms of the 1975 Act cannot and do not apply to limited companies.

For those reasons, I would, like Hirst and Peter Gibson LJJ, dismiss the appeal.

Appeal dismissed. Leave to appeal to House of Lords refused.

Allen Dyer (instructed by *Goodman Derrick*) for the company.
David Lord (instructed by *Payne Hicks Beach*) for the defendant.

Part II

Criminal Case-law

Regina
v
Pullum
and 8 other Appeals

Royal Courts of Justice
Tuesday, 1 November 1983

Before:
The Chief Taxing Master
(Master Horne)

Decision

(As approved by Master)

THE CHIEF TAXING MASTER: These are appeals by solicitors assigned under section 30 of the Legal Aid Act 1974. There are nine appeals, and they are from the determination of the costs of those solicitors in accordance with the Legal Aid in Criminal Proceedings (Costs) Regulations 1982 which are made under the authority of the Legal Aid Act 1974 (and I shall refer to them as "the Regulations" and to the Act as "the Act" throughout this decision). Being dissatisfied with the determination made by the determining officer in each case, the solicitors applied to him to review his decision pursuant to regulation 10. From this review they appealed to the then Chief Taxing Master and it has now fallen to me to hear the appeals.

In each appeal the Lord Chancellor pursuant to regulation 11(7) has arranged for oral representation to be made on his behalf. Pursuant to regulation 8, by letters dated 4 and 7 October 1983, the grounds on which such representations are made were disclosed, and written representations in reply were duly made on behalf of the appellants.

I am told that the principles which arise in these appeals are a matter of general importance and interest and that the parties before me desire my decision to be treated as given in open court. Regulation 11(13) requires me to communicate my decision and the reasons for it in writing to the appellants, the Lord Chancellor, and the appropriate authority or the determining officer. Therefore, though this decision that I give now verbally may be treated as given in open court, I will give the decision in writing subsequently, which may then be freely reported.

I propose to deal with the general submissions on matters of principle in this decision, and then I will adjourn into Chambers and deal with each of the nine appeals individually.

In a nutshell, I am required to interpret the Regulations, particularly those portions of the Regulations which provide for attendance at court and the payment therefor. Section 39(1)(*f*) of the Act gives the power to make the Regulations and to "prescribe rates or scales of payment of any costs payable in accordance with section 37(1) above and the conditions under which such costs may be allowed". Section 39(3) enunciates the principle which is to be applied in the Regulations, and it says:

> "The Secretary of State in making regulations under this section as to the amounts payable to counsel or a solicitor assigned to give legal aid under this Part of this Act, and any person by whom any such amount falls to be assessed, taxed or reviewed under the regulations, shall have regard to the principle of allowing fair remuneration according to the work actually and reasonably done."

The Regulations themselves are entirely new, and as they say in the explanatory note at the end of the Regulations:

> "These Regulations provide for the determination of the costs which may be paid to the legal representatives of a person given criminal legal aid, and prescribe rates and scales of payment for those costs."

(And revoke the previous Regulations, so far as we are concerned at any rate.)

> "Regulations 4, 5 and 6 in Schedule 1 deal with solicitors' costs, the principal change from the earlier Regulations being the provision of standard hourly rates for costs."

I am glad to say that I am not in any way concerned with the hourly rates which appear in the Schedule.

Mr Adrian Spencer-Ashworth appeared as counsel for the Lord Chancellor in the appeals, instructed by the Treasury Solicitors. Mr J M Wickerson appeared on behalf of the appellants in eight of the cases, that is all except *R* v *Chandler*. Mr Wickerson is a partner in Messrs Ormerod, Morris & Dumont. He is also a member of the Council of the Law Society, and I believe a member of more than one of the Standing Committees of the Society. Therefore I had particular regard to what he said as reflecting not only the view of his clients in this particular case but also reflecting the views of the Law Society in a matter of principle. Mr Carnell was instructed in the case of Chandler only. Mr Carnell is a partner in Messrs Offenbach & Co. Messrs Offenbach & Co are a specialist firm in criminal work, of whom I believe there are not many over this country. Mr Carnell's wide experience of criminal costing is again a matter which I found very helpful to me.

At the commencement Mr Wickerson wished to bring in the survey which was made by accountants on behalf of the Law Society and Lord Chancellor some little time ago. This was opposed by Mr Spencer-Ashworth, and I refused to look at that survey or the figures in it because it seemed to me that the survey was irrelevant to the considerations which arose before me in the appeals. Mr Spencer-Ashworth then invited me to look at the interim directions published by the Lord Chancellor's Department on 1 April 1983 in their latest form. His reason for that was that they could be distinguished from the survey in that they are subsequent to the Regulations. But they can be said to be equally irrelevant to these appeals in that they are directions for guidance and they contain at best the opinion of the Lord Chancellor's Department as to what the Regulations may mean. I should say that one of the reasons Mr Spencer-Ashworth gave for his objection to me looking at the survey was that "maybe the Regulations follow the survey and maybe they do not, but in the Lord Chancellor's submission the Regulations are plain and they have an interpretation section ...", and that is what I must deal with. It was also accepted at this stage that the Regulations cannot derogate from the Act.

Mr Wickerson then proceeded to deal with the written grounds submitted on behalf of the Lord Chancellor. They are in two letters, but in fact I think that one is simply a repetition of the other. Two letters arose because three additional cases were added after the first six had been dealt with. Mr Wickerson suggested that paragraph 3 of those written submissions is in fact asking me to reverse the whole of the taxation process as it has been known until now. Mr Wickerson also submitted to me, and maintained throughout, that in fact if a solicitor is represented at court by a fee-earner, in the proper performance of the solicitor's duty to the court, then under these Regulations it is never possible for a determining officer to say that no direct payment is to be made for that attendance.

Mr Wickerson went on to say, as was conceded by all concerned, that every case must be determined by the determining officer strictly on its own merits. Therefore the question for the determining officer is one of fact in every case.

Mr Wickerson put in a letter addressed to a Mr Buchan from the Lord Chancellor's Department dated 11 May 1983. I do not think it was really relevant, but it did show quite clearly that the vital question which has arisen between the solicitors' profession on the one hand and the Lord Chancellor's Department on the other is who or what is a fee earner. That letter by the Lord Chancellor's Department, and the interim directions, refer to the survey, and to the basis on which the survey was done; in fact the survey intruded into this matter at almost every stage in one way or another. Nonetheless, I maintain my view that the survey is not a matter for me and is irrelevant in this context.

Mr Wickerson then took me through the new Regulations and one or two helpful matters came out of that. Mr Wickerson said that the interpretation clause, clause 2, which contains the interpretation of what "fee earner" means, was quite satisfactory to the profession. Indeed, he considered it "well described". Mr Spencer-Ashworth, on behalf of the Lord Chancellor, seemed to find some difficulty with the interpretation of "fee earner", inviting me to look at it rather differently, and not to be as happy with it as the Law Society were.

Mr Spencer-Ashworth accepted that in accordance with a solicitor's duty somebody must always attend court with counsel; and that that person, whether he be a fee earner or not, must be a responsible representative.

Regulation 4 shows how a solicitor should claim, and 4(3)(*c*):

> "In the case of proceedings in the Crown Court or Court of Appeal the claim shall specify, where appropriate, the fee earner who undertook each of the items claimed."

It was agreed that the long-standing definition used in taxing costs in criminal cases would still apply in determination, namely, that the taxing officer has to find out who was the person who did the work, to decide whether that person or someone else ought to have done it, and to allow for whichever grade is the lower. The important words being "ought to have done it".

Regulation 5(1) is the enabling regulation which says:

> "The appropriate authority may allow work done by fee earners in the following classes:"

– and sets out the various classes of work, which appear to include just about everything which a fee earner would be expected to do in a criminal case. It was accepted by Mr Wickerson and by Mr Carnell that if work of any of those classes was not done by a fee earner, then it could not be charged for under the Regulations.

Mr Wickerson said of regulation 5(2) "It is ambiguous". The Lord Chancellor's Department seemed to think it was quite plain, and Mr Spencer-Ashworth subsequently pressed on me the interpretation which I should give to the subsection. Mr Wickerson and Mr Carnell said further that if a clause in a regulation is ambiguous and capable of more than one interpretation, then the interpretation which produces a sensible and reasonable result must be applied.

Mr Wickerson then took me through the interim directions at some length, and I will make some mention of them later in my decision. I think it is helpful just to note here that Mr Wickerson was quite content with paragraph 26 and paragraph 33 – a number of others he disagreed with, and in particular he said that paragraph 34 was the paragraph which really had caused the problems which led to these appeals.

Mr Wickerson then put to me his views with regard to the responsible representative who Mr Spencer-Ashworth had accepted must attend court. He said that such a person must always be treated as a fee earner and that is what the Regulations provide. Intervening, Mr Spencer-Ashworth, again recognising that a responsible representative or responsible person should attend, was unable to accept that he must always be treated as a fee earner; indeed, he might clearly not be a fee earner on the facts, and the Regulations do not provide that he should always be treated as a fee earner.

Mr Carnell then addressed me and broadly supported everything Mr Wickerson had said, particularly two matters: one was on the interpretation of regulation 5(2), I must apply a reasonable interpretation if I think that more than one interpretation is possible. The other was the concern, which is quite general in the solicitors' profession, that in cases which are well prepared by competent solicitors there is a somewhat higher risk of the solicitors being penalised, because then it may be said against them that there was no need for them to send a fee earner to court. I take note of that concern.

Mr Spencer-Ashworth, opening his submissions, which were made in accordance with regulation 11(7), that is "with a view to ensuring that the public interest is taken into account", began by stating the general law and practice with regard to the attendance of solicitors at court when counsel is briefed. The court requires that the solicitor shall provide responsible representation in every such case. Recognising that requirement of the court, the Code of Conduct for the Bar of England and Wales (edition of July 1980) at paragraph 142 deals with the matter in this way:

"A barrister may not appear in court, or discuss a case with or take instructions from or give advice to his lay client, unless the instructing solicitor or his representative is present."

And the solicitors' profession in their Guide to the Conduct of Solicitors (issued in 1974, paragraph 3(5), under the heading "Duty of solicitor to be present or represented in court") says:

"Where a solicitor is acting for a client in court proceedings and has instructed counsel to appear on behalf of his client, then it is the duty of the solicitor to be present or to arrange for the attendance of a responsible representative or agent, throughout such proceedings in which counsel is instructed."

Mr Spencer-Ashworth submitted that nonetheless the quality of the representation which a solicitor is required to provide may vary. It may vary because of the weight of the case and therefore of the level of duty which the representative may be called upon to perform. It may also vary with the availability of personnel in the solicitor's office. A solicitor may well send a responsible person who in fact is a non-fee earner. One must also always recognise that in the best, most well organised professions, there still may be cases where for one reason or another the person who is sent is not in fact a responsible person at all. The problem is one which has to be dealt with, and the question has to be answered in every case, whether the person is a fee earner or not. It is a question of fact. The circumstances surrounding that individual are relevant, as well as the other relevant circumstances related to the case.

Mr Spencer-Ashworth then submitted the Lord Chancellor's view of the interpretation clause. He suggested I should take certain words in the clause as being of more importance than others. Regarding the use of the word "appropriate", he said: "If it was unreasonable to send a fee earner in the circumstances of a particular case, one would say it would hardly be appropriate to make a direct charge to a client". He also strongly submitted that the word "regularly" is a vital word and the key to the whole interpretation.

The Lord Chancellor's Department was unable to agree with Mr Wickerson's contention that a solicitor is entitled to be remunerated on every occasion when a representative attends court, and pointed out there might well be circumstances where a solicitor would not be entitled to make a direct charge to his client for such an attendance.

Mr Spencer-Ashworth then referred to the difficult question which arises where the services of the person who attends court would appear to be charged for in the solicitor's general overhead expenses. The Lord Chancellor's Department was content that if a person attended court, the cost of whose services were not included in the computation of the solicitor's overheads, it would always be appropriate to make a direct charge to the client. This seemed to me to be leading directly into the area which Mr Spencer-Ashworth said I must not enter, and I heed Mr Spencer-Ashworth's injunction and shall not enter it, save to say there is no evidence before me with regard to the computation of standard charges in the Schedule to the Regulations, and I think that it is irrelevant to the task which I am required to perform.

Mr Spencer-Ashworth then referred me to the booklet entitled "The Expense of Time" published by the Law Society and in particular to Appendix E. He accepted that that publication is described as an aid to management for the use of solicitors in private practice. In my view it is equally irrelevant to the question with which I am concerned. However, I am grateful to Mr Spencer-Ashworth for bringing it to my notice and shall make reference to it at a later stage in my decision.

Mr Spencer-Ashworth drew attention to the danger of giving too much weight to the labels which appear in the Regulations. In other words to the descriptions of the grades of fee earner which appear therein. He agreed that the label is not a test at all, but accepted that the interim directions use a great many labels and appear to instruct the determining officer to use the label as an important part of the determining process. Mr Spencer-Ashworth submitted that although it may not be expressly stated in the Regulations, it is implicit in them that if a determining officer considers in all the relevant circumstances that the work actually done was not appropriate to any of the three grades, he is not empowered to hold that the work was reasonably done. He explained this by drawing attention to regulation 5(1) and said that the word "may" implies a discretion to disallow work actually done in circumstances in which it was not proper. He also said that, at the lowest end of the scale, it would not be within the duty of the determining officer to allow some work which had been reasonably done because (and I quote him) "it may be a case where it was not reasonable for the work, or any part of it, to be done by a fee earner". He illustrated that by saying that if an attendance was utterly unnecessary, it could not be reasonable. It must be contrary to the public interest to pay for the attendance of a fee earner where no fee earner's attendance is reasonable.

He wished me to take account of the *de facto* situation which is very much in the forefront of the Lord Chancellor's concern – that in certain cases quite inexperienced and unqualified people do attend court as the representatives of solicitors. The Lord Chancellor does not contend that it is inappropriate for such people to attend court, but that they should not then be paid as fee earners.

In reply both Mr Carnell and Mr Wickerson objected that Mr Spencer-Ashworth was elevating the exceptional to the general.

Mr Wickerson also drew attention to the fact that the definition of "fee earner" applies to all work and not just attending court, and this must be borne in mind when considering Mr Spencer-Ashworth's submission as to the importance and interpretation of the word "regularly".

In concluding the submissions, Mr Spencer-Ashworth stated the Lord Chancellor has never suggested that if it is not reasonable for a fee earner to attend court, the person who actually attends is not to be paid for such attendance. It is the Lord Chancellor's view that solicitors are paid in all cases – directly in the case of a fee earner, and in the overheads in the case of a non-fee earner.

Finally he submitted that the wording of regulation 5(2) demonstrates the indivisibility of the work of the fee earner, and it is work done by a fee earner and only by a fee earner that is provided for.

In reply Mr Wickerson reiterated that regulation 5(1) is an enabling section. It tells the determining officer the class of work for which payment is to be allowed. And then follows regulation 5(2), which says, in effect, provided the work was reasonably required to be done then the determining officer cannot disallow it. This interpretation keeps the principles exactly as they have been, and also accords with the general practice.

That is not an exhaustive recapitulation of the arguments. I think it is a sufficient indication of where the difficulty lies, and the opposing views; and I have also tried to indicate the happier situation where there is agreement.

The points on which my decision is required are really very short and only two in number. The first is the definition of "fee earner"; and the second is the meaning of regulation 5(2).

In my view the definition of a fee earner as contained in the Regulations is perfectly plain. It is very wide indeed. There are two words in it that I should discuss. The word "clerk" is a very well known and ancient word in the solicitors' profession. There is a comprehensive definition of it in Cordery on Solicitors, 7th edition. Broadly, the word "clerk" covers everyone who is employed in a solicitor's office who has no recognised legal qualifications.

The other word is "appropriate". I do not think the word itself presents any difficulty, but it is perhaps interesting to note that the Shorter Oxford

Dictionary says that "appropriate" in the legal connotation means "proper", and "proper" again is a word hallowed by long usage in the solicitors' profession which is well understood.

The regulation states quite clearly and categorically that "fee earner" means a solicitor, a legal executive or any clerk who regularly does work for which it is appropriate (or proper) to make a direct charge to a client. No one has suggested before me that it is not the universal practice of solicitors, who provide representation for their client in any court, to make a direct charge to the client for that service. This is something which clients in general accept and understand. I say that fortified by having conducted a large number of taxations between solicitors and their clients under the Solicitors Act.

So one must construe the Regulations that follow in accordance with that very wide definition. The determining officer must always keep in mind the requirements of the Act, about which he is reminded in regulation 3(5) – that he shall allow fair remuneration for work actually and reasonably done and shall take into account all the relevant circumstances of the case.

In my view regulation 5(2) is ambiguous, and could have been made clear. If it had been desirable to make the situation which Mr Spencer-Ashworth contended for a principle to be applied in general cases – let me say in normal cases – it would have been easy to do so. It should have been made clear because the determining officer is, I think I am right in saying, a new creation of these Regulations; and he has no authority beyond such as is vested in him by the Regulations. He does not appear to have any of the implied powers which are vested in a taxing officer acting in his judicial function. The determining officer is given a discretion as to the grade of fee earner which he is to apply by regulation 5(4); but sub-paragraphs (b) and (c) recognise and give effect to the wide definition of fee earner in regulation 2.

I would put the general principle in this way. A solicitor, as an officer of the court, has a duty to ensure that in all cases where counsel is instructed and appears at a trial the solicitor, or a responsible member of his staff, must attend. In my view the Regulations clearly provide that if that duty is performed, then providing the person actually attending regularly does that class of work, the determining officer must treat him as a fee earner. I would say with regard to regularity, it was accepted by the Lord Chancellor's Department that regularity is related to the solicitors' practice in that if a solicitor only has one case in court per annum, the person attending can still be said to be regularly attending.

I find myself unable to go the full distance with Mr Wickerson and the Law Society in their contentions as to the interpretation of regulation 5(2), because we are dealing here only with the lowest scale of case and there must be exceptional cases where the determining officer, in the proper exercise of his discretion, may be entitled or required to say either that it did not justify the attendance of a fee earner or that the individual who actually attended was not a fee earner. But these are exceptional cases, and the determining officer who proposes to exercise his discretion in that way would be well advised always to warn the solicitor of his intention and to give the solicitor the opportunity of making representations before the determination is actually made.

Thus I find that paragraph (2) of regulation 5 should be treated as meaning that the determining officer shall allow payment for all work which he considers has been actually and reasonably done and on which reasonable time has been spent, classifying the work in accordance with the classes specified in paragraph (1).

Therefore, assisted by the principles which have been set out earlier in this decision, a determining officer in the Crown Court or Court of Appeal who has to consider a claim for costs made pursuant to the Regulations should apply regulation 5 to each item or class of items of work for which payment is claimed by satisfying himself upon the following matters:

(a) Was the person who did the work a fee earner as defined in regulation 2?
(b) Did the work fall within the classes set out in regulation 5(1)?
(c) Was the work actually and reasonably done and was the time spent on it reasonable?

Having satisfied himself on these matters he must then decide which of the grades of fee earner set out in regulation 5(4) he considers reasonable to be applied when assessing the fees specified in Schedule 1.

I am well aware that the Regulations as they stand cannot entirely exclude the possibility of individual solicitors trying to claim double payment. The Law Society themselves are aware of this danger, and in Appendix E to "The Expense of Time" they endeavour to deal with it, at least in the case of articled clerks. It is clearly in the interests of the public that double payment should never be made. It is a difficult problem, and it is one that may well need to be considered when the next review of the standard fees for the lower grades of a fee earner takes place.

In my view it is clear that, in the form of costing now generally adopted by solicitors, the situation with regard to part-time fee earners is a difficult one. It may well be that reconsideration is already in hand. As I said, the actual standard fees are not a matter for me. But so long as the practice of the court in regard to representation by solicitors remains unchanged, and so long as the Regulations remain in their present form, it seems to me that the problem of double payment has to be dealt with in the context of the standard fees, and in the calculation of the expense rate which forms a basic element of those fees.

Lastly, I think it would be helpful if I made brief reference to the interim directions, which Mr Spencer-Ashworth accepted had their imperfections. Certain of those directions, in my view, clearly should immediately be withdrawn, because they do not comply with the Regulations; they do not reproduce what the Regulations say. And also because it is quite apparent in these appeals which are now before me that a number of determining officers have been misled by their reading of the interim directions; or at least have not received the guidance that they need from the interim directions.

I think that 14(*c*), 25(*c*), 27, 31 and 34 particularly require revision. I shall now adjourn into Chambers to deal with the individual appeals.

Mr Adrian Spencer-Ashworth (instructed by the Treasury Solicitor) appeared on behalf of the Lord Chancellor.

Mr J M Wickerson, Solicitor (instructed by the Law Society) appeared on behalf of eight appellants.

Mr R Carnell, Solicitor of Messrs Offenbach & Co, appeared on behalf of the appellant in *R* v *Chandler*.

Regina
v
Duxbury

Date of Determining Officer's Reasons
April 1983

Date of Taxing Master's Decision
November 1983

Regulation 6: Claim for Expenses of an Enquiry Agent for Attendance at Court

The solicitors claimed an amount as a disbursement for the attendance of their agent at court with counsel. The claim was disallowed, on the basis that an enquiry agent was not a fee-earner.

The taxing master referred to his decision in *R v Pullum*, **Costs LR (Core Vol) 413**, and disagreed with the determining officer. There was no rule or principle which stated that a part-time employee of a solicitor, who otherwise falls within the definition of a fee-earner in regulation 2, was disqualified from being a fee-earner for the purpose of the Regulations. It was a question of fact to be determined in each case whether the individual concerned was a fee-earner.

This enquiry agent, as part of the service offered, was prepared to provide representation at court with counsel. There was no suggestion that the solicitors did not regularly employ this method of complying with their duty to the court nor was there any suggestion that by using this method they failed to provide responsible representation for their client. The solicitors properly performed their duty to provide representation and they complied with the Regulations. The claim was allowed.

Regina
v
Ford-Lloyd

Date of Determining Officer's Reasons
May 1983

Date of Taxing Master's Decision
January 1984

Paragraph 3, Schedule 1: Rate per Hour where Exceptional Competence and Dispatch is Claimed

In this case the solicitors appealed against the rates per hour allowed for preparation work and travelling and waiting. The case was handled throughout by an articled clerk under supervision. When the bill was submitted for taxation the determining officer was asked to implement paragraph 3 of Schedule 1 to the 1982 Regulations. The reason for this was stated to be that the defendant was on life licence for manslaughter and that made the case exceptional. On the hearing of the appeal it was suggested that the articled clerk had done the work with exceptional competence and dispatch. The determining officer allowed only the standard rate but also allowed a claim for one hour supervision by a senior solicitor.

The taxing master held that the articled clerk acted with exceptional competence and dispatch and said that the hourly rate claimed, which was above the standard rate, was reasonable. However, having regard to the specific allowance made for supervision he made no increase.

The solicitors also claimed an increased rate for travelling and waiting but had to concede that exceptional competence and dispatch were not elements of these functions. The taxing master held that the standard rate must therefore apply. If paragraph 3(*b*) of Schedule 1 were appropriate different considerations might apply but that had not been argued before him.

Regina

v

Goodwin

Date of Determining Officer's Reasons
May 1983

Date of Taxing Master's Decision
January 1984

Regulations 5 and 6: Travelling and Waiting and Instruction of a Distant Solicitor

The solicitors appealed against the amount allowed for travelling and waiting time and expenses, their practice being based about a hundred miles from the defendant's home and the local court where the case was heard.

The taxing master held that the determining officer had correctly made his assessment on the basis of what should reasonably have been allowed to a local solicitor. The representation that the defendant had a free choice of solicitor, however, was incorrect. An assisted person was entitled to a reasonable choice of solicitors. The relevant regulations conferred on a person to whom legal aid was granted – the right to select any solicitor who was willing to act. The regulation further provided that "such solicitor shall be assigned to him" (regulation 8 of the Legal Aid in Criminal Proceedings (General) Regulations 1968).

There was therefore no power to refuse to assign a selected solicitor because he did not practice in the locality where the assisted person lived or was to be tried. As a general rule, a solicitor ought, if he was able, to accept instructions from an assisted person who had selected him, but there was nothing in the legislation which compelled him to and it would be a proper reason to decline a retainer that under the Regulations the costs involved in accepting could not be wholly recovered. There may be circumstances in which it was reasonable to instruct a solicitor at a distance but this case did not fall into that category.

Regina
v
Hussain and others

Date of Determining Officer's Reasons
April 1983

Date of Taxing Master's Decision
January 1984

Regulation 5: Amount of Preparation Time
Paragraph 3, Schedule 1: Claim for a Rate Above the
Standard Rate

This appeal arises out of a case of importing cannabis. The defendant was denied legal aid in the magistrates' court and was privately represented by the appellants and by junior counsel. He was committed to the Crown Court and was refused legal aid. An application was made on his behalf to the Crown Court, but was refused. The solicitors (the appellants) accordingly wrote to the defendant, who had been remanded in custody, and informed him that if he wished them to prepare his defence, he must arrange to fund them. He did not. It seems the defendant himself thereafter made unsuccessful applications for legal aid. The Crown Court, assuming the solicitors to have been instructed (though this was not so) sent them a copy of the warned list showing the case listed for pre-trial review, and later trial. The solicitors wrote to the court explaining that they were without instructions, and had in consequence taken no steps to prepare any defence or to brief counsel. The court telephoned to the solicitors to inform them that the trial judge had granted legal aid for solicitors and one counsel. The solicitors accordingly had a weekend and one working day to prepare for the pre-trial review which was a substantial matter as appears from the attendance notes. Thereafter there remained only eight working days to prepare for trial. These preparations were complicated by difficulties in proofing defence witnesses, the fact that the defendant could only be interviewed at the prison, the bulk of the documents and the service by the prosecution of notices of additional evidence. A very full and well prepared brief was delivered to counsel. Nevertheless there was considerable on-going work to be done during the long trial.

In the light of these facts the master was asked to review:

    (a) a total time of 79 hours for preparing and considering documents, 31 of which were allowed;

(b) a claim for a rate above the standard rate for senior solicitor, which
was rejected by the determining officer.

Preparation and consideration of documents

The claim was made up in this way: for perusing 1,400 pages of 2½ minutes
each, 58 hours; for ascertaining the law, 1 hour and for preparing the
defendant's statement, proofs of witnesses and the brief, running in all to 39
pages, 20 hours. The determining officer allowed 20, and 10 respectively. He
gave the following reason:

> "As your client was able to afford private representation by Junior Counsel at
> the lower court and by a Leader at Crown Court, and because of the evidence
> concerning his various bank accounts given at his trial, I take the view that at
> no time before the granting of Legal Aid was he, to say the least, destitute. The
> Prosecution, incidentally, was conducted by a Junior and a noting Junior. I
> therefore consider it reasonable that the vast majority of the preparation for his
> trial should properly have been done in the 47 days between committal and the
> granting of the Legal Aid Order, rather than in the 2 days between the granting
> of Legal Aid and the Pre-trial Review or the further 13 days to trial. The time
> allowed on determination – 10 hours – is of course an estimate but may I point
> out that you have not taken the opportunity when requesting redetermination
> or reasons of supplying further and better particulars of your claim, e.g. your
> bill gives dates for preparation work as 'various' which is unhelpful given the
> circumstances of the case.
>
> 59 hours was claimed for consideration of documents by a Senior Solicitor.
> This figure was reduced to 21 hours on determination.
>
> My reasoning in disallowing part of the time claimed is exactly the same as
> that set out in the previous paragraph. In addition I note that the brief to
> Counsel states that 'only 12 out of 33 witnesses relate to the defendant'. The
> grade of fee earner who did this work should be able to quickly distinguish
> between relevant and irrelevant statements, documents, etc, and considerable
> savings in time should result. Under these circumstances I do not think that the
> '3 minutes a page' estimate is really relevant."

THE TAXING MASTER: The first matter to be clarified is the question of
private representation. I have already set out the course of events. The
determining officer is concerned only with what work was actually and
reasonably done after the grant of Legal Aid since costs payable out of the
fund belong to counsel or solicitor and not the defendant. In making his
assessment the taxing officer must take account of any work actually done
prior to the grant of Legal Aid in order to satisfy himself whether what is
claimed for after the grant is reasonable. He is not entitled to reduce what
would otherwise have been a proper assessment because he concluded that
the defendant was in a financial position to instruct solicitors privately and
should have done so. The evidence in this case is that the defendant did not
do so and that the solicitors accordingly did not prior to the date of the
certificate do any of the relevant work. Accordingly the taxing officer ought,

but has failed, to make his assessment on the basis that all the work which had reasonably to be done was actually done either in the short time available between the grant of Legal Aid and the commencement of the trial or during the trial itself. While I accept that he does not in terms apportion the work reasonably done, the direction he gave himself leads me inevitably to conclude that that was in fact his reason for reducing the time claimed. To that extent his conclusions cannot stand and I have reconsidered the claim. I do not accept the notional calculation on a page/time basis as a reasonable method of estimation where actual time has not been recorded and I bear in mind that if the time had not actually been spent it would have consumed all and more of the working time available. Doing the best I can I allow a further 20 hours.

The rate to be allowed

The claim was for an "uplift" of 50%. As the determining officer correctly says, that was inept since there is no such provision in the Regulations. The relevant provision is paragraph 3 of Schedule 1 which states:

> "In respect of any item of work, the appropriate authority may allow fees at more than the relevant standard rate specified in paragraph 1 where it appears to the appropriate authority that, taking into account all the relevant circumstances of the case, the amount of fees payable at such specified rate would not reasonably reflect:
>
> (a)   the exceptional competence and dispatch with which the work was done; or
> (b)   the exceptional circumstances of the case."

Paragraph 3 thus contemplates two situations in which it is open to the determining officer to allow fees at more than the relevant standard rate. Under paragraph 3(*a*) he may do so if he is satisfied on the facts that there was both exceptional dispatch and exceptional competence. Those criteria are conjoined and both must be present. Under paragraph 3(*b*) he may do so if the circumstances of the case are exceptional. That second provision is much wider than the first. The determining officer correctly directed himself as to his task in considering the claim under paragraph 3 and rejected it for these reasons:

> "A mark up of 50% was claimed for preparation work. This uplift was disallowed on determination."

I believe that this claim is misconceived as the 1982 Regulations do not provide for an uplift on preparation work in the manner of "care and conduct" previously allowed under the 1968 Regulations. I would not, in any event, have allowed fees at more than the appropriate standard rate for the following reasons:

(1)   Paragraph 3 of Schedule 1 to the 1982 Regulations quotes two sets of circumstances under which the determining officer might consider

allowing fees at more than the relevant standard rate. The first of these is "The exceptional competence *and* dispatch with which the work was done". Exceptional in this context means exceptional in relation to the case as compared with other cases in the same general category. This was a reasonably straightforward, if somewhat lengthy, case of its nature and prepared in my view in a competent rather than an exceptionally competent manner.

Under the second limb of paragraph 3(*a*) I contend that there was no need for "exceptional dispatch" for reasons already rehearsed under "preparation of documents" and "consideration of documents".

(2) Paragraph 3(*b*) of Schedule 1 to the 1982 Regulations gives "the exceptional circumstances of the case" as the second reason for considering an increase to the standard rate. Again, I do not regard this as an exceptional case of its type in any way as in my experience all cases of this nature tend to last for several weeks. It was certainly much less complex than, say, a fraud trial of similar length.

The appellant's submission under paragraph 3(*a*) is that exceptional dispatch is self evident from the facts and timetable of events to which I have already referred and that exceptional competence should be inferred from the fact that a proper defence was prepared within a very limited time. I accept the first part of this submission but not the second, since to accept it would wholly erode what are clearly intended by the Regulations to be matters of separate consideration. Accordingly the determining officer was correct in rejecting the claim under paragraph 3(*a*) although, for the reasons I have already given under the first head of appeal, he misdirected himself in finding there was no exceptional dispatch.

As to paragraph 3(*b*) "exceptional" is to be construed in accordance with the well settled principle of taxation that the circumstances relied upon must be relevant to the particular case. The ordinary meaning of "exceptional" is given in the Oxford Dictionary as "creating an exception; unusual". In that context it seems to me clearly exceptional that solicitors should have impressed on them the burden of preparing a case of this weight within the limited time available. The determining officer has sought to equate the weight of the case with others of a similar nature but that overlooks the particular and as I say, exceptional circumstances of this case in relation to such other similar cases. Accordingly I allow the appeal in principle.

The more difficult question is how, once the principle is established to arrive at the rate other than the relevant standard rate which it is proper to allow. The Regulations are silent and afford no guidance. Moreover the relevant standard rate is a prescribed charging rate which is designed to cover not only what may be proper as an expense rate to cover the direct cost of the fee earner's time and overhead expenses but also any allowance for these factors which used to be considered under the general head of care and conduct including a commercial profit. The Regulations do not disclose how these components were assessed in arriving at the standard rate. Paragraph

37 of the Interim Directions for Determining Officers attempts to give guidance and (surprisingly to me) suggests that the standard rate includes an average profit element of 30% but goes on to say that that profit element is not to be confused with the percentage uplift formerly known as care and conduct. I do not know on what authority this paragraph is based and, in trying to assess a proper rate to allow I have not found it helpful. It seems to me that the taxing officer should proceed in accordance with the general principal that where any scale of costs is avoided by reason of the exercise of a discretion so to do, the allowance to be made should be fixed without reference to the scale item because the scale has ceased to be relevant. He should accordingly make his assessment in accordance with the directions contained in regulation 3(5) which provides

> "In determining costs the appropriate authority shall, subject to these Regulations:
>
>   (a) allow fair remuneration or work actually and reasonably done; and
>
>   (b) take into account all the relevant circumstances of the case including the nature, importance, complexity or difficulty of the work and the time involved"

save that he will ignore the limitation placed on his discretion by regulation 5(3) which would otherwise require him to allow fees in accordance with Schedule 1. To carry out that task he must assess a rate which reflects first the direct cost of the work at the time when it was done bearing in mind the status of the relevant fee earner, and secondly the burden of the relevant circumstances. The exercise is unavoidably arbitrary and can be no more than a value judgment based on experience.

Regina
v
Miller

Date of Determining Officer's Reasons
March 1983

Date of Taxing Master's Decision
January 1984

Regulation 5: Travelling Time to Local Court

The sole issue in this appeal was the disallowance of a charge for travelling time from the solicitors' office to the local court. The appeal was couched in the following terms:

> "The only question at issue is that of travelling time to our local Court. In addition to the submissions already made we would ask the Supreme Court Taxing Office to take into account the following paragraph.
>
> > 'Taxing officers must, by regulation 3(5)(a) allow fair remuneration for work actually and reasonably done. They must also allow reasonable travelling and waiting time in accordance with regulation 5(1)(d). There is nothing in the regulations suggesting that travelling time reasonably spent shall be disallowed on the grounds that the travelling is to a local court.
> >
> > The decisions under the old regulations to the effect that travelling time should not be allowed to a local court are now irrelevant. Those decisions were based on the fact that remuneration for attendances at court under the old regulations were at a daily rate'."

THE TAXING MASTER: I observe first of all that the word used in regulation 5(1)(d) is "may" and not "must". The regulation is permissive not mandatory. Accordingly the appellant is wrong in asserting that the masters' previous decisions on general principles of taxation do not apply to taxations under the 1982 Regulations. Those decisions continue to apply unless inconsistent with the 1982 Regulations.

The taxing officer has applied the principle set out in paragraph 90 of TONG and decision No 9 in the Digest but the question to be decided is whether that principle is consistent with the scheme of the 1982 Regulations.

The general principle of taxation applied in taxations under the 1968 Regulations was that the allowance for attending court was a daily allowance and not a time charge. Regulation 2(1) of those Regulations provides that subject to the other provisions of the Regulations, a solicitor is to be allowed basic fees in accordance with the Schedule. The Schedule provides for what were described as "daily fees" for attendance at court. The masters, in their decisions (see No 12 in the Digest) have held that, in applying that provision, the allowance to be made, when a certificate under regulation 7(6) was given, was to be a sum sufficient to reflect the broad average direct cost of the attendance based on the normal court day of 5 hours and including travelling time, waiting time and conferences at court. It was in the context of the total time engaged that taxing officers were required to discount time spent in travelling to the local court. The allowance of an attendance fee on this basis is referred to at paragraphs 98–100 of TONG and the correctness of the practice was affirmed by Goff J (as he then was) in *R* v *Wilkinson* [1980] 1 WLR 396.

The scheme of the 1982 Regulations is wholly different from that of the 1968 Regulations. Under regulation 5(1) the appropriate authority (i.e. the determining officer) may allow work done by a fee-earner in, inter alia, the following classes:

(c) attendance at court where counsel is assigned, including conferences with counsel at court and

(d) travelling and waiting.

Under regulation 5(2) what is to be allowed is:

(a) such work as appears to it to have been actually and reasonably done under the legal aid order by a fee-earner, <u>classifying such work according to the classes specified in paragraph (1)</u> as it considers appropriate and

(b) <u>such time in respect of each class of work</u> allowed by it ... as it considers reasonable.

Under regulation 5(3) fees are to be allowed in accordance with Schedule 1. The Schedule prescribes separate rates for travelling and waiting from those prescribed for attendance at court. The words I have underlined plainly indicate that under the 1982 Regulations travelling and waiting time is to be considered as a chargeable item on its own and separate from the time spent in court. That is quite a different basis from the treatment which it was proper to give to those items under the 1968 Regulations which required them to be taken together. It seems to me moreover that the whole intention of the 1982 Regulations is to provide a scheme for assessing at prescribed rates a charge for all the work reasonably done on a time basis: that is also different from the intention of the 1968 Regulations. Finally I observe that there is no limitation or restriction of the description of travelling or waiting time in regulation 5.

I conclude that the general principle excluding travelling time to the local court properly applies only where the allowance to be made is a daily allowance and that it is not consistent with the scheme of the 1982 Regulations. Accordingly all time reasonably spent in travelling to and waiting at court should be allowed without regard to the location of the court and the solicitor's relationship to it.

Regina
v
Osagie

Date of Determining Officer's Reasons
October 1983

Date of Taxing Master's Decision
January 1984

Paragraph 3, Schedule 1: Allowance of Fees at More Than the Standard Rate
Regulation 10: Supplying Written Reasons

In this case the taxing master was asked to review several items of the solicitors' bill, including the rate per hour. The rate for preparation claimed in the bill was in excess of the standard rate for a senior solicitor prescribed by the Regulations. The determining officer has a discretion under paragraph 3 of Schedule 1 to allow a rate greater than the standard rate if the standard rate would not reasonably reflect (a) the exceptional competence and dispatch with which the work was done or (b) the exceptional circumstances of the case.

The taxing master held that if the solicitors wished the determining officer to consider a claim under paragraph 3 of Schedule 1 it was incumbent on the solicitors to make a proper submission setting out the grounds relied upon. In this case, no such submission had been made at any time. The determining officer considered the case fit for a grade B fee-earner and allowed the appropriate rate. In the circumstances, he was correct in his assessment. The fact that the work was actually done by a senior solicitor was not relevant per se.

After the determining officer gave his reasons he engaged in further correspondence with the solicitors, and subsequently revised one of his decisions.

The taxing master commented that once the determining officer had given his reasons he was functus officio and no further correspondence ought to be entertained. If a solicitor was dissatisfied his remedy was to appeal.

Regina
v
Ali and others

Date of Determining Officer's Reasons
October 1983

Date of Taxing Master's Decision
February 1984

Regulation 5: Status of Fee Earner and Disallowance of Waiting Time

This appeal concerned the status of the fee-earner who did the work, it not being in issue that the gravity of the case merited the attention of a grade B fee-earner, and the amount of travelling and waiting time allowed for attendance at court. The fee earner was neither a solicitor nor a legal executive within the definition of the latter term contained in the Regulations. He was an unadmitted clerk, currently three quarters of the way through an external law degree course with four years experience of criminal practice. His employers were satisfied that he was able properly to conduct with only routine supervision, the middle range of cases. The determining officer felt himself constrained by the language used in paragraph 30 and 31 of the Interim Directions to classify him as grade C.

The taxing master did not agree. He said that the important sentences in paragraph 30 are these:

> "equivalent senior staff should be able to perform similar work to a solicitor or a legal executive, taking a similar time and performing to a similar standard. The majority of criminal cases will normally be conducted or supervised by this level of fee-earner."

He said that the determining officer had been misled by the use of the word "equivalent" into making the false assumption that an unadmitted clerk must have a length of experience equal to that required of solicitors or legal executives. The person concerned clearly had the experience and competence, and the allowable work should have been assessed at the rates claimed.

Turning to the other aspect of the appeal, the taxing master said that a claim was made for 125 minutes travelling to and waiting at court. He dealt with the travelling time which was 20 minutes. The determining officer allowed 1 hour waiting but on redetermination allowed a further 30 minutes thus leaving 15 minutes disallowed. He had done this because, as he says in his reasons, he considered it proper to allow only 30 minutes waiting prior to the listed time. The taxing master said that this item was truly the minimum, but he had been asked to allow it so as to make it clear that there was no absolute "half hour rule". He did so because the test was reasonableness and he did not think the Regulations required determining officers to be astute to prune off small amounts of time here and there when the overall sum claimed was moderate for the type of case. To do so encouraged applications for redetermination and appeals which were uneconomically time consuming for everyone concerned and wasteful in relation to the amounts in dispute.

Regina
v
Halcrow

Date of Determining Officer's Reasons
October 1983

Date of Taxing Master's Decision
February 1984

Regulation 5: Qualifications of a Senior Solicitor

The sole issue raised in this appeal concerns the qualifications required before a fee-earner can be considered to be a senior solicitor. The case involved three defendants on serious charges, and the determining officer took the view that the weight of the case merited preparation by a senior solicitor. He did not allow the relevant standard rate for a senior solicitor because he considered himself bound by paragraph 29 of the Interim Directions for Determining Officers issued by the Department, which reads "Senior Solicitor means a solicitor with at least ten years standing with substantial relevant expertise and experience".

The taxing master held that there was no authority for this statement. A senior solicitor is one who has the skill, knowledge and experience to deal with the comparatively small number of cases which fall within the higher categories of gravity or difficulty. It follows that he must have had a number of years relevant experience to acquire the skill and knowledge and "about ten" may well be a useful rule of thumb but it can be no more than that. Further, the experience may in certain circumstances have been acquired before admission. The taxing master quoted two examples: a legal executive of many years experience of crime who becomes admitted, or a former member of the criminal bar who becomes a solicitor. In this case, the solicitor concerned was admitted in 1979, but that was preceded by twenty years as a police officer, during which time he had extensive criminal experience. In consequence, the taxing master said that he qualified as a senior solicitor.

Regina
v
Moss

Date of Determining Officer's Reasons
December 1983

Date of Taxing Master's Decision
February 1984

Regulation 5: Disallowance of a Conference

In this matter the determining officer disallowed an attendance of 10 minutes as not being fee earners' work, because it had to do with questions of listing of the trial.

The taxing master said that the facts are that the defendant called uninvited and asked to see the fee-earner in charge of his case. The matters discussed were relevant. A solicitor or his clerk cannot be said to have been acting unreasonably under such circumstances. The taxing master allowed what he considered to be a trivial sum so as to underline his view that the Regulations do not require the determining officer to be astute to seek ways of snipping off small amounts of time here and there in a bill of costs.

Regina
v
Slessor

Date of Determining Officer's Reasons
May 1984

Date of Taxing Master's Decision
October 1984

Regulation 5: Travelling and Waiting Time
Regulation 6: Expenses of Travelling to and from Court

In this case the solicitors claimed an allowance for travelling and waiting time on the basis of the time actually spent in accomplishing the several journeys to court from their offices by motor car. They also claimed a mileage allowance at the standard rate then prescribed by the Costs in Criminal Cases (Allowances) Regulations 1977. The determining officer rejected that claim and allowed a notional amount for the time which would have been taken had the journeys been made by public transport together with the expense of train fares.

The taxing master in allowing the appeal set out the following rules which should be applied in assessing allowances to be made:

(a) prima facie the amount to be allowed is the cost of the time expended on and the expenses incurred in making the journey by public transport, provided that public transport is available and is reasonably convenient, having regard to the relevant circumstances in each case;

(b) a solicitor is not entitled to claim the cost of the time spent or cost incurred in travelling to his office from his home; the journey should be deemed to start from the solicitor's office, unless he in fact started from his home and that was nearer to the court than his office;

(c) allowance made should include the time spent and expense incurred in getting from the starting point to the railhead or coach station and also the time spent and expense incurred in getting from the terminus to the court;

(d) a solicitor travelling by train may claim the cost of first class travel if he has actually incurred that expense;

(e) if the journey is one which could have been made by public transport, but is accomplished by motor car purely as a matter of preference, then the allowance to be made for travelling time should be the notional time which would have been taken by public transport, or the time actually spent, whichever is the less: expenses should be calculated on the basis of the "public transport" mileage rate (that rate is calculated by reference to the average cost of public transport per mile) which is prescribed pursuant to the 1977 Regulations;

(f) if public transport is not available or not reasonably convenient, the actual time spent in travelling should be allowed and the expenses should be calculated on the basis of the standard mileage rate prescribed by the 1977 Regulations;

(g) what may be "not reasonably convenient" is a matter of discretion, dependent upon the relevant circumstances of each case, and what is reasonably convenient in one set of circumstances may not be in another; a factor which is always relevant is the time which may have been spent in getting from the starting point to the railhead, and from the terminus to the court; if it is considerable, the use of a car may be justified – the taxing master urged determining officers to adopt a flexible and broad approach to the problem.

Per curiam: so far as expenses only are concerned these rules apply equally to members of the Bar in cases in which it is appropriate to include an element for expenses in the fees allowed, but no allowance for the cost of time spent in travelling is made to them.

Regina
v
O'Brien

Date of Determining Officer's Reasons
October 1984

Date of Taxing Master's Decision
March 1985

Regulation 6: Claim for Out of Pocket Expenses Incurred in Travelling to a Local Court

The issue raised in this appeal related to a claim for out of pocket expenses by a solicitor for travelling to court from his office in London, a distance of 6 miles. The determining officer disallowed the claim on the basis that the solicitors' office was local to the court in question in which circumstances out of pocket expenses incurred in travelling to the court were not separately chargeable.

THE TAXING MASTER allowed the appeal and his decision, reported in full, is as follows: In an earlier Decision (No 11 of 1984) I made the following observations per curiam:

"Out of pocket expenses incurred in travelling to a local court were not chargeable under the 1968 Regulations but for different reasons. Small expenses of this nature are customarily included by solicitors in their general office overheads and not separately charged as disbursements. That being so they are subsumed into the relevant standard rate and the previous practice should be continued (see the decision of the Chief Taxing Master in R v *Pullum* reported in The Law Society's Gazette for 23 November 1983 [and **Costs LR (Core Vol) 413**]). Determining Officers should have regard however to the cost of travel and should bear in mind that the definition of what is a local court, while a matter for their discretion, should be reasonably narrow."

The important part of that observation is the last sentence. Masters have repeatedly stressed that a realistic and flexible approach should be made to the cost of travel and there is certainly no rule that a court in the London area is to be considered local if the solicitors' offices are within a radius of 8 miles of that court. The solicitors put their case in this way:

"Our understanding of the concept of a local court is that if a Solicitor is outside the area of a local Court then he is entitled to instruct Agents and, further, if he is not local to the Court but nevertheless travels to the Court he runs the risk that the additional claim that he makes for the additional travelling will not be allowed.

Further, so far as we are concerned the concept of a local Court refers more usually to out of London Courts where there is one Court per town, where the Solicitors' offices are situated near the Court and when normally the Solicitor can walk to Court."

It seems to me that there is considerable force in this argument. Moreover the 1982 Regulations do not limit a claim for disbursements unless they fall within the proviso to regulation 6(1)(*a*). In *R* v *Sandhu*, **Costs LR (Core Vol) 451**, (see Court Business 3/85) Mustill J (as he then was) pointed out that those Regulations provide an exclusive code for ascertaining what may be paid for and that the structure is radically different from the previous structure. The rates of remuneration are prescribed and no assistance is given to enable one to decide the basis of prescription.

The principle of not allowing expenses to a local court rests on the assumption that solicitors included them as an overhead in the calculation of their expense rate. If not so included, there would seem to be no reason why they should not be separately charged. In default of the requisite information it would be speculation to say, one way or the other, what the prescribed rates are intended to cover but it seems to me that the general tenor of the regulations is to permit a separate claim for all actual payments out of pocket and that the previous general rule ought no longer to apply. There is an inconsistency in allowing, on the basis of the quoted case, all the cost of travelling time but not all the concomitant out of pocket expense. Moreover, I do not think that any satisfactory definition of what is a local court can be given for the London area or any other large urban agglomeration.

Regina
v
Zemb

Date of Determining Officer's Reasons
April 1985

Date of Taxing Master's Decision
June 1985

Regulation 6: Payment for Photocopying

The solicitors in this case claimed a sum for photocopying as a disbursement. The determining officer allowed an amount which was considerably less than the sum claimed.

The taxing master held that the determining officer was wrong to allow anything. A disbursement is a payment of money out of pocket. Accordingly the cost of copies made in a solicitor's office cannot be a disbursement. It can be a profit charge only if reasonably done by a fee-earner but in general it is non fee-earners' work and in consequence subsumed into the solicitor's overhead expenses. In the recent case of *R v Sandhu*, **Costs LR (Core Vol) 451** (see Court Business 3/85 dated 22 March 1985), Mustill J made it plain that the powers to make allowances for any kind of work are created and exclusively defined by the Regulations. In the absence of express provision, the determining officer cannot and must not remunerate the services claimed even if he thought such a course would be reasonable.

Per curiam: If solicitors have copies made outside their office and make a payment for them, that is a disbursement. In such a case the determining officer would have to consider whether the course taken was reasonable, on the facts of the case, given that the making of copies in the ordinary way forms part of a solicitor's work.

Regina
v
Wanklyn

Date of Determining Officer's Reasons
May 1985

Date of Taxing Master's Decision
October 1985

Regulation 5(1)(c): Attendance at Court Where Counsel is Assigned

The issue raised in this appeal was (inter alia) whether solicitors should be paid at the attendance rate under regulation 5(1)(*c*) or the travelling and waiting rate under regulation 5(1)(*d*) while a jury is out considering its verdict.

For the period while the jury was out the solicitors had claimed at the rate for attending court and had been allowed the time at the travelling and waiting rate.

The solicitors relied in part on the judgment of Vaisey J in *Lawson* v *Tiger* (1953) 1 All ER 698 at page 699:

> "In my judgment so long as the judge is in court, either in open court or in his private room with the registrar in attendance waiting in court for the judge's return and no other case or cause is being tried in the court or receiving the attention of the judge, the whole of the time in ordinary court hours may be said to be occupied by the trial, even if some of that time is not being employed for the purposes of argument or the hearing of evidence of witnesses."

In allowing the appeal the master's reasons were as follows: Mr Justice Mustill, as he then was, in his decision in *R* v *Sandhu* (11 November 1984) **Costs LR (Core Vol) 451 at 452** said this:

> "Certainly regulation 5(1) creates an exclusive code for the ascertainment of the type of work which may properly be allowed. This does not mean, however, that nothing except what is explicitly described in the various sub-paragraphs can be claimed. The definitions of the type of work are contained (so far as concerns sub-paragraphs (*a*), (*b*) and (*c*)) in the words which precede the first comma what follows thereafter is added by way of illustration."

Thus in considering the present case it is necessary to differentiate between "attendance at Court where Counsel is assigned" (regulation 5(1)(*c*)) and "waiting" (regulation 5(1)(*d*)).

A trial begins when the jury is impanelled and the prisoner arraigned and it does not end until the judge records the jury's verdict and gives effect to it either by discharging the prisoner or sentencing him. The whole of the intervening period is "The Trial", except for any time when the judge adjourns (or releases solicitor or counsel for any reason), and is covered by "attendance at Court where Counsel is assigned" (regulation 5(1)(c)). The dictionary defines "attendance" as: "the action or condition of attending ... waiting the leisure, convenience or decision of a superior. The action or fact of being present at a meeting, etc. or when summoned. Waiting – expectation". The definition incorporates the act of waiting and further it seems to me that "waiting the ... decision of a superior" is on all fours with waiting for the decision of a jury.

Turning again to the Court Log it will be seen that when the jury retired at 12.02 the judge did not adjourn the case for lunch. It was not therefore open to counsel or solicitors to leave the court building since they might have been required at any time on a moment's notice. Thus, although counsel and solicitors were undoubtedly waiting for the jury's verdict, since the trial was still in progress, their presence constituted attendance at court under regulation 5(1)(c).

In those circumstances I find that it is proper for the solicitors to claim the time spent waiting for the jury to return at the rate for attendance at court.

Regina

v

Backhouse

Date of Determining Officer's Reasons
June 1985

Date of Taxing Master's Decision
March 1986

Paragraph 3 of Schedule 1: Assessment of Enhanced Hourly Rates

The issue raised in this appeal was the method of assessment of a solicitor's enhanced hourly rate under paragraph 3 of Schedule 1.

The solicitors claimed and the determining officer agreed that paragraph 3 of Schedule 1 applied to the case both because it was handled with exceptional competence and dispatch and also because of the exceptional circumstances of the case. The taxing master endorsed this assessment of the case.

Extracts from the master's decision are as follows: Under regulation 3(5) of the 1982 Regulations in determining costs the appropriate authority shall, subject to the Regulations, allow fair remuneration for work actually and reasonably done and take into account all the relevant circumstances of the case including the nature, importance, complexity or difficulty of the work and the time involved. No indication is given in the Regulations as to how fair remuneration for work actually and reasonably done is to be calculated once the prescribed rates are exceeded. Mr Justice Mustill (as he then was) in *Regina* v *Sandhu* (29 November 1984) **Costs LR (Core Vol) 451 at 452** said

> "I am not persuaded that it is altogether sound to invoke a concept of care and conduct which ex-hypothesi has been rendered obsolete by the new Regulations and then to draw inferences from the fact that it does not receive specific treatment in those Regulations; nor to my mind can it safely be assumed that the entirety of the factors which compromise care and conduct has been wholly absorbed into the prescribed rates. The Regulations have nothing to say on this point which is not surprising since they create a radically different structure."

In that case the learned judge was dealing with a claim for supervision but it is clear that the 1982 Regulations make no provisions for care and conduct.

Since the 1982 Regulations are silent as to the method of assessment of enhanced rates and since a point of principle was involved I invited the Lord

Chancellor to make representations with a view to ensuring that the public interest is taken into account.

The relevant part of the representations made on behalf of the Lord Chancellor was as follows:

"5. The Regulations make no provision for the calculation of the appropriate fees payable when the Determining Officer exercises his discretion under paragraph 3 of Schedule 1 to allow fees of more than the relevant standard rate. It is submitted, however, that this does not empower the Determining Officer wholly to disregard the 1982 Regulations and to proceed instead on the principles which govern Common Fund taxations. All costs payable to a Solicitor under section 37 of the Act are required to be determined in accordance with the 1982 Regulations. Since Schedule 1 does not prescribe rates for the purpose of paragraph 3, it is submitted that the correct approach is to apply the principles set out in regulation 3(5).

6. The question how, once it is established that paragraph 3 of Schedule 1 should apply, to arrive at the rate other than the relevant standard rate was considered by Master Clews in *R* v *Hussain* [**Costs LR (Core Vol)** 426] in his decision dated 3 January 1984, Case No 820498/9. The Master concluded that:

'... The Taxing Officer should proceed in accordance with the general principle that where any scale of costs is avoided by reason of the exercise of a discretion so to do, the allowance to be made should be fixed without reference to the scale item because the scale has ceased to be relevant. He should accordingly make his assessment in accordance with the directions contained in regulation 3(5) ... save that he will ignore the limitation placed on his discretion by regulation 5(3) which would otherwise require him to allow fees in accordance with Schedule 1. To carry out that task he must assess a rate which reflects first the direct costs of the work at the time when it was done bearing in mind the status of the relevant fee earner, and secondly, the burden of the relevant circumstances. The exercise is unavoidably arbitrary and can be no more than a value judgment based on experience ...'

It is submitted that this approach, applying the principles set out in regulation 3(5) rather than going outside the Regulations altogether, is the correct approach to take where the discretion available under paragraph 3 of Schedule 1 is exercised."

When the solicitors appeared before me to deal with the representations they confirmed that they felt it would be in order for me to reach a value judgment based on experience or to adopt the general principle of taxation set out by Mr Justice Robert Goff, as he then was, in *Regina* v *Wilkinson* [1980] 1 All ER 597 at 601, following *Re Eastwood (decd), Lloyds Bank Ltd* v *Eastwood* [1975] Ch 112, [1974] 3 All ER 603, **Costs LR (Core Vol) 50** and *Leopold Lazarus Ltd* v *Secretary of State for Trade and Industry* (1976) 120 SJ 268, **Costs LR (Core Vol) 62**, that

"... a solicitor's remuneration should consist of two elements: first, the sum computed on the basis of an hourly rate which represents the broad average direct cost of undertaking the work; and second, a sum, usually expressed as a percentage mark up of the broad average direct cost, for care and conduct. The first element is generally known as the A factor: the second is the B factor. The total of the A factor and the B factor (if any) constitutes the solicitors' total remuneration."

Counsel for the appellant solicitors argued that whichever approach was adopted the same result would be achieved.

I have considered the decision in *Regina* v *Hussain* and I notice that before expressing his view the learned master indicated that it was necessary to assess a rate which reflects first the direct cost of the work at the time when it was done bearing in mind the status of the relevant fee earner and, secondly, to assess the burden of the relevant circumstances, that is those circumstances set out in regulation 3(5) which are listed as including the nature, importance, complexity or difficulty of the work and the time involved. It seems to me that what the master was saying was that an A plus B calculation should be made in order to reach an enhanced rate. That seems to me to be the only possible and logical approach once the rates prescribed by the Regulations cease to apply, but I would go further and say that the proper approach is to arrive at an A figure for the broad average direct cost of the work and add to that a percentage uplift (the B figure) to take into account all the relevant circumstances of the case as required by regulation 3(5).

The Taxing Officer's Notes for Guidance at paragraph 8 recommended the taxing officer to take into account in every case the following factors:

(a) The importance of the case, including its importance to each defendant in terms of its consequence to his livelihood, standing or reputation even were his liberty may not be at stake.
(b) The complexity of the matter.
(c) The skill, labour, specialised knowledge and responsibility involved.
(d) The number of documents prepared or perused with due regard to difficulty or length.
(e) The time expended.
(f) All other relevant circumstances.

With regard to care and conduct paragraph 92 of TONG states:

"This is an allowance made to cover matters which have not been quantified in terms of a rate per hour (such as supervision and commercial profit). It should vary according to the professional skill and responsibility involved in the solicitor's work, having regard to the factors other than time set out in paragraph 8. This allowance may be expressed as a percentage of the total allowed for preparation."

The Taxing Officer's Notes give further guidance as follows:

"93.   In assessing the percentage to be added the Taxing Officer should have regard to:
(a)   The degree of responsibility accepted by the Solicitor and his staff;

(b) The weight of the case; (a complex case, or one which is protracted and time consuming, properly conducted will justify more than a simple one);

(c) The care, skill and thoroughness, speed and economy, with which the case was prepared.

94.   Where the Solicitor has exercised an unusual degree of skill, care or responsibility the percentage should be higher, but where the case has been badly handled the allowance should be less, or no addition at all should be allowed."

In my view there is nothing in the paragraphs cited above which in any way offends against the 1982 Regulations once the determining officer has decided to exercise his discretion to allow an enhanced rate and in those circumstances the principles therein contained ought to be applied when arriving at an enhanced rate under the 1982 Regulations.

In allowing the appeal the master applied the principles outlined above in assessing enhanced hourly rates for preparation and attendance at court.

In regard to the claim for an enhanced rate for travelling and waiting time the master said that in normal circumstances it was difficult to see how travelling and waiting time could attract an enhanced rate but in this case it was accepted that the circumstances were wholly exceptional and a modest increase in the standard rate was allowed.

Regina
v
Rycott

Date of Determining Officer's Reasons
16 January 1991

Date of Taxing Master's Decision
29 January 1992

Paragraph 3 of Schedule 1 Part I: Enhanced Rates

In this case the solicitors appealed against the composite hourly rates allowed under both regulation 7 of the Costs in Criminal Cases (General) Regulations 1986 and paragraph 3 of Schedule 1 Part I to the Legal Aid in Criminal Proceedings (Costs) Regulations 1986.

The solicitors represented the defendant who faced charges of conspiracy to obtain property by deception, conspiracy to defraud and fraudulent trading. The charges arose from the defendant's directorship of a company involved in the futures and options market. It was accepted by all concerned that the case involved matters of such weight and complexity that it was appropriate to allow enhanced rates by applying the principles laid down in *R v Backhouse* (TCS30) **Costs LR (Core Vol) 445.**

The Chief Taxing Master was asked to consider as a point of principle whether there is any difference between the broad average direct cost of a solicitor undertaking commercial work and of undertaking weighty criminal work of this nature and whether it is right to draw a parallel between them.

The Chief Taxing Master held that it is not wrong in principle to make a comparison between weighty and complex criminal cases, such as those described above, and commercial proceedings in appropriate cases. He went on to describe the type of case where it might be appropriate to draw a parallel as follows:

> "the recent past has seen an enormous increase in the number of lengthy fraud prosecutions. The amounts of money involved in the alleged offences run into many millions of pounds. Consequently, work which has to be undertaken is detailed, time-consuming and enormously expensive. The responsibility upon the legal representatives is enormous. The scale of work is such that it is normal to see a team of legal representatives working alongside experts in various disciplines. In this particular case the nature of the prosecution was such that it mirrored closely civil proceedings based on the same fact."

The Chief Taxing Master went on to say that for the purpose of conducting criminal litigation of this weight and complexity there is no significant difference in the broad average direct cost of doing work between this and similarly based civil litigation.

The Legal Aid in Criminal and Care Proceedings (Costs) (Amendment) (No 3) Regulations 1994 provide that in cases where a criminal legal aid order is granted on or after 1 October 1994 the appropriate authority may only make enhanced payments by way of an uplift to the prescribed legal aid rates. The amended Regulations also limit any enhancement to 200% in cases where the proceedings relate to serious or complex fraud; and in all other cases to 100%. Therefore, reference to broad average direct costs in this decision will not apply in respect of those criminal legal aid cases where legal aid was granted on or after 1 October 1994.

Regina

Plaintiff

and

Sandhu

Defendant

Royal Courts of Justice
Thursday, 29 November 1984

Before:
Mr Justice Mustill
(sitting with assessors)

Judgment

MUSTILL J: This review of taxation turns on a question of some general interest. Accordingly, with the consent of the parties, I have adjourned the matter into open court for judgment.

During December 1982 and January 1983 services were performed by solicitors in relation to the defence of a person appearing before the Crown Court. In due course the solicitors rendered a bill of costs for taxation. In addition to several items about which there is no controversy, there were modest sums in the bill attributed to –

> "Supervision of staff with regard to conduct of the case, allocation of counsel, listing difficulties, use of enquiry agents, evidence and other relevant matters"

and

> "Drawing Bill of Costs".

Each of these items was disallowed in full. After representations by the solicitors, the determining officer declined to make any alteration. An appeal by the solicitors to a taxing master of the Supreme Court was dismissed. They have now proceeded by Originating Summons to have the order of the taxing master set aside.

I will deal first with the item relating to supervision. By way of introduction, it is convenient to quote from the taxing master's summary of the way in which the solicitors manage their practice.

> "11.   ... On the question of supervision, he first explained to me the method by which he manages his specialised criminal practice. He employs a number of admitted assistants but they are committed daily to advocacy in the lower courts and not able to do much to supervise the unadmitted staff. He himself

allocates the cases to fee-earners who seem to him able to do the work. Some
of these persons are used partly for secretarial work and partly for fee-earning
work in preparing cases. They are, he claims 'clerks' within the definition of
fee-earners given in the Regulations. The senior solicitor himself reads the
brief prepared in each case and gives instructions for the allocation of counsel
and the grade of fee-earner who is to attend court. He does not permit the
delivery of a brief to a chambers clerk unmarked with the name of counsel
and, should the named counsel be unable to take the brief, he insists the brief
be re-referred to him for the selection of a named replacement. The senior
solicitor reminded me that it is the principal solicitor who is assigned under
the legal aid order and that it is he who must answer to the court for any
mistake. The senior solicitor's submission is that this active involvement in
each and every case goes beyond the general concept of supervision as a factor
which is fully taken account of in the relevant standard rate prescribed by the
Regulations."

Two different reasons have been assigned for the disallowance of this item.
First, it is said that the item relates to what would in the past have been
separately assessed as care and conduct. Under the regime recently created
by the Legal Aid in Criminal Proceedings (Costs) Regulations 1982, the
concept of care and conduct has disappeared, and remuneration for activities
which would previously have fallen under that heading must now be taken
to be subsumed in the standard rates provided for by the Regulations.

I would for my part feel some reservation about adopting this approach,
at least in its entirety. I am not persuaded that it is altogether sound to invoke
a concept of care and conduct which, ex hypothesi, has been rendered
obsolete by the new Regulations, and then to draw inferences from the fact
that it does not receive specific treatment in those Regulations. Nor, to my
mind, can it safely be assumed that the entirety of the factors which comprise
care and conduct has been wholly absorbed into the prescribed rates. The
Regulations have nothing to say on this point: which is not surprising, since
they create a radically different structure. The better course, I would suggest,
is simply to look at the Regulations and see what they have to say about the
kind of activity which the solicitors have described.

The second ground for disallowing the claim is this. If one looks at the
Regulations, one finds no express provision, either in regulation 5(1) or
elsewhere, for the appropriate authority to allow any sum for supervision.
The powers of the determining officer are created and exclusively defined by
the Regulations. In the absence of express provision, the determining officer
cannot and must not remunerate the services described by the solicitors, even
if he thought that such a course would be reasonable. Accordingly, he was
bound to disallow the item in question.

Again, I do not accept this argument in its entirety. Certainly regulation
5(1) creates an exclusive code for the ascertainment of the type of work
which may properly be allowed. This does not mean, however, that nothing
except what is explicitly described in the various sub-paragraphs can be
claimed. The definitions of the type of work are contained (so far as

concerns sub-paragraphs (*a*), (*b*) and (*c*)) in the words which precede the first comma. What follows thereafter is added by way of illustration. Thus, the fact that supervisory work of the type performed by the senior solicitor in this case cannot be fitted within any of the activities described in the latter part of sub-paragraph (*a*) does not mean that no fee can be allowed in respect of it. What matters is whether it constitutes "preparation". If it does, then the determining officer can and must allow, under regulation 5(2), (3) and (4), such fees in respect of it as he shall consider reasonable.

Plainly there are many considerations which the determining officer will have to bear in mind when deciding how to exercise this discretion. It would be undesirable to attempt in this judgment to lay down any fixed principles, or even to provide illustrations of what may or may not properly be allowed in taxation. Everything will depend on the circumstances of the individual case. It is sufficient for present purposes to say that –

(1) Many items of what may loosely be called supervision will not fall within the framework of the Regulations at all. Every senior solicitor will wish to keep an eye on what is going on in his office, to make sure that it is operating efficiently, and that the standards set by the senior solicitor, who bears the ultimate responsibility for the proper conduct of all work carried out by the practice, are being scrupulously maintained. Again, a senior solicitor who has proper regard for his broader responsibilities will find it necessary to discuss matters with his more junior staff, as a method of practical instruction, with a view of making them better fitted to perform their allotted work. Very often in both of these spheres the solicitor may occupy some time on a particular case. It would not, however, by any means necessarily follow that this time would be attributed to the preparation of that case, so as to entitle the solicitor to remuneration under paragraph 5(1). It would simply be part of the overhead expenses incurred by the solicitor in the proper conduct of his practice.

(2) The determining officer could properly have regard to the nature of the case and to the grade of fee-earner whose time is claimed for elsewhere in the bill when deciding whether it was reasonable for time to be spent by the senior solicitor on supervisory work. There must be many cases where, once the case has been allocated to a fee-earner of the appropriate grade, he or she can be allowed to carry on the work unaided, without any need for intervention by someone more senior. On the other hand, there may equally be cases where, even when the matter is in the hands of someone who could ordinarily be considered competent to deal with it, there might be an unexpected turn of events where the senior solicitor's extra experience and weight would be an essential reinforcement. Unqualified rules cannot be laid down. Thus, if the reasons given by the determining officer in the present case could be understood as asserting that questions relating to the allocation of counsel and the use of enquiry agents could never be the subject of a proper allowance to a senior solicitor, I would not agree. Often, and perhaps very often, they would not be allowable, but everything would

depend on the circumstances of the individual case.

(3) The determining officer can reasonably expect the senior solicitor to provide an explanation of the reasons why the nature of the case made his participation necessary; and of the occasions, duration and circumstances of such participation. Without such particulars, the determining officer might well consider that where an allowance has been claimed for a fee-earner of a particular grade, there was no case made out for a further allowance in respect of someone more senior.

Applying these conclusions to the facts of the present case, I cannot find that the determining officer erred in disallowing the claim for supervision. The bill itself showed no grounds for concluding that, once a fee-earner of Grade B had been assigned to the matter, there was any special call for the participation of a solicitor in Grade A. The determining officer invited further particulars of the "listing difficulties" referred to in the bill, but did not receive them. It seems to me that in the circumstances he was entitled to form the view as to what was reasonable, which he expressed when disallowing the item in question. What the position would have been if the claim had been thoroughly particularised is not now for me to determine.

Before leaving this part of the case, it is right to place on record that the views previously expressed do not differ, in any fundamental regard, from those advanced in helpful oral submissions made on behalf of the solicitors and the Lord Chancellor's Department. The former have not sought to assert that all instances of general oversight, which may have some connection with an individual case, can be recovered under the Regulations. Equally, the latter have not contended that supervision which can be specifically identified in a particular case can never be properly claimed under regulation 5. No doubt if individual cases were argued out, in the light of full particulars, differences of opinion might arise, but no such exercise has been possible, in the light of the information now before the court.

I turn to the second of the disputed items: "Drawing bill of costs". This may be dealt with very briefly. Under section 30(1) of the Legal Aid Act 1974, from which the 1982 Regulations derive, legal aid in relation to any proceedings:

> "... shall be taken ... as consisting of representation by a solicitor and counsel assigned by the court, including advice on the preparation of the person's case for those proceedings."

The drawing of a bill of costs, which by its nature takes place after the proceedings are concluded, could not possibly fall within this definition of legal aid. It is, therefore, not surprising to find that in the subordinate regulations, by which are defined in an exclusive manner the officer's powers to allow fees, there is no reference to time expended for this purpose. No doubt it has happened in the past that by statute, regulation or concession, an allowance for this purpose has been made in relation to certain types of business. Under the new regime governing legal aid costs in criminal matters, no such allowance is permissible. The item was rightly disallowed by the determining officer.

In the result, the order of the taxing master will be upheld.

Regina

v

Hudson

(Review of Taxation)

St Dunstan's House
Fetter Lane EC4
Thursday, 11 July 1985

Before:
Evans J

Judgment

(Revised)

EVANS J: The applicants are a firm of solicitors who represented the defendant Hudson in proceedings before the Southwark Crown Court under a Legal Aid Order No 2641 dated 5 November 1982. They appealed to the taxing master against the determination of their costs under the Legal Aid in Criminal Proceedings (Costs) Regulations 1982 pursuant to regulation 11 and their appeal was allowed in part. In relation to certain routine letters and telephone calls their appeal was unsuccessful, and they now seek to have the decision of the taxing master dated 18 January 1985 amended in this respect.

On 22 February 1985 the master certified pursuant to regulation 12(1) that the question which the applicants wish to have decided involves a point of principle of general importance. This is defined as follows:

> "Having regard to the fact that routine letters written and routine telephone calls, actually and reasonably dealt with by a fee earner, are work in respect of which fees may be allowed under Regulation 5(e) of the Legal Aid in Criminal Proceedings (Costs) Regulations 1982; should letters and telephone calls of the following nature be disallowed on the ground either, that they form part of the solicitor's overheads or that they should be assumed to be covered by a care and conduct element deemed to be included in the rates prescribed in the Regulations: Correspondence with and telephone calls to and from:
> (a) Counsel's chambers dealing with matters such as the availability of Counsel, arrangement of Conferences and listing difficulties
> (b) The Crown Court in connection with the listing and other administrative matters
> (c) Witnesses to arrange appointments?"

The Lord Chancellor's Department pursuant to regulation 11(6) was invited to make representations at the appeal proceedings but declined to do so and therefore did not appear at these review proceedings. Mr Girling, who has argued the matter most ably on behalf of the applicants, asked me to give this judgment in open court, and I have agreed to do so, having been informed that the Lord Chancellor's Department does not oppose his request.

The items which have been disallowed consist of three letters written by or on behalf of the applicants (whom I will call the solicitors) and nine telephone conversations received or made by them. All were concerned with the listing of the case for trial and the availability of counsel thereat. They are all within sub-paragraph (a) of the point of principle, as certified. It follows from this that no items within sub-paragraphs (b) and (c) of the certificate arise for decision in the present case. I am satisfied, however, that no material distinction needs to be made, as a matter of principle, between the three categories of communications referred to in the three sub-paragraphs. This judgment, therefore, is intended to apply equally to each of the three categories described in the certificate.

I approach the 1982 Regulations on the basis described by Mr Justice Mustill (as he then was) in *R* v *Sandhu* **Costs LR (Core Vol) 451**. He referred to "the regime recently created by" the Regulations, which "create a radically different structure" from what went before. The determination of solicitors' fees is provided for in regulation 5, sub-paragraph (1) of which, against quoting Mustill J, "creates an exclusive code for the ascertainment of the type of work which may properly be allowed". I should set out regulation 5 in full:

> "**Determination of solicitors' fees**
> 5. – (1)   The appropriate authority may allow work done by fee-earners in the following classes:
>
> (a) preparation, including taking instructions, interviewing witnesses, ascertaining the prosecution case, advising on plea and mode of trial, preparing and perusing documents, dealing with letters and telephone calls which are not routine, preparing for advocacy, instructing counsel and expert witnesses, conferences, consultations, views and work done in connection with advice on appeal or case stated;
> (b) advocacy, including applications for bail and other applications to the court;
> (c) attendance at court where counsel is assigned, including conferences with counsel at court;
> (d) travelling and waiting;
> (e) dealing with routine letters written and routine telephone calls.
>
> (2)   The appropriate authority shall consider the claim, any further particulars, information or documents submitted by the solicitor under regulation 4 and any other relevant information and allow:
>
> (a) such work as appears to it to have been actually and reasonably done under the legal aid order by a fee-earner, classifying such work

according to the classes specified in paragraph (1) as it considers appropriate; and

(b) such time in respect of each class of work allowed by it (other than dealing with routine letters written and routine telephone calls) as it considers reasonable.

(3) Subject to paragraph (4), the appropriate authority shall allow fees for the work allowed by it under this regulation in accordance with Schedule 1: provided that, where any work allowed was done after [30 June 1984], it may allow such fees as appear to it to be fair remuneration for such work having regard to the rates specified in Schedule 1.

(4) In the case of proceedings in the Crown Court and the Court of Appeal, the fees allowed in accordance with Schedule 1 shall be those appropriate to such of the following grades of fee-earner as the appropriate authority considers reasonable:

(a) senior solicitor;
(b) solicitor, legal executive or fee-earner of equivalent experience;
(c) articled clerk or fee-earner of equivalent experience."

It is important, in my judgment, to consider the regulation as a whole, before proceeding to answer the specific question regarding routine letters and telephone calls which is raised by the present application. Sub-paragraph (1) lists five classes, or types, of work done by fee-earners, and provides that the appropriate authority "may" allow (fees) for such work. Sub-paragraph (2) requires the authority to consider the claim and any supporting material and to allow ("shall ... allow") such work as was actually and reasonably done under the legal aid order by a fee-earner. The fee to be allowed is provided for in Schedule 1, and in relation to routine telephone calls this is a fixed, small amount per item, without reference to the time actually spent. There are at least two situations in which no fee may be paid even for work actually done. If any work is done, but by a person other than a fee-earner, then no question of remuneration can arise. Similarly, if work is done by a fee-earner but the taxing authority considers that it was not reasonable for that piece of work to be done by a fee-earner, then no remuneration can be allowed under sub-paragraph (2). Thus far, the construction of the regulation is in my view entirely clear.

If this simple, straightforward approach is adopted, then the only questions which arise when a claim for fees is made under regulation 5 are (1) what work was done? (2) Is the work within one of the classes listed in sub-paragraph (1)? (3) Was it done by a fee-earner? and (4) Was the work "reasonably done under the legal aid order" by the fee-earner? This is in effect a double requirement: was the work itself reasonably done under the legal aid order, and was it reasonable for the fee-earner to do it? A further, fifth, requirement under regulation (2)(*b*) regarding the time allowed for each class of work does not arise with regard to routine letters written and routine telephone calls with which this judgment is concerned.

Adopting this approach in the present case, the three letters and nine telephone calls were all of a nature which undoubtedly should be classified as "routine" within the normal meaning of that word. The master has found that they were all dealt with by a fee-earner and as I read his decision and his certificate he was satisfied that the work was reasonably done by the fee-earner concerned. There is certainly no indication that it was not reasonable for the fee-earner to do the work in this particular case. On the face of it, therefore, the claim for fees for this work under regulation 5 ought to succeed, and the items in question ought not to be disallowed.

The master's reasons for reaching the contrary conclusion, which I suspect that he did only with some reluctance, are set out in detail in his decision, and I can only attempt to summarise them here. He sought to apply the principles laid down in his own judgment in *R* v *Leonard & Stachini* (1984, unreported), where he allowed a claim for letters which were concerned with the arrangements for visiting defendants in prison. These were treated, and in my respectful view properly treated, as routine letters, but in the course of his judgment the master referred to what he called "the long-standing and well settled principles relating to letters and telephone calls exemplified by paragraph 91" of the Taxing Officer's Notes for Guidance (1982 version). Paragraph 91 reads as follows:

> "Routine letters should be allowed at the standard unit cost, other letters should be paid for according to the length and content. All routine telephone calls irrespective of length and whether or not they are timed should be allowed at the standard unit cost applicable at the relevant time. Only those calls which are timed and which represent attendances whereby material progress is made should be assessed on an hourly basis. Chargeable calls do not include unsuccessful attempts by Secretaries or telephonists to make outgoing calls or incoming attempts to contact fee-earners who are not available, all of which are part of normal office overheads."

So far as telephone calls are concerned, paragraph 91 effectively distinguishes "routine" calls from others which may be regarded as "attendances" and which should be remunerated on an hourly basis. It excludes from taxation what may be called "abortive calls" of the kind described in the last sentence. The taxing master clearly thought that the 1982 Regulations are intended to remunerate all "routine" calls, excluding only abortive calls, and in relation to letters he said "The Regulations are intended to remunerate at a standard rate the very simplest every-day correspondence". He also referred, however, to previous judgments in *R* v *Inniss* (1982), *R* v *Elliott* (1983), *R* v *Norman* (1984) and *R* v *Ford* (1984), and he concluded at the end of his judgment:

> "In summary, therefore, I think that the test is whether the letter or call ought to be treated as one in respect of which it would in normal practice not be proper for the solicitor to make a direct charge to the client and it seems to me that the number of items to be so treated will normally be extremely small and will fall within the compass set out by the Masters in their decisions which I have quoted, but applied on a very narrow basis."

It seems to me that in the present case the master felt constrained to interpret regulation 5(1)(*e*) in the light of paragraph 91 of TONG and of the other judgments referred to, and to hold that sub-paragraph (*e*) does not permit remuneration for certain routine letters and telephone calls, specifically those which were concerned with listing difficulties and the availability of counsel. This approach does receive some support from the other judgments referred to in R v *Leonard & Stachini*, though as I read that judgment the taxing master was disposed to interpret these judgments narrowly, as indeed his own summary, quoted above, clearly shows.

In my judgment, however, there is no justification in the terms of regulation 5 for excluding from paragraph (1)(*e*) any claim for routine letters written or for routine telephone calls made or received. It is necessary of course to establish what is meant by "routine" letters and "routine" telephone calls. They are distinguished by the regulation itself from the non-routine letters and calls referred to in sub-paragraph (*a*) under the heading "preparation" and for which an hourly charge may be made. They do not include, in my view, the kinds of abortive calls which are described in the last sentence of paragraph 91, either as a matter of language or of common sense. If there is any doubt about this so far as the language is concerned then it is permissible, in my judgment, to refer to the contemporary practice as stated in paragraph 91 in order to confirm the view that abortive calls are not to be regarded as "routine telephone calls" within sub-paragraph (*e*). But I can see no justification for going outside the regulation so as to exclude any kinds of routine calls or routine letters, properly so called, from the ambit of paragraph (1)(*e*). Moreover, even if reference is made to paragraph 91, as I read the paragraph it supports, rather than contradicts, the above interpretation of regulation 5(1). It does not seem to justify the disallowance of any routine letter written, or any routine telephone call, other than abortive calls which the last sentence expressly excludes.

The contrary argument, however, is that certain kinds of routine letters and routine calls should nevertheless be disallowed because under existing taxation practices they are regarded as forming part of the solicitors' office overheads or as being covered by the care and conduct allowance, and because the rates prescribed under the 1982 Regulations should be deemed to include an allowance of that sort. No doubt, the practical result of disallowing such claims would be that the cost of doing the item of work in question would have to be regarded by the solicitor either as part of his office overhead expenses, for which no remuneration may be claimed under the Regulations, or as having to be borne out of the fees which are allowed for work properly claimed under regulation 5. But I do not consider that this justifies disallowing an item which the regulation expressly allows. Even if there is, or was, a practice in other forms of taxation to disallow certain kinds of routine letters and routine telephone calls it would nevertheless be wrong, in my judgment, to interpret regulation 5(1)(*e*) in a way which would contradict its express terms.

As to whether the prescribed rates include or should be deemed to include a notional care and conduct allowance, I, for my part, prefer to adopt the approach described by Mr Justice Mustill in *R v Sandhu* **Costs LR (Core Vol) 451**. The 1982 Regulations do not provide for a care and conduct allowance. They establish a new regime, and one which is radically different from what went before. Regulation 5 permits and in my judgment requires the straightforward approach which I have attempted to describe. This means that all routine calls are within regulation 5(1)(*e*), but they will not be remunerated under the regulation unless the taxing authority is satisfied that the work in question was actually and reasonably done under the Legal Aid Order by a fee-earner. In practice, the scope of such work, particularly telephone calls, which is entitled to remuneration under the Regulations may be little or no different from what is allowed under other and earlier taxation procedures. To this extent I am in agreement with the taxing master's summary at the end of his judgment in *R v Leonard & Stachini*, which I have quoted above, but I would respectfully add the important qualification that the dividing line between allowable and non-allowable items in cases to which the 1982 Regulations apply is established by the terms of regulation 5 rather than by the present or former practices of taxation authorities in other kinds of case.

Regulation 5(1)(*e*) refers only to "routine letters written", and I express no view as to whether any sum may be allowed under regulation 5 for dealing with routine letters received other than, of course, the appropriate fee for writing a routine letter in reply.

For these reasons, I answer the certified question as follows:

> Correspondence and telephone calls of the kinds described in paragraphs (a) (b) and (c) of the question which are "routine letters written and routine telephone calls actually and reasonably dealt with by a fee-earner" should not be disallowed on the ground either that they form part of the Solicitor's overheads or that they should be assumed to be covered by a care and conduct element deemed to be included in the rates prescribed by the Regulations.

Mr Anthony Girling, of Messrs Girling Wilson & Harvie (Herne Bay) appeared for the applicant.

Regina
v
Panice

Date of Determining Officer's Reasons
October 1983

Date of Taxing Master's Decision
February 1984

Regulation 5: Transfer of Brief to Other Counsel

The defendant first appeared before the court in late 1982, when his counsel made an application to sever the indictment, which was granted. The trial proceeded on three counts, and ended 25 days later. The trial of the remaining counts was fixed for hearing in early 1983, when counsel was unable to attend. Someone was instructed in his place.

The taxing master said that counsel originally instructed undoubtedly prepared the case as a whole and would have been entitled to a re-reading fee and a refresher for the second trial if he had been able to appear thereon. He held that where the brief is transferred to other counsel on a further hearing or re-trial, the correct approach is set out in paragraph 53 of TONG. If the Taxing Authority had felt that the change of counsel was not necessary, the second counsel should have received the proper brief fee calculated in accordance with general principles and the brief fee for the first counsel should have been adjusted.

Regina
v
Ghadhim Gerhards

Date of Determining Officer's Reasons
September 1983

Date of Taxing Master's Decision
July 1984

Regulations 7 and 8: Counsel's Fees: Remuneration for Preparation Undertaken During the Course of a Trial

In this complex and heavy case involving several defendants, counsel appealed against the fees allowed by the determining officer. The documentation was heavy to begin with and increased as the trial progressed; additional evidence being put in by the prosecution on 6 separate days. The law involved was complex and some 7 days of court time was taken up with legal submissions. The trial lasted for 56 days. In consequence much preparation for trial had to be done in a short time and some of what would ordinarily have been pre-trial preparations had to be done after the trial started. In addition there was considerable on going preparation required notably because of the additional evidence put in and the legal submissions.

Those facts proved a difficulty, in the light of the 1982 Regulations, in the method of assessment of counsel's fees. Accordingly the taxing master adjourned the hearings of the appeals and invited the Lord Chancellor to intervene under regulation 11(7).

THE LORD CHANCELLOR made written representation as follows: These representations are made on behalf of the Lord Chancellor under regulation 11(7) of the Legal Aid in Criminal Proceedings (Costs) Regulations 1982 with a view to ensuring that the public interest is taken into account.

Background

It is unnecessary to recite the full background to this case since these representations are confined to a single issue of principle which concerns the method of remuneration for preparation undertaken during the course of a trial. Suffice it to say that this was a heavy and complex case which lasted some 60 days and counsel were required to prepare the case at comparatively short notice because of the condition of one of the defendants.

Further preparation work during the course of the trial was undertaken and in the circumstances it is not contended that this was unreasonable.

The taxing master has requested representation on how preparation work undertaken during the course of a trial should be remunerated.

Submissions

Prior to the commencement of the Legal Aid in Criminal Proceedings (Costs) Regulations 1982 it was the practice for further preparation reasonably undertaken during the course of a trial to be taken into account in assessing the brief fee. However, regulation 8(1)(*a*) of the 1982 Regulations provides for:

> "a basic fee for preparation, including preparation for a pre-trial review and, where appropriate, the first day's hearing including, where they took place on that day, short conferences ... and any other preparation;"

Regulation 8(1)(*b*) provides for:

> "a refresher fee for any day or part of a day during which a hearing continued, including, where they took place on that day, short conferences ... and any other preparation;"

It is submitted therefore that where further preparation work is reasonably undertaken on a day for which a refresher fee is allowed, the refresher fee should be fixed to take account of all work done on that day, including preparation work.

Paragraph 4 of Schedule 2 provides that "where a refresher fee does not relate to a full day, the appropriate authority shall allow such fee as appears to it reasonable having regard to the fee which would be allowable for a full day". It is submitted therefore that where further preparation work is undertaken in addition to a full day in court, the refresher fee should be increased to such an amount as appears reasonable having regard to the fee which would be allowable for a full day.

Regulation 8(2)(*b*) provides that where "it appears to the appropriate authority, taking into account all the relevant circumstances of the case, that owing to the exceptional circumstances of the case the amount payable by way of fees in accordance with Schedule 2 would not provide fair remuneration for some or all of the work it has allowed, it may allow such amount as appears to it to be fair remuneration for the relevant work." It is submitted that where further preparation is reasonably undertaken during the course of a trial on a day for which a refresher is paid and the amount payable in accordance with Schedule 2 for a full day in court and further preparation work would not provide fair remuneration, the determining officer has a discretion (owing to the exceptional circumstances of the case) to apply Regulation 8(2)(*b*) and allow such amount as appears to be fair remuneration for the relevant work.

It is further submitted that where preparation work is undertaken during the course of a trial on a day for which a refresher fee is not paid (e.g. during the weekend), account of this may properly be taken in assessing the brief fee.

This representation was made known to the appellants, and the taxing master gave them a further opportunity to be heard. They all accepted the representation as the proper construction of the relevant Regulations.

THE TAXING MASTER said as follows: It will be seen that the Regulations require a change in practice to this extent, that it is no longer open to those claiming fees to seek or to determining officers to make, in the brief fee, any allowance for work of preparation done after the commencement of the trial unless (and the proviso is important), the work in question was done on a day for which no refresher fee is payable. If any such work is done on a day when such a fee is payable then it can only be remunerated by the payment of an enhanced refresher for the day in question. This must be so even if the work was done outside normal court hours. If any properly chargeable work is done during the course of trial on a day for which no refresher fee is payable, then it must, and can only be claimed as part of the brief fee. Conversely, while short conferences at court remain to be subsumed into the ordinary refresher fee, a special conference outside the ambit of the ordinary refresher, will continue to be dealt with as a separate item. A determining officer cannot be expected properly to take these factors into account unless, when the claim is made, he is supplied with detailed information showing what additional work or conferences are claimed. A general statement, in support of a claimed brief fee, that the case entailed additional preparation during the course of the trial will not do. He must be told on which days it was done and whether or not it was done on days for which a refresher was payable. If the work was done on such a day then clearly a claim must be made that the provisions of regulation 8(2)(*b*) should apply. That will require counsel to explain under regulation 7(4), in respect of each such day, not only the time involved but the reason why the additional work became necessary, since unless there is some special circumstance, routine thinking work, and the ordinary work which counsel always does during a trial is covered by the brief fee or refresher without augmentation. In short, if proper remuneration is to be given, the burden on counsel accurately to record and to itemise and explain the work he has done, becomes very much heavier than was formerly the case.

Regina
v
Plews

Date of Determining Officer's Reasons
February 1984

Date of Taxing Master's Decision
November 1984

Schedule 2, Paragraph 6: Expenses of Travelling To and From Court

In this case heard at Ipswich Crown Court, counsel appealed against the amount allowed for hotel and travelling expenses incurred during the trial. The determining officer considered that the amounts claimed by way of expenses were excessive, and allowed lesser amounts.

Counsel argued that the total of the allowances in this case was inadequate because they did not recompense counsel for the expenses actually and reasonably incurred in respect of attendances at court. It was contended that the determining officer was under a duty to act fairly and that he had given no reasons in justification for his decision that the expenses claimed were excessive, save that other counsel in the case had incurred expenses of a lesser amount. Counsel argued that the nature of the case, a weighty conspiracy to steal and handle stolen goods, required him to hold several conferences after court hours. It was reasonable for him to stay in Ipswich on some occasions because the train services from London are inadequate and do not permit counsel to arrive at court at an appropriate time without leaving London unreasonably early. The use of a car was justified for the same reason.

The taxing master said that there was some confusion about the correct approach towards the allowance for travelling and hotel expenses incurred by counsel. Schedule 2, paragraph 6 to the 1982 Regulations permits the allowance of "an amount in respect of counsel's attendance at that court to cover travelling and hotel expenses actually and reasonably incurred and necessarily and exclusively attributable to counsel's attendance at that court, with a limitation on that amount which is not material to this case". The combination of the new claim and payment forms showing as a separate item the amount of actual travelling and expenses incurred has created the impression that the expenses should be paid in addition to and separate from the brief fee. The correct position is as set out in Decision Number II 68 in the Digest.

In assessing a proper fee under the Regulations the determining officer should take into account the reasonable expenses ascertained in accordance with paragraph 6 of the Regulations. The interim Directions issued by the Lord Chancellor's Department which at paragraph 55 say, "Any amount allowed is formally part of the fees for the relevant attendance but for convenience it is to be shown separately on claims and in determining fees" do not alter the correct approach but provide for a division of the fees when assessed for administrative convenience.

Before deciding by what amount the fees payable to counsel should be enhanced to reflect the expenses actually and reasonably incurred the determining officer should consider the reasonableness thereof. The reasonableness of any expenses claimed should be judged not by reference to the expenses incurred by other counsel involved in the same trial but in relation to the demands upon counsel in putting forward the claim of the case for the defendant for whom he acted and counsel's own particular circumstances in relation to the conduct of the trial. The determining officer misdirected himself by taking into account the level of the expenses claimed by other counsel and by making an arbitrary allowance without reference to the detail of the particular claim made in this case.

When making an allowance for counsel's travelling expenses there should normally be allowed the equivalent of a first class train fare from counsel's chambers or his residence, whichever is the nearer to the court. If counsel travels by car otherwise than for his own personal convenience the travel expenses should be allowed at a mileage rate equivalent to that prescribed for medical practitioners. In this particular case the court sat on most days at an earlier hour than normal. The latest train to Ipswich which would have allowed counsel to arrive at court in sufficient time not only to robe but to see his client and instructing solicitors to hold any necessary pre-hearing discussions with them and his opponent counsel left London at 07.15. It is unreasonable to expect counsel to leave at such an hour, bearing in mind that he has to travel from home to the station, when he is faced with a full day in court. It was therefore reasonable for counsel to travel by car and his claim, which was based on a mileage rate less than that prescribed for medical practitioners under the Costs in Criminal Cases (Allowances) Regulations 1977 at the relevant time was reasonable.

If counsel claims expenses for overnight accommodation and the cost is less than that of daily travel, then the determining officer should take into account in his assessment of the fees the additional hotel expenses incurred. If the hotel cost is more than the cost of daily travel the hotel expenses should be allowed if, having regard to the demands of the case on counsel, including the need for conferences after court and for overnight preparation, counsel could not have returned home at a reasonable hour.

Having considered counsel's claim for expenses on the above basis the taxing master said that the fee should be increased by a sum which, in broad terms, covered the expenses incurred. The determining officer was not, however, required by the Regulations to make an allowance in his assessment which is precise to a penny.

Regina
v
Thomas
Regina
v
Davidson
Regina
v
Hutton

Date of Determining Officers' Reasons
October/November 1984

Date of Taxing Master's Decision
March 1985

Regulation 8, Schedule 2(6): Travelling Expenses of Queen's Counsel

The Decision arises out of three appeals brought by leading counsel and relates to the allowance for travelling and hotel expenses incurred by them in connection with cases dealt with on the North Eastern Circuit.

The claims arose because the determining officer, applying paragraph 6 of Schedule 2, disallowed leading counsel's expenses on the basis that, either, there was an adequate local Bar or, an adequate local Bar was available at a lesser distance than leading counsel's chambers.

The basic argument put forward by leading counsel was that in order to make the circuit system work and to give solicitors a reasonable choice of Queen's Counsel, Circuit QCs are expected to and do appear anywhere on circuit. Expenses are inevitably incurred and, it is argued, the fact that leading counsel travels from Newcastle to Leeds (where there are a number of Silks in Chambers) should not be a reason for depriving counsel of any travelling and hotel expenses actually and reasonably incurred.

THE TAXING MASTER allowed the appeals and his decision in principle is as follows: Paragraph 6 of Schedule 2 provides,

> "Where Counsel is instructed to appear in a Court which is not within 25 miles of his Chambers, the appropriate Authority may allow an amount in respect of Counsel's attendance at that Court to cover any travelling and hotel expenses

actually and reasonably incurred and necessarily and exclusively attributable to Counsel's attendance at that Court; provided that the amount allowed shall not be greater than the amount, if any, which would be payable to Counsel practising from the nearest local Bar unless Counsel can justify his attendance having regard to all the relevant circumstances of the case."

That paragraph encapsulates the decision of the Chief Taxing Master in the case of *R* v *Crittenden*, a decision given under the 1968 Regulations [Decision II 68 in the "Digest of Taxing Master's Decisions"]. To the extent that there is no direct conflict with the 1982 Regulations, previous decisions of the taxing masters and the Taxing Officers' Notes for Guidance are still relevant.

Paragraph 67 of TONG provides,

> "*Travelling and Hotel Expenses*
> Counsel's fees should not be increased to reflect time taken in travelling to and from Court. When, however, it is necessary for a particular Counsel to travel to a 'distant court' then his brief fee, refresher or attendance fee should include a reasonable amount for any actual travelling and hotel expenses necessarily and exclusively attributable to the case or cases in question. In any case where it is proper to take into account expenses incurred by Counsel for rail travel, first class travel should be allowed if it has been incurred."

"Distant Court" for the purpose of paragraph 67 is considered to be one which is at a distance not less than 25 miles from a town in which there is a local Bar. Where this test is satisfied it is immaterial whether the court is one in which the individual counsel normally practises or not.

If counsel is instructed to appear in a distant court, the fees allowed should be no greater than those which would be allowed to counsel practising from the nearest local Bar, unless he can justify his attendance, having regard to the circumstances of the case in question. The allowance is based on the expense actually and reasonably incurred by counsel in travelling to the court from his home or the nearest local Bar town, whichever is the less.

The original decision in *R* v *Crittenden* related to junior counsel's fees. Paragraph 6 of Schedule 2 refers to "Counsel" Simpliciter. Expenses are only to be allowed where counsel can justify his attendance having regard to all the circumstances of the case. During the course of these appeals I was given details of the numbers of leading counsel practising from chambers on the North Eastern Circuit. I do not propose to set out those details here since they are inevitably constantly changing. Suffice it to say that whilst there appeared to be a sufficient number of leading counsel on the North Eastern Circuit as a whole to deal with the weightier cases, in one of the appeals now before me all the locally available leading counsel were engaged and a leader from the Northern Circuit had to be instructed. If one was to limit leading counsel to practising within 25 miles of their local Bar, there would be periods when no leading counsel would be available and other periods when the only work available would be at a distance and therefore at the penalty of paying the expenses out of the brief fee.

I am entirely satisfied, (and in this view I am fortified by the views of the presiding judges of the North Eastern Circuit), that leading counsel should not be regarded as being "local" to any particular city or area, even though his chambers are in one particular place. I find therefore that where leading counsel regularly practises on a circuit he should, as a general rule, receive an amount in respect of his travelling and hotel expenses actually and reasonably incurred and necessarily and exclusively attributable to his attendance at a court on that circuit. However, it seems to me that counsel who appear off circuit, whether leading or junior, can only expect to be reimbursed, if they can justify their attendance having regard to all the relevant circumstances of the case.

Regina
v
Davies

Date of Determining Officer's Reasons
July 1984

Date of Taxing Master's Decision
August 1985

Payment for Preparation Where Counsel is Unable to Conduct a Trial

In this case counsel was retained by the defendant's solicitors under a legal aid order but in the event he did not conduct the defence at the trial because he was detained at another Crown Court Centre in the case which overran its estimated length. Counsel submitted a claim for preparation for hearing and preparation for the pre-trial review at which he appeared. He was allowed a fee for attendance at the pre-trial review only, nothing being allowed for preparation.

The determining officer in his written reasons stated that if the change of counsel had been brought about by inconsiderate listing, the appellant counsel would have been entitled to payment for his abortive preparation. As that was plainly not the case the determining officer saw no justification in authorising payment for abortive preparation because another case exceeded its estimate.

It was submitted on behalf of counsel as a matter of principle that if there is a change of counsel due to unforeseen circumstances which arise through no fault of counsel, then he should be paid.

It was submitted on behalf of the Lord Chancellor's Department as a matter of principle that the barrister who carries out the actual work which is the subject of a brief or instructions shall, as between the barristers concerned, be entitled to the fee. When a barrister carries out part only of such work, division of the fee shall be a matter of arrangement between the barristers concerned (Code of Conduct for the Bar (1983) at paragraph 83). This basic rule is subject to certain exceptions but they can only be justified provided they are wholly exceptional to the rule.

Extracts from the Master's decision are as follows: I refer to regulation 8(1) of which only sub-paragraph (*a*) is relevant; and which provides as follows:

"8(1) The appropriate authority may allow any of the following classes of fee to counsel in respect of work allowed by it under this regulation:

(a) a basic fee for preparation including preparation for a pre trial review and, where appropriate, the first day's hearing including, where they took place on that day, short conferences, consultations and appearances (including bail applications), views and any other preparation."

The operative words are "a basic fee for preparation" and what follows thereafter is added by way of illustration. In this I adopt the words used by Mr Justice Mustill in *R v Sandhu* **Costs LR (Core Vol) 451** in a judgment delivered on 29 November 1984 when he was considering the interpretation of regulation 5(1). The words "brief fee" do not appear in the Regulations and in my respectful view the statement appearing in the Interim Notes for Guidance at paragraph 49(a), namely "basic fee: this is what is commonly known as the brief fee ..." is misleading. Clearly the term "basic fee" is wide enough to include a brief fee, but it is wider than that, and extends to all preparatory work properly carried out by counsel whether or not followed by a hearing. Thus preparatory work, properly done, must be paid for unless there is something in the subsequent conduct of counsel or that of his clerk which would justifiably deprive him of his entitlement to a fee, and unless there is any convention or rule of professional practice or conduct under which counsel is customarily so deprived. ...

Pursuant to the Legal Aid Act 1974, section 39(3) and regulation 3(5) the determining officer must follow the principle that he shall, subject to the regulations, "allow fair remuneration for work actually and reasonably done".

The purpose of the Taxing Officers' Notes for Guidance (TONG) is set out in the foreword as follows:

"These Notes seek to explain the main principles of taxation of costs as the law stands at present: they do not bind any taxing authority or limit judicial discretion in any way save where they accurately reflect a decision of the High Court or a statutory provision. They must be read in the context of the facts of each individual case."

The paragraphs relevant to change of counsel are 70, 70A and 71 and are as follows:

"70.   Care should be taken to see that preparation is not paid for than once, save when this was necessitated by reasons beyond the control of counsel or his clerk. Care must also be taken, however, to ensure that neither counsel is penalised, e.g. where, following a timely conference, the original counsel cannot for good reason hold the brief. (See also paragraph 71).

70A.   Where counsel has properly prepared a case which is a 'floater' but for reasons beyond control of counsel or his clerk he is prevented from appearing at the hearing so that a second counsel necessarily has to prepare the case again, it is proper for both counsel to be paid for the preparatory work carried out by them.

71. *Change of Counsel*

When a brief has been returned for some reason other than for the private or professional convenience of counsel, a fresh brief fee should be paid to the new counsel. This situation could arise where, for example, the first counsel has been dismissed by his client or is withdrawn from the case with the leave of the court. (For change of counsel on a retrial, see paragraph 53)."

Paragraph 70 appears under the heading "Devilling and cover" but is treated as being of general application. Determining officers are recommended to treat the principles contained in TONG as being applicable to determinations under the Regulations, save where they conflict with express provisions in the Regulations when the Regulations must prevail.

Each case must be considered on its own facts and where counsel has conducted himself responsibly and reasonably but for reasons beyond his control or that of his clerk, through no fault of his own, he is prevented from appearing at the trial so that a second counsel has to be retained, he is not to be penalised. In such circumstances each counsel should receive fair remuneration, subject to the Regulations, for the work actually and reasonably done by him.

In this case the master found that the circumstances in which the trial at the other Court Centre overran were wholly exceptional and could not possibly have been foreseen but he added that the examples referred to in argument as being "wholly exceptional" should be treated as illustrations of the circumstances in which the principle had been applied and not as limiting the scope of the principle. The appeal was allowed and it was ordered that the counsel be paid the basic fee for preparation originally claimed by him.

The master said that a second and entirely separate point of principle arose in the appeal as set out in the following extract from his decision:

"It is the responsibility of the counsel, who wishes to invoke the provision of regulation 8(2)(*b*), to satisfy the determining officer that exceptional circumstances exist and counsel must proceed in accordance with regulation 7 and in particular sub-paragraphs (4), (5) and (6) of that regulation. Decision No 50 (Digest Part II) draws attention to the fact that many appeals which might otherwise have succeeded have failed because the representations made to taxing authorities have been perfunctory and inexplicit. It cannot be too strongly emphasised that the provisions of regulation 11(11) are strictly applied and a taxing master will rarely accede to a request to adduce further evidence or to allow a ground of objection to be introduced which was not raised on the re-determination under regulation 10.

It is not sufficient to refer in general terms to counsel having been unavoidably detained on another case which overran its estimated time."

In the circumstances of this particular case and "with some hesitation" the master agreed to hear factual evidence from counsel in support of the claim notwithstanding that the evidence had not been disclosed to the determining officer.

Regina
v
(1) Neil
(2) Clements
(3) Martin
(4) Knight
(5) Walter & Breeze
(6) James

Date of Determining Officer's Reasons
February 1985

Date of Taxing Master's Decision
February 1986

Payment for Written Advice on Appeal

These six appeals related to the disallowance in each case of the fee claimed by junior counsel for a written opinion on an appeal against conviction and/or sentence; each opinion advised against an appeal.

The determining officer declined, on redetermination, to make any allowance in respect of the opinions and in his written reasons said that he considered that the work was unnecessary and not actually and reasonably done within the meaning of the Regulations. He referred to the Chief Taxing Master's Practice Direction No 2 of 1976 and in particular to the paragraph which reads as follows:

> "In the vast majority of cases advice on appeal is given during the normal '5 hour period' and there is in effect no additional fee for the work of advice on appeal."

The determining officer considered that these average matters fell within the category of "the vast majority of cases" and did not merit additional payment.

Counsel appealed against this decision on the following grounds:

(1)   That the advice was necessarily and properly given in accordance with the guidelines in the "Guide to Proceedings in the Court of Appeal Criminal Division" (the "Guide"); and

(2)   The 5 hour rule applied to oral advice given at the conclusion of the hearing resulting in conviction and/or sentence. This rule does not apply to

either positive or negative advice forwarded within 14/21 days of the hearing and does not apply where advice is requested under section 30(7) of the Legal Aid Act 1974.

It was submitted on behalf of the Lord Chancellor that a full and reasoned advice should be paid for in proper cases where it is appropriate for such an advice to be given in writing as a separate matter, but that a separate written advice is not required in every case. It was further submitted that the guidelines in the "Guide" did not preclude the giving of a short form of advice for which no separate fee is payable. It was argued on behalf of the Lord Chancellor that in the majority of cases advice on appeal could be given during the "normal 5 hour period" in accordance with the procedure set out in the Chief Taxing Master's Direction No 2 of 1976 so that there is in effect no additional fee for the advice on appeal. It was submitted that the "Guide" does not preclude the giving of a short form of written and reasoned advice endorsed on the form of Instructions to Counsel, payment for such "simple" advice being included within the brief fee, nor does section 30(7) of the Legal Aid Act 1974 require provision of separate written advice on appeal for which a separate fee is payable. It was suggested that this section only makes it clear that the scope of the Order granting legal aid extends to the giving of advice on the existence of reasonable grounds.

Counsel who appeared for the appellant did not seek to argue that, as a matter of principle, counsel was entitled to a fee for every written advice on appeal given by him. He accepted that in "simple" cases counsel would have complied with the spirit of the "Guide" by giving his advice in the form of a written endorsement on his instructions. He submitted that counsel should always act responsibly and only give a written opinion in the "more difficult" cases where the defendant has made a specific request for the written advice. He contended that these cases could not, on their particular facts be classified as "simple" but were "more difficult" as defined in the direction. The work involved in the preparation of opinion being done outside the "5 hour period" a separate fee was payable. He accepted the contentions made on behalf of the Lord Chancellor that in a simple case a responsible counsel would not expect a separate fee for an advice endorsed on his instructions, such being in his view a clear abuse of the system.

THE MASTER'S decision was as follows: Section 30(7) of the Legal Aid Act 1974 is in the following terms:

> "Legal Aid which may be ordered to be given to any person for the purpose of any proceedings by a Legal Aid Order under section 28(7) above shall, in the event of his being convicted or sentenced in those proceedings, include advice on the question of whether there appear to be reasonable grounds of appeal ..."

Counsel is entitled to be paid fair remuneration for any work actually and reasonably done by him within the scope of a Legal Aid Order granted pursuant to that section, the amount of which is determined in accordance with regulations 3(5) and 8 of the Legal Aid in Criminal Proceedings (Costs) Regulations 1982, which provides a comprehensive code for the allowance of fees of a nature wholly different to the provisions of the Legal Aid in Criminal Proceedings (Fees and Expenses) Regulations 1968. Regulation 8 provides for the allowance of fees for work done in three classes:

(a) the basic fee;

(b) refresher fee; and

(c) subsidiary fees, class (ii) of which includes written advice on evidence, pleadings, appeals, case stated or other written work.

Written advices do not fall within the work categorised under (a) above and should not therefore be taken into account in assessing the basic fee. If it is reasonable for counsel to give advice in writing a separate fee is payable even if the work is done on a day in respect of which a basic fee or a refresher fee has been earned.

The proper test to be applied to advices on appeal is whether it was reasonable to give that advice. The determining officer took into account the terms of the Practice Direction of 1976 and considered all these cases were average matters falling within the category of "the vast majority of cases" in which advice on appeal could be given within the "5 hour period" covered by the basic fees. This view was supported by the representations made on behalf of the Lord Chancellor. The Practice Direction of 1976 was made in the light of the then current practice of the Court of Appeal Criminal Division as set out in the pamphlet "Preparation of the Proceedings in the Court of Appeal Criminal Division" referred to in the Practice Note of the Lord Chief Justice [1974] 1 WLR 774, CA and provides machinery for giving of "advice in simple cases at little expense". The procedure was based on the use of forms set out in the Appendix to the pamphlet which if used had the result that "the negative advice situation" in simple sentence cases is then dealt with automatically and need not be the subject of separate fees. The current practice of the Court of Appeal is set out in the "Guide" prepared under the authority of Lane LCJ in May 1983. This does not include the same machinery for the giving of advice on appeal as is referred to in the 1976 Practice Direction.

Paragraph 1.1 emphasises that no one convicted or sentenced in the Crown Court should be without advice or assistance on appeal and that the practice set out in the following paragraphs should be followed in all cases.

Paragraph 1.3 requires counsel immediately after conviction and sentence to express orally a provisional view as to the prospects of a successful appeal and to inform the defendant that in any event he will receive written advice within 21 days. Counsel did not seek to argue before me that every advice given in accordance with this paragraph must be work reasonably done within the meaning of the Regulations, and accordingly I do not make any decision on this point of principle.

The test apparently applied by the determining officer to the opinion in each of these cases is whether it contained substantial content in an exceptional case. This is too narrow a test. The determining officer should have considered whether it was reasonable for counsel to have given a written advice. He should take into account the circumstances of the conviction, the length and nature of the sentence passed, the effect thereof on the defendant (a short sentence in a straightforward case can cause a defendant as much concern as a long sentence), any particular difficulties occurring in the trial, lack of impact which oral advice given immediately after the conclusion of the trial may have on the particular defendant's mind, and the fact that negative advice can prevent an unmeritorious appeal, which, if pursued, could cause the defendant to lose of the whole or part of his sentence. The Practice Direction of 1976 differentiates between "simple sentence cases" and "more difficult cases", including those where the defendant has been convicted after a "not guilty" plea and the conviction and sentence affects his liberty and livelihood. It is not reasonable to disallow a negative advice on appeal solely because counsel after consideration advises that no point of law arises and the only real issue is that of length of sentence.

If, on a date subsequent to this appearance in court, the defendant requests an advice in writing then the appropriate fee should be allowed to counsel in any event though the case could probably be classified as "simple".

Regina
v
Bellas
and five other appeals

Date of Determining Officer's Reasons
Appeal No 1 – June 1985
Appeal No 2 – September 1985
Appeal No 3 – September 1985
Appeal No 4 – September 1985
Appeal No 5 – September 1985
Appeal No 6 – October 1985

Date of Taxing Master's Decision
March 1986

Assessing a Brief Fee in Cases Prepared for Trial Where no Jury is Sworn

There are before me six appeals; Nos 1–4 arise under the Legal Aid in Criminal Proceedings (Costs) Regulations 1982 as amended by the Legal Aid in Criminal Proceedings (Costs) (Amendment) Regulations 1983, (No 2) 1984 and (No 3) 1985, and Nos 5 and 6 under the Costs in Criminal Cases (Central Funds) (Appeals) Regulations 1977 (which I shall refer to respectively as "the Legal Aid Regulations" and "the Central Funds Regulations").

Appeal Nos 1 to 4 are by counsel who are dissatisfied with the fees assessed by the determining officer in each of the cases in which they respectively appeared on behalf of the defendant. The appeals Nos 5 and 6 are by a prosecuting solicitor who is dissatisfied with the sums allowed to him by the taxing authority to compensate him for the expense of briefing counsel to prosecute in those two cases.

The prosecuting solicitor has authorised each counsel to pursue the appeal in the case with which counsel was concerned.

It having been suggested by the appellants that an important point of principle arises which is common to all the appeals, I agreed to hear representations before proceeding to determine each appeal individually on its own facts. At my invitation, the Lord Chancellor, pursuant to regulation 11 of the Legal Aid Regulations, caused written representations to be made on his behalf in appeal No 1.

All the appeals have a common factor in that the trial in each case went short. For the guidance of taxing and determining officers the general principle to be applied in such circumstances is stated at paragraph 39 of TONG as follows:

> "39. *For cases prepared as a plea of not guilty which run short.* If a case, which was justifiably prepared by counsel as a plea of not guilty, unexpectedly runs short, the brief fee should take account of the length of the hearing plus the full time taken for preparation, the weight of the case and the skill and responsibility involved in its conduct. Care must be taken to ensure that a fee appropriate to the work reasonably undertaken by counsel is allowed in those cases where a plea of guilty has been entered on his timely advice."

I will deal first with Appeals Nos 1–4 followed by Appeals Nos 5 & 6. Regulation 8(2) of the Legal Aid Regulations provides as follows:

> "8(2) ... the appropriate authority ... shall allow such work as appears to it to have been actually and reasonably done."

In each of Appeals Nos 2, 3 and 4 it is alleged that the brief fees allowed failed to provide fair remuneration for the work actually and reasonably done; the initial request for review in each case contained an allegation to the effect that the determining officer had disregarded "the recent decision of Stockley, Kennedy, Harrison and Baines" (which were written decisions of taxing masters and which I shall refer to collectively as "the Stockley decisions"). In Appeal No 1 the request for review did not refer to the Stockley decisions but the determining officer treated it as if it had done so. The relevant wording appearing in *R* v *Stockley* and reproduced in the remaining Stockley decisions is:

> "Where a case is properly prepared as a fight and the trial would have lasted a day the brief fee should not be reduced solely because the trial goes unexpectedly short."

This allegation has produced Reasons from the determining officers some of which contain lengthy discussion of the effect of the Stockley decisions on the general principle and of the duty of a determining officer who believes himself to be the recipient of conflicting "directions" from the appropriate authority and from taxing masters.

The description of the existing situation by counsel for the appellants was admirably succinct; he said "There is some confusion ... and no consistency of practice". He suggested that the initial cause of the confusion may have been that some counsel have sought to interpret the Stockley decisions as stating a new principle, which the determining officers have said is not a correct principle. Counsel accepted that the Stockley decisions do not state any new principle but he claimed that the determining officers are themselves failing to observe the existing general principle which is well established. He submitted that in effect the determining officers are applying a new principle of their own creation, which is just as erroneous as the so-called "principle" in the Stockley decisions.

That new principle is to assess the brief fee by deciding what figure would have been appropriate had the case not gone short and then making a deduction from that figure based on the proportion which the actual time in court bears to the anticipated time which would have been involved had the case been fought out.

Alternatively some determining officers assess the fee as if the case had been merely a plea and then make an addition on a time basis for the actual time spent in court. Either practice, in his submission, was equally wrong.

He suggested that in applying the general principle regard must be had to the work actually done by counsel and if an ordinary (one to two day) case goes short "by the efforts of counsel" the value of those efforts may well counter-balance any account which might otherwise be taken of the shortened hearing.

He drew attention to another well established principle of practice that counsel is not paid merely an hourly rate but a brief fee and he should not be placed in a situation where considerations of his own fee might obtrude on his duty to his client and to the court.

Lastly counsel pointed out that it can be seen from the Lord Chancellor's representations that he seems to think that the Stockley decisions were not wrong.

I turn now to the Lord Chancellor's representations which I have found most helpful as in my view they amplify and explain the general principle with admirable clarity. Counsel readily accepted that view and I therefore adopt the following paragraph from the representations as being generally applicable to cases covered by paragraph 39 of TONG. This paragraph does not replace or conflict with paragraph 39 but being set out in greater detail it affords additional assistance to those who have to apply paragraph 39. I shall proceed to use it as the basis for my decisions in these appeals:

> "It is submitted that the correct principle to be followed in these cases is that the brief fee should be determined having regard to the principle of fair and reasonable remuneration for work actually and reasonably done and taking into account all the circumstances of the individual case. The time spent in court is only one of a number of factors and should not be regarded as the sole, or even the major, criterion. The weight of a case has to be judged according to all its elements, and not simply to its weight as a fight. On this basis, it would be incorrect to determine the fee appropriate to a case of this nature by deciding what would have been allowed had there been a fight, and then applying a 'discount' to the figure thus reached in order to determine the brief fee. However, it is not accepted that these cases reveal any new principle, peculiar to cases prepared as a plea of not guilty which run short. Each case must be taken on its own facts, the determination being carried out on the basis of all the circumstances of the individual case."

As the Stockley decisions have been quoted at some length in the Reasons, I will refer to them in turn, but since it has been accepted that they do not involve any new principle, I shall deal with them quite shortly as being examples of cases where, on the particular facts, the taxing master was satisfied that the determining officer had failed to apply the general principle correctly.

In *R* v *Stockley* the taxing master seems to have concluded that the determining officer was "applying a discount" as quoted above and his written decision merely says that should not be done. In *R* v *Kennedy* the facts appear to have been similar, and the decision incorporated the words used in the Stockley decision. *R* v *Cribbin* was decided prior to the Legal Aid Regulations coming into force and has no current relevance. In *R* v *Baines* the facts were also similar to the *Stockley* case but the argument seems to have been centred on the meaning of "unexpectedly". The case of *R* v *Harrison* appears to have turned on its own particular facts which the taxing master thought had not been fully understood by the determining officer.

For the assistance of determining officers I set out below examples of the application of the principle in some actual cases. They are in no way comprehensive and I would warn against the danger of treating examples as if they are a complete catalogue of the circumstances in which the principle should be applied, thus limiting the exercise of discretion.

Cases where the efforts and skill of counsel are responsible for the case going short, thereby serving his client's best interest, saving the court's time and assisting the public interest by the prompt despatch of business. Examples of such cases are, counsel making a timely submission of law; advising a reluctant and obstinately unreasonable defendant to plead; persuading a prosecutor not to pursue some counts and to accept a plea on others; and in a case which would otherwise have had to be adjourned, assisting the prosecutor to amend the indictment to enable the case to be dealt with there and then by a plea. In these cases counsel's fee was assessed on the basis that the value of his service was no less (and in some circumstances it was even higher) than it would have been had the trial proceeded as originally anticipated and lasted a whole day.

Conversely there have been cases where the case has gone short for reasons entirely unconnected with the efforts or ability of counsel. Examples of such cases are, where the defendant changed his plea without the assistance of counsel; where the prosecution's main witness failed to attend; where the prosecution case was so plainly incompetent that a plea of no case should have been made at committal or it would obviously succeed at the trial. In these cases the value of counsel's services was considered less than it would have been had the trial proceeded as originally anticipated.

Appeals Nos 5 and 6 fall to be dealt with under the Central Funds Regulations and the Legal Aid Regulations have no relevance to them. In Appeal No 5 the determining officer, and in Appeal No 6 the appellant counsel, each appear to have overlooked this fact.

The power to award costs out of central funds in the Crown Court is derived from section 3 of the Costs in Criminal Cases Act 1973 and subsection (3) of that section provides:

"(3)   The costs payable out of Central Funds ... shall be such sums as appear to the Crown Court reasonably sufficient: –

(a) to compensate the prosecutor ... for the expenses properly incurred by him in carrying on the proceedings."

Where a prosecutor's costs are to be paid out of central funds the brief fee is assessed in accordance with the Bar's normal professional practice that the fee is agreed and marked on the brief before the trial. This applies even though, as often happens, an arrangement has been made between counsel and the prosecutor that counsel will accept whatever fee may be allowed on taxation in lieu of a fee being marked on the brief. The starting point for the taxing officer is to decide what fee the prosecutor would reasonably and properly agree to pay to counsel of the necessary competence on the assumption that counsel was properly and adequately briefed, and the brief was delivered at the normal and proper time. If the taxing officer finds all those conditions are satisfied then he allows the equivalent fee to compensate the prosecutor for the expense incurred. Thus the approach may of necessity be quite different from that applied in assessing a brief fee under the Legal Aid Regulations where the fee is assessed after the conclusion of the case and relates to work which has been actually and reasonably done. On the one hand the prosecutor may have chosen counsel of higher standing than is reasonably necessary or he may not have submitted proper and adequate instructions, nor delivered them at the normal and proper time, or he may choose to conduct the case in a way which requires counsel to do more work than is reasonable or proper, and in consequence although counsel may, as between himself and the prosecutor, have earned an enhanced brief fee, it will not be compensated for out of central funds. Indeed, counsel lacking the required experience or competence may have been briefed or the brief may have been so inadequate as to reduce the value of counsel's services at the trial, in which events the allowance will be reduced.

On the other hand the effect of events occurring at the trial which could not reasonably have been anticipated when the brief fee was notionally agreed, whether they increase counsel's responsibilities or decrease them, are normally to be ignored. This principle occasionally presents difficulties as to what should reasonably have been anticipated by the prosecutor or by counsel at the relevant time and this problem is a matter for the taxing officer to decide in his discretion after taking into account all the relevant circumstances of the case. He will find some help in this task in the general principles laid down in *Francis* v *Francis & Dickerson* (referred to at paragraph 78 of TONG).

In more than one of the present appeals the determining officer demonstrates a lack of understanding either of his basic function or of the proper use to be made of the material available to him when making his assessments.

When assessing fees the determining officer is called upon to form a value judgment by the exercise of judicial discretion. In so doing, in legal aid cases he must comply with the Legal Aid Regulations and with decisions of judges of the High Court which bear upon those Regulations.

The powers and duties of the appropriate authority are to be found in regulation 3 of the Legal Aid Regulations as follows:

> "3. – (1) Costs shall be determined by the appropriate authority in accordance with these Regulations.
>
> ...
>
> (4) The appropriate authority may appoint ... determining officers to act on his behalf under these Regulations in accordance with directions given by it or on its behalf.
>
> (5) In determining costs the appropriate authority shall, subject to these Regulations:
>
> (a) allow fair remuneration for work actually and reasonably done; and
> (b) take into account all the relevant circumstances of the case including the nature, importance, complexity or difficulty of the work and the time involved."

The powers under (1) and (4) are purely administrative, whereas the duty under (5) is to be performed by the exercise of judicial discretion. The duty is imposed on the person actually making the determination and the appropriate authority has no power, by discretion or otherwise, to restrict or fetter the exercise of that discretion.

In order to assist the determining officer in performing this duty, which may often be a difficult and onerous task, there are various sources of guidance available to him which are designed to help all determining and taxing officers to approach their task on the same basis and by this means to produce assessments which are broadly consistent. These include TONG, the Guidance to Determining and Taxing Officers in the Crown Court on Barristers' Fees, and the Interim Directions for Determining Officers in the Crown Court: all of which documents clearly indicate that they are issued for guidance, and stress the paramount duty of the determining officer in reaching his decision to take account of all the relevant circumstances in the particular case.

There are also the decisions of taxing masters on appeals made to them pursuant to the Regulations. It must be remembered that the Regulations require the taxing master to give a written decision in every case, and in the majority of appeals the decision is intended solely for the benefit of those to whom it is actually addressed. On the other hand certain decisions which are considered to be of general interest or importance, particularly those containing statements of principles of taxation, are set out in greater detail, and are published for the benefit of all those concerned with the determination and taxation of criminal costs. In general, only those decisions which are so published should be relied upon by determining officers and appellants. The other decisions will usually be of little supportive value to an appeal, although there can be no objection to their being quoted by appellants, who may have obtained permission to refer to them.

Thus "conflict" between "directions" from the appropriate authority and from taxing masters should rarely, if ever, occur. In these particular appeals it is apparent that the confusion to which counsel referred led some of the determining officers to the mistaken belief that they had detected a conflict in relation to the Stockley decision.

My function on each of the appeals before me is to decide whether the fees which were allowed in each case were reasonably sufficient, in the cases under the Legal Aid Regulations, to provide fair remuneration for counsel and, in the case under the Central Funds Regulations, to compensate the prosecutor for the expenses properly incurred by him in respect of counsel's fees. In so doing I shall endeavour to apply the principles which have been indicated above, but my primary duty is to ascertain and to take into account all the relevant facts and circumstances of each individual case.

Regina
v
Hindle

Date of Determining Officer's Reasons
November 1986

Date of Taxing Master's Decision
October 1987

Payment of Counsel's Travelling Expenses Incurred in Attending a Conference

The issue raised by this appeal was whether the Regulations contain any provision under which counsel may be reimbursed the expenses actually and reasonably incurred by him in travelling from his chambers to a prison or other place where the defendant is confined, for the purpose of holding a necessary conference with the defendant.

Counsel submitted that regulation 8(5)(*b*) conferred a discretionary power upon the determining officer to allow travelling expenses and claimed that it should be applied in the particular circumstances of this case.

It was submitted on behalf of the Lord Chancellor's Department that regulation 8(5)(*b*) could be applied and that in exceptional circumstances it might be proper for subsidiary fees payable under regulation 8(4)(*c*)(i) to be increased to take account of travelling expenses.

The master held, as a matter of principle, that regulation 8(5)(*b*) conferred upon the appropriate authority, in a case falling within that sub-paragraph, power to re-imburse counsel for travelling expenses incurred in attending a conference. This was subject to the expenses having been actually and reasonably incurred and having been necessarily and exclusively attributable to the attendance in question.

The master then went on to consider whether the circumstances in which counsel travelled to two conferences in this case (to a psychiatric hospital) were exceptional.

THE MASTER allowed the appeal and extracts from his decision are as follows: If it is necessary for counsel to have a conference with his client who is detained in prison or elsewhere and the prison authorities will only produce the client at the place of detention then counsel is under a duty to travel to attend the conference and it is an exceptional circumstance for him to have to do so. I do not consider the fact, referred to by the Lord Chancellor's Department, that in criminal proceedings this situation may often arise has any bearing on the question whether it is an exceptional circumstance so far as counsel is concerned, nor do I consider the size of the expenses to be relevant.

In this case I am satisfied that it was an exceptional circumstance for counsel to travel to the psychiatric hospital and that travelling expenses should have been taken into account in assessing his fees for the two conferences found to be necessary.

Regina
v
Huggett

Date of Determining Officer's Reasons
February 1987

Date of Taxing Master's Decision
January 1988

Assessment of Counsel's Basic Fee – Standard Fee Inappropriate (regulation 8(2))

The issue raised in this appeal, which was one of four involving the same point of principle, relates to the assessment of a basic brief fee under regulation 8(2), which provides:

> "Where the work allowed has been done by junior counsel in the Crown Court, the appropriate authority shall, subject to paragraph (3), allow such of the standard fees specified in Part I of Schedule 2 as may be applicable to that work, unless it appears to the appropriate authority that the standard fee would be inappropriate taking into account all the relevant circumstances of the case, in which case it shall allow fees in accordance with paragraphs (4) and (5)."

The taxing master found that the sole point in issue, arising from the appeal, was in what circumstances should it appear to the determining officer in the exercise of the discretion vested in him, that a standard fee would be inappropriate in a particular case.

The master upheld the submission made on behalf of the Lord Chancellor that the discretion must be exercised in accordance with the provisions to be found in the Regulations following the authority of *R v Sandhu* **Costs LR (Core Vol) 451** (per Mustill J Taxing Compendium SJI).

The master summarised the relevant provisions in the Regulations as follows:

The determining officer:
(a) shall allow such work as appears to him to have been actually and reasonably done (regulation 8(1));
(b) shall take into account all the relevant circumstances of the case to which the claim relates (regulation 8(2)) and these include the nature, importance, complexity or difficulty of the work and the time involved (regulation 3(5)(*b*));
(c) must, subject to the limitations imposed by the Regulations, allow

fair remuneration for work actually and reasonably done (regulation 3(5)(*a*)).

The master said

> "... these provisions contain the basic principle which must be applied by the determining officer and which may be stated very simply: 'If the standard fee would not provide fair remuneration for the work actually and reasonably done then it is inappropriate for the purposes of regulation 8(2)'. Nevertheless application of this simple principle gives rise to further difficulty if the fullest advantages of using standard fees in terms of simplicity of assessment and prompt payment are to be obtained. ..."

To meet this difficulty both the appellant and counsel for the Lord Chancellor were agreed that additional guidance was required and that such guidance may conveniently be encapsulated under the "swings and roundabouts" principle.

The master went on to say:

> "... the 'swings and roundabouts principle' must be operated within the limits imposed by the principles set out in the Regulations so that if the application of a standard fee would result in the award of remuneration which is plainly neither fair nor reasonable then the determination must be made on an ex post facto basis. Inevitably there will be cases which are marginal and in dealing with these the determining officer must make a value judgment as best he can having regard to all the relevant circumstances of the case before him.
>
> There is one further consideration to which the attention of the determining officer should be directed. Schedule 2 Part I paragraph 1 of the Regulations specifies the work which the standard fee shall cover and as it is with the work actually done that the determining officer is concerned, the word 'standard' has to be applied to that work; applied in this sense 'standard' means 'usual', 'normal' or 'of average quality'. Therefore any case falling within the categories to which standard fees are required to be applied must be a usual case of its kind, viewed as to weight, gravity or complexity. This applies equally to all cases falling within the categories without regard to the intrinsic weight, gravity or complexity which may be found in one class of case as distinct from another. Thus by way of illustration only, the simple theft of a bottle of milk from a doorstep and a case of causing death by reckless driving are both within the categories and comparisons between them are irrelevant for the purpose of deciding whether they are 'normal' for the purpose of applying the standard fee. It is in deciding whether an individual case is a normal one of its kind that the most difficult qualitative judgment has to be made. Using the illustration given above, in order to take the simple theft out of the standard, something very unusual or complex would have to exist whereas in the motoring case some comparatively minor problem of complexity or difficulty might be sufficient ..."

Regina

v

Sullivan

Date of Determining Officer's Reasons
July 1988

Date of Taxing Master's Decision
June 1989

Regulation 8(4)(*c*)(i): Views

In this case counsel claimed for a substantial number of hours spent inspecting prosecution statements made by persons not intended to be called as witnesses. They were disclosed to the defence in accordance with the guidelines issued by the Attorney General. Their number was such that the prosecution declined to make copies as is, in many cases, the normal practice, and insisted that they were inspected.

It was argued that this was "a view" and accordingly a separate fee was payable under regulation 8(4)(*c*)(i) of the Regulations which provides for the payment of a subsidiary fee for attendances at (inter alia) views not covered by the fees payable under sub-paragraphs (*a*) and (*b*) of the Regulations namely the basic fee and refresher fee. Those fees cover views which take place on the first day of the hearing or a subsequent day of the trial in respect of which a refresher is paid. That does not apply in this case. The issue is whether the attendance at the police station for the examination of the statements was a "view". The attendance was clearly not "an attendance at a conference or a consultation" nor can the work done be construed as "written advice" within the meaning of sub-paragraph (ii) of regulation 8(4)(*c*).

Counsel put details of his claim for this fee in box 7 on the claim form. He described the work as "prep 511/2 hours at the police station". In the written representations on behalf of the Lord Chancellor it was suggested that, as counsel had not claimed the fee specifically as a "view" under sub-paragraph (i), he was precluded from claiming that it was a view on appeal by virtue of regulation 11(11) which provides that "for the purposes of the appeal … no ground of objection shall be valid which was not raised on the re-determination under Regulation 10". The master held that to construe the Regulations in this way is to make the keyhole through which counsel has to pass too small. It was clear from the claim and from the explanatory schedule which was annexed thereto that counsel was claiming a separate fee for his attendance at the police station. The determining officer rejected the argument that a subsidiary fee was payable in respect of this work on the grounds that it was "preparation" which had to be considered within the basic fee and not remunerated separately.

The master accepted that it was reasonable and more economic for counsel to have considered these statements for himself than for his instructing solicitor to do so.

Counsel suggested that a "view" happens when a barrister was required to travel to look at something. A view was required in this case because counsel was required to look at the papers and a "view" was a form of preparation in any circumstances. The Lord Chancellor argued that preparation does not become a view merely because it is done at a particular location. It means more than doing work at a particular location, it means a visit to a place in order to see the place itself, or something, or some physical relationship between things at that place, which may have direct evidential value in the case. The master accepted and agreed with that interpretation "with one gloss only – a visit must occur because proper consideration can be given to the matters seen only at the place where they are situated". He added that in this case the documents could have been considered in counsel's chambers, or at the offices of his solicitors or any convenient location if copies had been available. It would have been otherwise if the examination of the documents required special equipment, for example they might have to be considered with special or other scientific equipment. In those circumstances the visit to the place where that equipment was located could properly be described as a view. That did not apply in this case. It follows that the determining officer was correct in considering this work in relation to the amount he allowed under regulation 8(4)(a) for the "basic fee". The fact that counsel had to carry out that work at a location away from his own chambers and at a time not wholly under his control are factors which the determining officer should take into account as being "exceptional circumstances" which places upon counsel an unusual burden which can properly be reflected in the basic fee.

Although the determining officer properly held that the time spent by counsel in this work was to be treated as preparation he made an allowance to compensate counsel for his travelling time and expenses for the eight days spent at the police station. It was argued on the behalf of the Lord Chancellor that counsel had made no claim in respect of this work, other than in respect of the hours he spent at the police station and had provided no information about travelling time. Accordingly, it was said, the determining officer misdirected himself in allowing this sum or his travelling time and expenses in connection with that work. It was however conceded that whilst there was no specific provision in the Regulations for payment of travelling time or expenses incurred, except when counsel travels to a distant court, it would be possible to enhance the fee allowed for that work under regulation 8(5)(b) to take account thereof. It is common practice, reflected by the Lord Chancellor's Departments Notes for Guidance to Taxing Officers, to take into account travelling time when assessing counsel's fees for a conference. It was clearly "out of the ordinary" for counsel to have to travel to the police station for the purpose of carrying out preparation which is remunerated as part of the basic fee. The determining officer should accordingly have enhanced that fee to take account of those exceptional circumstances, he should not have made a specific additional allowance in respect of that work. Counsel did not give any detail about the expenses which he incurred, but the determining officer in making the enhancement is entitled to take account of his own local knowledge of the time which it would take counsel to travel within the city and the expense of so doing in assessing a proper additional figure to be allowed.

Regina
v
Conboy

Date of Determining Officer's Reasons
November 1988

Date of Taxing Master's Decision
January 1990

Schedule 2 Part 1(11) and Schedule 2 Part 2(5): Travelling and Hotel Expenses of Queen's Counsel

This appeal related solely to the amount to be paid to counsel for his travelling expenses to court on the trial of the defendant.

Counsel lived in Wandsworth and practised from chambers in the Temple. The defendant appeared before the Crown Court at Canterbury on one occasion and at Maidstone on four occasions. Counsel travelled each day by car from his home to the court and claimed a sum for each day's travel equivalent to the amount which he would have incurred had he travelled by public transport from his chambers.

On determination of his claim counsel was allowed his travelling expenses based on the mileage from his home to the court each day at the relevant public mileage rate per mile. In his reasons the determining officer did not accept that counsel was entitled to mileage at the standard rate, that rate being payable where for good reason counsel used his car, for example where the case papers were heavy and bulky. He held no such reason existed in this case. Counsel chose to travel by car and was paid accordingly. The payment was based upon the distance between chambers and the court excluding any allowance for travel between counsel's home and his chambers.

The Lord Chancellor made representations under regulation 15(7) of the Legal Aid in Criminal and Care Proceedings (Costs) Regulations 1989 with a view to ensuring that the public interest was taken into account.

Schedule 1, Part 1 at paragraph 9 states:

"Where counsel is instructed to appear in a court which is not within 25 miles of his Chambers, the appropriate authority may allow an amount in respect of Counsel's attendance at that court to cover any travelling and hotel expenses actually and reasonably incurred and necessarily and exclusively attributable to Counsel's attendance at that Court; provided that the amount shall not be greater than the amount, if any, which would be payable to Counsel practising from the nearest local bar unless Counsel can justify his attendance having regard to all the circumstances of the case."

Counsel conceded that he had used his car for his own personal convenience and that there was available a convenient public transport service and accepted that the expenditure calculated in accordance with the standard rate was not reasonably incurred and not payable in accordance with the decision in *R* v *Slessor* (TC S23) **Costs LR (Core Vol) 438**. He therefore limited his claim to the notional costs of travel by public transport which is an expenditure which he contended was less than his actual expenditure.

It was represented on behalf of the Lord Chancellor that, as the public transport costs were not incurred, counsel could only be paid those costs which he did incur, namely travel by private car at the public transport mileage rate.

THE MASTER held that: The Regulations refer to "travelling expenses" and not to "travelling costs", the issue is therefore what expense has counsel incurred which is to be reimbursed to him under paragraph 9 of the Schedule. The "public transport mileage rate" the amount of which is prescribed by the Costs in Criminal Cases (General) Regulation 1986 is, according to paragraph v on page 17 of the Lord Chancellor's directions to Determining Officers, calculated by reference to the average cost of public transport per mile. Similarly the standard mileage rate is, I understand, calculated by reference to the average cost of running a motor car including such matters as depreciation, insurance, maintenance etc which are referable to the running of a car of the relevant engine capacity.

Neither rate is a precise measure of the actual cost of a particular form of transport but is intended to provide a mechanism for reimbursing expenses incurred for travelling by car in two separately defined situations: (a) when travel by public transport is available and reasonably convenient: or (b) when it is not. In the second situation, which does not apply here, the cost is calculated on the standard mileage rate even though some part of the elements in the calculation could be said to be referable to ownership of the vehicle rather than to the use for the particular journey undertaken. In the first situation, which is that applicable to the journey under question in this appeal, the amount of the expense *reasonably incurred* under the regulation is restricted under the rules laid down in the decision of *R* v *Slessor* to the cost of travel by public transport or to the notional cost calculated at the public transport mileage rate. The Regulations empower the appropriate authority to reimburse counsel for the expenditure "actually and reasonably incurred" (under the 1988 Regulations) or the expenditure reasonably incurred (under the 1989 Regulations). I do not know the reason for the alteration in the Regulations but the 1989 wording is in my view, wider than the wording of the 1988 Regulations. I can see nothing in either set of Regulations which restricts payment for a journey made by car to an amount calculated by reference to the public transport mileage rate, if the actual expenditure (calculated by reference to the standard mileage rate) would be greater than the cost which counsel would have incurred if he had travelled the whole distance from his chambers to the court by public transport. The amount claimed by counsel satisfies this test and accordingly I allow this appeal.

Regina
v
Clarke

Date of Determining Officer's Reasons
August 1989

Date of Taxing Master's Decision
June 1991

The Connection Between Delivery of the Brief and Payment of Brief Fee

In this case the defendant was privately represented until approximately two weeks before the hearing when legal aid was granted. As the solicitors were not put in funds, by the defendant, the brief to counsel was not delivered until after legal aid had been granted.

Counsel submitted his claim for costs and claimed his full brief fee under the legal aid order. The determining officer held that only work which was carried out under the legal aid order should be paid for from the legal aid fund. Any work done prior to the grant of legal aid was not recoverable from the legal aid fund.

Counsel argued that no brief fee becomes payable until a brief is delivered to counsel. He further argued that the fact that he may have undertaken some preparation work prior to the delivery of the brief is immaterial since if no brief were ever delivered that work would have been entirely wasted and he could not have claimed payment in respect of it at all. This, said counsel, is part of the way in which the Bar conducts itself. He went on to argue that it is only when the brief is delivered that the full brief fee becomes payable. Counsel suggests that a brief fee in a criminal legal aid case is not actually payable until the first day of the hearing.

On behalf of the Lord Chancellor it was submitted that payment can only be made for work done under a legal aid order and therefore payment can only be made for work done on or after the date of commencement of legal aid and any preparation done prior to the order being made cannot therefore be allowed. Regulation 4 of the Legal Aid in Criminal and Care Proceedings (Costs) Regulations 1989 provides:

"(1)   Costs in respect of work done under a Legal Aid Order shall be determined by the appropriate authority in accordance with these regulations.
    (2)   In determining costs the appropriate authority shall subject to and in accordance with these regulations: –

    (a)   take into account all the relevant circumstances of the case including the nature, importance, complexity or difficulty of the work and the time involved, and

    (b)   allow a reasonable amount in respect of all work reasonably done."

The master held that the contention put forward on behalf of the Lord Chancellor is entirely correct and that such preparation work as counsel undertook prior to the granting of the legal aid order was done entirely at his own risk.

    It was however necessary to assess exactly what work has been done after the issue of the legal aid order and to allow reasonable remuneration in respect of that.

Regina
v
Mills and Morris

Date of Determining Officer's Reasons
February 1992

Date of Taxing Master's Decisions
December 1993

Counsel's Refreshers for Week-end Sittings Regulation 9(5)(b)

The issue in this appeal was whether the fact that a court waiting for the jury's verdict on a Saturday and Sunday is, of itself, grounds for enhancement of a refresher.

In this case the court sat on Saturday 21 and Sunday 22 December in order to complete the trial by receiving the jury's verdict before the Christmas adjournment. The court sat between 10.05 and 5.10 on the Saturday and between 10.02 and 5.40 on the Sunday. On determination counsel was allowed the same enhanced refreshers as he had received for attending during the week. Counsel submitted that the refreshers should be further enhanced in respect of the sittings at the week-end.

On behalf of the Lord Chancellor it was submitted that where the appropriate authority, taking into account all the relevant circumstances of the case, considers that owing to the exceptional circumstances of the case the amount payable by way of the prescribed maximum would not provide reasonable remuneration, it is empowered to allow such amounts as appears to it to be reasonable remuneration for the relevant *work*: regulation 9(5)(*b*) of the Legal Aid in Criminal and Care Proceedings (Costs) Regulations 1989.

It was also submitted that the relevant test is not just whether there is an exceptional circumstance (sitting on the Saturday and Sunday before Christmas) but also that the prescribed maximum will not reasonably remunerate the *work* done, the responsibility borne or the hours involved on those days (TONG paragraphs 57 to 65). It was submitted that the *work* done on the Saturday and Sunday would be the same as would have been done if it had taken place on a weekday and was, accordingly, reasonably remunerated at the same rate as that which was allowed for the comparable weekdays.

The master held that barristers being in private practice are not wage earners but professionals and that it is in the nature of a professional's work that, from time to time, he or she will be expected to work unsocial hours without being remunerated at a higher rate in the way that a salaried person would be. However, in coming to his decision the master made clear that it was not arrived at due to the fact that for the two days in question counsel was simply waiting for the jury to return its verdict. He said there could be no justification for paying less for such a day's work than for a day when counsel is cross-examining strenuously throughout.

Reasons for Decision in Regina v Mills

Crown Courts do not normally sit on Saturdays and Sundays but in this case the court did sit on Saturday 21 December and Sunday 22 December 1991 from 10.05 am to 5.10 pm on the Saturday and from 10.02 am to 5.40 pm on the Sunday in each case to receive and consider the jury's verdict.

The sole question, and it is a very important one of principle in this case, is whether counsel should be paid an enhanced refresher for those two days.

The case was originally assigned to Master Prince who invited the Lord Chancellor to put in written submissions which he has done. Before Master Prince could hear the appeal however, he sadly died and thus it falls to me to dispose of the appeal in his place.

The determining officer allowed Mr Jeffrey £360 for each of the two days in question and Mr Lodder, his fully led junior, £180, that is half the above fees. Mr Jeffreys claimed enhanced refreshers at the rate of £650 for the Saturday and Sunday but at the oral hearing before me he resiled from that claim and said that he would limit his claim in the event of success to £500.

As this is a test case and of general interest, and not just to the parties, I think it right that I should set out the arguments in some detail.

The written submissions of Mr Jeffreys and Mr Lodder read as follows:

"Counsel is appealing against the Taxing Officer's refusal to increase the refreshers paid in relation to Saturday and Sunday, 21 and 22 December. Counsel is content with the brief fee allowed which properly reflects the serious nature of the work involved in the case.

The trial lasted longer than expected and because of the impending Christmas holiday, the jury was sent out to consider their verdicts on Saturday, 21 December. As this could not have been anticipated, counsel was left with little choice but to be in full attendance during the entire time the jury were in retirement which totalled two full days.

The Taxing Officer does not consider that attendance at court over a full week-end, prior to Christmas week merits any payment in addition to an ordinary refresher. The fact that for the majority of the two days counsel was waiting for a jury to return verdicts, rather than on his feet in court does not detract from the fact that he had no choice but to be in court.

Whilst it is of course accepted that the professional life of a barrister often involves working unsocial hours, there is some degree of choice. Court hours are relatively predictable and confined to five days a week. It appears that there is provision in the guidelines to enable Taxing Officers to pay enhanced refreshers when a court day extends beyond 5.30 pm, therefore it is assumed that such a provision takes into account the additional burden of a long day and to some extent the unsocial nature of such long hours.

In this case, counsel would submit that a court sitting the entire week-end prior to Christmas places far more burden upon those concerned than a longer than average day during the week. In this particular case, the trial having commenced the previous week in fact meant that counsel had been in court for seven full, consecutive days with no break. It seems fair to suggest that in most other jobs when people are expected to work on their days off, there is some benefit paid over and above a basic day's wage. The added burden of the week-end prior to a Christmas holiday inevitably meant that plans had to be cancelled.

The purpose of this appeal is on a point of principle. It would seem entirely appropriate for some guidance to be given to Taxing Officers to clarify the situation which will inevitably occur again at some point in the future."

The written representations put in on behalf of the Lord Chancellor read as follows:

"1.   These representations are made on behalf of the Lord Chancellor under Regulation 15(7) of the Legal Aid in Criminal and Care Proceedings (Costs) Regulations 1989.

POINT IN ISSUE
2.   The issue is whether the fact that a court sits on a Saturday and Sunday prior to Christmas is, of itself, grounds for enhancement of a refresher. As mentioned in paragraph 4 below, enhanced refreshers were allowed by the Determining Officer at a rate exceeding the maximum prescribed by the Regulations; counsel, however, seek a further enhancement of the refreshers for the Saturday and Sunday.

THIS PARTICULAR CASE
3.   Mills' trial lasted over 11 days in December 1991. In order to complete the trial before the Christmas adjournment, the court sat on both Saturday 21 and Sunday 22 December. On Saturday, the court sat at 10 am, the jury retiring to consider their verdict at 10.05 am. Having yet to reach a verdict by the end of the day, the jury retired to a hotel and the court adjourned at 5.10 pm. On Sunday, the court sat 10.02 am to give the jury further directions, followed by 20 minutes of legal argument relating to the Court's powers to take verdicts and a sentence on a Sunday. As a result of this, verdicts were taken with the sentence for this defendant being postponed to a suitable weekday. The court rose at 5.40 pm on the Sunday.

4.   Leading counsel claimed enhanced refreshers in this case at £400 for the week days, with a further enhancement for the week-end sitting at £650 per day. He was allowed the same enhanced refreshers as he had received for attending during the week, namely £360 per day.

COUNSEL'S SUBMISSIONS

5.   David Jeffreys QC the leader in Silk, and his junior Peter Lodder, submit that:

(i)   A court sitting at the week-end places far more of a burden on those concerned than a longer than average day during the week;

(ii)   That they had been in court for seven full consecutive days with no break. That they submit that in most other jobs, when people are expected to work on their days off, there is some benefit paid over and above the basic days wage;

(iii)   The added burden of sitting the week-end prior to a Christmas holiday inevitably meant that plans had to be cancelled and they submit that it would be entirely appropriate to allow considerably enhanced refreshers for the inconvenience, additional burden and unsocial nature of this week-end sitting.

LCD'S SUBMISSIONS

6.   Where the appropriate authority, taking into account all the relevant circumstances of the case, considers that owing to the exceptional circumstances of the case the amount payable by way of the prescribed maximum would not provide reasonable remuneration, it is empowered to allow such amounts as appears to it to be reasonable remuneration for the relevant work: Regulation 9(5)(*b*) of the Legal Aid in Criminal and Care Proceedings (Costs) Regulations 1989.

7.   The relevant test is not just whether there is an exceptional circumstance (sitting Saturday and Sunday on the week-end prior to Christmas) but also that the prescribed maximum will not reasonably remunerate the *work* done, the responsibility borne or the hours involved on those days (TONG paragraphs 57 to 65). We submit that in fact the work done on the Saturday and Sunday was the same as would have been done if it had taken place on a weekday and was, accordingly, reasonably remunerated at the same rate as that which was allowed for weekdays.

8.   We do not accept that overtime payment is common for members of the profession. Counsel are not salaried employees and their fees are not assessed on that basis. It has not been the practice of the Bar to seek enhanced refreshers for unsocial hours.

9.   Greenslade on Costs (Section 6.50) supports our submission that the circumstances of a court sitting at the week-end does not of itself merit any automatic enhancement:

'The jury retired to consider its verdict on the previous day, returning to Court to continue their deliberations throughout the Saturday. Verdicts were reached during the afternoon, and the Court adjourned at 3.35 pm. Counsel claimed that the refresher paid for that day would be at an enhanced rate, saying that it was general practice in the whole world to pay for work on a Saturday and that Court sittings on that day are sufficiently unusual to justify payment at the higher rate.

The argument that the refresher should be enhanced solely because it relates to a Saturday is not founded on authority nor on the practice of the Bar which has never sought an enhanced refresher for work done on a particular day.'

10. We also submit that the proximity to Christmas and the fact that the sitting extended to a Sunday whilst increasing the unusualness of the circumstances of the case and inconvenience caused did not significantly affect the work done.

CONCLUSION
11. The Taxing Master is asked to dismiss this aspect of the appeal by agreeing that the fact that the sittings extended over the week-end does not of itself justify further enhancement of the refreshers allowed for the Saturday and Sunday."

Mr Jeffreys appeared at the oral hearing of these appeals, both on his own behalf and on behalf of his junior, and very ably expanded on the submissions set out above.

He quite properly pointed out that the golden thread running throughout the Regulations, which alone determine remuneration in these cases, is that of reasonableness.

The relevant regulation is regulation 9(5) which I will quote in full:

"In the case of proceedings in the Crown Court or Magistrate's Court, the appropriate authority shall, except in relation to work for which a standard fee is allowed under paragraph (2), allow such fees in respect of such work as it considers reasonable in such amounts as it may determine in accordance with Part II of Schedule 2; provided that:

(a) Where any work allowed was done after 30 June 1994, the appropriate authority may allow such fees in such amounts as appears to it to be reasonable remuneration for such work having regard to the amount specified in Part II of Schedule 2; or
(b) Where it appears to the appropriate authority, taking into account all the relevant circumstances of the case, that owing to the exceptional circumstances of the case the amount payable by way of fees in accordance with Part II of Schedule 2 would not provide reasonable remuneration for some or all of the work it has allowed, it may allow such amounts as appears to it to be reasonable remuneration for the relevant work."

As to what might amount to exceptional circumstances Mr Jeffreys cited the case of *R v Ford-Lloyd* (S6 in the Taxing Compendium) **Costs LR (Core Vol) 424.** In that case the solicitors appealed against the rates per hour allowed for preparation work and for travelling and waiting. The case was handled throughout by an articled clerk under supervision. When the bill was submitted for taxation the determining officer was asked to implement paragraph 3 of Schedule 1 to the 1982 Regulations. The reason for this was stated to be that the defendant was on life licence for manslaughter and that made the case exceptional. On the hearing of the appeal it was suggested that the articled clerk had done the work with exceptional competence and dispatch. The determining officer allowed only the standard rate, but also allowed a claim for one hour supervision by a senior solicitor.

The taxing master held that the articled clerk acted with exceptional competence and dispatch and said that the hourly rate claimed, which was above the standard rate, was reasonable. However, having regard to the specific allowance made for supervision he made no increase.

Mr Jeffreys freely conceded that this was a "solicitor's case" and the wording of the Regulations is not identical and that he could only draw limited benefit from that case in support of his submissions.

Next, Mr Jeffreys submitted that the introduction to Butterworth's costs written by the present Chief Master indicated that exceptional cases such as treason and terrorism qualified for enhanced rates but there was nothing in that commentary which confined the right to pay enhanced rates to the facts of the particular case.

As to the quotation from Greenslade on Costs, which is cited in the Lord Chancellor's written submissions, Mr Jeffreys indicated that it was not of particular help, since, although it referred to a case, there is no reference to that case which could in any way be followed up.

Finally, Mr Jeffreys referred me to paragraphs 7, 20 and 57 of TONG. The first two deal with general principles and repeat the word "reasonable".

So far as paragraph 57 was concerned, interestingly the expression there used is "fair remuneration" rather than reasonable remuneration.

In answer to questions from me, Mr Jeffreys conceded that the fact that the week-end in question was just before Christmas really added nothing to his submissions. Although it was a particularly inconvenient time to be in court, he accepted that there could be other equally inconvenient times at other times of the year and he did not therefore seek to rely on the fact that this was the week-end immediately preceding Christmas.

He also conceded, as of course he had to do, that magistrates' courts do sit on a Saturday and counsel does not claim enhanced rates for such work but he pointed out that it is very rare indeed for a magistrates' court to sit on a Saturday having previously sat throughout the preceding five week days. Finally Mr Jeffreys said that he did not seek to draw any distinction between the refreshers to be paid on a Saturday and the Sunday on the basis that there was some research into the question of whether the judge could pass sentence on the Sunday. (In the event the judge indicated to the defendant what the sentence would be, but it was formally passed in the New Year).

Although I find the arguments finely balanced I have come to the conclusion, not without some regret, that the Lord Chancellor's submissions should prevail. Barristers in private practice are not wage earners but professionals, and, in my view, it is in the nature of a professional's work, that, from time to time, he or she will be expected to work at unsocial hours without being remunerated at a higher rate or indeed any rate for that extra work in the way that a salaried person would be. I should perhaps add that in coming to this conclusion I am deliberately not resting my decision on the fact that for the two days in question the barristers concerned were simply waiting for the jury to return its verdict. There can be no justification for paying less for such a days' work than for a day when counsel is cross-examining strenuously throughout.

Reasons for Decision in Regina v Morris

Mr Feinberg, the junior counsel but now in Silk, was led by Mr Rock Tansey QC for the defence of Paul Morris, who, with a co-defendant Thomas Mills, was charged with murder and unlawful possession of a sawn-off shotgun.

Counsel's principal ground of appeal is that he should be allowed enhanced refreshers for Saturday 21 and Sunday 22 December 1991 when the court sat for two complete days to receive the jury's verdict. This is an identical argument to that advanced by Mr Jeffreys on behalf of himself and Mr Peter Lodder his junior for Morris' co-defendant Mills, and I have dealt with and dismissed that appeal in separate reasons and do not therefore intend to repeat those reasons here. On that point the appeal must fail for the same reasons.

Counsel however seeks an increase in his basic fee of £3,750 and other refreshers. The £3,750 which was allowed to him was precisely half that allowed to his leader Mr Tansey who has not appealed. Miss Kincade, who appeared on Mr Feinberg's behalf, accepted that there were no special features which distinguished this case from the ordinary case which is of course governed by paragraph 49 of TONG which states that a fully led junior should normally receive half his leader's fees.

In those circumstances, there being no other grounds of appeal, this appeal in respect of the basic fee and other refreshers must also fail and is hereby dismissed.

Regina
v
O'Brien and Ollife

Queen's Bench Division
20 December 1984

In this case two defendants applied to the magistrates' court for legal aid for the Crown Court. The magistrates' court granted legal aid for each defendant jointly with the other, the legal aid order for each reading "legal aid granted shall consist of representation by solicitor and counsel jointly with the co-defendant …". The solicitor assigned, instructed counsel for trial who advised that the two men should be represented by separate counsel and at their trial both men were separately represented.

On legal aid taxation the fees of the second counsel were disallowed. On appeal, the taxing master also disallowed the fees because the legal aid order did not authorise separate counsel to be instructed for the two defendants. On appeal to Queen's Bench Division, Mr Justice Hobhouse in his judgment said:

> "The court has the power to assign the solicitor; it does not as well have the power to assign the counsel to be instructed by the solicitor to appear in the Crown Court, it cannot by its order fetter the right of the solicitor to select counsel. It is wrong to construe regulation 14 (of the Legal Aid in Criminal Proceedings (General) Regulations 1968 as amended) as giving a power to assign counsel when that power is not to be found in some other regulation; still less should it be construed as giving the court the power to make a legal aid order which requires the assisted persons to be represented by the same counsel when the authority making the order has not even got the power to assign counsel at all."

The Lord Chancellor was invited to make representations to the appeal to ensure that the public interest was taken into account and appropriate representations were made on his behalf.

Court staff are asked to ensure that they do not make legal aid orders which purport to limit the right of selection of counsel, or which might be thought to do so.

Section 30(6) is clear in its terms. The Legal Aid Order extends to giving advice on the existence of grounds of appeal and the making of an application for a case to be stated.

Rule 26 of the Crown Court Rules 1982 sets out the procedure for making an application; rule 26(2) provides that the application shall state the ground on which the decision of the court is questioned. Rule 26(5) provides for a communication of the judge's decision on the application. Sub-paragraph 7 and subsequent sub-paragraphs set out the procedure to be adopted if the judge grants the application. Counsel argued that as the heading to the rule is entitled "Application to Crown Court to State Case" and the body of the rule refers throughout to "applicant" the whole of the procedure created by the rule is part of the application referred to in section 30(6). This is a construction I cannot accept. In my judgment the section extends legal aid so as to cover all procedural steps prescribed by paragraphs 1–6 of the Rules and that the scope of Legal Aid Order does not extent to any work done after the date of the decision on the application.

It may be that in some cases it is reasonable for counsel to draft a case as part of the application under paragraph 2 of the Rules so that, for example, the judge can see the reason behind the formulation of the grounds. Counsel drafted the case stated after the application had been granted and therefore the work done by him was outside the scope of the Order.

Regina
v
Boswell
Regina
v
Halliwell
(Taxation Review)

Royal Courts of Justice
Tuesday, 3 February 1987

Judgment
(As Approved)

LEGGATT J: Before the court are applications by two counsel, Mr Normal Jones, QC, and Mr Jeremy Barnett, for review of their fees and costs under legal aid orders dated respectively 29 February 1984 and 28 November 1984. By reason of the importance of the applications, I directed that they be adjourned into court for judgment.

In each case counsel had prepared his brief in the expectation of a full hearing in the Crown Court, which had then gone short. A lesser fee was allowed than that claimed. On re-determination the Chief Clerk adhered to his original decision. On appeal to Master Devonshire the appeal was allowed in both cases and an appropriate additional payment, the amount of which is not challenged, was added to the fee.

When the matter first came before the taxing master, Mr Barnett appeared both on his own behalf and on behalf of Mr Jones, but when the substantive argument occurred both counsel were represented by Mr Bartfield, as they were in this court.

To the sums awarded to the appellants was added the sum of £66 for counsel's expenses in attending the appeals. Each counsel now applies for an order that the decision of Master Devonshire contained in his certificate dated 4 July 1986 of his review of the taxation of the appellant's bill of costs payable under the legal aid order be reversed, and that there be substituted a finding that counsel is entitled to a professional fee or other remuneration for preparing and attending an appeal on his own behalf to a taxing master under regulation 11 of the Legal Aid in Criminal Proceedings (Costs) Regulations 1982 ("the 1982 Regulations") or on behalf of another member of the Bar on appeal under the same Regulations, in addition in either case to his actual out of pocket expenses incurred. The taxing master certified that the question to be decided involves a point of principle of general importance.

Regulation 10 of the 1982 Regulations deals with the re-determination of costs by an appropriate authority, which in this case was the Chief Clerk of the Crown Court.

Regulation 11 of the 1982 Regulations deals with appeals to a taxing master, and so far as material provides as follows:

> "(1)   Where the appropriate authority has given its reasons for its decision on a re-determination under Regulation 10, a solicitor or counsel who is dissatisfied with that decision may appeal to a Taxing Master.
>
> ...
>
> (5)   The notice of appeal shall state whether the appellant wishes to appear or to be represented or whether he will accept a decision given in his absence.
>
> ...
>
> (14)   Save where he confirms or decreases the sums re-determined under Regulation 10, the Taxing Master may allow the appellant a sum in respect of part or all of any reasonable costs (including any fee payable in respect of an appeal) incurred by him on connection with the appeal."

From these paragraphs it is plain that (a) for purposes of an appeal to a taxing master, the solicitor or counsel concerned (as the case may be) is treated as the appellant, (b) an appellant can elect to be represented at the hearing of an appeal, and (c) an appellant may be awarded a sum in respect of part or all of any reasonable costs incurred by him in connection with the appeal.

The reference in paragraph (14) to "any fee payable in respect of an appeal" is to the fee which an appellant must pay for the privilege of appealing: if he wins it is returnable, whereas if he loses it is forfeited.

By force of regulation 2 of the 1982 Regulations:

> "In these Regulations, unless the context otherwise requires –
> 'The Act' means the Legal Aid Act 1974.
> 'Costs' means, in the case of a solicitor, the fees and disbursements payable under Section 37 of the Act and, in the case of counsel, the fees payable under that Section."

Section 37 of the Legal Aid Act 1974 ("the 1974 Act") is concerned exclusively with the costs of the legal aid given to a legally assisted person. Section 37(2) of the 1974 Act provides that:

> "Subject to regulations under Section 39 below the costs of legal aid ordered to be given to a legally assisted person for the purpose of any proceedings shall include sums on account of the fees payable to any counsel or solicitor assigned to him and disbursements reasonably incurred by any such solicitor for or in connection with those proceedings."

Section 39 of the 1974 Act empowers the Lord Chancellor to make regulations. Such regulations may:

"(f)   prescribe rates or scales of payment of any costs payable in accordance with Section 37(1) above and the conditions under which such costs may be allowed.

(g)   provide for the assessment and taxation of such costs and for the review of any assessment made or taxation carried out under the Regulations."

On the hearing of these appeals, it has not been argued by Mr Sankey on behalf of the Lord Chancellor that he is not thereby empowered to provide for the payment of costs incurred by or on behalf of appellants appearing before the taxing master.

The taxing master's power under regulation 11(14) of the 1982 Regulations is to "allow the appellant a sum in respect of part or all of any reasonable costs ... incurred by him in connection with the appeal". Since such costs must have been incurred by the appellant solicitor or counsel personally rather than by their legally assisted client, and since such costs cannot but be incurred after the conclusion of the proceedings in respect of which legal aid is paid under section 37 of the 1974 Act, it follows that the "costs" referred to by regulation 11(14) must be costs other than as defined by regulation 2. In the language of regulation 2, the context of regulation 11(14) requires "costs" to mean something other than the definition in regulation 2. Since the "fee payable in respect of an appeal" is expressed to be included in the reasonable costs which may be allowed, the term "costs" is not confined to a fee so payable.

Though Master Devonshire was not so informed, the Bar Council had at its meeting on 22 May 1986 approved amendments to paragraph 50 of the Code of Conduct so that it now reads as follows:

"50(*a*)   Subject to sub-paragraph (*b*) of this paragraph and to such exceptions as may be authorised by custom of the Bar Council (including Annex 17), a barrister may not act in a professional capacity except upon the instructions of a solicitor, or in appropriate cases of a Parliamentary Agent or Patent Agent or Trade Mark Agent ...

(*b*)   A barrister may accept instructions with or without fee directly from and represent another barrister on that other barrister's appeal as to his fees before a Taxing Master without the intervention of a solicitor."

It is plain from an earlier ruling of the Professional Conduct Committee of the Bar Council that the practice referred to under sub-paragraph (*b*) had for some time past been treated by the Bar as approbated by custom. Although the taxing master was told of that ruling, he was not told of the relevant amendment to rule 50 of the Code of Conduct. On 25 March 1986 the Bar Council approved in principle the ruling of the Professional Conduct Committee: "that there was no impropriety on the hearing of a barrister's appeal on his fees before a Taxing Master concerning his own fees for that barrister to pay a fee to counsel other than himself." Where a taxation of counsel's fees is reviewed, the barrister concerned has since 1968 had a right to appear in person, created by the Regulations governing legal aid in criminal proceedings.

In written representations made to the taxing master on behalf of the Lord Chancellor, it was submitted "that the approach to be adopted in applying regulation 11(14) is to consider, according to the facts of the particular case, whether the costs in question were reasonably incurred; where costs have been reasonably incurred then the appellant may be allowed a sum in respect of part or all of them". By necessary implication from this passage it was admitted that costs would be recoverably, provided that they were reasonable. In this court Mr Sankey accepted that implication.

Master Devonshire accepted the argument advanced before him that the term "costs" in regulation 2 is so defined as to be incapable of applying to "costs" such as are the subject of regulation 11(14). The argument was apparently not put to the taxing master that the context of the latter paragraph must accordingly require a different meaning from that afforded by regulation 2. With regard to the scope of "costs" in regulation 11(14), the taxing master concluded that:

> "The practice and custom of the Bar does not entitle a barrister to claim a fee when he appears on his own behalf. When he does so he has to be treated as a litigant in person and is only entitled to recover his out of pocket expenses when he appears on an appeal under the Regulations in respect of his own fees."

The taxing master was therefore not prepared to allow a barrister to recover a fee for appearing on his own appeal. In relation to cases where one barrister appears on behalf of another to argue the appeal of that other, the taxing master, as I have indicated, was not told of the amendment to rule 50 of the Bar's Code of Conduct, though he was, of course, aware that taxing masters do permit an appellant counsel to be represented by another in certain circumstances. The taxing master concluded that:

> "If a fee which is paid to counsel does not fall within the definition (in regulation 2) then, however reasonably the appellant counsel may have acted, the fee cannot be allowed."

The basis upon which the taxing master nevertheless felt able to allow to Mr Bartfield, who appeared before him on behalf of both appellants, a sum "for counsel's expenses for attending the appeal" was unexplained. Whilst it is obvious that out of pocket expenses may be paid to counsel who argues his own appeal, if he falls to be treated as a litigant in person, it is less obvious why it is permissible to treat one counsel who appears on behalf of another in the same way since one litigant in person cannot appear for another.

In this court Mr Bartfield argued that a fee paid by one lawyer to another for legal representation must constitute part of the "costs", however defined, of the person paying. Mr Sankey did not seek to controvert this proposition, but argued that the incurring of such costs would only be reasonable in exceptional circumstances, for example where the appellant counsel is ill or abroad for a protracted period.

In my judgment a professional fee payable by one barrister to another for conducting the appeal of the former is capable of constituting part of the costs incurred by the appellant, within the meaning of regulation 11(14) of the 1982 Regulations. Whether such costs constitute "reasonable costs" within the meaning of that paragraph is a matter within the discretion of the taxing master.

Mr Sankey argues that because a barrister may not appear as counsel in a matter in which he himself is a party or has a significant pecuniary interest, counsel appearing on his own behalf before a taxing master is to be viewed as a litigant in person. This however disregards a barrister's long-standing right, referred to earlier in this judgment to appear on his own behalf by way of exception to the rule where taxation of his fees is concerned.

Mr Bartfield invokes the decision of the Court of Appeal in *London Scottish Benefit Society* v *Chorley* (1884) 13 QBD 872, in which it was held that where an action is brought against a solicitor who defends it in person and obtains judgment, he is entitled upon taxation to the same costs as if he had employed a solicitor, except in respect of items which the fact of his acting directly renders unnecessary. At 876 the Master of the Rolls said this:

> "The true rule seems to be that when a solicitor brings or defends an action in person, he is entitled to the same costs as an ordinary litigant appearing by a solicitor, subject to this restriction, that no costs which are really unnecessary can be recovered. Of this kind are the costs of instructions and attendances."

(I have read this passage as corrected by the errata immediately before the Table of Cases in this volume of the Law Reports.) The reference to "instructions and attendances" is to a solicitor's instructions to and attendances upon himself, which could only notionally occur.

At 877 Bowen LJ said this:

> "Professional skill, when it is bestowed, is accordingly allowed for in taxing a bill of costs, and it would be absurd to permit a solicitor to charge for the same work when it is done by another solicitor and not to permit him to charge for it when it is done by his own clerk."

That the result would be the same if the work were done not by the solicitor's clerk but by himself is plain from the Lord Justice's approval of a passage from Dixons Lush's Practice, where it was said that:

> "An attorney regularly qualified is allowed to make the same charges for business done when he sues or defends in person, as when he acts as attorney for another."

In reliance upon this authority Mr Bartfield has only to add the submission that the costs recoverable where one counsel instructs another must be the same in principle as where one solicitor instructs another.

In my judgment this submission is correct. Indisputably an appellant solicitor or counsel can conduct his own appeal. An attempt to equate such a professional person with a litigant in person is unhelpful because the

Regulations do not limit the scope of the remuneration recoverable by an appellant, and such an appellant brings to bear professional skill and labour, the value of which can as readily be assessed as if they were performed for him by another lawyer.

In relation to both appeals the taxing master ought therefore to have concluded that he did have power to allow costs to such extent as in the exercise of his discretion he considered reasonable.

In assessing the costs he would no doubt be entitled to take account of time and skill expended by the appellant or his counsel in the drawing of grounds of appeal to the taxing master, in the preparation of appeals and in the conduct of the hearing, together with travel and subsistence costs. In addition, a successful appellant must ordinarily be entitled to the return of the fee of £25 payable in respect of the appeal.

Because the question raised by these appeals is one of law, responsibility for the answer to it is mine alone. But I am grateful to both assessors for their support, and fortified by their concurrence in my conclusion.

At first sight the conclusion may appear unexpected, especially to older practitioners, since before the advent of legal aid there was no one to whom counsel could charge a fee for appearing on his own behalf. Thereafter some time elapsed before counsel was permitted, as a matter of professional etiquette, to argue in his own cause, and it is only lately that one counsel has been permitted to instruct another and pay him a fee, without the intervention of a solicitor. It may well be, therefore, that the draftsman of the 1982 Regulations did not have in mind or foresee that concatenation of events which has resulted in the present appeals being allowed.

Both cases will be remitted to the taxing master to determine what sum to award in respect of part or all of any reasonable costs (including any fee payable in respect of an appeal) incurred by each appellant in connection with his appeal.

In relation to costs, I am not satisfied that the arguments which prevailed in this court were sufficiently presented to the taxing master. Had they been so, the need for these appeals might have been avoided. There will therefore be no order as to the costs of the appeals to this court.

Mr R Bartfield appeared on behalf of counsel.

Index